MOZART
A DOCUMENTARY BIOGRAPHY

By the same Author
HANDEL: A DOCUMENTARY BIOGRAPHY
SCHUBERT: A DOCUMENTARY BIOGRAPHY
SCHUBERT: MEMOIRS BY HIS FRIENDS

MOZART

A DOCUMENTARY BIOGRAPHY

BY

OTTO ERICH DEUTSCH

TRANSLATED BY
ERIC BLOM, PETER BRANSCOMBE
AND JEREMY NOBLE

STANFORD UNIVERSITY PRESS
STANFORD, CALIFORNIA

Library of Congress Catalog Card No: 64–12077

FIRST PUBLISHED 1965
SECOND EDITION 1966

PRINTED IN GREAT BRITAIN BY R. AND R. CLARK LTD, EDINBURGH

CONTENTS

PREFACE

THIS collection of all the available documents relevant to Mozart's life has been compiled on the same principles as my earlier biographies of Schubert and Handel, published in London in 1946 and 1955. It does not include Mozart's letters, however ; these are too numerous, and a new edition of the Mozart family's correspondence—the first complete one—has just been published *. Certain events, however, such as the details of Mozart's journeys, which are established by these letters and journals but could not be indicated through other documents, have been inserted here in chronological order. The annotations to individual documents and events are given, as in my previous documentary biographies, not in footnotes but in the body of the text, immediately following the item to which they refer. Reference from one document or event to another is made by means of dates, since the page-numbers were not available until the book had been made up.

The present book was commissioned by A. & C. Black, the publishers of the Handel biography, as long ago as 1948. For personal and technical reasons, however, it first appeared in a German edition as a supplement to the Neue Mozart-Ausgabe published (like the letters) by the Internationale Stiftung Mozarteum, Salzburg. In the German edition the documents in languages other than German were given in their original form ; here all are translated into English.

The long delay in the appearance of this English edition is due to a succession of misfortunes in completing the translation. My friend the late Miss Emily Anderson kindly agreed to make this her next undertaking after the preparation of her great edition of Beethoven's letters, but her ill-health sadly prolonged that task and after some years she reluctantly withdrew. Dr. Eric Blom was then engaged to make the translation and he was still at work upon it when he died in 1959. I am grateful to Mr. Jeremy Noble and Mr. Peter Branscombe for finding time from their other commitments to revise very thoroughly Dr. Blom's first draft of some three-quarters of the whole book, to complete the translation, and to see the work through the press. The delay has not been without its compensations. Since 1961 a number of inaccuracies have been discovered and are here corrected. Moreover thirty-eight new documents have come to light, and these are indicated in the present edition by a star (*) in front of the heading.

Original sources are given, in principle, at the beginning of each note. Where it seemed necessary and was in fact possible, these sources have been consulted afresh. In each instance the first publication is specified, and often

---

* *Mozart. Briefe und Aufzeichnungen. Gesamtausgabe.* Collected and annotated by Wilhelm A. Bauer and Otto Erich Deutsch. 4 vols. (Bärenreiter-Verlag, Kassel, 1962–3).

later ones as well, with the exception of extracts from Count Karl Zinzendorf's diaries and the official *Wiener Zeitung*. Where no previous publication is mentioned in the notes it may be taken that the document concerned is here printed for the first time. However it is not on claims to priority but on the work of collecting, arranging and elucidating the documents that I would wish my contribution to be assessed.

Petitions by Mozart and his father, and also Leopold's letters to publishers in so far as these seemed to me to have any biographical significance, have been included among the documents, although they are of course also printed in the new edition of the letters. Surviving letters to the Mozarts from outside the family circle and other letters concerning Mozart have been included on biographical grounds.

The series of documents extends as far beyond Mozart's death as I considered useful, and for the first time brings together all the memoirs of him that are worthy of credence or consideration and were written or published during the ensuing hundred years.

In Appendices I and II are given an annotated list of the subscribers to Mozart's Vienna concerts in 1784 and the documents pertaining to Mozart's estate, with precise identification of the books and music mentioned therein. Jahn's Mozart biography is, unless otherwise stated, quoted in the third edition (1889–1891) revised by Hermann Deiters ; references to E. H. Müller von Asow's edition of the letters use the original numeration as Vols. II and III.

It is a pleasant duty for me to thank those who have helped me. Of those from whose kindness my work has benefited, the public institutions are named in the text. It would be impossible to thank all the many private individuals, among them both friends and colleagues, but their names shall at least be enumerated, and if there are any omissions the blame must be ascribed to a memory that is no longer so receptive of the twentieth century : the late Emily Anderson (London), Erna Felmayer (Vienna), Hilde Glück (Vienna), Dr. Monika Holl (Vienna), Ruth Larsen (Copenhagen), Josefa Morbioli (Vienna), Auguste Roth (Vienna), Lidia F. Wendelin (Budapest), Gertrud Wernigg (Vienna) ; Dr. Wilhelm A. Bauer (Vienna), the late Dr. Eric Blom (London), Dr. Alexander Buchner (Prague), Dr. Josef Heinz Eibl (Munich), the late Dr. Rudolf Geyer (Vienna), Professor Walter Hummel (Salzburg), Charles Humphries (London), Hans Jörgen Hurum (Oslo), Dr. Hanns Jäger-Sunstenau (Vienna), Ds. W. C. de Jong (The Hague), A. Hyatt King (London), Hofrat Dr. Herbert Klein (Salzburg), François Lesure (Paris), A. W. Ligtvoet (The Hague), Dr. C. B. Oldman, C.B. (London), D. E. Olleson (Peterborough), Christopher Raeburn (London), Professor Géza Rech (Salzburg), Dr. Wolfgang Rehm (Cassel), Albi Rosenthal (Oxford), the late Dr. Ernst Fritz Schmid (Augsburg), Dr. Wolfgang Schmieder (Frankfurt on Main), Otto Schneider (Markt Piesting) and Dr. Luigi Ferdinando Tagliavini (Bologna).

Of Mr. Raeburn, who is preparing a study of Mozart's operas, it must be added that by not withholding his discoveries in the periodicals of Mozart's Vienna period he has made a considerable contribution to the collection of documents.

The indexes of the German edition were compiled by Dr. Holl ; those of the present English edition are the work of my daughter, Mrs. Gitta Holroyd-Reece.

Vienna, Spring 1964   O. E. D.

NOTE TO THE SECOND EDITION

ADVANTAGE has been taken of the opportunity to correct a number of misprints. The translators are especially grateful to Mr. Bernard E. Wilson of the Newberry Library, Chicago, for many suggested improvements. Among factual corrections the chronology of the Mozarts' visit to Switzerland and Germany in 1766 (p. 66) has been revised according to information kindly supplied by Dr. Joseph H. Eibl. References to the Schiedermair edition of Mozart's letters have been allowed to stand since an extensive resetting of type would have been necessary to replace them by references to the recent edition by Bauer and Deutsch (Bärenreiter: Kassel and London, 4 vols., 1962-63).

1966

P. J. B.
J. J. N.

TRANSLATORS' NOTE

IN the considerable amount of work that the late Eric Blom was able to do on this book before his death in 1959, he established one guiding rule—that the translation should seek above all to retain the character of the original texts, and not to reduce their immense diversity of tone and diction to a flavourless common denominator. With this in mind we have adopted certain working principles, a knowledge of which may save the reader some surprise.

(1) The spelling of personal names is retained exactly as it stands in each document, so that Mozart, for instance, may appear in such unfamiliar guises as Mozzard, Mozhart or even Mozer. Except where specifically noted, however (e.g. in the signatures of Maria Thekla Mozart's letters), the customary feminine suffix " -in " added to German surnames has been tacitly suppressed, as liable to lead to confusion.

(2) As a reminder of the wide diversity of languages in which the original documents were written, we have also retained titles in their original form, so that Mozart himself appears not only as Herr and Kapellmeister (in various spellings) but also as Monsieur, Signore, Chevalier and in other ways. In Latin documents, however, in order to avoid undue pomposity, " Dominus " has usually been translated into the appropriate modern language. Unless otherwise stated, the originals are in German.

(3) Within the documents geographical names have also in general been retained in their original form, though not in the original spelling where this might lead to confusion. In the notes, however, current modern place-names have been preferred, even when these would have been unrecogniz-able to Mozart.

(4) In the same way the titles of all stage works are given in the language and spelling of the original documents, so that *Le nozze di Figaro*, for example, often appears as *Die Hochzeit des Figaro*. For easier reference they have, however, been italicized, except in the English-language documents, whose original typography has been retained.

It is to be hoped that in refusing to impose upon the immense amount of documentary material that Prof. Deutsch has assembled a uniformity and consistency that is foreign to it we have served the reader's interest, however much we may have strained the patience and credulity of our ever-helpful publishers and printers. To them, as to the necessarily anonymous legal and masonic experts who were so kind as to check our renderings of the relevant documents, we should like to express our gratitude.

P. J. B.
J. J. N.

1965

A NOTE ON CURRENCY

THE intricacies of eighteenth-century currency in the German-speaking countries are formidable, but a note on the denominations most frequently found in the following documents may perhaps prove helpful. The gulden (fl., florin), in use throughout the Austrian empire and southern Germany, consisted of 60 kreutzer (kr., xr.), though its absolute value was not consistent as between one region and another (cf. the note on 10 October 1787). The thaler, when not specified, may be either the Reichsthaler (Imperial thaler, $=1\frac{1}{2}$ fl.$=90$ kr.) or the Spezies- or Konventionsthaler ($=2$ fl.$=120$ kr.). The ducat seems at this period generally to have been calculated as the equivalent of $4\frac{1}{2}$ fl., but at times (cf. 18 March 1767, 27 November 1769) we find it$=5$ fl., and at times (cf. 16 July 1782) as low as $4\frac{1}{4}$ fl.

It could only be misleading to attempt to give a modern equivalent for these coins. It seems more useful to bear in mind certain sums as a yardstick of their value. Thus Leopold Mozart's basic annual salary as Vice-kapell-meister at Salzburg was 300 fl., with 54 fl. subsistence allowance ; Wolfgang's annual salary as Imperial kammermusicus was 800 fl. ; the standard fee he received for composing an opera for the Imperial theatres was 100 ducats (450 fl.).

This is the currency most frequently mentioned in these documents. Anyone who wishes to explore its vagaries in more detail is recommended to consult W. H. Bruford's *Germany in the Eighteenth Century* (Cambridge, 1935). It is not possible to give hard and fast conversion rates into the currencies in use in northern Germany (1 mark lübisch$=16$ schillings$=$about $\frac{2}{3}$ fl.), in Italy (1 lira$=20$ soldi ; 1 zecchino$=$about 12 lire), in France (1 livre tournois$=20$ sous ; 1 livre parisis$=25$ sous) or in England (1 pound$=20$ shillings ; 1 guinea$=21$ shillings).

THE DOCUMENTS

ANTECEDENTS

WEDDING OF MATERNAL GRANDPARENTS
(in Latin)
From the Marriage Register of the Parish of St. Gilgen, 22 November 1712

United in matrimony the noble and industrious Nicolaus Wolfgangus Pertl, learned in both laws [canon and civil], secretary to the Salzburg Exchequer, and the noble Euphrosina Puxbaum, widow ; in the presence of the aforementioned [Wolfgang Philipp Wendlinger, vicar] and witnesses : Joannes Andreas Schnedizeni, prefect, and Martinus Pertl.

> Communicated by Dr. Wilfried Keplinger, Salzburg.—Johann Andrä Schnedizeni was Prefect of Hüttenstein on the Krottensee ; the official seat was the Neue Schloss there. It lay north-east of St. Gilgen (on the Aber- or Wolfgang-See). Wolfgang Nikolaus Pertl was at the time Secretary to the Exchequer at Salzburg and in 1716 succeeded Schnedizeni as Deputy Prefect. The Prefect or, when the office was provisionally filled, Deputy Prefect was the highest administrative and judiciary official of a prefecture—in this case that of Hüttenstein-St. Gilgen.

WEDDING OF PATERNAL GRANDPARENTS
From the Records of the Augsburg Marriage Registry, 1 May 1718

Joh. Georg Mozer, bookbinder, widower, and Anna Maria Sulzer, spinster, both of this place, his witness Johann Georg Mozer, master-mason, her witness Christian Sulzer, weaver.

> Vol. 21, fol. 233 of the records.—Communicated by Dr. Ernst Fritz Schmid. —The bookbinder Mozart had previously been married to Anna Maria Peter, who only died on 18 March 1718. The church ceremony took place on 16 May 1718 (*cf.* next document). His witness was an uncle, hers her father, who had come to Augsburg from Baden-Baden (*cf.* 11 December 1766).

From the Marriage Register of the Parish of St. George, Augsburg, 16 May 1718
(in Latin)

On the 16th day of this month Father Ignatius Seefelder, after the customary declarations had been made, asked the most honourable widower, Joannes Georgius Mozarth, bookbinder, and the modest and virtuous maiden Anna Maria Sulzer, both of Augsburg, and having obtained the mutual consent of both parties by word of mouth, there being no canonical hindrance or impediment, joined the same in holy matrimony ; there being present as witnesses the reverend, most noble and famous Josephus de Schilling, canon of the chapter of St. Maurice, and the reverend and famous Joannes Georgius Grabherr, canon of the chapter of St. Peter.

Liber Parochialis, p. 257.—Communicated by Dr. Ernst Fritz Schmid.—St.
Maurice and St. Peter were both Augsburg foundations.

FATHER'S BIRTH AND BAPTISM
From the Augsburg Baptismal Register of the Parish of St. George, Augsburg,
14 November 1719
(in Latin)

On the 14th day of this month the same [Father Ignatius Seefelder] baptized a son born to Joannes Georgius Mozarth, bookbinder, and his wife
Anna Maria, about the first hour of the morning. The godparents were the
most reverend and famous Joannes Georgius Grabher, canon of St. Peter's,
Augsburg, and Maria Schwarz. Name of child—Joannes Georgius Leopoldus.

> Ernst Fritz Schmid, *Ein schwäbisches Mozart-Buch* (Lorch-Stuttgart, 1948), Plate
> IVb and p. 378, note 56.—For Grabherr, see Schmid in the *Mozart-Jahrbuch*
> *1950* (Salzburg, 1951), pp. 108 f.—Leopold Mozart left Augsburg for Salzburg
> in 1737, to study philosophy and law at the University there. In 1738 he was
> publicly commended at an examination, but in 1739 sent down for lack of
> application. In 1740 he entered the service of Count Johann Baptist Thurn-
> Valsassina and Taxis, President of the Salzburg Consistory, as valet and
> musician ; he dedicated his first work to him, six church sonatas for 2 violins
> and bass, which he himself engraved. In 1743 the Prince-Archbishop Leopold
> Anton Eleutherius, Baron Firmian, admitted him as fourth violinist into his Hof-
> kapelle ; he was promoted second in 1758 and soon afterwards first, becoming
> Vice-Kapellmeister in 1763, but never reaching the full appointment.

MOTHER'S BAPTISM
From the Baptismal Register of the Parish of St. Gilgen, 25 December 1720
(partly in Latin)

Anna Maria Walburga, legitimate daughter of the industrious Wolfgangus Nicolaus Pertl, Deputy Prefect of this place, and of Eva Rosina Alt-
man his wife. Godmother : Gertrud Seywalter, stewardess of the Chapter
and St. Peter's, and inn-keeper in the Strobl. Minister as above [Franz
Anton Kaltenbrunner, vicar].

> Communicated by Dr. Keplinger.—Already in the eighteenth century an
> unknown hand added to this entry : "mother of the famous Mozart". On
> 27 April 1720 the Prefect of Hüttenstein had removed to the new official resi-
> dence at St. Gilgen (now the district court).

PARENTS' WEDDING
From the " Liber Matrimonialis " of the Cathedral Parish, Salzburg
(in Latin)

Year 1747, November
21. The noble Leopold Mozarth, violinist [" Chelista "] to the Court,
legitimate son of the most virtuous Johann Georg Mozart, book-binder, of

Augsburg, and of Maria Anna Sulzer his wife, to the noble and chaste maiden Maria Anna, legitimate daughter of the noble Nicolaus Pertl, Deputy Prefect at Hildenstein and Eva Rosina Altmann his wife, there being present as witnesses the most reverend and learned Sebastian Seyser, Metropolitan vicar-choral, and the noble Franz Spetzner, Court Chamberlain and dancing-master, I, Leopold Joly, Civic Chaplain, being present.

> Alfred Orel, in *Mitteilungen der Internationalen Stiftung Mozarteum* (Salzburg, June 1956), p. 3. The inaccurate translation quoted by Jahn (II, 695) probably stems, like that of the entry of Wolfgang's baptism (28 Jan. 1756), from the Salzburg cathedral vicar Balthasar Schitter, dating from 1841.—The marriage register, where this entry appears on p. 115, had been in use since 1740. "Hildenstein" should be Hüttenstein ; "Spetzner" should be Speckner.— The erroneous supposition that Mozart's parents were married at Aigen, near Salzburg, is attributable to a jocular reference of Leopold Mozart's in a letter of 27 November 1764 to Lorenz Hagenauer ; they had made a vow there.

From the Records of the Augsburg Marriage Registry, 10 February 1748

Actum 10 February

Johann Georg Leopold Mozhard, son of a book-binder of this place, and at present *valet-de-chambre* to the Prince of Salzburg, has paid 9 florins for the favour of permission, by decree of the hon. Council of 6 February *praes :* *Anni*, to marry and be wedded at Salzburg.   C :   *Actum :*   10 February.
He will live at Salzburg.   [Signed] J. E. C. Herwart

> Augsburg City Archives : Vol. 25, p. 361 ; exhibited in the Mozart-Haus, Augsburg.—*Cf.* Ernst Fritz Schmid, *Ein schwäbisches Mozart-Buch* (Lorch-Stuttgart, 1948), p. 103 : at Leopold Mozart's " obedient request and petition " he obtained from the City Council of Augsburg written permission " to live abroad and to get married without loss of his civic rights ".—Herwart was Deputy at the Marriage Registry.

BIRTH OF THE FIRST CHILD

From the Baptismal Register of the Cathedral Parish, Salzburg, 18 August 1748

18. hora 4 mane	Joannes	Leopoldus	Maria Cordula	Leopoldus
natus et hora 5	Leopoldus	Mozard Chelista	Pergmayrin Mer-	Joly
vesperi renatus	Joachimus Filius	Aulicus et Maria	catrix loco	capellanus
	Legitimus	Anna Pertlin	Mariti Amadaei	civicus
		conjuges	Pergmayr	

> The extracts from the registers of baptisms and deaths at Salzburg Cathedral (*cf.* Jahn II, 695 f.) were communicated by Dr. Herbert Klein, Salzburg.—In the first column of the Baptismal Register are given the times of birth and baptism, in the second the child's name, in the third the parents', in the fourth the god-father or god-mother, and in the last the priest.—The parents lived in the Getreidegasse on the third floor of the grocer Lorenz Hagenauer's house.

DEATH OF THE FIRST CHILD
From the Register of Deaths of the Cathedral Parish, Salzburg, 2 February 1749

Infans Leopoldus, Leopoldi Motshart Chelistae Aulici fil[ius] leg[itimus]
aetatis 23 heb[domadarum] ad S. Petrum.

The child was buried in the churchyard of St. Peter's.

BIRTH OF THE SECOND CHILD
From the Baptismal Register, 18 June 1749

18. hora 5 vesperi nata et hora 6ta renata	Maria Anna Cordula Filia Legitima	Leopoldus Motsart Chelista Aulicus et Maria Anna Pertlin Conjuges	Amadaeus Pergmayr mercator civicus loco uxoris Mariae Cordulae	P.R.D. Sebastia[nus] Seyser Chori Metropol. Vicarius

DEATH OF THE SECOND CHILD
From the Register of Deaths, 24 June 1749

Infans Maria Anna Cordula, Leopoldi Mozart Chelistae Aulici fil[ia]
leg[itima] aetatis 3 dierum ad S. Petrum.

It should read " six days ", not " three ".

BIRTH OF THE THIRD CHILD
From the Baptismal Register, 13 May 1750

13. hora 9 mane nata et hora 5 pomerid[iàna] renata	Mar[ia] Anna Nepomuzena Walpurgis Filia Legitima	Leopoldus Mozart Musicus Aulicus et Maria Anna Pertlin Conjuges	Cordula Pergmayrin Mercatrix Civica	Leopoldus Josephus Joly Cap. Civicus

DEATH OF THE THIRD CHILD
From the Register of Deaths, 29 July 1750

Infans Joanna, Leopoldi Mozart Chelistae Aulici filia legitima aetatis 16
hebdom[adarum] ad S. Petrum.

It should read " Maria Anna " not " Joanna ", and " eleven weeks ", not
" sixteen ".

BIRTH OF THE FOURTH CHILD
From the Baptismal Register, 30–31 July 1751

30. med. 12 noctu nata et 31. hora 4 pomeridiana renata	Maria Anna Walburga Ignatia Filia Legitima	Leopoldus Mozart Chelista Aulicus et Maria Anna Pertlin Conjuges	Mar[ia] Cordula Bergmayrin Mercatrix Civica	Ferdinandus Joly cap[ellaniae] ivicae Coadiutor

" Nannerl ", the first surviving child.

BIRTH OF THE FIFTH CHILD
From the Baptismal Register, 4 November 1752

4. Horâ 8vâ mane natus et horâ 4tâ pom[eridiana] renatus est	Joannes Carolus AmaDeus F[ilius] L[egitimus]	Leopoldus Mozhart Musicus Aulicus et Maria Bertlin Conjuges	Joannes AmaDeus BergMayr Mercator Civicus	Ferd[inandus] Joly Coad[iutor]

This is the first appearance of the name Amadeus.

DEATH OF THE FIFTH CHILD
From the Register of Deaths, 2 February 1753

Joan[nes] Bapt[ista] Carolus Theophilus, fil[ius] leg[itimus] Leopoldi Mozart Musici Aulici. aet[atis] 1/4 ann[i]. ad S. Petrum.
The name Amadeus is given in its Greek form, Theophilus.

BIRTH OF THE SIXTH CHILD
From the Baptismal Register, 9 May 1754

9. med. 10 antemer[idiana] Baptizata est, natâ pridie med[ia] 5. Vespert[ina]	Maria Crescentia Francisca de Paula fil[ia] leg[itima]	D. Leopoldi Mozzard Aulae Musici hic, et Mariae Annae Pertlin Conjugum	D. Maria Cordula Pergmayrin mercatrix civica, loco eiusdem stetit Josepha Wagnerin soluta	L eopoldus Lamprecht Capellanus Civicus

DEATH OF THE SIXTH CHILD
From the Register of Deaths, 27 June 1754

Maria Francisca, fil[ia] leg[itima] D[omini] Leopoldi Mozard Aulae musici. aet[atis] 7 Hebdomad[arum]. ad S. Petrum.
parv[a]   tempore nocturno

LEOPOLD MOZART TO JOHANN JAKOB LOTTER IN AUGSBURG

Salzburg, 15 October 1755.

I hope that your dear wife is meanwhile happily delivered of her burden.
. . . My own dear one sends the same sincere wish ; about the end of
January she has the same task before her.

LEOPOLD MOZART TO LOTTER

Salzburg, 26 January 1756.

My wife will soon be starting her journey.
For Lotter *cf.* 9 February 1756, note.

DOCUMENTS OF MOZART'S LIFE

1756

BIRTH OF THE SEVENTH CHILD

From the Baptismal Register of the Cathedral Parish, Salzburg,
28 January 1756

| Januarius. 28. med[ia hora] 11. merid[iana] baptizatus est : natus pridie h[ora] 8. vesp[ertina] | Joannes Chrysost[omus] Wolfgangus Theophilus fil[ius] leg[itimus] | Nob[ilis] D[ominus] Leopoldus Mozart Aulae Musicus, et Maria Anna Pertlin coniuges | Nob[ilis] D[ominus] Joannes Theophilus Pergmayr Senator et Mercator Civicus p[ro] t[empore] sponsus | Idem [Leopoldus Lamprecht Capellanus Civicus] |

Facsimile in L. Schiedermair's *Mozart-Ikonographie* (Munich, 1914), p. 52. Alfred Orel, *op. cit.*, p. 2.—The entry is on page 2 for January 1756. The hour of the christening was 10.30, not 10 o'clock, as given in most sources, including the translation quoted by Jahn (Vol. II, page 696) which the Salzburg cathedral vicar Balthasar Schitter produced on 16 December 1841.—27 January is the saints' day of St. John Chrysostom (Goldmouth), Father of the Church and Patriarch of Constantinople (d. 407), a brilliant preacher and patron saint of pulpit orators.—In Italy, from 1770, Mozart called himself " Wolfgango Amadeo ", and from about 1777 " Wolfgang Amadè ".

LEOPOLD MOZART TO JOHANN JAKOB LOTTER AT AUGSBURG

Salzburg, 9 February 1756.

. . . Moreover, I must inform [you] that on 27 January, at 8 p.m., my dear wife was happily delivered of a boy; but the placenta had to be removed. She was therefore astonishingly weak. Now, however (God be praised) both child and mother are well. She sends her regards to you both. The boy is called Joannes Chrisostomos, Wolfgang, Gottlieb.

Augsburg City Archives.—Arthur Schurig, *Mozart*, 2nd ed. (Leipzig, 1923), Vol. I, p. 64.—Lotter was the publisher of Leopold Mozart's *Violinschule*, published at Augsburg in 1756. In 1793 this house published one of Mozart's works posthumously, the *Missa Brevis* in D (K. 194). Leopold Mozart, who was particularly attached to his brother Franz Alois, bookbinder at Augsburg, had remained a citizen of that town, so that Nannerl and Wolfgang, though born at Salzburg, were actually Augsburg citizens.

LEOPOLD MOZART TO LOTTER

Salzburg, 12 Feb. 1756.

. . . I can assure you, I have so much to do that I sometimes do not know where my head is. Not, to be sure, because of composition, but because of

M.—1 *a*

the many pupils and the operas at Court. And you know as well as I do that, when the wife is in childbed, there is always somebody turning up to rob you of time. Things like that cost money and time.

Original in the Austrian National Library, Vienna. Facsimile in Schiedermair's *Mozart-Ikonographie*, p. 48a.

1757

FROM FRIEDRICH WILHELM MARPURG'S "HISTORISCH-KRITISCHE
BEYTRÄGE ZUR AUFNAHME DER MUSIK", BERLIN, 1757
VERSUCH EINER GRÜNDLICHEN VIOLINSCHULE
[A THOROUGH VIOLIN SCHOOL ESSAY'D], DEVISED AND FURNISHED WITH
FOUR COPPER-PLATES, AS WELL AS A TABULATION, BY
LEOPOLD MOZART, CHAMBER MUSICIAN TO THE COURT OF
SALZBURG. PUBLISHED BY THE AUTHOR. AUGSBURG, PRINTED BY
JOHANN JACOB LOTTER,
1756.

A work of this kind has long been wished for, but one had hardly dared to expect it. Those who are most adept at wielding the bow are not always in control of the pen, and the few who possess equal facility in both often lack the will to write. How much the greater, then, is our obligation towards the author of the present work. The thorough and accomplished virtuoso, the reasonable and methodical teacher, the learned musician—these characteristics, each of which alone makes a man of merit, are all here revealed in one. We may not only congratulate lovers of this instrument on now having the opportunity of making greater progress at little expense than might otherwise be achieved at great cost in the course of many years ; for many of those, too, who profess the violin will here find instruction, and will do well to profit by this great master's teaching, so as no longer to spoil their pupils with bad precepts . . . [here follow details of the contents].

These are the matters of which Herr Mozart treats in the best and most natural order and in a pure German diction. He never fails to support his precepts with the most convincing reasons, and all rules are duly exemplified. What the famous Geminiam [Geminiani] was able to do for the English nation, the excellent Mozart has done for us Germans, and in providing us with a work of this nature has proved himself worthy of general approbation.

Vol. III, Part ii, pp. 160-3. Francesco Geminiani (1687-1762), pupil of Corelli and a distinguished violinist, settled in England and Ireland, and published *The Art of Playing on the Violin*.

FROM THE SAME
REPORT ON THE PRESENT STATE OF MUSIC
AT THE COURT OF HIS SERENE HIGHNESS
THE ARCHBISHOP OF SALZBURG
IN THE YEAR 1757.
THE COURT COMPOSERS.

. . . . 4. Herr Leopold Mozart from the Imperial City of Augsburg. 1st violinist and leader of the orchestra. He composes both church and chamber music. He was born on the 14th of November [*Wintermonat*], 1719, and soon after completing his studies in Natural and Legal Science entered the princely service in the year 1743. He has made himself known in every branch of composition, without however, issuing anything in print, but only himself engraved in copper 6 Sonatas à 3 in the year 1740 ; principally in order to gain experience of engraving. In July [*Heumonat*] 1756 he published his Violin School.

Among the compositions by Herr Mozart which have become known in manuscript, numerous contrapuntal and other church pieces are especially noteworthy ; moreover a large number of Symphonies, some only à 4, but some with all the generally current instruments ; likewise more than thirty grand Serenades, in which are introduced solos for various instruments. Apart from these he has composed many Concertos, especially for transverse flute, oboe, bassoon, horn, trumpet, &c., countless Trios and Divertimenti for divers instruments ; also twelve Oratorios and a host of theatre pieces, even Pantomimes and especially music for certain special occasions, such as a military piece with trumpets, kettle-drums, side-drums and fifes, together with the ordinary instruments ; a Turkish piece ; a piece with a steel clavier ; and music for a sleigh-ride with five sleigh-bells ; not to mention marches, so-called notturnos [*Nachtstücke*], many hundreds of minuets, opera dances and suchlike smaller pieces.

Vol. III, Part iii, p. 184 f.—This information was doubtless provided by Leopold Mozart himself.

1759

FROM MARPURG'S " KRITISCHE BRIEFE ÜBER DIE TONKUNST ",
BERLIN, 1759

FIRST LETTER TO HERR LEOPOLD MOZART,
COMPOSER TO THE COURT OF SALZBURG

Berlin, 23 June 1759.
. . . a certain musical society here, whose secret correspondent I have the pleasure of being, wishes to produce a musical weekly. . . . The society is minded to publish its periodical articles in the form of letters, and it proposes to take the liberty of addressing its letters to persons of merit, insight and taste. Could the aforesaid, in this endeavour, Sir, make a more auspicious beginning than with you ? . . .

Hypographus.

Part i, Letter 1, pp. 1-8.—Letter 4 was addressed to Carl Philipp Emanuel Bach. All the letters appeared under a pseudonym ; the one addressed to Leopold Mozart was probably written by Marpurg himself, whose name does not appear on the title-page of the periodical either.

FROM FRIEDRICH WILHELM MARPURG'S " HISTORISCH-KRITISCHE BEYTRÄGE
ZUR AUFNAHME DER MUSIK ", BERLIN, 1759

AUGSBURG.   Recently issued here by Lotter's publishing-house : " Morning and Evening, proclaimed in melody and harmony to the Inhabitants of
the City of Salzburg " ; or " Twelve Musical Pieces for the Clavier, whereof
one is played daily, morning and evening, on the so-called ' Horn Work '
in the Fortress of Hohensalzburg ; published at the request of many amateurs, together with a Short Account of the Origin of the Fortress of Hohensalzburg, by Leopold Mozart, Chamber Musician to His Serene Highness
the Archbishop of Salzburg. Augsburg, 1759." . . . From time immemorial
only a single piece was played. To this, for the sake of change, the worshipful *Regional Council* caused another eleven to be added. . . . Since many
music-lovers wished to have these pieces for the pianoforte, Herr *Mozart* has
been so kind as to make them available for printing. The pieces for January,
April, August, November and December are by his Highness's *Kapellmeister*,
Herr Johann Ernst Eberlin, and those for February, May, June, July, September and October, as well as the variations upon the piece for March, by
the Court Composer, Herr *Mozart*. These variations, however, are not to
be heard on the " horn work ", but have only now been made by the
aforesaid for lovers of the clavier. The piece for March is the ancient one,
whose composer no man knows. The names of the above two famous
masters of music can only bring lustre to this collection of small pieces. We
could wish that Breitkopf's new musical type might soon become known at
Augsburg too, and the old one be done away with.

    Vol. IV, Part v, pp. 403-5.—Music printing from type was introduced by
Immanuel Breitkopf at Leipzig in 1755, but Lotter had also used this process.

1761

LEOPOLD MOZART'S NOTE IN NANNERL'S MUSIC BOOK, BELOW A
SCHERZO BY GEORG CHRISTOPH WAGENSEIL

    This piece was learnt by Wolfgangerl on 24 January 1761, 3 days before
his 5th birthday, between 9 and 9.30 in the evening.

    Mozarteum, Salzburg.—*Nannerl-Notenbuch*, edited by Erich Valentin (Mu-
nich, 1956), p. 40 f., No. 27.—Against Nos. 1 to 8 (pp. 13-16) of this practice-
book written in 1759 Leopold has noted : " The preceding 8 Minuets were
learnt by Wolfgangerl in his 4th year " [*i.e.* at the age of four]. Against No.
19 (p. 24) : " This Minuet was also learnt by Wolfgangerl in his fourth year ".
And against No. 37 (p. 68 f.) : " This Allegro was learnt by Wolfgangerl in
his 4th year ".

IBID.

This Minuet and Trio was learnt by Wolfgangerl within half an hour on 26 January 1761, a day before his 5th birthday, at about half past 9 at night.
  Op. cit., p. 18 f., No. 11.

IBID., BELOW A MARCH

Learnt by Wolfgangerl on 4 February 1761.
  Op. cit., p. 27, No. 21.

IBID., BELOW A SCHERZO BY WAGENSEIL

This was learnt by Wolfgangerl on 6 February 1761.
  Op. cit., p. 42 f., No. 28.—Against Mozart's two earliest compositions, an Andante and an Allegro written between February and April 1761 (before K.1), Leopold noted : " Compositions by Wolfgangerl, in the first three months after his 5th birthday ". (*Der früheste Mozart*, with facsimiles, edited by Erich Valentin (Munich, 1956), p. 25.)

FROM THE PRINTED LIBRETTO OF THE LATIN PLAY " SIGISMUNDUS HUNGARIAE REX ", PERFORMED ON 1 AND 3 SEPTEMBER 1761

AUCTOR OPERIS MUSICI.
  Praenobilis ac Strenuus D. Joannes Ernestus Eberlin, Celsissimi ac Reverendissimi Archi-Episcopi, & S[acri] R[omani] I[mperii] Principis Salisburgensis &c. &c. Dapifer & Capellae Magister.

PERSONÆ MUSICÆ .   .   .   [5]
ACTORES   .   .   .   .   .   [8]

SALII
Illustriss[imus] ac Generosiss[imus] D. Antonius S.R.I. Comes de Seeau, Celsiss[imi] ac Reverendiss[imi] Archi-Episc[opi] & S.R.I. Principis Salisburgensis &c. &c. Ephebus, Philos[ophiae] Baccalaureus, & Physices Studiosus.
Illustr. ac Generosiss. D. Cajet. S.R.I. Comes de Sauer, Celsiss. . . . Ephebus, AA. LL. [Artium Liberalium] et Phil[osophiae] Magister, ac Jurium Auditor.
Illustriss. ac Generosiss. D. Christoph. L.B. [Liber Baro] de Waidmanstorf, Celsiss. . . . Ephebus, Rhetor.
Illustriss. ac Generosiss. D. Maximil. S.R.I. Comes de Lamberg, Celsiss. . . . Ephebus, AA. LL. & Phil. Magist. ac Jurium Auditor.

Illustriss. ac Generosiss. D. Josephus L.B. de Cless, Celsiss. . . . Ephebus, Syntaxista.

Illustriss. ac Generosiss. D. Casimirus S.R.I. Comes de Schenk, Celsiss. . . . Ephebus, Grammatista.

Illustriss. ac Generosiss. D. Carolus L.B. de Freyberg, Celsiss. . . . Ephebus, Grammatista.

Illustriss. ac Generosiss. D. Mauritius S.R.I. Comes de Berchtold, Celsiss. . . . Ephebus, Rudimentista.

Illustriss. ac Generosiss. D. Ernestus S.R.I. Comes de Wildenstein, Celsiss. . . . Ephebus, Principista.

Perill[ustris] ac Generos[us] D. Joannes Baptista L.B. de Bositzio. Illustr[is] Coll[egii] Virgiliani Convictor, Rhetor.

Praen[obilis] D. Antonius de Moelk.

Nob[ilis] et Spectatiss[imus] D. Franciscus Spoeckner, artis Saltatoriae Magister.

Wolfgangus Mozhart.

MINISTRI IN SALTV.

Ex Syntaxi omnes

Adamer, Herndl, Kaserer, Neisser, Proetz, Rebmann, Schafleutner, Voelker.

IN INTERLVDIIS . . . . [8]

MILITES . . . . . . [65]

IN CHORIS . . . . . [40]

> Salzburg, Studienbibliothek.—Communicated by Dr. Herbert Klein.—Performed as end-of-term play (*commoedia finalis*) for the academic year 1760/61. The double date of performance is explained by the fact that Prince-Archbishop Schrattenbach had on this occasion for the first time commanded separate performances for men and women on moral grounds.—The author of the text was Father Marian Wimmer, a Benedictine of Seeon, Prefect and Professor of the Gymnasium.—The drama had for subject the wooing of Maria, daughter and heiress of King Ludwig of Hungary, by Sigismund, later Emperor ; this was a spoken play. Interwoven with it, however, was a second play (Tobias's wooing of Sarah), which was set to music. (*Cf.* 13 May 1767). The presence of dancers (Salii) indicates that there was a ballet, but the programme does not make clear with which of these two themes it was connected, or whether, like the Interludes, it was independent of both.—The dancers were predominantly young noblemen (Ephebi) who were either studying at the University (law, science) or attended the Academic Gymnasium (rhetoric, syntax, grammar, rudiments, principals). Also taking part were a member of the aristocratic Collegium Virgilianum, a private student (Mölk), the dancing-master Franz Speckner (*cf.* 1747) and the five-year-old Mozart, whose name here appeared for the first time in print.—The performances took place in the great theatre of the university ; the libretto was printed by Mayr. (*Cf. Allgemeine musikalische Zeitung* [Leipzig, 4 March 1874], col. 139 f.)

1762

Leopold Mozart, with his two children, left on 12 January 1762 for a three weeks visit to Munich, where Nannerl and Wolfgang appeared before the Bavarian Elector Maximilian III Joseph.

> No details of this journey have come to light. Leopold Mozart had also been at Munich in mid-January 1761, when his friend Georg Joseph Robinig von Rottenfeld was buried there.

On 18 September 1762 Leopold Mozart went to Vienna with his wife and children, remaining away until 5 January 1763.

The Mozarts arrived at Passau at 5 p.m. on 20 September ; they stayed at the Red Crayfish (now the White Hare) until the morning of the 26th. During their stay Wolfgang played at the house of Bishop Joseph Maria, Count Thun-Hohenstein.

On 26 September the family sailed down the Danube to Linz, arriving at 5 p.m. and putting up at the Trinity (Hofgasse 14), kept by the sisters Kiener.

> They met with Ernst Johann, Count Herberstein, a canon of Passau Cathedral, travelling to Linz by the same boat.—It was in this inn at Linz, on 1 October, that Wolfgang gave his first public performance. The Governor of Upper Austria, Count Leopold Schlick, and his wife took the family under their protection.

At 4.30 p.m. on 4 October the Mozarts continued their journey on the Danube and at 7.30 p.m. reached Mauthausen, where they spent the night. Wolfgang suffered from catarrh on this journey.

On 5 October they continued to Ybbs, and on to Stein, where they arrived in the evening and spent the night.

> At Ybbs Wolfgang played the organ.

At 3 p.m. on 6 October their post-boat arrived at Vienna.

> Whether the family spent the first night or the first few days at the White Ox on the Fleischmarkt is uncertain. In any case, in mid-October they were living in the Tiefe Graben at the house of Johann Heinrich Ditscher (now No. 16).

FROM KARL COUNT ZINZENDORF'S DIARY, 9 OCTOBER 1762
(in French)

. . . In the evening, at 8 o'clock, I called for Lamberg, and we went to Colalto's together, where la Bianchi sang and a little boy, who, it is said, is but five and a half years of age, played the harpsichord. . . .

> The sixty volumes of diaries of Count Karl von Zinzendorf (1739–1813), who later became a high state official, are preserved in the Vienna State Archives and have been often quoted from in musical literature (C. F. Pohl, Oskar Teuber, Arthur Schurig, Robert Haas and others), most recently as the bulk of Gustav Gugitz's "Mozartiana" in *Wiener Geschichtsblätter*, 1956, No. 1, pp. 17–19. A transcription of the Mozart references was published by O. E. Deutsch in the *Schweizerische Musikzeitung* (Zürich), August 1962.—The palace of Count Thomas Collalto stood, and still stands, next to the Jesuit Church, Am Hof (No. 13).—Lamberg is probably the statesman Anton Franz

de Paula, Count Lamberg (1740–1823).—Marianna Bianchi had sung Eurydice in Gluck's *Orfeo ed Euridice* at the Burgtheater on 5 October 1762.

On 10 October the Mozarts paid a visit to Count Johann Joseph Wilczek, to whom they were introduced by Eleonore Elisabeth, Countess Sinzendorf, *née* Hardegg. In the evening Leopold Mozart went to hear Gluck's new opera [*Orfeo ed Euridice*] which was preceded by the comedy *La surprise de l'amour italienne.*

On 11 October the two children performed before the Vice-Chancellor of the Realm, Rudolf Joseph, Prince Colloredo-Melz and Wallsee, again introduced by Countess Sinzendorf.

> Leopold Mozart, in his report to Salzburg of 16 October 1762 calls the Vice-Chancellor of the Realm " Count " ; Rudolf Joseph's eldest son, Franz de Paula Gundaccar I, Count Colloredo (a brother of the later Archbishop Hieronymus), did not become a Prince and Vice-Chancellor of the Realm until 1788, in succession to his father.

From 3 to 6 p.m. on 13 October the Mozarts were at Schönbrunn Palace, where they were received by Maria Theresa and her consort, the Emperor Francis I, in the presence of the Archduchess Maria Antonia (Marie-Antoinette) and the composer Wagenseil. In the evening they were guests of the music-loving Prince Joseph Friedrich of Saxe-Hildburghausen at what later became the Auersperg Palace (formerly Rofrano Palace, now 1 Auerspergstrasse), where the contralto Vittoria Tesi lived.

On 14 October the family visited the Countess Maria Theresia Kinsky, *née* Marchesa Rofrano, in her palace on the Freyung ; they later went on to the Minoritenplatz to visit the Lord High Steward, Corfiz Anton, Count Ulfeld, whose young daughter Wilhelmine was the wife of Count Franz Joseph Thun.

FROM ZINZENDORF'S DIARY, 14 OCTOBER 1762
(in French)

. . . At the Princess Trautson's. I saw Mme de Martinitz there, friend of the late Mme de Dünewald. Talked to the Nuncio about the opera. He is very critical of its poem. Also about that little boy who played yesterday at Schönbrunn and to-day at Uhlefeld's . . .

> Marie Karoline, Princess Trautson (1701–93), born Baroness Haager von Altensteig, was lady-in-waiting to Maria Theresa and later Mistress of the Household to the (2) Archduchesses ; she took a lively interest in music and the theatre.—Marianne Martinez, pupil of Johann Adolph Hasse, Joseph Haydn and Nicolò Porpora, and friend of Metastasio, was a very talented musician.——The Papal Nuncio was Vitaliano Borromeo.—The opera in question was evidently Gluck's *Orfeo* ; the libretto is by Raniero de' Calzabigi. Zinzendorf had already criticized the text after the first performance on 5 October (*cf.* Robert Haas, *Gluck und Durazzo im Burgtheater* [Vienna, 1925], p. 62).

In the morning of 15 October, gala attire for Nannerl and Wolfgang was delivered at the family's residence by the Imperial Paymaster, Johann Adam Mayr. Wolfgang's dress, in which he was painted, had originally been intended for the Archduke Maximilian, who was of the same age. Between 2.30 and 3.45 the Mozarts paid an unrecorded visit, from which they were collected by a young courtier, Count Johann Hardegg. Later, until 5.30, they visited an unnamed lady, and from 6 until about 9 they were guests of the Chancellor, Wenzel, Count Kaunitz-Rietberg, who then sent them home in a carriage.

Kaunitz was not made a prince until 1764.

From 2.30 to 4 p.m. on 16 October the Mozarts visited the youngest archdukes, Ferdinand and Maximilian (probably at the Hofburg), and later they were the guests of Count Nikolaus Pálffy in what is now No. 6 Josefsplatz.

Count Pálffy was Hungarian Chancellor in Vienna.

IBID., 17 OCTOBER 1762

(in French)

. . . Then at *Thurn's*, where the little child from Salzburg and his sister played the harpsichord. The poor little fellow plays marvellously, he is a Child of Spirit, lively, charming, his sister's playing is masterly, and he applauded her. Mlle de Gudenus, who plays the harpsichord well, gave him a kiss, and he wiped his face . . .

> If the name Thurn is right, the reference is probably to the statesman Franz, Count Thurn-Valsassina (1718–66) (*cf.* 14 November 1719) ; but it has also been read as Thun, which would indicate Franz Joseph, Count Thun (see 14 October 1762). Nothing is known about Fräulein von Gudenus. In his letter of 24 November 1781 Mozart mentions a " Baron Godenus " in Vienna.

In the morning of 19 October Mayr, the paymaster, presented an honorarium of 100 ducats from the court, with the request to prolong their stay in Vienna. In the afternoon the children performed before the French Ambassador, Florent-Louis-Marie, Comte du Châtelet-Lomont, who invited the Mozarts to Versailles.

In the afternoon of 20 October the family was called for at 4 o'clock and taken by coach to the near-by palace of Count Ferdinand Harrach on the Freyung. After two hours there, they attended a concert (*Akademie*) at the house of another wealthy nobleman, where the children were given 6 ducats for performing with several " virtuosi ".

At 7 p.m. on 21 October the Mozarts were received at Schönbrunn for the second time. That same evening Wolfgang fell ill with a rash (*erythema nodosum*), which kept him in bed until 31 October.

> The illness, which Leopold regarded as a kind of scarlet fever, was first diagnosed by Hans Holz (*Mozarts Krankheiten und sein Tod*, dissertation, Jena, 1939). It has recently been confirmed by Dr. Johannes Dalchow and Professor Aloys Greither.—Wolfgang's doctor, recommended by Countess Sinzendorf, was Dr. Johann Anton von Bernhard, as Alfred Orel and Erich Schenk discovered almost simultaneously.

An invitation from the Postmaster-General, Count Wenzel Paar, for 25 October had to be refused, as well as a few other invitations for the end of October.

On 31 October, Wolfgang's name-day, Leopold Mozart presented his son, now well again, with a music exercise-book similar to that which Nannerl had received in 1759 (see 24 January 1761).

By 4 November Wolfgang was able to go out again. They viewed the Karlskirche on the Glacis and took a walk to the Josefstadt suburb. (The Glacis was the open ground outside the walls of the Inner City.)

On 5 November the children performed at Dr. Bernhard's as an expression of gratitude for his treatment of Wolfgang.

FROM ZINZENDORF'S DIARY, 9 NOVEMBER 1762
(in French)

. . . At M. de Pacheco's in the Windischgraetz house near the Schwarze Thor. The little Salzburger played, Nicolini sang to admiration . . .

Vincenzia, Marchesa Pacheco, wife of the chamberlain Melchior Telles Giron, Marchese Pacheco, was a confidante of Maria Theresa's. She is also mentioned in Leopold Mozart's letter to Hagenauer of 10 November 1762.—The house of Count Joseph Windischgrätz was in the Vordere Schenkenstrasse (now Bankgasse 7), next to the house "Zum schwarzen Thor" (corner of Bankgasse and Petrarcagasse). The house at the corner of Bankgasse and Abraham-a-Santa-Clara-Gasse, opposite the Liechtenstein Palace, later became part of the great Starhemberg Palace ; the small house was later rebuilt when the Ministry of Education occupied it.—The singer Carlo Niccolini had appeared in opera and oratorio.—That evening Count Collalto (see 9 October 1762) handed Leopold Mozart a poem in manuscript, which was not distributed in print until 25 December (q.v.).—Mozart's name does not reappear in Zinzendorf's diary until 30 July 1782.

In the evening of 19 November they were allowed to attend, as standing spectators, a gala dinner (presumably at the Hofburg) in celebration of the name-day of the late Dowager Empress, Elisabeth Christine ; Maria Theresa inquired from Leopold Mozart about the health of Wolfgang, who was ailing again.

On 22 November, St. Cecilia's Day, which according to custom was celebrated with church music, the family took lunch at the Court Kapellmeister Georg Reutter's.

On 23 November the Mozarts lunched with a Herr von Wahlau (or Wallau) and in the evening, accompanied by Dr. Bernhard, they had a box at the Burgtheater for an opera.

On 8 December, the Feast of the Immaculate Conception, a gala dinner was held (presumably at the Hofburg) in celebration of Emperor Francis I's birthday, and the Mozarts again attended as spectators.

On 11 December the family left for Bratislava (Pressburg), presumably by Danube boat.

No details of the stay at Bratislava are known.

On 24 December they returned to Vienna in a private carriage, the journey taking from 8.30 a.m. to 8.30 p.m.

THE FIRST POETIC TRIBUTE TO MOZART

ON THE LITTLE SIX-YEAR-OLD CLAVIER-PLAYER FROM SALZBURG. DISTRIBUTED AT HIS CONCERT BY THE HON. COUNT VON COLLALTO. VIENNA, 25 DECEMBER 1762.

Ingenium coeleste suis velocius annis
Surgit, et ingratae fert mala damna morae.

Ovid.

Child, worthy our regard, whose ready skill we praise,
Who, small in stature, like the greatest plays ;
For thee the art of sound will hold no pain,
Full soon wilt thou to mastery attain.
But may thy frame the soul's exactions bear,
And not, like Lübeck's child,* too soon outwear.

* This learned wonderchild of Lübeck, who was the talk of all Germany, and at the age of six was master of many languages and sciences, died a few years later and by his example proved the principle : *Fructus esse idem diuturnus ac praecox nequit.*

Puffendorff.

The only known copy of this print is in the German State Library, Berlin.—Nissen, p. 27.—Richard Petzoldt and Eduard Crass, *W. A. Mozart. Sein Leben in Bildern* (Leipzig, 1956), plate 13.—The motto is on page 2 of the broadsheet, title and poem on pages 1 and 3.—Since Leopold had been given a manuscript copy of the poem by Count Collalto at Marchese Pacheco's as early as 9 November, which he sent to Salzburg the next day, the occasion may have been the concert held at Collalto's house on 9 October. On 25 December the Mozarts do not seem to have been at Collalto's, but the poem may have been printed for Christmas Day.—Konrad Friedrich von Pufendorf was an Aulic Councillor, and later Grand Master of the Masonic National Lodge of Austria ; his wife, Anna, born a von Posch, subscribed to Mozart's concerts in 1784 and on 13 March 1786 sang Ilia in the private performance of *Idomeneo*. The writer Johann Andreas von Pufendorf, however, is another possible claimant to authorship of this poem. The quotation from Ovid is *Ars amandi*, I. 185 f. The dictum at the end is reminiscent of Quintus Curtius Rufus, *Historiae Alexandri Magni regis Macedonum*, VIII. 5. 15 (pointed out by Professor Franz Stoessl, Vienna).

On 27 December Countess Kinsky gave a dinner in honour of Field-Marshal Leopold Count Daun, at whose desire the Mozart family was also invited.

Cf. 14 October 1762.

1763

On 31 December 1762 the Mozarts set out in their carriage on their journey home. They arrived at Linz in the evening of 2 January 1763 but did not reach Salzburg till the evening of the 5th. Wolfgang had to stay in bed for a week owing to rheumatism.

FROM FATHER PLACIDUS SCHARL'S " EPHEMERIDES DIURNIAE ",
6 JANUARY 1763
(in Latin)

There was present at lunch Herr Starke and at supper Herr Adlgasser, who spoke about Herr Mozart's child, telling how he had rushed up and would have embraced the Empress, saying that he loved her with all his heart.

Andechs, Monastery Archives, MS. No. 70.—Romuald Bauerreiss, "Mozart und die Benediktiner ", in *Studien und Mitteilungen zur Geschichte des Benediktiner-Ordens und seiner Zweige*, Vol. 57 (Munich, 1939), p. 84.—The Benedictine

Scharl taught from 1759 to 1770 at the Salzburg Gymnasium.—Anton Kajetan Adlgasser was the Court organist.

FROM THE SALZBURG COURT CHRONICLE

28 February (Birthday of the Prince Archbishop Sigismund von Schrattenbach) 1763

After Mass the following promotions took place : . . . Herr Lolli, Vice-Kapellmeister was to-day nominated to the full rank, and Herr Mozart, musician, to that of Vice-Kapellmeister. . . .

At 5 p.m. the whole Court . . . was commanded to appear in gala, whereupon His Serene Highness received congratulations from all in the audience chamber, and then, towards 6 o'clock, and after the Ave Maria had been sung, he went out into the council chamber with them all and, instead of a gathering, attended a musical performance, that is to say vocal music by several virtuosi, among whom were, to everyone's astonishment, the new Vice-Kapellmeister's little son, aged 7, and daughter, aged 10, performing on the harpsichord, the son likewise on the violin, as well as one could ever have hoped of him, so that the birthday celebrations came to a happy end.

> Salzburg Provincial Archives.—Franz Martin, " Vom Salzburger Fürstenhof um die Mitte des 18. Jahrhunderts ", offprint from *Mitteilungen der Gesellschaft für Salzburger Landeskunde* (1952), p. 122 f.—Giuseppe Lolli succeeded Johann Ernst Eberlin, and Leopold Mozart was given Lolli's post.

FROM THE " AUGSBURGISCHER INTELLIGENZ-ZETTEL ", 19 MAY 1763

CURIOSITIES. That the Germans in this century have become very prominent in the art of music, and have not only happily learnt from the Italians what is agreeable and charmingly harmonious, but also, since Germany now has such excellent virtuosi to show, they have excelled the latter in many respects, will scarcely be doubted any longer by those who understand music ; more especially as now kings, princes and rulers endeavour to contest the primacy of the Italian virtuosi once so famous in music. In instrumental music we could mention many virtuosi among the Germans and thereby prove, supposing that were our intention, that they are to be preferred even to the most celebrated Italians as virtuosi on various instruments and at the same time as composers. But we content ourselves for to-day with a favourable mention in these pages of what is particularly curious in two admirable children whose father is a very famous virtuoso and an especially skilful and fortunate composer : and this in the form of a letter which has been sent from Vienna to a good friend resident in this city.

Sir,

I am perhaps the first to have the honour of imparting news to you which may soon be the object of the greatest admiration all over Germany and perhaps also in distant countries. I speak of the two children of the famous Mozart, Vice-Kapellmeister at Salzburg. Just imagine a girl 11 years of age who can perform on the harpsichord or the fortepiano the most difficult sonatas and concertos by the greatest masters, most accurately, readily and with an almost incredible ease, in the very best of taste. This alone cannot fail to fill many with astonishment. But we fall into utter amazement on seeing a boy aged 6 at the clavier and hear him, not by any means toy with sonatas, trios and concertos, but play in a manly way, and improvise moreover for hours on end out of his own head, now *cantabile*, now in chords, producing the best of ideas according to the taste of to-day ; and even accompany at sight symphonies, arias and recitatives at the great concerts.— Tell me, does this not exceed all imagination ?—And yet it is the simple truth ! What is more, I saw them cover the keyboard with a handkerchief ; and he plays just as well on this cloth as though he could see the keys. Furthermore, I saw and heard how, when he was made to listen in another room, they would give him notes, now high, now low, not only on the pianoforte but on every other imaginable instrument as well, and he came out with the letter or the name of the note in an instant. Indeed, on hearing a bell toll or a clock, even a pocket-watch, strike, he was able at the same moment to name the note of the bell or time-piece. I was also present in person when a clavier player on several occasions played a few bars of melody for him, which he then repeated and had to fit a bass to of his own ; and every time he carried this out so beautifully, accurately and well that everybody was astounded. These two extraordinary children had to appear twice before H.M. the Emperor and H.M. the Empress-Queen, and then again before the younger members of the imperial family ; they were favoured with grand presents and then invited to concerts by the highest nobility of the Court and everywhere handsomely rewarded.

P.S. I am credibly informed that the boy can now not only play from the violin clef, but also from the soprano and bass clefs, and takes part in everything on a small *violino piccolo* made specially for him, having already appeared with a solo and a concerto at the Court of Salzburg. Has he then learnt this since the New Year ?

E. F. Schmid, *Augsburger Mozartbuch* (1943), p. 96.

On 9 June 1763 the Mozart family set out on their great journey across Europe, which kept them away from home until 29 November 1766. They travelled in their own carriage, with changes of post-horses, and were accompanied by a servant named Sebastian Winter.

Just after midnight on 10 June they arrived at Wasserburg, where they alighted at the Golden Star, and where Mozart played the church organ.

In the morning of 12 June they moved on to Munich, where they arrived in the evening and put up at Störzer's inn, the Golden Stag, in the Theatinerstrasse.

On a trip to Nymphenburg on 13 June they met Prince Karl August von Zweibrücken, who arranged for the Mozarts to appear at 8 o'clock that evening in the Elector Maximilian's palace, where Wolfgang performed on the clavier and the violin. The concert lasted until nearly 11 o'clock.

On 14 and 15 June they visited Duke Clemens of Bavaria where Nannerl also performed.

On 18 June the family were present as spectators at the Elector's gala dinner at the palace.

On 19 June Nannerl too performed at court. Whether the Mozarts again performed before the Duke and the Elector is uncertain.

They left Munich on 22 June and arrived that evening at Augsburg, Leopold's birthplace, where they alighted at the Three Moors.

The children gave public concerts at Augsburg on 28 and 30 June and 4 July.
Cf. 19 July 1763.

FROM THE " AUGSBURGISCHER INTELLIGENZ-ZETTEL ", 30 JUNE 1763
(Arrived on 22 June :)

Herr Mozard and wife arrive with the post from Munich and lodge at the Three Moors.

✓Leopold bought a travelling clavier from Johann Andreas Stein.

On 6 July the Mozarts left for Ulm, where they alighted in the evening at the Golden Wheel inn. In the morning of the 7th Wolfgang played on the organ in the minster, and in the afternoon the family continued their journey.

In the evening of 9 July they reached Ludwigsburg by way of Cannstatt. They lodged at the Golden Hunting-Horn inn, facing the castle. Unfortunately the Duke of Württemberg, Karl Eugen, was not in residence.

Here the family met Pietro Nardini and the opera composer Niccolò Jommelli.

At 8 a.m. on 12 July the journey was continued to Bruchsal, where the Mozarts arrived in the evening and stayed at the Giant.

On 14 July they arrived at Schwetzingen, the country seat of Karl Theodor, the Elector-Palatine, and lodged at the Red House.

The Elector was the founder of the famous Mannheim orchestra. His Director of Music was Karl, Baron Eberstein.

On 18 July the children performed in the palace at Schwetzingen.

FROM THE " EXTRACT-SCHREIBEN, ODER . . . EUROPAEISCHE ZEITUNG,
AUS VERSCHIEDENEN ORTEN, UND DER ZEITEN NEUESTER BEGEBENHEITEN ",
SALZBURG, 19 JULY [1763]

Augsburg, 9 July

The day before yesterday, in the morning, the Vice-Kapellmeister to the
Court of Saltzburg, Herr Leopold Mozart, left here for Stuttgard with his
2 wonderful children, to continue his journey to France and England by way
of the greatest German Courts. He afforded the inhabitants of his native
city the pleasure of hearing the effect of the extraordinary gifts which the
Great God has bestowed on these two dear little ones in such abundant
measure ; gifts of which the Herr Kapellmeister has, as a true father, taken
care with such indefatigable zeal, as to present the musical world with a girl
of 11 and, what is incredible, a boy of 7 years at the harpsichord, as a marvel
of our own and past time. All connoisseurs have found what a friend in
Vienna wrote some time ago about these celebrated children, and what was
inserted in the local *Intelligenz-Zettel*, to be not only true, incredible as it had
seemed, but even more worthy of admiration.

> No. 57.—*Mozarteums-Mitteilungen*, Year 3, Pt. 1, November 1920, p. 29
> (Rudolf von Lewicki). The *Augburgischer Intelligenz-Zettel* is quoted above
> under 19 May 1763.

After 19 July the Mozarts paid a visit to Heidelberg (the Three Kings inn), where
Wolfgang played the organ at the Church of the Holy Ghost ; they then travelled on
to Mannheim (the Prince Frederick), where they stayed for three days, and Worms
(the Swan).

The itinerary from 19 July to 2 August is uncertain.

On 3 August the family arrived at Mainz and lodged at the King of England inn
(Markt 37). A few days later the children performed at the King of Rome inn
(Grebenstrasse), where the main room was used as a theatre. The reigning Elector,
Emmerich Joseph, Count Breidbach-Burresheim, was ill at this time.

> *Cf.* Adam Gottron, *Mozart und Mainz* (Mainz, 1951).—Whether the family's
> excursions from Mainz to Wiesbaden, Biebrich and Kostheim took place at
> the beginning of August or only after their return from Frankfurt early in
> September is uncertain. In the meantime they left their large luggage behind
> at Mainz.

About 10 August the Mozarts sailed by market boat to Frankfurt on Main, where
they stopped at the Golden Lion inn.

SCRATCHED BY LEOPOLD MOZART ON A WINDOW-PANE AT
HIS FRANKFURT LODGINGS, 3 BENDERGASSE

Mozart Maitre de la Musique de la Chapelle de Salzbourg avec Sa Famile
le 12 Aout 1763.

Preserved in the Historisches Museum, Frankfurt.

FROM THE " ORDENTLICHE WOCHENTLICHE FRANCKFURTER FRAG- UND ANZEIGUNGS-NACHRICHTEN ", 16 AUGUST 1763

Avertissement

Lovers of music, and all those who find some pleasure in extraordinary things, are herewith apprized that on Thursday next, 18 August, at Scharf's Hall on the Liebfrauenberg, a concert will be held at 6 o'clock in the evening, at which two children, namely a girl of 12 and a boy of 7, will be heard to play with incredible dexterity concertos, trios and sonatas, and then the boy also the same on the violin. And if this be unheard-of and incredible in such young children and with such power, since the boy is complete master of the keyboard ; so much so that these two children's skill not only astonished the Electoral Courts of Saxony, Bavaria and the Palatinate, but also afforded exceptional entertainment to His Imperial and Royal Majesty during a 4 months' visit to Vienna, and were the object of general wonderment : so we hope the more readily to procure some pleasure to the public of this city ; for we know of no-one in a position to say truthfully that he has ever seen or heard the like from children of such tender years. Further be it known that this will be the only concert, since they are immediately afterwards to continue their journey to France and England. Admission, a small thaler per person.

> Saxon Electoral Court is doubtless an error for Archiepiscopal Court of Salzburg. The concert of 18 August was followed by four others, on 22, 25, 26 and 30 August (*cf.* Karl Woelcke, " Mozart in Frankfurt " in *Alt-Frankfurt* [Frankfurt/Main, 1917], pp. 103-121).

FROM THE HOUSEHOLD BOOKS OF THE IMPERIAL COUNCILLOR JOHANN KASPAR GOETHE

(in Latin)

Frankfurt on Main, 18 August 1763

4 florins, 7 kreutzer for the musical concert of two children.

> Goethe, then aged fourteen, remembered the seven-year-old boy's appearance as late as 1830—his " hair-style " (wig) and his " sword "—much as the little Mozart had been painted (*cf.* 3 February 1830).

FROM THE " ORDENTLICHE WOCHENTLICHE FRANCKFURTER FRAG- UND ANZEIGUNGS-NACHRICHTEN ", 30 AUGUST 1763

Avertissement

The general admiration aroused in the souls of every auditor by the skill, never before either seen or heard to such a degree, of the two children of the Kapellmeister to the Court of Saltzburg, Herr Leopold Mozart, has already entailed a threefold repetition of the concert planned for one single occasion. Indeed, this general admiration and the request of several great connoisseurs and amateurs is the cause of the concert (which, however, will quite definitely be the last) to-day, Tuesday, 30 Aug., in Scharf's Hall on the Liebfrauenberg, at 6 o'clock in the evening ; whereat the girl, who is in her twelfth year, and the boy, who is in his 7th, will not only play on the harpsichord or forte-piano, the former performing the most difficult pieces by the greatest masters ; but the boy will also play a concerto on the violin, accompany symphonies on the clavier, completely cover the manual or keyboard of the clavier, and play on the cloth as well as though he had the keyboard under his eyes ; he will further most accurately name from a distance any notes that may be sounded for him either singly or in chords, on the clavier or on every imaginable instrument including bells, glasses and clocks. Lastly he will improvise out of his head, not only on the pianoforte but also on an organ (as long as one wishes to listen and in all the keys, even the most difficult, that may be named for him), in order to show that he also understands the art of playing the organ, which is entirely different from that of playing the pianoforte. Admission, a small thaler per person. Tickets to be had at the Golden Lion.

Frankfurt City and University Library.—Jahn, Vol. I, p. 33 f.

On 31 August, after a fifth concert in Frankfurt, the Mozarts returned to Mainz, where they remained until mid September.

At midday on 17 September they landed at Coblenz, where they put up at the Three Imperial Crowns inn.

On 21 September the children gave a concert at Coblenz.

They left Coblenz at 10 a.m. on 27 September and reached Bonn in the evening ; their inn was the Golden Carp (Rheinstrasse).

From Bonn they continued their journey on 28 September by way of Brühl (the Annunciation inn) to Cologne (the Holy Ghost, Rheinstrasse).

On 30 September they left Cologne for Aachen (the Golden Dragon).

At 7 a.m. on 2 October they journeyed on from Aachen to Liège, where they arrived at 9 p.m. and stayed at the Black Eagle.

In the evening of 3 October they reached Tirlemont.

On 4 October they lunched at Louvain (the Wild Man inn) and reached Brussels, where they stayed at the Hôtel de l'Angleterre for more than a month.

> Unfortunately not much is known about this long sojourn. On the 4th the Mozarts attended a " free ball " in the theatre. The children appeared on the 7th before the Governor-General of the then Austrian Netherlands, Prince Karl Alexander of Lorraine, a brother of the Emperor Francis I.

In the evening of 15 November the family arrived at Mons, in the evening of the 16th at Bonavis and in the evening of the 17th at Gournay.

At last, at 3.30 p.m. on 18 November, they arrived in Paris, where they remained for five months. They did not stay at the house where the Basle copper-engraver, Christian von Mechel, lived (rue Saint-Honoré, *vis-à-vis* the rue d'Échelle, at the notary Le Noir's) and where they had booked lodgings ; but at the special invitation of the Bavarian Ambassador, Count van Eyck, they immediately came to his house, the Hôtel Beauvais, rue Saint-Antoine (now 68 rue François-Miron). His wife, *née* Countess Arco, was a native of Salzburg.

Mechel must soon afterwards have engraved the well-known group portrait by L. C. de Carmontelle, which shows the two children at the keyboard and the father with his violin, standing. But the engraving is signed by J. B. Delafosse, and it is not so far known how the two engravers divided the work between them.—The Countess van Eyck presented Mozart on the evening of 26 January 1764 with a pocket calendar printed in Liège (in 1892 this was in the possession of Count Viktor Wimpffen, Vienna).

FROM FRIEDRICH MELCHIOR VON GRIMM'S " CORRESPONDANCE LITTÉRAIRE "
(in French)

1 December 1763.

True prodigies are sufficiently rare to be worth speaking of, when you have had occasion to see one. A Kapellmeister of Salzburg, Mozart by name, has just arrived here with two children who cut the prettiest figure in the world. His daughter, eleven years of age, plays the harpsichord in the most brilliant manner ; she performs the longest and most difficult pieces with an astonishing precision. Her brother, who will be seven years old next February, is such an extraordinary phenomenon that one is hard put to it to believe what one sees with one's eyes and hears with one's ears. It means little for this child to perform with the greatest precision the most difficult pieces, with hands that can hardly stretch a sixth ; but what is really incredible is to see him improvise for an hour on end and in doing so give rein to the inspiration of his genius and to a mass of enchanting ideas, which moreover he knows how to connect with taste and without confusion. The most consummate Kapellmeister could not be more profound than he in the science of harmony and of modulations, which he knows how to conduct by the least expected but always accurate paths. He has such great familiarity with the keyboard that when it is hidden for him by a cloth spread over it, he plays on this cloth with the same speed and the same precision. To read at sight whatever is submitted to him is child's play for him ; he writes and composes with marvellous facility, without having any need to go to the harpsichord and to grope for his chords. I wrote him a minuet with my own hand and asked him to put a bass to it ; the child took a pen and, without approaching the harpsichord, fitted the bass to my minuet. You may imagine that it costs him no trouble at all to transpose [*transporter*] and to play the tune one gives him in any key one may ask ; but here is something more I have seen, which is no less incomprehensible. A woman asked him the other day whether he was able to accompany by ear, and without looking at it, an Italian cavatina she knew by heart ; and she began to sing. The child tried a bass that was not absolutely correct, because it is impossible to prepare in advance the accompaniment to a song one does not know ; but when the tune was finished, he asked her to begin again, and at this repeat he not only played the whole melody of the song with the right hand, but with the other added the bass without hesitation ; whereafter he asked [her] ten times to begin again, and at each repeat he changed the style of his accompaniment ; and he could have repeated this twenty times, if he had not been stopped. I cannot be sure that this child will not turn my head if I go on hearing him often ; he makes me realize that it is difficult to guard against madness on seeing prodigies. I am no longer surprised that Saint Paul should have lost his head after his strange vision. M. Mozart's children have excited the admiration of all who have seen them. The Emperor and Empress have overwhelmed them with kindnesses ; and they have already met with the same reception at the Court of Munich and the Court of Mannheim. It is a pity that people are so ignorant of music in this country. The father proposes to go on from here to England, and afterwards to take his children back through lower Germany. . . .

> The Paris *Correspondance littéraire, philosophique et critique adressée à un souverain de l'Allemagne* (1753-90) was circulated in manuscript by Grimm until 1768 and afterwards by Diderot, Mme d'Épinay and Meister ; first collected in 1813, it was published complete by Maurice Tourneux in 1877-82. The letter of 1763 is taken from Vol. V, pp. 410-12, of this edition (Jahn, Vol. III, p. 367 f). A German translation of the letter appeared on 10 October 1821 in the Leipzig *Allgemeine musikalische Zeitung*, later in Nissen's Mozart biography, pp. 46-8. Grimm, a gifted writer from Germany, was at the time secretary to the Duke of Orleans and became Mozart's champion in Paris.— " The Court of Mannheim " refers to the electoral court at Schwetzingen.

FROM FATHER RUPERT VON GUTRATH'S " ANNALES SAN-PETRENSES SEU VARIARUM RERUM NOTABILIUM . . . ANNOTATIO "
(in Latin)

[End of December, 1763]

Just as the noble and most respectable Leopold Mozart, a musician of the Court of Salzburg, has spent some time in foreign parts, travelling at his Highness's expense with the aim of broadening his studies in the art of music, so too the noble and worshipful Anton Cajetan Adlgasser, Court organist, will shortly and to the same end travel to Italy, likewise at His Highness's expense, who will surely acquire the highest praise for himself if he shows similar generosity on behalf of letters, science and the other arts. Meanwhile, regarding Mozart, it should be noted that on his travels he has with him, beside his wife and ten-year-old daughter, who is highly skilled in the musical art, his seven-year-old son, who shows as much skill in the art of playing the organ as many adults, and whose like we have not hitherto seen or heard for expertness in matters musical. This young Apollo is considered a prodigy of nature and art in Vienna, Munich, Augsburg, Strasbourg, Brussels, Paris and other places.

Salzburg, Archives of St. Peter's. MS. A 152, Part iii, p. 239.—Herbert Klein
in the *Mozart-Jahrbuch 1957* (Salzburg, 1958).—Gutrath's baptismal names
were Karl Joseph ; Salzburg, 1732–77, from 1741 at St. Peter's, from 1761 a
Professor at the University.—The Mozarts did not visit Strasbourg on this
journey.

On 24 December the Mozarts went to Versailles for two weeks (see 19 November
1762), where they stayed " au Cormier, rue des bons enfants ".

1764

On New Year's Day 1764 they were present at the court dinner. They were
graciously treated by Louis XV and his consort, Queen Marie Leszczyńska, by the
Dauphin Louis and his consort, Maria Josepha of Saxony, by Madame Adélaïde, the
queen's eldest daughter, and by Madame Adrienne-Catherine de Tessé, lady-in-
waiting to the Dauphine, but Madame de Pompadour behaved haughtily.

The children were given presents by Mme de Tessé and by Marie-Thérèse
Louise de Savoie-Carignan. Wolfgang also performed on the organ in the
court chapel.

On 8 January, at half past 8 in the evening, the Mozarts arrived back in Paris.

FROM FATHER PLACIDUS SCHARL'S " EPHEMERIDES DIURNIAE ",
26 JANUARY 1764
(in Latin)

Herr Hagenauer told me various things about Herr Mozart and sent me
two of his letters.
Cf. 6 January 1763.

FRIEDRICH KARL VON BOSE PRESENTS A BOOK TO WOLFGANG,
PARIS (? JANUARY) 1764

Take, little Orpheus of seven years, this book from the hand of thy
admirer and friend ! Read it often,—and experience its divine songs, and
lend them (in those blessed hours of perception) thy irresistible harmonies ;
so that the unfeeling despiser of religion may read,—and attend !—that he
may hear them—and bow down, and pray to God.
                                    Friedrich Carl, Baron von Bose.

This dedication is quoted in Leopold Mozart's letter to Hagenauer of 1 April
1764. The book in which it was inscribed is lost. It was probably Christian
Fürchtegott Gellert's *Geistliche Oden und Lieder* (Leipzig, 1757), perhaps in the
third edition (Berlin, 1764), containing compositions by C. P. E. Bach.—Bose
was one of two Saxon barons whose journey from Munich to Paris coincided
with that of the Mozarts.

FROM THE " COMPTES DES MENUS PLAISIRS DU ROI", MIDDLE OF
FEBRUARY 1764
(in French)

Sieur Mozart 1200 livres for having had his children perform before the
royal family.

> Paris, National Archives : Maison du roi. O¹2886 : Dépenses des Menus,
> f.47ᵛ.—J. G. Prod'homme, *Mozart raconté par ceux qui l'ont vu* (Paris, 1928), p.
> 52.—1200 livres equalled 50 louis d'or.

In the middle of February Wolfgang suffered seriously from quinsy.

TITLE AND DEDICATION OF OPUS I, PARIS, MARCH 1764
(in French)

Sonatas For the Harpsichord
Which can be played with Violin Accompaniment
Dedicated To Madame Victoire of France
By J. G. Wolfgang Mozart of Salzburg Aged Seven years.
Opus I . . . Paris, at the usual addresses . . .

To Madame Victoire of France
Madame

The attempts I lay before your feet are no doubt mediocre ; but since
Your goodness permits me to adorn them with Your August Name, their
success is in no further doubt, and the Public cannot fail to exercise indulgence
for their seven-year-old Author since he appears under Your auspices.

I could wish, Madame, that the language of Music were that of gratitude ;
I should then be less embarrassed in speaking of the impression which Your
benefits have left on my heart. I shall carry their remembrance to my
country ; and so long as Nature, who has made me a Musician as she makes
the nightingales, shall inspire me, the name of Victoire shall remain engraved
on my memory with the same ineffaceable strokes which mark it upon the
hearts of the French nation.

I am, with the most profound respect,
    Madame,
        Your very humble, very obedient and very small Servant,
                                J. G. Wolfgang Mozart.

> Köchel Nos. 6 and 7. The first of these two sonatas was written at Salzburg,
> Brussels and Paris in 1762-64, the second in Paris during the winter of 1763–64.
> They were engraved together with Op. II in Paris in February 1764 (score and
> violin part), at Leopold Mozart's expense, and sold in London under a common
> title-page. " Mme Vendôme ", named on the Paris title-pages, was in all
> probability Marie Charlotte Vendôme, an outstanding music engraver.
> —The Princess Victoire was the King's second daughter.—The dedication
> was written by Baron Grimm.

On 3 March Sebastian Winter left the family to go to Donaueschingen.
Until 4 March the Mozarts lived with Count van Eyck.

FROM THE "AVANT-COUREUR", PARIS, 5 MARCH 1764
(in French)

It is within the province of our journal to devote itself to extraordinary phenomena.

Herr Mozart, director of the music of H.H. the Prince-Archbishop of Salzburg, has been in this capital for several months with two children who cut the most delightful figure. His daughter, aged eleven, plays the harpsichord in a distinguished manner ; no one could have a more precise and brilliant execution. His son, who this month reached his eighth year, is a veritable prodigy. He has all the talent and all the science of a maître de chapelle. Not only does he perform in a surprising manner the *concertos* by the most celebrated European masters ; but he composes himself. He plays from memory for hours together and, giving rein to the inspiration of his genius, he joins the most valuable ideas to the most profound science of harmony. All those who know about music were in the highest degree surprised to see a child carry out what they would have admired in the most consummate maître de chapelle. This astonishing child may be put to any test. Let him be given a piece without a bass, and let him be asked to write a bass underneath, he will do it without resorting to a harpsichord or a violin, which few composers can do without when they write. Let him be given a violin part, and he will play it on the harpsichord and at once fit the required bass to it ; often he will even add intermediate parts. He will accompany by ear tunes that are sung to him, and he will even vary them on the spot in endless ways. He is so much accustomed to the keyboard that it may be covered with a napkin without this preventing him from playing with the same precision and the same speed.

These children have had the honour of playing several times before Monseigneur the Dauphin, Mme the Dauphine and Mesdames of France, as well as before a large number of distinguished persons, of the Court and of the town. Young Mozart has also had the honour of playing the organ in the royal chapel at Versailles for an hour and a half before this august assembly. . . .

> Paris, Bibliothèque nationale.—*Mozart en France* (Paris, 1956), No. 29. Probably written by Grimm.—The Dauphin was Louis, his consort Maria Josepha of Saxony ; the Princesses were Mmes Adélaïde and Victoire.

On 10 March 1764 the children gave their first concert in Paris, in the private theatre of M. Félix, rue et porte Saint-Honoré.

> The admission ticket cost " a foliage or feather thaler [6 francs], four of which make a *louis d'or* ", according to Leopold Mozart's report to Salzburg. The receipts came to 112 *louis d'or*.

A POEM ON THE MOZART CHILDREN, PARIS (? MARCH) 1764
(in French)

ON THE CHILDREN OF M. MOZART

Mortals belov'd of Gods and Kings,
What pow'r doth harmony possess !
When modulated sounds your playing brings,
What taste, what science do you not profess !
Silence alone can serve to praise you best.
With what emotion doth dead wood vibrate !
With sound and sense dumb things you can invest.
Nothing's impossible to you, O mortals blest,
For touch itself with grace you animate.

This anonymous poem is preserved in a copy by Leopold Mozart, which came
to the Gesellschaft der Musikfreunde from the Viennese collection of Aloys
Fuchs.—Jahn, Vol. II, p. 717.

FROM THE " HOCHFÜRSTLICH-BAMBERGISCHE WOCHENTLICHE FRAG- UND ANZEIGE-NACHRICHTEN ", 30 MARCH 1764

News

Paris, 20 Martii.

[There follows a German translation of the *Avant-Coureur's* report, cf. 5
March 1764.]

The Princess Victoire has been graciously pleased to accept the most submissive dedication of a few sonatas, which are shortly to appear in print,
composed by this master, a child.

At the head stands this address : [there follows a German translation of
the dedication—cf. p. 29 above].

From the State Library, Bamberg.—The first two paragraphs, translated from
L'Avant-Coureur, also appeared on 4 April 1764 in the *Wienerisches Diarium*,
the precursor of the official *Wiener Zeitung*, where, however, the family's
name is printed as " Muzart ". The whole report was also reprinted in 1764
in *Kurzgefasste Historische Nachrichten*, Regensburg.

TITLE AND DEDICATION OF OPUS II, PARIS, APRIL 1764
(in French)

Sonatas for the Harpsichord
Which can Be played with Violin Accompaniment
dedicated to Mme la Comtesse de Tessé,
Lady-in-Waiting to Madame la Dauphine.
By J. G. Wolfgang Mozart of Salzburg Aged Seven years.
Opus II . . . Paris . . .

To Madame la Comtesse de Tessé,
Lady-in-Waiting to Madame la Dauphine.

Madame, Your taste for Music and the kindnesses with which You have loaded me entitle me to devote my feeble talents to You. But since You accept their homage, is it possible that You will forbid a Child the expression of the sentiments of which his heart is full ?

You do not wish me, Madame, to say of You what all the Public says. This severity will diminish the regret I feel in leaving France. If I no longer have the happiness of complimenting You, I am going to a country where at least I may speak as much as I shall wish, both of what You are and of what I owe to You.

I am, with the most profound respect,
        Madame,
                Your very humble and very obedient little servant,
                                J. G. Wolfgang Mozart.

> Köchel Nos. 8 and 9. The first sonata was written during the winter of 1763–1764, the second early in 1764.—Concerning the engraving cf. Op. I (March 1764).—This dedication too was written by Grimm.

The second concert in Paris took place on 9 April 1764 at the Félix theatre. The violinist Pierre Gaviniès and the singer Clémentine Picinelli took part.

On 10 April 1764 the Mozarts left Paris, but the banker Hummel took care of a large part of their luggage during their stay in England.

Not till 23 April did they reach London, via Calais (the 19th), where they left their own carriage, and Dover. They stayed at first at the White Bear inn, Piccadilly, but on the 24th they found lodgings with a barber, John Couzin, in Cecil Court (now No. 19), St. Martin's Lane.

CLAUDE ADRIEN HELVETIUS TO (?) FRANCIS, 10TH EARL OF HUNTINGDON,
LONDON, END OF APRIL 1764
(in French)

Allow me to ask your protection for one of the most singular beings in existence. He is a little German prodigy who has arrived in London these last few days. He plays and composes on the spot the most difficult and the most agreeable pieces for the harpsichord. He is the most eloquent and the most profound composer in this kind. His father's name is *Mozart* ; he is maître de chapelle at Salzburg ; he lodges with this prodigy aged seven with Mr. Couzin, *hare cutter in Cecil Court, St. Martins Lane.* All Paris and the whole French Court were enchanted with this little boy. I do not doubt that the King and the Queen will be charmed to hear him. London is good pasture-land for talent. It is to the Apollo of England that I turn to beg for protection.

> San Marino, California, Henry E. Huntington Library.—*Report on the Manuscripts of the late Reginald Rawdon Hastings*, ed. by Francis Bickley (London, 1934), Vol. III, p. 143 f.—The phrase in italics appears thus in the French original.

On 27 April, from 6 to 9 p.m., they were received by King George III and his consort, Queen Sophia Charlotte, *née* Princess of Mecklenburg-Strelitz. Leopold received 24 guineas for his children's performance.

FROM THE "PUBLIC ADVERTISER", 9 MAY 1764
(in English)

For the Benefit of Sig. GRAZIANI.

HICKFORD's Great Room, in Brewer-Street, Thursday, May 17, will be a Grand Concert of Vocal and Instrumental MUSIC. The Vocal Parts by the Signoras Sartori, Cremonini, and Signor Maziotti. First Violin, and a Concerto, by Sig. Giardini. Concerto and Solo on the Violoncello, by Sig. Graziani. Concerto on the German Flute by Sig. Florio. Concerto on the Harpsichord by Master Mozart, who is a real Prodigy of Nature ; he is but Seven Years of Age, plays any thing at first Sight, and composes amazingly well. He has had the Honour of exhibiting before their Majesties greatly to their Satisfaction. The Whole to conclude with a Full Piece. Tickets, Half a Guinea each, to be had of Sig. Graziani, at the Warwick-street Coffee-house.

> Most of the announcements and notices about the Mozarts published in the London papers in 1764–65 were reprinted in C. F. Pohl's *Mozart und Haydn in London* (Vienna, 1867, Part I : "Mozart in London"), most of them in a German translation only. The original texts have been checked and completed for the present work by Mr. Charles Humphries of the British Museum. Repeated announcements are not cited.—Carlo Graziani was also a composer. Felice de Giardini's opera *Enea e Lavinia* was then in the repertory of the Little Theatre in the Haymarket, of which the famous violinist was the manager. Pietro Grassi Florio was a renowned flautist. The singers were those of the opera-house.

IBID., 17 MAY 1764
(in English)

By Permission of the LORD CHAMBERLAIN.

For the Benefit of Sig. GRAZIANI.

HICKFORD's Great Room, in Brewer-Street, Tuesday Morning, May 22, at Twelve o'Clock, will be a Concert of Vocal and Instrumental MUSIC. The Vocal Parts by the Signoras Sartori, Cremonini, and Signor Maziotti. First Violin, and a Concerto, by Sig. Giardini. Concerto and Solo on the Violoncello, by Sig. Graziani. Concerto on the Harpsichord by Master Mozart, a Boy, who is Seven Years old, and allowed by every body to be a Prodigy for his Age.

** Tickets, 10s 6d each, to be had of Signor Graziani, at Warwick-street Coffee-house.

N.B. Signor Graziani is obliged to postpone his Concert to next Tuesday

M.— 2

Morning, on account of the Opera Band being engaged for that Night ; when Tickets given out for the 13th will be taken on Tuesday next.

> Giardini's opera was again given on 17 May. The date 13 May for the day originally fixed for the concert is clearly wrong.

On 19 May the children performed at court for the second time, Wolfgang also playing the organ. The honorarium was again 24 guineas.

FROM THE "PUBLIC ADVERTISER", 21 MAY 1764
(in English)

By Permission of the LORD CHAMBERLAIN

For the Benefit of Sig. GRAZIANI

HICKFORD's Great Room, in Brewer-Street, To-morrow Morning, May 22, at Twelve o'Clock, will be a Concert of Vocal and Instrumental MUSIC. The Vocal Parts by the Signoras Sartori, Cremonini, and Signor Maziotti. First Violin, and a Concerto, by Sig. Giardini. Concerto and a Solo on the Violoncello, by Sig. Graziani. Concerto on the German Flute by Sig. Florio. I had declared in the Public Advertiser, of May 17, Mr. Mozard, but as he is sick I cannot promise that he will play.

** Tickets, 10s 6d each, to be had of Signor Graziani, at Warwick-street Coffee-house.

> Mozart was unable to appear ; he was probably taken ill on 20 May, but not indisposed for more than ten days.

IBID., 31 MAY 1764
(in English)

At the Great Room in Spring-Garden, near St. James's Park, Tuesday, June 5, will be performed a grand Concert of Vocal and Instrumental MUSIC. For the Benefit of Miss MOZART of eleven, and Master MOZART of seven Years of Age, Prodigies of Nature ; taking the Opportunity of representing to the Public the greatest Prodigy that Europe or that Human Nature has to boast of. Every Body will be astonished to hear a Child of such tender Age playing the Harpsichord in such a Perfection—It surmounts all Fantastic and Imagination, and it is hard to express which is more astonishing, his Execution upon the Harpsichord playing at Sight, or his own Composition. His Father brought him to England, not doubting but that he will meet with Success in a Kingdom, where his Countryman, that late famous Vertuoso Handel, received during his Life-time such Particular Protection. Tickets, at Half a Guinea each ; to be had of Mr. Mozart, at Mr. Couzin's, Hair-Cutter, in Cecil Court, St. Martin's Lane.

> These announcements were evidently written or drafted by Leopold Mozart. Spring Garden is near Charing Cross ; the exhibitions of the Society of Artists were held there at the time.

IBID., I JUNE 1764
(in English)

At the Great Room in Spring-Garden, near St. James's Park, Tuesday, June 5, at Twelve o'Clock, will be performed a grand Concert of Vocal and Instrumental MUSIC.

For the Benefit of Miss MOZART of Eleven, and Master MOZART of Seven Years of Age, Prodigies of Na[ture]. This Method is therefore taken to shew to the Public the greatest Prodigy that Europe or that even Human Nature has to boast of. Every Body will be struck with Admiration to hear them, and particularly to hear a young Boy of seven Years of Age play on the Harpsichord with such Dexterity and Perfection. It surpasses all Understanding or all Imagination ; and it is hard to say whether his Execution upon the Harpsichord, and his playing at Sight, or his own Compositions, are most astonishing. His Father brought him to England, not doubting but that he must meet with Success in a Kingdom, where his Countryman Handel received during his Life-time such particular Protection.

† Tickets, at Half a Guinea each, to be had of Mr. Mozart, at Mr. Couzin's, Hair-Cutter, in Cecil-Court, St. Martin's Lane.

IBID., 4 JUNE 1764
(in English)

AT the Great Room in Spring Garden, near St. James's Park, To-morrow, June 5, at Twelve o'Clock, will be performed a grand Concert of Vocal and Instrumental MUSIC.

For the Benefit of Miss MOZART of Eleven, and Master MOZART of Seven Years of Age, Prodigies of Nature. The Vocal Parts by Signora Cremonini and Sig. Quilici. The First Violin with a Solo by Sig. Barthelemon. Violoncello with a Concerto by Sig. Cyri. Harpsichord and Organ by Miss Mozart and Master Mozart. † Tickets at Half a Guinea each, to be had of Mr. Mozart, at Mr. Couzin's, Hair-Cutter in Cecil Court, St. Martin's Lane.

> On that day the King's birthday was celebrated in London. This induced many members of society to return to the capital after the end of the season, a fact Leopold Mozart had borne in mind in fixing the date of the concert for 5 June.—François Hippolyte Barthélémon and Giovanni Battista Cirri were also composers.

IBID., 5 JUNE 1764
(in English)

By Permission of the Lord Chamberlain.

AT the Great Room in Spring Garden, near St. James's Park, This Day, June 5, at Twelve o'Clock, will be performed a grand Concert of Vocal and Instrumental MUSIC.

For the Benefit of Miss MOZART of Eleven, and Master MOZART of Seven
Years of Age, Prodigies of Nature. The Vocal Parts by Signora Cremonini
and Sig. Quilici. The First Violin with a Solo by Sig. Barthelemon. Violoncello with a Concerto by Sig. Cyri. Harpsichord and Organ by Miss Mozart
and Master Mozart. † Tickets at Half a Guinea each, to be had of Mr.
Mozart, at Mr. Couzin's, Hair-Cutter in Cecil Court, St. Martin's Lane.

> Leopold Mozart's expenses amounted to 20 guineas, but the receipts to 100
> guineas.

FROM THE " WIENERISCHES DIARIUM ", 23 JUNE 1764

When the Vice-Kapellmeister to the Court of Salzburg, Herr Leopold
Mozart, after a sojourn of 5 months in Paris with his two children, left there
for England, the little seven-year-old composer received, apart from the
present the Court had made the two children, a gold snuffbox worth 80
Louis d'or, because of the clavier sonatas composed by him and dedicated to
Madame Victoire of France. To what an astonishing degree, even at the
tenderest age, will taste and an innate urge for fine art of one sort or another
develop.

> It is true that there was a gold snuff-box among the presents received in Paris
> which Leopold Mozart enumerated for his Salzburg friends, but Wolfgang
> had received it from Mme de Tessé before the dedication of his Op. II.

FROM THE " PUBLIC ADVERTISER ", 26 JUNE 1764
(in English)

For the Benefit of a Public useful Charity.

AT RANELAGH HOUSE, on Friday next, will be performed (beside the usual
Entertainments of Music and Singing).

At the End of the third Act, a very favourite Chorus in ACIS and GALATEA :
Oh the Pleasures of the Plains, &c. End of Act Four, The Song and Chorus
in ALEXANDER'S FEAST : Happy Pair, &c. To conclude with the Coronation
Anthem, God save the King, &c. In the course of the Evening's Entertainments, the celebrated and astonishing Master MOZART, lately arrived, a Child
of 7 Years of Age, will perform several fine select Pieces of his own Composition on the Harpsichord and on the Organ, which has already given the
highest Pleasure, Delight, and Surprize to the greatest Judges of Music in
England or Italy and is justly esteemed the most extraordinary Prodigy, and
most amazing Genius that has appeared in any Age.

☞ A Porter belonging to the above deserving Charity, being employed
to distribute Tickets for this Purpose, having lost a large Packet of 800 of
them, it becomes therefore necessary to give this Notice, the Benefit designed
for Wednesday the 27th, is, on that Account, postponed to Friday the 29th
instant, when Tickets for the Oratorio of SAMSON cannot be taken ; but

those Ladies and Gentlemen who have paid for them, are desired to send for fresh Tickets for Friday next. Tickets at 5s. to be had at Arthur's, the Smyrna, and at Ranelagh, each Night of Performance.

' And Christ said unto him, one Thing thou yet lackest, give Charity to the Poor, and thou shalt have Treasure in Heaven.'

It has been thought a Truth, beyond Contradiction, that if the Rich, Affluent, and Compassionate, were more thoroughly acquainted with the Wants and Distresses of the Poor ; if their vast Variety of Miseries and Afflictions were more known to them, it would not be possible in the Nature of Things, for any Person, unless totally divested of every Sympathetic Feeling for their Fellow Creatures, to pass them by indifferently, or as altogether unconcerned for their painful agonizing Sufferings. The Almighty Superintendant of all Things has wisely and providentially imprinted a compassionate Sense of the Misfortunes of others deeply in our Nature ; so that when we once stare them in the Face, we cannot avoid being melted to real Pity, and a Readiness to relieve and comfort. The Success of the above Benefit depends only upon this Heavenly and Godlike Virtue ; which Christ himself says, covers a Multitude of Sins.

> The charitable object of this concert was the Lying-in Hospital, the foundation stone of which was laid in 1765. Ranelagh Gardens were on the Thames at Chelsea. Friday was 29 June. The three oratorios and the Coronation anthem mentioned are by Handel.

On 6 August the Mozarts took up residence with the Randal family in Five Fields Row, on the borders of Chelsea, and stayed there until about 25 September, as Leopold Mozart had fallen dangerously ill on 8 July.

The address is now 180 Ebury Street.

On 25 October the Mozarts were received at Court for the third time.

GRIMM TO ERNST LUDWIG OF SAXE-GOTHA
(in French)
[Paris,] 13 December 1764.

. . . Your Highness has perhaps heard some talk about little children whose talent for music, and particularly for the harpsichord, has been admired by all Paris last winter ; their portrait will be enclosed in the first packet. These children have been in London since last April. Although they arrived much too late, they did well at the beginning ; they were summoned before the Queen two or three times, and the little virtuoso is going to dedicate to her a book of sonatas composed at her command. But the summer is an absolutely dead season in London ; the father has moreover had a serious illness, and thought he would die, and it took him three months to recover. It is therefore a question of recovering this winter the losses sustained during the summer, and the father's plan is to give a subscription concert at each assembly at Mrs. Cornelys's in Soho Square. Now the Duke of York, the King's father, is one of the chief members of this assembly, and if His Royal Highness were to patronize these children, whose name is Mozart, their concert would doubtless be welcomed by the whole assembly and their fortune would be made. As things are, I have the firmest belief that you will have the goodness, Monseigneur, to cause the happiest and best of mothers, the next time she writes to the Princess of Wales, to say a word in favour of these children, and to beg Her Royal Highness to recommend them to her son, the Duke of York.

> *Correspondance littéraire*, Vol. XVI, p. 420 f.—The addressee was Ernst Ludwig, later Duke of Saxe-Gotha and Altenburg, whose mother, Louise Dorothea regularly received Grimm's journal.—Prod'homme, p. 56 f., who quotes this letter, observed that the Duke of York was the King's brother, not his father : *père* should thus read *frère*. (The Duke of York whom Leopold Mozart met with a Prince of Saxe-Gotha at Milan in 1771 was the brother of this Duke, who had died in the meantime.) Teresa Cornelys, properly Imer-Pompeati, an opera singer from Venice, had bought Carlisle House, Sutton Street, off Soho Square in 1760, where from 1764 she organized subscription concerts for the members of society. From 1765 these concerts were managed by Johann Christian Bach and Karl Friedrich Abel.

1765

FROM THE SALZBURG COURT DIARIES, 3 JANUARY 1765

At 6 o'clock in the evening there was a party at Court, in the course of which was performed a small *Cammer-Musique*, composed by the young son of Mozart, the resident Vice-Kapellmeister here, who is at present in London together with his son.

> Friedrich Pirkmayer, " Über Musik und Theater am f.e. salzburgischen Hofe, 1762–1775 " in *Salzburger Zeitung*, 1886, offprint, p. 11.—Martin, *op. cit.*, p. 125.—The music by Wolfgang performed at this time was probably one or another of his Paris sonatas (? K. 7 or 8), played by the tenor Franz Anton Spitzeder, who was also a clavier player, and the violinist Wenzel Hebelt (*cf.* Leopold Mozart's letter to Hagenauer, 27 November 1764).

TITLE AND DEDICATION OF OPUS III, LONDON, 18 JANUARY 1765
(in French)

Six Sonatas for the Harpsichord
which can be played with the accompaniment of Violin, or Transverse
Flute Very humbly dedicated To Her Majesty Charlotte
Queen of Great Britain
Composed by I. G. Wolfgang Mozart Aged eight Years
Opus III. London. Printed for the Author and Sold at his
Lodgings At Mr. Williamson in Thrift Street, Soho.

To the Queen. Madam,

Full of pride and joy at daring to offer a homage to You, I finished these Sonatas in order to lay them at the feet of Your Majesty ; I was, I confess, intoxicated with vanity and ravished with myself when I perceived the Genius of Music at my side.

" Thou art very proud ", he said to me, " of knowing how to write at an age when others are still learning to spell." " I, proud of thy Work ? ", I answered him. " No, I have other causes for vanity. See in me the favourite of the Queen of these Fortunate Isles. Thou deemest that, if she had been born far from the Supreme rank that distinguishes her, her talents would have brought her glory : set upon the throne as she is, She honours and protects them. Let Her permit thee to make her an offering, thou art avid of glory, thou wouldst that all the world should know it ; more philosophical, I entrust my pride to my harpsichord, which becomes a little more eloquent thereby, that is all." " And that eloquence produces Sonatas ! . . . Is it quite certain that I have ever inspired a maker of Sonatas ? "

This provoked me. " Fie, father ", I said to him, " thou speakest like a pedant this morning. . . . When the Queen deigns to listen to me, I surrender myself to thee and I become sublime ; far from Her, the charm grows weak, her August image gives me a few ideas which art then takes charge of and completes. . . . But let me live, and one day I shall offer Her a gift worthy of Her and of thee : for with thy help I shall equal the glory of all the great men of my fatherland, I shall become immortal like Handel, and Hasse, and my name will be as celebrated as that of Bach."

A great burst of laughter disconcerted my noble confidence. Let Your Majesty judge of the patience I need to live with so whimsical a Being ! . . . Did he not also wish me to dare to reproach Your Majesty with that excess of kindness which is the object of my pride and my glory ? I, Madam, reproach You with a fault ? That glorious fault ! Your Majesty will never in a lifetime cure herself of it.

It is said that everything should be allowed to Genius ; I owe mine the happiness of pleasing You, and I forgive it its caprices. Deign, Madam, to receive my poor gifts. You were from the first destined to reign over a free people ; the children of Genius are so no less than the British People ; free above all with their offerings, they take pleasure in surrounding Your throne. Your virtues, Your talents, Your benefactions will for ever live in my memory ; wherever I live, I shall consider myself Your Majesty's subject.

I am, with the most profound respect,
    Madam,
        Your Majesty's
            Very humble and very obedient little servant
                J. G. W. Mozart.

London, 18 January 1765.

Köchel Nos, 10-15, written in 1764, almost entirely in London. It was at
Thrift Street (now 20 Frith Street) that the family settled after their return to
London from Five Fields Row. Williamson was a corset-maker.—The copy
in the Royal Music Library, deposited at the British Museum, also contains the
rare violoncello part, engraved but not mentioned in the original title ; in this
case the words "et d'un Violoncelle" have been added to the title.—The
Bach mentioned is Johann Christian, the "London" Bach.

PROPOSAL OF THE VIENNA COURT CHANCERY, 19 JANUARY 1765
(CONCERNING THE EARLIEST AGE AT WHICH JEWISH CHILDREN SHOULD
BE ALLOWED TO BE BAPTIZED)

. . . as only in the past year certain children, born at Salzburg, were conducted round the world at the age of 7, so experienced in music as even to
compose, which calls for more than a *iudicium discretivum*.

> Gerson Wolf, *Judentaufen in Österreich* (Vienna, 1869), p. 53.—Eduard Hanslick,
> *Geschichte des Concertwesens in Wien* (Vienna, 1869), p. 121.—A. F. Přibram,
> *Urkunden und Akten zur Geschichte der Juden in Wien* (Vienna, 1918), p. 384 f.—
> Maria Theresa decided on 15 February 1765 that Jewish children should not
> be baptized before completion of their seventh year.

FROM THE "PUBLIC ADVERTISER", 6 FEBRUARY 1765
(in English)

For the Benefit of Miss MOZART of Twelve and Master MOZART of Eight
Years of Age ; Prodigies of Nature.

LITTLE Theatre in the Haymarket, Friday, Feb. 15, will be a Concert of
Vocal and Instrumental MUSIC.

Tickets, at Half a Guinea each, to be had of Mr. Mozart, at Mr. Williamson's in Thrift street, Soho.

> The same announcement appeared on 9 February in *The Gazetteer and New
> Daily Advertiser*.

IBID., 14 FEBRUARY 1765
(in English)
HAYMARKET, Little Theatre,

ON Account of Dr. ARNE's Oratorio of JUDITH and the same Reason for
want of some principal Assistants of Performers, Master and Miss MOZART
are obliged to postpone the Concerts which should have been Tomorrow,
the 15th instant, to Monday the 18th instant. They desire that the Nobility
and Gentry will be so kind to excuse them for not performing according to
the Time first proposed.

Tickets to be had of Mr. Mozart, at Mr. Williamson's in Thrift street,
Soho, and at the said Theatre.

Tickets delivered for the 15th will be admitted.

A Box Ticket admits two into the Gallery.

To prevent Mistakes, the Ladies and Gentlemen are desired to send their Servants to take Places for the Boxes, and give in their Names to the Box-keepers on Monday the 18th, in the Afternoon.

> Thomas Augustine Arne's oratorio *Judith* was first performed in the chapel of the Lock Hospital on 29 February 1764.

IBID., 15 FEBRUARY 1765
(in English)

HAYMARKET, Little Theatre,

THE CONCERT for the Benefit of Miss and Master MOZART will be certainly performed on Thursday the 21st instant, which will begin exactly at six, which will not hindering the Nobility and Gentry from meeting in other Assemblies on the same Evening.

Tickets to be had of Mr. Mozart, at Mr. Williamson's in Thrift-street, Soho, and at the said Theatre.

Tickets delivered for the 15th will be admitted.

A Box Ticket admits two into the Gallery.

To prevent Mistakes, the Ladies and Gentlemen are desired to send their Servants to keep Places for the Boxes, and give in their Names to the Box-keepers on Thursday the 21st in the Afternoon.

> An almost identical announcement appeared in *The Gazetteer* for 16 February.

FROM THE " OPRECHTE SATURDAGSE HAERLEMSE COURANT ",
16 FEBRUARY 1765
(in Dutch)

Great Britain, (London, 8 February)

Also arrived here is a composer and master of music of about eight years of age, who is truly a wonder, such as was never known before.

This youngster is a German, named Wolfgang Mozart :

He plays on the harpsichord with incredible precision, not only concertos and sonatas by various masters, but also in a wonderful manner the most difficult Fantasias, worthy of being played by the greatest masters, and entirely by heart. Let only a piece be put before him, and he will vary it and also play it in a different key. Let him be shown an aria, and he will sing it, accompanying himself at the same time, without ever having seen the aria before. Let him be given a piece without a bass, and he will play it effortlessly to the end, adding the bass and the middle part.

On the other hand, if a bare bass part is given him, he will easily complete it with the required melody. And if he is asked to play on the organ, he will play a beautiful fugue or one of the most difficult pieces on it. In short, to what test soever he may be put, he will never fail to convince everybody

M — 2a

of his splendid and inconceivable talent. Furthermore, he writes his own compositions without touching the harpsichord.

He has on three occasions had the honour of playing before Their Majesties, the King and Queen, and has received permission to write six sonatas for the harpsichord with accompaniment for violin and violoncello for her Majesty the Queen, who was not only pleased to accept them but also expressed her royal approbation, after the young composer had played the pieces to Her Majesty. This musical wonder submits boldly to the judgment of all the masters of music and expects of the honesty of their hearts that they will deal justly with him. The whole world must agree that he is an example without precedent, that they should see and hear him in order to be fully and fittingly convinced of his astonishing ability.

Copy in the Enschedé Museum, Haarlem.

FROM THE " PUBLIC ADVERTISER ", 21 FEBRUARY 1765
(in English)

HAYMARKET, Little Theatre

. . . All the Overtures will be from the Composition of these astonishing Composers, only eight Years old. . . .

The wording of the announcement otherwise corresponds with that of 15 February. In an N.B. in *The Gazetteer* of 21 February the error that Nannerl was also a composer is further emphasized : " . . . who are only Eight Years of Age ". Among the " Overtures " performed at this concert, from parts in Leopold Mozart's hand, may have been the " Sinfonia " KE. 19a (formerly K. App. 223), known only from 15 bars of the first violin part.

FROM THE " MERCURE DE FRANCE ", FEBRUARY 1765
(in French)

To be found at the Sieur *Bordet's*, author and music-dealer, Rue Saint-Honoré, facing the Palais Royal, between the Rue Saint Thomas du Louvre and the Quinze-Vingts, at " Modern Music ", two books of harpsichord sonatas composed by *J. G. W. Mazart*, aged seven.

The first work by this child, who was the admiration of all Paris last winter and has since been no less successful in London, contains the sonatas dedicated to *Madame Victoire de France*. The second contains the sonatas dedicated to the Comtesse de *Tessé*. The price of each work is 4 livres 4 sols, but only very few copies remain, the edition being out of print and the plates no longer in France.

Those who would like to join the portrait of the little author to the sonatas will find it at the same address. Price 24 sols. This child-master is seen on it playing the harpsichord, his sister at his side, looking at a sheet of music, and his father behind him, accompanying him on the violin ; the resemblance is perfect. This plate is engraved after the picture by M. *de Carmontelle*.

> G. de Saint-Foix, "Les éditions françaises de Mozart" (*Hommage à L. de La Laurencie*, 1933), p. 249. The advertisement of the new firm of Toussaint Bordet mentions K. 6-9 (referred to as keyboard sonatas) and the engraving of the Paris group portrait.

FROM THE "PUBLIC ADVERTISER", 11 MARCH 1765
(in English)

BY DESIRE

For the Benefit of Master MOZART, of eight Years, and Miss MOZART, of Twelve Years of Age, prodigies of Nature, before their Departure from England, which will be in six Weeks Time.

THERE will be performed at the End of this Month, or the Beginning of April next, a Concert of Vocal and Instrumental MUSIC.

Tickets at Half a Guinea each.

To be had of Mr. Mozart, at Mr. Williamson's in Thrift-street, Soho ; where those Ladies and Gentlemen, who will honour him with their Company from Twelve to Three in the Afternoon, any Day in the Week, except Tuesday and Friday, may, by taking each a Ticket, gratify their Curiosity, and not only hear this young Music Master and his Sister perform in private ; but likewise try his surprising musical capacity, by giving him any Thing to play at Sight, or any Music without Bass, which he will write upon the Spot, without recurring to his Harpsichord.

The Day and Place of the Concert will be advertised in the Public Advertiser eight Days before.

IBID., 20 MARCH 1765
(in English)

NEW MUSIC Extraordinary.

This Day are published, Price 10s 6d.

Dedicated, by Permission, to HER MAJESTY,

SIX SONATAS for the HARPSICHORD, with Accompaniment for a Violin, or German Flute and a Violoncello. Composed by I. G. WOLFGANG MOZART, Eight Years of Age.

Printed for the Author, and sold at his Lodging at Mr. Williamson's in Thrift-street, Soho.

Where may be had, his first Set of Sonatas for the Harpsichord, with Accompaniment for a Violin, &c. Price 6s and a Family Print, Price 2s 6d

Ladies and Gentlemen, who will honour him with their Company from Twelve to Three o'Clock in the Afternoon, any Day in the Week, except Tuesday and Friday, may, by taking each a Book of Sonatas, or a Ticket for his Concert, gratify their Curiosity, and not only hear this young Composer and Music Master and his Sister perform in private, but likewise try his surprising Musical Capacity by giving him any thing to play at Sight, or any Music without Basse, which he will write upon the Spot, without recurring to his Harpsichord.

> *Cf.* 18 January 1765.—Copies of the two Paris books of sonatas, which were given a new joint title-page in London, and of the Paris engraving, were taken home by Leopold Mozart or sent after him. A similar announcement, but without the last paragraph, appeared in *The Gazetteer* of 9 April.

FROM THE "PUBLIC ADVERTISER", 9 APRIL 1765
(in English)

MR. MOZART, the Father of the celebrated young Musical Family, who have so justly raised the Admiration of the greatest Musicians of Europe, intending soon to leave England, proposes, before his Departure, to give to the Public in general an Opportunity of hearing these young Prodigies perform both in public and private, by giving at the End of this Month a CONCERT.

Which will chiefly be conducted by his Son, a Boy of Eight Years of Age, with all the Overtures of his own Composition.

Tickets may be had, at 5s each, of Mr. Mozart, at Mr. Williamson's, in Thrift-street, Soho ; where such Ladies and Gentlemen, who chuse to come themselves, and take either Tickets, or the Sonatas composed by this Boy, and dedicated to her Majesty, (Price 10s 6d) will find the Family at home every Day in the Week from Twelve to Two o'Clock, and have an Opportunity of putting his Talents to a more particular Proof, by giving him any thing to play at Sight, or any Music without a Bass, which he will write upon the Spot without recurring to his Harpsichord.

Notice of the Day, and Place of the Concert, will be given in due Time.

> The same announcement appeared in *The Gazetteer* of 16 April.—Admission this time was only 5s.

IBID., 10 MAY 1765
(in English)

For the Benefit of Miss MOZART of Thirteen, and Master MOZART of Eight years of Age, Prodigies of Nature.

HICKFORD'S Great Room in Brewer Street, Monday, May 13, will be A CONCERT of MUSIC.

With all the OVERTURES of this little Boy's own Composition. . . .

IBID., 13 MAY 1765
(in English)

For the Benefit of Miss MOZART of Thirteen, and Master MOZART of Eight years of Age, Prodigies of Nature.

HICKFORD's Great Room in Brewer Street, this Day, May 13, will be A CONCERT of VOCAL and INSTRUMENTAL MUSIC.

With all the OVERTURES of this little Boy's own Composition.

The Vocal Part by Sig. Cremonini ; Concerto on the Violin Mr. Barthelemon ; Solo on the Violoncello, Sig. Cirii ; Concerto on the Harpsichord by the little Composer and his Sister, each single and both together, &c.

Tickets at 5s each, to be had of Mr. Mozart, at Mr. Williamson's, in Thrift-street, Soho.

> About the " Overtures " *cf.* 21 February 1765. The four-handed concerto was KE. 19d.—For the performers *cf.* 4 June 1764.

IBID., 30 MAY 1765
(in English)

MR. MOZART, the father of the celebrated young Musical Family, who have so justly raised the Admiration of the greatest Musicians of Europe, begs Leave to inform the Public, that his Departure from England is fixed for the Beginning of next Month. Such Ladies and Gentlemen who desire to hear these young Prodigies perform in private, will find the Family at Home at his Lodgings at Mr. Williamson's, in Thrift-street, Soho, every Day in the Week from One to Three o'Clock, and may have an opportunity of putting his Talents to a more particular Proof, by giving him any Thing to play at Sight. The Terms are 5s each Person, or else to take the Sonatas composed by this Boy, and dedicated to Her Majesty (Price 10s 6d) which he had the honour of performing many Times before their Majesties.

In June the Mozarts met Daines Barrington (*cf.* 28 November 1769).

IBID., 8 JULY 1765
(in English)

MR. MOZART, the Father of the celebrated young Musical Family, who have so justly raised the Admiration of the greatest Musicians in Europe, has been obliged by the Desire of several Ladies and Gentlemen to postpone his Departure from England for a short Time, take this Opportunity to inform the Public, that he has taken the great Room in the Swan and Harp Tavern in Cornhill, where he will give an Opportunity to all the Curious to hear these two young Prodigies perform every Day from Twelve to Three. Admittance 2s 6d each Person. He begins To-morrow the 9th instant.

> Pohl, *op. cit.*, p. 134, erroneously has " Swan and Hoop ".

IBID., 9 JULY 1765
(in English)

To all Lovers of Sciences.

THE greatest Prodigy that Europe, or that even Human Nature has to boast of, is, without Contradiction, the little German Boy WOLFGANG

MOZART ; a Boy, Eight Years old, who has, and indeed very justly, raised the Admiration not only of the greatest Men, but also of the greatest Musicians in Europe. It is hard to say, whether his Execution upon the Harpsichord and his playing and singing at Sight, or his own Caprice, Fancy, and Compositions for all Instruments, are most astonishing. The Father of this Miracle, being obliged by Desire of several Ladies and Gentlemen to postpone, for a very short Time, his Departure from England, will give an Opportunity to hear this little Composer and his Sister, whose musical Knowledge wants not Apology. Performs every Day in the Week, from Twelve to Three o'Clock in the Great Room, at the Swan and Harp, Cornhill. Admittance 2s. 6d. each Person.

The Two Children will play also together with four Hands upon the same Harpsichord, and put upon it a Handkerchief, without seeing the Keys.

    This announcement was repeated on 11 July.

THE SECRETARY OF THE BRITISH MUSEUM TO LEOPOLD MOZART
(in English)

Sir. I am ordered by the *Standing Committee* of the Trustees of the British Museum, to signify to You, that they have received the *present of the musical performances of your very ingenious Son* which You were pleased lately to make Them, and to return You their Thanks for the same.

British Museum   *M. Maty*
July 19. 1765   Secretary

    Original in the Mozarteum at Salzburg.—The words printed in italics are inserted by hand in the engraved form.—Leopold Mozart and his children had shortly before visited the Revd Andrew Joseph Planta, the Assistant Keeper of Printed Books, in the British Museum and presented the manuscript of the motet " God is our refuge " (K. 20), which is preserved there, together with the three engraved volumes of sonatas and the Paris group portrait engraved after Carmontelle. For Maty *cf.* 28 November 1769.

FROM THE " HISTORISCH-MORALISCHE BELUSTIGUNGEN DES GEISTES ODER ERMUNTERNDE BETRACHTUNGEN ÜBER DIE WUNDERBARE HAUSHALTUNG GOTTES IN DEN NEUESTEN ZEITEN ", HAMBURG, 1765.

·   ·   ·   ·   ·

§ 2.

A Musical Artist of 7 Years and his Sister of 11 Years.

Curious as the preceding example of nature and art has been, the more curious are the following two. In March 1764 Herr Mozart, Musical Director to His Serene Highness the Archbishop of Salzburg, had been for some months in Paris with two most agreeably cultivated children. His daughter, aged 11, played the clavier to perfection. His son, 7 years of age, represented

a veritable miracle. He had all the knowledge and skill of a Kapellmeister.
He not only performed the concertos of the most celebrated masters in
Europe with such art as to astonish, but he also himself composed. For
whole hours he extemporized, uniting the most rare notions to the most profound science of harmony. All those who have the least idea of what music
is were as if spellbound to find in a child what they would not without
surprise and admiration have seen in the most accomplished Kapellmeister.
This wonderchild could be tried in any manner one desired ; pieces without
a bass were put before him so that he might write it in underneath, which he
did without using clavier or violin, which after all few composers can dispense with when they write. If he were given a violin part, he would play
it on the clavier and immediately add a bass as it should be ; indeed, now
and again he let admirably fitted middle parts be heard as well. Arias sung
to him he accompanied by ear and modified the same in a variety of ways.
His familiarity with the clavier was so great that for him too, as for the preceding musical artist, the keys could be covered with a napkin, without this
preventing him from playing with the same correctness and rapidity. These
children had the honour of playing on several days in succession before the
Dauphin, the Dauphine, the Princesses of France and many other aristocratic
persons of the Court and the town. Likewise had young Mozart the honour
of playing the royal organ at Versailles for an hour and a half, in the presence
of this august company. But is it conceivable that a child of 7 should, thanks
to an adroit dedication, appear in public print ? This young artist had produced some sonatas and himself caused them to be published, and that with
a most submissive dedication to the Princess Victoire, which the latter very
graciously deigned to accept.
      [Here follows the dedication translated into German]
   These children, with their father, remained in France until the end of the
year and then went to England. In the year 1765 the young artist had the
particular honour of playing three times before the King and Queen. The
Queen he presented with six clavier sonatas of his own composition, with
accompaniment of a violin and violoncello, which Her Majesty not only
very graciously accepted, but also caused to be played before her by the
young composer and favoured with her especial royal approbation.

> Part vii.—The original of this periodical can no longer be found in the Hamburg
> libraries.—Jahn (1st ed., Vol. I, pp. 163-5), from a copy formerly owned by
> the Mozart family which had come into the Aloys Fuchs collection in Vienna.
> Cf. Nottebohm, Mozartiana, p. 113 f.—The wonder-child discussed in the
> preceding section was Marie Magdalena Gräf of Mainz, born 1754, who played
> the clavier and the harp at a Frankfurt concert in 1764, sometimes both
> together. She too seems to have played on a covered keyboard, as Wolfgang,
> however, had already done at the Vienna Court in 1762.

On 24 July 1765 the Mozarts left London and spent the night in Canterbury.

From 25 to 30 July they stayed at Bourn Place, near Canterbury, the country seat
of Sir Horace Mann, a nephew of Horace Walpole's friend of the same name.

The night of 30–31 July was spent at Canterbury, where they attended a horse-race.

At 10 a.m. on 1 August they embarked at Dover, and at 1.30 p.m. they reached Calais, where they stayed at the Hôtel d'Angleterre.

On 3 (?) August they reached Dunkirk, having taken to their own carriage again, and lodged " à St.-Catherine ".

On 5 (?) August they arrived at Lille and alighted at the Hôtel de Bourbon, on the Grand' Place. During a month's stay there Wolfgang was taken ill again (quinsy), and so was Leopold after him.

FROM THE " EUROPÆISCHE ZEITUNG ", SALZBURG, 6 AUGUST 1765

London, 5 July 1765. The very famous clavier maker Burkard Thudy [sic] of this city, a Swiss by birth, had the honour of making for the King of Prussia a wing-shaped instrument with two manuals which was very much admired by all who saw it. It has been regarded as particularly note-worthy that Mr. Thudy connected all the stops [*Register*] to a pedal, so that they can be drawn by treading, one after another, and the decrease and increase of tone may be varied at will, which *crescendo* and *decrescendo* has been long wished for by clavier players. Mr. Thudy has moreover conceived the good notion of having his extraordinary instrument played for the first time by the most extraordinary clavier player in this world, namely by the very celebrated master of music Wolfg. Mozart, aged nine, the admirable son of the Salzburg Kapellmeister, Herr. L. Mozart. It was quite enchanting to hear the fourteen-year-old sister of this little virtuoso playing the most difficult sonatas on the clavier with the most astonishing dexterity and her brother accompanying her extempore on another clavier. Both perform wonders !

> No. 63.—The original of this paper (*cf.* 19 July 1763) was not accessible.—Pohl, *op. cit.*, p. 127. Jahn, Vol. I, p. 45. Abert, Vol. I, p. 62 (all incomplete). The quotation in Köchel-Einstein, p. 13, probably wrongly dated, concerns the Paris and London sonatas (K. 6–15).—Franz Josef Hirt, *Meisterwerke des Klavierbaus* (Olten, 1955), p. xvi, quotes the report complete from Georg Kinsky (*Acta Musicologica* [Copenhagen, 1940], Vol. XII, p. 1 f.) and also has a picture of Frederick II's instrument (p. 22), which came to the Kunstgewerbe Museum, Wrocław. *Cf.* W. Rehm, Critical Commentary to the *Neue Mozart-Ausgabe*, IX/24/2, *Werke für Klavier zu 4 Händen*, p. 55 f.—Burkhard Tschudi made this instrument in 1765. It was the first to which he had fitted the newly invented mechanism for changing the registration by means of a pedal (Hirt). —The two children are said to have played it at the concert of 13 May 1765. Kinsky surmised that the report was written by Leopold Mozart and perhaps first printed in the *Augspurgische Postzeitung*.

Emperor Francis I died at Innsbruck on 18 August.

On 4 September the Mozarts travelled from Lille to Ghent, where they arrived in the evening and alighted at the Hôtel Saint-Sébastien on the Place d'Armes. In the afternoon of the 5th Wolfgang played on the organ of the Cistercian monastery.

They left Ghent on 6 September and stayed at Antwerp on the 7th and 8th, where Wolfgang played the organ in the cathedral.

At 6.30 a.m. on 9 September they left Antwerp, where they had to leave their carriage.

By way of Moerdijk they reached Rotterdam at 8 p.m. on the same day ; on the 10th they proceeded by canal, arriving at 7 p.m. at The Hague, where they put up at the Ville de Paris.

The house, which stood on the Nieuwe Markt, was demolished in 1890.

On 12 September Nannerl fell ill with intestinal typhoid. The first concerts at court, on the 12th and 18th, had to be given without her.

> Prince William V of Orange was only seventeen and still under the guardian-ship of Duke Ludwig Ernst of Brunswick, who had been Regent of the Netherlands since 1759. The Prince was the son of Princess Anne, daughter of King George II of England, Handel's pupil, and consort of William IV of Orange. The two concerts took place at the house of his sister, Princess Caroline of Nassau-Weilburg, who was on the brink of a confinement (*cf.* 23 January 1778). Wolfgang played at the Prince's on an unspecified day.

FROM THE " LEYDSE COURANT ", 20 SEPTEMBER 1765
(in Dutch)

The celebrated musician J. G. Wolfgang Mozart of Salzburg is here at the moment, who is but eight years of age and most marvellously performs the most difficult concertos and solos by the most famous masters, as well as several of his own. This young musician has exhibited his excellent talents at the Court of the Stadholder and in other places, exciting the admiration and earning the applause of all.

> D. F. Scheurleer, *Mozart's verblijf in Nederland* (The Hague, 1883), p. 62, quotes from the Leyden *Courant* in Dutch. William V did not become hereditary Stadholder of the seven Netherlands Provinces until 1766.

FROM THE " 'S-GRAVENHAEGSE VRIJDAGSE COURANT ", 27 SEPTEMBER 1765
(in Dutch)

By permission, Heer Mozart, Capel-Meester to the Prince Archbishop of Salzburg, will have the honour of giving, on Monday, 30 September 1765, a Grand Concert in the hall of the " Oude Doelen " at The Hague, at which his son, only 8 years and 8 months old, and his daughter, 14 years of age, will play concertos on the harpsichord. All the overtures will be from the hand of this young composer, who, never having found his like, has had the approbation of the Courts of Vienna, Versailles and London. Music-lovers may confront him with any music at will, and he will play everything at sight.   Tickets cost 3 florins per person, for a gentleman with a lady 5.50 fl. Admission cards will be issued at Heer Mozart's present lodgings, at the corner of Burgwal, just by the " City of Paris ", as well as at the " Oude Doelen ".

Scheurleer, *op. cit.*, p. 63.

On 21 October Nannerl was given extreme unction.

A week after Nannerl's recovery, on 15 November, Wolfgang in turn was taken ill with intestinal typhoid ; he remained in danger for nearly two months.

1766

FROM THE " 's-GRAVENHAEGSE VRIJDAGSE COURANT ", 17 JANUARY 1766
(in Dutch)

By permission, Heer MOZART, Capel-Meester to the Prince Archbishop of Salzburg, will have the honour of giving, on Wednesday, 22 January 1766, a grand concert at the " Oude Doele " at The Hague, at which his little son, 8 years and 11 months of age, and his daughter, aged 14, will play concertos on the harpsichord.   All the overtures will be from the hand of this young composer, who, never having found his like, has had the approbation of the Courts of Vienna, Versailles and London.   Admission is 3 gulden per person, for a gentleman with a lady 1 ducat.   Tickets are issued at Heer Mozart's lodgings at the house of Monsr. Eskes, master watchmaker, on the Hof-Spuy, The Hague, where the " Court of Utrecht " is situated.

Scheurleer, *op. cit.*, p. 80a.

IBID., 20 JANUARY 1766
(in Dutch)

By permission, the children of Heer Mozart will have the honour of giving a grand concert on Wednesday, 22 January 1766 at the " Oude Doelen " at The Hague, at which his little son, 8 years and 11 months of age, and his daughter, aged 14, will play concertos on the harpsichord.   All the overtures will be from the hand of this young composer, who, never having found his like, has had the approbation of the Courts of Vienna, Versailles and London. Admission is 3 gulden per person, for a gentleman with a lady 1 ducat. Tickets are issued at Heer Mozart's lodgings at the house of Monsr. Eskes, master watchmaker, on the Hof-Spuy, The Hague, where the " Court of Utrecht " is situated, and also at the " Oude Doele ".

Scheurleer, *op. cit.*, p. 80b.

FROM THE "AMSTERDAMSCHE DINGSDAGSCHE COURANT",
21 JANUARY 1766
(in French)

Sieur Mozart, Kapellmeister to the Prince-Archbishop of Salzburg, will have the honour of giving, on Wednesday, 29 January 1766, a grand Concert at the hall of the Riding-School in Amsterdam, at which his Son, aged 8 years and 11 months, and his Daughter, aged 14, will perform Concertos on the Harpsichord. All the Overtures will be of the Composition of this little Composer, who, never having found his like, was the Admiration of the Courts of Vienna, Versailles & London. Music-lovers may submit Music to him at will; he will perform everything from the open Book. The Price is 2 florins per Person. Tickets will be distributed at J. J. Hummel's, Music Dealer, on the Vygendam. Will the Gentry kindly procure tickets, because no Money will be received at the Door.

> Scheurleer, *op. cit.*, p. 93.—The Amsterdam newspapers, whose advertisements appeared in French, are preserved in the Oud-archief der gemeente Amsterdam.—Vygendam, properly Vijgendam, means "Fig Dam".—A similar announcement appeared in the *Haerlemse Courant* for 22 January.

About 26 January 1766 the Mozarts moved from The Hague to Amsterdam, where they lodged at the Golden Lion inn, Warmoesstraat.

FROM THE "AMSTERDAMSCHE DINGSDAGSCHE COURANT",
28 JANUARY 1766
(in French)

Sieur MOZART . . . will have the honour of giving, on Wednesday, 29 January 1766, a grand Concert . . . at which his Son and his Daughter, the one aged 8 years & 11 months, the other aged 14, will perform Concertos on the Harpsichord. All the Overtures will be of the Composition of this little Composer, who, never having found his like, was the Admiration of the Courts of Vienna, Versailles and London. Music-lovers may submit pieces of Music to him at will, which he will perform entirely from the open Book.

The Price per Person is two florins. The public is requested to obtain its tickets at Sieur Mozart's lodgings at the Golden Lion in the Warmoestraat, or from J. J. Hummel, on the Vygendam. No Money will be received at the entrance to the Hall. N.B. They will play with four hands on a Harpsichord.

> Scheurleer, *op. cit.*, p. 80.—A similar announcement appeared the same day in the *Haerlemse Courant*.—At the concert of 29 January the Symphony in B♭ major (K. 22), written at the end of December, may have been performed and conducted by Wolfgang.

FROM THE "AMSTERDAMSCHE DONDERDAGSCHE COURANT",
20 FEBRUARY 1766
(in French)

The universal Contentment & Satisfaction given by the Children of Sieur
MOZART has induced the Lovers of Music to desire a second Concert, which
will be held on Wednesday, 26 February, at the Hall of the Riding-School.
Tickets, at 2 fl. per Person, to be had at the said M. Mozart's, at the Golden
Lion in the Warmoestraat, & at Hummel's, on the Vygendam.

Scheurleer, *op. cit.*, p. 98 f.

FROM THE "AMSTERDAMSCHE DINGSDAGSCHE COURANT",
25 FEBRUARY 1766
(in French)

By request, the Children of Sieur Mozart will have the Honour of giving
a Second Concert on Wednesday, 26 February, at the Hall of the Riding-
School, at which these two Children will not Only Perform Concertos To-
gether on different Harpsichords, but also on the same with 4 hands, and the
Son will Play at the End on the Organ his own Caprices, Fugues and Other
Pieces of the most profound Music. The Price is 2 Florins per Person.
Tickets may be had of Sieur Mozart, at the Golden Lion in the Warmoes-
straat, and of Hummel, on the Vygendam, where is sold Opus 1, 2 & 3,
Sonatas for the Harpsichord with Accompaniment of a Violin, Composed
by this little Composer. No Money will be received at the Entrance to the
Hall.

> Scheurleer, *op. cit.*, p. 99.—The "Caprices" were probably identical with the
> "Capricci" repeatedly mentioned by Constanze Mozart in about 1800; they
> were contained in a lost music-book of Wolfgang's (*cf.* K. 32a).

At the beginning of March the Mozarts returned to The Hague, where they again
took lodgings with the watchmaker Eskes, 44 Spui.

FROM THE "'S-GRAVENHAEGSE VRIJDAGSE COURANT", 7 MARCH 1766
(in Dutch)

Of the music-dealers J. J. Hummel in Amsterdam, on the Vijgendam, and
B. Hummel, at The Hague, in the Spuystraat, are to be had to-morrow:
1. A Dutch Song on the Installation of His Serene Highness Willem V,
Prince of Orange &c. &c. &c. Set to music by C. E. *Graaf*, and furnished
with eight artful variations by the celebrated young composer *J. G. W.
Mozart*, aged 9, at 12 stivers. 2. The words of the Cantata by C. E. *Graaf*,
to be sung in Italian on 8 March on the occasion of the Installation of His
Serene Highness, with French and Dutch translations, at 6 stivers. And *3.*

the well-known ditty *Wilhelmus van Nassau &c.*, varied for the clavier by the aforesaid young *Mozart*, at 6 stivers.

> Scheurleer, *op. cit.*, p. 126.—An identical announcement appeared in the *Haerlemse Courant* for 8 March. On that day occurred the solemn installation of the Prince, who was now eighteen and declared of age. There was an "astonishing illumination", as Leopold Mozart reported to Salzburg. The festivities lasted from 7 to 12 March.—The variations on a song by the Court Kapellmeister Christian Ernst Graaf (actually Graf) are K. 24, those on the Dutch national hymn K. 25. This tune was also used by Wolfgang for the final fugue of the quodlibet, *Galimathias musicum* (K. 32), written in March 1766.

On 11 March the children performed at court.

> On this occasion the above-mentioned quodlibet may have been performed, and certainly the two sets of variations.

At the end of March the family left The Hague. Early in April they stayed at Haarlem, where they lodged at the Golden Fleece. Joannes Enschedé presented Leopold with the finely printed Dutch edition of the latter's *Violinschule*. Wolfgang played on the great organ. The next stage was Amsterdam once more, where the Mozarts again stayed at the Golden Lion.

> The *Violinschule* had already been presented to the Prince during the festivities at The Hague, but was not advertised in the *Haerlemse Courant* until 13 May (*Mozart in Haerlem* [1956], p. 31). It was then stated that "the name of Mozart and his two children, especially the little son aged nine, this prodigy of music, is sufficiently known".

FROM THE "AMSTERDAMSCHE DINGSDAGSCHE COURANT", 15 APRIL 1766
(in French)

The Children of Sieur Mozart will have the honour of giving A Concert on Wednesday, 16 April, at the Hall of the Riding-School. These two children will perform Concertos together not only on different Harpsichords, but also on the same at four hands. The Price per Person is two Florins. Tickets may be had of Sieur Mozart, at the Golden Lion in the Warmoestraat, and of Hummel, on the Vygendam.

> Scheurleer, *op. cit.*, p. 139 (incomplete).

FROM THE "'S-GRAVENHAEGSE WOENSDAGSE COURANT", 16 APRIL 1766
(in Dutch)

By B. Hummel, in the Spuystraat at The Hague, and by J. J. Hummel, on the Vygendam in Amsterdam, are published today : Six new Sonatas for the Clavier, with Violin Accompaniment, *i.e.* Opus 4, by the celebrated young composer J. G. Wolfgang Mozart, nine years of age ; the price is 3 florins.

> Scheurleer, *op. cit.*, p. 125 (erroneously dated 16 March).—These sonatas (K. 26-31), composed in February, were dedicated to the Princess Caroline of

Nassau-Weilburg as " Op. IV ". The publishers Burchard and Johann Julius
Hummel were brothers.

FROM THE MINUTES OF THE COLLEGIUM MUSICUM ULTRAJECTINUM [UTRECHT]
(in Dutch)

18 April. Monsieur Mozart, Virtuoso, having asked the college for the
use of the orchestra and instruments, has been granted this after deliberation
according to old usage and custom.

Jahn, Vol. II, p. 834 (revised).

PRESENTATION OF CLAVIER SONATAS BY GEORG BENDA TO THE MOZART CHILDREN, 18 APRIL 1766
(in French)

Monsieur Kuhlman presented them to Monsieur Mozart's Children as a
token of Remembrance on their departure from Amsterdam today, 18
April 1766.

> Copy in the National Library, Vienna.—Benda's " Sei Sonate per il Cembalo
> solo " had been published in Berlin in 1757 by Georg Ludwig Winter.—Herr
> Kuhlmann, on whom no further information could be discovered in Holland,
> is mentioned in Leopold Mozart's travel diary and in his letter to Hagenauer
> dated Paris, 16 May 1766 ; he had forwarded the Hague Mozart editions to
> Salzburg.—Mozart himself later came to value Benda's melodramas *Medea* and
> *Ariadne auf Naxos*, and wrote to his father (12 November 1788) that " among
> the Lutheran Kapellmeisters Benda was always my favourite ".

On 18 April the Mozarts left Amsterdam for Utrecht, again in their own carriage,
and alighted at the Plaets-Royal hotel in the Minnebroederstraat.

FROM THE " UTRECHTSCHE COURANT ", 18 APRIL 1766
(in Dutch)

Sieur *Mozart*, Capelmeester of His Highness the Prince-Archbishop of
Salzburg, will have the honour of giving a grand *Concert* next Monday
afternoon, 21 April, in the music-room of the Vreeburg at Utrecht, at which
his little son, aged 9, and his daughter, aged 14, will perform sonatas and
concertos on the harpsichord. All the symphonies will be of the composition
of this little composer, who has won the admiration of the Courts of Vienna,
France, England and Holland. Price for a gentleman with a lady 3 gulden
and for a single person 2 gulden. The tickets are to be had of the aforesaid
Sieur *Mozart*, who lodges with Sieur *Mos* in the Plaets-Royal, Utrecht.

> Copy in Gemeente Archief, Utrecht.—P. T. A. Swillens, " Mozart in
> Utrecht " in *Mens & Melodie* (Utrecht), December 1955, p. 386.—The concert
> took place on 21 April.

FROM THE " DIARIUM PATRIS BEDAE HÜBNER ORDINIS SANCTISSIMI PATRIS
BENEDICTI IN ANTIQUISSIMO MONASTERIO AD SANCTUM PETRUM
APOSTOLUM SALISBURGI PROFESSO AC SACERDOTE INDIGNISSIMO ",
26 APRIL 1766

I cannot forbear to remark, by way of diversion, that in the town of
Salzburg there are very many people of fame and renown, who, however,
are not appreciated here, since no prophet is acceptable to his own country,
whereas elsewhere people are never at an end of marvelling and in every
place would wish to have such artists as Salzburg possesses.   And most
famous of all is a certain Mozart, who is *de facto* Vice-Kapellmeister here,
and has two little children, a boy and a girl.   This Mozart has already
travelled almost all over Europe with his children, and although the father
himself is an excellent musician, especially on the violin, he nevertheless
seldom appears himself, or indeed never, but only his children, who are to
be called veritable wonders of the world.   The girl, with her 11 years, and
the boy with 7, are such virtuosi on the clavier that the world can only stand
amazed at it.   The boy is an accomplished composer who, during the time
he was in Paris, himself composed such beautiful, artful and precious music
for a certain festivity of the Dauphiness, that not only the whole Parisian
Court but the whole world was amazed thereat, the more so as all the music
at once appeared in public print in Paris.   Dear God, it is incredible how far
all the sciences have advanced !   A boy of seven years to be such an
artist in music already, that even the most excellent in Paris freely admitted
that they did not dare to enter into competition with this boy in music :
and there is no saying how much money this Leopold Mozart may be
gaining in the world with his son Wolfgang and his little daughter, who
plays the clavier even more brilliantly than her small brother : the most
valuable honours and presents he has obtained everywhere at all the
Courts : and every moment one has learned from the publicly printed newspapers about these children, where Herr Mozart now was with them, and
how the world could not sufficiently wonder over them : this is already the
third year that they are absent from here, they have already been in England
and France, and now they are staying in Holland, because the Dutch Republic
invited them to Holland at its own expense.

    Salzburg, St. Peter's Abbey Library : MS. b VIII, 36, p. 452.—Herbert Klein
in *Mozart-Jahrbuch 1957* (Salzburg, 1958), p. 174 f.—Hübner was Librarian of
St. Peter's and secretary to his uncle, the Abbot Beda Seeauer.

At the end of April the Mozarts left Utrecht and travelled to Brussels by way of
Moerdijk, Antwerp and Malines. In Antwerp the children gave a concert on the 30th.

On 8 May they arrived in Brussels and spent Ascension Day there.

At 9 a.m. on 9 May they left Brussels for Valenciennes, where they arrived at 8 p.m.

On 10 May they returned to Paris via Cambrai, arriving in the evening and putting
up at the bath proprietor Brie's in the rue Traversière facing rue Clos Georgeot.

From 28 May to 1 June they stayed at Versailles, again lodging " au Cormier ".

They left Paris about 8 p.m. on 9 July.

> Not much is known about this second visit of the family to Paris (*cf.* Grimm's letter of 15 July below). It was at this time that Michel-Barthélemy Ollivier's picture in oils (Louvre, Paris) was painted, which shows Wolfgang at the harpsichord in the drawing-room of Louis-François de Bourbon, Prince de Conti, in the midst of a large tea-party—and therefore looking very small.

On 12 (?) July the Mozarts reached Dijon, where they remained for a fortnight.

FROM GRIMM'S " CORRESPONDANCE LITTÉRAIRE "

(in French)

[Paris] 15 July 1766

We have just seen again here the two lovable children of M. Mozart, maître de chapelle to the Prince-Archbishop of Salzburg, who had such a great success during their visit to Paris in 1764. Their father, having spent nearly eighteen months in England and six months in Holland, has just brought them back here, to return hence by way of Switzerland to Salzburg. Whereever these children have stayed awhile, they have won everyone's approval and caused astonishment among the connoisseurs. They were dangerously ill at The Hague ; but their good star at last delivered them both from the illness and from the doctors. Mlle Mozart, now thirteen years of age, and moreover grown much prettier, has the most beautiful and most brilliant execution on the harpsichord. Her brother alone is capable of robbing her of supremacy. This marvellous child is now nine years old. He has hardly grown at all ; but he has made prodigious progress in music. He was already a composer and the author of sonatas two years ago. He has since had six engraved in London, for the Queen of Great Britain. He has published another six in Holland for the Princess of Nassau-Weilburg. He has composed symphonies for full orchestra which have been performed and generally applauded here. He has even written several Italian arias, and I have little doubt that before he has reached the age of twelve, he will already have had an opera performed at some Italian theatre. Having heard Manzuoli in London all one winter, he profited so well from this, that although his voice is excessively weak, he sings with as much taste as soul. But what is most baffling of all is the profound knowledge of harmony and its most recondite progressions which he possesses to a supreme degree, and which caused the Hereditary Prince of Brunswick, a very competent judge in this matter, as in many others, to say that many Kapellmeisters who have reached the summit of their art will die without ever knowing what this child of nine knows. We have seen him for an hour and a half on end withstand the assaults of musicians, and while they sweated blood and had the hardest struggle in the world to keep even with him, the child came out of the combat unfatigued. I have seen him at the organ, disconcerting and silencing

organists who thought themselves very highly skilled.   In London Bach took
him between his knees and they played alternately on the same keyboard
for two hours together, extempore, before the King and the Queen.   Here he
went through the same trial with M. Raupach, an able musician who was for
a long time in St. Petersburg and who improvises in a very superior manner.
One could talk interminably about this singular phenomenon.   He is, moreover, one of the most lovable of creatures imaginable, who puts wit and
spirit into everything he says and does, with all the grace and sweetness of
his age.   He even reassures one with his gaiety against the fear that so premature a fruit might fall before it has come to maturity.   If these children live,
they will not remain at Salzburg.   Before long monarchs will vie for their
possession.   The father is not only a gifted musician, but a man of sense and
good nature, and I have never seen a man of his profession who united so
much talent to so much merit.

> *Correspondance littéraire*, Vol. VII, p. 81 f.—Jahn, Vol. II, p. 722 f., mistakenly
> quotes the letter, following Nannerl's account, as from a Paris "journal
> de cabinet".—German translation in Nissen, pp. 112-14.—Giovanni Manzuoli
> of Florence was a famous male soprano, who had given Wolfgang free singing-
> lessons in London.—Karl Wilhelm Ferdinand, heir to the Duchy of Brunswick,
> who was on a visit to France, was an admirable violinist.—The "London"
> Bach, Johann Christian, had a great influence on Wolfgang's musical develop-
> ment.—Hermann Friedrich Raupach of Stralsund, who composed operas and
> chamber music, was only temporarily in Paris (*cf*. K. 37, 39 and 41).

ANNOUNCEMENT OF THE CONCERT AT DIJON
(in French)

BY PERMISSION
Of H.S.H. Monseigneur
LE PRINCE DE CONDÉ.

WHO WILL HONOUR THE CONCERT WITH HIS PRESENCE

The Sieur Mozart, Master of the Music in the Chapel of the Prince-
Archbishop of Salzburg, will have the honour of giving to-morrow, 18 July
1766,

A GRAND CONCERT
IN THE ASSEMBLY ROOM OF THE TOWN HALL,

at which his Son, aged 9 years, & his Daughter of 14, will perform Concertos
on the Harpsichord composed by the greatest Masters.   They will also perform Concertos on two Harpsichords, & Pieces together on the same for
four hands.

He will sing an air of his own composition, & all the Overtures will be
by this young Child, a great Composer, who, never having found his
match, has excited the admiration of the Courts of Versailles, of Vienna &

of London. Music-lovers will, if they wish, be able to submit to him any
Music, and he will play everything from sight.

To begin at eight o'clock.

The charge is 3 livres.

Dijon, Municipal archives.—*Mozart en France* (Paris, 1956), No. 61 (facsimile
on Plate VII).—Louis-Joseph de Bourbon, Prince de Condé, had invited the
Mozarts to Dijon, where an assembly of the Burgundian Estates was being held.

On 26 (?) July the Mozarts reached Lyons, where they remained for four weeks.

FROM THE " PETITES AFFICHES ", LYONS, 13 AUGUST 1766

(in French)

This evening at the Grand Concert will be performed *L'Acte d'Hilas* by
M. de Bury, sung by Mme Charpentier and M. Lobreau.

M. J. G. Wolfgang Mozart, a child of nine years, composer and master of
music, will perform several pieces for harpsichord alone.

The concert will conclude with *L'Acte de la Danse des Talents lyriques*, by
M. Rameau.

Lyons, Bibliothèque de la Ville.—Prod'homme, *op. cit.*, p. 75.—*Mozart en
France* (Paris, 1956), No. 63.—The concert was one of the series that took place
every Wednesday in the hall on the Place des Cordeliers, opposite St. Bona-
ventura's church.

JOHANN RUDOLF FORCART TO ISAAC ISELIN AT BASLE

(in French)

Lyons, 15 August 1766.

Sir and very dear Brother-in-Law

. . . There is here M. Mozart, maître de chapelle to the Prince of Salzburg, who is touring Europe with his son and his daughter, who are prodigies
on the harpsichord ; you may perhaps remember having read about it in
the Basle Gazette some years ago, at the time he was in Paris ; the son is 9
years old and the daughter 14. They gave a concert here in the last few
days, at which they played the most difficult pieces, and all the symphonies
that were played were of the composition of this little *virtuosus*, and he pre-
luded for a quarter of an hour with the most skilled local master, yielding in
nothing to him ; in short, he must be seen to be believed, just as the poster
announced, and truly I was enchanted by him like everyone else ; there were
more than 300 persons at this concert at 3 livres a head, for they say that he
earned nearly 1,000 livres that day. If by any chance he should be tempted
to go to Basle, he would not earn as much as that, although in proportion
there are more people there able to afford it than there are here.

Basle, State Archives.—Lucas A. Staehelin, " Neues zu Mozarts Aufenthalten in
Lyon, Genf und Bern ", in the *Schweizerische Musikzeitung* (Zürich), February
1956, p. 46.—The writer was a ribbon manufacturer of Basle, the recipient his

brother-in-law, the well-known philanthropist.—The report on the Mozart children in a Basle newspaper has not been traced so far.

On 20 August the Mozarts arrived at Geneva, where they remained until 10 (?) September.

They probably stayed at the Hôtel Balance.—The dates for the Swiss sojourn in Max Fehr's pamphlet (*Die Familie Mozart in Zürich*, Zürich, 1942) differ somewhat from those given here, which are based on L. Caflisch's study of 1952 (in Caflisch & Fehr, *Der junge Mozart in Zürich*).

GABRIEL CRAMER TO JOHANN RUDOLF SINNER
(in French)

Geneva, 5 September 1766.

We have here a young German who is strongly recommended to me from Paris, nine years of age ; he plays the harpsichord as it has never been played ; he reads everything at sight in a moment ; he composes instantly on every possible theme ; with all that he is gay, child-like, high-spirited, in short one dare not describe him for fear of not being believed.

Berne, Burgerbibliothek. Staehelin, *op. cit.*, p. 46.—Cramer was Voltaire's publisher ; Sinner, Sieur de Ballaigues, was a librarian.

On 11 September the Mozarts reached Lausanne, where they remained for seven days ; the children gave concerts on the 15th and 18th.

At Lausanne they met, among others, the music-loving Prince Ludwig Eugen of Württemberg, brother of the Duke Karl Eugen, and the famous physician Tissot (see 11 October 1766).

On 19 or 20 September the family went on to Berne, where they remained for a week.

FRANÇOIS MARIE AROUET DE VOLTAIRE TO MADAME LOUISE D'ÉPINAY
(in French)

Ferney, 26 September 1766.

. . . Your little Mazar, Madame, chose, I am afraid, a rather unfavourable time to bring harmony into the temple of Discord. You know that I live two leagues from Geneva : I never go out ; and I was very ill when this phenomenon shone on the black horizon of Geneva. In short, he has left, to my great regret, without my having seen him. I cheered myself up by having comic operas played in my little theatre at Ferney during my convalescence ; the whole company from Geneva, to the number of fifty, was kind enough to give me this pleasure.

Voltaire, *Œuvres*, ed. Garnier, Vol. XLIV, p. 452 f.—The Mozarts had intended to visit Voltaire from Geneva at the Château de Ferney, with recommendations from Madame d'Épinay, Grimm's mistress (*cf.* 7 July 1770), and the encyclopedist Damilaville (see 7 November 1766), both Paris acquaintances.

HANS CONRAD OTT, ACTUARY OF THE COLLEGIUM MUSICUM IN ZÜRICH, CIRCULATES A MINUTE, 30 SEPTEMBER 1766

Insomuch as a few days ago the young Herr Mozart, a 9-year-old virtuoso in Composition and at the keyboard, who has won fame at the first courts of Europe and has been marvellously extolled in various papers and journals, together with his 14-year-old sister, who also plays the clavier, and their father, Herr Kapellmeister Mozart of Salzburg, arrived here : the Worshipful Collegium, meeting in the Music-room, permits them, at their request and upon the presentation of good references, to perform publicly on the coming Tuesday the 7th and Thursday the 9th of October in the said Music-room. The Worshipful Collegium moreover deems it proper and incumbent upon them to inform thereof those of Your Excellencies who have upon previous occasions shown yourselves patrons and lovers of Music, and to invite Your Excellencies graciously to honour the Collegium with your presence, if it so please you. Wherefore the Steward, Herr Meister, is instructed on behalf of our distinguished members to present this written invitation to all highly respected lovers of music with due and seemly deference.

Passed Tuesday 30 September 1766. Present : Guildmaster Werdmüller and other members of the Collegium in the Music-room.

Ott, Actuary.

Caflisch and Fehr, *op. cit.*, p. 9, with facsimile.—Hans Jakob Meister, a musician, was " Stubenverwalter " (steward) of the Collegium ; Hans Caspar Werdmüller was Quaestor, later President.—The programmes of these concerts are not known.

By way of Baden in Aargau they arrived at Zürich in the evening of 28 (?) September, staying until 10 October.

They probably stayed at the Sword on the Weinplatz. At the music-room on the Limmat the children each gave a concert, on 7 and 9 October (*cf.* November 1766).

SALOMON GESSNER'S DEDICATION OF HIS " SCHRIFTEN " TO THE MOZART FAMILY

Take, most valued friends, this present with the same friendship with which I give it to you, and may it be worthy of keeping my memory ever alive with you ! Continue long to enjoy, honourable parents, the fairest fruits of education in the happiness of your children : may they be as happy as their merits are extraordinary. At the tenderest age they are the pride of the nation and the admiration of the world. Fortunate parents ! fortunate children ! Do not, any of you, ever forget the friend whose high regard and love for you will remain as lively all his life as it is today.

Zürich, 3 October 1766.

S. Gessner.

Salzburg, Mozarteum (*cf.* Estate documents, List of books 13).—Facsimile in Fehr, *op. cit.*, facing p. 16, with the attestation of Nannerl's son, Leopold von Berchtold zu Sonnenburg. Apart from the edition in 4 volumes of S. Gessner's *Schriften*, published in 1765 with four title vignettes and twenty-four others, by the author's hand, the Mozarts received among other things Christoph Martin Wieland's *Poetische Schriften* with similar copper engravings, all published by " Orell, Gessner u. Comp.".—In the collection *Zürichs musikalische Vergangenheit im Bild* (Zürich, 1945), a drawing by Gessner is reproduced on Plate 28, supposed to represent Wolfgang at a party with his violin.

FROM THE " DONNSTAGS-NACHRICHTEN ", ZÜRICH, 9 OCTOBER 1766

From Herren Orell, Gessner and Co., below the Cobblers' Guild hall are to be had :

An engraving, wherein the celebrated Mozart family, at that time visiting the city, is portrayed. Herr Mozart, the father, stands leaning against the chair on which his 9-year-old son sits at the clavier ; beside him stands Mlle Mozart, his sister. This well executed portrait is signed by the very same artist who made the engraving of the Calas family. For a cash payment of 30 kreuzer.

Caflisch and Fehr, *op. cit.*, p. 11 f., with facsimile.—The engraving is the one made in Paris in 1764 by Delafosse after Carmontelle, which Leopold Mozart sold everywhere on this journey.—Carmontelle had also portrayed the Huguenot Calas family, of whom the father, Jean Calas, a victim of religious fanaticism, was only rehabilitated by Voltaire's efforts in 1765.

FROM THE PERIODICAL " ARISTIDE OU LE CITOYEN ", LAUSANNE
(in French)

XVIth DISCOURSE

11 October 1766.
Edera crescentem ornate poetam.
VIRG.

Throw some flowers to this young artist.

I do not doubt, Gentlemen, that you have heard the young MOZARD, & I am convinced that he made the same impression on you as on anyone endowed by nature with organs capable of appreciating the products of the fine arts. You will have seen, with as much surprise as pleasure, a child of nine play the harpsichord like the great masters ; & what will have astonished you even more was to hear from trustworthy persons that he already played it in a superior manner three years ago ; to know that almost everything he plays is of his own composition ; to have found in all his pieces, and even in his improvisations, that character of force which is the stamp of genius, that variety which proclaims the fire of imagination, & that charm which proves an assured taste ; and lastly, to have seen him perform the most difficult pieces with an ease and a facility that would be surprising even in a musician of thirty ; & you will perhaps have put the same question to yourselves that I have heard asked of many people : can you understand it ?

It seems to me as stupid to be surprised by nothing as it is to be surprised by everything : to witness all these phenomena without seeking to account for them is sheer imbecility. I have seen much of our young musician, I have observed him attentively, & I may here hazard a few ideas that will perhaps not be as strange to you as I imagine they may seem at first. The explanation of young Mozard, if you will allow this expression, is connected with the general question of the relationship between moral man and physical man, & it is the more interesting in that it serves to explain what is extraordinary in all other children in whom precocious talents in some branch of science or in one of the fine arts have been admired ; & at the same time to account for those men in whom some small event has developed, quite late sometimes, very superior gifts hidden until then.

The same cause that would not permit Ovid, when still a child, to speak in prose to his father, asking his pardon for making too many verses ; & which obliged Molière to write comedies instead of upholstering chairs, has formed young Mozard ; they were born Poets, he a Musician. But what is it that lets anyone be born a Poet, a Musician, or a Painter ? Metaphysics alone can tell us. But if on the one hand it leaves us in ignorance about the influence of exterior objects on our senses, communicating it to our soul, & leaves on our brain impressions it is able to reproduce in images, on the other hand it reveals to us several truths of experience which, admitted as principles, throw a keen light on the most interesting questions of human science.

One of these truths is that differences in the organs make a given person more receptive to impressions received by one of his senses than to those received by the others. Of two men leaving a picture exhibition for a concert-hall, one who has been captivated by the masterpiece of some great painter will continue to be under its spell and will not hear the music ; the other, having looked at the pictures without seeing them, will be compensated by keenly perceiving all the beauties of the concert.

Thus one who is entranced by an image turned into music may often be little affected by it if it is in verse ; & Iphigenia at the altar seen on a picture may move another to tears who may have seen RACINE's play unmoved.

Another truth, which is perhaps but the corollary of the first, is that the greater or lesser receptivity of a sense, and the greater or lesser mental disposition to be affected by ideas appealing to that sense, causes the same object to be perceived very differently by different persons. There are some who care for pictures without seeing more in them than an array of colours that pleases them, while the painter's eye at once seizes all their beauties ; or, to leave the fine arts, an ordinary child looking with pleasure at a carnation will notice only whether it is red or white, while the child destined by nature to be a botanist will be aware of several characteristics ; but he will miss a larger number than [Joseph Pitton de] TOURNEFORT perceived at a glance at the age of seven.

Another important observation is that, although it is neither certain nor even probable that different classes of ideas have their particular locations in the brain, nature nevertheless decreed that there should be a close link between ideas of a similar kind, between those we received through the same sense, between those that have reached us at the same time, at the same place, in the same circumstances, so that one that has been awakened recalls all the others.

It is moreover proved that, as one part of the body acquires by the frequent repetition of certain movements the ease of executing them with an astonishing quickness, force and precision, the organism—a word by which I mean all that is concerned with the faculty of thought—the organism, I repeat, which is almost wholly occupied with sensations and ideas of a certain kind, may take an advantage of it such as those less occupied with that object, or whose particular part of the organism is less developed, are incapable of understanding.

I will add, as a fifth truth, that very strong impressions act automatically on a receptive brain and produce involuntary reactions that cannot be repressed. The sight of a new machine whose secret has been concealed from him worries the great Engineer until he understands it ; why then should not a sound, and more especially any sort of sound, force a brain keenly affected by sound to occupy itself with music ?

Well, I may here assert, on the strength of a few examples, that in men gifted with a very superior talent it seems that whatever in the brain is the cause of this talent is the key to all the others that show themselves only when it is fully developed. CORNEILLE was a pitiful Advocate, and was considered to be a very mediocre man when he wrote his first verse ; and how this verse developed ! [Edmond] STONE at the age of 28 was a gardener's assistant who could not read ; he saw a mason calculate and was born to calculate too, and three years later he was a distinguished scientist able to enlighten the greatest Geometricians on the most difficult mathematical problems ; at the age of fifteen the greatest Engineer of our day was no good at anything, and when his mother took him to see his headmaster he waited for him in an anteroom where there was a great clock ; the ticking of the pendulum attracted his attention, he caught sight of the wheel through the cracks in the case, and soon made the masterpieces that astonished Europe, where he is today one of the first of the Academicians. The father of one of the most agreeable Poets in Germany, despairing of being able to teach his son anything, sent him as a last resort into the country to a man famous for the education of his kind, who had no better luck with him than his first masters ; but a book of Poetry fell into the young man's hands; the shell covering the Poet burst, he wrote verse and quickly acquired all the knowledge needful to this art. I shall cite no other examples, which would take me too far from our little Orpheus, to whom it is high time to return.

He was born with an exquisite ear & an organism disposed to be strongly affected by music ; the son of a father who is a great Musician, & younger brother of a sister whose playing claimed a share of your admiration, the first sounds he heard were harmonious ones ; the sensitive cord was struck in him from infancy, it gave forth music on the instant, & he must have made music from the moment that he heard it.   This dominion with which the soul sways everybody through the organs of the voice, without being aware of them, in a musician it does so through the fingers &, one may say, the whole body ; the instrument is so well adapted to its needs that it soon gets to know all its uses.   It has received at birth this organic precision and delicacy which suffers from the least falsity of intonation.   It is thus that the poetic ear is at once hurt by bad verse, while he who labours at verse and has no other Apollo than rules, loses the greater part of his time in trying to discover if he has broken them.   Aural sensibility and justness are so keen in young Mozard that wrong, harsh or too loud notes bring tears to his eyes. His imagination is as musical as his ear, for it is always conscious of a multitude of sounds all together ; a given single note calls up the same instant all those that may form a melodious succession & a complete symphony.   With people who possess a certain very superior talent all the ideas occur in the relationships they may have with this talent ; it is this that was so noticeable in our young man ; he was sometimes involuntarily driven to his harpsichord, as by a hidden force, & he drew from it sounds that were the living expression of the idea that had just seized him.   One might say that at such moments he is an instrument at the command of music, imagining him like a set of strings, harmoniously arranged with such art that a single one cannot be touched without all the others being set in motion ; he plays all the images, as a Poet versifies and a Painter colours them.

This young child is very natural, he is charming, he has knowledge outside music ; yet if he were not a musician, he would perhaps be quite an ordinary child.   Were he not a musician's son, his talent would perhaps not have had a chance to develop until later, & his other faculties would have remained buried until then.

It may be predicted with confidence that he will one day be one of the greatest masters of his art ; but should we not be afraid lest, developed so young, he should age very early ? It is only too true that precocious children have often been used up at full bloom ; the too hard-worn fibres become callous and incapable of functioning any longer ; but one has also sometimes had the experience of seeing men born with a special talent for one of the arts maintaining themselves for a very long time ; the organism constituted to carry this talent works with such ease that practice hardly strains it at all, & it is to be noticed that work in no way tires young Mozard.   The shortsighted eye loses itself in looking at the stars, the long-sighted one used for the observation of insects destroys itself ; but each kind of sight fixed on the objects within its range preserves itself much better.   Ch. MARATTI was a great painter from the age of eleven until 90, and at 70 CORELLI, who had been able to play the violin as soon as he could talk, still swayed the souls of his hearers as he wished.

I have detained you long, Gentlemen, on the subject of the child-musician ; I should fail to do justice to what is due to your views if I did not spend a moment on recalling the moral child to you, since he has an even greater right to your interest. A well-ordered mind appears to be made for a virtuous soul and sweet ways ; experience has verified this in several great artists, & little Mozart supplies a new proof of it ; his heart is as sensitive as his ear ; he has modesty such as is rare at his age, and rare combined with such superiority ; it is truly edifying to hear him attribute his talents to the giver of all things and to conclude from this, with a charming candour and an air of the most intimate conviction, that it would be unpardonable to pride himself on them. One cannot see without emotion all the evidence of his tenderness for a father who seems most worthy of it, who has taken even greater care over the formation of his character than the cultivation of his talents, & who speaks of education with as much sagacity as of music ; who thinks himself well rewarded by success, & regards it as sweet for him to see his two lovable children better rewarded by a glance of approval from him, which they seek with tender anxiety in his eyes, than by the plaudits of a whole audience. This trait alone seems to me to characterize all three of them most advantageously, & they furnish two reflections on education which are new, I admit, only in practice : one is that many men who could excel in a particular thing do only very middlingly well, because what they have been set to is not what suits them ; and this consideration, the first one should study on deciding on the choice of a vocation, is the one that is hardly ever studied ; instead of trying a child with various things to profess, as one tries metal with a touchstone in order to discover its nature, parents as a rule suppose their wishes to be an easy means to efficiency ; with what success may be deduced from the results. A second reflection is that it is much to be wished that the fathers whose children show outstanding talents should emulate M. Mozard, who, far from pressing his son, has always been careful to moderate his fire and to prevent him from giving way to it ; the opposite principle daily stifles the fairest genius and can render the most superior talents abortive.

I have the honour to be, &c.

A copy of this rare weekly, which was published by François Grasset & Cie, is in the Paul Hirsch Library in the British Museum.—German translation in A. Leitzmann, *W. A. Mozart. Berichte der Zeitgenossen und Briefe* (Leipzig, 1926). Reprint in *Revue Musicale*, Paris, January 1938 (Mathias Morhardt). Facsimile in *Notes*, Washington, December 1950, with a translation (Richard S. Hill). Another English translation in A. Hyatt King's *Mozart in Retrospect* (London, 1955).—There is an early German translation (Mozarteum, Salzburg), which an anonymous admirer (B.B.) sent in 1771 to Mozart, by then a Konzertmeister at Salzburg, with a comment (see 1771) showing that the unknown sender ascribed the anonymous original to some "highness", evidently Prince Ludwig of Württemberg. It may perhaps be supposed that the Prince assisted the true author, Professor Samuel (Simon) André (David) Tissot, whose interests included the nervous system of genius, especially in children, and as an author called himself Auguste Tissot (1728–97 or –98).

On 10 October the Mozarts left Zürich for Winterthur, where they spent the night with the town clerk, Wolfgang Dietrich Sulzer, and on the 11th they went on to Schaffhausen, where they remained for four days.

On 16 October they left Schaffhausen for Donaueschingen, where they remained from the 17th to the 28th; on 29 October they continued their journey to Messkirch, Ulm and Günzburg, reaching Dillingen on 3 November. The children gave a concert there in the presence of Joseph, Landgrave of Hesse and Prince-Bishop of Augsburg. On the 6th they went on by way of the Fuggers' pilgrimage church at Biberbach to Augsburg, where they stayed one day (at the Three Moors); and finally on the 8th they reached Munich, where they arrived in the evening and again stayed at Störzer's inn.

> At the almost daily concerts held at the Court of Prince Joseph Wenzeslaus von Fürstenberg at Donaueschingen (where the Mozarts' servant Sebastian Winter had been hairdresser since 1764 and later valet), the *Galimathias musicum* may have been performed.—At Biberbach Wolfgang competed with the twelve-year-old Swabian Sigismund (later Pater Sixtus) Bachmann on the organ of the pilgrimage church (see 24 November 1790).

FROM THE PERIODICAL "ARISTIDE OU LE CITOYEN", LAUSANNE, 18 OCTOBER 1766
(in French)

When I see the young Mozart jokingly create these tender and sublime symphonies which one would take for the language of immortals, every fibre of my being takes up the theme, so to speak, of immortality, just as all the powers of my spirit despair of it. Carried away by a delightful illusion, beyond the narrow sphere which confines my senses, I could almost take this child, so blest by heaven, for one of those pure spirits who inhabit the happy realm destined for me.

> Discours XVII, p. 201.—*Revue Musicale*, Paris, January 1938, p. 13.—*Cf.* 16 October 1766.—These lines too, and perhaps with more justification, have been ascribed to Prince Ludwig Eugen of Württemberg (1731-95).

VOLTAIRE TO ÉTIENNE-NOËL DAMILAVILLE
(in French)

Ferney, 7 November 1766.

. . . How could I have seen your young harpsichord player? Mme Denis was ill; I have been bedridden for more than six weeks. Ah! we are far from festive here!

> Voltaire, *Œuvres*, Vol. XLIV, p. 493.—Mme Denis was Voltaire's niece and housekeeper.

On 9 November Wolfgang played before Maximilian III Joseph, Elector of Bavaria, and improvised a piece (? K. 33c).

Wolfgang was ill again between 12 and 21 November.

It is to be supposed that he again suffered from rheumatism.

FROM THE " AUGSBURGISCHER INTELLIGENZ–ZETTEL ", 13 NOVEMBER 1766

Note of the gentry and passengers arrived [on the 6th] . . . Herr Mozart, Kapellmeister, comes with family from France ; lodges at The Three Moors.

Hardly recovered, Wolfgang played again at the Bavarian court on 22 November ; Nannerl also performed on this occasion.

FROM JOHANN ADAM HILLER'S " WÖCHENTLICHE NACHRICHTEN UND ANMERKUNGEN DIE MUSIK BETREFFEND ", LEIPZIG, 25 NOVEMBER 1766

Vienna.

The sciences have had precocious scholars who were rightly regarded as miracles of nature. Music has likewise boasted such precocious scholars, or *virtuosi*, as they have to be named in musical terminology. Some time ago Herr Mozart, a chamber musician in princely service, who apart from his compositions has earned much fame with his *Violin School*, made not a little stir with a daughter of nine and a son of seven years, in England and in France. This musical family has even been represented and perpetuated by a neat engraving. Herr *Mozart*, the father, plays the violin, his son accompanies on the harpsichord, and the daughter sings, holding the music in her hand. We regard this example of young musicians as indeed extraordinary ; especially as the son, a child of seven, is already so adept in composition that in Paris half a dozen clavier sonatas of his have been engraved. Such precocious virtuosi certainly do much honour to their father, since they have attained to all this through his instruction ; and since he knew how to discover easy ways and means of making a matter comprehensible and easy for children which at times is not readily grasped by older and adult persons.

> This was the first mention of Wolfgang in a specifically musical periodical, this being the first published in German. The article closes with a report on the appearance of Franz Lamotte (*c.* 1757–81), " aged 12 ", who on 15 October had played a violin concerto of his own composition at the Viennese Court.

On 29 November 1766 the family arrived back at Salzburg ; they had left there on 9 June 1763.

FROM HÜBNER'S " DIARIUM ", 29 NOVEMBER 1766

I cannot forbear to remark here also that today the world-famous Herr Leopold Mozart, Vice-Kapellmeister here, with his wife and two children, a boy aged 10 and his little daughter of 13, have arrived to the solace and joy of the whole town. It may well be that I have already elsewhere given a report on this Mozart family ; especially as these past two or three years

nothing has been more frequently discussed in the newspapers than the wonderful art of the Mozart children : the two children, the boy as well as the
girl, both play the harpsichord, or the clavier, the girl, it is true, with more
art and fluency than her little brother, but the boy with far more refinement and with more original ideas, and with the most beautiful harmonic
inspirations, so that even the most excellent organists wondered how it was
humanly possible for such a boy, who was already so good an artist at the
age of 6, to possess such art as to astonish the whole musical world. This
Mozart family has now been absent from Salzburg for nearly four years
and has traversed the greater part of Europe ; for they first went to France,
where the boy, who was then seven years of age, himself composed a complete *Tafelmusique* for a great gala day at the French royal court in the
presence of persons of the highest rank, which music for that gala day was
publicly performed and what is more issued in public print : indeed a
portrait of the whole family was engraved, the boy playing the clavier, the
daughter singing an aria, and the father accompanying on the violin (for he
is at the same time a celebrated violinist and has also published in print a
book on the fiddle, which book was only last year, in Holland, translated
into the Dutch language, although he never travelled particularly to make
himself famous for his art on the violin, but only because of his children, who
may be called veritable wonders of the world), in which portrait are introduced, with the following inscription in the French language : Léopold
Mozart Père de Marianne Mozart, virtuose âgée de onze ans, et de J. G.
Wolfgang Mozart Compositeur, et Maitre de Musique âgé de sept ans.
Which being translated is : Leopold Mozart father of Marianne Mozart,
artist and virtuoso, aged eleven years, and father of Johan Georg Mozart,
composer and master of music, aged seven years : this copperplate, however,
I did not wish to include here, because I have had it framed. They were in
France nearly a whole year, receiving countless honours and the most valuable appreciations, which I shall report elsewhere, *i.e.* on 8 December. From
France they went to England, where they made very much money : they
never cease to relate how dreadfully expensive everything is in England,
and adduced the following in proof thereof : He, Mozart, heard in England,
at Court, among other things some very fine music, perhaps a ballet or an
opera ; he therefore wished to have this copied there, but asked what they
charged for copying per sheet, for which here they ask 4 or at the very most
6 kreuzer, in England they receive 12 groats, *i.e.* 36 kr., per sheet, and he
thereupon gave up the copying, for it would have cost him approximately
100 thalers ; indeed he added that, had he sent the whole of this music from
England to Salzburg, had it copied at Salzburg, and had it brought from
Salzburg to England again, it would not have cost him nearly so much as
the copying alone would have cost him in England. He appeared in England
exactly as in other countries, appearing with his children on public stages, and
at theatres, just as foreign play-actors appear : now if here we pay a 6, 12
or 24 kreutzer piece, going to the comedy, in England they pay nothing

but *chinée* [guineas], which is a gold coin similar to the Max *d'or* or *Carolin* here, so that it is easy to imagine the amount of money this Herr Mozart must have made in England, where moreover all presents are given purely and solely in ready cash. In England too they stayed a whole year, and Herr Mozart in particular, who has in any case a very learned head and possesses great knowledge, as well as a very exalted mind and energetic disposition, acquired a complete knowledge of the English language, having already known Italian and French by reason of his art. From England they went to Holland, and that at the request of the Republic, where again they received very many presents and collected much money. And there again, Herr Mozart, having once learnt the English language, acquired Dutch quite easily. From Holland they went to Switzerland, then to Augsburg, Bavaria, and so on, until at last they once again arrived back at Salzburg in good health, at the keenest desire of the whole town, to the solace, joy and pleasure of everybody of high and low degree, and to their own honour, fame and praise ; although nearly all the members of the whole family, especially the wife in England, now and again suffered very dangerous and almost fatal illnesses. The boy is now rather over 10 years of age and the little daughter over 13 : the boy Wolfgangl, by the way, has not grown very much during this journey, but Nannerl has become tolerably tall and almost marriageable already. There is a strong rumour that the Mozart family will again not long remain here, but will soon visit the whole of Scandinavia and the whole of Russia, and perhaps even travel to China, which would be a far greater journey and bigger undertaking still : *de facto*, I believe it to be certain that nobody is more celebrated in Europe than Herr Mozart with his two children, for indeed, after God, it is his children whom he has to thank for his fame and his great riches. The journey now accomplished is said to have cost them something near 20,000 florins : I can well believe it ; but how much money must he not have collected ?

> Klein, *op. cit.*, pp. 175-7.—Cf. 26 April 1766.—It was not Mozart's mother but his father who was ill in London (*cf.* 6 August and 13 December 1764).

FROM THE ANNUAL ACCOUNTS OF THE ZÜRICH MUSICAL SOCIETY
(NOVEMBER ?) 1766

Paid by order to a Salzburger for symphonies and notturni 28 [Pfund].

> Fehr, *op. cit.*, p. 12. Written by the treasurer of the " Musikgesellschaft beim Kornhaus ", Hans Caspar Werdmüller.—The amount is doubtless for music sold at Zürich by Leopold Mozart.

FROM HÜBNER'S " DIARIUM ", 8 DECEMBER (IMMACULATE CONCEPTION)
1766

This very day I found myself, quite unexpectedly, at the Mozart family's, where to my utmost and particular delight I heard the harpsichord, or clavier, played by the boy Wolfgangerl, about whom I reported on the twenty-ninth of last month, but also saw with my eyes and touched with my hands all the presents and tributes they had received on the whole of their journey. Astonishing it is, concerning the boy, how this boy treats the harpsichord : the like will not soon be heard again, nor seen ; and I declare that this boy, to say nothing of his youth and still childish years, has not his like in the whole of Germany, indeed I daresay in the whole Continent of Europe—although that is saying a good deal—in art, rapidity, delightful ideas and curious manipulations. During the four and a half years that he was travelling he so improved and perfected himself in clavier playing that no score nor drawing-room piece can be put in front of him to play, be it as difficult as may be imagined, which he will not play without ado, without preparation, and half by heart, to everyone's astonishment, indeed even far more excellently and more artfully than it is written down, by the application of inventions and manipulations of his own. Nobody can believe it, and it is indeed inconceivable, except those who have themselves heard him play, who can and must believe it. And what is even more surprising is that this boy, because his little hands are still too small, cannot stretch an octave on the keyboard, but always has to spread it, which only makes his art the more exceptional and admirable ; all the organists here, among whom there are certainly great artists in our Court music, especially Herr Adlgasser and Herr Haydn, freely admit and confess that they would not dare to enter into competition with this boy on the clavier, although they may surely be called organists matched by but few. About composition, which this boy already understands like an artist, new turns of phrase and eulogies would have to be invented anew, for he has already composed very much and today especially, at High Mass in the Cathedral for a great festivity, a symphony of his was done which not only found great approbation from all the Court musicians, but also caused great astonishment : one could only wish that this boy were able to compose more.

I afterwards saw all the tributes and presents which the aforesaid Herr Mozart and his children had received from the great monarchs and princes during their costly journey : of gold pocket watches he has brought home 9 ; of gold snuff-boxes he has received 12 ; of gold rings set with the most handsome precious stones he has so many that he does not know himself how many ; ear-rings for the girl, necklaces, knives with golden blades, bottle-holders, writing-tackle, toothpick boxes, gold *objets* for the girl, writing-tablets and suchlike gewgaws without number and without end ; so much, that merely to see all this *raptim* and *obiter*, you would have to spend several hours doing nothing but look, and it is just like inspecting a church treasury, not perhaps because of its value, but because of its rarity, for so many things from various countries are rarely to be seen collected together, as they are at Herr Mozart's ; but the most valuable and the most beautiful I have seen is the snuff-box from the King of France, filled by the King with his own hands with 50 *Louis d'or*, *i.e.* 500 florins, with this express rider :

should he, Mozart, be obliged by necessity to sell this snuff-box, he was to return it to the King to buy, and he would give him 100 *Louis d'or*, *i.e.* 1000 florins for it ; but Herr Mozart brought it home with him : what is more, I believe that Herr Mozart's gewgaws, brought home by him, are worth 12,000 florins if they are worth 10 kreuzer. In addition, he had bought very many things cheaply in these foreign countries, which he will sell here at a high price, and in this way make even more money on the spot ! For this Herr Mozart has such a clever, inventive, energetic and sensible head that I am sure there are few who would have thought all this out and managed it as Herr Mozart has done.

    Klein, *op. cit.*, p. 178 f.—On the " symphony " *cf.* Minos E. Dounias, Critical Commentary to the *Neue Mozart-Ausgabe* VI/16, *Sonaten für Orgel und Orchester*, p. i/4.

On 11 December Leopold's mother, Anna Maria Mozart, died at Augsburg.

FROM THE SALZBURG COURT DIARIES

21 December [The Archbishop's consecration day] 1766 . . . after Ave Maria in the evening . . . His Serene Highness . . . betook himself to the Italian comedy, performed by the company then resident. This was entitled *Il cavaliere di Spirito*, and was followed by an *intermezzo* with music for four voices, entitled *Li tre gobbi rivali per amore di Madame Sazzesa* [?] and lastly there was a *licenza* consisting of a recitative and aria, the music of which was composed to everybody's admiration by young Wolfgang Mozard, son of the Vice-Kapellmeister and a remarkable boy ten years of age, complete master of the harpsichord, only just arrived here from England ; the whole lasting until half past eight o'clock.

    Salzburg Provincial Archives.—Pirkmayer, *op. cit.*, p. 23 f. Martin, *op. cit.*, p. 132.—Pirkmayer read the Italian name as " Vezzosa ".—That Sunday was the anniversary of the consecration (1753) of the Prince-Archbishop Sigismund, Count Schrattenbach.—The entertainment described here followed the " Ave Maria " sung at the cathedral.—Wolfgang's contribution was K. 36 : the recitative " Or che il dover " with the aria " Tali e cotanti sono ".—Hubner on this occasion omits to name Mozart in his " Diarium ".

1767

FROM HÜBNER'S " DIARIUM ", 26 FEBRUARY 1767
(partly in Latin)

On the 26th of this month, being Thursday, there was again, at half past six in the afternoon, or evening, a rather large company in our refectory, and music.

Today there also took place in the palace at 4 o'clock the public rehearsal of the Italian opera entitled *Vologeso*, which however will not be properly performed until next Sunday in honour of the joyful occasion of the Archbishop's birthday, for on the 28th of February he completes his 69th year. This opera was performed once or twice last year.

> Klein, *op. cit.*, p. 181 f.—Giuseppe Sarti's opera *Vologeso* had already been performed at the end of 1765 and the beginning of 1766. The " licenza " for the new performance was clearly Mozart's recitative and aria K. 70, which Einstein considered probably to have been written for 28 February 1769.

FROM HÜBNER'S " DIARIUM ", 1 MARCH 1767
(partly in Latin)

1st March, Sunday . . .

Our very reverend Abbot was invited to Court ; for today was a double festivity there, and there was a banquet in the Imperial Hall : first to celebrate the Archbishop's birthday, and secondly because a wedding took place today between a certain Count Lodron and a certain Countess Firmian, whom the Archbishop united in the Cathedral oratory. There was moreover an incomparable Italian opera performed at the Court today, of which I made mention under the 26th of February. This opera began at 6 o'clock in the evening and did not end until 10 o'clock at night ; but it was a magnificent masterpiece of music, likewise its singers, though many were our own people and the Archbishop's court musicians.

> Klein, *op. cit.*, p. 182.—The Imperial Chamberlain and Lieutenant-Colonel, Kaspar, Count Lodron, married Maria Nothburga, the daughter of the High Steward at the Salzburg court, Franz Lactantius, Count Firmian.

FROM THE MINUTES OF THE UNIVERSITY GYMNASIUM, SALZBURG
(in Latin)

1767, 12 March, Thursday : holiday. (After dinner.) At half past six in the Hall there was sung an oratorio set to music by D. Wolfgang Mozart, aged 10 years, greatly skilled in composition.

> *Protocollum Praefecturae Gymnasii Universitatis Salisburgensis* in the Provincial Library, Salzburg ; written, as established by Alfred Orel, by Placidus Scharl (*cf.* 6 January 1763).—A. J. Hammerle, *Mozart und einige Zeitgenossen* (Salzburg, 1877), p. 5.—As in Vienna, so at Salzburg, the University at that time had a Gymnasium attached to it as a preparatory school.—Wolfgang composed the first part of the sacred singspiel or oratorio *Die Schuldigkeit des ersten Gebots* (K. 35), the text of which was by Ignaz Anton von Weiser (*cf.* January 1770). The distribution of the composition to three composers was by no means unusual. The performance, probably a concert one, took place in the Knights' Hall of the palace during Lent, with artists of the Court Chapel : first part (Mozart) on 12 March ; second part (M. Haydn) on 19 March ; third part (Adlgasser) probably on 26 March.

FROM HÜBNER'S "DIARIUM", 12 MARCH 1767

12 March, Thursday : Today after evening prayers there took place at Court in the so-called Knights' Hall an oratorio set to music for five persons, that is to say three women and two men, namely Herr Meisner and Herr Spizeder. The German text was by Herr Weiser, a merchant and a councillor, the music by Wolfgang Mozart, a boy of ten years old.

Klein, *op. cit.*, p. 182.

TITLE-PAGE OF THE LIBRETTO OF "DIE SCHULDIGKEIT DES ERSTEN GEBOTS"

The Obligation of the first and foremost Commandment (Mark XII. v. 30) And thou shalt love the Lord thy God with all thy heart, and with all thy soul, and with all thy mind, and with all thy strength. In three Parts set forth for Consideration by J. A. W. Part I set to music by Herr Wolfgang Motzard, aged 10 years. Part II by Herr Johann Michael Heiden, Concert Master to His Serene Highness. Part III by Herr Anton Cajetan Adlgasser, Chamber Composer and Organist to His Serene Highness. Salzburg, Printed by the heiress of the late Johann Joseph Mayr, Court and Academic Printer and Bookseller, 1767.

Copy in the Studienbibliothek, Salzburg.—Hammerle, *op. cit.*, p. 52 f.—Facsimile (together with cast-list) in *Neue Mozart-Ausgabe* I/4/1, *Die Schuldigkeit des ersten Gebots*, p. xvii.

CAST-LIST FROM THE SAME

The action takes place in a pleasant landscape with a garden and a small wood.

Singers :

A lukewarm and afterwards ardent Christian : Herr Joseph Meisner.
The Spirit of Christianity : Herr Anton Franz Spitzeder.
The World Spirit : Jungfer Maria Anna Fesemayr.
Divine Mercy : Jungfer Maria Magdalena Lipp.
Divine Justice : Jungfer Maria Anna Braunhofer.

Jahn, Vol. I, p. 56 f.—Meissner had nothing to do in the first part. Fräulein Fesemayer married Adlgasser and Fräulein Lipp later became the wife of Michael Haydn, the younger brother of the great Joseph, who lived at Salzburg as first Kapellmeister in the Court Chapel and was a highly gifted composer.

FROM THE REGISTER OF THE SALZBURG PRIVY PURSE, 18 MARCH 1767

On the 18th, to little Mozartl, for the composition of the music to an oratorio, a gold medal of 12 ducats . . . 60.-fl.

M.—3*a*

Salzburg Provincial Archives.—Martin, *op. cit.*, p. 137.—This medal, the weight of twelve ducats, was paid for from the Archbishop's privy purse.

FROM HÜBNER'S "DIARIUM", 19 MARCH (ST. JOSEPH'S DAY) 1767

There was also a great gala day at Court today, because very many of the highest nobility, of both sexes, bear the name of Joseph. Today, too, at Court, in the so-called Knights' Hall, there was a repetition of the oratorio written in German verse, whose music was composed by that very famous man, Michael Haydn, virtuoso and Concert Master of our Court.

Klein, *op. cit.*, p. 182.

IBID., 28 MARCH 1767

On Saturday, 28 March, Prince Colloredo, a brother of the Bishop of Gurk and Imperial Envoy to Spain, was here, and lodged with his brother the Bishop of Gurk.

Klein, *op. cit.*, p. 183.—The Imperial Ambassador in Madrid was Franz de Paula Gundaccar I, Prince Colloredo. His brother was the later Archbishop of Salzburg, Hieronymus, Count Colloredo.

IBID., 29 MARCH 1767

29 inst., the fourth Sunday in Lent, there was an uncommonly noble and costly dinner at Court in the Imperial Hall, arranged by the Archbishop in honour of the envoy to Spain, Prince von Colloredo ; and music at which all the resident virtuosi, of whom not a few and no bad ones are to be met here, had to perform by special command : my gracious lord, who not only today but all through Lent was invited to eat meat at Court three times a week, namely on Sundays, Tuesdays and Thursdays, told me that he had never yet seen the Archbishop giving precedence to anyone at table, except this time, or that moreover such splendid table music had ever been given at Court ; however, the Archbishop was by no means approved of for having given precedence to the envoy to Spain, especially as he was not here in his capacity as Spanish or Imperial envoy.

Klein, *op. cit.*, p. 183.—Mozart will probably have been among the virtuosi, and perhaps his sister too.—Hübner's "lord" was Abbot Beda Seeauer.

FROM THE MINUTES OF THE SALZBURG GYMNASIUM
(in Latin)

1767, 2 April, Thursday : holiday. The music of the first oratorio repeated in Hall.

Hammerle, *op. cit.*, p. 6.—Only on this occasion was the first part of the oratorio (K. 35) repeated.

The Paris publishers Le Menu & Boyer announced Wolfgang's sonatas for pianoforte and violin (K. 26-31), composed in Holland, in the *Avant-Coureur* of 6 April 1767.

> Cari Johansson, *French Music Publishers' Catalogues of the Second Half of the Eighteenth Century* (Stockholm, 1955), p. 111 f.—This Paris reprint, the first of a work by Mozart, bears the note " Ces pièces peuvent s'exécuter sur la Harpe " (*cf.* 27 January 1768).

On Good Friday, 17 April, the Passion cantata (K. 42) was probably performed in the cathedral.

IBID.
(in Latin)

13 May, Wednesday. In the morning short schools on account of phlebotomy. After dinner was given the Syntaxists' comedy written by the Very Reverend Professor, and by desire performed by his students, which gave me the greatest pleasure. I congratulate the Professor on the public applause. The music for it, composed by Wolfgang Mozart, a youngster of eleven, delighted everybody, and at night he gave us notable proofs of his musical art at the harpsichord.

> Salzburg Provincial Archives.—Hammerle, *op. cit.*, p. 7 f.—The Latin school comedy performed by the Syntax class was *Clementia Croesi* by Father Rufinus Widl of Seeon Monastery, the Professor mentioned in the minutes ; the musical " intermedium " to it was *Apollo et Hyacinthus* (K. 38).—It was customary at Salzburg University in the seventeenth and eighteenth centuries to arrange scenic performances by students, both at the end of the academic year, before the prize-giving, and as here, within the academic year, on the stage built in 1661 next to the great hall.

FROM HÜBNER'S " DIARIUM ", 13 MAY 1767
(in Latin)

Yesterday after dinner there was produced at the University a comedy by the Rev. Father Ruffinus, of Seeon, Professor of Syntax. The music for this comedy was composed by the celebrated eleven-year-old boy, Wolfgang Mozart, son of Herr Leopold Mozart, Kapellmeister here at Salzburg.

> Klein, *op. cit.*, p. 183.

FROM THE PROCEEDINGS OF THE THEOLOGICAL FACULTY, SALZBURG,
13 MAY 1767
(in Latin)

On the same day there was performed a comic play by the Very Reverend Father Ruffinus, Professor of Syntax, in the Great Hall, the actors presenting his characters most excellently.

> Salzburg Provincial Archives.—Communicated by Dr. Herbert Klein.

FROM THE PRINTED LIBRETTO OF THE LATIN COMEDY " CLEMENTIA CROESI " AND THE MUSICAL INTERMEZZO "APOLLO ET HYACINTHUS ", SALZBURG, 1767
(in Latin)

. . . the author of the work is the noble D. Wolfgangus Mozart, aged eleven, son of the noble and vigorous D. Leopoldus Mozart, Kapellmeister.

PERSONS IN THE MUSIC

Oebalus, King of Lacedaemonia	The Most Illustrious and Learned D. Mathias Stadler (Scholar in Theology, Morals and Law).
Melia, daughter to Oebalus	Felix Fuchs, of the Chapel (Grammar).
Hyacinthus, son to Oebalus	Christianus Enzinger, of the Chapel (Rudiments).
Apollo, received by Oebalus as a guest	Joannes Ernst, of the Chapel.
Zephyrus, friend of Hyacinthus	Josephus Vonterthon (Syntax).
First Priest of Apollo	Josephus Bruendl (Poetics).
Second Priest of Apollo	Jacobus Moser (Syntax).

Salzburg, Studienbibliothek.—Abert, Vol. I, p. 110.—Facsimile in *Neue Mozart-Ausgabe* II/5/1, *Apollo und Hyacinth*, p. XXVI.—Melia and Hyacinthus are parts for soprano, Apollo and Zephyrus for alto, Oebalus for tenor.

FROM HÜBNER'S " DIARIUM ", 2 JUNE 1767
(partly in Latin)

Today, after the singing of the third office for the dead, about nine o'clock, our lately deceased and dearly beloved brother P. Thaddaeus Haydn was buried in the Chapel of St. Vitus, at the gospel side of the altar there ; the coffin was carried by the Fellows of the University. Then, at about eleven o'clock, the meal-time reading was cancelled, since all the University and all the Professors who had participated in the funeral procession were invited to join us, and a memorial tribute [Todten solatium] to the late P. Thaddaeus was made ; also on two subsequent days, namely the seventh and thirtieth, which three requiems were celebrated as is customary by Rev. Father Prior. Prominent among the mourners was Herr Mozart and his wife, who were on somewhat friendly terms with the deceased P. Thaddaeus. I have mentioned this Herr Mozart on 8 December of last year and elsewhere.

Klein, *op. cit.*, p. 184.—Father Thaddäus Haiden (baptismal names : Johann Adam), of St. Peter's Abbey, died on 31 May. *Cf.* P. Lindner's Book of Professions in the *Mitteilungen der Gesellschaft für Salzburger Landeskunde* (1906), Vol. 46, p. 140.

On 11 September 1767 the family set out on a second journey to Vienna and travelled as far as Vöcklabruck.

On 12 September they reached the monastery of Lambach at midday and in the evening arrived at Linz, where they alighted at the Green Tree in the suburbs.

On Sunday, 13 September, they passed the day on the Strengberg ; at midday on the 14th they reached Melk and in the evening St. Pölten.

On 15 September they went by way of Purkersdorf to Vienna, where they found lodgings on the second floor of the house of a goldsmith, Johann Schmalecker, in the Weihburggasse (the building now occupying the site is No. 3).

> Soon after their arrival they attended Johann Adolf Hasse's new opera, *Partenope*, at the Burgtheater.

In the afternoon of 23 October they left Vienna for Brno [Brünn].

> Leopold Mozart's hopes of the festivities in honour of King Ferdinand IV, King of Naples and Sicily, and his betrothed, the sixteen-year-old Archduchess Maria Josepha, were frustrated by her death on 15 October. Since smallpox was raging in Vienna, the family left the city precipitately.

After two days at Brno they went to Olomouc [Olmütz] on 26 October, where they alighted at the Black Eagle. Wolfgang fell ill with smallpox.

On 28 October the family moved to the deanery, the official residence of Leopold Anton, Count Podstatzky, dean of the cathedral and rector of the university.

By 10 November Wolfgang had recovered, thanks to Dr. Joseph Wolff's treatment, but the Mozarts remained at Olomouc until 23 December.

On 24 December they were back at Brno, where they found lodgings with Count Franz Anton Schrattenbach, a brother of the Prince-Archbishop of Salzburg (Krapfengasse 4).

> Schrattenbach later became Governor of Moravia.

FROM THE DIARY OF AURELIUS AUGUSTINUS, PRIOR OF STERNBERG,
BRNO, 30 DECEMBER 1767
(in Latin)

In the evening, persuaded by his Excellency the Governor, I attended a musical concert in a house in the city known as the " Taverna ", at which a Salzburg boy of eleven years and his sister of fifteen years, accompanied on various instruments by inhabitants of Brunn, excited everyone's admiration ; but he could not endure the trumpets, because they were incapable of playing completely in tune with one another.

> Brno, State Archives. MS. 701, fol. 64. Photographed by Dr. Robert Smetana, Olomouc.—Sternberg, where there was a college of Augustinian canons, lies close to Olomouc.—The concert, arranged by Schrattenbach, took place in the " Taverne ", where the Assembly Rooms now stand, with the collaboration of Brno musicians.—Abraham Fischer, leader of the town waits, referred to this occasion in a petition made to the Brno magistrates in 1768 : " The Kapellmeister of Salzburg, Herr Mozart, was very pleased with the orchestra here and would not have believed that my colleagues could accompany so well at the first rehearsal ". (City Archives, Brno.—Bohumir Štědroň in the report

of the "Internationale Konferenz über das Leben und Werk W. A. Mozarts, Prague, 1956" [Prague, 1958], p. 53.)

1768

On 9 January 1768 the Mozarts left Brno, spent the night at Poysdorf and arrived back in Vienna on the 10th, where they took lodgings in the Red Sabre house on the Hohe Brücke (now Wipplingerstrasse 19, corner of Färbergasse). *Cf.* 23 July 1782.

Between 2.30 and 4.30 p.m. on 19 January the Mozarts were at last received at court again by Maria Theresa and her son Joseph II, the new Emperor.

FROM HILLER'S "WÖCHENTLICHE NACHRICHTEN", LEIPZIG,
27 JANUARY 1768
(partly in French)

Continuation of the new practical works which appeared in France in the year 1767

. . . Six Sonatas for Harpsichord with accompaniment for a Violin, by J. G. Wolfgang *Mozart*, nine years of age, Op. IV. Cost 7 *livres* 4 *sols*. These Sonatas may also be played on the Harp.

Cf. 6 April 1767.

THE ARCHIEPISCOPAL EXCHEQUER TO THE PAY OFFICE
Decretum
To the Archiepiscopal Court Pay Office

His Serene Highness has graciously ordered by word of mouth, that the Court musicians at present absent by his most gracious permission, namely Kapellmeister Motzhard, Meissner and Küffl, unless they report here again in the coming month of April, are not to be handed any further salary.

Herewith entrusted to the Court Pay Office for obedient execution, Decreed by the Princely Council *18* March 1768.

Salzburg Provincial Archives.—Friedrich Pirkmayer, "Zur Lebensgeschichte Mozart's" in *Mitteilungen der Gesellschaft für Salzburger Landeskunde* (1876), Vol. XVI, pp. 130-51 ; p. 19 of offprint.—This was the first official reprimand for Leopold Mozart's frequent unauthorized extensions of leave. Schrattenbach was at this time still Prince-Archbishop of Salzburg.—Joseph Niclaus Meissner was a bass singer, Ignaz Küffel a cellist in the court band.—Leopold Mozart's salary was withheld from April to December 1768 (*cf.* Leopold's letter to Hagenauer of 11 May 1768 and his petition to the Archbishop of early March 1769).

About 24 March the children performed before the Russian Ambassador in Vienna, Dimitri, Prince Galitsin.

Schenk observes in his Mozart book (p. 201 f.) that, according to the *Wiener-isches Diarium*, an " excellent dinner music [Tafelmusik] " was given at Court on 6 April, on the eve of the marriage by proxy of the Archduchess Maria Carolina to the absent King of Naples, and believes that the Mozart children took part in it.

MARIE-THÉRÈSE GEOFFRIN TO PRINCE WENZEL KAUNITZ
(in French)

Paris, 27 April 1768.

I have heard that someone named the little Mozart, called the little prodigy of music, was in Vienna with his father, who is so much touched by the kind treatment of the Imperial Court that he has resolved to settle in Vienna under your Highness's protection. The father, and the rest of the family, being most honest people, they were generally esteemed in Paris, and in particular by several persons among my friends, who thought a great deal of the qualities of the father and the talent of the children.

Be pleased, your Highness, to take this worthy family under your wing ; they will be happy, and will be so far more than I, to whom nothing remains but a sad remembrance of my past felicity.

Kaunitz family archives, Jaroměrice, Moravia (about 1890).—Alfred von Arneth and Jules Flammermont, *Correspondance secrète du Comte de Mercy-Argenteau avec l'Empereur Joseph II et le Prince de Kaunitz* (Paris, 1889–91), II, 334, note 2.—Communicated by Dr. Wilhelm A. Bauer, Vienna.—Mme Geoffrin (1699–1777) was known as " la reine des salons ". Her salon in the rue Saint-Honoré was for sixty years the meeting-place of all persons prominent in literature, the arts and society, including Baron Grimm. The meetings took place on Mondays, sometimes on Wednesdays too. Kaunitz addressed the lady as " maman ". On her journey to Warsaw she spent a week in Vienna in June 1776 and was received at Court. Pierre de Ségur says in his book *Le Royaume de la rue Saint-Honoré, Madame Geoffrin et sa fille* (Paris, 1897), p. 60 : " A little later, when the eight-year-old Mozart came with his family on his first visit to Paris, the salon in the rue Saint-Honoré was one of those where he first performed ; Mme Geoffrin was struck with admiration for this amazing child, took a lively interest in him and his, and when they left Paris to take up residence in Vienna, she wrote a warm letter of recommendation on their behalf to Prince Kaunitz, the prime minister of Austria ".

FROM HILLER'S " WÖCHENTLICHE NACHRICHTEN ", LEIPZIG,
1 AUGUST 1768

Fourth Continuation of the Suggestions for a Music Library

. . . Herr *Mozart's Violin School* and Herr *Quantz's Instruction on the Flute* should not remain unknown to lovers of these instruments : here once again are a couple of books which in thoroughness and clearness surpass everything that had been written on these matters by our neighbours in their own languages. Fingering, and the various kinds thereof, use of the bow, expression, in short everything calculated to make a good violinist, is taught with all truth and exactness in the said work by Mozart. It is, moreover, cleanly and beautifully printed ; and perhaps this, apart from the exceptional usefulness of the book, may encourage its reading, even if the author's use of language might not always do so. He was born at Augsburg, and is in the service of His Serene Highness at Salzburg as Court Composer and Concert Master.

> Johann Joachim Quantz, Frederick the Great's flute master, had published his flute method in 1752, before Leopold Mozart's *Violinschule*. Both works are still highly esteemed after more than two centuries.

On 12 September, the Most Holy Name of Mary, the Mozarts visited Dr. Ignaz Parhamer, the spiritual director of the Orphanage in the Rennweg, in the Landstrasse suburb.

> Parhamer had occupied this post since 1759. The foundation stone of the orphanage church was laid in the summer of 1768, in the presence of the Emperor and the Mozarts.

LEOPOLD MOZART'S PETITION TO THE EMPEROR JOSEPH II, VIENNA, 21 SEPTEMBER 1768
SPECIES FACTI.

Many of the nobility resident here having been convinced of my son's extraordinary talents, both by report from elsewhere and through trials and tests undertaken by themselves, it has been everywhere regarded as one of the most astonishing events of these and earlier times that a boy of 12 should write an opera and conduct it himself. A learned paper from Paris has confirmed this opinion by declaring, after an exhaustive description of my son's genius, that *there was no doubt that this child would at the age of twelve write an opera for one or the other of the Italian theatres ;* but everybody thought that a German should reserve such glory for his own country alone. I was unanimously encouraged therein ; I paid heed to the general voice, and the Dutch Minister, Count Degenfeld, was the first to make this proposal to the theatre impresario Affligio, since he had already become abundantly acquainted with the boy's capacity in Holland. The singer Carattoli was the second to propose it to Affligio ; and the matter was agreed with the impresario at the house of the physician-in-ordinary Laugier in the presence of young Baron van Swieten and the two singers Carattoli and Caribaldi, the more so as they all, but especially both the singers, declared most emphatically that the whole town would be drawn to the theatre even by very mediocre music composed by so young a boy because of the extraordinary wonder, and if only in order to see this child conduct his work from the keyboard in the orchestra. I therefore allowed my son to write.

No sooner was the first act finished than I begged Carattoli to hear the same and to judge it, in order to confirm my opinion. He came, and so great was his astonishment that he called on me again the very next day, bringing

Caribaldi with him. Caribaldi, no less surprised, a few days later brought Poggi to me. They all professed such uncommon approval that on my asking repeatedly : *whether they really thought it was good ?—whether they considered that he ought to continue ?*—they were annoyed at my misgivings and repeatedly explained with great emotion in their native Italian : What? How ? this is a prodigy ! this opera will reach the stars ! it is a marvel ! —have no doubts, let him go on writing!—&c. : with a deal of other expressions. And the same was told me by Carattoli afterwards in his own room.

Assured of the desired success by the approval of the singers, I let my son continue with his work ; but I also requested the physician Logier to set things in order with the impresario in the matter of payment. This was done ; *and Affligio promised 100 ducats.* Now, in order to shorten my expensive stay in Vienna, I then proposed that the opera should be performed before Your Majesty's departure for Hungary ; but some alterations which the poet had to make in the text hindered the composition ; and Affligio declared that he would have it performed on Your Majesty's return.

The opera had now been ready for some weeks. They began to copy ; and the first act was distributed to the singers, with the second following immediately : and in the meantime my son was on various occasions asked by the nobility to perform one or other of the arias, and even the finale of the first act, at the clavier; and this was admired by them all, as Affligio himself witnessed with eyes and ear at Prince Kaunitz's. The rehearsals were now to begin ; only—how was I to suspect such a thing ?—this was where the persecutions of my son also began.

It occurs very rarely that an opera succeeds immediately at the first rehearsal and has not to be subjected to some alterations here and there. This is the very reason why one begins with the keyboard alone, until the singers have studied their parts, and especially the ensembles in the finales, and never with all the instruments. Yet here the very opposite happened. The parts had not been sufficiently studied, no keyboard rehearsal had been held with the singers, the finales had not been studied together, and yet the rehearsal of the first act was held with the full orchestra, simply to give the thing a mean and confused aspect from the beginning. Nobody who was present would be able to call this a rehearsal without blushing ; and of the unkind behaviour of those who will be accused by their own consciences I will say nothing. May God forgive them.

After the rehearsal Affligio said to me : *it was all right ; but as this or that was pitched too high, some alterations would have to be made here and there : I was only to have a talk with the singers ; and as His Majesty would be here in a mere 12 days, he would give the opera in 4 weeks' time, or 6 at the most, so as to have time to get everything into proper shape. I was not to worry about it at all ; he was a man of his word, and would keep all his promises ; there was nothing new in that ; other operas too had to be altered, &c.*

Thereupon the alterations demanded by the singers were made, and two new arias were written for the first act : but in the meantime *La Caschina* was performed at the theatre. By this time the appointed term was past, and I heard that Affligio had again had another opera distributed. There was even some talk that Affligio would not perform the opera at all, that he had been heard to utter that *the singers were quite unable to sing it :* those who had themselves not only approved of it, but exalted it to the skies.

To safeguard me against this gossip, my son had to perform the whole opera at the clavier at young Baron van Swieten's in the presence of Count Spork, the Duke of Braganza and other connoisseurs of music. They were all highly astonished at the behaviour of Affligio and the singers ; they were all greatly perturbed and declared with one accord that such un-Christian, untruthful and wicked proceedings were utterly incomprehensible ; that they preferred this opera to many an Italian one and that, instead of encouragement held out to so heavenly a talent, a cabal was being instigated which had no other aim than that of barring for this innocent boy the way to the honour and happiness he deserved.

I betook myself to the impresario to learn the real truth of the matter. He said to me : *that he was never against performing the opera ; but that I must not hold it against him if he considered his interests ; some doubts had been uttered to him that perhaps it would not please ;* he had the Caschina *and would now also try the* Buona figliuola, *and after that at once have the boy's opera performed : if it should then not please as desired, he would at least be provided with two other operas.* I protested against my already long stay, and its further prolongation. He retorted : *Come come ! What are 8 days more or less ? I shall then have it done at once.* It was then left at that. Carattoli's arias were altered ; with Caribaldi everything was settled ; the same with Poggi's and Laschi's, &c. : each assured me particularly more than once *that he had nothing to object to ; everything depended only on Affligio.* Meanwhile more than a month went by. The copyist told me he had not yet had any order to copy the revised arias ; and hearing at the dress rehearsal of the *Buona figliuola* that Affligio again proposed to take on another opera, I tackled him myself. Whereupon, in my presence and that of the poet Coltellini, he ordered the copyist to have everything distributed in a couple of days, and said the opera should be rehearsed with the orchestra in a fortnight at the latest.

But the poor child's enemies (whoever they may be) have again prevented it. On the same day the copyist was ordered to cease writing : and a few days later I heard that Affligio had now decided not to give the boy's opera at the theatre at all. Wishing to know the true state of affairs, I called on him, and received the information that *he had called the singers together, and that they confessed that although the opera was composed incomparably well, it was untheatrical and therefore could not be performed by them.* Such talk was altogether incomprehensible to me. For would the singers really dare without blushing for shame to despise that which they had previously extolled to the stars, in which they had themselves encouraged the boy, and which they had themselves recommended to Affligio as being good ?—I replied to him that *he could not expect the boy to have taken the pains to write an opera for nothing. I reminded him of his agreement ; I gave him to understand that he had kept us hanging about for four months and thus involved us in expenses of more than 160 ducats. I pointed out the time I had myself lost, and assured him that I should hold him responsible for the 100 ducats he had agreed to with the physician-in-ordinary Laugier, as well as the extra expenses.* To this my reasonable demand he gave me an incomprehensible answer, which betrayed his embarrassment, with which he endeavoured, I know not how, to rid himself of the whole thing, until at last he left me with the most shamelessly unkind expressions : *if I wished to see the boy prostituted, he would see to it that the opera was laughed to scorn and hissed.* Coltellini heard all this. Was this, then, to be the reward offered to my son for the great labour of writing an opera (*the original of which amounts to 558 pages*), for lost time and for the resulting expenses ?— and last, what of that which I have most at heart, my son's honour and fame, now that I no longer dare to insist on the performance, since I have been given to understand plainly enough that no pains would be spared to perform it as wretchedly as possible ; and since furthermore they say, now that the composition was unsingable, and now that it was untheatrical ; now that it did not fit the words, and now that he was unfit to write music of this kind— in short, whatever this sort of foolish and self-contradictory chatter may be; wherefore I humbly and obediently beg for a close examination of the musical powers of my child, above all for the sake of his honour, that the shamefully envious and dishonouring calumniators may vanish like smoke and everyone be convinced that their only endeavour is to suppress and cause unhappiness in the capital of his German fatherland to an innocent creature whom God has endowed with an extraordinary talent, and whom other nations have admired and encouraged.

Original in the University Library, Glasgow (Zavertal Collection).—Nissen, pp. 145 ff. Accurately printed in Henry George Farmer & Herbert Smith, *New Mozartiana* (Glasgow, 1935), pp. 113-19 (*cf.* also pp. 16-23).—The draft is undated, but it is clear from Leopold Mozart's letter to Hagenauer of 24 September (Ludwig Schiedermair's edition of the Mozart letters [Munich and Leipzig 1914], IV, 287) that he handed the fair copy to the Emperor at an audience on the 21st. The occasion for this unsuccessful petition was the Emperor Joseph's wish that Wolfgang should write an Italian opera for Vienna. Marco Coltellini altered a libretto by Carlo Goldoni, *La finta semplice*, which Wolfgang composed between April and June (K. 51) ; but the new lessee of the Burg and Kärntnertor Theatres, the unscrupulous Giuseppe d' Affligio, prevented the performance (*Cf.* Leopold Mozart's letter to Hagenauer, 30 July 1768).—The "learned paper from Paris" was Grimm's open letter of 15 July 1766.—Friedrich Christoph, Count Degenfeld was Ambassador in Vienna.—Among the singers for whom Wolfgang had written parts in his first opera were the *buffo* bass Francesco Coratoli, the tenor Gioacchino Garibaldi, Domenico Poggi and Laschi, the father of the first Contessa (*cf.* 1 May 1786).—Alexander Ludwig Laugier was imperial physician ; Gottfried van Swieten, who was later to play an important part in Mozart's life, was the son of the famous physician, at that time on leave from diplomatic service, and interested in music.—The Emperor went to Hungary in mid-April, but returned before the summer.—Wenzel, Prince Kaunitz-Rietberg, was Chancellor of State.—*La cecchina* was the alternative title of Nicola Piccinni's successful opera *La buona figliuola*, which was revived at the Burgtheater ; its sequel, *La buona figliuola maritata*, was not given.—Count Johann Wenzel Sporck was Director of Entertainments, but could do little to influence the manager d'Affligio. Duke Johann Carl of Braganza, who had abandoned the Portuguese royal family, lived in exile in Vienna at that time.—This document obviously belongs with Leopold's list of Wolfgang's childhood works which Mozart's sister on 4 August 1799 sent to the Leipzig publishers Breitkopf & Härtel, and which later passed to the library of the Paris Conservatoire (reprinted in Nissen, App., pp. 3 ff. and in Köchel-Einstein, p. xxiv f.).

In September or October 1768 Wolfgang's one-act German Singspiel *Bastien und Bastienne* (K. 50), composed during the late summer, was performed at Dr. Anton Mesmer's.

Alfred Orel, in the *Schweizerische Musikzeitung* (Zürich) for April 1951, doubted that this work had already been finished at that time ; certainly the *secco* recitatives for the early scenes were written later for a performance that had been planned at Salzburg. In any case the Singspiel was not given in the magnetist's garden theatre, which did not yet exist, but in his house, probably in a garden room, in the Rauchfangkehrer- (now Rasumofsky-) Gasse in the Landstrasse suburb.—The libretto by Friedrich Wilhelm Weiskern (1764) was a translation of that for Jean-Jacques Rousseau's *Le devin du village* (1752).

★ FROM THE "PROTOKOLLUM AULICUM IN CEREMONIALIBUS DE ANNO 1768"

Wednesday the 7th inst [7 December]

Excursion of Her Majesty the Queen and Empress to the Orphanage, with members of the Royal Family.

This day Her Royal and Imperial Apostolic Majesty with Their Royal Highnesses the two Archdukes Ferdinand and Maximilian, also the Archduchesses Elisabeth and M. Amalia, was graciously pleased to visit the Orphanage on the Rennweg to attend the first solemn consecration of the newly built church there, and also divine service.

Vienna, State Archives. Fol. 411b and 412a.—Karl Pfannhauser in the *Kirchenmusikalisches Jahrbuch* (Vienna, 1959), Jahrgang 43 (p. 37 of the off-print "Mozarts kirchenmusikalische Studien im Spiegel seiner Zeit und Nachwelt").

FROM THE "WIENERISCHES DIARIUM", 10 DECEMBER 1768

On Wednesday the 7th Her Imperial and Royal Majesty was graciously pleased to visit the orphanage on the Rennweg, to be present there at the first solemn consecration and service in the newly built church. . . . The whole of the music for the orphans' choir at High Mass had been new composed throughout for this solemnity by Wolfgang Mozart, the little son aged 12 (but already well known for his talents) of Herr Leopold Mozart, Kapellmeister in the service of the Prince-Archbishop of Salzburg, performed by himself to general applause and admiration, and conducted with the greatest accuracy ; and apart from this he also sang in the motets.

> Before the Feast of the Immaculate Conception, the new but as yet unfinished church of the Nativity of the Blessed Virgin Mary was consecrated. Maria Theresa and the Archbishop of Vienna, Count Christoph Bartholomäus Anton Migazzi, were present. Three new works by Wolfgang, now probably lost, were performed : a Mass, an Offertory and a trumpet concerto (K. 47 a–c). The suffragan bishop Franz Anton Marxer celebrated.

FROM THE " PRIORATS-EPHEMERIDEN ", MELK, 28 DECEMBER 1768
(in Latin)

At six o'clock came Dom. Mozart, with his wife, his daughter, and his famous twelve-year-old son, already a noted composer and a most highly praised organist, for whom luncheon was prepared outside with the Reverend Choirmaster in attendance. At dinner they were joined by the Most Reverend Lord Abbot, who also brought me, the Father Prior, at his invitation. Also present was his reverence the Parish Priest from Heinrichstein [?].

> Melk, Abbey Archives.—Communicated by Father Edmund Kummer and Dr. E. F. Schmid.—The Abbot was Urbanus Hauer, the Prior Petrus Boratzky, the Choirmaster Robert Kimmerling.—The exact date of the departure from Vienna at the end of December is not known.

IBID., 29 DECEMBER 1768
(in Latin)

At 7.15 Herr Mozart (*maestro di capella à* Salzburg) left here for Linz accompanied by his family, with four swift horses.

> Melk, Abbey Archives.

In December 1768 two German songs by Mozart were published by Rudolf Gräffer of Vienna in the *Neue Sammlung zum Vergnügen und Unterricht* : " An die Freude' (K. 53, words by J. P. Uz) and " Daphne, deine Rosenwangen " (K. 52, No. 11 from *Bastien und Bastienne* with altered words).

> This periodical for the young, edited by Christian Gottlob Stephanie, the elder, appeared without a date.

1769

On 4 January 1769, during their journey home, the Mozarts probably again stayed at the Benedictine monastery of Lambach nears Wels.

> The visit to Lambach is assumed to have taken place because there is a manuscript copy there (in parts) of the Symphony K. App. 221 (KE. 45a) composed in Vienna early in 1768, with the inscription " Dono Authoris 4ta Jan. 769 ".— Cf. 12 September 1767 and 27 (28) October 1783.

On 5 January 1769 the family, who had left home on 11 September 1767, arrived in Salzburg again.

FROM THE MS CALENDAR OF FATHER DOMINIKUS HAGENAUER,
SALZBURG, 5 JANUARY 1769
(in Latin)

Today Herr Mozart returned from Vienna with his wife and children, after an absence of a year and four months.

> Cajetan Hagenauer was the son of the Mozarts' landlord. This childhood friend of Wolfgang's, born in 1746, entered the Benedictine abbey at Salzburg as Father Dominikus in 1764 and in 1786 became abbot of the foundation. His calendar for 1769 is preserved there (Monastery Archives, MS. A 166, f. 484-526), and the passages concerning Mozart were published by Sigismund Keller in the *Monatshefte für Musikgeschichte* for 1873 (No. V, pp. 122 ff.). The orthography was corrected by Romuald Bauerreiss in *Studien und Mitteilungen zur Geschichte des Benediktiner-Ordens und seiner Zweige* (Munich, 1939), Vol. LVII, p. 71 f. The original was only rediscovered by Franz Martin in 1943, and the Mozart passages revised by Herbert Klein in 1957.

FROM HAGENAUER'S MS CALENDAR, 5 FEBRUARY 1769
(in Latin)

At 9 o'clock in the Collegiate Church his Reverence celebrated Mass in the presence of the Prince. The music of the Mass was composed by Dom. Wolfgangus Mozart, a youth of thirteen.

> The *Missa brevis* (K. 65), composed on 14 January, was sung at the opening of the forty hours prayer in the University (Collegiate) Church.

EPIGRAM IN HONOUR OF HERR WOLFGANG MOZART

To ancient poets' dreams that wearied her
Too long had Nature listened with annoy :
Of Orpheus taming beasts and rocks and trees,
Which with his lute he taught to dance in joy ;
Or of Apollo, banished from Olympus
And punished for his guilt, to spend his days
On earth in shepherd's guise, by mortals known
As one who 'mong his flock sings his first lays ;
Of Mercury, whose song compels to sleep
The Watchful Argus with his hundred eyes ;
Fables and myths, a chaos of rare things,
Spun by the brain of one who sleepless lies,
Learned abortions, which in idle hours
The poet's fancy lured from heated brain,
Defying Nature, making sport of beauty,
The readier the stupid crowd to gain.

Thus did mankind, 'gainst Nature's law offending,
Debase all art, till she resolved to strike
And, meeting pride with pride, all trickery ending,
A wonder made that never had its like.

Here, where the Salza springs from gloomy rocks
And greets the open land with waters fair,
Cutting in two the happy land's fair town,
Whose castle now with it the name can share,
A child, by Nature formed a work of art,
A wondrous boy one fortunate day was born,
Whose genius turned the fables of the past
To foolish stories, justly laughed to scorn.
O child ! by noble mind so lofty raised
That all too lowly writes my feeble pen,
If e'er thy merits can be duly praised,
Thy fame itself will be a poem then.
Who would have thought a child of seven years
Could equal music's greatest names in fame ?
Who will believe that what but few attain
By industry, for thee was childish game ?
But no ! immediate fame, reward of rarest gifts,
Already has flung far and wide thy name ;
Proofs of thy skill, to many races known,
Thy art to all eternity proclaim.
Nature in thee has passed her wonted bounds,
The greatest of this world thy worth maintain,
The Frenchman, German and the thoughtful Briton
Take pride that thou to visit them didst deign ;
They praise the happy land that gave thee birth
And look with envy on thy native town ;
Lamenting thy departure, still they recollect
Thy art, for ever in their memory written down.
To chance I owe the honour of thy knowledge,
Thy lively mind like others I enjoyed :
A happy deed was thine to call me friend,
Would I were longer in thy company employed !
Now let me wish (indeed, if wish I may)
That thou may'st live for ever in men's heart,
Nay, would that, for thy parents' sake I'd say
Thou couldst thyself be immortal, like thy art.

> Your faithful Servant and Friend
> Christoph von Zabuesnig, of Augsburg,
> a passer-by.

Salzburg the 2nd. March [1769]

Nissen, p. 153 f. Jahn, Vol. II, p. 717 f. (without reference).—Johann Christoph von Zabuesnig (1747–1827) was a merchant of Augsburg, then on a visit to Salzburg. He more than once tried his hand at poetry and prose (*cf.* 21 October 1777).

LEOPOLD MOZART'S PETITION TO THE PRINCE-ARCHBISHOP,
EARLY MARCH 1769

Your Serene Highness
Most Worthy High-born Prince of the
Holy Roman Empire,
Most Gracious Prince and Lord !

Your Serene Highness was recently most graciously pleased benevolently to permit me to remain some months longer in Vienna with my family, but your Highness gave orders that my salary should be withheld until my return ; since, however, this stay of mine in Vienna was made against my will and turned out to my disadvantage and to safeguard my and my child's honour I was unable to leave Vienna earlier, and since, moreover, I myself as well as my son have composed sundry things for the Church, and especially for the use of the archiepiscopal Cathedral Church : I now therefore most humbly address to Your Serene Highness the request that I should not only be paid for the past month, but that you will also be most graciously pleased to give your gracious command that the arrears should also be handed to me. The greater this beneficence may now be, the more shall I endeavour to render myself worthy of it, and to pray God for the well-being of Your Serene Highness. Most humbly recommending myself with my children in this as in all things to your Princely Grace,

I am, Most Gracious Prince
and Lord,
Your Serene Highness's

most submissive and obedient
Leopold Mozart, *m.p.*
Vice Kapellmeister.

[Appended]
Herr Mozard's salary at 28 fl., from which however 3 fl. had already been paid to another for instruction in the Chapter House, together with wine money at 4 fl. 30 kr., was cancelled as from April 1768. This information as requested. *Actum, 8 Martii ao. 1769.*

Joseph Ignati Schwarz, *m. p.*
Court Pay Office Assistant.

[On the verso] (*pro nota : de prioribus* was not to be found.)

To

His Serene Highness the

Archbishop of Salzburg, &c.

most submissive and obedient Supplication by

Leopold Mozart, His Serene Highness's Vice-Kapellmeister,

for his especial and most gracious

Assent to supply the arrears of some Months

of his Salary.

[Endorsement] By decree of his Highness : 8th March 1769. The Exchequer is to pay to the petitioner his salary for the months of January and February.

In consilio camerae, 10 March 1769.

For the immediate attention of *Secretarius* von Mayregg

In Consilio Camerae the 8th inst. Instruction by decree.

Salzburg Provincial Archives. (A draft of the decree accompanies the document.)—Pirkmayer, *op. cit.* (1876), p. 19 f.—*Cf.* 18 March 1768 and Leopold's letters to Hagenauer of 30 March and of 11 May 1768.—As early as 1762 Leopold had handed over his work as violin teacher at the Salzburg *Kapellhaus* to Wenzel Hebelt, and in Vienna made the best of the fact that his salary as Vice-Kapellmeister had been stopped for as long as he overstayed his leave.

PROGRAMME OF THE FIRST PERFORMANCE OF " LA FINTA SEMPLICE "

SALZBURG, 1 MAY 1769

(in Italian)

La Finta Semplice, Comic Drama in Music,

To be performed at Court by order of His Most Reverend Highness

Monsignor

Sigismund Archbishop

and Prince

of Salzburg.

Prince of the Holy Roman Empire

Hereditary Legate of the Sacred and Apostolic See

Primate of Germany and of the most ancient family

of the Counts of SCHRATTENBACH, etc., etc.

Salzburg, at the Court Printing-Office, 1769.

CAST

Fracasso, Hungarian Captain	Ninetta, Chambermaid
Sig. Giuseppe Meisner.	Sig^{ra}. Maria Anna Fösomair.
Rosina, Baroness, Sister to Fracasso, who feigns simplicity	Don Polidoro, a Foolish Gentleman, Brother to Cassandro
Sig^{ra}. Madalena Haydn.	Sig. Francesco Antonio Spizeder.

Giacinta, Sister to Don Cassandro   Don Cassandro, a Foolish and Avari-
and Don Polidoro   cious Gentleman, Brother to Poli-
Sig^{ra}. Maria Anna Braunhofer.   doro.
                                   Sig. Giuseppe Hornung.
                                   Simone, Lieutenant to the Captain,
                                   Sig. Felice Winter.

All in Actual Service of His Most Reverend Highness, etc.
The Music is by Sig. Wolfgango Mozart, aged Twelve Years.

Jahn, Vol. I, p. 108 f.—On the Archbishop's name-day the opera written for Vienna (see 21 September 1768) was given at the Salzburg court. However, since the Archbishop, according to Abbot Seeauer's diary, was then at Hallein, the date seems questionable. The singers were—correctly spelled—Meissner, Frau Haydn (*née* Lipp), Fräulein Braunhofer, Fräulein Fesemayer (later Frau Adlgasser), Spitzeder, Hornung and Winter.

FROM THE MARRIAGE REGISTER OF SALZBURG CATHEDRAL PARISH,
19 JUNE 1769
(in Latin)

June 19, in
the church of the Most Holy
Body of Our Lord

In the aforesaid church of the Most Holy Body of Christ by licence of the Most Reverend Director of the Consistory granted to me by word of mouth, the following celebrated marriage :

HUSBAND : Noble and ingenious Dom. Caietanus Antonius Adlgasser, Harpsichord Composer and Organist to the Court, widower ;

WIFE : Noble, chaste and virtuous maiden Maria Anna, Court Singer, legitimate child of the honourable Matthias Fesemayr, Master of Horse to His Highness, and of Maria Theresa Rauscher his wife, both living.

MINISTER ASSISTING : Leopoldus Lamprecht, civic chaplain.

WITNESSES : Noble Domm. Nicolaus Strasser, Secretary and Registrar to His Highness's Council ; Leopoldus Mozart, His Highness's Vice-Kapellmeister, with his son Wolfgang as groomsman ; Josephus Nicolaus Meissner and Antonius Spizeder, both musicians of the Princely Court.

Communicated by Dr. Herbert Klein.—The Church of the Fellowship of Corpus Christi in the Kaigasse is no longer standing. The best man (*paranymphus sponsae*) is not named elsewhere in the Register of Marriages. The priest who celebrated the wedding is the same who baptized Mozart and who, on 3 January 1769, furnished evidence on his birth.—Schenk's biography of Mozart (Vienna 1955), p. 39, mentions that the thirteen-year-old Mozart acted as a witness.—Adlgasser had first been married to Maria Eberlin, then to Maria Barbara Schwab ; for Maria Anna Fesemayer, his third wife, *cf.* 12 March 1767.

FROM THE MINUTES OF THE SALZBURG GYMNASIUM
(in Latin)

1769. 6 August. (Menstrual Sunday). At night, in honour of the Professor of Logic, music composed by the most excellent boy Wolfg. Mozart.

> Salzburg Provincial Archives.—Hammerle, *op. cit.*, p. 8.—The music was probably the serenade in D major (K. 100), written in the summer of 1769. The Professor of Logic was Father Rufinus Widl, for whom see 13 May 1767. —The "dominica menstrualis" was the first Sunday of the month.

FROM HAGENAUER'S MS CALENDAR, 6 AUGUST 1769
(in Latin)

Today was the Logicians' *Final-Musik*, composed by young Wolfgangus Mozart.

> See the previous note. For *Final-Musiken* see note to 9 August 1775.

FROM THE MINUTES OF THE SALZBURG GYMNASIUM
(in Latin)

1769. 8 August. Tuesday. Holiday. The Physicians' music, written by the same boy.

> Hammerle, *op. cit.*, p. 8.—The music was probably the serenade in G major (K. 63), written early in 1769.

FROM HAGENAUER'S MS. CALENDAR, 8 AUGUST 1769
(in Latin)

Today there was the Physicians' *Final-Musik*, also composed by Wolfgangus Mozart.

FROM LEOPOLD MOZART'S "PRELIMINARY NOTICE" TO THE SECOND EDITION OF HIS "VIOLIN SCHOOL", 24 SEPTEMBER 1769

. . . However, the first edition of this book having become very scarce these last five years, being already completely sold out nearly three years ago, will not an apology be expected of me for the late appearance of the second edition ? Will not the reason for this delay be asked ?—The fact is that I have been little at home since 1762. The extraordinary musical talent with which merciful God has blessed my two children in full measure was the cause of my travelling through the major part of *Germany* and my very long sojourn in *France, Holland* and *England,* &c. &c. I might here take the opportunity of entertaining the public with a story such as probably appears but once in a century, and which in the domain of music has perhaps never yet appeared *in such a degree of the miraculous* ; I might describe the wonderful genius of my son ; circumstantially relate his unbelievably rapid progress in the whole extent of musical science from the fifth to the thirteenth year of his age ; and I might, in so incredible a matter, call to witness the unanswerable testimony of many of the greatest masters, indeed even the testimony of envy itself. But since I am to write but a short preliminary notice and not a circumstantial story, I hope that after my return from Italy, where I now intend to go with God's blessing, I may not only entertain the public with this story, but also keep the promise of which I have already hinted something in § 22 of the first edition at the end of the Violin School.

> Lotter of Augsburg published this edition too. Leopold's reference at the end of this extract is to a remark at the end of the first edition (p. 264), where he said that he might perhaps follow up this School for " beginners " with one for " concert artists ". Nothing came of this, or of the projected history of his wonder-child. That Leopold never gave up the idea of a biography of Wolfgang may be gathered from the careful way in which he collected the family letters and made his wife, son and daughter preserve them.

JOHANN ADOLPH HASSE TO GIOVANNI MARIA ORTES AT VENICE
(in Italian)

Vienna, 30 September 1769.

I have made the acquaintance here of a certain Sig. Mozard, *maestro di capella* to the Bishop of Salzburg, a refined man of spirit and of the world ; and who, I believe, knows his business well, both in music and in other things. This man has a daughter and a son. The former plays the harpsichord very well, and the latter, who cannot be more than twelve or thirteen years of age, is already a composer and a master of music. I have seen the compositions that must be his own, which certainly are not bad and in which I have found no trace of a boy of twelve ; and I dare not doubt that they are by him, seeing that I took him through various tests on the harpsichord, on which he let me hear things that are prodigious for his age and would be admirable even for a mature man. Now, his father wishing to take him to Italy to make him known there, therefore wrote to me asking me to give him at this moment some letters of recommendation, and I shall take the liberty of sending him one for you. You see how much I presume to rely on your kindness. This letter shall, however, have no other aim than that you might permit him to make your acquaintance and that you will consent to give him your usual wise counsel, such as you may judge useful and necessary for him in your country ; and if, apart from this, you should introduce him to and let him be heard by some lady of your acquaintance : that will be much more than I shall have led him to expect. The father says that he will leave Salzburg on 24 October, so he may be with you at the end of the month.

The said Sig. Mozard is a very polished and civil man, and the children are very well brought up. The boy is moreover handsome, vivacious, graceful and full of good manners ; and knowing him, it is difficult to avoid loving him. I am sure that if his development keeps due pace with his years, he will be a prodigy, provided that his father does not perhaps pamper him too much or spoil him by means of excessive eulogies ; that is the only thing I fear.

The famous opera composer Hasse (see 15 September 1767) lived in Vienna as Court Composer round about 1770. His friend Ortes, a secular priest with the title of Abbate, was a wealthy opera-lover and political author in Venice; during the summer he lived at his country seat near Bologna.—The correspondence between the two is in the Museo Correr in Venice, which kindly furnished photographs of Hasse's three letters ; Dr. Luigi Ferdinando Tagliavini very kindly helped to decipher these. The passages concerning Mozart were first used by Hermann Kretzschmar, but he only published Hasse's letters of 30 September 1769 and 23 March 1771, in Italian and German, in the *Zeitschrift der Internationalen Musikgesellschaft* (Leipzig) for April 1902. These letters, together with Hasse's of 4 October 1769 and Ortes's of 2 March 1771, were reproduced by Carl Mennicke, first in German in the Berlin *Musik* for 1 January 1906 and then in the original in his book *Hasse und die Brüder Graun als Symphoniker* (Leipzig, 1906), without reference to Kretzschmar. The collected work *Mozart in Italia* (Milan, 1956), p. 28, contains the two Hasse letters published by Kretzschmar, translated back into Italian from the German. —Kretschmar, *op. cit.*, p. 263, Mennicke, p. 430.

HASSE TO ORTES
(in Italian)

Vienna, 4 October 1769.

Reverting to what I have already told at length about Sig. Mozard in my last letter, about his family and his virtuoso son, I content myself in this one with presenting him to you, as he will himself be its bearer. Thus without returning to what I have explained to you about the father's and the son's qualities, I will only beg you again that you will kindly consider them my friends and assist them with your good advice, and with such hints and warnings as you may deem useful and necessary to one newly arrived in the country, who wishes to appear before the public in some way and make himself known. Forgive me if I seem so pressing and dare hope to obtain for them the accustomed kindness with which you have favoured me on all occasions. For the rest, I hope that you will not be displeased to know a father who has the merit of having known how to form and give so good an education to a son who, for all that he is still almost an infant, is certainly admirable in what he knows, writes and performs on the harpsichord.

Mennicke, *op. cit.*, p. 431.

FROM HAGENAUER'S MS CALENDAR, 15 OCTOBER 1769
(in Latin)

Today P. Dominicus celebrated his first mass [*prymitia*] . . . . At a quarter before nine o'clock nones were sung. Mass then followed . . . . Music for the Mass composed by Dom. Wolfgangus Mozart, 14 years of age, which in every one's opinion was most elegant. The Mass lasted

over two hours, which was necessitated by the great number of worship-
pers ; the offertory amounted to 656 florins, 55 kreuzer . . . dinner was at
12 o'clock . . . and then Dom. Wolfgangus Mozart played on the great
organ for half an hour to the astonishment of all.

> The so-called " Dominicus Mass " (K. 66) was written by Wolfgang for his
> friend's induction. It was sung at St. Peter's.

FROM THE OFFICIAL DIARY OF ABBOT BEDA SEEAUER OF ST. PETER'S, 15 OCTOBER 1769
(in Latin)

Solemn mass with the most splendid and ingenious music.

Salzburg, Archives of St. Peter's.

FROM HAGENAUER'S MS CALENDAR, 16 OCTOBER 1769
(in Latin)

The neophyte celebrated Mass at the Nunberg.   Afterwards he was
invited by his father to a dinner held at his house in the Nunthal.   There were
about 50 persons seated at table, among them our Most Reverend Lord,
the Most Reverend Abbot of Ettal, the Rector Magnificus, Father Con-
stantinus Langheider, three Most Reverend Consistorial Councillors, Dom.
Empl, Dom. Mayr, Confessor to His Grace, Dom. Mairle[r], Regent of
His Grace's alumni.   Dinner began at 12.30 and lasted until about a quarter
past four.   When it was over, Dom. Mozart, Second Master of the Court
Chapel Music, with his two famous children, held a concert.   The daughter
first played the clavier, then Wolfgangus, a youth aged thirteen, sang [and]
played the violin and the clavier to everyone's astonishment.   Which
things finishing at about 5.30, the Most Reverend Abbots departed.

> The elder Hagenauer owned a house in the suburb of Nonntal, which still
> stands as Hauptstrasse 24.   The original Latin uses the word " pandura " for
> violin.

FROM THE REGISTER OF THE SALZBURG TREASURY, 1769

27 [November] : to Mozarth and his son presented for the journey to Italy
120 ducats .   .   .   . 600.-[fl.]

> Salzburg Provincial Archives.—Martin, *op. cit.*, p. 138.—The Prince-Arch-
> bishop had not only granted leave to Leopold, but gave him financial support
> for the first Italian journey.

FROM HAGENAUER'S MS CALENDAR, 27 NOVEMBER 1769
(in Latin)

Today Dom. Wolfgangus Mozart, a youth of fourteen years, received
permission to travel to Italy and also an official letter granting him the title

of *Concert-Maister* and promising him, upon his return from Italy, the remuneration due to that office.

> On 14 November (according to Schenk, *Mozart*, p. 230) Schrattenbach had appointed Wolfgang, aged thirteen, by patent to the unpaid post of third Concert Master of the Court Chapel, doubtless not only in order to bestow a title on him for the Italian journey, but also to tie him to Salzburg. From 1770 onwards Wolfgang appears in this capacity in the Salzburg court calendar.

DAINES BARRINGTON'S REPORT ON MOZART
(in English)

Received November 28, 1769.

ACCOUNT OF A VERY REMARKABLE YOUNG MUSICIAN.

In a Letter from the Honourable Daines Barrington,
F.R.S. to Mathew Maty, M.D. Sec. R.S.

Read Feb. 15, 1770.

SIR,

If I was to send you a well attested account of a boy who measured seven feet in height, when he was not more than eight years of age, it might be considered as not undeserving the notice of the Royal Society.

The instance which I now desire you will communicate to that learned body, of as early an exertion of most extraordinary musical talents, seems perhaps equally to claim their attention.

Joannes Chrysostomus Wolfgangus Theophilus Mozart, was born at Saltzbourg in Bavaria, on the 17th of January, 1756[1].

I have been informed by a most able musician and composer, that he frequently saw him at Vienna, when he was little more than four years old.

By this time he not only was capable of executing lessons on his favourite instrument the harpsichord, but composed some in an easy stile and taste, which were much approved of.

His extraordinary musical talents soon reached the ears of the present empress dowager, who used to place him upon her knees whilst he played on the harpsichord.

This notice taken of him by so great a personage, together with a certain

---

[1] I here subjoin a copy of the translation from the register at Saltzbourg, as it was procured from his excellence Count Haslang, envoy extraordinary and minister plenipotentiary of the electors of Bavaria and Palatine :

"I, the under-written, certify, that in the year 1756, the 17th of January, at eight o'clock in the evening, was born Joannes Chrysostomus Wolfgangus Theophilus, son of Mr. Leopold Mozart, organist of his highness the prince of Saltzbourg, and of Maria Ann his lawful wife (whose maiden name was Pertlin), and christened the day following, at ten o'clock in the morning, at the prince's cathedral church here ; his godfather being Gottlieb Pergmayr, merchant in this city. In truth whereof, I have taken this certificate from the parochial register of christenings, and under the usual seal, signed the same with my own hand.

Saltzbourg,   Leopald Comprecht,
Jan. 3, 1769.   Chaplain to his Highness in this city."

consciousness of his most singular abilities, had much emboldened the little musician. Being therefore the next year at one of the German courts, where the elector encouraged him, by saying, that he had nothing to fear from his august presence ; Little Mozart immediately sat down with great confidence to his harpsichord, informing his highness, that he had played before the empress.

At seven years of age his father carried him to Paris, where he so distinguished himself by his compositions, that an engraving was made of him.

The father and sister who are introduced in this print, are excessively like their portraits, as is also little Mozart, who, is stiled " Compositeur et Maitre de Musique, agé de sept ans."

After the name of the engraver, follows the date, which is in 1764 ; Mozart was therefore at this time in the eighth year of his age.

Upon leaving Paris, he came over to England, where he continued more than a year. As during this time I was witness of his most extraordinary abilities as a musician, both at some publick concerts, and likewise by having been alone with him for a considerable time at his father's house ; I send you the following account, amazing and incredible almost as it may appear.

I carried to him a manuscript duet, which was composed by an English gentleman to some favourite words in Metastasio's opera of Demofoonte.

The whole score was in five parts, viz. accompaniments for a first and second violin, the two vocal parts, and a base. I shall here likewise mention, that the parts for the first and second voice were written in what the Italians stile the *Contralto* cleff ; the reason for taking notice of which particular will appear hereafter.

My intention in carrying with me this manuscript composition, was to have an irrefragable proof of his abilities, as a player at sight, it being absolutely impossible that he could have ever seen the music before.

The score was no sooner put upon his desk, than he began to play the symphony in a most masterly manner, as well as in the time and stile which corresponded with the intention of the composer.

I mention this circumstance, because the greatest masters often fail in these particulars on the first trial.

The symphony ended, he took the upper part, leaving the under one to his father.

His voice in the tone of it was thin and infantine, but nothing could exceed the masterly manner in which he sung.

His father, who took the under part in this duet, was once or twice out, though the passages were not more difficult than those in the upper one ; on which occasions the son looked back with some anger pointing out to him his mistakes, and setting him right.

He not only however did complete justice to the duet, by singing his own part in the truest taste, and with the greatest precision : he also threw in the accompaniments of the two violins, wherever they were most necessary, and produced the best effects.

It is well known that none but the most capital musicians are capable of accompanying in this superior stile.

As many of those who may be present, when this letter may have the honour of being read before the society, may not possibly be acquainted with the difficulty of playing thus from a musical score, I will endeavour to explain it by the most similar comparison I can think of.

I must at the same time admit, that the illustration will fail in one particular, as the voice in reading cannot comprehend more than what is contained in a single line. I must suppose, however, that the reader's eye, by habit and quickness, may take in other lines, though the voice cannot articulate them, as the musician accompanies the words of an air by his harpsichord.

Let it be imagined, therefore, that a child of eight years old was directed to read five lines [1] at once, in four [2] of which the letters of the alphabet were to have different powers.

For example, in the first line A, to have its common powers.

In the second that of B. In the third of C. In the fourth of D.

Let it be conceived also, that the lines so composed of characters, with different powers, are not ranged so as to be read at all times one exactly under the other, but often in a desultory manner.

Suppose then, a capital speech in Shakespeare [3] never seen before, and yet read by a child of eight years old, with all the pathetic energy of a Garrick.

Let it be conceived likewise, that the same child is reading, with a glance of his eye, three different comments on this speech tending to its illustration ; and that one comment is written in Greek, the second in Hebrew, and the third in Etruscan characters.

Let it be also supposed, that by different signs he could point out which comment is most material upon every word ; and sometimes that perhaps all three are so, at others only two of them.

When all this is conceived, it will convey some idea of what this boy was capable of, in singing such a duet at sight in a masterly manner from the score, throwing in at the same time all its proper accompaniments.

When he had finished the duet, he expressed himself highly in its approbation, asking with some eagerness whether I had brought any more such music.

Having been informed, however, that he was often visited with musical ideas, to which, even in the midst of the night, he would give utterance on his harpsichord ; I told his father that I should be glad to hear some of his extemporary compositions.

The father shook his head at this, saying, that it depended entirely upon

---

[1] By this I mean, The two parts for the violins. The upper part for the voice. The words set to music. And lastly, the base.

[2] By this I mean, The violin parts in the common treble cleff. The upper part for the voice in the contralto cleff as before-mentioned. The words in common characters. And the base in its common cleff.

[3] The words in Metastasio's duet, which Mozart sung, are very pathetic.

M.— 4

his being as it were musically inspired, but that I might ask him whether he was in humour for such a composition.

Happening to know that little Mozart was much taken notice of by Manzoli, the famous singer, who came over to England in 1764, I said to the boy, that I should be glad to hear an extemporary *Love Song*, such as his friend Manzoli might choose in an opera.

The boy on this (who continued to sit at his harpsichord) looked back with much archness, and immediately began five or six lines of a jargon recitative proper to introduce a love song.

He then played a symphony which might correspond with an air composed to the single word, *Affetto*.

It had a first and second part, which, together with the symphonies, was of the length that opera songs generally last : if this extemporary composition was not amazingly capital, yet it was really above mediocrity, and shewed most extraordinary readiness of invention.

Finding that he was in humour, and as it were inspired, I then desired him to compose a *Song of Rage*, such as might be proper for the opera stage.

The boy again looked back with much archness, and began five or six lines of a jargon recitative proper to precede a *Song of Anger*.

This lasted also about the same time with the *Song of Love* ; and in the middle of it, he had worked himself up to such a pitch, that he beat his harpsichord like a person possessed, rising sometimes in his chair.

The word he pitched upon for this second extemporary composition was, *Perfido*.

After this he played a difficult lesson, which he had finished a day or two before [1] : his execution was amazing, considering that his little fingers could scarcely reach a fifth on the harpsichord.

His astonishing readiness, however, did not arise merely from great practice ; he had a thorough knowledge of the fundamental principles of composition, as, upon producing a treble, he immediately wrote a base under it, which, when tried, had very good effect.

He was also a great master of modulation, and his transitions from one key to another were excessively natural and judicious ; he practised in this manner for a considerable time with an handkerchief over the keys of the harpsichord.

The facts which I have been mentioning I was myself an eye witness of ; to which I must add, that I have been informed by two or three able musicians, when Bach the celebrated composer had begun a fugue and left

---

[1] He published six sonatas for the harpsichord, with an accompaniment for the violin, or German flute, which are sold by R. Bremner, in the Strand, and are intituled, Oeuvre Trois*me*.

He is said in the title page to have been only eight years of age when he composed these sonatas.

The dedication is to the Queen, and is dated at London, January 8, 1765.

He subscribes himself, " tres humble, et tres obeissant *petit* serviteur."

These lessons are composed in a very original stile, and some of them are masterly.

off abruptly, that little Mozart hath immediately taken it up, and worked it after a most masterly manner.

Witness as I was myself of most of these extraordinary facts, I must own that I could not help suspecting his father imposed with regard to the real age of the boy, though he had not only a most childish appearance, but likewise had all the actions of that stage of life.

For example, whilst he was playing to me, a favourite cat came in, upon which he immediately left his harpsichord, nor could we bring him back for a considerable time.

He would also sometimes run about the room with a stick between his legs by way of a horse.

I found likewise that most of the London musicians were of the same opinion with regard to his age, not believing it possible that a child of so tender years could surpass most of the master in that science.

I have therefore for a considerable time made the best inquiries I was able from some of the German musicians resident in London, but could never receive any further information than he was born near Saltzbourg, till I was so fortunate as to procure an extract from the register of that place, through his excellence count Haslang.

It appears from this extract, that Mozart's father did not impose with regard to his age when he was in England, for it was in June, 1765, that I was witness to what I have above related, when the boy was only eight years and five months old.

I have made frequent inquiries with regard to this very extraordinary genius since he left England, and was told last summer, that he was then at Saltzbourg, where he had composed several oratorios, which were much admired.

I am also informed, that the prince of Saltzbourg, not crediting that such masterly compositions were really those of a child, shut him up for a week, during which he was not permitted to see any one, and was left only with music paper, and the words of an oratorio.

During this short time he composed a very capital oratorio, which was most highly approved of upon being performed.

Having stated the above-mentioned proofs of Mozart's genius, when of almost infantine age, it may not be improper perhaps to compare them with what hath been well attested with regard to other instances of the same sort.

Amongst these, John Barratier hath been most particularly distinguished, who is said to have understood Latin when he was but four years old, Hebrew when six, and three other languages at the age of nine.

This same prodigy of philological learning also translated the travels of Rabbi Benjamin when eleven years old, accompanying his version with notes and dissertations. Before his death, which happened under the age of twenty, Barratier seems to have astonished Germany with his amazing extent of learning ; and it need not be said, that its increase in such a soil, from year to year, is commonly amazing.

Mozart, however, is not now much more than thirteen years of age, and it is not therefore necessary to carry my comparison further.

The Rev. Mr. Manwaring (in his *Memoirs of Handel*) hath given us a still more apposite instance, and in the same science.

This great musician began to play on the clavichord when he was but seven years of age, and is said to have composed some church services when he was only nine years old, as also the opera of Almeria, when he did not exceed fourteen.

Mr. Manwaring likewise mentions that Handel, when very young, was struck sometimes whilst in bed with musical ideas, and that, like Mozart, he used to try their effect immediately on a spinnet, which was in his bed-chamber.

I am the more glad to state this short comparison between these two early prodigies in music, as it may be hoped that little Mozart may possibly attain to the same advanced years as Handel, contrary to the common observation that such *ingenia praecocia* are generally short lived.

I think I may say without prejudice to the memory of this great composer, that the scale most clearly preponderates on the side of Mozart in this comparison, as I have already stated that he was a composer when he did not much exceed the age of four.

His extemporary compositions also, of which I was a witness, prove his genius and invention to have been most astonishing ; least however I should insensibly become too strongly his panegyrist, permit me to subscribe myself, Sir,

Your most faithful
humble servant,
Daines Barrington.

This report was handed on 28 September 1769 to the Secretary of the Royal Society in London, Dr. Mathew Maty (*Cf.* 19 July 1765) and read on 15 February 1770, but not published till 1771 in the *Philosophical Transactions* of this learned society (Vol. LX pp. 54-64). It was reprinted, revised, in Dr. Barrington's *Miscellanies* on various subjects (London, 1871), pp. 279 ff., supplemented by a communication from Charles Burney (see 21 January 1780), (Burney reported to the same society on William Crotch, the English wonder-child of music ; see 18 February 1779).—The extract quoted by Barrington from the Salzburg Cathedral birth register was obtained from Leopold Lamprecht, town chaplain of that city (see 28 January 1756) through Count Joseph Haslang, the Bavarian Ambassador in London. (Information kindly supplied by the Bavarian State Archives in Munich.)—Barrington concerns himself with the time of June 1765, during the Mozarts' sojourn in London. A portrait of Wolfgang at the age of seven appeared in his book, engraved by T. Cook from a portion of the group-portrait by Carmontelle-Delafosse (Paris, 1764). Beneath this engraving are quoted three lines (440-442) from the so-called Homeric Hymn to Hermes :

ἦ σοί γ' ἐκ γενετῆς τάδ' ἄμ' ἕσπετο θαυματὰ ἔργα,
ἠέ τις ἀθανάτων ἠὲ θνητῶν ἀνθρώπων
δῶρον ἀγαυὸν ἔδωκε καὶ ἔφρασε θέσπιν ἀοιδήν;

Salzburg did not actually belong to Bavaria but, as an independent principality, to the Bavarian circle of the German Empire.—The Bach named here is, of course, Johann Christian, the " London " Bach.—The " oratorio " Wolfgang is supposed to have written in confinement at Salzburg, is probably the *Grabmusik* or Passion cantata, K. 42, dating from Holy Week 1767, and not (as Jahn assumed) *Die Schuldigkeit,* K. 35.—Benjamin ben Jonah's travel book *Massaoth schel Rabbi Binjamin,* was published at Constantinople in 1543.— John Mainwaring published in 1760, a year after Handel's death, a biography of that master (the first of any composer in book form).—Handel's opera *Almira* was not performed till 1705, when he was already nineteen years of age.

On 13 December 1769 Leopold Mozart left Salzburg with Wolfgang, this time without his wife and daughter, but with a servant. They arrived at Keitl bei Reichenhall at 1 p.m. and at Lofer at 7 p.m.

Herbert Klein, " Mozart in Reichenhall " in *Reichenhaller Heimatsblatt,* 1959, No. 4. The first Italian journey lasted until 28 March 1771.

FROM HAGENAUR'S MS. CALENDAR, 13 DECEMBER 1769
(in Latin)

Today Dom. Mozart, with his only son, left for Italy.

At noon on 14 December the two Mozarts reached St. Johann in the Tyrol, and in the evening Wörgl.

On 15 December they reached Schwaz at midday and Innsbruck at 5.30 p.m., where they alighted at the White Cross inn.

On Sunday, 17 December, at 5 p.m., Wolfgang played at Count Leopold Künigl's, Vice-President of the Tyrolean administration.

Wolfgang played, *inter alia,* a concerto dedicated to the Count by another composer.

FROM THE " INNSBRUCKER MONTÄGIGE ORDINARI ZEITUNG ", 18 DECEMBER 1769

On Friday, *i.e.* the 14th inst., have arrived here at the White Cross inn Herr Leopold Mozart, Kapellmeister to the Prince of Salzburg, with his son Herr Wolfgang Mozart, at this time actual Concert Master to His Serene Highness of Salzburg, who has already since his sixth year made himself famous for his extraordinary musical science, both at the all-highest Imperial Court and in England, France, Holland and also throughout the entire Roman Empire.

Yesterday he was invited to a concert organized by the high nobility, at which he gave the most splendid proofs of his quite peculiar skill. This young musician, who is at present 13 years of age, has thus lent new lustre to his fame here and by his extraordinary talents united the voices of all musical connoisseurs in his praise. To-morrow he will continue his journey to Italy.

Nissen, p. 157, from a cutting sent home by Leopold Mozart. Jahn, Vol. I p. 119.—This newspaper is not to be found at Innsbruck.—Friday was 15 December.

On 19 December they travelled from Innsbruck to Steinach, on the 20th by way of Sterzing to Bressanone [Brixen], and on the 21st by way of Atzwang, where they took lunch, to Bolzano [Bozen], where they alighted in the evening at the Sun inn and spent two nights.

On 23 December the travellers left Bolzano and arrived at Egna [Neumarkt] ; on the 24th they went by way of Trento [Trient] to Rovereto, where they put up at the Rose inn.

On 25 December Wolfgang played at the house of Baron Giovanni Battista Todeschi ; in the afternoon of the 26th he tried the organ at the Church of San Marco at Rovereto.

On 27 December father and son arrived at Verona, where they stayed at the Two Towers inn.

1770

FROM THE " HOCHFÜRSTLICH-SALZBURGER KIRCHEN- UND HOF-KALENDER " FOR 1770

HIS SERENE HIGHNESS'S COURT MUSIC

.   .   .

VICE CHAPEL MASTER

Herr Leopold Motzart, 28 February 1763.

CONCERT MASTERS

Herr Ferdinand Seidl.
Herr Johann Michael Hayden.
Herr Wolfgang Motzart.

This is the first appearance of Wolfgang's name in the Salzburg Court Calendar. The leading artists in the court music remained the same for the next three years, Seidl not disappearing from the list in the Calendar till 1774. The date against the name of Mozart's father is that of the day on which he became vice-Kapellmeister, at a salary of 25 gulden a month and 4½ gulden for his board. Giuseppe Maria Lolli had been appointed Kapellmeister at the same time, at a monthly salary of 30 gulden with 8 gulden board and lodging allowance.

On 5 January 1770 Wolfgang gave his first concert in Italy, at the Accademia filarmonica of Verona.

INSCRIPTION ON THE FRAME OF THE PORTRAIT OF MOZART BY SAVERIO DALLA ROSA, PAINTED AT VERONA, 6–7 JANUARY 1770

AMEDEO VOLFANGO MOZARTO SALISBVRGENSI
PVERO DVODENNI
IN ARTE MVSICA LAVDEM OMNEM FIDEMQ. PRAETERGRESSO
EOQ. NOMINE GALLORVM ANGLORVMQ. REGIBVS CARO
PETRVS LVIATVS HOSPITI SVAVISSIMO
EFFIGIEM IN DOMESTICO ODEO P.[INGERE]C.[VRAVIT]
ANNO MDCCLXX.

This portrait of the young Wolfgang, the first important portrait, was painted on 6 and 7 January. Formerly ascribed to one of the brothers Felice and then, with greater plausibility, to Gian Bettino Cignaroli, it is now regarded as the work of the Felices' nephew, Saverio dalla Rosa (Raffaello Brenzoni in *Studi storici veronesi*, 1954). Over the keyboard of the harpsichord are the words : " Ioannis Celestini veneti MDLXXXIII [1583] ". The *Molto Allegro* on the desk is probably by Wolfgang (K. 72a). The Latin inscription on the frame may have been by Giuseppe Torelli (Erich Schenk's Mozart book, p. 239). The picture was commissioned by the Mozarts' Veronese host, Pietro Lugiati, and was in Alfred Cortot's collection at Lausanne.—An authentic collotype was published in 1957 by Bärenreiter-Verlag (Cassel, Basle, London).—*cf.* 22 April 1770.

On Sunday 7 January he played both the organs in the Church of San Tommaso.

THE VERONESE POET MESCHINI'S ADDRESS TO MOZART, JANUARY 1770
(in Latin and Italian)

TO AMADEO MOZART
SWEETEST CHILD
AND MOST ELEGANT PLAYER
FROM ANTONIO MARIA MESCHINI
OF VERONA.

If Orpheus enraptured the forests, if Tartarus he moved,
Now thou stealest men's hearts, child, and movest the stars.

————

So, as thou dost for us,
Did fair Apollo play,
Shedding celestial ray,
Upon his lyre thus.
But no : thou with thy singing
Dost set all music ringing.

Nissen, *op. cit.*, p. 163.—At Verona two poems on Wolfgang were indited. One of them, probably the second, is likely to have been the one which was sung extempore by the Academy Professor Daniele Barba at Verona. Ignaz Anton von Weiser, the half-brother of Frau Maria Theresia Hagenauer and Burgomaster of Salzburg from 1772 to 1775, made a German paraphrase, not precisely dated, of Meschini's poem ; this has been preserved in a manuscript copy made by Aloys Fuchs (Jahn, Vol. II, p. 719). It is here freely paraphrased at two removes in English :

If woods and Hades bowed of old to Orpheus' strains,
    Thy music, wondrous boy, our hearts and senses gains,
The stars themselves, where he but moved the world ; in sooth
    That which he showed in dreams thy art has turned to truth.
If Orpheus' ancient lyre the underworld could capture,
    Thy later taste, O child, affords us greater rapture !
High though the ancient minstrel's art did once aspire,
    Low must he bow to thee, as one aspiring higher.

That Orpheus should today be heard and seen in thee
    Our ears and eyes proclaim, no need for poetry.
Of old 'twas Greece alone experienced Orpheus' ways,
    While thou, prodigious boy, knowest universal praise.
O Orpheus, when this child the lyre plays, and sings,
    Believe us, thine own lyre and song but feebly rings.
Then let not too ambitious sound thine ancient fame ;
    Hear but this youthful voice, which silences thy fame.
Behold the wonders done by this precocious youth
    And say if thou canst match his worth, in very truth.
Learn, Orpheus, what music can attain today,
    And wilt thou enter then against this wonder, say ?
'Tis true that Orpheus brought the stones to life, we learn,
    But list'ning to this boy himself to stone he'll turn.
Compare of these two artists' lives the mortal span,
    Then judge that Orpheus is a child, our child a man.

Another version of Weiser's poem, preserved among Nissen's Collectanea at the Salzburg Mozarteum, is printed on pp. 520-21 of the German edition of this book.

THE VERONESE POET BETTI'S ADDRESS TO MOZART, JANUARY 1770
(in Italian)

TO SIG. AMADEO MOZART,
THE ADMIRABLE LITTLE BOY.
AN EXTEMPORANEOUS SONNET.

If with his lyre from celestial heights
Cupid divine awakens lovely strains,
Then how can we on earth, with all our pains
And errors ever set our songs to rights ?
Well may we, charming boy, accord thee praise,
If thou reformest music with thy art ;
May nature shape for better in thy heart
The strains the god's inspired plectrum plays.
You, who for years have struggled to attain
The blessing and the favour of your art,
And hoped harmonious mastery to gain,
I am not wrong, you know it in your heart,
If I declare that his enchanting strain
Alone is god-like in its ev'ry part.

In token of admiration and love,
Zaccaria Betti.

Nissen, *op. cit.*, p. 162 f.—Betti was a Veronese occasional poet.

On 10 January father and son left Verona for Mantua, where they arrived at 5 p.m. and alighted at the Green Anchor inn ; the same evening they attended a performance of Hasse's *Demetrio*.

Hasse's opera dates from 1732 ; its second version was first given in Vienna, as *Cleonice*, in 1734. At Mantua *Demetrio* was being revived after a long interval.

FROM THE " GAZZETTA DI MANTOVA ", 12 JANUARY 1770
(in Italian)

VERONA, 9 January.

This city cannot do otherwise than declare the amazing prowess in music possessed, at an age still under 13 years, by the little German boy Sig. Amadeo Wolfango Motzart, a native of Salzburg and son of the present *maestro di cappella* to His Highness the Prince-Archbishop of that city. On Friday, the 5th inst., this youth gave, at one of the halls of the noble Philharmonic Academy, in the presence of the civic authorities and a crowded concourse of nobles of both sexes, such proofs of his expertness in the aforesaid art as to astonish everyone. In the company of a number of distinguished performers he was able to exhibit first of all a most beautiful overture of his own composition, which deserved all its applause. He then splendidly played a harpsichord concerto at sight, and afterwards sonatas that were entirely new to him. This was followed by four verses submitted to him, on which he composed on the spot an aria in the best of taste in the very act of singing it. A subject and a finale proposed to him, he marvellously improvised upon according to the best rules of the art. He also played a trio by Bocherini very well at sight, and a theme given him on the violin by a professor he admirably composed in score. In short, on this and other occasions, subject to the most arduous trials, he overcame them all with an inexpressible skill, and thus to universal admiration, especially among the music-lovers ; among them were the Signori Lugiati, who, after enjoying and allowing others to enjoy yet finer proofs of this youth's ability, in the end wished to have him painted from life for a lasting memorial. Nor is this a new idea, considering that, having travelled all over *Europe* with his father to exhibit himself, he caused so much wonder everywhere, up to the tender age of 7 years, that his portrait was taken everywhere, in *Vienna*, in *Paris*, where in fact there are portraits of his whole family, in *Holland* and in *London*, where his portrait was placed in the famous British Museum, with an inscription commemorating his stupendous skill in music at the green age of 8 years, which was all he was then. For the rest, we have no doubt that as he progresses on the journey he is now taking through *Italy*, he will cause the same astonishment wherever he will go, especially among the experts and the intelligentsia.

Enclosure in Leopold Mozart's letter to his wife of 11 January 1770. The report from Verona of 9 January appeared at Mantua on the 12th (not 19th, as generally given) ; the *Gazzetta* was a weekly. The same report appeared also in the *Gazzetta di Pesaro*—Facsimile in *Mozart in Italia* (Milan, 1956), Plate VI, from the copy in the Biblioteca Comunale, Mantua. Nissen, *op. cit.*, p. 169 f.

PROGRAMME OF MOZART'S CONCERT AT THE TEATRO SCIENTIFICO,
MANTUA, 16 JANUARY 1770
(in Italian)

SERIES OF MUSICAL COMPOSITIONS TO BE PERFORMED AT THE PUBLIC
PHILHARMONIC ACADEMY OF MANTUA IN THE EVENING OF THE 16TH
OF THE PRESENT MONTH OF JANUARY 1770
ON THE OCCASION OF THE ARRIVAL OF THE MOST HIGHLY SKILLED YOUTH
SIGNOR AMADEO MOZART.

1. Symphony composed by Sig. W. Amadeo Mozart, Parts 1 and 2.
2. Concerto for Harpsichord presented and performed by him at sight.
3. Aria contributed by the tenor of the Opera, Sig. Uttini.
4. Sonata for Harpsichord performed at sight by the youth and Variations of his invention extemporized and subsequently repeated in a key other than that in which it is written.
5. Concerto for Violin *obbligato* by a Professor.
6. Aria composed and sung at the same time by Sig. Amadeo extempore, with the proper Accompaniments performed on the Harpsichord, to words made for the purpose, but not previously seen by him.
7. Another Harpsichord Sonata, both composed and performed by the same, on a musical theme proposed to him extempore by the first violin.
8. Aria contributed and sung by Signorina Galliani.
9. Concerto for Oboe *obbligato* by a Professor.
10. Musical Fugue, composed and performed by Sig. Amadeo on the Harpsichord and led to a proper conclusion according to the laws of counterpoint, on a simple theme for the same submitted to him extempore.
11. Symphony by the same, performed with all the parts on the Harpsichord from a single Violin part, openly submitted to him extempore.
12. Duet of Professors.
13. Trio in which Sig. Amadeo will play an improvised Violin part.
14. Final Symphony by the same Sig. Mozzard.

Original MS. in the Accademia Virgiliana, Mantua. The printed programme is somewhat different (*cf.* the volume *Mozart und seine Welt* . . . in the *Neue Mozart-Ausgabe*, X/32, No. 194).—Nissen, *op. cit.*, p. 173 f.—Erich Schenk, " Mozart in Mantua " in *Studien zur Musikwissenschaft* (Vienna, 1955), Vol. XXII, p. 23.—The concert took place in the theatre of the Reale Accademia di scienze, lettere e arti (also known as the Accademia filarmonica, and now as the Accademia Virgiliana), which had been opened only six weeks before. Among the works performed by Wolfgang Nos. 1, 11 and 14 in the programme have been identified, with fair probability, as the symphonies KE. 66c, e and d (formerly K. App. 215, 218 and 217), written at Salzburg at the end of 1769. The aria, No. 3, was sung by the tenor Uttini ; the violin concerto, No. 5, was played by Angelo Orsi ; another aria, No. 8, was performed by Angiola Galliani ; Luigi Livraghi was the soloist in the oboe concerto, No. 9 ; and a duet, No. 12, was sung by Leonora Ambreville and Uttini. Schenk mentions a handwritten invitation to this concert (*cf. Mozart und seine Welt in zeitgenössischen Bildern*, No. 195), in the possession of Count Giovanni Battista Arco and quotes (in Italian) the following notice from Stefano Gionta's *Fioretto delle Cronache di Mantova* (1844), p. 272 :

"In 1770, being on his way through Mantua, Amedeo Wolfango Mozart, a youngster of 13, gave, in the evening of 16 January, a pianoforte concert in the scientific theatre, to the wonder of those who heard him, having improvised various pieces from which it became clearly apparent to what heights of glory he has attained in musical science."

FROM THE "GAZZETTA DI MANTOVA", 19 JANUARY 1770
(in Italian)

MANTUA, 19 January.

Last Tuesday evening, the 16th inst., in the Theatre of the Royal Academy, the public Philharmonic Academy of the month was given before its time, in order opportunely to catch the incomparable boy Sig. Wolfango Amadeo Mozart, who is passing through here, with the express aim of letting this town admire the amazing talent and extraordinary mastery which he already possesses in music at the age of 13. To write at a desk (as the best masters do) in as many parts as you wish, concertato or obbligato, vocal and instrumental, is so easy for him that he can do it just as well at the harpsichord, even extempore. On the evening here mentioned, apart from opening and closing symphonies of his composition, he performed, in the presence of the illustrious personages who hold office in every rank of political, military and ecclesiastical Government, all the Nobility and Citizens, the Body of the Academy itself, and a select assembly of amateur and professional Members of the said Academy, concertos and sonatas for harpsichord, extemporized, with most judicious variations, and with the repetition of a sonata in another key. He sang a whole aria extempore, on new words never before seen by him, adding the proper accompaniments. He improvised two sonatas on two themes successively given him on the violin by the leader of the orchestra, elegantly linking them both together the second time. He accompanied a whole symphony with all the parts from a single violin part submitted to him on the spot. And what is most to be esteemed, he composed and at the same time extemporaneously performed a fugue on a simple theme given him, which he brought to such a masterly harmonic interweaving of all the parts and so bold a resolution as to leave the hearers astounded ; and all these performances were on the harpsichord. Finally he also played marvellously well the violin part in a Trio by a famous composer. After various private trials to which our Masters and Professors of music have subjected him these last few days that he has stayed here, they cannot sufficiently assert that this youth appears to them to be born to vanquish all the experts in the art ; and this view accords well with that of a noted literary man of Verona, written to the Secretary of our Philharmonic Academy in recommendation of Sig.

Wolfango ; namely that he *is a miracle in music, and one of those freaks Nature causes to be born, a Ferracina to humiliate the Mathematicians, and a Corilla to degrade the Poets.* Meanwhile he now tours Italy with Sig. Leopoldo, his Father, who is also a man of talent and a Chapel Master of repute ; and they both have that which will cause wonder on Italian soil, though it is the true habitation of good taste in this matter especially. The concert was thus a most brilliant success and altogether satisfactory, having moreover been interspersed with two arias, and a duet, and two concertos, one for violin, the other for oboe, performed by these Professors : one and all things of great exquisiteness and perfection.

> Facsimile in *Mozart in Italia*, Plate IX, from the copy at Mantua.—Schenk, "Mozart in Mantua", *op. cit.*, p. 26 f.—A free German translation of this notice appeared in the *Europaeische Zeitung* printed at Salzburg (but no longer to be found there), probably at Leopold Mozart's instigation (*cf.* Nissen, pp. 170-2 ; Nottebohm, pp. 114 and 117). The report of an aurora borealis was also translated by mistake.—Bartolomeo Ferracina (1692-1777) was an inventive engineer ; "Corilla Olimpica" was the pseudonym of the poetess Maria Maddalena Morelli Fernandez (Ernst Fritz Schmid, "Auf Mozarts Spuren in Italien" in *Mozart-Jahrbuch 1955*, p. 25). *Cf.* 4 April 1770.

SIGNORA SARTORETTI : POEM TO MOZART, MANTUA, JANUARY 1770
(in Italian)

TO SIGNOR AMADEO WOLFGANGO MOZART
ANACREONTIC

Spirits of gaiety,
Spirits of mirth,
Quick, I invite you,
Descend to the earth,
Tribute to render
To music so tender.

No, I deceive me not,
You are the rare ones,
Charming and amiable,
Courteous and fair ones,
Who in a merry round
Ever are gladly found.

Venus, the Graces, shall
Come down with you,
Pleasure to share in him,
Worthy and true,
Whose love to you he gives,
Who but for music lives.

Who, with his golden hair,
Gentle of nature, he
One of your company
Almost appears to be,
And in his roguish eyes
Spirit to yours replies.

Rosy his cheeks and round,
Soft as the down of swan.
Does he not please you, then ?
Does he not lure you on ?
Do not, then, bind and hold
His pretty wings of gold.

Do you not love him for
His vital song,
Languid and fierce by turns,
Now soft, now strong ?
Nay, vieing oft
With Phoebus aloft !

See how his fingers move,
Hear with what art
He makes the keys respond
In ev'ry part ;
How he to you imparts
All his accomplished arts.

If noble harmony
Can turn to naught
The soul's affliction and
Troublesome thought,
If its perfection
Can waken affection,

Europe has witnessed him,
Where, as a child,
Her ev'ry region
He newly beguiled.
Woe ! if to them he's near,
Let not the Sirens hear.

If it can rouse you
And give you delight,
So it may bridle your
Fugitive flight.
Nay, once you hear him,
You will stay near him.

Why then not stay awhile,
Where is the harm ?
Let him but kindle your
Flames with his charm.
Spirits, he enthralls you,
Plays for you, calls you.

With flowers, O Spirits,
Let's tribute bring ;
Oh, do not leave him,
Do not take wing.
Return not above,
To him give your love !

Spirits, regard me not,
Who'eer I may be.
So much more noble
And worthy is he,
Far more than I renowned,
Who is by genius crowned.

Nissen, *op. cit.*, p. 174 f ; Jahn, Vol. II, p. 720.—The author, Signora Sartoretti, who had treated Wolfgang's frozen hands with pomade, sent a present of money with this poem.

On 19 January the Mozarts left Mantua and arrived at Bozzolo at 6 p.m. ; here they stayed at the Post inn (*cf.* 26 January). On the 20th they continued to Cremona, where they heard Hasse's opera *La clemenza di Tito*. On the 23rd, at noon, they reached Milan, where they found accommodation in the Augustine monastery of San Marco. Before the 26th they heard Niccolò Jommelli's *Didone abbandonata* (1741) at the Scala.

Leopold Mozart probably brought with him a letter of recommendation from the Augustinian monastery of Mülln, Salzburg (Schmid, *op. cit.*, p. 27).

FROM THE " GAZZETTA DI MANTOVA ", 26 JANUARY 1770
(in Italian)

They write from *Bozolo* that towards one o'clock at night on the 19th of the current month the celebrated boy Sig. Wolfango Amadeo Mozart arrived here, who had no sooner alighted at the coaching inn of this town,

than he was most courteously received by the Archpriest Don Carlo Saragozzi, Professor of Music, and then taken by the same in a carriage to his
house ; and that the said famous little boy in the course of some two hours
gave proofs of his amazing talent, sight-reading at the harpsichord various
sonatas by several worthy composers, and especially a Trio composed by Sig.
Giuseppe Saragozzi, also a Master and Professor of Music, giving unspeakable
pleasure and satisfaction to both the Political and the Military authorities
there, and many other Gentlemen who happened to be present ; and that
when, on the following morning, he had fully satisfied the people of that
place, he departed in the direction of Cremona.

> E. F. Schmid, *op. cit.*, p. 26 f. ; *Mozart in Italia*, p. 288.—" One o'clock at
> night " (" un' ora di notte ") meant, in January, six in the evening (*cf.* Goethe's
> *Italian Journey*, 17 September 1786).

On 2 February Mozart met Nicola Piccinni at the dress rehearsal of the latter's
opera *Cesare in Egitto*.

On 7 February father and son dined with Count Karl Joseph Firmian, Governor-
General of Lombardy, who presented Wolfgang with the Turin edition of Pietro
Metastasio's works. Mozart played for the guests, who included Giovanni Battista
Sammartini.

> Count Firmian was one of the four nephews of the former Archbishop of
> Salzburg, Leopold Mozart's first prince. His brothers were Leopold Ernst,
> Prince-bishop of Passau, Vigil Maria August, Suffragan Bishop of Lavant,
> and Franz Lactantius, Chief Steward and Inspector of the Court Music at
> Salzburg.

On 15 February 1770 Daines Barrington read his report on Mozart before the
Royal Society in London (see 28 November 1769).

On 18 February Mozart again played at Count Firmian's, in the presence of Ercole
IV Rainoldo d' Este, Duke of Modena, and his daughter Beatrice Ricciarda ; father
and son afterwards went to the opera and a ball.

On 23 February Mozart gave a public concert.

On 12 March Mozart played at an evening party at Count Firmian's which was
attended by 150 guests from the nobility. Four new soprano arias by him, to words
by Metastasio (K. 78, 88, 79, 77), were performed.

> Unfortunately nothing further is known about this.

COUNT KARL JOSEPH FIRMIAN TO COUNT GIAN LUCA PALLAVICINI
AT BOLOGNA
(in Italian)

Your Excellency,

Seeing that Sig. Leopoldo Mozart, Chapel Master in the service of the
Prince-Archbishop of Salzburg, and with him his son, is making his way to
your city, I take the liberty of recommending them warmly to Your Excellency, moved by the assurance I have of your well-known generosity and
kindness, and by the thought that perhaps you will not be displeased to
find in young Mozart one of those musical talents but rarely produced by

nature, inasmuch that at his tender age he not only equals the Masters of the art, but even exceeds them, I believe, in readiness of invention. I hope therefore that Your Excellency will be pleased to honour them with your protection during their stay there and to find them means of appearing in public, as I also urgently beg you will help them in the matter of their prudent and most advantageous conduct. Please expect of me in exchange any service I may render you, anxious as I ever am to do justice to all my obligations and to assure you, more than ever of the great respect with which I pass on to subscribe myself,

Your Excellency's   Milan, 14 March 1770

Most Devoted and Obliged Servant,
Carlo, Count Firmian.

To His Excellency the Marshal Count Pallavicini,
Bologna.

Original in State Archives, Bologna, Fondo Pallavicini—E. F. Schmid, *op. cit.*, p. 29 ; Andrea Ostoja, *Mozart e l'Italia* (Bologna, 1955), p. 24. Facsimile in the monthly *Città di Milano*, December 1955, p. 690.—Field-Marshal Pallavicini-Centurioni was a keen patron of the arts.—Firmian on the same day wrote an almost identical letter to Guglielmo du Tillot, Marchese di Felino, a patron of the arts at Parma (Archivio di Stato, Parma ; *Mozart in Italia*, pp. 74 and 227 f.). A third letter of the kind, addressed to the Tuscan Minister of State, Franz Xaver Wolf, Count Orsini-Rosenberg, at Florence, has not so far been found.

On 15 March the travellers left Milan and went to Parma and Modena by way of Lodi and Piacenza.

This journey took from 15 to 24 March. At Parma they were guests of the singer Lucrezia Agujari, nicknamed " La Bastardella ".

GUGLIELMO DU TILLOT TO COUNT KARL JOSEPH FIRMIAN
(in Italian)

Parma, 20 March 1770.

With Your Excellency's most valued letter Sig. Leopoldo Mozart has presented himself to me, together with his young son, from whose conversation I have been able to recognize the lively mind and the singular talent with which he is gifted in the difficult art of Music. While I have sought to show them my most sincere endeavour to be of use to them both and to exhibit their merits in a favourable light, particularly in view of their enjoyment of Your Excellency's protection, I await (since they are also availing themselves of this Baron de Knebel's enthusiastic assistance) further opportunities of showing the high regard in which I hold Your Excellency's recommendation, and the constant devotion of which I have the honour to assure you.

State Archives, Parma.—Referred to in *Mozart in Italia*, p. 75.—Reply to Firmian's letter of 14 March.—Franz Philipp, Baron Knebel, was Imperial Ambassador at Parma in 1769-70.

On 24 March father and son arrived at Bologna and alighted at the Pilgrim of St. Mark inn.

This house is still a highly esteemed hotel.

On 26 March a concert took place at Field-Marshal Count Pallavicini's, lasting from 7.30 to 11.30 p.m.

This *soirée* had been arranged in honour of Count Joseph Clemens Kaunitz, son of the Chancellor of State Wenzel, Prince Kaunitz. Apart from Wolfgang, two castrati, Giuseppe Aprile and Giuseppe Cicognani, took part in the concert. A hundred and fifty noble guests were present, but Padre Giambattista Martini also attended the concert.

FROM THE COPY-BOOK OF THE PALLAVICINI HOUSEHOLD,
26 MARCH 1770
(in Italian)

Sig. Leopoldo Mozart, Master of Music in the service of the Prince-Archbishop of Salzburg, and his son, Giovanni Giorgio Wolfango Mozart, Master of Music and Composer now 13 years of age, having been recommended by a letter from His Excellency Count Carlo di Firmian on their way through Bologna, a Musical Concert was held this day, the 26th. . . .

Bologna, State Archives.—E. F. Schmid, *op. cit.*, p. 31 f. ; Ostoja, pp. 24 ff., where the list of the invited guests is also shown.—Johann Georg were the Christian names of Wolfgang's Augsburg grandfather.

FROM THE PALLAVICINI DOMESTIC ACCOUNTS, 26 MARCH 1770
(in Italian)

Costs incurred for a musical Concert with refreshments held in the house on the evening of the 26th inst. when Count Joseph, son of Prince Kaunitz Rittberg, lodged here.

. . . To the celebrated Leopoldo Mozart, Master of Music, 13 years of age, who conducted the Concert, L. 205. . . .

To the German Chapel Master Sig. Leopoldo Muzard, 20 sequins.

Bologna, State Archives.—Ostoja, p. 29.—In the first entry " Leopoldo " should of course read " Wolfango ". The total costs of the concert, including singers and orchestra, amounted to L. 763.15.

COUNT GIAN LUCA PALLAVICINI TO COUNT KARL JOSEPH FIRMIAN
(in Italian)

Bologna, 28 March 1770.

Your Excellency,

Hardly had Messrs. Mozart, Father and Son, handed me your Excellency's most kind letter, and told me that they intended to make but a short stay at Bologna, wishing to proceed with all speed to Florence in order to be in Rome for Holy Week, than I immediately hastened to give effect to your justified desire that this city should know and admire young Mozart's rare talent. To this end a conversazione was held in my house on Monday evening, at which 70 ladies were present as well as the Cardinale-Legate, the Princes of Holstein and almost all the nobility, and the young professor gave such admirable proofs there of his knowledge, as would at his tender age seem incredible to anyone who had not witnessed them ; they were all surprised and took infinite pleasure in knowing a boy of such singular merit. He is about to depart together with his father, and I am giving him letters for Rome addressed to the Cardinal Pallavicini, Secretary of State, and to Prince Doria ; and I find it easy to believe that the Cardinal will enable him to be heard by His Holiness. So much I thought it my duty to do, not less because of the merits of those I recommend than in order to act upon Your Excellency's most valued commendations, in the hope of the continuation of which I remain in constant and cordial devotion

Your Excellency's

Most devoted, most obliged

and true servant. . . .

Draft in State Archives, Bologna.—E. F. Schmid, *op. cit.*, p. 34 f.—This was the reply to Firmian's letter of recommendation of 14 March.—Among the Field-Marshal's guests were the Cardinal-Legate in Bologna, Antonio Colonna-Branciforte, and the Cardinal-Archbishop Vincenzo Malvezzi ; also the two young Princes Wilhelm August and Peter Friedrich Ludwig of Holstein-Gottorp, who had lost both their parents and were studying at Bologna. The hostess, Countess Maria Caterina Pallavicini, born Fava di Ferro, had invited sixty-six ladies.

COUNT GIAN LUCA PALLAVICINI TO CARDINAL COUNT LAZZARO OPIZIO
PALLAVICINI IN ROME

(in Italian)

Bologna, 28 March 1770.

Count Firmian has most assiduously recommended to me Sig. Leopoldo Mozart, chapel master in the service of the Prince-Archbishop of Salzburg, and his son, a boy of such uncommon merit in music that at his tender age he not only equals the masters of the art, but perhaps even exceeds them in readiness of invention. To make this singular merit of his known to the Cardinal-Legate and to the nobility here I held a conversazione at my house on Monday evening, where to great admiration he was pronounced a prodigy, and as such was judged by the celebrated master Padre Martini, who was present. The said professors are now leaving for Tuscany, where they will stay only a few days, in order to find themselves in Rome for Holy Week, and I urgently recommend them to Your Eminence, begging you to honour them with your protection during their sojourn there.

Since I recognize in the boy Mozart a truly extraordinary merit, I beg to suggest to Your Eminence that you let him be heard by our Lord, the more so because without the noise of instruments and in the presence of a single chapel master, who may examine him at the harpsichord, he will be able to give such proofs of his prowess that I flatter myself he will meet with His Holiness's entire satisfaction. I shall be greatly beholden to Your Eminence if you will extend these favours to Messrs. Mozart, of which you will find them very worthy, and also give them your attention as being recommended by me ; and with constant, cordial and unwavering devotion I subscribe myself

Your Eminence's

Most devoted and most obliged

servant and cousin C. P.

> Draft in State Archives, Bologna.—E. F. Schmid, *op. cit.*, p. 36 f.—These two Counts were only distantly related, and not real cousins. The Roman Pallavicini had recently become Secretary of State to the Vatican ; the Mozarts met him on 11 April.—At the same time the Field-Marshal sent similar letters to Prince Andrea Doria Pamphili-Landi and to Matthäus Dominicus, Baron de Saint-Odîle, Tuscan Ambassador to the Holy See. Leopold Mozart took the three letters to Rome with him.

On 29 March the travellers left Bologna ; they reached Florence on the 30th where they stayed at the Eagle inn.

> As early as 30 March Wolfgang was to play at Earl Cowper's, but he had caught cold on the journey and had to be excused (see 7 April).

On 1 April the Mozarts were received by Grand Duke Leopold of Tuscany, a son of Maria Theresa's, at the Palazzo Pitti.

> They had already called upon the High Steward, Count Orsini-Rosenberg (later " Director-General of Entertainments " in Vienna), and upon the High Chamberlain, Averardo, Duke of Salviati.

In the evening of 2 April Mozart played in a concert at Poggio Imperiale, the Grand Duke's summer residence (*cf.* 4 April).

On 3 April there was a reunion with the male soprano Giovanni Manzuoli, whom the Mozarts had already met in London.

On the same day they visited Signora Morelli, a poetess writing under the name of Corilla Olimpica (*cf.* 19 January 1770), where they met the young English violinist Thomas Linley (1756–78), who had studied under Pietro Nardini and on 30 March had appeared at Lord Cowper's, when Mozart was too ill to perform.

COUNT ROSENBERG'S ORDER OF PAYMENT, 4 APRIL 1770

(in Italian)

No. 17

The Accountant of the Royal Household issues the order to pay three hundred and thirty-three Lire & 6.8 to Mozard as his fee for having played at a Concert held at Poggio Imperiale in the quarters of Their Royal Highnesses.

Executed 4 April 1770.   f. Orsini Rosenberg.
L. 333.6.8.

> Florence, State Archives.—*Mozart in Italia*, Plate XVI (facsimile). *Cf.* 2 April.

THE MAJOR-DOMO'S ORDER TO PAY FOR A CONCERT GIVEN BY
LEOPOLD MOZART, WITH THE LATTER'S SIGNED RECEIPT
(in Italian)

Major-Domo-in-Chief
of the Royal Court   No. 43
                                              4 April 1770

Sig. Domenico Martin, Cashier to the Royal Court, is to pay the Musician Mozard the sum of three hundred and thirty-three Lire & 6.8 as his fee for having played at a Concert held at Poggio Imperiale in the Quarters of Their Royal Highnesses according to the Order in File III numbered 17. Due receipt of this sum is required at the foot of this Order, and it is to be posted as an outlay in the expenses of the Department of the Major-Domo-in-Chief of the Royal Court.   L. 333.6.8.

                                           Rosenberg.

The undersigned has received of Sig. Giud. La Guerre, Vice-Cashier of the R. Court, twenty-five Florentine sequins, amounting to Lire three hundred and thirty-three & 6.8 as honorarium benignly granted me by His Royal Highness for having played at the last Concert held at Court.
5 April 1770   Say L. 333.6.8
                                     Leopoldo Mozart

        Ibid.—Mozart in Italia, Plate XVI (facsimile) and p. 93.

In the afternoon of 4 April Mozart and Linley played duets for two violins at the Eagle inn.

On 5 April Mozart and Linley played at the house of Gavard, the administrator of archducal finances.

ON THE DEPARTURE OF SIGNOR W. A. MOZART
FROM FLORENCE
(in Italian)

E'er since I by Fate was divided from thee,
In thought I have followed thy journey in vain ;
To tears then were laughter and joy turned for me,
Scarce allayed by the hope I may see thee again.

What ecstasies open to music my heart,
By harmony wafted to Eden, forsooth !
To Heaven transported by love of thy art,
I seem for the first time to contemplate truth.

O fortunate instant ! O thrice blessed day,
When first I beheld thee, and wondering heard,
By thy music enchanted more than I can say,

Was happy to find myself loved and preferred.
May the gods grant that I shall remember alway
To resemble thy virtues in deed and in word.

In token of sincere esteem and affection
Thomas Linley.

Nissen, p. 195 f.—This sonnet, brought to Wolfgang by Linley on the morning
of 7 April, had been written by Corilla Olimpica the previous day on behalf
of the English youth. Leopold sent it to Salzburg on 21 April.

FROM THE " GAZZETTA TOSCANA ", FLORENCE, 7 APRIL 1770
(in Italian)

Finding himself at Florence, Sig. Volfang Motzhart, the excellent Player
of the harpsichord at present in the service of His Highness the Bishop of
Salzburg, had the honour of performing last Monday before the Court,
where he received all the applause due to his ability. He has not yet completed his fourteenth year, but is so well-grounded in music that already two
years ago he composed an opera which was performed in Vienna. After an
excursion to Rome he will go to Milan, whither he has been expressly
called to set to music the opera that is to be staged in the coming Carnival.
The most learned Professors cannot do otherwise than admire this boy, in
whom they recognize the rarest capacity for profiting as much as is possible
in this art.

Milord Covvper, in the evening of the 30th ult., having invited the highest
Nobility, gave a musical Concert with his usual splendour, at which was also
present Milady Heshet with her husband, who has been staying in the City
of late. Among the various Professors, Messrs. Guarducci and Niccolini
sang a duet, and a concerto was played on the violin by Sig. Linley, a youth
of great merit, who more than once has shown himself a worthy pupil of
Sig. Pietro Nardini.

Mozart in Italia, Plate XV, pp. 90 and 92.—Lady Harriet Hesketh was the wife
of Sir Thomas Hesketh, Bart, and a cousin of the poet William Cowper.—
Tommaso Guarducci and Carlo Niccolini were male sopranos ; Wolfgang
had met the latter on 9 November 1762 at Pacheco's in Vienna.

COUNT KARL JOSEPH FIRMIAN TO COUNT GIAN LUCA PALLAVICINI
(in Italian)

Your Excellency,

You have deigned, Your Excellency, to receive with so much kindness
the Father and Son Mozart recommended by me, and to bestow such signal
favours on them, that I find myself in the most urgent need to render the
utmost gratitude I am capable of to Your Excellency for the perfect goodness
with which it has pleased you to receive my urgings on this occasion as on
others.

I beg Your Excellency in return to dispose of me most freely in anything in which I can be of service to you, and I would only assure you that
I shall always hold in special regard the honour of your commands, since
they will afford me at once the pleasure of discharging in some sort my many
obligations and, what is more, of expressing the great devotion with which I
ever am

Your Excellency's
Most devoted and most obliged servant,

Milan, 7 April 1770.   *Carlo*, Count *Firmian*.

> Bologna, State Archives.—Ostoja, p. 37.—This was the reply to the Field-
> Marshal's letter of 28 March.

On 6 April the travellers left Florence and went by way of Siena and Orvieto to
Viterbo, where they arrived on the 10th.

They arrived in Rome at midday on Ash Wednesday, 11 April.

> For three days they occupied a room with a double bed ; from the 14th they
> were lodged with the wife of the absent papal courier, Steffano Uslenghi, at the
> Palazzo Scatizzi, a wing of the Collegium Clementinum on the Piazza Nicosia.

On the afternoon of the 11th they both went to St. Peter's in order to hear Allegri's
Miserere sung in the Sistine Chapel ; Mozart later wrote it out from memory. On
the 16th they presented letters of recommendation from Field-Marshal Pallavicini,
and on the 19th they were guests of a Neapolitan prince named San Angelo.

On 20 April Mozart played at a social evening arranged by Prince Chigi.

> This evening party was probably held in the Golden Hall of the Palazzo
> Chigi, which still survives. Among those present were Cardinal Pallavicini,
> Baron Saint-Odile and Charles Edward Stuart, the pretender to the English
> throne, who lived in Rome as the Earl of Albany.

CARDINAL PALLAVICINI TO FIELD MARSHAL PALLAVICINI AT BOLOGNA
(in Italian)

Your Excellency,

I reckon as my particular good fortune any occurrence which brings me
your valued commands, since the devotion which I owe you always equals
the pleasure I experience in obeying you. You may thus understand the
satisfaction I have had in acting upon your praiseworthy requests on behalf
of Sig. Leopoldo Mozart, Chapel Master in the service of the Prince-
Archbishop of Salzburg, and of his Son. The testimonial which your most
sensitive discernment procured me about the latter's extraordinary talent for
Music only enhanced the interest I shall take on all occasions in everything
that is of advantage to you and which makes me hope that I may deserve
the honour of further commands from you ; in expectation of which, and
with the accustomed respectful and unvarying regard, I kiss your hands from
my very heart.

Your Excellency's . . .
Rome, 21 April 1770.

It is certainly not often the case that Pontiffs hear musical virtuosi in their chambers ; however, I addressed myself to the gentlemen amateurs, and last night, at my instigation, Prince Chigi engaged the one recommended by you to play.

I was present, and no less than all the others there assembled admired the incomparable singularity of the enormous progress this boy has made at such a tender age in the difficult science and performance of music.

The said youth is truly amazing.

May Your Excellency continue to love me and to believe me when I truthfully declare myself

Your true servant and most affectionate cousin,
Lazzaro, Cardinal *Pallavicini*.

Bologna, State Archives.—E. F. Schmid, *op. cit.*, p. 39 ; Ostoja, p. 37 f.—This was the reply to the Field-Marshal's letter of 28 March. The lines following the date are a postscript in the Cardinal's own hand.

PRINCE ANDREA DORIA PAMPHILI TO FIELD MARSHAL PALLAVICINI
(in Italian)

Your Excellency,

The commands with which Your Excellency is pleased to honour me are, as you are yourself well aware, most precious to me on every occasion, since I have no other major ambition than to profess, by obeying you, the respect and the obligation which I owe you. It was with the most intense pleasure, therefore, that I received Your Excellency's most valued letter introducing to me Sig. Leopoldo Mozart, present Chapel Master of the Prince-Archbishop of Salzburg, who in the company of his Son has journeyed to this capital, and with equal pleasure that I offered both of these artists, whom you recommended to me so highly, all such services as would match your wishes and at the same time proclaim to you the value I attach to your requests.

I appreciate the Son's prodigious Talent and the Father's singular ability in the Profession of Music, and I shall not fail further to admire them myself and to seek ways and means to oblige them apart from what I am able to to do for them myself—in order to continue to merit Your Excellency's commands and to show most clearly in their execution that great devotion with which I wish to express the profound gratitude for the goodness Your Excellency deigns to show me, which I think myself the more fortunate in accepting for the glory of remaining unalterably

Your Excellency's
Most devoted and most obliged Servant,
Andre Doria Pamphili.
Rome, 21 April 1770.

Bologna, State Archives.—Ostoja, p. 38 f.—This too was a reply.

BARON SAINT-ODÎLE TO FIELD-MARSHAL PALLAVICINI
(in Italian)

Your Excellency,

To Sig. Leopoldo Mozart and his Son, who have been introduced to me by the most valued letter whereby Your Excellency has recommended them to me, I have proffered my best services, and I shall certainly not fail to do all that may depend on me to assist them during their stay in the capital.

Last night I heard Young Mozart at the House of Prince Chigi ; he is truly a prodigy of nature, all those present at the Conversazione immensely admiring his excellence in music. I beg Your Excellency to give me preference in the execution of your most valued commands on any other occasion whatever, that I may have the advantage ever more actively to prove to you the most perfect devotion with which I have the honour to be

Your Excellency's

Most devoted and most obliged Servant,

Saint-Odîle.

Rome, 21 April 1770.

Bologna, State Archives.—Ostoja, p. 39.—Another reply (see 7 May).

In the morning of 21 April the travellers took a walk in the park of the Villa Medici with William Beckford, whom they had known in London, and other Englishmen.

On the same day the *Diario dell' Archivio Capitolinum* mentions the " giovanetto tedesco . . . di anni 12 ", whose astounding gifts the members of the Papal Chapel unreservedly acknowledged (Elisabeth I. Luin in *Studien zur Musikwissenchaft* [Vienna, 1955], p. 38)—This William Beckford was the cousin of the author of *Vathek*.

PIETRO LUGIATI TO ANNA MARIA MOZART AT SALZBURG
(in Italian)

Madame,

Since the beginning of the present year this our City has been admiring the most highly prized person of Signor Amadeo Volfango Mozart, your Son, who may be said to be a miracle of nature in Music, since Art could not so soon have performed her Mission through him, were it not that she had taken his tender age into account.

I was certainly among his admirers, although, however much pleasure I have always taken in music and much as I have heard of it on my travels, I cannot hope to be an infallible judge of it ; but I have certainly not been mistaken in the case of so amazing a boy, and I have conceived such a regard for him that I had him painted from life with the inscription copied on the end of the Cantata—which he will be pleased to read.

This charming likeness of him is my solace, and serves moreover as incitement to return to his Music now and again, so far as my public and private occupation will permit, though I have not lost track of Sig. Amadeo and of

Sig. Leopoldo, his most amiable Father, having with pleasure received news of them from Mantua, Milan and last from Florence, reporting universal applause, as no doubt we shall before long hear from Rome, where I have already put him in touch with the most illustrious people.

I do but recall to you, Madam, the pleasure you experienced in taking him, at a still tenderer age, to the first cities of Europe together with your astonishing Daughter, whose virtuosity excited general admiration, as his does at present. I can only assert herewith the esteem I have for the one as for the other, and consequently how much I value their Parents, who have with such careful education fostered such rare talents that having afforded you abundant pleasure, they will yet give the world cause for universal admiration.

Please receive these sentiments, born of good intentions and true esteem, since while expressing them I take the opportunity to discharge an understanding entered into with your Son to let him have two pieces of Music, seen by him while he was staying with me, which I have had copied to please him, and that he may make much use of them. You will receive these at the hands of a merchant, Sig. Soldini, who promises me to deliver them safely to you, and which I shall be glad if you will kindly acknowledge at your convenience.

I conclude by wishing you and your most valued Family every great happiness, and meanwhile subscribe myself, with sincerely devoted esteem, Madame,

Your most devoted and most obliged Servant

Verona, 22 April 1770.   Pietro Lugiati.

Salzburg, Mozarteum.—Erich H. Müller von Asow, *Briefe Wolfgang Amadeus Mozarts* (Berlin, 1942), Vol. II (Vol. i of text), p. 11 f.—*Cf.* 6-7 January 1770.

After a visit to the Palazzo Barberini (*c.* 25 April) the Mozarts were received on 28 April by the Maltese ambassador, on the 29th in the palace of Giuseppe Maria Altemps, Duca di Gallese, and on the 30th in the Augustinian monastery.

At Princess Barberini-Colonna's they again met the English Pretender as well as Prince Xaver of Saxony, who at that time lived in Italy as the Comte de la Lusace (Count of Lusatia). The Ambassador of the sovereign order of St. John of Malta was probably Cavaliere Santarelli, master of the papal chapel. The reception at Altemps's palace was given by Baldassare Odescalchi, Duke of Bracciano and Geri. The prior of the monastery, Padre Vasquez, was General of the Augustinians.

FROM THE " DIARIO DELL' ARCHIVIO CAPITOLINUM ", ROME,
26 APRIL 1770
(in Italian)

Much applause was gathered at these first conversazioni by the little German boy, son of the chapel master of the cathedral and metropolitan church of Salzburg, who at the age of only 12 years shows consummate science in music and in playing the harpsichord, and as much knowledge in the one and the other kind as all the most renowned professors have not been able to acquire in their maturity.

Elisabeth I. Luin in *Neues Mozart-Jahrbuch* (Regensburg, 1943), Vol. III, p. 47.

COUNT KRAFT ERNST OETTINGEN-WALLERSTEIN TO HIS MOTHER, COUNTESS CHARLOTTE JULIANE THERESE, NÉE COUNTESS OETTINGEN-BALDERN, ROME, 28 APRIL 1770
(in French)

I have seen to-day, but did not hear him play the harpsichord, young Mozard of Salzburg ; he knows Beeke ; he is to compose this year, at the age of 13, an opera for Milan.

Wallerstein, Archives of Prince Oettingen-Wallerstein.—Communicated by Dr. Volker von Volckamer, director of the library, art collection and archives at the family seat, Schloss Harburg bei Donauwörth.—The Count (1748–1802) became a Prince of the Realm in 1774. *Cf.* 26 October 1777. His father was Philipp Karl Dominicus, Count Oettingen-Wallerstein.

On 2 May Mozart played at the Collegium Germanicum, facing the Palazzo Altemps, where the bass Joseph Meissner (from Salzburg) also appeared.

COUNT OETTINGEN-WALLERSTEIN TO HIS MOTHER, ROME, 5 MAY 1770
(in French)

On Thursday, the 3rd, I went in the evening to the Princess Doria, and Count Gunsco [?] took me to a certain Mme Doria, a bourgeoise, where I heard young Mozart ; he does astonishing things.

See 28 April.

BARON SAINT-ODILE TO GIUSEPPE BONECHI AT NAPLES
(In Italian ; P.S. partly in French)

Most Illustrious Sir, Most Worshipful Patron,

Sig. Leopold Mozart, Chapel Master of His Highness the Prince of Salzburg, has a son of his with him, who at a tender age has made such great progress in Music that he surprises all those who hear him, as much by his excellence as by his consummate facility in extempore composition. They have been particularly recommended to me by Count Rosenberg and by Marshal Pallavicini. I thought of sending them to you, Illustrious Sir, knowing the value you set on Persons of virtuosity ; hence I do not doubt that during their sojourn there, you will not fail to favour them with your accustomed kindness. And assuring you that I shall remain immensely beholden to you for this, I subscribe myself, with the highest esteem,

Rome, 7 May 1770.

[To:] Sig\u02b3. Giuseppe Bonechi, Naples.

P.S. that you will receive from the said Mozarts two copies of the "Giornale Enciclopedico" for 15 March, one for yourself, the other, together with a "Mercurio" for the Month of February, for the Prince della Roccella, to whom I beg you to hand them.

I beg you, Sir, to make some especial effort on behalf of my little Mozart, who is full of the best qualities. He well deserves to become known in the house of Tanucci, at least by the two young married people, to whom I beg you to remember me, asking them to receive my sincere good wishes for their especial happiness.

Most devoted and most obliged Servant,
Saint-Odile.

Florence, State Archives.—Discovered by Bernhard Paumgartner, published by Erich Schenk in *Neues Mozart-Jahrbuch* (Regensburg, 1943), Vol. III, p. 36 f.—Facsimile in *Mozart in Italia*, Plate XX.—Bonechi was secretary to the Imperial Ambassador at Naples, Count Ernst Christoph Kaunitz-Rietberg. Marchese Bernardo Tanucci was the famous Neapolitan statesman.

At 10 a.m. on 8 May the travellers left Rome and lunched at the Augustinian monastery of Marino on Lake Albano. By way of Terracina they reached Sessa on the 11th and Capua on the 12th, taking shelter in both places at the Augustinian hospices.

At Capua they were present on the 13th at the ceremony of a nun's taking the veil.

COUNT OETTINGEN-WALLERSTEIN TO HIS MOTHER, ROME, 9 MAY 1770
(in French)

In the evening I was at the Governor's to discuss Monica; thence to the Venetian Ambassadress, where I heard young Mozart.

See 28 April.—The letter evidently refers to a previous evening, round about 7 May—The Monica referred to was the sister of the painter Georg Caspar von Prenner; he had died in 1766, and she came to Rome to attend to his estate.

On 14 May the Mozarts reached Naples.

On 18 May they were received by the Prime Minister, Tanucci, at Portici, and on the same day by William Hamilton, the British Ambassador.

Hamilton's first wife, *née* Catherine Barlow, was an excellent keyboard player. He was not knighted until 1772.

On 20 May they again visited Tanucci and on the 21st went to an opera buffa.

On 28 May Mozart performed at a concert held by the Imperial Ambassador, Kaunitz, and arranged by Mrs. Hamilton.

COUNT OETTINGEN-WALLERSTEIN TO HIS MOTHER, NAPLES, 29 MAY 1770
(in French)

In the evening we went to a concert given by young Mozart, who is a very Prodigy in Music.

See 28 April.—This refers to 28 May.—In the accounts of the young Count's major-domo we find an item (in French) : "To two tickets distributed by Mme. la Comtesse de Kaunitz for Mozart's concert . . . 60 L." (Elisabeth Luin in the *Neues Augsburger Mozartbuch* [1962], p. 474 f.).

On 30 May, at the Teatro San Carlo, they heard Jommelli's *Armida*, with Aprile as Rinaldo.

On 10 June they lunched at the Augustinian monastery of San Giovanni a Carbonaro, on the 13th they visited Pozzuoli and Baiae, on the 16th they lunched with the Carthusians of San Martino, on the 18th and 19th they visited Vesuvius, Pompeii, Herculaneum, Caserta and Capodimonte.

On 25 June they left Naples and, travelling post-haste, reached Rome in 27 hours, at 8 p.m. on the 26th.

ENACTMENT FROM THE PAPAL SECRETARY OF STATE TO CARDINAL ANDREA NEGRONI
(in Italian)

From the Secretariat of State

26 June 1770.

In that His Holiness has deigned to confer the Cross of the Golden Spur on Giovanni Amadeo Wolfango Mozart of Strasbourg, the certificate shall herewith be forwarded to Signore Cardinale Negroni, in order that he may dispatch the appropriate patent.

Signore Cardinale Negroni

Rome, Vatican Archives.—Elisabeth I. Luin, in *Studien zur Musikwissenschaft* (Vienna, 1955), p. 46 f.—Cardinal Pallavicini was president of the State Secretariat, Cardinal Negroni of the Segretaria dei Brevi.—The description of Wolfgang as being from Strasbourg, instead of Salzburg, is an error that is also to be found in the draft for the patent, but not in the fair copy (see 4 July).

On 29 June, the feast of St. Peter and St. Paul, the Mozarts attended a public festivity with illuminations.

THE PAPAL PATENT, ROME, 4 JULY 1770
(in Latin)

To Our beloved Son Joannes Amadeus Wolfgangus Mozart of the City and Diocese of Salzburg.

Clement P.P. XIV.

To Our beloved Son greetings and apostolic benediction. Inasmuch as it behoves the beneficence of the Roman Pontiff and the Apostolic See that those who have shown them no small signs of faith and devotion and are graced with the merits of probity and virtue, shall be decorated with the honours and favours of the Roman Pontiff and the said See : We, therefore, wishing to honour thee with fitting tokens of our grace and beneficence on account of thy sincere faith and devotion to us and the aforesaid See, together with thy other merits, hereby absolve thee, in so far as shall give effect and consequence to these presents, from any sentence of excommunication, suspension and interdict, or other censures and penalties of the Church, imposed by law or man for whatever occasion or cause, if in any way whatsoever thou art enmeshed in them : And deeming thee to be thus absolved, and hearkening to the supplications humbly submitted to us on thy behalf in this matter, we hereby make and create thee—whom we understand to have excelled since thy earliest youth in the sweetest sounding of the harpsichord—Knight of the Golden Order, by the Apostolic authority and the terms of these presents : Receiving thee favourably into the number of Knights of the said Order, especially that thou mayst in like manner freely and lawfully use and enjoy each and all of the privileges and prerogatives which the other Knights of the Order enjoy by law usage, custom or in any other way, and shall in future enjoy (excepting such as have been abolished by the Council of Trent), notwithstanding any apostolic or other constitutions or ordinances to the contrary whatsoever.

Wherefore it is our wish that thou shalt at all times wear the Golden Cross (for otherwise there is no present grace in the object itself) according to the manner and form laid down by our predecessor Benedict P.P. XIV of happy memory, of which we command a copy to be presented to thee.

Given at Rome at S. Maria Maggiore under the Fisherman's ring, the 4th day of July 1770, in the second year of our Pontificate.

A. Card[inal] Nigornus

> The original is lost. One of the two copies made by Leopold Mozart for Archbishop Schrattenbach of Salzburg and for Padre Martini of Bologna is to be found in the library of the Bologna Conservatory. Schmid, *op. cit.*, p. 44 f. —The draft in the Vatican Archives, published by Elisabeth Luin, *op. cit.*, pp. 44 ff., differs in several places from the final version ; it is signed " Placet L." by the Pope, " L." standing for Laurentius, his former monastic name. The original of the patent, probably lost by Mozart in 1778 together with the order, would be sealed with the Fisherman's Ring.—The first line here stands on the verso of the document. The signature of Cardinal Negroni (Nigronus) was no doubt incorrectly copied by Leopold Mozart.—Gluck, who thenceforth called himself " Ritter ", and Ditters (later von Dittersdorf) had received this papal order before Wolfgang, but not with the high rank of " Knight of the Golden Order ", which had hitherto been awarded to only one musician, Orlando di Lasso.—The brief was made out on 3 July and signed by the Pope on the 4th. Mozart was excused the customary fee.

On 5 July Cardinal Pallavicini, at his residence in the Palazzo Quirinale, presented Mozart with the insignia of the papal order : a golden cross on a red sash, sword and spurs.

> The robe of the order had to be provided for Wolfgang by his father.—On the 6th they dined with Baron Odîle.

ABBÉ FERDINANDO GALIANI TO MADAME D'ÉPINAY
(in French)

Naples, 7 July 1770.

I think I wrote to you that little Mosar is here, and that he is less of a miracle, although he is always the same miracle ; but he will never be anything else than a miracle, and that is all.

Galiani, *Correspondance avec Madame d'Épinay* (Paris, 1881), p. 191 f.—He was a national economist and statesman, had been in touch with the encyclopaedists in Paris and now lived at Naples. Cf. 16 September 1766.

On 8 July Mozart, wearing the insignia presented to him, was received in audience by the Pope at his temporary residence, the Palazzo Santa Maria Maggiore.

The necessary witness at Wolfgang's appointment was probably his later master, Hieronymus, Count Colloredo, then Bishop of Gurk. It is possible that he was present at the audience.

On 10 July the travellers left Rome, reaching Cività Castellana on the morning of the 11th, where Wolfgang tried the organ, and continued their journey in the afternoon by way of Terni, Spoleto and Foligno. They arrived at Loreto on the 16th, went on by way of Ancona, Senigallia, Pesaro, Rimini and Forlì as far as Imola, where they arrived on the 19th, and eventually returned to Bologna (St. Mark's inn) on the 20th.

From 10 August to 1 October they stayed at " Alla croce del Biacco ", the country seat of Field-Marshal Pallavicini, near Bologna.

The house still exists. Leopold Mozart was still suffering from an abrasion on the right shin received in a carriage accident during the precipitate journey from Naples to Rome.

FROM CHARLES BURNEY'S TRAVEL NOTES, BOLOGNA, 30 AUGUST 1770
(in English)

Thurs. Aug. 30 . . . After seeing a Church or two on my way, I went to S. Giovanni in Monte to hear the Philharmonic performances. There was a great deal of Company . . . and among the rest who should I meet but the celebrated little German, Mozart, who in 1766 astonished all hearers in London by his premature musical talent. I had a long conversation with his father. I find they are inmates of the Palace of Prince Palaviccini. The little man is grown considerably, but is still a little man. He has been at Rome and Naples, where he was much admired. At Rome the Pope has conferred on him the Order of the *Speron d' Oro*, or Gold Spur, the only civil or military order in the gift of his Holiness. He astonished the Italian musicians wherever he stopt. He is now at the age of 12, ingaged to compose an Opera for Milan, on occasion of the marriage of the Principessina of Modena, with one of the Arch-Dukes of Austria. There are to be 3 new Operas composed on this occasion. I know not yet who are his concurrents ; but shall be curious to know how this extraordinary boy acquits himself in setting words in a language not his own. But there is no musical excellence I do not expect from the extraordinary quickness and talents, under the guidance of so able a musician and intelligent a man as his father, who, I was informed, had been ill five or six weeks at Bologna.

Percy A. Scholes, *The Great Doctor Burney* (London, 1948), Vol. I, p. 170, and his edition of Burney's *Musical Tours in Europe* (London, 1959), Vol. I, p. 161 f. —In 1770 Burney travelled in France and Italy, in 1772 in Germany and the Netherlands, to collect material for his *History of Music* (1776–89) ; but he published reports on these journeys as early as 1771 and 1773 (our quotations from which are placed at the ends of those years).—The solemn performance of a Mass and Vespers, arranged at the Church of S. Giovanni in Monte by the Accademia filarmonica of Bologna, consisted of works by ten of its members. For the opera written by Wolfgang for Modena see 26 December 1770. He was in fact fourteen by now.

On 4 October the Cathedral of San Petronio celebrated its nominal patron with a concert by the Bolognese musicians.

On 6 October Wolfgang played the organ in the Church of San Domenico.

MINUTES OF MOZART'S EXAMINATION FOR ADMITTANCE TO THE
ACCADEMIA FILARMONICA OF BOLOGNA
(in Italian)

This day, 9 October *1770*

At the electoral Assembly of the Gentlemen Academicians, under the Presidency of Sig. Petronio Lanzi, the following were present, *viz.:*

Sig. Co[nte] : Baldassare Carrati, Hereditary	Sig : Pietro Gionima
Sig : Petronio Lanzi, President	Sig : Antonio Mazzoni
Sig : B[aron]e Luigi Ferri, Secretary	Sig : Bernardino Ottani
Sig : Angelo Antonio Caroli	Sig : Angelo Galasi
Sig : Lorenzo Gibelli	Sig : Barone Nesselrode
Sig : B[arone] Giuseppe Corsini	Sig : Giovanni Piantanida
Sig : Antonio Montroni	Sig : Girolamo Bernia
Sig : Melchiore Prosperi	Sig : Gaetano Poggi
	Sig : Petronio Vecchi

First of all, memorials were read presented by Francesco Piantanida, Professor of the Violoncello, who petitioned for admission to the Academy in the capacity of Player : and after a secret ballot it was revealed that he had been favourably received with all white votes, and he was admitted :

Afterwards was read another memorial presented on behalf of Sig. Wolfgang Amadeo Mozart of Salzburg, aged fourteen years, who petitioned for admission to the Academy in the capacity of composer, submitting himself to every trial according to the Statutory form ; the Antiphonary being then opened by the President, there was found the Antiphon in the first mode, " Querite primum Regnum Dei ", &c., which was given him to make his trial upon ; whereupon he, retiring alone to the customary room, set himself to the task.

At the end of less than an hour, the said Sig. Mozart completed his trial, which, considering the circumstances, was judged to be sufficient, whereupon it was put to the vote whether he should be enrolled in the Academy in the capacity of Master, which when counted was found to be in his favour ; the Assembly resolved that the usual Patent should be sent to him.

> Bologna, Accademia filarmonica.—C. Rizzi, in *Gazzetta Musicale di Milano*, 9 August 1891. Jahn, Vol. II. p. 724 f. Facsimile in Robert Bory, *W. A. Mozart. Sein Leben und sein Werk in Bildern* (Geneva, 1948), p. 81.—The antiphon composed by Wolfgang in confinement is K. 86.

DIPLOMA OF THE ACCADEMIA FILARMONICA OF BOLOGNA
(in Latin)

The President [Princeps] and other members of the Accademia filarmonica. To each and every reader of these presents, greeting.

Although virtue wins reward for itself and those who cultivate it, yet for the greater dignity of the same it is fitting that it should be brought to the public notice. Hence it is that, in the intention of increasing the reputation of our Philharmonic Academy and of bringing to light the knowledge and achievements of each of its members, we bear witness that *Domin. Wolfgangus Amadeus Mozart e Salisburgo* on the 9th day of *October* in the year 1770 was enrolled among the *Magistri Compositores* of our Academy. Wherefore we, the undersigned fellow Academicians, in order to honour virtue and merit with a permanent mark of our esteem, issue these letters patent, signing them with the seal of our Assembly. Given in our City of Bologna this 10th day of the month of *October* in the year 1770.

President. *Petronius Lanzi*
P. Aloysius Xav. Ferri
Secretary.
Registrar [Camplonerius]
Cajetanus Croci.

Registr. in Libro Camplon[eri]o G pag. 147

> Salzburg, Mozart Museum.—Nissen, p. 226 f. Jahn, Vol. II, p. 725. Facsimile in Schiedermair, Vol. 5, Plate 58.—The original is a printed form, into which the words here shown in italics were written in ink.

PADRE MARTINI'S TESTIMONIAL
(in Italian)

Bologna, 12 October 1770.

I, the undersigned, attest that, having seen some Musical Compositions in various styles, and having several times heard [him play] the Harpsichord, the Violin, and sing, Sig. Cav. Giov. Amadeo Wolfgango Mozart of Salzburg, Master Chamber Musician to His Highness the eminent Prince Archbishop of Salzburg, aged 14 years, to my particular admiration, was found by me most highly versed in all the musical qualities indicated, he having passed every test whatever, above all in playing on the Harpsichord various subjects given him to improvise, which with great mastery he carried out according to all the conditions demanded by Art. In token whereof I have written and subscribed this in my own hand.

F. Giambattista Martini
Minor Conventual.

Bologna, Conservatorio G. B. Martini.—Jahn, Vol. II, p. 727.

On 13 October the travellers left Bologna, reaching Parma on the 14th, Piacenza on the 16th and Milan at 5 p.m. on the 18th.

The first three of these four dates are not completely certain.

RECEIPT OF DON DOMENICO ZANARDI, COUNCILLOR OF THE
ACCADEMIA FILARMONICA OF BOLOGNA, 4 NOVEMBER 1770
(in Italian)

Received at the hands of Padre Maestro Martini forty lire on behalf of Sig. Wolfgang Mozart of Salzburg, knight of the Golden Spur, for his admission into the Academy and his election as a foreign member in the rank of composer, namely L. 40.

Nestore Morini, *La R. Accademia filarmonica di Bologna* (Bologna, 1930), p. 56.—Padre Martini seems to have paid this fee out of his own pocket.

During the week-end of 17-19 November the Mozarts stayed at the country seat of Leopold Troger, Count Karl Joseph Firmian's secretary, near Milan.

Leopold Mozart made use of Troger's address for his post from Salzburg, which Troger visited in 1771.

On 26 November an orchestral concert was held at the residence of Count Firmian, Governor of Lombardy.

For the performance of the opera *Mitridate*, which had been commissioned from Mozart for the Milan season, the second recitative rehearsal was held on 8 December. The first rehearsal with reduced orchestra took place on the 12th, one with full orchestra was held at the Assembly Hall on the 17th with a second in the theatre on the 19th, a third complete one on the 22nd and the dress rehearsal on the 24th.

On 26 December *Mitridate* was performed at the grand-ducal castle (Teatro Regio Ducal) for the first time.

The libretto by V. A. Cigna-Santi was based on G. Parini's Italian translation of Racine's tragedy ; it had already been set by Q. Gasparini in 1767. Mozart's first opera composed for Italy had twenty-two consecutive performances. Wolfgang conducted the first three performances at the harpsichord, Giovanni Battista Lampugnani playing the second harpsichord. The performance lasted six hours.

TITLE-PAGE OF THE LIBRETTO OF " MITRIDATE "

M I T R I D A T E
Re di Ponto,
Dramma per Musica
da rappresentarsi
Nel Regio-Ducal Teatro
di Milano
Nel Carnovale dell' Anno 1771
dedicato
A Sua Altezza Serenissima
il
Duca di Modena
Reggio, Mirandola ec. ec.
Amministratore,
e Capitano Generale
della Lombardia Austriaca
ec. ec.
in Milano, MDCCLXX

Nella Stamperia di Giovanni Montani
Con Licenza de' Superiori

Copies of the libretto are in the Biblioteca musicale Santa Cecilia in Rome, the Conservatorio Giuseppe Verdi in Milan, and in the German State Library in Berlin.—Facsimile of the title-page in Bory, *op. cit.*, p. 82.

CAST OF " MITRIDATE "
(in Italian)

Dramatis Personae:

Mithridates, King of Pontus, and other
kingdoms, in love with Aspasia.
Sig. Cavaliere Guglielmo D' Ettore, Chamber
Virtuoso to His Serene Highness
the Elector of Bavaria.

Aspasia, Betrothed to Mithridates,
and already proclaimed Queen.
Signora Antonia Bernasconi.

Sifare, son of Mithridates and Stratonica,
in love with Aspasia.
Sig. Pietro Benedetti, known as *Sartorino.*

Farnace, elder son of Mithridates,
in love with the same.
Sig. Giuseppe Cicognani.

Ismene, the King of the Parthians' daughter,
in love with Farnace.
Signora Anna Francesca Varese.

Marzio, Roman Tribune, friend of Farnace.
Sig. Gasparo Bassano.

Arbate, Governor of Nymphaea.
Sig. Pietro Muschietti.

Composer of the Music
Sig. Cavaliere Amadeo Wolfgango Mozart,
Philharmonic Academician of Bologna, and
Master of Chamber-Music to His Highness the
Prince and Archbishop of Salzburg.

Facsimile in Bory, *op. cit.,* p. 82.

FROM THE MANUSCRIPT REGISTER OF THE TEATRO REGIO DUCAL,
MILAN, 1770
(in Italian)

26 December / do. / *Mitridate Re di Ponto* / Cav. Amadeo Mozart /
Pietro Benedetti known as Sartorino / Antonia Bernasconi / Cav. Guglielmo
d' Ettore, chamber virtuoso to His Electoral Highness of Bavaria / Gius.
Cicognani Anna Francesca Varese Gaspare Bassano Pietro Muschietti /
Francesco Caselli / Above-mentioned [Ant. Galli-Bibiena] Galleari / Above-
mentioned lease-holders.

Milan, State Archives.—Facsimile in *Mozart in Italia* (1956), Plate XXVI.—The
eleven columns of the table show, after the composer, the names of the *primo
uomo,* the *prima donna* and the other singers, the ballet master, the stage designer
and others concerned (information kindly supplied by Dr. L. F. Tagliavini).—
Giuseppe Galliari and his brother were stage designers.

1771

FROM THE " GAZZETTA DI MILANO ", 2 JANUARY 1771
(in Italian)

On Wednesday last the Teatro Regio Ducal reopened with the performance of the drama entitled *Mitridate, Re di Ponto,* which has proved to the
public's satisfaction as much for the tasteful stage designs as for the excellence
of the Music, and the ability of the Actors. Some of the arias sung by
Signora Antonia Bernasconi vividly express the passions and touch the
heart. The young *Maestro di Cappella,* who has not yet reached the age of

fifteen, studies the beauty of nature and exhibits it adorned with the rarest of Musical graces.

> Müller von Asow, *op. cit.*, Vol. II, p. 101.—*Mozart in Italia*, p. 133 : compiled by Giuseppe Parini.

On 3 January 1771 the Mozarts dined with Frau Marianne d' Asti von Asteburg, Troger's daughter ; on the 4th Mozart played a concerto at a small concert in Count Firmian's house, where they dined again on the 5th.

> Frau d'Asti, who came from Salzburg, served Wolfgang his favourite dish : sauerkraut and dumplings.

NOMINATION AS HONORARY MAESTRO DI CAPELLA BY THE
ACCADEMIA FILARMONICA OF VERONA, 5 JANUARY 1771
(in Italian)

The 5th day of the month of January 1771, Convocation of the Hon. Philharmonic Academy of Verona, in the usual Place, in the presence of the Worshipful Members.

The Noble Count Murari Brà, Governor, stated that it was an ancient principle of this Academy to promote the honour of virtuosi in order that their distinguished Qualities might lend ever greater lustre and dignity to the said Academy ; wherefore, note having been taken of the remarkable gifts possessed by the wonderful youth Sig. Amadeo Wolfgango Mozart of Salzburg, Concert Master to His Rev. Highness the Archbishop and Prince of Salzburg, Knight of the Golden Spur, decorated by the Reigning Supreme Pontiff, who deigned to hear him and to applaud the merits of this Youth. He may truly pride himself as one of the most admirable prodigies in the profession of Music, which this city of Verona can also affirm, in that during the few days he spent here he gave, on several occasions, such proofs of his skill at playing the most difficult things at sight on the harpsichord with great readiness and elegance ; setting on the spot certain poetical passages that were shown him to very fine concerted music for several instruments, to the amazement of those most versed in the said Art. Apart from which this our Academy can also offer the most truly sincere acknowledgments of the incomparable merit of this Youth, who in January of last year in the Hall of the Academy, in the presence of Ladies, Gentlemen and Public Representatives, miraculously overcame the greatest Musical Tests with complete mastery and to the astonishment of all this Noble Gathering. And this in addition to the multitudinous notices received from many parts of Italy, where this expert person has performed to the Principal Professors and lovers of Music, earning praise and applause from all : in short, his fair Talent promises ever further outstanding progress, apt to strike all those destined to hear him in future ; since at so early an age his keen-witted Genius has succeeded, and will in the sequel succeed, in reaching such a degree of knowledge as, in its progress, shall surpass those who most excel in Music.

It would therefore be to the great advantage of our Academy, which has always and everywhere had the most signal and distinctive reputation in Music, Poetry and *Belles-Lettres*, that this famous Youth should be enrolled as *Maestro di Capela* by the aforesaid Philharmonic Academy ; in the hope that this token of esteem will be accepted by him.

This worthy proposal having been submitted to the Academy and discussed with learned eloquence, it was unanimously acclaimed by the Academicians, and the Young Virtuoso Sig. Amadeo Wolfgango Mozart was consequently enrolled as *Maestro di Capela* of the Hon[ble] Philharmonic Academy of Verona.

The Philharmonic Academicians
Dr. Antonio Tommasi, Sec[y].

Salzburg, Mozart-Museum.—Jahn, Vol. II, p. 726, with textual differences. Facsimile in Bory, *op. cit.*, p. 83.

On 14 January the travellers went to Turin, where they stayed for a fortnight at the Dogana nuova.

On 31 January they returned to Milan, where Count Firmian gave a farewell luncheon for them on 2 February.

On 4 February they left Milan and went by way of Canonica, Brescia, Verona, Vicenza and Padua to Venice, where they arrived on Carnival Monday, 11 February, and took lodgings at the Casa Cavaletti on the Rio San Fantino al Ponte di Barcaroli.

On 12 February, at the Teatro San Moisè, from 2 to about 7 p.m., they attended Antonio Boroni's opera *Le contadine furlane*.

On 18 February they took lunch with Giovanni Antonio Dolfin.

On 21 February they took lunch with Signora Caterina Corner, and on the 24th and 25th with Giovanni Bragadino, the Patriarch (Archbishop) of Venice, and again with Dolfin.

ORTES TO HASSE, VENICE, 2 MARCH 1771
(in Italian)

I do not think, however, that they [the Mozarts] are very much pleased with this city, where they probably expected that others would seek after them, rather than they after others, as will have happened to them elsewhere. The truth is that it is not much the custom here to go out of one's way to esteem others, however meritorious and estimable they may be, and they tend on the contrary to admire those who go in search of admiration. What a curious thing it is, this unconcern with which the boy notes this difference, whereas the father appears to be somewhat piqued by it.

Mennicke, *op. cit.*, p. 431. *Cf.* 30 September and 4 October 1769, and 23 March 1771.

On 3 March the Mozarts were the guests of Count Giacomo Durazzo, the former intendant of the court theatres in Vienna, now Imperial Ambassador to Venice ; and on the 4th they visited the Maffei family.

THE NEW OPERA CONTRACT FOR MILAN
(in Italian)

It is agreed that Sig. Amadeo Mozart will set to music the first drama to be performed in the Teatro Regio Ducal of Milan in the Carnival of the year 1773 and as honorarium for his artistic services are to be assigned to him one hundred and thirty *Gigliati* viz. 130 g. and furnished lodgings.

It is further agreed that the said Maestro is to deliver all the recitatives set to music within the month of October of the year 1772 and to be in Milan again at the beginning of the subsequent month of November to compose the arias and be present at all the rehearsals required by the said opera. With the usual reservations in case of theatrical misfortunes and Princely intervention (which God forbid).

Milan, 4 March 1771.

The Associates of the Lessee of the Theatre
Federico Castiglione

Jahn, Vol. II, p. 727.—The new opera for Milan was *Lucio Silla*.

On 5 March Mozart held a concert in Venice.

No details are known of this " great " and " beautiful " concert.

On 12 March the travellers left Venice and sailed on the Brenta to Padua, where they arrived on the evening of the same day and spent two nights at the Palazzo Pesaro.

At Padua Wolfgang played on Maestro Giovanni Ferrandini's harpsichord at the Santo Church and on the organ of that of Santa Giustina. It was there on 13 March that he received the commission to compose an oratorio, *La Betulia liberata*, to words by Metastasio, but this was not performed at Padua so far as is known. *Cf.* 23 May 1775.

On 14 March they continued to Vicenza, where their host was Bishop Marco Giuseppe Cornaro.

JOHANNES WIDER TO MARIA ANNA MOZART AT SALZBURG

Madame,

As I have now had the Honour of doing my poor best to serve Your dear husband and your most delightful son Herr *Amadeus* for a month here, I can do no less than take the Liberty of reporting to You, that I also had the pleasure of accompanying these my Dear Acquaintances and good Friends as far as *Padua* with a good Part of my *famille*, where we then had to part Early yesterday, Thank God all hale and well ; to-morrow evening is to be their Arrival at *Verona*, where there is to be no long delay, but the journey towards the dear Fatherland is to be continued, may the good God thus be their Companion everywhere, and convey these good and dear Friends happily and healthily to their Home, of which I in good time expect to hear with an uncommonly great Desire, begging meanwhile to be kindly *excused* having made so free as to forward this wretched scrawl to yourself, none the less do I beg your continued Goodwill, in Which Expectation I also offer You my feeble services with every Urgency, whatever may befall, so that You may indeed know me as remaining with the most obedient *Respect*, with that of my dear Wife, also to the most worthy *Mademoiselle* your Daughter, in all Devotion

Madame

your most devoted true Servant

Johannes Wider

Venice, 15 March 1771   *V. S. V. P.*

P. S. This very moment I received from Herr Hagenauer, to whom I send my most sincere *Compliments*, a missive for your most worthy husband, which I shall forward to him at *Verona* to-morrow evening.

> Salzburg, Mozarteum.—Müller von Asow, *op. cit.*, Vol. II, p. 110.—Wider was a merchant in Venice, to whom Lorenz Hagenauer, Leopold Mozart's Salzburg landlord, had recommended him. He looked after the Mozarts during their stay at Venice.

On 16 March the travellers reached Verona, where they alighted at Pietro Lugiati's ; on the 17th Mozart played there to invited guests.

On 20 March they arrived at Rovereto and then continued their journey by way of Bressanone.

HASSE TO ORTES

(in Italian)

Vienna, 23 March 1771

Young Mozard is certainly marvellous for his age, and I do love him infinitely. The father, as far as I can see, is equally discontented everywhere, since here too he uttered the same lamentations. He idolizes his son a little too much, and thus does all he can to spoil him ; but I have such a high opinion of the boy's natural good sense that I hope he will not be spoilt in spite of the father's adulation, but will grow into an honest fellow.

> *Cf.* 30 September and 4 October 1769, and 2 March 1771.—Kretzschmar, p. 265. Mennicke, p. 431 f.

In the evening of 25 March the Mozarts reached Innsbruck, where they stayed for one day.

On Maundy Thursday, 28 March 1771, father and son returned home after an absence of some 15½ months.

On 19 July Leopold Mozart wrote to Field-Marshal Pallavicini concerning the projected second journey to Italy.

> Ostoja, *op. cit.*, p. 42 ; facsimile, pp. 30-2.

On Tuesday 13 August 1771 father and son began their second Italian tour, which was to last only four months. They travelled by way of Kaltern and Waidring to arrive at St. Johann in the evening, at midday on the 14th they stopped at the Post at Kundl, and in the evening they reached Innsbruck. On the 15th they were at Steinach at midday and at Bressanone by the evening ; on the 16th they took lunch at Bolzano and supper at Trento ; on the 17th they arrived at Rovereto at 9 a.m., where they remained for an hour and a half, and at Ala at 1 p.m.

THE OPERA CONTRACT FOR VENICE
(in Italian)

The 17th day of the month of August 1771.

Venice.

With this present private agreement, which the parties wish to have the same force and effect as though it were drawn up by a Public Notary of this or any other City, Sig. Michele dall'Agata, entrepreneur of the heroic opera that is to be produced in the coming Carnival of the year 1773, the performances to begin on St. Stephen's Day in the magnificent and noble theatre of San Benedetto, hereby confirms and establishes that Sig. Wolfgang Amadeo Mozart, maestro di capella, is to write the second opera, to be given in the said Carnival, with the obligation not to write for any other theatre in the capital without having first carried out the present commission. With the further obligation to present himself in Venice by 30 November 1772 in order to be present at all the rehearsals and performances to be held at that time. And in recompense for his artistic services he is to be paid by Sig. dall' Agata seventy sequins in cash or their just equivalent, which the undersigned promises to discharge punctually without reservation of any other kind than the usual conditions governing matters theatrical, in witness whereof sequins 70 in cash,

Michele dall' Agata.

Jahn, Vol. II, p. 727 f.—This opera never materialized.

On Sunday 18 August the travellers left Ala at 7 a.m., having attended early mass, and arrived at Verona at noon, where they were again Pietro Lugiati's guests. On the 20th they continued to Brescia, where they arrived at 3 p.m. and spent the night. On the 21st they were at Canonica at lunch-time and in Milan by 7 p.m.

In the evening of 23 August they met the Purveyor Johann Georg Zinner at the house of the Court Steward Don Fernando Germani and his wife Therese : on the 31st they visited Hasse, who had arrived the day before.

On the 29th Wolfgang received the libretto of the opera *Ascanio in Alba*, which he was to compose for Milan.—Burney mentions in his notes for August 1772 that Venanzio Rauzzini, then still at Munich, was to sing in Mozart's Milan opera ; this came about at the end of 1772, with *Lucio Silla* (see also end of 1773).

On 27 September the choruses of the new opera were rehearsed, on the 28th the first complete musical rehearsal took place, and on 4, 8, 11 and 14 October the last four rehearsals were held in the theatre.

DECREE

To the Princely Court Pay Office.

Whereas His Serene Highness has been graciously pleased to order by word of mouth that no salary is to be paid to His Highness's Vice Kapellmeister Leopold Mozart so long as he shall be absent from here, . . . which further instruction from His Highness is herewith conveyed to the Princely Court Pay Office and to be punctually carried into effect.

Decretum in Consilio Camerae.
16 October 1771.

Draft in Salzburg Provincial Archives.—Pirkmayer, *op. cit.*, 1876, p. 20 f.—
See 28 December 1771.

On 17 October *Ascanio in Alba* was produced at the Teatro Regio Ducal in Milan, to celebrate the wedding of Archduke Ferdinand of Austria and Princess Maria Beatrice Ricciarda d' Este of Modena.

The Archduke was Governor and Captain-General of Lombardy, a brother of Leopold, Grand Duke of Tuscany and later Emperor, and third son of Maria Theresa (*cf.* 12 December 1771). The principal opera on this occasion was Hasse's *Ruggiero*, his last opera, with libretto by Metastasio. It was given on 16 October. Wolfgang's *festa teatrale* was in two acts ; his librettist was Abbate Giuseppe Parini. The title-part was sung by Giovanni Manzuoli, Venus by Signora Geltrude Falchini, the Nymph Silvia by Signora Antonie Maria Girelli-Aguilar, the Priest Aceste by Giuseppe Tibaldi and the Shepherd Fauno by the male soprano Adamo Solzi. Parini, in his description of the wedding festivities (Milan, 1825, p. 21), says : " The music of the said drama was composed by Signor Amadeo Volfgango Mozart, a youth already known for his ability in various parts of Europe ". The words attributed to Hasse, " This boy will put us all into the shade ", are apocryphal. Mozart's *serenata* was repeated on 19 and 24 October, probably also on the 27th and 28th.

TITLE-PAGE OF THE LIBRETTO OF " ASCANIO IN ALBA "

ASCANIO
IN ALBA

Festa Teatrale
da rappresentarsi in musica
per le felicissime nozze
DELLE LL. AA. RR.
il Serenissimo
FERDINANDO
Arciduca d' Austria
e
La Serenissima Arciduchessa
MARIA BEATRICE
D' ESTE
Principessa di Modena

Semper ad Aeneadas placido pulcherrima vultu
Respice, totque tuas Diva tuere nurus.

Ovid. Fast. lib. 4.

In Milano MDCCLXXI.
Appreso Gio. Batista Bianchi Regio Stampatore

Copies in the Santa Cecilia library in Rome and the Raccolta delle Stampe del Castello in Milan. Facsimile in *Mozart in Italia*, Plate XXX, and in the *Neue Mozart-Ausgabe* II/5/5, *Ascanio in Alba*, p. xx.

FROM THE MANUSCRIPT REGISTER OF THE TEATRO REGIO DUCAL, MILAN, 1771.

(in Italian)

16 do. [October] / As above [for the wedding of Their Royal Highnesses the Archduke Ferdinand, son of the Empress Maria Theresa, and the Archduchess M. Beatrice, Princess of Modena] / Ascanio in Alba / Amadeo Mozart / aforesaid [Giov. Manzoli] aforesaid [M. Girelli Aguilar, chamber virtuosa to His Royal Highness the Duke of Parma and Piacenza] / aforesaid [Giuseppe Tibaldi] / — / aforesaid Favier with dances and choruses / the aforesaid / as above [? at the expense of the Royal Exchequer].

Cf. 26 December 1770.—16 October should read 17 October.—Giovanni Favier was a ballet-master.

On 22 October Field-Marshal Pallavicini wrote from Bologna to congratulate Leopold Mozart on his son's success, and Leopold answered his letter on the 30th.

Ostoja, *op. cit.*, p. 43 f. ; facsimile of Leopold Mozart's letter on p. 40 f.

On 8 November the Mozarts and Hasse lunched at Count Firmian's.

On 22 (? 23) November Mozart gave a concert at the house of Johann Adam Mayr.

Although no particulars of this concert are known, it is likely that the E♭ major divertimento (K. 113), composed in November, was played.—This Mayr was the younger son of the Court Paymaster of the same name, for whom *cf.* 15 and 19 October 1762.

On 30 November the Mozarts were received by Archduke Ferdinand.

On 5 December they left Milan, in the evening of the 6th they arrived at Brescia, in the evening of the 7th at Verona, and at 4 p.m. on the 8th at Ala, where they stayed until noon on the 9th, reaching Trento that evening ; in the evening of the 11th they arrived at Bressanone [Brixen], whence they continued their journey on the morning of the 13th.

At Verona they probably lodged with Lugiati again, at Ala with the Pizzini brothers and at Bressanone with Count Spaur (see the following document).

FROM THE BRESSANONE COURT CHRONICLE, 11 & 12 DECEMBER 1771

On the 11th, Wednesday, Mass at 7 o'clock and continued the cure, at 6 o'clock confession : Canon Count Ignati made music with the 2 Mozarts and took supper with them.

On the 12th December, Thursday, Mass after 7 o'clock and continued the cure, the Mozarts ate with Canon Count Ignati and made music in the afternoon, and also supped with the Canon.

Bressanone, Court Archives.—Discovered by Walter Senn, published by Erich Schenk in the *Sitzungsberichte* of the Österreichische Akademie der Wissenschaften, Philosophico-Historical Section, Vol. 225, (Vienna, 1947), p. 8.—Leopold Maria Joseph, Count Spaur, was Bishop of Bressanone from 1747 to

1776 ; he was succeeded by his nephew, the canon Ignaz Joseph, Count Spaur. The "cure" (spelt *Khur* or *Chur*) consisted of baths in milk and cold water.

MARIA THERESA TO THE ARCHDUKE FERDINAND AT MILAN: VIENNA, 12 DECEMBER 1771
(in French)

. . . you ask me to take the young Salzburger into your service [.] I do not know why, not believing that you have need of a composer or of useless people[.] if however it would give you pleasure, I have no wish to hinder you[.] what I say is intended only to prevent your burdening yourself with useless people and giving titles to people of that sort[.] if they are in your service it degrades that service when these people go about the world like beggars[.] besides, he has a large family.

Alfred Arneth, *Briefe der Kaiserin Maria Theresia an ihre Kinder und Freunde* (Vienna, 1881), Vol. I, p. 92.—Facsimile in *Mozart in Italia*, Plate XXXI.— This was the postscript to a letter. Leopold Mozart's family consisted of only four persons. The Archduke did not engage Wolfgang.

In the evening of 13 December father and son arrived at Innsbruck and on the 15th they returned to Salzburg.

The day after the Mozarts' arrival the Prince-Archbishop Sigismund, Count Schrattenbach, died.

LEOPOLD MOZART'S PETITION TO THE SALZBURG CATHEDRAL CHAPTER

Most Reverend, most Highborn Lords ; my Lords, Cathedral Provost, Cathedral Dean, entire Sovereign and Worshipful Cathedral Chapter of the Archbishopric of Salzburg, my most gracious and mighty Lords !

Your most reverend and most noble Excellencies will not be unaware that Her Imperial and Royal Majesty was most graciously pleased to summon my son to Milan to compose a theatre *serenata* to be performed on the occasion of the Milanese wedding celebrations, in pursuance whereof his Excellency Count Carl *Firmian*, in a letter to his esteemed brother, the Chief Steward, formally requested His Serene Highness of sacred memory to allow me most graciously to betake myself to Milan with my son. It is true that His Serene Highness most considerately granted us permission to travel, but withheld my salary which in any case amounts to only 28 florins 30 kreuzer, though by an oversight I was paid for another month and a half.

When, however, in a letter from his Excellency Count *Sauerau*, addressed to the Court Chancellor, the former thought to acquaint His Serene Highness with the good news of the general applause and honour accorded to my son, His Serene Highness at once gave orders for my salary to be stopped.

Your most reverend and most noble Excellencies are accordingly most humbly requested and besought graciously to have paid to me this deduction of only 2 months at 59 florins, *i.e.* for October and November ; for which, as for all other high favours I tender my and my family's most humble devotion.

Your most reverend and most noble
Excellencies'
my most gracious Lords'
submissively obedient
Leopold *Mozart*
Vice Kapellmeister

To

The most worthy Cathedral Chapter of the Archbishopric of Salzburg, reigning *Sede Vacante*,

A most submissive and obedient petition,

from, Leopold Mozart, Archiep[I] : Vice Kapellmeister for the gracious favour herein requested

[Endorsement]

EX DECR[O] ILL[MI] ET REVD[MI] CAPIT : REG[TIS] DED[O].   *28. Xbris 1771.*

Exchequer : Granted, but without precedent for the future, nor for other court musicians absenting themselves.

Ferd. Truchses, Count Zeyl, Dean.
Carl Hannibal, Count Dietrichstain.

In Cons[i]l[io] C[ame]rae
7 January 1772
Instruction by Decree

Salzburg, Provincial Archives.—Pirkmayer, *op. cit.* (1876), p. 5 f.—*Cf.* 16 October 1771.—Franz Lactantius, Count Firmian, was Chief Steward ; Joseph Gottfried, Count Saurau (if he is meant), was a canon of the cathedral ; Franz Felix von Mölk was Court Chancellor and Director of the Privy Chancery. Ferdinand Christoph, Count Zeil, was Dean of the cathedral, and Karl Hannibal, Count Dietrichstein, was a canon.—Only the discharge of the petition is dated.

LETTER ACCOMPANYING A TRANSLATION OF TISSOT'S ARTICLE, 1771

The Translator
to Herr Wolfgang Mozart
Concert Master to
the Prince-Archbishop of Salzburg.

Do not be surprised, Sir, that I should have translated an essay from the French, written in your honour by an exalted pen (as is supposed) on the occasion of your journey through Switzerland.

I do not endeavour thereby to increase your fame, which you have acquired from crowned heads some time ago : no, indeed, this were folly on my part and no better than if I wished to hang a little night-light on Vesuvius in full eruption, to make it more visible. What induced me thereto was only the fact that the enlightened speaker observed and found in you not only a natural but a moral human being ; a splendid object, in truth, worthy of study, and one rarely or never to be encountered in the case of great artists.

What do we see on examining great artists thoroughly ? One is as disdainful and boastful as a Spanish mountebank, another as lazy and unfriendly as a Greenland bear, a third as greasy and impudent as a northern Laplander, a fourth goes as far as to believe that art will die out with him, and fools of that sort there are generally among all artists.

But you, Sir, are represented as a model of art and virtue in this essay : what solace, pleasure and honour for your dear parents, who have known so well how to unite and nurture in you the moral and the natural man.

May God bless you and protect you for many years yet from all misfortune and every adversity, so that a rational world may eternally admire through you the hand of the Almighty (from whom and through whom you possess both art and virtue).

Farewell and enjoy contentment !

> Salzburg, Mozarteum.—Gustav Nottebohm, *Mozartiana* (Leipzig, 1880), p. 112.—Tenschert, *Mozart* (Amsterdam, 1931), p. 24 f.—In the translation by " B. B." Tissot's *Discours* (see 11 October 1766) is called *Sinn-Rede*.

FROM CHARLES BURNEY'S " THE PRESENT STATE OF MUSIC IN FRANCE AND ITALY, ETC.", LONDON, 1771
(in English)

. . . I must acquaint my musical reader, that at the performance just mentioned, I met with M. Mozart and his son, the little German, whose premature and almost supernatural talents astonished us in London a few years ago, when he had scarce quitted his infant state. Since his arrival in Italy he has been much admired at Rome and Naples ; has been honoured with the order of the *Speron d' Oro*, or Golden Spur, by his Holiness ; and was engaged to compose an opera at Milan for the next Carnival.

> Burney here refers to the church music at Bologna on 30 August 1770 (*q.v.*).

1772

LEOPOLD MOZART TO BREITKOPF & SON, LEIPZIG

[Salzburg,] 7 February 1772.

. . . We arrived on 15 December from Milan, and as my son has again earned much fame by the composition of a theatrical *serenata*, he has once more been commissioned to write the first Carnival opera for the coming year at Milan and immediately after, the second opera for the same Carnival at the Teatro San Benedetto at Venice. We shall therefore remain at Salzburg until the end of the coming September and then leave again for Italy, which will be for the third time.

Should you wish to have something of my son's to print, the time until then would be the best : you need only say what would suit you most. It may be things for the clavier, or trios for 2 violins and violoncello, or quartets, *i.e.* for 2 violins, one viola and violoncello ; or symphonies with 2 violins, viola, 2 horns, 2 oboes or transverse flutes and bass. In short, whatever kind of composition it may be that will seem suitable to you, he will produce it all, provided only that you let us know soon.

> Original sold by auction at Munich on 5-6 October 1951 by Karl & Faber (with J. A. Stargardt). Copy in the German State Library, Berlin (at present in the University Library, Tübingen).—Emily Anderson, *Letters of Mozart and his Family* (London, 1938), p. 306.—The transverse flutes (*Querflöten*) are here called *Zwerchflauten*.—Breitkopf published nothing of Mozart's during his lifetime. *Cf.* 12 February 1781.

On 14 March 1772 Hieronymus, Count Colloredo, was elected Prince-Archbishop of Salzburg.

FROM GRIMM'S " CORRESPONDANCE LITTÉRAIRE ", 1 APRIL 1772
(in French)

. . . Today the first performance of *Le Bal masqué*, a comic opera in one act, took place at the same theatre of the Comédie-Italienne. The music of this piece is by a little rascal aged twelve named Darcis, who on the poster is described as a pupil of M. Grétry. . . . This child was born in Vienna, I believe, of a French father and a German mother. . . . His parents took him to Paris two or three years ago to make him a successor to young Mozart, that amiable and marvellous child of Salzburg, who left so great and so well-merited a reputation in Paris, in London and in Vienna, and who now, having not yet completed his fifteenth year, is in Italy, where, as I have heard tell, he has composed the opera for Milan with the greatest success. The connoisseurs made no mistake about the talent of young Darcis and did not do the young and charming Mozart the wrong of comparing him with this little abortion. . . .

> Tourneux edition, Vol. IX, p. 481.—*Mozart en France* (Paris, 1956), No. 65. —François Joseph Darcis, another wonderchild, failed to live up to his earlier promise.—His first composition had been given at Versailles the day before, 31 March.

On 29 April the new archbishop made his solemn entry and received homage.

At the beginning of May Mozart's *serenata drammatica* : *Il sogno di Scipione* was performed at the archiepiscopal residence in honour of Colloredo.

> The date is uncertain. The piece had been composed for this occasion to a text by Metastasio which had originally been written for Charles VI's birthday

(composed by Angelo Predieri, 1735) and again used for the name-day of
Francis I (composed by Giovanni Porta, 1743).

INSTRUCTION TO THE SALZBURG EXCHEQUER

Inasmuch as His Serene Highness has by his most gracious decree of 9
hujus granted one hundred and fifty florins annually at the most submissive
supplication of His Highness's Concert Master Wolfgang Amade Mozart,
the Princely Court Pay Office is herewith instructed to pay this monthly
pro rata and to post it in the accounts.

Decretum in Consilio Camerae

21 August 1772.

Salzburg, Provincial Archives.—Pirkmayer, *op. cit.* (1876), p. 21.—Wolfgang
had so far borne only the title of " Konzertmeister ", which carried no salary.

On Saturday 24 October 1772, father and son began their third Italian tour, which
was to keep them away for nearly five months. In the evening of the 24th they
reached St. Johann. They left there at 7 a.m. on the 25th, to arrive at 10 p.m. at
Innsbruck, where they stayed at the Golden Eagle. In the afternoon of the 26th
they visited Hall in the Inntal, where Mozart played the organ at the convent church.

On the 27th they left Innsbruck for Bressanone and at midday on the 28th reached
Bolzano. On the 29th they departed at 5 a.m., getting to Trento at midday and to
Rovereto in the evening ; on the 30th they went to see the brothers Pizzini at Ala,
where on the 31st Mozart celebrated his name-day ; in the evening of 1 November
they moved on to Verona, where they again stayed with Lugiati, on the 3rd to Brescia
and at last, on the 4th, to Milan, where they lodged near the d' Astis.

It seems that Baron Pizzini (of Thürberg) in Rovereto and the " Piccini "
brothers at Ala, also mentioned in Leopold's letters, were related. For Frau
d' Asti *cf.* 3 January 1771.

On 21 November Leopold and his wife commemorated their silver wedding.

Anna Lucia de Amicis, the *prima donna* engaged for Mozart's new opera *Lucio Silla*,
arrived in Milan on 4 December. The first recitative and orchestral rehearsals were
held on the 12th, the first full orchestral rehearsal followed on the 19th, the second on
the 20th, the third on the 22nd and the dress rehearsal on the 24th.

On 18th December the Mozarts were present at the function organized by Count
Firmian to celebrate the cardinalate of his brother Leopold Ernst, Prince-Bishop of
Passau. On the 19th they dined with Johann Adam Mayr. On the 21st, 22nd and
23rd Mozart took part in the concerts at Firmian's house ; these lasted from 5 to
11 p.m. ; the Mozarts spent Christmas Eve with the Germanis (see 23 August 1771) ;
on the 26th they lunched at Frau d'Asti's.

For Mayr, *cf.* 22 November 1771.

On 26 December Mozart's three-act opera *Lucio Silla* was performed for the first
time at the Teatro Regio Ducal. The libretto was by Giovanni de Gamerra, with
alterations by Metastasio.

The cast was as follows : Lucio Silla—Bassano Morgnoni ; Giunia—Anna de
Amicis ; Cecilio—Venanzio Rauzzini ; Lucio Cinna—Felicità Suardi ;
Celia—Daniella Mienci ; Aufidio—Giuseppe Onofrio. This was the third

and last opera Mozart wrote for Italy. It was given 26 times during the Carnival of 1772–73. The first performance began at 8 o'clock instead of 6 o'clock, because the Archduke was delayed by official matters, and lasted until 2 a.m.—Gamerra translated *Die Zauberflöte* into Italian after Mozart's death.

TITLE-PAGE OF THE LIBRETTO OF " LUCIO SILLA "

LUCIO SILLA

Dramma per Musica
da rappresentarsi
Nel Regio-Ducal Teatro
di Milano
Nel Carnovale dell' anno 1773
dedicato

ALLE LL. AA. RR.

Il Serenissimo Arciduca

FERDINANDO

Principe Reale d' Ungheria, e Boemia, Arciduca d' Austria,
Duca di Borgogna, e di Lorena ec., Cesareo Reale
Luogo-Tenente, Governatore, e Capitano
Generale nella Lombardia Austriaca,
e la
Serenissima Arciduchessa
MARIA RICCIARDA
BEATRICE D' ESTE

Principessa di Modena

In Milano

Presso Gio. Batista Bianchi Regio Stampatore
Con licenza de' Superiori.

Copy in the Liceo Musicale in Bologna.—Facsimile in *Mozart in Italia*, Plate XXXII.

FROM THE LIBRETTO OF " LUCIO SILLA "

The Poetry is by Sig. De Gamera Poet
of the Regio-Ducal Theatre.

Composer of the Music.

Sig. Amadeo Wolfango Mo-
zart, Knight, Philharmonic Academician of Bologna, and of Verona, and Master of the
Chamber Music of His Serene and Most Reverend Highness
the Archbishop, and Prince of Salzburg.

Designers and Scene Painters
The Brothers Galliari.

Dress Designers
Francesco Motta, and Gio. Mazza.
Facsimile in *Mozart in Italia*, Plate XXXII.

FROM THE MANUSCRIPT REGISTER OF THE TEATRO REGIO DUCAL,
MILAN, 1772

26 December / The aforementioned [The Archduke Ferdinand and the
Archduchess] / Lucio Silla / Amadeo Mozart / Venanzio Rauzzini / Anna de
Amicis / Bassano Morgnoni / —/ Carlo de Picq / Aforementioned / Afore-
mentioned.

> *Cf.* 26 December 1770.—An allusion to Carlo de Picq, who danced in the
> ballet of this opera (*Le gelosie del seraglio*, K. App. 109), is found in the bass
> aria " Rivolgete a lui lo sguardo " (K. 584), originally intended for *Così fan
> tutte.*

1773

FROM JOHANN GOTTLIEB NAUMANN'S DIARY, 2 JANUARY 1773

I went to Colloredo's and heard the news of the Opera at Milan.

> Jahn, Vol. I, p. 159.—The composer to the Saxon court had himself often
> visited Italy and had recently composed four operas for Venice and one for
> Parma.—The Archbishop had been taken ill about the New Year in Vienna,
> and it seems that Naumann met him there.

On 17 January 1773 Mozart's new motet " Exsultate, jubilate " (K. 165) was sung
by Venanzio Rauzzini at the Theatine Church in Milan.

On 30 January the Mozarts were present, in Germani's box, at the production of the
second Carnival opera commissioned for Milan, Giovanni Paisiello's *Sismano nel
Mogol.*

About 4 March the Mozarts left Milan for Verona, by way of Brescia, and then
went on to Ala.

> On the 6th they were again at Lugiati's and on the 8th at Pizzini's.

On 10 March they left Ala for Trento ; on the 11th father and son continued to
Bressanone, on the 12th to Innsbruck, and on the 13th they were home again.

> Soon after their return home the family must have moved to the large new
> lodgings on the Hannibal-Platz (now Makart-Platz), opposite the theatre.
> The " Tanzmeister-Saal " has been turned into a memorial hall.

On 14 March the first anniversary of the archbishop's enthronement was celebrated.

> It has been suggested that Mozart's C major divertimento (K. 187), a re-
> working of pieces by Starzer and Gluck, was performed on this occasion.

TOBIAS PHILIPP, BARON GEBLER, TO CHRISTOPH FRIEDRICH
NICOLAI IN BERLIN

Vienna, 31 May 1773.

. . . Should my *Thamos* have the honour of being performed there,
I could oblige with the music for the choruses, which have been not at all
badly set and were thoroughly revised by the Chevalier Gluck.

> Richard Maria Werner, *Aus dem Josephinischen Wien* (Berlin, 1888), p. 51.—
> Gebler's drama *König Thamos* was published in Prague and Dresden in 1773
> and was first performed on 11 December 1773 in Bratislava by the Karl Wahr
> company (with unspecified music), and subsequently in Vienna on 4 April 1774
> at the Kärntnertor Theatre. The first two choruses were composed by Johann
> Tobias Sattler, who died in Vienna on 19 December 1774. His music was
> revised by Gluck. Meanwhile in Vienna Mozart had set both these choruses
> afresh, and they appear to have been sung there in his version. Not until the
> performance at Salzburg by the Karl Wahr company on 3 January 1776 was
> Johann Andreas Schachtner's setting of the final chorus performed. Mozart's
> complete music—three choruses (the first two in new versions) and five
> entr'actes—was probably first used during the 1779–1780 season at Salzburg
> by Johann Böhm's company.—Cf. 13 December 1773, 24 March, 13 April and
> 19 May 1774, 3 and 17 January 1776.—See Alfred Orel in *Acta Mozartiana*
> (Augsburg, 1957), Year IV, Nos. 3 and 4 ; H. Heckmann in the Preface and
> Critical Commentary to the *Neue Mozart-Ausgabe* II/6/1 (*Chöre und Zwischen-
> aktmusiken zu Thamos, König in Ägypten*) ; and Ervin Major in *Mozart in Ungarn*
> (Budapest, 1958) pp. 38 and 41.

On 14 July father and son left for Vienna, where they arrived in the evening of
the 16th and remained for more than two months ; they stayed at the house of Gottlieb Friedrich Fischer in the Tiefe Graben (No. 322 in the Inner City). On 17 July
the Mozarts took supper with the magnetist Dr. Anton Mesmer in the Landstrasse
suburb, and on the 18th with his cousin Joseph Mesmer, a headmaster ; on the 19th
they spent the whole day at Dr. Mesmer's ; on the 20th they lunched with one
Porta (their erstwhile servant ?) and in the afternoon of the 21st they visited Herr von
Mayr senior (*cf.* 15 and 19 October 1762 ; he had been ennobled since then).

The Empress returned from Eisenstadt on 24 July ; on the 26th, St. Anne's Day,
the Mozarts again spent the day at Dr. Mesmer's.

The Archbishop of Salzburg arrived on 31 July and went on to Laxenburg on 2
August. On the 4th (?) the Mozarts were invited to lunch by Dr. Leopold Auen-
brugger.

> About 1 August Wolfgang's new serenade in D major (K. 185) was performed
> at Salzburg, probably (according to Dr. H. Klein) as the logic students' "Final-
> musik" commissioned by Judas Thaddäus von Antrettern.—The famous Dr.
> Auenbrugger was, like Dr. Mesmer, a music-lover ; he later wrote the libretto
> of Antonio Salieri's German Singspiel *Der Rauchfangkehrer*.

On 5 August the Mozarts were received in audience by the Empress.

> Since the actual purpose of this journey to Vienna has remained unknown, it
> is impossible to say whether Leopold Mozart had some special request to make
> at Court.

On 7 August, St. Cajetan's Day, father and son visited the neighbouring monastery
of St. Cajetan, where Mozart played a violin concerto in the choir of the church.

On 8 August Leopold Mozart conducted Mozart's Dominicus Mass (K. 66) in the Jesuit Church in the square named "Am Hof".

See 15 October 1769.—The Jesuit Order was suppressed in Austria on 10 September.

After the Archbishop's return from Laxenburg on 12 August the Mozarts were received by him on the same day and their leave of absence was extended.

The Archbishop returned to Salzburg on the 17th.

At midday on 18 August there was a "grand concert" in Dr. Mesmer's garden.

Alfred Orel (*Mozart-Jahrbuch 1951* [Salzburg, 1953], p. 43) conjectures that Wolfgang's D major divertimento (K. 205) was performed on this occasion.

The Mozarts spent the week-end of 21-23 August with the Fischers and the Teyber family at Baden, near Vienna.

The Fischers were the Mozarts' hosts. The Teybers' daughter Therese was the first Blonde in *Die Entführung*.

On 25 August the Mozarts visited the Salzburg Court Chancellor von Mölk, who was staying in Vienna, and lunched with Joseph Mesmer. On the 27th they lunched with Aeodat Joseph Philippe du Beyne de Malechamp, a retired councillor and a music-lover, and on the 29th with the ballet-master Jean Georges Noverre.

The Mozarts also visited (dates not precisely known) the Hofkapellmeister Giuseppe Bonno and the pianist Marianne Martinez (see 14 October 1762).

On 6 September the Mozarts paid their respects to the Salzburg doctor, Franz Joseph Niderl von Aichegg, who had come to Vienna for an operation, and who died under it on the 10th ; he was buried at 8 p.m. on the 12th.

On 22 September the Mozarts and Frau Mesmer, wife of the headmaster, drove to Rothmühl, Dr. Mesmer's summer residence near Schwechat, and in the evening they dined at Joseph Mesmer's.

On 24 September the Mozarts travelled by way of St. Pölten, Linz and Lambach back to Salzburg, where they arrived on the 26th.

The return journey had originally been planned to lead by way of Mariazell, St. Wolfgang and St. Gilgen. The date of departure is unknown.

GEBLER TO NICOLAI

Vienna, 13 December 1773.

. . . I . . . enclose the music for *Thamos*, in any case, as set not long ago by a certain Sigr. Mozzart. It is his own original score, and the first chorus very fine.

Cf. 31 May 1773.

FROM CHARLES BURNEY'S " THE PRESENT STATE OF MUSIC IN GERMANY, . . . ", LONDON, 1773
(in English)

. . . The first singer in the serious opera here [Munich], is Signor Rauzzini, a young Roman performer, of singular merit, who has been six years in the service of this court ; but is engaged to sing in an opera composed by young Mozart, at the next carnival at Milan ; ...

Vol. I, p. 126.—The passage refers to Munich, summer 1772 (*cf.* 23 [29] August 1771).

IBID.
(in English)

... The archbishop and sovereign of SALTZBURG is very magnificent in his support of music, having usually near a hundred performers, vocal and instrumental, in his service. This prince is himself a *dilettante*, and good performer on the violin ; he has lately been at great pains to reform his band, which has been accused of being more remarkable for coarseness and noise, than delicacy and high-finishing. Signor Fischietti, author of several comic operas, is at present the director of this band.

The Mozart family were all at Saltzburg last summer ; the father has long been in the service of that court, and the son is now one of the band ; he composed an opera at Milan, for the marriage of the arch-duke, with the princess of Modena, and was to compose another at the same place for the carnival of this year, though he is now but sixteen years of age. By a letter from Saltzburg, dated last November, I am informed, that this young man, who has so much astonished all Europe by his premature knowledge and performance during infancy, is still a great master of his instrument ; my correspondent went to his father's house to hear him and his sister play duets on the same harpsichord ; but she is now at her summit, which is not marvellous ; " and ", says the writer of the letter, " if I may judge of the music which I heard of his composition, in the orchestra, he is one further instance of early fruit being more extraordinary than excellent."

Vol. II, p. 322 f. (2nd ed.).—The passage refers to Salzburg, summer 1772. —Domenico Fischietti was engaged by Colloredo as second Kapellmeister of the Salzburg Court Music on 5 September 1772, Giuseppe Maria Lolli being no longer regarded as capable.—The above is the text of the second, slightly revised, edition of Burney's book (1775) ; the only significant difference in the first is the description of Mozart as " this young man, who so much astonished all Europe by his infant knowledge and performance, ..."

1774

FROM THE " HOCHFÜRSTLICH–SALZBURGER KIRCHEN– UND
HOF-KALENDER " FOR 1774
HIS HIGHNESS'S COURT MUSIC.

.   .   .   .

Vice Kapellmeister
Herr Leopold Motzart, 28 Feb. 1773.

Konzertmeister
Herr Johann Michael Hayden.
Herr Wolfgang Motzart.

Cf. early 1770 and 21 August 1772.—1773 in the document is a misprint for 1763.—Seidl, the first Konzertmeister, had left ; Michael Haydn and Wolfgang —now salaried—had advanced.   Until 1777 inclusive the list remained unchanged for these three musicians.   In 1778 Wolfgang was not a member of the Court Music ; in 1779 he became Salzburg Court Organist, but only for a short time.

FROM THE " HISTORISCH-KRITISCHE THEATERCHRONIK VON WIEN ",
24 MARCH 1774

On Easter Monday the German playhouse will be opened with the new tragedy by the author of *Der Minister* (Baron Gebler), entitled *Thamos, König in Egypten,* with choruses set for it by Herr Starzer.   I await with pleasure the moment at which I shall be able to spend more time with this fine piece.

The editor of this short-lived periodical was Christian Hieronymus Moll, a theatre writer.—*Cf.* 31 May 1773.   The paper seems originally to have confused Johann Sattler with Josef Starzer, but it was wrong in any case. (Alfred Orel in *Mozart-Jahrbuch 1951* [Salzburg, 1953], p. 48)

IBID., 13 APRIL 1774

On 4 April the German playhouse was opened with *Thamos, König von Egypten,* together with a . . . ballet by Herr Angiolini. . . . *Thamos,* an heroic drama in five acts, is by the well-known and well-favoured poet of *Der Minister* and of *Clementine.*   As in all the other plays by this author, his virtuous heart speaks through Thamos.   The whole tragedy is full of warmth, of dignity in heroic poetry, it has not the excessive length of other tragedies written here, and recommends itself for this very reason to our local poets, and also for its no less finely pithy and thoughtful dialogue.

It consists of only five and a half folded sheets.

In the Preface the author at once meets, with his own peculiar modesty, all the objections with which some wiseacres might confront him, if they were intent on judging everything in a false light.

The apology made for the choruses in the first and the fifth acts is no less praiseworthy, although in my opinion there was no need for it.   They made their effect—for the music by Herr *Karl Mozzart* is beautifully written—and more than that I think the author did not expect.—The pity is only that it was not better sung. . . .

Gasparo Angiolini had again become ballet-master at the Vienna Court Theatre after Noverre's departure.—*Der Minister* and *Clementine, oder das Testament* were earlier plays by Gebler, each performed twice at the Burgtheater after 1775.

IBID., 13 APRIL 1774

The *Theaterchronik* committed a great sin in its No. 1 by stating, under "Miscellaneous News", that the choruses in *Thamos* were composed by Herr Starzer. It was not Herr Starzer, but Herr Mozart, who wrote the music. This correction appeared in the same number as the criticism of the piece.

IBID., 9 MAY 1774

Our German actors will this year have the honour of playing before the Imperial Court, and that four times a week. *Thamos* made a beginning on Wednesday last [the 4th]. The management receives the usual fee of 50 ducats for each performance.

> Alfred Orel in *Acta Mozartiana* (Augsburg, 1957) Year IV, Part 4, p. 76.—These performances doubtless took place in Schloss Laxenburg, a summer residence south of Vienna.

CHRISTOPH MARTIN WIELAND TO GEBLER

Belvedere near Weimar, 19 May 1774.

Receive, . . . dearest friend, my most sincere thanks . . . for the beautiful music for *Thamos* which you sent me.

Our Schweizer, whom I believe to be incomparable in his kind, has found much that is fine in this music, and in general a great *ability* in its author, although he *guessed* immediately that he must be still a beginner.

> Wieland, *Auswahl denkwürdiger Briefe*, edited by his son Ludwig (Vienna, 1815), Vol. II, p. 30.—Anton Schweitzer, the theatre composer in Weimar, had set Wieland's *Alceste* and *Rosamunde*.—Gebler had sent Mozart's music to Wieland, although the choruses could not have been performed at the Weimar theatre.

On 6 December father and son went by way of Frabertsham to Wasserburg, where they arrived at 9 p.m., leaving for Munich at 8 a.m. on the 7th. They arrived in Munich at 4 p.m. and took lodgings with Johann Nepomuk von Pernat, a canon at the Church of Our Lady, in the so-called Bellvalli house, where they remained for three months.

FROM JOACHIM FERDINAND VON SCHIEDENHOFEN'S DIARY, 6 DECEMBER 1774

Herr Mozart travelled to Munich with his son this very day, in order to produce the *opera buffa* composed by the latter.

> This diary (1774–78), which Jahn knew only from extracts and from which he quoted only a small portion of the passages relevant to Mozart, now belongs to Frau Michaela Grimburg, Schloss Töllerberg, Post Völkermarkt, Carinthia, and is at present on loan to the Salzburg Provincial Archives. Dr. Herbert Klein, Director of the Salzburg Provincial Archives, rediscovered the diary in 1956 and placed it at the present editor's disposal. J. F. von

Schiedenhofen auf Stumm und Triebenbach was, like his father before him, a Salzburg councillor. He and his sister Aloisia, as well as their widowed mother, lived at Getreidegasse 1 and were among the close friends of the Mozart family. *Cf.* O. E. Deutsch in the *Mozart-Jahrbuch 1957* (Salzburg, 1958), pp. 15 ff.—The opera was *La finta giardiniera.*

The first performance of the new opera, planned for 29 December, was postponed till 5 January 1775.

1775

Leopold Mozart's *Litaniae de venerabili altaris sacramento* and W. A. Mozart's setting (K. 125) of the same text, were performed at the canonical hours on New Year's Day in Munich.

This probably took place in the Frauenkirche.

FROM SCHIEDENHOFEN'S DIARY, 3 JANUARY 1775

Today the Robinigs and M^{selle} Mozart left for Munich.

For Robinig see 12 January 1762 and 7 January 1781.

On 4 January 1775 Nannerl arrived in Munich and was given lodgings at the widow von Durst's "in the Spatzenreiter-Haus on the Square". Father and son, having taken a meal with Wenzel Andreas Gilowsky of Salzburg at Starzer's inn, spent the evening with Nannerl at Frau von Durst's. On the 5th, the opera première having again been put off, Nannerl went to coffee at Canon Johann Nepomuk von Pernat's. On the 10th all three Mozarts went to a "masked academy" [concert].

On 13 January the three-act opera buffa *La finta giardiniera* was performed at the Assembly Rooms in the Prannerstrasse. The libretto by Raniero de' Calzabigi, composed by Pasquale Anfossi for the Carnival in Rome the preceding year, had been revised by Marco Coltellini.

No libretto of this version has come to light. Of the cast only three names are certain : Sandrina—Rosa Manservisi, Ramiro—Tommaso Consoli and Serpetta—Teresina Manservisi. Rossi as the Podestà Anchise is not authenticated. For the second performance, attended by the Elector Palatine Karl Theodor in February, the opera was cut because the *seconda donna* (Manservisi) was ill. On 3 March the third and last performance was given at Munich. In the German translation by Stierle the work was perhaps given as early as the 1779–80 season at Salzburg by Johann Böhm's company, which certainly produced it as *Die verstellte Gärtnerin* at Augsburg on 1 May 1780. See also 2 April 1782 and 30 April 1789.

FROM THE DIARY OF THE SAXON LEGATION SECRETARY J. F. UNGER, ### MUNICH, 15 JANUARY 1775 (in French)

On Friday Their Electoral Highnesses were present at the first performance of the *opera buffa* : *La finta giardinera* ; the music was generally applauded ; it is by young Mozart of Salzburg, who is here at the moment. He is the same who went to England and elsewhere at the age of 8 to be heard on the harpsichord, which he plays supremely well.

> Dresden, State Archives.—Jahn, Vol. I, p. 165.—The reigning Elector Palatine was Maximilian III Joseph of Bavaria.

On 21 (?) January a musical concert was held in Munich in honour of Archbishop Hieronymus, who was on a visit there.

> The Archbishop was on a visit to Munich from 14 (?) to 26 January, and thus had no opportunity of hearing Mozart's opera. Whether the latter took part in the concert is uncertain.

On Sunday 12 February Leopold Mozart conducted a short mass by his son in the Munich court chapel, probably the *Missa brevis* in F (K. 192).

GEBLER TO NICOLAI

Vienna, 14 February 1775.

. . . The good *Magister* Sattler, who had written the first music for it (I believe, however, that I sent the better music by Mozart to your Excellency) has died in the meantime from consumption.

> Werner, *op. cit.*, p. 65.—Cf. 31 May 1773.

On 14 February the three Mozarts attended a masked ball at the Assembly Rooms.

On 19 February Leopold Mozart again conducted a mass by his son at the court chapel, probably the *Missa brevis* in D (K. 194).

On Sunday, 5 March, Mozart's *Offertorium de tempore* " Misericordias Domini " (K. 222), composed at Munich, was performed there.

> This was probably also in the Court Chapel.—Wolfgang sent this motet to Padre Martini at Bologna on 4 September 1776, explaining to him the occasion for which it had been written ; Martini praised it highly. See 18 December 1776.

The three Mozarts left Munich on 6 March and arrived home on the 7th.

FROM SCHIEDENHOFEN'S DIARY, 19 APRIL 1775

In the evening Councillor Mölck came to me, with whom I went to the Mozarts', where I met the castrato Consoli and the transverse-flute player Becke, both from Munich.

> Consistorial Councillor Albert von Mölk was a son of the Chancellor, for whom see 28 December 1771.—For Consoli see 13 January 1775. Like the flautist Johann Baptist Becke he had been engaged from Munich, probably through Leopold Mozart, for the two concerts held at the archiepiscopal residence on 22 and 23 April in honour of the Archduke Maximilian.

IBID., 20 APRIL 1775

. . . Afterwards I went to the 9.30 Mass and thence to Court, where the Serenade by Mozart was rehearsed. Thence I accompanied the Robinigs home.

> See 23 April.

FROM SCHIEDENHOFEN'S DIARY, 22 APRIL 1775

In the evening I went with the Town Syndic to the Serenade at Court, which was by Sigr. Fischietti and for which the castrato Consoli and the transverse-flute player Becke of Munich were engaged.

> See 23 April. The Town Syndic was Joseph Benedikt Loës (later von Loës).

IBID., 23 APRIL 1775

To the Court in the evening for the Serenade, which had been composed by young Mozart.

> The often composed libretto of *Il rè pastore* by Metastasio had been considerably altered for the present purpose. The part of Aminta was sung by Consoli ; the other singers belonged to the Court Chapel.

FROM THE ARCHDUKE MAXIMILIAN'S TRAVEL JOURNAL, SALZBURG, 23 APRIL 1775

Sunday the 23rd. . . . Moreover, the evening was again concluded, as on the day before, with a *musique-concert* and supper at the Palace, and as regards the concert the difference was made for a change that, as the music for the past day had been written by the well-known Kapellmeister *Fischietti*, so the *musique* for the cantata sung this evening was by the no less famous *Mozart*.

> Vienna, Austrian State Archives, Familien-Akten, Karton 87, No. 15, fol. 4, verso.—The Archduke Maximilian, later Elector of Cologne, was Maria Theresa's youngest son (see 15 October 1762). The journal, which describes the Archduke's journey from Vienna to Italy, was probably written by Count Johann Hardegg, at that time the officer supervising the Archduke's travelling arrangements. Maximilian had been in Paris for the carnival ; he arrived in Salzburg on 21 April and stayed at the archiepiscopal residence. In the evening of the 22nd all the nobility of the town attended dinner and the concert, which was directed by Fischietti. It is curious that the journal should describe Mozart's *dramma per musica* as a cantata.

IBID., 24 APRIL 1775

Monday the 24th. . . . In the evening . . . as on the preceding days, *musique* was chosen for the entertainment, in such a way, however, that Countess *Lützau*, a niece of the Archbishop's, as well as another lady, performed on the clavier, and were accompanied, apart from the Archduke, by the Archbishop and by Counts Ugarte, Czernin and Hardegg. Also, at the end of the *musique*, the famous young *Mozart* was heard on the clavier and played various things by heart with as much art as pleasantness. Thus ended the day, and because of the Archduke's impending departure everyone retired early.

> *Ibid.*, fol. 5 recto.—Jahn, Vol. I, p. 169.—Colloredo's niece was Antonie, Countess Lützow, born Countess Czernin-Chudenitz, probably a pupil of Leopold Mozart's. Johann Wenzel, Count Ugarte, later became *Hofmusikgraf* and in 1791 Director-General of the Court Theatres ; like Count Johann Hardegg (see 15 October 1762), he was at the time in the Archduke's retinue. Johann Rudolf, Count Czernin von Chudenitz, the Archbishop's nephew and Countess Lützow's brother, studied law at Salzburg University and cultivated music and poetry.

FROM ABBOT BEDA SEEAUER'S DIARY, SALZBURG, 24 APRIL 1775

In the evening, at the party, the Prince himself condescended to fiddle *violino 2do*, and many of the high nobility *utriusque Sexus*, with the gracious Lord himself *in capite*, as happens almost every day, proved their skill in the art of music.

> Salzburg, Archives of St. Peter's.—Communicated by Dr. Herbert Klein.— The " prince " is the Archduke, the " gracious lord " the Archbishop.

FROM CHRISTIAN FRIEDRICH DANIEL SCHUBART'S " DEUTSCHE CHRONIK ", AUGSBURG, 27 APRIL 1775

Extract from a Letter from Munich

. . . I also heard an *opera buffa* by that wonderful genius *Mozart* ; it is called *La finta giardiniera*. Flashes of genius appear here and there ; but there is not yet that still altar-fire that rises towards Heaven in clouds of incense—a scent beloved of the gods. If *Mozart* is not a plant forced in the hot-house, he is bound to grow into one of the greatest musical composers who ever lived.

Just think, brother, what a delight that was ! In Munich last winter I heard two of the greatest clavier players, Herr *Mozart* and Captain *von Beecke* ; my host, Herr Albert, who is enthusiastic about all that is great and beautiful, has an excellent fortepiano in his house. It was there that I heard these two giants in contest on the clavier. Mozart's playing had great weight, and he read at sight everything that was put before him. But no more than that ; Beecke surpasses him by a long way. Winged agility, grace, melting sweetness and a quite peculiar, self-formed taste are clubs which nobody is likely to wrest from this Hercules. . . .

Y.

> Year II, No. 34, p. 267.—Copy in the Mozart-Gemeinde, Augsburg.—Ernst Holzer (*Schubartstudien* [Ulm, 1902], p. 9, and *Schubart als Musiker* [Stuttgart, 1905], p. 20) has pointed out that Schubart is here quoting a correspondent, not writing on his own account.—Ignaz von Beecke was music director to Prince Kraft Ernst of Oettingen-Wallerstein. The Mozarts had already met

this composer and clavier player in Paris in 1766. The competition must have taken place in the winter of 1774-75 at the house of the " learned " host Franz Albert in the Kaufinger-Strasse, with whom the Mozarts later made friends.

FROM THE ACCOUNTS OF THE GENERAL ARCHIEPISCOPAL RECEIVER

Salzburg, 15 May 1775

To Leop. Mozart, Princely Kapellmeister, for food, drink, etc., served by the Sternbräu to the two virtuosi engaged from Munich.

98 fl. 47 kr.

Salzburg, Provincial Archives.—Pirkmayer, *op. cit.* (1876), p. 138.—This entry seems to show that the engagement of the castrato Consoli and the flautist Becke from 23 April 1775 had been arranged by Leopold Mozart.

On 23 May an oratorio, *Betulia liberata*, was performed at Munich.

In Unger's diary (see 15 January 1775) the work is mentioned, without a composer's name, as an *oratoire ou opérette* (Abert, Vol. I, p. 365). See 12-13 March 1771. This was probably the first performance of the work, but it may have been another of the numerous settings of this text (Abert, Vol. I, p. 286).

FROM SCHIEDENHOFEN'S DIARY, 9 AUGUST 1775

After dinner to the *Final-Musik* composed by Herr Mozart. I went to Mirabell first, and then to the University, with Herr von Luidl and my sister. The acquaintances I met were the Barisannis, the Loeses and the Robinigs.

Perhaps the D major serenade (K. 204), which was finished on 5 August (1775 ?). Jahn and Abert (Vol. I, p. 479) believed that the work in question was the D major serenade (K. 185), written in Vienna in the summer of 1773. The so-called *Final-Musiken,* usually given on Wednesday since there was a school holiday on Thursday, were serenades which the students of the philosophical faculty's two courses (logic and natural science) offered about the end of the academic year to the Prince at his summer residence of Mirabell and to their professors in front of the University. (See 6 and 8 August 1769, 31 July and 1 August 1773 and the following entry.)—The rehearsal for this *Final-Musik* given by the logicians took place on 8 August. (See *Nannerl Mozarts Tagebuchblätter,* edited by Walter Hummel [Salzburg, 1958], p. 15.)

IBID., 23 AUGUST 1775

After dinner to the *Final-Musik,* which was by Mozart. I saw there the Robinigs, Barisannis, Daubrawas and Mozarts.

This was the first or a repeat performance of K. 284.—Silvester Barisani was the Archbishop's physician. Johann Baptist Anton Daubrawa von Daubrawaik was syndic of the Cathedral Chapter ; his elder brother Virgil Christoph was a Councillor of the Exchequer and Master of the Mint. Schiedenhofen married Virgil's daughter Anna (Nanette) in 1778.

1776

IBID., 3 JANUARY 1776

In the evening . . . to the comedy, in the stalls. A curtain-raiser was played, and afterwards *Tamos König in Egipten* by Baron Gebler.

> According to Alfred Orel the music was Mozart's, complete with the new final chorus.

FROM THE "THEATERWOCHENBLATT FÜR SALZBURG", 17 JANUARY 1776

On 3 January. *Thamos*, a tragedy in five acts by Baron von Gebler . . . He has made an attempt, following Klopſtock, to bring the choruses of the ancients into heroic tragedy, and to link them up with it in such a way as not to impair the interest of the action. The composer of the choruses has prolonged the fifth act unduly by repetitions. The choruses ought to be sung straight through and would be better interchanged. They might also be entirely omitted without robbing the piece of anything, as was done in Vienna.

> Konstantin Schneider, *Geschichte der Musik in Salzburg* (Salzburg, 1935), p. 120 f.—*Cf.* 31 May 1773 and (4) 13 April 1774.—Friedrich Gottlieb Klopstock (1724–1803), best known for his great epic *Der Messias*, also wrote dramas on biblical and historical themes.

FROM THE MINUTE-BOOK OF THE COLLEGIUM MUSICUM OF THE CITY OF MEMMINGEN, 15 FEBRUARY 1776

His Excellency Senator von Heuss auf Trunkelsberg submitted a symphony by young Mozart, which excited applause and amazement : the former on account of its beautiful composition, the latter because Mozart, when he wrote it, can scarcely have been twelve years old.

> Memmingen, City Archives.—E. F. Schmid, *Ein schwäbisches Mozart-Buch* (Lorch-Stuttgart, 1948), pp. 170 and 428.—Tobias von Heuss had been a member of the Collegium since 1760.—The symphony has not been identified.

FROM SCHIEDENHOFEN'S DIARY, 18 FEBRUARY 1776

At 7 in the evening to the Marshal of the Household, where I supped. Then in company to the rout, driving there with the Chief Equerry as a lady, the Marshal as a cavalier, Baron Lilien as a gallant, Count Micha as a courier, Herr Schmid, B. Lilien's companion, as a hairdresser, the elder Mozart as a porter and the younger as the hairdresser's boy, Count Überacker as a moor and myself as a lackey . . .; apart from that there was a remarkable company of gods among the masqueraders . . . they made an entry and then a country dance. About 420 persons were present today. I stayed until 4 a.m.

> The High Chamberlain was Nikolaus Sebastian, Count Lodron ; his wife was Maria Anna, born Countess Harrach. The Chief Equerry was Leopold Joseph, Count Kuenburg. Polycarp, Baron Lilien, was at that time a student at Salzburg University. Wolf Joseph, Count Uiberacker was a Councillor at the Exchequer.

FROM SCHIEDENHOFEN'S DIARY, 19 FEBRUARY 1776

In the evening I again went to the rout, where there were 320 masqueraders. I went at first as a Tyrolese girl. Among the curiosities was an operetta by Mozart, and a peasants' wedding. I remained until 4.30, and dancing continued until 5.30.

> *Die Bauernhochzeit* is the title of a humorous piece of programme-music by Leopold Mozart (for strings, wind, bagpipe and hurdy-gurdy). The " operetta ", probably a comic interlude, was in any case presumably by him.

IBID., PALM SUNDAY, 31 MARCH 1776

To the Cathedral with the Dicasteries at 5 o'clock in the afternoon, for the festal sermon. Remained also for the following sermon by Fr. Simpert Schwarzhueber, and for the new Litany by Mozart.

> The *Litaniae de venerabili altaris sacramento* (K. 243). On the two following days new Litanies by Adlgasser and Michael Haydn were performed (*cf.* 23 May 1776, 14 April 1778, 30 March 1779 and 13 April 1783). During these three days the forty hours' prayer was observed, with sermons and concluding litanies. Schwarzhuber belonged to the monastery of Wessobrunn in Bavaria.

IBID., EASTER SUNDAY, 7 APRIL 1776

. . . Afterwards to the Cathedral, where His Grace the Prince pontificated. The Mass was a new one by young Mozart.

> " His Grace the Prince " was, of course, the Archbishop.—The C major Mass, (K. 262), was thus not composed as late as May 1776, and was not performed at St. Peter's, as has been supposed (see Köchel-Einstein, pp. 314 and 316).

On 23 May 1776 Mozart's litany (K. 243) was again performed at Mirabell Palace· *Nannerl Mozarts Tagebuchblätter*, p. 27.—*Cf.* 31 March 1776.

IBID., 18 JUNE 1776

After dinner to the music composed by Mozart for Countess Ernst Lodron.

> The Countess Antonia, born Countess Arco, was the wife of the Salzburg Hereditary Marshal Ernst, Count Lodron. Her house was a centre of the

town's musical life. As well as the divertimento in F (K. 247) of 1776, Mozart wrote another for her in 1777 (see 13 June 1777). These "Lodron Serenades" were given on 13 June, the Countess's name-day.

IBID., 7 JULY 1776

[Evening] Afterwards we went together to the music-making at Frau von Antretter's. Thence I went home in the company of the Mozarts.

> Johann Ernst von Antrettern, whose wife is frequently mentioned in the Mozart family's letters, was Provincial Chancellor and a councillor in the War Department. Cf. 31 July (1 August) 1773.

IBID., 21 JULY 1776

After dinner I went to the bridal music which young Herr Hafner had made for his sister Liserl. It was by Mozart and was performed in the summer-house at Loreto.

> Elisabeth, daughter of the deceased wholesale merchant and Burgomaster of Salzburg, Siegmund Haffner, married the forwarding-agent Franz Xaver Spaeth. Her brother, the younger Siegmund, had ordered the Haffner serenade (K. 250), which was played in the garden of his summer residence in the Paris-Lodrongasse. Cf. 29 July 1782. Elisabeth Spaeth died in 1781.

On 26 July, as usual, Nannerl celebrated her name-day, and on the 30th her twenty-fifth birthday.

> It is supposed that Wolfgang wrote the D major divertimento (K. 251) for the first occasion. Schiedenhofen mentions no serenade for this day.

IBID., 22 AUGUST 1776

At night, until 12 o'clock, I went . . . for a walk with Carl Agliardi and others, and there was also music at Mozart's.

> Karl von Agliardis was one of the Councillors in the Salzburg administration.

* IBID., 23 AUGUST 1776

In the evening, late, to the Mozarts.

KARL, FREIHERR VON PETERMANN, TO COUNT PROKOP ADALBERT CZERNIN IN PRAGUE
(in French)

[Salzburg, 13 December 1776]

. . . I shall always consider myself fortunate if I am able to execute to your satisfaction such commissions as you are kind enough to entrust to me.

Wherefore I have spoken to little Motzard about the annual payment of 20 ducats, and he leaves it entirely to your judgement. So I await your orders. He also told me that he will send the Symphony and the other pieces at the earliest opportunity. . . .

> Discovered by E. F. Schmid in the erstwhile Czernin Archives at Jindřichův Hradec [Neuhaus].—Petermann was a Lieutenant-Colonel in the Imperial Army living in Salzburg, an intimate friend of the Archbishop's with bachelor quarters in the Residenz. He had supervised the education of the very musical young Count Johann Rudolf Czernin, who was a son of the addressee, a brother of Countess Antonia Lützow and a nephew of the Archbishop, as well as being on friendly terms with Mozart. The old Count Czernin's settlement on Mozart of an annual sum of 20 ducats (90 gulden) carried the obligation to provide compositions, and in the first instance a symphony. Although this sum must have been paid at least once before the Count's death at the beginning of 1777 (cf. 1 February 1777), Mozart seems not to have written anything for him, or at any rate no new symphony. Cf. his letter to his father from Munich, 19 December 1780, whose reference to the old Count can only be explained by the above document.

PADRE MARTINI TO MOZART
(in Italian)

Bologna, 18 December 1776.

Together with your most kind letter, which reached me by way of Trent, I received the Motet. . . . It was with pleasure that I studied it from beginning to end, and I can tell you in all sincerity that I was singularly pleased with it, finding in it all that is required by Modern Music : good harmony, mature modulation, a moderate pace in the violins, a natural connexion of the parts and good taste. I am delighted with it and rejoice that since I had the pleasure of hearing you at Bologna on the harpsichord you have made great strides in composition, which must be pursued ever more by practice, for Music is of such a nature as to call for great exercise and study as long as one lives.

> Vienna, National Library.—Müller von Asow, op. cit., Vol. III (text vol. II), p. 315.—Facsimile in Città di Milano, 12 December 1955, p. 706.—This draft appears below Mozart's letter of 4 September. Cf. 5 March 1775.—It appears that in the fair copy of this letter Martini expressed the wish to receive portraits of Leopold and Wolfgang. Not until 22 December 1777 did Leopold so far fulfil this wish as to send to Bologna, by means of Haffner, the portrait of Wolfgang with the insignia of the papal order, the work of a Salzburg painter. The original is now in the Conservatorio G. B. Martini at Bologna; a modern copy hangs in the Mozart-Museum at Salzburg.

1777

FROM SCHIEDENHOFEN'S DIARY, 1 FEBRUARY 1777

At home in the afternoon. Then to Loreto, thence to Barisani's, where I found no one, as everyone was at Lizzau's for the country dance practice. Then to the Mozarts', where I saw nobody but the mother and daughter, who told me that on Carnival Monday a ballet, *Apollo et les Muses*, was to be performed, at which Count Czernin and further Countess Aursperg, Herr von Miller, the 4 Barisanis, Robinig, Mölck and Mozart are to be present.

> Carnival Monday was 10 February. Because Countess Antonia Lützow's father, Count Prokop Adalbert Czernin, had died in Prague on 31 January, this plan was abandoned.

IBID., 22 FEBRUARY 1777

In the evening I was visited by Wolfgang Mozart, Councillor Mölck, and Weirotter.

> Schiedenhofen had been taken ill and was confined to bed for some time.— Privy Councillor Franz von Mölk was a brother of the Consistorial Councillor (see 19 April 1775) ; Gottlieb von Weyrother was Master of the Horse.

On 14 March 1777 Leopold Mozart addressed a petition to the Archbishop.

> This unanswered document is known only from Wolfgang's petition of August 1777, and is thus probably lost. It clearly concerned leave for father and son to travel once again.

IBID., 26 FEBRUARY 1777

In the forenoon I was visited by Kapellmeister Mozart.

IBID., 20 APRIL 1777

In the morning I was visited by . . . ., in the afternoon by young Mozart and Helbnreich.

> " Helbnreich " is Joseph Ernst von Helmreichen zu Brunnfeld.

On 23 April *Bastien und Bastienne*, a singspiel, was performed at Augsburg by Franz Joseph Moser's theatrical company.

> *Augsburger Mozartbuch* (1943), p. 283.—Hermann Endrös supposed that this was Wolfgang's singspiel of the autumn of 1768 ; but since no performance of this early work is known for certain to have taken place until 122 years later (Berlin, 2 October 1890), what was performed at Augsburg was probably *Les Amours de Bastien et Bastienne* by Charles Simon Favart, Marie Justine

Benoîte Favart and Harny de Guerville, a parody of Jean-Jacques Rousseau's
Le devin du village which had been given on many German stages since 1763.

FROM SCHIEDENHOFEN'S DIARY, 8 MAY 1777 (ASCENSION DAY)

In the morning to the Robinigs', where I [met] Mozart and Abbé Pol-
linger, and then Kolb, and we made music together. Fr. Louise played a
clavier concerto.

> Abbé Joseph Bullinger, the amateur violinist Andrä (?) Kolb, and Aloisia
> Robinig.

IBID., 4 JUNE 1777

In the evening after 7 o'clock went for a walk with Herr von Loes and
the Mozarts.

> Joseph Benedikt von Loës was the Town Syndic (see 22 April 1775).

IBID., 13 JUNE 1777

. . . In the afternoon I went to the Mozarts' with Moll, where he rehearsed the Serenade he wishes to perform at the Countess Lodron's.

> Ludwig Gottfield Moll was Acting Privy Councillor at the Salzburg Court.—
> The second "Lodron Serenade" was probably the divertimento in B♭ major,
> (K. 287) (cf. 18 June 1776).—Wyzewa and Saint-Foix (*Mozart*, Vol. II, pp. 367
> and 429) supposed that the divertimento was the incompletely preserved
> K. 288, which, it is true, does date from June and not, like the divertimento in
> question, from early 1777. The Countess's name-day was 13 June.

IBID., 16 JUNE 1777

Supper as early as 6 o'clock today. Herr von Luidl, the two young
ladies of the house and I then went to the Barisanis' to hear the music which
young Mozart had written during the Octave for Countess Ernst von
Lodron ; it was quite beautiful. There were many people at Barisani's,
among others Frl. Nannette Dauwrawaick, whom I saw home afterwards.

> Rochus Sebastian von Luidl was Director of the Exchequer. The two young
> ladies of the house were Schiedenhofen's sister Aloisia and her cousin Nanette
> von Kranach. The Barisanis lived in the garden wing of the Palais Lodron.—
> An "octave" is the week after a feast-day.

JOHANN ANDREAS STEIN TO LEOPOLD MOZART

To Mozart   [Vienna, Summer 1777.]
The esteem in which I hold you and your musical family grows daily,
and so strongly in particular now that I find myself here in Vienna, that it
has truly brought me to the point of performing some enthusiastic action.

Draft in Stein's notebook owned by the Streicher family of Krumpendorf, Carinthia.—*Augsburger Mozartbuch*, p. 89.—The esteemed organ and clavier maker of Augsburg was visiting Vienna with his daughter Nanette, who later married the Viennese pianoforte maker Johann Andreas Streicher. Stein had known the Mozarts since 1763.

FROM SCHIEDENHOFEN'S DIARY, 25 JULY 1777

[In the morning] . . . to Gusseti's, where the music by young Mozart, which he wanted to perform for his sister in the evening, was rehearsed. It consisted of a symphony, a violin concerto, played by young Mozart, a concerto for transverse flute, played by the violone-player Herr Castel, and everything was young Mozart's work. Herr von Moll, both the von Molcks, Edlenbach, Carl Agliardi, Baron Pappius and I were present, and lunched together afterwards at Sauerwein's. Then Councillor von Mölk and I went to Frl. and Frau von Dauwrawaick in the Mint, then to pay our compliments to Frau von Mayern, the Mozarts, Nannerl Barisani and Felix Agliardi at Court.

The rehearsal took place at the house of Johann Baptist Gusetti, a grocer (now Siegmund Haffnergasse 7-9); the performance was presumably given in the garden courtyard behind the " Tanzmeisterhaus ". The " symphony " was clearly only an overture. The violin concerto was probably that in D major (K. 271a) of 16 July 1777, if it is genuine ; it is known only in a questionable version. The flute concerto has not been identified. Johann Thomas Cassel, double-bass player in the Court Chapel, also played the violin and flute.—At Salzburg, as in Vienna, Anna was a common name : there were two in the Mozart family, and three in the Barisani family.—Gusetti seems to have played the horn.—Councillor Felix von Agliardis was the elder brother of Karl (*cf.* 22 August 1776).

IBID., 11 AUGUST 1777

In the afternoon . . . with Gilowski to the Robinighof, Concertmeister Mozart coming with us. We chatted in the garden until 7.30 and the Robinigs then accompanied us a good way.

The Robinig estate was in the neighbourhood of Gnigl, close to Salzburg.

IBID., 15 AUGUST 1777

In the afternoon I went with the same Dauwrawaik and her father to Mozart's *accademia*, where Mme Toucheck, *petite fille* of the merchant Weiser and married to M. Toucheck, the famous clavier master in Prague, kindly consented to sing to us. The voice was uncommonly clear and agreeable, she had taste and sang very nicely. Herr Colb played a violin concerto, he has a good tone, great strength and agility, but was somewhat out of tune now and again. M. and Mlle Mozart played together on one *clavecin*.

M.—6

The concert evidently took place in the Mozart family's "Tanzmeister-Saal".
Josepha Dušek was the grand-daughter of the ex-Burgomaster of Salzburg,
Ignaz Anton von Weiser (see 12 March 1767 and January 1770), whom she
and her husband were visiting (*cf.* 12 April 1786).—It is not known whether
Kolb played the B♭ concerto (K. 207).—Duet playing on the same keyboard
was unusual.

MOZART'S PETITION TO ARCHBISHOP HIERONYMUS, COUNT COLLOREDO
[AUGUST 1777]

Your Serene Highness
most worthy Prince of the Holy Roman Empire,
most gracious Ruler
and
Lord !

I have no need to importune Your Serene Highness with a circumstantial
description of our sad situation : my father, in all honour and conscience,
and with every ground of truth, has declared this in a petition most submissively placed before Your Serene Highness on 14 March last. Since however
Your Highness's favourable decision did not ensue, as we had hoped, my
father would have submissively begged Your Serene Highness as early as
June graciously to allow us a journey of several months, in order somewhat
to rehabilitate us, had not Your Highness been pleased to command that all
members of his Music hold themselves in readiness for the impending
visit of His Majesty the Emperor. My father again humbly asked for this
permission later ; but Your Serene Highness refused him this and graciously
observed that I, being in any case only on part-time service, might travel
alone. Our circumstances are pressing : my father decided to send me off
by myself. But to this too Your Serene Highness made some gracious objections. Most gracious Sovereign Prince and Lord ! Parents takes pains
to enable their children to earn their own bread, and this they owe both
to their own interest and to that of the State. The more of talent that
children have received from God, the greater is the obligation to make use
thereof, in order to ameliorate their own and their parents' circumstances,
to assist their parents, and to take care of their own advancement and future.
To profit from our talents is taught us by the Gospel. I therefore owe it
before God and in my conscience to my father, who indefatigably employs
all his time in my upbringing, to be grateful to him with all my strength, to
lighten his burden, and to take care not only of myself, but of my sister
also, with whom I should be bound to commiserate for spending so many
hours at the harpsichord without being able to make profitable use of it.
May Your Serene Highness graciously permit me, therefore, to beg most
submissively to be released from service, as I am obliged to make the best
use of the coming September, so as not to be exposed to the bad weather of

the ensuing cold months. Your Serene Highness will not take this most submissive request amiss, since already three years ago, when I begged for permission to travel to Vienna, Your Highness was graciously pleased to declare
that I had nothing to hope for and would do better to seek my fortune elsewhere. I thank Your Serene Highness in the profoundest devotion for all
high favours received, and with the most flattering hope that I may serve
Your Serene Highness with greater success in the years of my manhood, I
commend myself to your continuing grace and favour as

Your Serene Highness's
my most gracious Sovereign Prince
and
Lord's
most humble and obedient
Wolfgang Amade Mozart.

[On the verso :]
To
His Serene Highness
The Archbishop of Salzburg,
the most humble and submissive
Petition
of Wolfgang Amade Mozart.

By His Highness's decree, 28 August 1777.
To the Exchequer with the observation that father and son have permission
to seek their fortune elsewhere, according to the Gospel,
In Cons[ili]o C[ame]rae, 1 September of this year.
Instruction by Decree.

> Salzburg, Provincial Archives.—Pirkmayer, *op. cit.* (1876), pp. 11-13. Müller
> von Asow, *op. cit.*, Vol. III, p. 325 f.—*Cf.* 14 March 1777.—The Emperor
> Joseph II made a brief visit to Salzburg on 31 July, according to Dr. H. Klein.
> Leopold Mozart's second petition must have been submitted to the Archbishop
> in audience. Whether Wolfgang had really asked for leave again since his
> last visit to Vienna (14 June to 26 September 1773), "three years ago", *i.e.* in
> 1774, is doubtful ; *cf.* 12 August 1773.—The petition was probably drawn up
> by Leopold Mozart. The reference to the Gospel received a sarcastic reply
> from Colloredo. According to Dr. Klein the Archbishop's own pencilled
> comment can still be read beneath the quittance : "Father and son herewith
> granted permission to seek their fortune according to the gospel."—The petition
> is undated, and Ludwig Schiedermair's date, 1 August, is an arbitrary one
> (*Mozart-Briefe*, Vol. I, p. 54).

DECRETUM

to His Highness of Salzburg's Conzertmeister Wolfgang Amade Mozart.
    Whereas it has pleased His Highness to receive the humble petition of the
above-named for release from His Highness's service with the gracious

decree that father and son shall have permission to seek their fortune elsewhere : the above-named Mozart herewith informed accordingly.

Decretum in Consilio Camerae Salzburgensi
Die 1ᵐᵃ Septembris 1777.

DECRETUM

The Court Pay Office herewith informed, to enable it to regulate the
salary in the event of his leaving service.
Decretum ut supra

Salzburg, Provincial Archives.—Pirkmayer, *op. cit.*, p. 21. Müller von Asow,
Vol. III, p. 326 f.—Leopold Mozart remained in the Archbishop's service, but
Wolfgang was dismissed.

FROM SCHIEDENHOFEN'S DIARY, 6 SEPTEMBER 1777

In the afternoon I visited the Mozarts, where I found the father ill, because
he and his son are dismissed the service because of the request which the
latter made to His Grace for permission to travel.

IBID., 19 SEPTEMBER 1777

In the afternoon. . . . Finally . . . to the Mozarts for a farewell visit,
because young Mozart and his mother are to depart next Monday, the
former to look for foreign service. I find old Mozart ill with a heavy
catarrh.

The departure was not on Monday, 22 September, but on the 23rd.

At 6 a.m. on 23 September 1777 Mozart and his mother set out for Germany, on
the way to Paris, whence he was not to return until mid-January 1779, and alone.
Their route at first took them to Waging, Stein, Frabertsham and Wasserburg, where
they spent the night at the Star ; then to Munich, where they arrived at 4.30 p.m. on
the 24th and alighted at the Black Eagle.

For Albert, the landlord of the inn in the Kaufingerstrasse, see 27 April 1775

IBID., 24 SEPTEMBER 1777

In the evening I went to the market at first, then to Mozart, because the
mother and son had left the day before.

On the morning of 25 September Mozart waited, in vain, on Count Joseph Anton
Seeau, supervisor of entertainments at the Bavarian court. On the 26th he waited on
Count Ferdinand Christoph Zeil, Prince-Bishop of Chiemsee ; on the same day he
met Seeau. On the 28th he again visited Seeau, and on the 29th Zeil. On the 28th
and 29th the Mozarts were visited by Franz Xaver Woschitka, cellist in the *Hofkapelle*.
On the 30th Wolfgang was received by the Elector Maximilian III Joseph.

On 30 September and 1 and 2 October Mozart played at Count Joseph Salern's, intendant of the Court Opera.

It is assumed that the divertimenti K. 247, 251 and 287 were performed.

On 3 October, the day before the court left Munich, Mozart played at the house of a Frau von Tosson, the mother-in-law of the merchant Philipp Hepp.

On 4 October Mozart gave a private concert at the innkeeper Franz Albert's ; it lasted from 3.30 to 8 p.m.

The pianoforte concertos K. 238, 246 and 271 (the last written for Mlle Jeune-homme in January 1777) were played there, and probably also the divertimenti K. 287 and 254 (piano trio), in which Mozart played the violin.

After another visit to the ailing Joseph Mysliveček on 10 October, Mozart left Munich with his mother on the 11th. They arrived at 9 p.m. at Augsburg, where they stayed at the White Lamb.

Mozart had first met the Czech opera composer at Bologna in 1770.

In the morning of 12 October Mozart's uncle, the bookbinder Franz Alois Mozart, introduced him to the city governor, Jakob Langenmantel vom Wertheim and Ott-marshausen ; on the 13th and 14th he visited Langenmantel's son, Jakob Alois Karl. On 12 October he also visited the pianoforte maker Stein, at whose house he met Music Director Friedrich Hartmann Graf. On the 13th he and his uncle visited prelate Bartholomäus Christa at the Canonry of the Holy Cross ; in the evening of the 14th Mozart and his mother went to the theatre, and on the 15th he visited Graf, with whom he met Anton Christoph Gignoux, manufacturer and art-lover.

At the theatre Mozart and his mother saw Karl Ludwig Reuling's singspiel Der Teufel ist los [The Devil to Pay], a translation from the French, and the ballet Der betrunkene Bauer [The Drunken Peasant] (Augsburger Mozartbuch, illustration 28).—Graf was a brother of Christian Ernst Graaf, whom Mozart had met at The Hague (see 7 March 1766).

MARIA ANNA THEKLA MOZART TO LEOPOLD MOZART IN SALZBURG

Dearest Cousin :

I cannot express our pleasure at the happy arrival of your dear wife and your darling son, but only regret we must lose such precious friends again so soon, who show us so much friendship. We are sad not to see you as well as your dear wife. My parents send their dutiful regards to you and your daughter, and hope you find yourselves well and wish it ever. Please give my regards to your dear daughter and ask her to think of me always as a friend, as I also flatter myself that I retain your goodwill, I have the honour to send you my regards, and to close with all respect : [your]

Obedient servant
and kinswoman M A
Mozartin

Augspurg 16 Oct. 1777

My father cannot remember whether he told you he gave Herr Lotter 4 Violinschulen on 31 May 1777 and a further two on 13 August 1777.

Salzburg, Mozarteum.—Schiedermair, *Mozart-Briefe*, Vol. IV, p. 387.—The letter was enclosed with Mozart's written to his father on 17 October.—The " Bäsle " at Augsburg, daughter of Franz Alois Mozart, became very friendly with Mozart. Her father kept Leopold's *ViolinSchule*, published by Lotter, in stock in unbound sheets and supplied it either in that form or bound.—Maria Thekla signs herself with the customary feminine form of her family name. Her style and spelling are more idiosyncratic than can safely be conveyed in a translation.

In the evening of the same day, 16 October, at the end of a concert of the Augsburg " Musikkränzchen ", Mozart played a pianoforte concerto followed by the pianoforte sonata in G major (K. 283).

The concert took place in the " Geschlechterstube ", opposite the Town Hall. Wolfgang wore the cross of the papal order of the Golden Spur.

On 17 October Mozart ate at the merchant Valentin Alois Gasser's and afterwards again visited Herr Stein ; on the 18th he again went to the Holy Cross monastery, dined at Stein's and examined the organ at St. Ulric's Minster ; on Sunday the 19th, after attending mass, there was an orchestral rehearsal at Stein's, at 10 a.m., for Mozart's own concert ; in the evening at the Holy Cross monastery he played the G major violin concerto (K. 216), a pianoforte sonata, the variations for pianoforte on a minuet by Johann Christian Fischer (K. 179) and, lastly, an improvisation.

Gasser looked after the supply of Leopold Mozart's *ViolinSchule* to the Frankfurt Fair free of charge.

FROM THE " AUGSBURGISCHES INTELLIGENZ-BLATT ", 20 OCTOBER 1777

(Visitors' List, 11 October 1777)

Mme Mozart with her son arrive by post from Salzburg and lodge at the White Lamb.

Ernst Fritz Schmid in the *Augsburger Mozartbuch*, p. 138.

FROM THE " AUGSBURGISCHE STAATS- UND GELEHRTEN ZEITUNG ",
21 OCTOBER 1777

Something for Lovers of Art and Music !

An honour for us, dear Patriot ! To have a composer, a compatriot here with us whom the whole of England, France and Italy envies us.

Those who know a little about political newspapers will be aware that this can be nobody else than Herr Chevalier Wolfgang Amadee Mozart, who did such great wonders before the above nations in his tenderest youth.

Let us see whether he will do it for us too.

To-morrow, Wednesday, 22 October, Chevalier Mozart will hold a concert in the concert-hall of the noble Counts Fugger, where, to defray the costs, one florin for a first place and 30 kreuzer for a second will be paid immediately on admission. The compositions will be entirely by this author, and will appear in the following order : (1) Symphony with the proper instruments. (2) Clavier Concerto for 3 pianofortes. A very rare case, but here made possible by a fortunate chance. (3) Clavier Sonata without accompaniment. (4) A single Clavier Concerto *con stromenti*. (5) If time permits, a freely fugued Fantasy in the church style. (6) Final Symphony. Herr Mozart will use his best endeavour to entertain his compatriots right royally for a few hours.

> *Ibid.*, p. 145.—The announcement was written by Herr von Zabuesnig (see 2 March 1769).—The concerto for three pianofortes was the Lodron concerto (K. 242), the pianoforte sonata K. 284, the pianoforte concerto K. 238, the fantasy was in C minor, and then came another sonata in C major.—The three-piano concerto was played by the cathedral organist, Johann Michael Demmler, Mozart and Stein.

IBID., 22 OCTOBER 1777

To yesterday's announcement about Herr Chevalier Mozart is yet to be added that the concert to-night will begin at 6 o'clock.

> *Ibid.*, p. 145.—Baron Grimm, on his way to Paris, attended the concert (see 21 February 1778).—Mozart earned $83\frac{1}{2}$ florins in all on 16 and 22 October (100 florins, less 16 fl. 30 kr. expenses) ; the sojourn at Augsburg cost 27 florins more.

MOZART'S ENTRY IN HIS COUSIN'S ALBUM, AUGSBURG, 25 OCTOBER 1777

Si vous aimés ce que j'aime
Vous vous aimés donc vous même
votre
Tres affectioné Neveu
Wolfgang Amadée Mozart

Augspourg le 25 oct. 1777

> Original in possession of Dr. Curt Sluzewski, London.—Paul Nettl in *Acta Mozartiana* (Augsburg, 1956), Vol. III/ii, p. 9 (incomplete and with erroneous ascription) ; E. F. Schmid in the *Neues Augsburger Mozartbuch* (1962).—The " Bäsle " later added the inscription " Your friend [Freundin] Mozart 1793 " for some unknown recipient.

On the same day, 25 October, Mozart paid a farewell visit to Bartholomäus Christa, the prelate at the Holy Cross, whom he had seen the day before. On the 26th, at 7.30 a.m., he and his mother left Augsburg and went on to Hohen-Altheim, the country-seat of Prince Kraft Ernst von Oettingen-Wallerstein (see 28 April 1770). On 27 October Mozart played the pianoforte sonatas K. 281 and K. 284 to Ignaz von Beecke, the prince's director of music.—The prince was in mourning for his young wife.

FROM THE " AUGSBURGISCHE STAATS- UND GELEHRTEN ZEITUNG ", 28 OCTOBER 1777

AUGSBURG, 24 Oct. The evening of Wednesday last was one of the most agreeable for the local music-lovers. Herr Chevalier Mozart, a son of the famous Salzburg musician, who is a native of Augsburg, gave a concert on the fortepiano in the hall of Count Fugger. As Herr Stein happened to have three instruments of the kind ready, there was an opportunity to include a fine concerto for three claviers, in which Herr Demler, the Cathedral organist, and Herr Stein himself played the other two clavier parts. Apart from this the Chevalier played a sonata and a fugued fantasy without accompaniment, and a concerto with one, and the opening and closing symphonies were of his composition as well. Everything was extraordinary, tasteful and admirable. The composition is thorough, fiery, manifold and simple ; the harmony so full, so strong, so unexpected, so elevating ; the melody, so agreeable, so playful, and everything so new ; the rendering on the fortepiano so neat, so clean, so full of expression, and yet at the same time extraordinarily rapid, so that one hardly knew what to give attention to first, and all the hearers were enraptured. One found here mastery in the thought, mastery in the performance, mastery in the instruments, all at the same time. One thing always gave relief to another, so that the numerous assembly was displeased with nothing but the fact that pleasure was not prolonged still further. Those patriotically minded had the especial satisfaction of concluding from the stillness and the general applause of the listeners that we know here how to appreciate true beauty—to hear a virtuoso who may place himself side by side with the great masters of our nation, and yet is at least half our own—and to hear instruments which according to the judgment of strangers by far surpass all others of the kind. And Stein also belongs to us : he himself plays, and has a taste for the more refined music.

Augsburger Mozartbuch (1943), p. 158 f. ; Müller von Asow, *op. cit.*, Vol. II, p. 271 f. This notice too may have been written by Zabuesnig.—In 1778 Mozart recommended Johann Michael Demmler for the post of cathedral organist at Salzburg, which he afterwards obtained himself.

In the morning of 28 October they continued their journey from Hohen-Altheim by way of Nördlingen and Ellwangen to Mannheim, where they arrived on the 30th and alighted at the "Pfälzischer Hof" (Paradeplatz Lit. D 1).

On 31 October Mozart visited Christian Danner, the son of the court violinist Johann Georg Danner, and the Kapellmeister Christian Cannabich ; he then attended part of the rehearsal for the concert that was to be given at court the following day. On Sunday the 2nd he heard a mass by Ignaz Holzbauer, was received by Count Louis Aurel Savioli, the director of court music, and played for Cannabich and others the six piano sonatas, K. 279-284. During the festivities in honour of the name-day of the Elector Palatine, Karl Theodor, from the 4th to the 7th, Mozart attended Holzbauer's opera *Günther von Schwarzburg* on the 5th. On the 6th, in a concert at court, he played a concerto, a sonata and improvisations. He was again at court on the 7th, when he heard a French comedy. On Sunday the 9th he played the organ in the court chapel. During the five days of festivities for the name-day of the Electress Maria Elisabeth Auguste, from the 19th to the 23rd November, Mozart heard a mass by Abbé Georg Joseph Vogler on the 19th, and the Konzertmeister Ignaz Fränzl on the 21st. On the 7th and 8th and again on the 28th and following days he visited the Elector's four natural children at the Palais Heydeck, and on 1 December played them a (lost ?) Rondeau, and the Fischer variations (K. 179) ; on the 3rd he visited them yet again. On the 5th he heard Rosa Cannabich, the Kapellmeister's gifted daughter, play the C major sonata he had written for her (K. 309). On the 8th he attended another concert at court. On the 12th or 13th he moved with his ailing mother from the inhospitable inn to the house of Councillor Serrarius. On the 18th, in Mozart's presence, Abbé Vogler tried out the new organ in the Protestant Church.

On 21 December 1777 Mozart's *Missa brevis* in B♭ major (K. 275) was performed in the church of St. Peter's abbey at Salzburg.

> Mozart wrote the Mass shortly before his journey to Paris. The castrato Francesco Ceccarelli, who was a member of the Court Chapel from 1778 to 1788, sang the soprano part.

On 21 December the cathedral organist Kajetan Adlgasser died at Salzburg.

> He had a stroke while playing the organ.

On 30 December Maximilian III Joseph, Elector of Bavaria, died.

FROM ERNST CHRISTOPH DRESSLER'S "THEATER-SCHULE FÜR DIE DEUTSCHEN, DAS ERNSTHAFTE SING-SCHAUSPIEL BETREFFEND", HANOVER AND CASSEL, 1777

. . . I cannot possibly refrain from drawing the attention of Germans to Messrs. *Mozart* and *Schröder*, two extraordinary geniuses, musicians, clavier players and composers ; not we alone, but foreigners too know their merits.

> " Schröder " is Johann Samuel Schröter (1750–88), who was born in Warsaw and became pianist to the Prince of Wales in London, where he died. He was a brother of the singer Corona Schröter and of the violinist Johann Heinrich Schröter (*cf.* Köchel-Einstein 626a, App. D, F, G and H). His widow became Haydn's friend in London.

1778

On 1 January 1778, at 10 p.m., the Elector-Palatine Karl Theodor left his official residence at Mannheim in order to proceed to Munich for his accession as Elector of Bavaria.

> Karl Theodor was now both Elector-Palatine and Elector of Bavaria.

On 14 January Serrarius, the Mozarts' host, gave a domestic concert at which the Abbé Vogler and Mozart played.

FRANZ VON HEUFELD TO LEOPOLD MOZART

Most valued friend !

Your highly appreciated letter of the 16th inst. has duly reached me. I thank you most cordially for your valued remembrance and rejoice at your general well-being. That your son should have left a place too narrow for his genius is indeed expedient. I am sure that he will be received more decently everywhere ; moreover it will serve to perfect his education and

M.—6 *a*

give him the needful knowledge of the world, if he looks round the world a little. I trust in the good principles implanted in him early by his honest parents to guard him from being easily caught in bad society.

Now, dear friend, I am obliged to discover to you, with the frankness with which I am accustomed to act towards my friends, my ideas about the suggestion that I should act on behalf of your son in the way you have proposed to me. What has happened is that His Majesty the Emperor, to whose hands his mother has entirely entrusted the theatre, intends to start a German Comic Opera. All commands proceed from His Majesty to the company through the Chief Chamberlain, Count von Rosenberg, and a kind of council consisting of the leading actors and actresses has been established for the sharing and distribution of the pieces and parts. For the Opera, which is to be united to the national company, those engaged as extra singers are D^{lle} Cavalier and Schindler's daughter, whose married name is Lange, as well as a bass whose name escapes me. They recently had the first rehearsal for the first opera, for which Herr Weidmann has furnished the text and the violist of the theatre orchestra, Herr Umlauf, has composed the music ; the performance is to take place soon. All this is for the moment only a trial, to see whether anything is to be done with the Germans in this department. What is certain, however, is that for the present no musical composer will be specially taken on, particularly as *Gluck* and *Salieri* are in the Emperor's service. To recommend anyone to the sovereign would be a sure means of not finding a place for the person recommended. Nor is there any middleman through whom he could be approached, since, being himself a connoisseur, he arranges and chooses everything according to his own idea and fancy. Everybody knows this, and no one dares to come forward with suggestions and recommendations. In this way His Majesty has made his own choice of *Gluck, Salieri*, and for some time now, of most of the people in his service. I might give you some examples, too, of people who appealed straight to the sovereign and failed to succeed. I cannot approve of the way in which you intend to go about it, and that is the reason why I refrained from taking any steps by means of a petition, because I am convinced in advance that it would be useless and indeed disadvantageous. At the same time, another, more laudable and surer way remains open whereby good talents may find their fortune with the sovereign, namely by their works, for in this respect all men are considered eligible. If your son will take the trouble of setting some good German comic opera or other to music, to submit it, to leave his work to the imperial judgment and then to await a decision, he may succeed in being admitted, if the work pleases. In that case, however, it would probably be necessary to be here in person. About Benda and Schweizer your son need not worry. I am ready to guarantee that they will not be admitted. They have not the reputation here that is theirs elsewhere. Perhaps even Wieland has since his visit to Mannheim relinquished some of the high opinion he had had of these people. I read a letter from him of the 5th inst., in which he admits that he had come to see music in a very different light at Mannheim than he had ever done before. He announces that the Opera there is finished and that he is on the point of returning to Weimar.

To contrive a letter of recommendation to the Queen of France for my dear Wolfgang is scarcely possible for me, my friend. The friends who might have been able to do it are no more. I prefer to tell you this straight out, rather than give you false hopes. If he were present, perhaps something could more easily be done in one way or another, but as it is I am helpless. I have abandoned the theatre altogether, and I never approach the great ones now, being tired of bowing and scraping. On the other hand I am on good terms with a man who can do much with the Empress these days and who (fortunately for our case) is a passionate lover of music, plays and sings himself, and whom nothing pleases more than a good little musical composition ; only I cannot expect him to do anything for your son, whom he does not know, although if he did know him he would certainly exert himself on his behalf.

Only a word about myself. I have been married eighteen months, have a son already and something more on the way. My wife is a Zach von Garberstein, and I live very contentedly with her. I enjoy the satisfaction of my superiors and the favour of my Sovereign Lady, of which you will find a token in my signature. Remember me to your dear family, and keep up your friendship for me, as I emphatically confirm mine for you. I remain with undiminished high regard

your most devoted
Franz, Edler von Heufeld.

Vienna, 23 January 1778

With *Director* Messmer I shall have high words
as soon as I meet him.
I now live at No. 416 Wildwerkerstrasse.

Salzburg, Mozarteum.—Müller von Asow, *op. cit.*, Vol. II, p. 377 f.—Heufeld, a dramatist, was Auditor of the Court Accounts and in 1769, and again in 1773–75, manager of the German Theatre in Vienna ; he was a friend of both the Mesmers and had been acquainted with the Mozarts since 1773.— In 1776 Joseph II had brought the Burgtheater under the special management of the court as a German National Theatre, and caused the Italian singers, dancers and musicians to be dismissed. Count Rosenberg (see 23 April 1775) took on the supreme directorship of the Court Theatres (April 1776 to January 1791), including, from the autumn of 1785 onwards, the Kärntnertor Theatre, which had been leased until then. On 17 December 1777 the Emperor had decreed the additional establishment of a German Opera at the Burgtheater, which began in February 1778 as the German National Singspiel under the musical direction of Ignaz Umlauf, but survived only until March 1783. During these five years the Kärntnertor Theatre was not allowed to stage any operas. In April 1783 the Italian Opera returned to the Burgtheater.—Caterina Cavalieri, the first Constanze in *Die Entführung aus dem Serail* (1782), Anna Maria Elisabeth Lange, daughter of the miniature painter Philipp Ernst Schindler and the first wife of the Court actor Lange, and also the bass Fux (or Fuchs) were members of the first German opera ensemble.—

The first German opera was Umlauf's *Die Bergknappen*, libretto by Paul Weidmann.—Gluck was Imperial and Royal Chamber Composer, Salieri first Kapellmeister of the Court Opera.—Georg Benda's melodrama *Medea* was given at the Burgtheater at the end of 1778, and other works of his soon after ; in March 1779 he gave a concert in the Kärntnertor Theatre. Nothing by Anton Schweitzer was performed in Vienna at that time.—Dr. Mesmer had to leave Vienna early in 1778 ; his cousin Joseph had taught Marie-Antoinette calligraphy.—Heufeld had been ennobled. The Wildwerkerstrasse was part of the later Wipplingerstrasse.—Leopold Mozart sent this letter to Wolfgang on 29 January and enclosed a copy of the following letter from Joseph Mesmer, which had accompanied Heufeld's.

JOSEPH MESMER TO LEOPOLD MOZART, VIENNA, c. 23 JANUARY

. . . My cousin Dr Messmer, who leaves for Paris in the next few days, and was going to take my son to you for better or worse, was to have made this rebuke [for not answering] to you. Now everything is dropped again, as your son is no longer at Salzburg. . . . Why did you not send your son at once to Vienna ? Or why do you not send him even now ? . . . I assure you herewith most faithfully that he will have board, lodging and everything with me as long as he likes, and that I and all our other friends would endeavour to render him other good services before long : nothing can be done here without his personal presence. After all, there is always a good opening here for a great talent, even if one does not always succeed at once ; but with the support of good friends one achieves one's object all right— and when all is said, Vienna is still the best place to live in. You know your Swabian friends, and the place itself. Make your choice—and let me know.

Salzburg, Mozarteum (copy in Leopold Mozart's letter of 29 January).— Schiedermair, *op. cit.*, Vol. III, p. 334.—Mesmer wished to have his musically gifted son taught by Leopold Mozart. The Mesmers, Heufeld and other acquaintances of the Mozarts in this circle came from Swabia, the region to the NE of Lake Constance.

In the morning of 23 January 1778 Mozart accompanied Fridolin Weber and his daughter Aloisia to Kirchheimbolanden, where they spent several days at the court of Princess Caroline of Nassau-Weilburg (see 12 November 1765).

About 25 January Nannerl at Salzburg played her brother's divertimento in B♭ major, a trio for pianoforte, violin and 'cello (K. 254), with the Wallerstein musicians Anton Janitsch and Joseph Reicha. *Cf.* 4 October 1777.

The musician Weber lived at that time at Mannheim with his wife, Maria Cäcilia, née Stamm, and their four daughters. Aloisia, the most gifted, with whom Mozart fell in love, sang two arias from his *Lucio Silla* (Nos. 4 and 11) before the Princess during this visit.

From 29 January to 2 February Mozart stayed with the Webers at Worms ; on the 2nd he returned to Mannheim and his mother.

The Dean of St. Paul's cathedral in Worms, Father Joseph Benedikt Stamm, was Weber's brother-in-law.

On 13 February, in a concert at Cannabich's, Aloisia Weber sang two arias (Nos. 11 and 16) from *Lucio Silla*, Rosa Cannabich played the pianoforte concerto in B♭

major (K. 238), Mozart that in D major (K. 175), Friedrich Ramm the oboe concerto in D major (K. 314), and lastly Mozart conducted the overture to *Il rè pastore*.

PADRE MARTINI TO LEOPOLD MOZART, BOLOGNA, 14 FEBRUARY, 1778
(in Italian)

Developments in Bavaria, and the departure of His Electoral Highness of the Palatinate from Mannheim, will perhaps hinder them in making a good impression upon him ; however, delay is not failure.

> Mozarteum, Salzburg (copy in Leopold Mozart's letter of 29 April).—Schieder-mair, *op. cit.*, vol. IV, p. 21.—*Cf.* 1 January 1778.—In the part of this letter that was not copied (the original is lost) Martini had sent thanks for the portrait of Wolfgang (see 18 December 1776).—*Cf.* 6 September 1778.

On 20 February Mozart was temporarily indisposed.

GRIMM TO LEOPOLD MOZART
(second half in French)

I had your letter of 25 December only a few days ago, and just as I was going to answer I received your 2nd letter of 9th January. It is quite true that I was at Augsburg when Herr Amadeo gave his concert, I was going to leave again immediately—but I even went to the concert, and I put myself so into the line of sight that he and Mme Mozart could see me, but neither he nor *Mme sa mère* recognized me : and as I was in a great hurry to depart, and everyone told me that they were on the point of going to Paris, I decided to remain unknown, since we should meet in Paris. I shall be very glad to see him again ; but I am very sorry that he is coming without his father. According to your letter, he should now be on the way, and I thus hope to see him any day now, and then I shall hear from him and see what I shall be able to do for him. It is true that he is in good hands, as he is with Herr Wendling, who can be useful to him ; yet nobody can take the true place of a father. It is now 3 months that I have been back from my travels, and I do not yet know whether this recent journey from Russia will not have been my last. It should be time to think of rest. I send you my address herewith, so that your letters no longer risk going astray. I am overwhelmed with business and writing, and therefore a very bad correspondent ; but when your son is here, he shall be my secretary, and we shall keep you informed. Meanwhile do not worry. I believe your son's conduct to be sufficiently good to have no fears for him from the dangers of Paris. If he were inclined to libertinage, he might no doubt run some risks ; but if he is reasonable, he will take precautions against all trouble, without thereby leading the life of a hermit. I am very sorry that you are tied to Salzburg. Goodbye, Sir, you know what sentiments I have always professed for you, and I beg you to regard them as unchangeable. Paris, 21 February 1778.

Mozarteum, Salzburg (copy in Leopold's letter to his wife and son of 28 February to 2 March).—Schiedermair, *op. cit.*, Vol. III, p. 382 f.—The concert at Augsburg took place on 22 October 1777.—Like Ramm, the flautist Johann Baptist Wendling belonged to the Mannheim orchestra ; both were outstanding woodwind players, who wished to travel to Paris with Mozart.

On 23 February Frl. Therese Pierron, one of Mozart's pupils, played the Lutzow concerto (K. 246) at a French Monday concert.

On 12 March, at a farewell concert for Mozart at Cannabich's, Aloisia Weber sang the aria " Aer tranquillo ", No. 3 from *Il rè pastore*, and the recitative and aria "Alcandro lo confesso—Non so d' onde viene " (K. 294) recently written for her ; the Misses Rosa Cannabich, Aloisia Weber and Therese Pierron, housekeeper at Serrarius's, played the Lodron concerto for three pianofortes (K. 242).

Aloisia, who had by then become Lange's second wife, sang the aria K. 294 again on 11 March 1783 in Vienna.—Abert (I. 586) says that Therese Pierron was Serrarius's 15-year-old daughter.

LEOPOLD MOZART TO JOHANN GOTTLOB IMMANUEL BREITKOPF
AT LEIPZIG

Salzburg, 13 March 1778

. . . My son has left the Salzburg service, and will now, as you read this, be in Paris. Things look very sad for us ; but where do they not look critical now ?—Our mutual friend, Herr von Grimm, but now *Baron von Grimm, Ministre plenipotentiaire de Saxe-Gotha*, wrote to me a week ago from Paris, where he has returned from Russia. I commended my son to him. . . .

Darmstadt, Hessian Provincial Library.—Facsimile in the annual *Der Bär* (Leipzig, 1924) after p. 46.—*Cf.* 7 February 1772 and 12 February 1781.

In the evening of 13 March Mozart took leave of the Weber family.

On this occasion Fridolin Weber presented him with Molière's comedies in the translation by Friedrich Samuel Bierling (Hamburg, 1752). Only the third of the four volumes remained in Mozart's possession at the time of his death (No. 12 in the list of his books).

On 14 March, after a stay of four and a half months, Mozart and his mother left Mannheim for Paris, where they arrived on the 23rd, at 4 p.m., and where they took lodgings with one Mayer in the rue Bourg l'Abbé.

On the 19th they were at Clermont ; apart from this nothing is known of the journey. Mayer was an agent of the Augsburg merchant Joseph Felix Arbauer.

On 25 March Mozart visited Baron Grimm, whom he had missed the day before, and Count Karl Heinrich Joseph von Sickingen, Ambassador of the Palatinate. On 9 April Grimm visited Mozart's mother.

On 12 April the divertimento in B♭ major (K. 287), one of the two cassations written for Countess Lodron, was performed in a concert at Count Czernin's (see 24 April 1775 and 13 December 1776).

FROM SCHIEDENHOFEN'S DIARY, 14 APRIL 1778

At 4 o'clock at the dicastery service. Stayed until the litany, which was by young Mozart.

> K. 243, cf. 31 March 1776. The litanies by Adlgasser and Michael Haydn were performed on the two preceding days (Palm Sunday and Monday).

In mid-April mother and son moved to new quarters in the rue du Gros Chenêt.

> These lodgings had been found for them by Mme d'Épinay (see 26 September 1766 and 7 July 1770).

In Holy Week parts of Holzbauer's Miserere, arranged by Mozart (K. App. 1), were given at the Concert spirituel.

On 17 May, at Salzburg, Leopold Mozart performed the Missa brevis with solo organ (K. 259), on the occasion of the consecration of the Archbishop of Olomouc [Olmütz], Count Anton Theodor Colloredo.

> The cousin of the Salzburg Archbishop had been elected on 6 October 1777.

On 31 May Wendling, who had reached Paris before the Mozarts, returned to Mannheim.

FROM GRIMM'S " CORRESPONDANCE LITTÉRAIRE ", 3 JUNE 1778
(in French)

. . . The performance of the *Finte gemelle* (by M. Piccini) was followed by a new ballet-pantomime composed by M. Noverre, *Les Petits Riens* . . .

> Tourneux edition, Vol. XII, p. 117.—Nicola Piccinni's opera *Le finte gemelle*, conducted by the composer, was performed on the same evening as Noverre's ballet ; Grimm does not mention Mozart's music (K. App. 10) in this preliminary announcement. *Cf.* 11 and 12 June.

On 11 June Mozart's mother bled herself, and from the 19th on never rose from her bed.

On 11 June, at the Grand Opéra, Noverre's ballet *Les petits riens*, with music by Mozart, was performed after Piccinni's opera.

> The programme was repeated on 20 and 25 June and 2, 5 and 7 July, the ballet also on 13 August, this time with Pasquale Anfossi's opera *Il curioso indiscreto*. —Noverre's ballet had already been given at the Burgtheater in Vienna on 5 January 1768, probably with music by Franz Asplmayr.

FROM THE " JOURNAL DE PARIS ", 12 JUNE 1778
REPORT ON NOVERRE'S BALLET-PANTOMIME " LES PETITS RIENS "
(in French)

It consists of three episodic scenes almost detached from each other. The first is purely Anacreontic : Cupid taken in the net and caged ; it is very agreeably composed. Mlle Guimard and the younger M. Vestris display all the grace contained in the subject. The second is the game of blind-man's buff ; M. d'Auberval, whose talent the public finds so agreeable, plays the principal part.   The third is one of the rogueries of Cupid, where he shows two shepherdesses another shepherdess disguised as a shepherd.   Mlle Asselin plays the shepherd and Mlles Guimard and Allard the two shepherdesses.   The two shepherdesses fall in love with the supposed shepherd, who, to undeceive them, eventually bares her breast.   This scene is made very piquant by the intelligence and the grace of these three famous dancers. We must add that at the moment where Mlle Asselin enlightens the two shepherdesses several voices cried *bis*.   The varied figures with which this ballet ends were much applauded.

> V. Wilder, *Mozart* (Paris, 1889), p. 105.—Here again the music is not mentioned. "According to Grimm, the questionable dénouement displeased a part of the public" (Jahn).—Auguste Vestris was the son of the ballet master Gaetano Vestris.

On the same day, 12 June, Mozart played his new symphony in D major (K. 297) at Count Sickingen's.

> This later became known as the Paris symphony.—The Mannheim tenor Anton Raaff, who was still in Paris, was present on this occasion.

On Corpus Christi Day, 18 June, the Concert spirituel opened with this symphony.

FROM THE "COURRIER DE L'EUROPE", LONDON, 26 JUNE 1778
(in French)

The Concert Spirituel on Corpus Christi Day began with a symphony by M. Mozart.   This artist, who from the tenderest age made a name for himself among harpsichord players, may today be ranked among the most able composers.

> Copy in the Bibliothèque Nationale, Paris.

At 10 p.m. on 3 July Mozart's mother died, aged 57.   The following day she was interred in the cemetery of Saint-Eustache.

> The burial ground has since been abandoned.

FROM THE CHURCH REGISTER OF SAINT-EUSTACHE, PARIS
(in French)

Saturday. – 4 July 1778.

On the said day, Marie-Anne Pertl, aged 57 years, wife of Leopold Mozart, *maître de chapelle* at Salzburg, Bavaria, who died yesterday at Rue du Groschenet, has been interred in the cemetery in the presence of Wolfgang Amédée Mozart, her son, and of François Heina, trumpeter in the light cavalry in the Royal Guard, a friend.

> [signed] Mozart.   F. Heina.   Irisson, Vicar.

> Original destroyed in 1870.—*Revue française* (Paris, 1856), Vol. II, No. 7, p. 37 ; Jahn, Vol. II, p. 697 ; *Mozart en France*, No. 91.—Heina was the husband of the music publisher Gertrude Heina, *née* Brockmüller.—Mozart at once,

on 3 July, wrote to the Abbé Joseph Bullinger, a friend of the family's, to tell him the sad news, and only then wrote to his father. Soon after his mother's death Mozart moved to the house of Grimm and Mme d'Épinay in the rue de la Chaussée d'Antin.

On the evening of 4 July Andrä (?) Kolb directed a cassation (K. 287) in front of the house of the Antrettern family in Salzburg; and in the evening of the 9th he played a *Final-Musik* (K. 204 or 251 ?) by Mozart and one of his violin concertos (K. 271ᵃ ?) in front of the Mayr family's house.

> Mozart had written five violin concertos (K. 207, 211, 216, 218 and 219) in 1775, probably for his own use in the first place, but perhaps also for Kolb and the Salzburg Konzertmeister Antonio Brunetti.—Mozart's father and sister heard this concert by chance across the river Salzach.—For Kolb see 15 August 1777.

On 10 July Raaff returned to Mannheim from Paris.

BARON GRIMM TO LEOPOLD MOZART
(in French)

Paris, 27 July 1778.

He is *zu treuherzig* [too trusting], too inactive, too easy to catch, too little intent on the means that may lead to fortune. To make an impression here one has to be artful, enterprising, daring. To make his fortune I wish he had but half his talent and twice as much shrewdness, and then I should not worry about him. For the rest, he can try but two ways here to make a living. The first is to give harpsichord lessons ; but, not to mention that one cannot get pupils without a great deal of activity and even mountebankery, I am not sure that his health would be good enough for him to sustain that profession, for it is a very tiring thing to run to the four corners of Paris and to exhaust oneself in explanations. And then this profession will not please him, because it will keep him from writing, which is what he likes above all things. He might therefore give all his time to that ; but in this country the great public knows nothing about music. Consequently everything depends on names, and the merit of a work can be judged by only a very small number. The public is at the moment ridiculously divided between Piccini and Gluck, and all the argument one hears about music is pitiable. It is thus very difficult for your son to succeed between these two parties. . . . You see, my dear *maître*, that in a country where so many mediocre and even detestable musicians have made immense fortunes, I very much fear that your son will not so much as make ends meet. . . . I have given you the facts faithfully, not to distress you, but in order that we may together decide on the best course. It is unfortunate that the death of the Elector of Bavaria should have prevented your son from finding a place at Mannheim. . . .

> Jahn, Vol. I, p. 556. Müller von Asow, Vol. II, p. 510.—This report is known only through having been copied into Leopold Mozart's letter to Wolfgang of 13 August (Mozarteum, Salzburg).—The quarrel between Gluck's and Piccinni's adherents was then at its height in Paris.

On 11 August the archiepiscopal Hofkapellmeister Giuseppe Maria Lolli was buried at Salzburg.

> Leopold Mozart, Vice-Kapellmeister since 1763, was unsuccessful in his application for Lolli's post ; but since the vacancy gave him more work, he received an increase of 100 florins a year.

On 15 August, the Feast of the Assumption, Mozart's Paris symphony (K. 297) was again performed at the Concert spirituel, with a new Andante.

> The original middle movement, an Andantino, had failed to please. The Andante written to take its place was printed in the first edition (*c.* 1788) of the Paris publisher Jean Georges Sieber. (*Cf.* Hermann Beck in *Mozart-Jahrbuch 1955* [Salzburg, 1956] and in the *Neue Mozart-Ausgabe* IV/11, *Sinfonien, Band 5*, pp. 128 ff., also the Preface and Commentary.)

From 19 to about 28 August Mozart and the male soprano Ferdinando Tenducci stayed with Louis, Duc de Noailles, at Saint-Germain.

> The Duke, Marshal of France, maintained a private orchestra.—Tenducci, with Johann Christian Bach, was on a visit to Paris from London, where the Mozarts had already met him in 1764.

PADRE MARTINI TO LEOPOLD MOZART, BOLOGNA, 6 SEPTEMBER 1778
(in Italian)

. . . I am delighted. Sig. Raff having returned to Mannheim, I have written with all the power at my command, recommending your son to him, as I am still very anxious that he should be suitably and advantageously placed ; but since Sig. Raff has not replied to so pressing a letter of mine, I am writing again by this post to urge this matter upon him as best I know and am able. I grieve to hear of the loss of your worthy spouse.—Rest assured, I am deeply concerned that you should find solace, and I hope that God will grant you his contentment. Bologna, 6 September.

> Müller von Asow, Vol. III, p. 319.—Reply to Leopold Mozart's letter of 21 August, in which he requested Martini to recommend Mozart at Mannheim or Munich. *Cf.* 14 February 1778. This document too owes its preservation to having been copied in one of Leopold Mozart's letters to his son (17 September 1778), now at the Salzburg Mozarteum.

FROM THE "JOURNAL DE PARIS", EARLY SEPTEMBER 1778
(in French and Italian)

The concert will begin with a new symphony *del signor Amadeo Mozart.*

> Wilder, *Mozart*, p. 115 ; Jahn, Vol. I, p. 350.—Announcement of the concert on 8 September.

On 8 September, the Nativity of the Virgin, a symphony by Mozart was performed at the Concert spirituel.

> Probably the lost second Paris symphony (see Mozart's letter of 11 September 1778). An earlier supposition that it might have been the " Ouvertüre " in Bb major (K. App. 8 ; KE. 311a) has turned out to be erroneous : this work

is not by Mozart (*cf.* Ernst Hess in *Schweizerische Musikzeitung*, Zürich, February 1956).

On 11 September Mozart broke with Baron Grimm.

On 26 September Mozart left Paris after a sojourn of six months. He reached Nancy on about 3 October and Strasbourg on about the 14th.

On Saturday 17 October he gave a solo subscription concert, and on the 24th and 31st two concerts with orchestra, at the Strasbourg theatre.

> These concerts were poorly attended. At the first of them Prince Max of Zweibrücken was present.

> In early November 1778 the six sonatas for violin and clavier, K. 301-306 (KE. p. 361) were published in Paris by Jean Georges Sieber as *Oeuvre Premier*.

On 3 November Mozart left Strasbourg ; he arrived at Mannheim on the 6th, where he stayed with the wife of Christian Cannabich, the Konzertmeister of the Mannheim orchestra. Cannabich himself was at this time in Munich.

MOZART'S ENTRY IN THE VISITORS' BOOK OF THE MANNHEIM OBSERVATORY

Mozart maitre de chapelle den 16ten nov^bre [1778]

> The observatory belonged to the Jesuit College. Its visitors' book is now preserved at the Heidelberg observatory.—Friedrich Walter in *Mannheimer Geschichtsblätter*, Year XVI, Nos. 11-12, p. 137 f. Facsimile in Robert Haas, *Mozart* (Potsdam, 1933 [1950]), p. 22.

On 22 November Mozart's divertimento in D major (K. 251) was performed at the Salzburg court.

At 8.30 a.m. on 9 December Mozart left Mannheim and travelled by way of Heidelberg, Schwäbisch-Hall, Crailsheim, Dinkelsbühl, Wallerstein and Nördlingen to Kaisheim monastery, near Donauwörth ; he arrived on the 13th and stayed with Coelestin Angelsprugger, prelate to the Diet. On the 24th he left for Munich via Neuburg and Ingolstadt. He arrived in Munich on the 25th and stayed with the Weber family.

> Fridolin Weber had removed to Munich with the Mannheim orchestra in September, and Aloisia was engaged at the Opera there.

JOHANN BAPTIST BECKE TO LEOPOLD MOZART, MUNICH, 29 DECEMBER 1778

Monsieur mon très cher Ami !

This day I count among my most pleasant. I have the good fortune to see your very dear son at my house almost all day long. He arrived here safely on the 25th, and since the 26th we have been almost constantly together : he burns with desire to embrace his dearest and most cherished father, which will ensue as soon as his circumstances here will permit ; but he almost made me dispirited too, since for a whole hour I hardly succeeded in staying his tears : he has so good a heart. Never have I seen a child who carried more feeling and love for his father in his bosom than does your son.

He is assailed by some fear lest your reception of him may not be as tender as he wishes. I, however, hope for something very different of your paternal heart. He surely deserves to enjoy all love and happiness at his father's side : his heart is so pure, so childlike, so frank towards me, how much more must it be so towards his father.

Only to hear him speak is to accord him justice as the best of characters, the most honest and upright of men. But how many such are there in this world ? Best of fathers, it is you and your 2 children who deserve such praise, such laud and fame.

If circumstances permitted, I should myself accompany your son to Salzburg. . . . Pray write to us soon and assure us of your true fatherly love : for your son is a little out of sorts through sheer affection for his father : do but make his stay at Salzburg truly agreeable and friendly : his whole pleasure and delight are centred in his father and sister, apart from them the world holds nothing more for him : such things I write to you alone. . . .

> Salzburg, Mozarteum.—Enclosure in Wolfgang's letter of 29 December ; dated in another hand.—Jahn, Vol. I, p. 582 f ; Müller von Asow, Vol. II, p. 572 f.—For Becke *cf.* 19 and 22 April and 15 May 1775.

1779

FROM HEINRICH AUGUST OTTOKAR REICHARD'S " THEATER-KALENDER ", GOTHA 1779

Mozard . . . Kapellmeister at Salzburg ; begins *Semiramis*, a musical drama by Baron Gemmingen.

> P. 137.—Jahn, Vol. I, p. 581.—In November 1778, at Mannheim, Mozart had begun to compose music for this melodrama by Baron Otto von Gemmingen. The fragment (K. App. 11 ; KE. 315e) is lost ; but in the following yearly issues of the *Theater-Kalender* the melodrama was listed as one of Mozart's finished works. In 1782 Gemmingen moved to Vienna, where Mozart, as a fellow freemason, got to know him well.

FROM C. G. RÖSSIG'S " VERSUCHE IM MUSIKALISCHEN DRAMA ", BAYREUTH, 1779

Semiramis, a musical drama by Baron Gemmingen, is now occupying Herr Mozard, Kapellmeister at Salzburg.

> P. 17.—Jahn, Vol. I, p. 848.

On 7 January 1779 Mozart presented the Electress Maria Elisabeth, consort of Karl Theodor, with the sonatas for violin and pianoforte (K. 301-6), dedicated to her and engraved in Paris.

Sieber had published the sonatas in Paris as Op. I early in November 1778.

MARIA ANNA THEKLA MOZART TO LEOPOLD MOZART, 8 JANUARY 1779

Monsieur mon très cher oncle

I hope you are in good health and also my cousin, I had the honour to meet your son in Munich in excellent good health, he wants me to go with him to Salzburg, but I do not yet know whether I shall have the honour of seeing you : but my kinsman is a regular fool, you see : I wish you all happiness, mon cher oncle, and 1000 compliments to ma cousine. Je suis de tout mon coeur

Mozartin

Munich, the 8th January 1779

> Salzburg, Mozarteum. Postscript to Mozart's letter of the same day, with humorous additions in his hand (not shown here).—Jahn, Vol. II, p. 755 ; Schiedermair, Vol. IV, p. 387 f. ; Müller von Asow, Vol. II, p. 576. Facsimile in *Augsburger Mozart-Buch*, illustration 43.

On 11 or 12 January Mozart heard Schweitzer's *Alceste* in the Residenztheater.

On 13 or 14 January he left Munich and travelled with the " Bäsle " to Salzburg, where they arrived on the 15th.

> The " Bäsle " was to have followed in the stagecoach on the 20th, but seems to have accompanied Mozart.—Mozart now lived with his father again for nearly two years.

MOZART'S PETITION TO THE ARCHBISHOP HIERONYMUS, COUNT COLLOREDO, WITH DISCHARGE

Your Serene Highness !
Most Reverend Prince of the Holy Roman Empire !
Most Gracious Sovereign Prince and Lord ! *

Your Serene Highness was most graciously pleased after the decease of Cajetan Adlgasser most graciously to take me into your service : I therefore most submissively beg that I may be graciously assigned the post of Court Organist in your Exalted Service ; to which end, as for all other high favours and graces, I subscribe myself in the most profound submission,

Your Serene Highness,
my most gracious Sovereign Prince
and Lord's
most submissive and
most obedient Wolfgang Amade Mozart.

[On the verso]
  To
His Serene Highness
the Archbishop of Salzburg etc., etc.
most submissive and obedient
petition of Wolfgang Amade Mozart
    for the favour of his decree.

• *Ex Decreto Nostro 17ᵐᵃ Januarii 1779.*

Whereas We by these presents have graciously admitted and accepted the
suppliant as Our Court Organist, that he shall, like Adlgasser, carry out his
appointed duties with diligent assiduity and irreproachably, in the Cathedral
as well as at Court and in the Chapel, and shall as far as possible serve the
Court and the Church with new compositions made by him ; We decree
him therefor, like his predecessor, an annual salary of four hundred and fifty
gulden, and command Our Court Pay Office to discharge this by monthly
instalments, and to render account for each outlay in the appropriate place.

Hieronymus *m.p.*
praes : ad Cameram the 25th February *ao.* 1779
In Consº Crae : 26 Eiusdem
Instruction by Decree.

Salzburg, Provincial Archives.—Pirkmayer, *op. cit.* (1876), p. 18.—Müller
von Asow, Vol. III, p. 328 f.—Adlgasser had died at the end of 1777. Leopold
Mozart must have drafted the petition before his son's return home, so as
to be able to write and submit it immediately. Mozart was now paid three
times as much as his salary as second Konzertmeister during the years 1772–77.

FROM CHARLES BURNEY'S DISCOURSE ON WILLIAM CROTCH,
LONDON, 18 FEBRUARY 1779
(in English)

. . . his [Samuel Wesley's] extemporary performance on keyed instruments, like Mozart's, was so masterly in point of invention, modulation, and
accuracy of execution, as to surpass, in many particulars, the attainments of
most professors at any period of their lives. Indeed Mozart, when little
more than four years old, is said to have been "not only capable of executing
lessons on his favourite instrument, the harpsichord, but to have composed
ome in an easy style and taste, which were much approved" : . . . Here
the difference of education appears : little Crotch, left to nature, has not
only been without instructions but good models of imitation ; while
Mozart and Samuel Westley, on the contrary, may be said to have been
nursed in good music : . . . the German infant, living in the house of his
father, an eminent professor, and an elder sister, a neat player on the harpsi-

chord, and constantly practising compositions of the first class for that instrument, had every advantage of situation and culture joined to the profusion of natural endowments. Of Mozart's infant attempts at music I was unable to discover the traces from the conversation of his father; who, though an intelligent man, whose education and knowledge of the world did not seem confined to music, confessed himself unable to describe the progressive improvements of his son during the first stages of infancy. However, at eight years of age, I was frequently convinced of his great knowledge in composition by his writings ; and that his invention, taste, modulation, and execution in extemporary playing, were such as few professors are possessed of at forty years of age. . . .

> Michael Raeburn in *The Musical Times*, London, October 1956, p. 519 f.— Submitted on 9 February 1779, read on the 18th before the Royal Society and printed in its *Philosophical Transactions* for 1779, Vol. LXIX, pp. 183-206, London. *Cf.* 28 November 1769 and 21 January 1780.—Crotch was born at Norwich on 5 July 1775 and already played the organ in London at the age of four. In 1790 he became organist and in 1797 Professor of Music at Oxford. —Wesley was born at Bristol on 24 February 1766, learnt to play the organ at the age of six and at eight composed his first oratorio. Both lived to a ripe old age.—This discourse was reprinted in 1809 in *Philosophical Transactions . . . abridged* (Vol. 14, pp. 513-521).

On 20 February the Paris publisher Sieber, in the *Annonces, Affiches et Avis divers*, opened a subscription list for various symphonies, among which were two by Mozart.

> *Mozart en France* (Paris, 1956), p. 70.—Of these two symphonies the one in D major (K. 297)—the Paris symphony—appeared between 1782 and 1788 under the heading " Du Répertoire du Concert Spirituel ".

★ FRANZ ANTON SPITZEDER TO ARCHBISHOP COLLOREDO,
SALZBURG, *c.* 20 FEBRUARY 1779

Most excellent and noble Prince of the Holy Roman Empire, Gracious Lord, Sir,

    After it pleased your princely Grace to nominate Wolfgang Mozart to take the keyboard lessons in the Kapellhaus, I myself however attended to it at your gracious command for more than a whole year : I therefore in all respect and obedience request your Grace to vouchsafe me, of your gracious discretion, something for my pains, and prostrate myself most respectfully at your feet.
Your princely Grace's
our Sovereign Lord's

                    most humble and obedient
                    Franz Anton Spitzeder
                            tenor

[Address]   To
        Your Princely Grace the Archbishop of Salzburg
        most humble and obedient memorandum
                        from
        The Princely Court Pay Office
                            on behalf of Anton Spitzeder
                            Court Tenor : payment for
                            instruction in the Kapellhaus

[Endorsements]
        By His Highness's decree, 22 February 1779
        Referred to the Court Pay Office, herewith
        to show what Adlgasser received for instruction
        in the Kapellhaus, and whether after his death
        someone else did not receive this payment.

        By His Highness's Decree, 25 February 1779
        To the Exchequer, with the order
        to pay to Spitzeder the sum of fifty gulden, against a receipt,
        as recompense for instruction given in the
        Kapellhaus for one year.

        In Con[silio] C[ame]rae : 27 February 1779

   With reference to the memorandum submitted by the Court Pay Office
under the 24th inst. : graciously decreed that the petitioner shall be paid
50 florins against receipt as recompense for the clavier instruction given by
him in the Capellhaus during one year ; which decree herewith intimated to
His Grace's Court Pay Office.

   Decr[etum] in C[onsilio] C[amerae] S[alisburgensis,] 27 Febr[uary] 1779

        Salzburg, Provincial Archives.—Cf. Mozart's petition of the previous month.
        This document makes it clear that during his period as an organist at Salzburg
        Mozart also had the job of giving keyboard lessons in the choirboys' Kapell-
        haus.

THE EXCHEQUER TO THE COURT PAY OFFICE

Decretum

to the Princely Court Pay Office of this place.

   Whereas His Serene Highness, by virtue of the decree of 17 January last,
has admitted and accepted the most submissively supplicating applicant
Wolfgang Amade Mozart as His Highness's Court Organist, and most
graciously granted him, like his predecessor, an annual salary of four hundred
and fifty gulden ; these are to be remitted to the suppliant in monthly instalments, and account is to be rendered for each outlay in the appropriate place.

        Decretum in Consilio Camerae Salisburgensis
                Die 26 Februarii 1779.

Salzburg, Provincial Archives.—Pirkmayer, *op. cit.*, p. 22.—Müller von Asow, Vol. III, p. 329 f.

At the Paris Concert spirituel symphonies by Mozart were performed on 18 and 28 March, 23 May and 3 June.

Georges de Saint-Foix, *Les Symphonies de Mozart* (Paris, 1932), p. 102. Apart from the Paris symphony (K. 297) and the lost one, the Sinfonia concertante in E♭ major (K. App. 9 ; KE. 297b) was probably performed.

On 30 March 1779 the Litany K. 243 was performed in the cathedral again.

Nannerl's diary for 1779 (*Wiener allgemeine Musik-Zeitung*, 20 June 1846). The litanies by Adlgasser and Michael Haydn were repeated on the two previous days. *Cf.* 31 March, 1776.

FROM THE " MERCURE DE FRANCE ", PARIS, 5 JUNE 1779
(in French)

. . . the other [symphony] by Amédeo Mosartz. He is perhaps as learned and as majestic as the former [Sterkel] ; but he did not excite the same interest.

Communicated by H. C. Robbins Landon.—Johann Franz Xaver Sterkel, court organist at Mainz, wrote a number of symphonies.—The symphony mentioned above was probably the lost second Paris one.

IBID., 15 JUNE 1779
(in French)

This concert began with a symphony for full orchestra composed by Amadeo Mozards. We remarked great character in the first two movements, great richness of ideas, and motifs followed through. As regards the third, in which all the science of counterpoint shines forth, the Author obtained the suffrages of Lovers of the kind of music that may interest the mind, without ever touching the heart.

Ibid.—Corpus Christi Day in 1779 was 3 June. The symphony was probably the " Paris " (*cf.* 18 June and 15 August 1778), and the date of the concert 23 May.

In the evening of 24 September the Haffner serenade (K. 250) and one of the two marches (K. 335) for the most recent serenade (K. 320) were played in the Kollegienplatz (now Universitätsplatz) in Salzburg.

Walter Hummel, *Nannerl Mozarts Tagebuchblätter*, p. 61.

On 14 December Mozart saw Goldoni's comedy *Il bugiardo* played at the Salzburg theatre in German (*Der Lügner*) by Johann Böhm's company.

The company played there in the 1779–80 season. A leaf from a theatre diary of this December testifies to Nannerl's and Wolfgang's interest in the performances, which were directed by Böhm. Mozart gave him the E♭ major symphony (K. 184) of 1773 as an overture to Karl Martin Plümike's play *Lanassa*

and finished his music for Gebler's *König Thamos* for him (see 31 May 1773).
Böhm later used music from *König Thamos* for the last act of *Lanassa* also.—
The libretto for Mozart's opera *La finta semplice* (K. 51, 1768) had been adapted
from Goldoni by Coltellini, and in 1783 Mozart planned to compose Goldoni's
Il servitore di due padroni in a translation begun for him by Johann Nepomuk
Friedrich, Baron Binder von Kriegelstein. The arias K. 433 and 435 may
possibly be connected with this project.

FROM PAUL VON STETTEN's " KUNST-, GEWERB- UND HANDWERKS-GESCHICHTE DER REICHS-STADT AUGSBURG ", 1779

Music.

. . . But some excellent good geniuses, too, have tried their fortune
abroad, the mention of a couple of whom must not be omitted.

One such is Herr Leopold Mozart, Kapellmeister to the Prince-Archbishop
of Salzburg, the son of a local citizen. Not fine compositions alone, but also
his Violin School, or Instruction for the Violin, which was printed here,
have made his name famous. But he became particularly well known in
Germany, France and England when he visited these countries in 1769 and
1770 with his two extraordinarily skilled children, a daughter of eleven and
a son of nine years, and earned their admiration for them.* In Paris they
had so much success that the father and the children were portrayed in the
actual performance of a concert, engraved in copper.

This son, Herr Chevalier Wolfgang Amadeus Mozart, has over several
years become celebrated for his exceptional power on the clavier, and has
obtained the post of Conzertmeister at the aforesaid Salzburg Court, which
however he has again resigned, resolved to seek his fortune in other places.
On passing through Augsburg in 1777, he displayed the whole of his powers
at a public concert.

* Burney, Vol. I, p. 170 ; Vol. III, p. 262.

Vol. I, p. 553 f.—Abert, Vol. I, p. 544.—The reference to Burney is to the
German translation of his travel journals (see end of 1771 and end of 1773).—
Stetten wrote the text of the cantata *Deucalion und Pyrrha*, composed by Demmler (see 28 October 1777). The second volume of Stetten's book is cited below
under the end of 1788.

1780

Early in 1780 father and son Mozart each ordered a copy of the *Sammlung Vermischter
Clavierstücke für geübte und ungeübte Spieler . . . von Georg Benda. Erster Theil.
Gotha, beym Verfasser und in Commission bey C. W. Ettinger. 1780.*

Discovered by Ernst Fritz Schmid. Copies in the British Museum, London,
and in the Moravian Provincial Library, Brno.—In the list of subscribers

appears the entry : " Salzburg 2 copies Hr. Capellm[eister] Mozart. Hr. Tonk[ünstler] Mozart."—Five further parts to this work appeared in the next fifteen years ; the Mozarts may have subscribed for them too.—For Benda *cf.* 23 January 1778.

POSTSCRIPT TO DAINES BARRINGTON'S " MISCELLANIES ", LONDON, 1781

(in English)

Jan. 21. 1780

On this republication of what appeared in the LXth volume of the Philosophical Transactions, it may be right to add, that Mozart (though a German) hath been honoured by the pope with an order of merit called the Golden Spur, and hath composed operas in several parts of Italy. I have also been favoured by D. Burney with the following account of one of his latest compositions.

" Mozart being at Paris, in 1778, composed for Tenducci a scene in 14 parts, chiefly obligati ; viz. two violins, two tenors, one chromatic horn, one oboe, two clarinets, a Piano forte, a Soprano voice part, with two horns, and a base di rinforza.

It is a very elaborate and masterly composition, discovering a great practice and facility of writing in many Parts. The modulation is likewise learned and recherchée ; however, though it is a composition which none but a great master of harmony, and possessed of a consummate knowledge of the genius of different instruments, could produce ; yet neither the melody of the voice part, nor of any one of the instruments, discovers much invention, though the effects of the whole, if well executed, would, doubtless, be masterly and pleasing."

P. 288.—C. F. Pohl, *Mozart in London* (Vienna, 1867), p. 122.—*Cf.* 28 November 1769.—Mozart wrote this scena for Tenducci, now lost (K. App. 3; KE. 315b), at Saint-Germain (see 19 August 1778) at the end of August 1778, probably stimulated by a similar piece written by Johann Christian Bach for the same castrato. *Cf.* C. B. Oldman in *Music & Letters* (London, January 1961), pp. 44-52.

On 18 March 1780, during the Böhm company's season, there was a concert in the Salzburg theatre which opened with the Haffner serenade (K. 250).

W. Hummel, *Nannerl Mozarts Tagebuchblätter*, p. 69 ; O. E. Deutsch, " Ein scherzhaftes Konzertprogramm von Mozart " in *Mitteilungen der Internationalen Stiftung Mozarteum* (Salzburg), June 1958, p. 2 f. ; W. Hummel, *ibid.*, December 1958, p. 8.—According to Mozart's entry in his sister's diary No. 6 of the programme, an aria, was also his, but not No. 8, a rondo sung by Ceccarelli. It seems that Mozart himself directed the concert.

On 1 May Johann Böhm's company performed *La finta giardiniera*, translated into German by Franz Xaver Stierle (as *Die verstellte Gärtnerin*), in Augsburg.

Unless Böhm had already given this opera in the 1779–80 season at Salzburg, this performance was the first of any opera by Mozart given on a stage for which it was not originally written.—Stierle was an actor in Böhm's company.

FROM THE " ALMANACH MUSICAL POUR 1781 ", PARIS
(in French)

1780, 14 May. Whit Sunday. Concert Spirituel, begun with a symphony *del Signor Amadeo Mozartz*, followed by the " Veni Sancte Spiritus " by Jomelly.

> P. 102.—The almanach was published by Pierre Joseph François Luneau de Boisjermain (information from Mme Nanie Bridgman, Paris).—J. B. Weckerlin, *Dernier Musiciana* (Paris, 1899), p. 29.—On Whitsunday the Paris symphony was probably repeated.—The hymn by Niccolò Jommelli was a great favourite.

On 2 and 4 September Mozart played at the archiepiscopal court ; on the 3rd he and Nannerl played a concerto for two claviers there (either an arrangement of K. 242, originally written for three claviers, or K. 365) and a four-hand sonata, K. 381.

On 6 and 7 September Leopold Mozart took both his children to the St. Zeno Augustinian canonry, and to Reichenhall.

> W. Hummel, *Nannerl Mozarts Tagebuchblätter*, p. 96 f., wrongly given under 1783.

FROM THE " LITTERATUR- UND THEATER-ZEITUNG ", BERLIN, 1780
Extract from a Letter to Herr André

Yesterday I received the new *Singspiel* by Herr Grossmann, just published : *Adelheit von Veltheim*, and found to my astonishment that the two of us, without in the least knowing anything about each other, have by coincidence worked on almost identical lines. Much as the plan and details of my Singspiel *Belmonte und Constanze, oder Die Entführung aus dem Serail* (which I sent you to compose last July), differs from Herr Grossman's Singspiel, the pieces nevertheless resemble each other by both dealing with a story of a harem, and both contain an elopement. As I should not care to have my piece printed before its performance, and yet wish to escape any reproach of plagiarism, I beg you to publish this information in the *Litteratur- und Theater-Zeitung*. According to your promise, I await the score of this piece shortly. Leipzig, 4 October 1780.

C. F. Bretzner.

> Part III, No. 43, p. 672.—This periodical, published since 1775 by Christian August von Bertram, was later continued as *Ephemeriden der Litteratur und des Theaters* (1785–87) and *Annalen des Theaters* (1788–97).—Christoph Friedrich Bretzner's singspiel was set by Johann André and performed in Berlin on 25 May 1781. The singspiel *Adelheit von Veltheim* composed by Christian Gottlieb Neefe to words by Gustav Friedrich Wilhelm Grossmann, produced at Frankfurt on 23 September 1780, was one of the earliest German operas with a Turkish subject. *Cf.* Bretzner's protests against Mozart (end of 1782) and Gottlieb Stephanie (21 June 1783), the Viennese adapter of his libretto.

On 31 October Aloisia Weber married the court actor Joseph Lange in Vienna.

> The Weber family had left Munich for Vienna in September 1779, where the father, Fridolin, died in the following month. Aloisia was engaged at the German Opera. Lange (see 23 January 1778), a widower since March 1779, had similar experiences with Aloisia's mother as Mozart was to have in 1782, when he married her sister Constanze. (*Cf.* Lange's petition to the Chamberlain, Eugen, Count Wrbna-Freudenthal, published by Emil Karl Blümml, *Aus Mozarts Freundes- und Familien-Kreis* [Vienna, 1923], p. 23.)

On 5 November Mozart travelled to Munich, where he arrived at 1 p.m. on the 6th and took lodgings at Herr Fiat's in the house known as the " Sonneck ", Burggasse 6.

> Mozart's leave for the performance of his *Idomeneo* was valid until 18 December ; but he remained in Bavaria until 12 March 1781, when the Archbishop summoned him to Vienna.

In the morning of 7 November Mozart, accompanied by Becke, called on Count Seeau. Archduke Maximilian arrived in Munich on that day. In the evening Mozart attended the gala performance at the court theatre, where the tragedy *Graf Essex* (Christian Heinrich Schmidt's translation of *The Unhappy Favourite* by John Banks), and a ballet with an overture by Cannabich, were performed. On 8 November Mozart went to a concert held by the singer Gertrud Elisabeth Mara-Schmehling.

On Sunday 12 November Mozart was presented to the Elector Karl Theodor by Count Seeau. On the 13th a discussion of Mozart's opera was held at the Count's.

Maria Theresa died on 29 November.

> Her eldest son, the Emperor Joseph II, succeeded her as sovereign of Austria, Bohemia and Hungary.

On 1 December the first orchestral rehearsal for *Idomeneo* was held. On the same day, at the Salzburg theatre, Fräulein Adelheid sang the aria (since lost) by Mozart interpolated into Gozzi's play *Le due notti affannose* (K. App. 11ᵃ).

> Mozart wrote this aria for Schikaneder's company, which visited Salzburg in the 1780–81 season. The translation of the play was by F. A. C. Werthes.

On 16 December the second rehearsal for *Idomeneo* was held, and on the 23rd the Elector attended the third rehearsal.

FROM THE CHRISTMAS SALT LISTS OF THE SALZBURG EXCHEQUER, 1780

COURT MUSICIANS

Leopold Motzard, Kapellmeister
Joh : Michael Haiden, Konzertmeister
Wolfg : Amade Motzard, Court Organist.

> Salzburg Provincial Archives.—The handwritten " Christmas salt lists ", filed with the Exchequer documents (" Catenicheln "), contained the names of those officials who received a yearly present of salt from the archiepiscopal mines.

1781

On 8 January 1781 Frau Maria Viktoria Robinig, the first of the visitors from Salzburg, arrived in Munich.

The ironmonger Georg Joseph Robinig von Rottenfeld, a friend of Leopold Mozart's, had died at Munich in 1760 (see 12 January 1762). His son Georg Sigismund arrived there before the widow.

On 13 January the third act of *Idomeneo* was rehearsed for the first time ; on the 18th the recitative rehearsals began.

On 20 January Dr. Silvester Barisani, the archiepiscopal physician-in-ordinary, arrived in Munich with his wife, Maria Anna Theresia ; on the 26th Leopold Mozart arrived with Nannerl.

The oboist and composer Joseph Fiala of the Court Chapel was also among the visitors from Salzburg.

On 27 January, Mozart's birthday, the dress rehearsal of *Idomeneo* took place.

The first performance, planned for the 22nd and then for the 27th, had again to be postponed for two days. It was finally performed on the 29th.

FROM THE LIBRETTO OF THE OPERA " IDOMENEO "
(in Italian and German)

IDOMENEO.

Dramma
per
musica
da rappresentarsi
nel Teatro nuovo di
Corte
Per Comando
di s. a. s. e.
CARLO TEODORO

Conte Palatino del Rheno, Duca dell' alta, e bassa Baviera, e del Palatino Superiore, etc. etc. Archidapifero, et Elettore, etc. etc. nel Carnovale 1781.

The poetry is by Signor Abate Gianbattista Varesco Chaplain to the Court of His Serene Highness the Archbishop and Prince of Salzburg.

The music is by Signor Maestro Wolfgango Amadeo [in the German copy: Wolfgang Gottlieb] Mozart, Academician of Bologna and of Verona, in actual service of His Serene Highness the Archbishop and Prince of Salzburg.

The translation is by Sig. Andrea Schachtner, also in actual service of His Serene Highness the Archbishop and Prince of Salzburg.

MUNICH.
Francesco Giuseppe Thuille.

CHARACTERS.

Idomeneo, King of Crete. Sig. Raaf, Chamber Virtuoso to His Electoral
    Highness the Duke Palatine of Bavaria, etc. etc.

Idamante, his Son. Sig. Dal Prato.

Ilia, Princess of Troy, Daughter to Priam. Sigra Dorothea Wendling, Chamber
    Virtuosa to His Electoral Highness, etc. etc.

Elettra, Princess, Daughter to Agamemnon, King of Argos. Sigra Elizabetha
    Wendling, Chamber Virtuosa to His Electoral Highness, etc. etc.

Arbace, Confidant to the King. Sig. Domenico Panzachi, Chamber Virtuoso
    to His Electoral Highness, etc. etc.

High Priest of Neptune. Sig. Giovanni Valesi, Chamber Virtuoso to His
    Electoral Highness, etc. etc.

Supernumeraries and Chorus

Of Priests.
Of Trojan Prisoners.
Of Cretan Men and Women.
Of Mariners from Argos.

The dances are of the invention of Sig. Le Grand, Ballet Master to His
Electoral Highness the Duke Palatine of Bavaria.

.   .   .   .   .

The scenery is of the invention of Sig. Lorenzo Quaglio, Councillor to the
Chamber of Finance, Professor of the Academy of Fine Arts at Düsseldorf,
and Theatre Architect to H. E. H.

> The Bavarian State Library at Munich possesses a copy of the edition with
> Italian words and one of the bilingual edition. Facsimile of the title-page in
> Bory, *op. cit.*, p. 111. The singers were : Anton Raaff, Vincenzo del Prato,
> Dorothea and Elisabeth Wendling, Domenico de' Panzacchi and Giovanni
> Valesi. (The Wendlings were sisters-in-law : Dorothea the wife of the
> flautist Johann Baptist Wendling, Elisabeth of the violinist Franz Wendling.)
> The " New Electoral Opera House " was that later known as the Residenz-
> theater.—The conductor was probably Cannabich.—The opera was repeated
> on 3 February and 3 March ; according to the *Münchner Stats-, Gelehrte und
> Vermischte Nachrichten* of 9 January, repeat performances were originally
> planned for 5, 12, 19 and 26 February (four more Mondays).

FROM THE " MÜNCHNER STATS-, GELEHRTE, UND VERMISCHTE
NACHRICHTEN ", 1 FEBRUARY 1781

On the 29th day of last month the first performance of the opera *Idomeneo* took place at the new Opera House here. The text, music and
translation—all are by natives of Salzburg. The ornamentations, among
which the views of the sea-port and the temple of Neptune are especially
effective, were masterpieces of our local and famous theatre architect, the

Court Councillor Herr Lorenz Quaglio, which attracted everyone's admiration.

> Jahn, Vol. I, p. 654.—This notice was copied by the *Augsburgische Ordinari-Postzeitung* of 5 February.

FROM THE "ANNALEN DER BAIERISCHEN LITTERATUR VOM JAHRE 1781", NUREMBERG, 1782

Short Description of the Theatre Personalities at Munich

The Intendant of the music as well as the drama is His Excellency Joseph Anton, Count Seeau. Herr Marchand is Director . . .

At the so-called Grand Opera the singers are Dal Prato, Hartig, Zonga, Raff, Wallesi, Mme Wendling, sen., Mme Wendling, jun., Mlle Schierlinger. The music for this season is by the younger Herr Mozzard of Salzburg. The scenery is in the care of the Court Councillor and Theatre Architect, Herr Quaglio.

> Pp. 340-46.—Copy in the Munich City Library.

★ FROM FRANZ XAVER RIEGER'S TRAVEL NOTES, STRASBOURG, 9 FEBRUARY 1781

[In a room belonging to Princess Maria Christina of Saxony, Abbess of Remiremont.]

In this room there was lying on the table the opera that was performed at Munich this Carnival. The Italian words are by Varesco, the translation by Herr Schachtner, and the music by the young Mozart, all three of Salzburg.

> Salzburg, Museum Carolino-Augusteum.—Herbert Klein in the *Mozart-Jahrbuch 1959* (Salzburg, 1960), p. 227.—Rieger was a graduate of the Salzburg seminary.—The "opera" was the libretto of *Idomeneo*.

LEOPOLD MOZART TO JOHANN GOTTLOB IMMANUEL BREITKOPF AT LEIPZIG; MUNICH, 12 FEBRUARY 1781

I have long wished that you would put something by my son into print. You will surely not judge him by the clavier sonatas he wrote as a child? It is true that you cannot have seen a note of what he has written these last few years, unless it were the 6 sonatas for clavier with a violin, which he had engraved in Paris, for we allow little to appear. You might make a trial with a few symphonies or pianoforte sonatas, or with quartets, trios, &c. You would only have to give us some copies in exchange so that at least you get an idea of my son's way of composing. Not that I wish in the least to persuade you; this idea has often come to me merely because I see many things engraved and printed which seem pitiable to me.

Jahn, Vol. I, p. 687.—*Cf.* 7 February 1772.—Although Christoph Gottlob Breitkopf came to Vienna in the autumn of 1786 and transacted business with Haydn, he does not appear to have got into touch with Mozart.

Between 7 and 10 March the Mozarts, father, daughter and son, paid a visit to Augsburg.

The visit lasted at least four days.

DAVID BARTHOLOMÄUS STROBL OF AUGSBURG TO HYACINTH LECH AT MUNICH

Noble, learned, and right honoured Cousin,

May it please you, Sir, to draw your own conclusions from the enclosed, and to see to the necessary. We have these days had the privilege and pleasure of doing the honours to Herr Mozart, Kapellmeister [of] Salzburg, whose two children, from Wednesday till today have incessantly entertained us with almost more than heavenly music on two fortepianos. You would have recovered your health and hearing, had you listened to them for only a quarter of an hour, for it was indescribably enchanting. I hope your health is in the best of ways. I remain meanwhile with my courteous compliments,

Your worship's

Most devoted

D. Strobl.

Monastery of the Holy Cross, Augsburg, 10 March 1781

Munich, Bavarian State Archives.—Richard Schaal, in *Acta Mozartiana*, Vol. I/i, p. 8 (Augsburg, 1954).—Strobl was treasurer of the monastery of the Holy Cross at Augsburg, and Lech its legal representative with the Privy Council at Munich.—10 March was a Saturday, so that the Mozarts probably spent four days at the monastery, or at any rate at Augsburg.

On 12 March Mozart left Munich and, in obedience to the Archbishop's orders, went to Vienna. On the 14th Leopold and Nannerl returned to Salzburg.

It is to be supposed that the Mozarts returned from Augsburg to Munich on 10 or 11 March and that the father and daughter went home to Salzburg, while Wolfgang travelled by way of Altötting, Braunau and Linz to Vienna.—The Archbishop, with his staff, was staying on in Vienna with his ailing father, the Imperial Vice-Chancellor Rudolf Joseph, Prince Colloredo (see 11 October 1762). When Mozart had already long overstayed his leave the Archbishop ordered him to come immediately to Vienna, where as Court organist he was required to serve as clavier player.

At 9 a.m. on 16 March Mozart arrived in Vienna, where he lodged at the house of the Teutonic Order (now Singerstrasse 7), and at 4 p.m. he was already taking part in a concert.

While the Konzertmeister Brunetti and the castrato Ceccarelli were allowed to lodge independently, Mozart was obliged to stay in the house where the Archbishop had his quarters, like the staff and the servants. The Archbishop's uncle, Karl, Count Colloredo, was District Commander of the Austrian bailiwick of the Teutonic Order, but lived for the most part in Italy.

At 7 p.m. on 17 March the Archbishop's musicians performed at Prince Galitsin's (see end of March 1768) and on the 24th Mozart played at Councillor Johann Gottlieb von Braun's on the Judenplatz.

The Councillor was the father of Peter von Braun, who later became a theatre manager.

FROM THE " DEUTSCHES MUSEUM ", LEIPZIG, 1781

Vienna, 31 March 1781.

. . . Of the Operetta I must after all tell you this much, that anything more stiff, wooden and puppet-like than the acting of these people is not to be imagined. I cannot understand why the operettas are not turned into concerts. Herr Adamberger has sung to great applause in London and in several Italian cities. That is enough to say in his honour, I should think ; but he seems to me to be soulless in his singing as well as his acting Herr Fischer, who was formerly at Mannheim, is known to be the foremost bass in Germany, and, after Günther, he also acts the best. This Günther happens to be the one who so often played Jobsen Teckel at Hanover, and no bad Merry Andrew. Mme Lange, formerly Mlle Weber, the *prima donna*, has a very agreeable voice, which is however too weak for the stage. Mlle Cavalieri's is incomparably stronger, but most peculiar in quality ; apart from that she is frightfully ugly, has only one eye, and both of them act pitiably.—Mlle Teyber, the third voice, acts best among the women. Mme Weiss's singing is of no use, she can act a little, but without intelligence, but is adored by the Viennese in the part of the Fair Cobbler's Wife because she is a handsome woman. Apart from these there are a lot of others, of both sexes. Thus you see that there is no lack of personnel in the Operetta any more than in the Comedy. After Easter Glück's *Iphigenie en Aulidé* is to be given in German.

> Vol. I, Part xii, p. 528 f.—The journal had been published by Heinrich Christian Boie since 1776.—The anonymous report from which this section is taken bears the heading " Bemerkungen über das Pariser und Wiener Theater " (Part x, pp. 316-30), the second part " Schluss des Beitrages zur Geschichte der deutschen Schaubühne " (Part xii, pp. 512-29). It is here interpolated under the correspondent's date to show the conditions Mozart encountered at the German Opera in the Vienna Burgtheater.—Of the singers Valentin Joseph Adamberger, tenor, Ludwig Karl Fischer, bass, and Friedrich Günther, bass, had belonged to the company since 1780 ; Aloisia Lange, soprano, since 1779 ; Caterina Cavalieri, soprano, and Therese Teyber, soprano, since 1778 (Teyber was married to the tenor Ferdinand Arnold, who had been a member in 1778-79), and Anna Maria Weiss, soprano, from 1779 to 1781.—Umlauf's singspiel *Die pucefarbenen Schuhe, oder Die schöne Schusterin* was first performed at Schloss Laxenburg in 1779 and then in the Burgtheater ; a portrait of Fräulein Weiss in the title-part is in the possession of the Gesellschaft der Musikfreunde in Vienna. Gluck's *Iphigénie en Aulide* was not given in Vienna until 1808, but his *Iphigénie en Tauride* was played at the Burgtheater on 23 October 1781.

FROM THE PROGRAMME OF A CONCERT IN THE KÄRNTNERTOR THEATRE

INFORMATION.

To-morrow, Thursday, 3 April 1781, will be held
in the I. & R. priv. Playhouse next the Kärntnertor

FOR THE BENEFIT OF

the newly established Society of Musicians

A GRAND MUSICAL CONCERT,

which will commence with

a Symphony of the composition of Herr Wolfgang Amadi Mozart, Knight,
in actual service of His Serene Highness the Archbishop of Salzburg.

Herr Mozart, Knight, will then be heard on the pianoforte all by himself.

He was already here himself as a boy aged seven, and even then earned the
general applause of the public, partly in the matter of composition and
partly in that of art altogether, as well as for his especial skill and delicacy
of touch. . . .

To begin at 6.30.

> Vienna, National Library (Music Collection), and Museum of the City of
> Vienna.—Jahn, Vol. I, p. 693. Facsimile in Robert Haas, *Mozart*, p. 26.—The
> Society of Musicians for the benefit of the widows and orphans of musicians
> had been founded in 1771 in imitation of the London one. (In 1785 Mozart
> could not be admitted as a member, apparently because he had not submitted
> a birth certificate, *cf.* 11 February 1785.) Since 1772 concerts had been given
> during Advent in the Kärntnertor Theatre, usually with oratorios, for the
> Society's benefit. Already on 1 April 1781 Johann Georg Albrechtsberger's
> musical drama, *Die Pilgrime auf Golgatha*, had been given in concert perform-
> ance there, with Cavalieri, Teyber, Adamberger and Fischer as soloists.
> Before the repeat performance on the 3rd Mozart, with the Archbishop's
> grudging permission, made his first public appearance in Vienna. The Em-
> peror himself was present at this concert. The symphony played by a large
> orchestra under Giuseppe Bonno's direction was probably that in C major
> (K. 338) ; the pianoforte piece the variations on Antoine-Laurent Baudron's
> " Je suis Lindor " from Beaumarchais's *Barbier de Séville* (K. 354). It is unlikely
> that Mozart also played a pianoforte concerto, which would have been a
> complete novelty for Vienna (Pohl, *Haydn*, Vol. II, p. 145). The Stein grand
> pianoforte had been lent to him by Countess Wilhelmine Thun.

On Sunday 8 April, at Prince Rudolf Joseph Colloredo's, the rondo in C major for
violin and orchestra (K. 373), the G major sonata for pianoforte and violin (K. 379)
and the recitative and aria for soprano "A questo seno deh vieni — Or, che il cielo a me
ti rende " (K. 374) were performed.

> Brunetti, Mozart and Ceccarelli took part. (It is not true that the concerto-
> rondo in Eb major for horn [K. 371], was given on this occasion.) On account
> of this concert held at the house of the Archbishop's father Mozart missed
> another at Countess Thun's, at which the Emperor was present.

On 11 April Mozart went to confession at the Theatine Church (Kajetanerkirche) ;
on the Maundy Thursday following, the Archbishop administered the sacrament
to his household.

The Theatine monastery in the Tiefe Graben was well known to Mozart (see 7 August 1773).

On 27 April the Salzburg musicians gave their last concert before the Archbishop in Vienna.

Probably again at the house of his father, Prince Colloredo. Brunetti had already left. At the end Mozart had to play variations on the pianoforte on a theme proposed by the Archbishop.

On 1 or 2 May Mozart was obliged to leave his lodgings at the house of the Teutonic Order ; he moved to Frau Cäcilie Weber's at the house called " The Eye of God ", Am Peter (now No. 11), 2nd floor.

He originally intended to stay there for only a week.

On 9 May Mozart broke with the Archbishop and on the 10th he handed his resignation to the Chief Steward, Karl, Count Arco.

Mozart's departure for Salzburg had been postponed from 9 May to the 12th.

After a second interview with Arco at the end of May, Mozart was finally dismissed by the Count on 8 June with a kick.

In July Mozart repeatedly visited the Reisenberg, the summer residence of Johann Philipp, Count Cobenzl, Court Vice-Chancellor and Chancellor of State.

The Count had already made Wolfgang's acquaintance in Brussels in the autumn of 1763, and his cousin, Marie Karoline, Countess Thiennes de Rumbeke, became Mozart's first pianoforte pupil in Vienna.—The Reisenberg, now known as Cobenzl, is the eastern spur, facing Vienna, of the Kahlengebirge in the Wienerwald. The Count's country house was not turned into a castle until after 1781 ; but it already boasted a garden, a pond and an artificial grotto, as may be seen from entries in Zinzendorf's diary under 2 May 1781 and 31 July 1783, which speak of " an earthly paradise " with " all kinds of animals ". (Cf. Alfred von Arneth's biography of Cobenzl [Vienna, 1885], p. 45.) Mozart spent one night there early in July, and nearly the whole time from the 11th to the 31st.

On 30 July Gottlieb Stephanie gave Mozart the libretto of the singspiel Die Entführung aus dem Serail.

Cf. 4 October 1780.—Stephanie had been with the Burgtheater as producer and dramatist since 1769.

LEOPOLD MOZART TO BREITKOPF, SALZBURG, 10 AUGUST 1781

As regards my son, he is no longer in service here. He was called to Vienna by the Prince, who was there while we were at Munich. . . . Now since His Serene Highness quite uncommonly ill-treated my son there, and since on the contrary the whole of the high nobility did him especial honour, they easily persuaded him to resign a post entailing a miserable salary and to remain in Vienna.

People tried to persuade us to have the opera published, either printed or engraved, the complete score or a clavier arrangement. Subscribers to some 20 copies had already made themselves known, among them His Serene Highness Prince Max of Zweybrücken, &c. ; but my son's journey to Vienna and the events that happened in the meantime, caused everything to be postponed. . . .

The 6 sonatas dedicated to the Electress of Bavaria and the Palatinate are published by Herr Sieber in Paris. He acquired them from my son in Paris for 15 *Louis neufs*, 30 copies and a free dedication.

> Original in the German State Library, Berlin (at present University Library, Tübingen).—Jahn, Vol. I, pp. 552, 572, 706 f. (footnotes) ; Schiedermair, Vol. IV, p. 290.—*Cf.* 12 February 1781.—The opera was *Idomeneo*. "Printed" means type-set. Full scores of operas were rarely printed or engraved at that time ; nor did a vocal score of this opera of Mozart's appear in his lifetime.— The "Œuvre premier" [*sic*] published by Sieber was the set of pianoforte and violin sonatas, K. 301-6 (see 7 January 1779).

On 5 September (or shortly before) Mozart moved to a room in the Graben in the Inner City, No. 1175 (now No. 17), 3rd floor.

> The house was near the Platz Am Peter, where Mozart had until now been living at Frau Weber's.

On 15 October, St. Theresa's Day, the E♭ major serenade for wind instruments (K. 375), written by Mozart for the court painter Joseph Hickel's sister-in-law, was performed.

> This Frau Therese was Hickel's wife's sister. Among his numerous portraits is one of Lange as Hamlet (now in the Gallery of Honour of the Burgtheater). —The serenade was played again the same evening for two other Thereses.

Mozart's name-day, 31 October, was celebrated at midday at Baroness Martha Elisabeth Waldstätten's, Leopoldstadt No. 360 (Jägerzeile, later Praterstrasse) ; in the evening his new serenade (K. 375) was played outside his lodgings in the Graben.

> The Baroness, who was separated from her husband, was a good pianist and became an active benefactress to Mozart.

On 16 November Archduke Maximilian presented Mozart to Duke Friedrich Eugen of Württemberg, his consort Friederike and his daughter Elisabeth, and he played to them.

> The Archduke, whom Mozart had last seen at Munich (see 7 November 1780), had become coadjutor of the Elector-Archbishop of Cologne, whom he later succeeded. The Duke was a brother of Prince Ludwig Eugen (*cf.* 11 September and 11 October 1766).—Princess Elisabeth, who was fourteen, had just been betrothed to the Archduke Franz, aged thirteen, nephew of Joseph II and later to become Emperor. The wedding did not take place until the beginning of 1788, and Elisabeth died two years later. Mozart's hope of becoming her music-master was not fulfilled.

On 23 November Mozart played at Auernhammer's house with his host's daughter Josepha, a pupil of his ; they performed the concerto in E♭ major (K. 365), and the sonata in D for two pianofortes (K. 448).

> The Economic Councillor Johann Michael Auernhammer, who died four months later, and his wife Elisabeth, had only one daughter, Josepha. She was musically highly gifted but ugly ; she fell in love with her teacher, but he did not respond. She later married the Town Councillor Johann Bessenig. —Mozart had added 2 clarinets, 2 trumpets and drums to the outer movements of the concerto ; the sonata was written specially for this concert. Among

the guests were Countess Thun, the Court Librarian and President of the Education Commission Gottfried van Swieten (see 21 September 1768) and the baptized Jewish banker Karl Abraham Wetzlar, Baron von Plankenstern— two men who were destined to play a part in Mozart's life.

On 25 November Mozart attended a gala performance of Gluck's *Alceste* in the theatre at Schönbrunn Palace ; it was given in honour of Grand-Duke Paul and his consort, Maria Feodorovna, *née* Princess of Württemberg.

> The guest of honour was the future Tsar Paul I.—Gluck's opera was newly produced and was staged a week after this festival performance, on 3 December 1781, at the Burgtheater. On both occasions it was sung in Italian by the members of the German Opera. *Cf.* 12 January 1779.

FROM THE " WIENER ZEITUNG ", 8 DECEMBER 1781

Announcement

At the art establishment of Artaria & Co. on the Kohlmarkt, opposite St. Michael's Church, are newly published and to be had : 6 Sonatas for the clavier with accompaniment for a violin by the sufficiently well-known and celebrated Herr Wolfgang Amadee Mozart, *Op.* 2.

5 fl. -

> The official *Wiener Zeitung*, formerly called *Wienerisches Diarium*, was the only regular and permanently published newspaper in Vienna (it still exists), and was therefore used by the music publishers for their advertisements. The firm of Artaria & Co. was the most distinguished of them. It was the first in Vienna to publish a work by Mozart, the sonatas K. 376, 296, 377-80. On 26 April 1783 Mozart wrote to Sieber in Paris, in reference to this work, that he was " not very well pleased with the way in which engraving is done here ". Fräulein Auernhammer, to whom this work was dedicated, later read the proofs of works by Mozart published in Vienna. This one had appeared before the end of November 1781. On the opus numbers arbitrarily given to works by Mozart, see O. E. Deutsch & C. B. Oldman in *Zeitschrift für Musikwissenschaft* (Leipzig, April 1932). This was already the third Op. 2.

On 11 December Noverre's ballet *Les petits riens* was performed at the King's Theatre in London.

> *Cf.* 11 June 1778.—The music, which has not survived, was by François Hippolyte Barthélemon, but perhaps based on Mozart's. (Deryck Lynham, *The Chevalier Noverre* [London, 1950], pp. 102 and 170.)

On 24 December, before Joseph II and the Grand Duchess, a pianoforte contest was held at the Vienna Hofburg between Mozart and Muzio Clementi.

> The Emperor proposed a theme for the two composers, " which we had to vary, accompanying each other in turn " (Clementi). Mozart played, *inter alia*, variations, Clementi a sonata and a toccata. When he published these two pieces with Breitkopf & Härtel in 1804, in the " Cahier VI " of his " Œuvres complettes ", he prefixed this note (in French) to the sonata : " This Sonata, with the Toccata that follows, was played by the author before His Imperial Majesty Joseph II in 1781, Mozart being present." (Sonata II, pp. 20-32 ; Toccata, pp. 33-36.) The same note appeared in the Viennese edition of Clementi's Op. 41, T. Mollo & Comp. (beginning of 1804).—See 5 December 1782.

1782

FROM JOHANN NIKOLAUS FORKEL'S " MUSIKALISCHER ALMANACH
FÜR DEUTSCHLAND AUF DAS JAHR 1782 ", LEIPZIG

LIST

of Composers now living in Germany.

.   .   .   .   .

Mozart (J. G. Wolfgang), son of the preceding, musician at the Archiepiscopal
Chapel at Salzburg ; born—.*Six Sonatas pour le Clavecin, avec l'accompagnement d'un Violon. à Paris* 1767. (These sonatas were composed by
him in his ninth year.) *Two similar Sonatas.* London.—2 do. 6 do.
6 Trios. Amsterdam.

> P. 73.—This was the first year of the almanach, probably printed in 1781.—
> The works referred to are K. 6-9, 10-15, 301-6, and 26-31. In Paris four
> sonatas of the years 1762–64 appeared in 1764, and Wolfgang was described
> as seven years of age on the title-pages. In London not two but six sonatas
> of the " eight-year-old " Wolfgang were published. The Amsterdam edition
> too contained pianoforte-and-violin sonatas, as did the Vienna one. The total
> of 22 is correct.

On 1 January 1782 Johann Christian Bach died in London.

On 3 March 1782 Mozart held a concert at the (? Burg) Theatre, at which parts
of *Idomeneo* were given and Mozart himself played the D major pianoforte concerto
(K. 175), with the new rondo finale (K. 382), and improvised a fantasia.

> This was the first of the " Lent Concerts " Mozart gave in Vienna. The date,
> 23 January, given in Köchel-Einstein, p. 244, is wrong.—Mozart had already
> played extracts from *Idomeneo* at Countess Thun's in May 1781.—He included
> the improvised fantasy especially for the benefit of Clementi, his rival in this
> art, who soon afterwards left Vienna without having given the concert he had
> planned.

On 2 April Johann Böhm's company performed *La finta giardiniera* in German
(under the title *Sandrina, oder Die verstellte Gräfin*) at Frankfurt on Main.

> Such performances brought the authors no royalties ; they received only a
> lump sum for the first performance.—*Cf.* 13 January 1775.

On 12 April Pietro Metastasio died in Vienna.

CONSTANZE WEBER TO MARIA ANNA MOZART, VIENNA, 20 APRIL 1782

Most worthy and treasured Friend !

Never should I have been so bold as to abandon myself so frankly to the
urge and desire of writing to you, most worthy friend, had not your brother
assured me that you would not resent a step taken owing to the great
eagerness to converse at least in writing with a person who, though unknown,
is already highly valued by me through the name of Mozart.—Will you be
angry when I presume to tell you that I value and love you above all things,

without having the honour of knowing you personally, merely as the sister
of a brother so worthy of you—and venture to beg you for your friendship ?
—Without being presumptuous I may say that I half deserve it, wholly—I
shall endeavour to deserve it !—may I offer you mine in return (which I
have long ago secretly given to you in my heart) ?—Oh yes ! I hope so.—
and in this hope I remain

most worthy and treasured friend

your

most obedient servant

and friend

Constanze Weber

Pray kiss your Papa's hand for me :

> Salzburg, Mozarteum.—Schiedermair, Vol. IV, p. 379.—This letter was an
> enclosure in one from Mozart to his sister, written on the same day. He had
> already reported his engagement to Constanze to his unrelenting father, and
> was evidently hoping that Nannerl would help to win him over.

LEOPOLD MOZART TO BREITKOPF'S SON & CO.

Salzburg, 29 April 1782.

. . . My son is in Vienna and will remain there. At Herr *Artaria's* some
of his *clavier sonatas* have appeared. . . .

> Original in the Bonn University Library.—Schiedermair, Vol. IV, p. 290.—
> *Cf.* 10 August 1781.—The sonatas were K. 376, 296 and 377-80, published in
> November 1781.

On 7 May Mozart played the second act of *Die Entführung aus dem Serail* to Countess
Thun on the pianoforte.

> He had played through the greater part of the first act on 7 August 1781 (see
> 30 May 1782).

Early in the morning of 26 May Mozart took part in the first concert in the
Augarten ; a rehearsal had taken place the evening before. The C major symphony
(K. 338, see 3 April 1781) with the supplementary minuet (K. 409) was performed,
and Mozart again played the E♭ concerto for two pianofortes (K. 365) with Fräulein
Auernhammer (see 23 November 1781).

> The programme included a symphony by Gottfried van Swieten. The Arch-
> duke Maximilian and many members of the Viennese nobility attended the
> concert.—These concerts were from now on generally held during May in the
> refreshment pavilion of this imperial park, which Joseph II had opened to the
> public in 1775. The caterer was Ignaz Jahn, the organizer of the twelve sub-
> scription concerts Philipp Jakob Martin, who in summer was also allowed to
> arrange serenades on the Neue Markt (see 7 August 1782). This was the only
> occasion on which Mozart took part. The " admission card to the concert of
> W. A. Mozart " preserved in the Mozart Museum at Salzburg, probably refers
> not to this occasion, but to a subscription concert held at the Trattnerhof
> in the spring of 1784 or one in the " Mehlgrube " in 1785 (see 1 June 1782).

On 30 May Mozart played the third act of *Die Entführung* to Countess Thun.

Cf. 7 May.

FROM THE " WIENER ZEITUNG ", I JUNE 1782

Home Events.

. . . Our favourite place of recreation, the Augarten, whose daily increasing embellishment our Sovereign still proves by the best of arrangements to have much at heart, has acquired new value by the enterprise of two private persons. . . . Thus Herr Martin too has for the summer transplanted his Amateur Concert, recently established in the Mehlgrube in town, to the Augarten ; where we shall now have the pleasure every Sunday of admiring many a virtuoso and virtuosa, and of finding the most agreeable entertainment amid the best society, for a small outlay.

> The Mehlgrube (Flour-store) was a casino on the Mehlmarkt, also known as the Neue Markt, which had a hall used for lottery draws, balls and concerts.

On 3 June the first rehearsal for *Die Entführung* was held at the Burgtheater.

BURGTHEATER POSTER

New Singspiel.
The Imperial and Royal National Court Actors
will perform to-day, Tuesday, 16 July 1782 :
(for the first time)
DIE ENTFÜHRUNG AUS DEM SERAIL
A Play with Music in three Acts,
freely adapted from Bretzner and arranged for the I. & R. National Theatre.
Set to Music by Herr Mozart, Kapellmeister.
The Librettos may be had at the Box Office at 17 kr.
To begin at 6.30.

> Oskar Teuber, *Die Theater Wiens*, Vol. II/ii, Part i, p. 71 (facsimile).—After April 1782 the programmes (placards) of the Burgtheater showed the casts less frequently, and they were at last dropped altogether.—The cast was : Constanze—Caterina Cavalieri (later Aloisia Lange) ; Blonde—Therese Teyber ; Belmonte—Johann Valentin Adamberger (later Friedrich Karl Lippert) ; Pedrillo—Johann Ernst Dauer (alternating with Gottfried Heinrich Schmidt) ; Osmin—Ludwig Karl Fischer ; Bassa Selim (speaking part)—Dominik Jautz. —The adapter of the text, not named on the programme, was Gottlieb Stephnie.—Mozart's report on the first performance is unfortunately lost, but on 19 July he wrote to his father about the second. The first two performances brought in 1200 florins.—The work was repeated at both the Burg and Kärntnertor Theatres, according to the custom then prevailing. The dates during Mozart's lifetime were as follows : 1782 : 19, 26 and 30 July, 3, 6, 20 and 27 August, 6 and 20 September, 8 October and 10 December ; 1783 : 7 January, 4 and 16 February ; 1784 : 25 January, 1 February and 5 November; 1785 : 25, 27 and 30 November ; 1786 : 1 and 20 January, 2 February, 7 and 10 May, 21 July, 18 August, 9 and 21 November and 1 and 19 December ; 1787 : 9 January, 6 February, 8 June, 13 and 31 July, 26 August, 13 and 20 November and 14 December ; and lastly 4 February 1788. The performances of 1782-83

M.—7 *a*

were in the Burgtheater, the others in the Kärntnertor Theatre, except that of 21 July 1786.—During Mozart's lifetime this work was also his greatest stage success outside Vienna.

TITLE-PAGE OF THE LIBRETTO OF "DIE ENTFÜHRUNG"

DIE ENTFÜHRUNG AUS DEM SERAIL
A Singspiel
in three acts
freely arranged after Bretzner
for the I. & R. National Court Theatre.
Set to music
by
Herr Mozart.
Performed in the I. & R. National Court Theatre.
Vienna,
to be had of the Keeper of the Boxes, 1782.
Copy in the National Library, Vienna.

FROM THE ACCOUNT BOOKS OF THE COURT THEATRES

To Stephanie, jun., for adaptation of the Singspiel *Die Entführung aus dem Serail*   100.–
Expenses for composition and copying of music

.   .   .   .   .

To Tyron, Franz, *Kapellmeister*, for a band supplied from the Artillery for *Die drei Sultaninnen*   12.–
Item for do. for the opera *Die Entführung aus dem Serail*   32.–
Together, as No. 155   44.–
To Mozart, Wolfgang, for composition of the music for the opera *Die Entführung aus dem Serail* 100 Imperial Ducats, or as No. 166

426.40

Vienna, State Archives.—13th and 14th half-yearly accounts, 1782–83, pp. 52, 54, 56.—The lump sums paid to librettist and composer were the customary ones of the time.—Tyron was bandmaster of the 2nd Field Artillery Regiment. —*Soliman second, ou Les trois Sultanes*, a play with songs by Charles Simon Favart, after Marmontel, music by Paul César Gibert and others, had been given in French at the Burgtheater in 1765, in 1770 at the Kärntnertor Theatre and in 1776 at the Burgtheater in German. The oriental setting of both works required Turkish music ; it was provided by a military band.

On 20 July Count Karl Zichy called for Mozart and drove with him to Laxenburg Palace to present him to the Chancellor, Prince Wenzel Kaunitz-Rietberg.

The imperial summer residence lay to the south of Vienna—Count Zichy was Court Councillor of the Royal Hungarian Transylvanian Chancellery and the husband of the Countess Anna Maria, born Countess Khevenhüller-Metsch, another of Mozart's pupils.

On 23 July Mozart removed from the Graben to the house called the " Red Sabre " on the Hohe Brücke (*cf.* 10 January 1768).

On 29 July Johann Thorwart, Constanze Weber's guardian, applied to the Senior Court Marshal's office, the appropriate authority, for permission for her marriage with Mozart. The official consent, signed by Ferdinand von Fetzer, the secretary of the department, was made out shortly afterwards.

> The petition, in private possession first in Vienna and later in London, has been lost since about 1950.—Thorwart, " Inspector of Court Music and the Theatre Directorate ", was at one with Frau Weber in her desire to tie Mozart down.— As in the record of his marriage (4 August) he is here called Wolfgang Adam —evidently a mistake of Thorwart's.

On 29 July Siegmund Haffner the younger was ennobled with the title von Imbachhausen (Jenbachhausen).

> This Salzburg wholesale merchant, who was an exact contemporary of Mozart's but died even younger in 1787, was the son of the former burgomaster of the same name, who came from Imbach (Jenbach) in the Tyrol. The frivolous youth had developed into a public benefactor. For the celebration in Salzburg of his ennoblement Mozart wrote the D major symphony (K. 385). *Cf.* 21 July 1776.

FROM ZINZENDORF'S DIARY, 30 JULY 1782
(in French)

. . . To-night at the theatre *Die Entführung aus dem Serail*, an opera the music of which is pilfered from various others. *Fischer* acted well. Adam Berger is a statue. . . .

> See 9 October 1762.—Pohl, *Haydn*, Vol. II, p. 123 (where instead of " est une statue " we read " me depluit ").

MOZART'S MARRIAGE CONTRACT

In the name of the Most Holy Trinity, God the Father, Son, and Holy Ghost. Amen.

THIS DAY, the date given hereunder, between the *well and nobly born Herr Wolfgang Mozart*, Kapellmeister, bachelor, as *bridegroom* of the one part, and the *noble spinster Constantia Weber*, the legitimately begotten daughter of minor years of the *noble Herr Fridolin Weber*, I. & R. Court *Musicus*, deceased, and his still living consort in marriage, the *well and nobly born Frau Cecilia Weber*, as *bride* of the other part, in the presence of the witnesses bidden therefor, the following Marriage *Contract* has been agreed upon and concluded with gracious official *consent*, viz :

FIRSTLY the aforesaid spinster *Constantia* Weber has been promised to the suitor at his proper application pending priestly *confirmation*.

SECONDLY the said spinster *bride* assigns to her *bridegroom* five hundred *gulden*, which

THIRDLY the latter has promised to augment with one thousand *gulden*, in such wise that the dowry and the augmentation together amount to 1,500 fl., which sum to pass to the survivor.

FOURTHLY that whatever the *consorts* shall during their marriage jointly earn, inherit, acquire and rightfully gain for themselves by the rich blessing of God to constitute and be called their common property ; likewise both parties shall equally benefit from and have custody of any land they may receive.

FIFTHLY each party shall be entitled to increase the other's possessions by will, *codicil* or gift. Wherefore

FINALLY two identical *copies* of this marriage *contract* shall be drawn up, signed with their own hands by the *contractors*, the Mother, the Guardian and Witness (the last however without prejudice), and each shall be handed a copy. *Actum*. Vienna, 3 *Augusti* 1782.

Maria Costanza Weber as bride.	Wolfgang Amade Mozart as bridegroom.
Maria Caecilia Weber as bride's mother.	Franz Gilowsky De Urazowa *Magister Chirurgiae Et*
Johann Carl Cetto von Kronstorff I. & R. District Councillor for Lower Austria as witness invited thereto.	*Anatomiae.*
Johann Thorwart Auditor to the I. & R. Court Theatres, as guardian.	

Original in the Stefan Zweig Collection, London (deposited at the British Museum).—Jahn, Vol. II, p. 699 f. Facsimile in Schiedermair, *op. cit.*, Vol. 5, supplement.—Mozart's witness at the marriage was the son of the Salzburg Court Surgeon Wenzel Andreas Gilowsky, brother of the "Katherl" mentioned in the Mozart letters.—Of the seals on this document Mozart's is the only one without a coat of arms.—On the wedding-day the Baroness Waldstatten gave the bridal pair a "princely" supper (Mozart's letter to his father, 7 August 1782).

FROM THE MARRIAGE REGISTER OF THE PARISH OF ST. STEPHEN
VIENNA, 4 AUGUST 1782

The noble Herr Wolfgang Adam Mozart, a Kapellmeister, bachelor, native of Salzburg, legitimate son of Herr Leopold Mozart, Kapellmeister there, and Maria Anna, his late wife, born Bertl, *cons[ensum] ab exc[elsissimo] Regim[ine] tulit*, resident at present for 12 days on the Hohe Brücke, No. 387, formerly for 5 months in the Graben, and ere that for 1 year under the

Tuchlauben, at The Eye of God, altogether resident here for 16 months continuously, *ita testatus D[omi]nus tutor, et testis sp[on]sae.*

To the noble J. [*Jungfrau, Jungfer . .* spinster] Konstanzia Weber, born at Zell in Lower Austria, legit. daughter of the late Herr Fridolin Weber, I. & R. Court *Musicus,* and Cecilia, his wife, born Stam, *cons[ensum] tutor[ium] a judicio Mareschal aulico tulit,* resident for 2 years by St. Peter's at The Eye of God, No. 577, *ita testatur tutor, et testis.*

Testis sp[on]sae Herr Johann Thorwarth, I. & R. Court Auditor and Herr Johann Cetto von Cronstorf. I. & R. Lower Austrian Government Councillor, *et sp[on]si* Herr Franz Gilowsky, *Medicinae Doctor.*

[Marginal Note]
> *Dispensati in tribus denunc. [denunciationibus]*
> *Depos[ito] libert[atis] Juram[ento]*
> *Cop[ulavi]* 4 Aug : Wolff.

> Marriage register (" Copulationsbuch ") No. 74, fol. 270.—Cited by Jahn, Abert and Müller von Asow according to an extract made in 1847 ; reproduced with reasonable accuracy in Otto Schneider's *Mozart in Wirklichkeit* (Vienna, 1955), p. 214.—The Eye of God house was a " Durchhaus ", *i.e.* it gave on to two streets. The use of both its addresses, one for Mozart and one for Constanze, was probably intentional, though it happened fairly frequently that bridal couples came from the same house. Mozart had lived only about four months with Frau Weber, but almost eleven on the Graben. Constanze was born on 5 January 1762 at Zell im Wiesenthal, Breisgau, which was part of Lower (or Further) Austria. Mozart needed the consent of the Lower Austrian authorities because his place of residence did not come within the jurisdiction of the cathedral ; she, however, as a minor without living father, needed the consent of her guardian and his legal representatives, the Lord Chamberlain's office (*cf.* 29 July 1782). Exemption from the calling of banns, which the authorities also granted, was made use of only in urgent cases ; the couple then had to declare on oath that they knew of no impediment to the marriage.—Ferdinand Wolf was a curate.

On 6 August *Die Entführung* was repeated at Gluck's request.

> Gluck afterwards congratulated Mozart and invited him to dinner on the 8th. Gluck lived at this time in the Michaelerplatz (Inner City No. 3, demolished).

FROM THE " WIENER ZEITUNG ", 7 AUGUST 1782
Notice.

The undersigned, who had the good fortune of earning the gracious approbation of an esteemed and distinguished public by means of several serenades on the Neue Markt, rejoices in the honour of being able to inform everyone that most of his patrons and subscribers have decided to furnish him with a small monetary contribution for the continuation of these entertaining serenades ; on condition, however, that they should be able to listen to this music in closer proximity and greater comfort than heretofore. In pursuance of this the undersigned has provided a large, closed circle of stalls for the subscribers, and for those who still intend to subscribe, and has thus contrived every imaginable arrangement for their comfort. He flatters himself that he will thus increase ever further the favour and confidence of his patrons, and also maintain the same. The extra amount of the subscription is 1 fl. 20 kr., against which 4 grand serenades will be given during the month of August ; and on Sunday, 11 August, the new serenade by the undersigned, recently received with gracious applause, will be given at general request, while on the 18th, recently arranged for wind music, the newly composed opera by Herr Kapellmeister Mozart, entitled *Die Entführung aus dem Serail*, while the other music will be announced in due course. He therefore hopes for as large attendances as he has always had the happiness to enjoy. Subscriptions tickets are to be had before the serenade at the entrance to the circle, next to the lemonade stall, as also from me,

> P. J. Martin, Director of the Amateur Concert in Vienna, resident in the Mehlgrube, 1st floor.

Cf. 26 May and end of 1782.—In late July Mozart hurriedly arranged extracts from *Die Entführung* for wind instruments, to forestall anyone else (? Martin). But it is still uncertain whether he wrote these for Martin, whether he completed them, and whether his version is identical either with the manuscript one announced by Laurent Lausch on 10 July 1784 (for 2 oboes, 2 clarinets, 2 horns and 2 bassoons) or with that of which a copy was discovered in the Schwarzenberg archives at Český Krumlov [Krumau] in 1955 with 8 numbers from the opera (for 2 oboes, 2 cors anglais, 2 horns and 2 bassoons). (*Cf.* Franz Giegling in the programme-book of the fifth German Mozart Festival [Ludwigsburg, 1956], p. 71 and Ernst Fritz Schmid in the *Mozart-Jahrbuch 1956* [Salzburg, 1957], p. 41.)

In the autumn of 1782 Karl Wahr's company performed *Die Entführung* in Prague.

The date of this first performance outside Vienna is unknown. A libretto (" freely adapted from Bretzner ") was published in Prague in 1784. For Wahr *cf.* 31 May 1773. At this period the scores of operas were sold by the copyists attached to the theatres which gave the original production.

FROM THE " LITTERATUR- UND THEATER-ZEITUNG ", BERLIN,
5 OCTOBER 1782

Fragments from Viennese Letters.

. . . I must not forget an opera by Kapellmeister Mozart, *Die Entführung aus dem Serail*. It has an extraordinary amount of happily inspired song, and was very prettily performed. It is a pity that so much diligence should not have been employed on a better product, and as Herr Brezner's work, such as it lay to hand, was useless to the composer, the adapter would have done better to manipulate *Adelheit von Veltheim*, which in every respect except for the musical part is an excellent opera. But then a better adapter would also have been desirable, poetically and morally speaking ; what do you say, for instance, to the way in which the servant addresses the soubrette :

> Did not Osmin perchance
> Exert a master's will
> And make thee do his drill ?

It is said that the adapter is Herr Stephanie, the Younger ; I do not believe it, for he is a member of the board !

> Cf. 4 October 1780.—The two Stephanie brothers were among the five " inspectors " (i.e. stage-managers) of the Burgtheater.

On 8 October Mozart conducted *Die Entführung* at the Burgtheater in honour of Grand-Duke Paul and his consort.

> Cf. 25 November 1781.—The couple stayed in Vienna until 18 October under the assumed name of Count and Countess du Nord.

On 3 November Mozart took part in a concert held by Fräulein Auernhammer at the Kärntnertor Theatre.

> The programme of this concert is unknown.

On 13 November Mozart postponed the journey to Salzburg planned for the celebration of his father's name-day, the 15th.

> Not until the summer of 1783 was he able to introduce his wife to his father and sister.

In December Mozart removed to another apartment at the Hohe Brücke, No. 412 (now Wipplingerstrasse 14), 3rd floor ; his landlord was Raimund Wetzlar, Baron Plankenstern, and the house was known as the Little Herberstein House.

> The couple occupied two rooms there, with an ante-room and a kitchen.

FROM ZINZENDORF'S DIARY, 5 DECEMBER 1782

(in French)

[At Countess von Pergen's.]

I remained until about 9 o'clock, having been unable to leave because of the arrival of the Emperor, who talked endlessly about music, and the contest between Mozhardt and Clementi.

> See 24 December 1781.—Ernst Benedikt, *Kaiser Joseph II* (Vienna, 1936), p. 348 (in German).—The Countess was presumably Philippine Gabriele, wife of Count Johann B. Anton Pergen, President of the Lower Austrian Government.

FROM THE " KURFÜRSTLICHE MAINZISCHE GNÄDIGST PRIVILEGIERTE ANZEIGEN ", 9 DECEMBER 1782

At the Court music engraver's, Herr Schott, resident in the Kapuzinergasse, are for sale all the latest Viennese musical works, viz. . . . Sonatas by Mozard, Hayden, . . .

Communicated by Dr. Adam Gottron, Mainz.—The firm of Bernhard Schott had been founded about 1770.

FROM ZINZENDORF'S DIARY, 14 DECEMBER 1782
(in French)

In the evening at Mme von Thun's, where Mozhard played.

This was in the drawing-room of Countess Wilhelmine Thun.

FROM THE " WIENER ZEITUNG ", 21 DECEMBER 1782
Announcement.

Johann Traeg, at the Pilate House, 1st floor, has the honour of announcing new manuscript music to the highly to-be-honoured public, namely : Symphonies by Mozart, . . . etc. . . . Concertos for clavier by Haydn, Mozart. . . .

Traeg retailed music in manuscript copies, parts in this case.

FROM BENEDIKT SCHWARZ'S PAMPHLET " UIBER DAS WIENER DILEKTANTEN-KONZERT ", VIENNA, 1782

When last winter I attended the Vienna Dilettante Concert . . . Frl. von Aurenhammer, a great dilettante on the pianoforte, Frl Desideria von Pauler, and Mlles Weber and Berger, who as dilettantes of singing raise much hope, were magnanimous enough to open the delights of the local Dilettante Concerts, and were honoured with the warmest and most heartfelt gratitude by the society. . . .

Herr Mozart, Kapellmeister, one of the greatest virtuosi in Europe, obliged the society no less, since at his incomparable pianoforte he several time caused us to feel the sweetest enchantment and the admiration due to him for his brilliant performance.

Schwarz was a Viennese musician (1750–95). The passages quoted above are to be found on pp. 7 and 8 of his pamphlet (copy in the City Library, Vienna).— The organizer of these " amateurs' concerts " was P. J. Martin (see 26 May and 7 August 1782). For this purpose he had had a special podium erected in the tavern " Zur Mehlgrube ".—Among the violinists occurs the name " v. Hering ", *i.e.* Johann Baptist von Häring (*cf.* 9 April 1790). The Fräulein Weber mentioned above must have been one of Aloisia Lange's sisters, but hardly Constanze. Fräulein Berger is mentioned in Mozart's letter of 25 May 1782.—The concerts took place on Fridays from 6.30 to 8.30.—*Cf.* Hanslick, *Geschichte des Concertwesens in Wien* (Vienna, 1869), p. 69, and Robert Haas in the *Festschrift Alfred Orel* (Vienna, 1960), pp. 77-80.

FROM JOHANN FRIEDRICH SCHINK'S " DRAMATURGISCHE FRAGMENTE ",
GRAZ, 1782

Entführung aus dem Serail
comic opera
in three acts, by Brezner,
the music by Mozard.

Brezner's comic operas are on the whole among our better plays of this
kind, and next to the admirable gifts bestowed on our comic-lyric theatre
by Weise, Engel and Götter, unquestionably our most considerable possession
in this category. At least they lack neither fancy nor entertainment, nor light
dialogue and pleasing song. His *Entführung aus dem Serail*, however,
happens to be the most inept of his lyric pieces. It is much inferior to Grossmann's opera on a similar subject,* for all that this opera of Grossmann's is
not worth a quarter of the fanfares which its author has blown with such
exemplary modesty in his announcement of it. Herr Brezner seems to me
to have unnecessarily stretched his theme over three acts. What is more, his
characters are here deficient in attraction and vitality. Belmont's and Julia's
tenderness is very much apt to become tedious, while wit and humour
limp along pretty feebly.

The improvements that have been made in it are not of the best either.
What pleases me least is the alteration of Brezner's catastrophe. In Brezner
the Bashaw forgives Belmont because he recognizes in him his son ; but
in the Viennese improvement he does so because it is a far greater thing to
forgive an enemy than to take revenge : a motive which is indeed more
noble, but also—as is ever the case with such exaltations—incomparably less
natural. The worst of it is that by this improvement Brezner's reason for
making a renegade of the Bashaw is entirely removed and the alteration made
even more absurd thereby.

Altogether these eternal magnanimities are a loathsome thing, and no
longer the fashion upon any stage except our own. Yet one may count
almost with certainty on a raging success for a piece in which there is plenty
of magnanimizing, bestowing, reconciling and forgiving, even if such results
are arrived at in the most unnatural way.

This taste benefits the poet's purse, of course, but art correspondingly
less ; and the people's education suffers the greatest loss.

The stage has clearly the most evident influence on this education. If
taste is wrongly formed in this direction, it is vitiated thereby, so that the
endeavours of the best of authors go for nothing. The drama has a greater
effect as a living influence than any books ; and those who come to literature
with a taste already corrupted will receive no impression from even the most
tasteful of books. And this is quite natural : how am I to recognize truth
and nature if I have no feeling for truth and nature ?

* *Adelheit von Veltheim.*

Thus true art too is led to ruin. Its great object, to instruct, to make people wiser and better, to hold up a mirror to human nature and to show the morals of every age in their true shape, is thus entirely nullified. In place of a picture of life we are given tales of adventure which are of no service but to teach us to admire false greatness and, despite all these examples of adventure and magnanimity, to keep us from acquiring so much as a glimmer of magnanimity above that which we already possess, since all these magnanimities are too unnatural for us to emulate.

Indigenous morality and the formation of national character are thus undone by such plays. We are and we remain un-German, and shall never become anything but the eternal apes of other nations, the eternal reproach of foreigners, the eternal object of their scorn.

Truly, it is irksome to witness this and very hard to refrain from giving vent to one's irritation. However, one grows tired at last of quarrelling about one and the same thing. So let us return to Brezner.

Die Entführung aus dem Serail has been received with very notable applause in Vienna. Applause it owes not to itself, but to the excellent music of Herr Mozard and the very good performance by the singers of the National Theatre.

I am no real connoisseur of music ; of the true artistic rules of composition I have no understanding whatever ; I do not even know the notes. I judge music merely by the general principles of all the fine arts, by the principles of truth and nature. Music which affects the human heart and the human passions, which stirs joy, sorrow and in short every kind of sentiment, which is something more than ear-tickling, namely nourishment for the soul : such music has excellence in my eyes and is the undeniable product of musical genius. Judged by these principles, then, Herr Mozard's music has my entire approval, and I confess with pleasure that Benda and Gluk alone are capable of touching and moving my heart more strongly than Herr Mozard has done with his lovely music.

I cannot praise this still youthful artist's work in detail ; for that I am too little of a true musical expert. I can only say that his declamation is correct, his song uncommonly eloquent as the language of the heart and of nature, and that he shows altogether the right ideas of the true purpose of the most beautiful of all the human arts.

The singers of the national stage here deserve praise for having felt what they sang ; for having put their whole soul into what Mozard wrote ; their song too came from the heart ; they did not merely gurgle, but spoke ; and I am convinced that Mozart's work will not be so perfectly felt and represented on any German stage as it has been on our national stage here.

It is therefore no wonder, either, that, in spite of all the defects with which it has been saddled by the poet and by the unwise alterations, this *Entführung aus dem Serail* should have been received with general approbation, and continues to be received with this general approbation. If composer and singers thus work with combined forces at the fulfilment of the true purpose of music, our hearts too must needs be interested thereby ; and where art interests our hearts, its impression will also be durable and lasting. . . .

Vol. IV, Part ii, pp. 1001-25.—Schink, born at Magdeburg in 1755, had lived in Vienna in 1780 and from 1782 at Graz. He was an opponent of Schikaneder and made use of an orthography peculiar to himself. His notice of Mozart's singspiel related, of course, to the Vienna performance.—The librettists mentioned at the beginning are Christian Felix Weisse, Johann Jakob Engel and Friedrich Wilhelm Gotter.—For Grossmann cf. 4 October 1780.—Interesting and imaginative as Schink's essay on librettos and operas is, only the introduction, which is concerned with Die Entführung itself, can be given here.

BRETZNER'S PROTEST, 1782

A certain individual, Mozart by name, in Vienna has had the audacity to misuse my drama Belmonte und Constanze for an opera text. I herewith protest most solemnly against this infringement of my rights, and reserve the right to take the matter further.

Christoph Friedrich Bretzner,
Author of Das Räuschgen.

The date of this protest has so far remained unknown. It did not appear in the Leipziger Zeitungen as it was first quoted in C. von Wurzbach's Biographisches Lexikon des Kaiserthums Österreich (Vienna, 1868), Vol. XIX, p. 284.—Das Räuschchen was a comedy, not printed till 1786. In 1787 Bretzner published anonymously the novel Das Leben eines Lüderlichen in which Mozart's Figaro is repeatedly mentioned and one of Cherubino's two arias is quoted (Aloys Greither, Die sieben grossen Opern Mozarts [Heidelberg, 1956], p. 86). Bretzner translated Così fan tutte for Leipzig in 1794, and in the preface to his frequently performed Weibertreue, oder Die Mädchen sind von Flandern the "charming and altogether admirable music of this masterpiece by the immortal Mozart" is praised.—Cf. 4 October 1780 and 21 June 1783.

1783

FROM FORKEL'S " MUSIKALISCHER ALMANACH FÜR DEUTSCHLAND AUF DAS JAHR 1783 ", LEIPZIG

Supplement to the List of Composers now living in Germany

Mozart (J. G. Wolfgang) at Salzburg. Nothing new.

P. 52.—See beginning of 1782.

On 4 January Mozart played in a concert held by Councillor Anton von Spielmann.

Spielmann, a friend of van Swieten's, was in the Court and State Chancery and was thus one of the closest colleagues of the Chancellor of State, Prince Kaunitz. He lived in the Herrengasse, Inner City No. 22, a government building.

On 11 January 1783 Aloisia Lange sang the scena and rondo " Mia speranza adorata —Ah, non sai, qual pena " (K. 416) at a concert in the " Mehlgrube ".

> Mozart wrote this aria for his sister-in-law and finished it on 8 January. The concert was doubtless one of those arranged by Martin (cf. 26 May 1782).

In mid-January Mozart organized a private ball at his lodgings.

> Wetzlar, who took part, had placed empty rooms at the disposal of the partici- pants, among whom were also Dr. Gilowsky and the Adambergers, the Langes and the Stephanies. Each of the " chapeaus " (Gentlemen) contributed 2 gulden. It lasted from six in the evening until seven the next morning.

FROM THE "WIENER ZEITUNG", 15 JANUARY 1783

Musical Announcement.

Herr Kapellmeister Mozart herewith apprizes the highly honoured public of the publication of three new, recently finished pianoforte concertos. These 3 concertos, which may be performed either with a large orchestra with wind instruments or merely *a quattro*, viz. with 2 violins, 1 viola and violoncello, will not appear until the beginning of April of this year, and will be issued (finely copied and supervised by himself) only to those who have subscribed thereto. The present serves to give the further news that subscription tickets may be had of him for four ducats, counting from the 20th of this month until the end of March. His dwelling is on the Hohe Brücke in the Little Herberstein House, No. 437, third floor.

> This announcement may be connected with that of Traeg on 21 December 1782, but the works concerned here were the new concertos in F major, A major and C major (K. 413-15). The subscription was evidently unsuccessful, nor has any of these copies been preserved (*cf.* 27 September 1783). On 26 April Mozart offered these three concertos to the Paris publisher Sieber for 30 *louis d'or*, but they were eventually published by Artaria & Co. in Vienna early in 1785.

FROM KARL FRIEDRICH CRAMER'S " MAGAZIN DER MUSIK ", HAMBURG, 15 JANUARY 1783

Reviews, Announcements, Advertisements.

Mozart, W. A. 1 Clav[ier] Divertim[ento]. with 1 Violin & Violon- cel[lo]. Op. 3. Paris   2 mks. 8 sch.

Mozart, W. A. 3 Clav[ier] Son[atas]. Op. 4, *ibid.* [Paris] 4 mks. 4 sch.

> Vol. I, pp. 118 and 126.—Op. III was the divertimento (pianoforte trio) in B♭ major (K. 254), Op. IV the three pianoforte sonatas in C major, A minor and D major (K. 309-11), all engraved and published by Mme Gertrude Heina in Paris (*c.* 1782 and 1778). *Cf.* 4 July 1778.

In February Mozart temporarily removed to the Kohlmarkt, No. 1179 in the Inner City (now Kohlmarkt 7).

Wetzlar, who required the lodgings in the Wipplingerstrasse, paid the expenses of the removal and the rent of the emergency quarters. Mozart was already in debt at that time.

FROM CRAMER'S " MAGAZIN DER MUSIK ", HAMBURG, 2 MARCH 1783

Information from the Cologne Electoral Hofcapelle at Bonn
Louis van Beethoven

. . . This young genius deserves support to enable him to travel. He would be sure to become a second Wolfgang Amadeus Mozart, if he progressed as he has begun.

Christian Gottlieb Neefe.

Vol. I, p. 394 f.—A. W. Thayer, *Beethoven* (Leipzig, 1917), Vol. I, 3rd ed., p. 150. This was the first printed report on Beethoven. Neefe was his first teacher.

On Carnival Monday, 3 March, Mozart and his friends performed in the Assembly Room of the Hofburg a " Masquerade "—a pantomime with music (K. 446) devised by himself. It was presented during the half-hour's interval in the public masked ball.

The cast was the following : Columbine—Aloisia Lange ; Harlequin—Mozart ; Pierrot—Joseph Lange ; Pantaloon—the dancing-master " Merk " (? the French dancer Louis Mergery) : Doctor—the painter Josef Grassi.—The dancing-master had rehearsed the pantomime. The programme, distributed by a masquer dressed as a " Rattle-Postman " (*Klepperpost*), with doggerel verses written by the Burgtheater actor Johann Heinrich Friedrich Müller, has not come down to us. (The *Klepperpost*, or more correctly *Klapperpost*, got its name from the rattles or clappers with which the messengers who delivered local letters were provided.)

On 11 March Mozart took part in Aloisia Lange's concert at the Burgtheater : The Paris symphony in D major (K. 297) was given ; Mozart played the C major pianoforte concerto (K. 415) and gave two performances of the concerto-rondo in D major (K. 382) ; and Aloisia sang the recitative and aria " Alcandro, lo confesso—Non so d' onde viene " (K. 294).

On the symphony *cf.* 18 June 1778 and 14 May 1780 ; on the concerto *cf.* 23 and 30 March 1783 ; on the rondo (the new finale for the D major concerto, K. 175) *cf.* 30 March 1783 ; on the aria *cf.* 12 March 1778.—Gluck, who sat in the box next to that shared by Lange and Mozart's wife, praised the symphony and the aria, and invited the Mozarts and the Langes to dinner for the following Sunday, the 16th.—Lange painted Mozart's portrait in 1783.

On 12 March Mozart played at Count (? Johann) Esterházy's.

On 16 March the Mozarts and the Langes took lunch with Gluck.

Cf. 6 (8) August 1782.

On Sunday 23 March Mozart's grand concert took place at the Burgtheater in the presence of the Emperor. The orchestra played the Concertante (No. 3) from the serenade in D (K. 320) and the new version of the Haffner symphony (K. 385); Mozart himself performed the D major pianoforte concerto (K. 175) with the new rondo finale (K. 382) and the C major concerto (K. 415), as well as, improvised, the Paisiello and Gluck variations (K. 398 and 455) and a small fugue. Therese Teyber sang Giunia's aria (No. 16) from *Lucio Silla*, "Parto, m' affretto", Aloisia Lange Ilia's aria (No. 11) from *Idomeneo*, " Se il padre perdei " and the recitative and rondo (K. 416); and Johann Valentin Adamberger the scena and aria " Misera, dove son ! —Ah ! non son' io che parlo " (K. 369), originally written for soprano.

> See 9 May 1783. The finale of the Haffner symphony was played separately at the end of the concert.

FROM CRAMER'S " MAGAZIN DER MUSIK ", HAMBURG, 27 MARCH 1783

Vienna. December 1782. *Die Entführung aus dem Serail* appeared here this year ; the music for this opera has been made by Herr *Mozart* the younger. It is full of beauties, which we intend to dissect another time at a better opportunity. It surpassed the public's expectation, and the author's taste and new ideas, which were entrancing, received the loudest and most general applause.

> Vol. I, p. 352.

On 30 March, at Therese Teyber's concert at the Burgtheater, Mozart played the pianoforte concerto in C major (K. 415) and a free fantasia.

> Joseph II was again present.

On 3 April Mozart entrusted portraits of himself and Constanze to Councillor Johann Baptist Anton von Daubrawa and Dr Franz Wenzel von Gilowsky ; they took them to Salzburg and gave them to Leopold Mozart on the 6th.

> These were evidently the portraits by Lange, probably in smaller copies.

FROM CRAMER'S " MAGAZIN DER MUSIK ", HABMURG, 4 APRIL 1783

Six Sonatas pour le Clavecin, ou Piano Forte avec l'accompagnement d'un Violon par Wolfg. Amadei Mozart. Œuvre II. chèz Artaria Comp. à Vienne.

These sonatas are unique in their kind. Rich in new ideas and traces of their author's great musical genius. Very brilliant, and suited to the instrument. At the same time the violin accompaniment is so ingeniously combined with the clavier part that both instruments are constantly kept in equal prominence ; so that these sonatas call for as skilled a violinist as a clavier player. However, it is impossible to give a full description of this original work. Amateurs and connoisseurs should first play them through for themselves, and they will then perceive that we have in no way exaggerated.

N. N.

> Vol. I, p. 485.—The sonatas are K. 376, 296, 377-80.

On 13 April Mozart's Litany K. 243 was again sung in Salzburg Cathedral.

> From leaves of Nannerl's diary preserved in the Royal Archives at The Hague. —As at the first performance (31 March 1776) and the repeat in April 1778 the litanies by Adlgasser, Michael Haydn and Mozart (then all new) were sung on successive days.

On 24 April Mozart removed from the Kohlmarkt to the Judenplatz, No. 244 in the Inner City (now Judenplatz 3), 1st floor.

In May and June Mozart was ill.

In May, parts of Holzbauer's Miserere were again performed in Paris (cf. April 1778), probably in Mozart's arrangement (K. App. 1).

> According to the *Mercure de France*, discovered by Dr. Robert Münster (cf. *Mozart-Jahrbuch 1959* [Salzburg, 1960], p. 242 f.).—An inexact extract in German from this report appeared in 1783 in Cramer's *Magazin der Musik*, Vol. I, pp. 834 ff.

On 8 May *Die Entführung* was performed in German in Warsaw.

> Cf. 25 November 1783.

FROM CRAMER'S " MAGAZIN DER MUSIK ", HAMBURG, 9 MAY 1783

Vienna, 22 March 1783. . . . To-night the famous Herr Chevalier *Mozart* held a musical concert in the National Theatre, at which pieces of his already highly admired composition were performed. The concert was honoured with an exceptionally large concourse, and the two new concertos and other fantasies which Herr M. played on the fortepiano were received with the loudest applause. Our Monarch, who, against his habit, attended the whole of the concert, as well as the entire audience, accorded him such unanimous applause as has never been heard of here. The receipts of the concert are estimated to amount to 1,600 gulden in all.

> Vol. I, p. 578 f.—Jahn, Vol. I, p. 817.—The date of the correspondence from Vienna should have been 23 March.—The Emperor had sent 25 ducats.

FROM THE " WIENER ZEITUNG ", 24 MAY 1783
Of Artaria and Company,

Dealers in Copper Engravings, Maps and Music in Vienna, are to be had : . . . W. A. Mozart, 2 Sonatas for four hands on one Clavier, *Opera* III
2 fl.

> They were the sonatas in D major and B♭ major (K. 381 and 358).

On 17 June Mozart's first child, Raimund Leopold, was born.

> His godfather was Raimund von Wetzlar, the Baron's eldest son ; but Philipp Martin appeared for him by proxy in the Church Am Hof.—See 19 August 1783 (Emil Karl Blümml, " Mozarts Kinder " in his book *Aus Mozarts Freundes- und Familienkreis* [Vienna, 1923]).

FROM THE " LITTERATUR-UND THEATER-ZEITUNG ", BERLIN, 21 JUNE 1783
Information.

An unnamed person in Vienna has been pleased to adapt my opera, *Belmont und Constanze*, for the I. & R. National Theatre, and to have the

piece printed in this altered shape. The changes in the dialogue being in-
considerable, I ignore this altogether ; but the adapter has at the same time
interpolated a mass of songs in which occur truly heartbreaking and edifying
verselets. I should not like to deprive the improver of the fame due to his
work, and I therefore find myself under the necessity to specify here the
songs interpolated by him according to the Viennese edition and Mozart's
composition :

Interpolations as follows :

Belmont's first aria : Hier soll ich dich dann sehen, etc.
The duet for Belmont and Osmin, p. 5 : Verwünscht seyst du, etc.
Osmin's aria, p. 9 : Solche hergelaufene Laffen, etc.
Osmin's duet, p. 25 : Ich gehe, doch rathe ich dir, etc.
Osmin's recitative, p. 27 ; up to the beginning of the aria.
Constanze's aria, p. 30 : Martern aller Arten, etc.
Blonde's aria, p. 34 : Welche Wonne, welche Lust !, etc.
Belmont's aria, p. 41 : Wenn der Freude, etc.
The quartet and finale, pp. 42-46.
Belmont's aria, p. 49 : Ich baue ganz auf, etc.
Osmin's aria, p. 57 : O wie will ich triumphiren !
The recitative and duet, p. 61 : Welch Geschick, etc.
The whole finale, p. 65 to the end.

To finish with, a sample of the improver's work from the quartet, p. 43.

Pedrillo : But Blonde, woe ! The ladder !
    Wilt thou be worth as much ?
   (*shows that he will risk being hanged.*)

Blonde : Jack Pudding ! Art thou mad ?
    Forsooth, thou hadst done better
    To turn the question round.

Pedr. : But Osmin, Sir . . .

Blon. : Let's hear it !

Constanze : Wilt thou then not explain it ?

Belmonte :   Pedrillo :

      (*simultaneously*)

I will, but do not grieve.   Did not Osmin perchance,
A rumour some believe,   ('Twere easy to believe)
I trembling ask if true   Exert a master's will
The Bashaw's loved by you,   And make thee do his drill ?
His favours you receive ?   I'd no such bargain make.
   Constanze (*weeping*)   Blonde (*boxing his ears*)
Oh, how you make me grieve !   To that my answer take.

Pedr. : Now know I how we stand.

Bel. : Constanza, oh, forgive !

Blon. : Thou art not worth my hand

Con. : For you alone I live.

Blon. : The rascal dares to ask
　　　　If I to him were true.

Con. : The Bashaw's love I had,
　　　　Belmonte thought he knew.

Pedr. : My Blonde's honesty
　　　　I'll swear to, out and out.

Bel. : Constanza's true to me,
　　　　Of that there is no doubt ! &c.

That is what I call improvement!

Leipzig, 27 April 1783.　　　　　　　　　　　　　C. F. Bretzner.

> Part i, No. 25, pp. 398-400.—Jahn, Vol. I, p. 754 (incomplete).—The unnamed
> person was Gottlieb Stephanie.—Bretzner's protest against Mozart may have
> appeared at Leipzig as early as 1782 (*Cf.* end of 1782).

FROM THE LIBRETTO OF PASQUALE ANFOSSI'S OPERA " IL CURIOSO
INDISCRETO ", VIENNA, 30 JUNE 1783
(first part in Italian)

Notice.

The two arias on p. 36 and on p. 102 have been set to music by Signor
maestro Mozart to oblige Signora Lange, those written by Signor maestro
Anfossi not being commensurate with her ability, but meant for someone
else. This must be notified, so that honour should be accorded where it is
due, and this without prejudice to the reputation and fame of the already
well-known Neapolitan.

Notice.

The music of the two arias by Herr Anfosi, viz. pp. 36 and 102, having
been written for someone else, and not being suited to the eminent abilities
of Mme Lange, Mr. Mozztzrt furnished new music for them to oblige the
said Mme Lange. This is herewith made known to all, in order that honour
should be done to whom it is due, without in any way doing harm to the
fame of the already sufficiently well-known Neapolitan.

> A copy of the bilingual libretto is in the National Library in Vienna. The
> Italian version is on p. 142, the German one opposite. Mozart wrote three
> additional arias for this performance at the Burgtheater (K. 418-20), two
> for Aloisia Lange and one for Adamberger. The second soprano aria had to
> be repeated, but the tenor aria was not sung at all—according to Mozart's
> report to his father " through a trick of Salieri's "—nor does it even appear in
> the printed libretto. The words of the two soprano arias appear there on pp.
> 36 and 102, the second erroneously assigned to the Count instead of Clorinda.
> Both singers were appearing for the first time at the Italian Opera.

Continuation of Information about the Theatre in Vienna.

. . . On the 30th [June] *Il curioso indiscreto.* For the first time. Mme Lange sang at the Italian Opera for the first time today, and the public showed, in the face of every intrigue, how much it values her talent. . . .

> Part i, No. 35, p. 559.

In June *Die Entführung* was performed at Bonn.

> The day is not known.

At the end of July Mozart went to Salzburg with his wife to introduce her to his father and sister.

> They arrived before the 29th. The visit was originally planned for the previous autumn (see 11 November 1782). Mozart had not been in his home town since 5 November 1780. As the family were together for the next three months (for the last time), we know none of the particulars about this period, which might otherwise have been preserved in their letters. Some compensation is provided by the excerpts published by W. Hummel in *Nannerl Mozarts Tagebuchblätter*, pp. 87 f. and 99 f.

On 2 August *Die Entführung* was given at Frankfurt on Main, with Aloisia Lange making a guest appearance as Constanze.

On 19 August Mozart's son, Raimund, died of intestinal cramp [" Gedärmfrais "]

> The child was not at Frau Weber's, but with a fostermother in the Neustift suburb, No. 250 (now Lerchenfeldstrasse 65, Vienna VII). It is possible that the parents knew nothing of the child's death until their return to Vienna in the autumn.

Report on the Performances of Bondini's Company of Actors at Leipzig, Michaelmas 1783.

.   .   .   .   .

Die Entführung aus dem Serail, a comic opera in three acts by Herr Bretzner, with the music of Herr Mozart, which to my mind is too artificial.

> Part i, No. 45, p. 717.—The first Leipzig performance took place on 25 September. Pasquale Bondini, whom we shall meet again in Prague, was the director of a travelling company.—The Michaelmas trade fair was held at the end of September.

New Music.

At Johann Traeg's in the Vinegar-maker's House, No. 654, first floor, new manuscript music is again to be had, viz. the 3 latest pianoforte concertos by Mozart, at 10 fl.

Probably the concertos K. 413-15, the parts of which Mozart had himself wished to sell by subscription (see 15 January 1783).

On 27 and 28 September Maria Theresia Paradies and Leopold Mozart called upon one another in Salzburg.

The blind pianist from Vienna was on a European concert tour with her mother.

On 26 October Mozart performed his C minor mass (K. 427) in the Church of St. Peter's abbey in Salzburg, with Constanze as one of the two soprano soloists.

Mozart had vowed before his wedding to celebrate his marriage in this way, and perhaps also the reunion with his placated father. The mass was not quite ready for the occasion and was never completed. A rehearsal for the performance had been held on the 23rd at the Kapellhaus near by. Mozart was especially familiar with St. Peter's through Fr. Dominikus Hagenauer (see 5 January 1769). A fragmentary diary of Nannerl's, offered by Gabriel Charavay of Paris in 1881 and now in the Royal Archives at The Hague, notes that the mass was performed at the Sunday mass on the 25th (actually 26th) by the Hofmusik. The dates hitherto given for the rehearsal and performance, respectively 23 and 25 August, appear to stem from faulty readings of Nissen's. *Cf.* O. E. Deutsch in *Acta Mozartiana* (Augsburg, 1957), Vol. I, and Walter Hummel in *Nannerl Mozarts Tagebuchblätter* (Salzburg, 1958), p. 126 f.—See *Davidde penitente*, under 13 March 1785.

On 27 October Mozart and Constanze left Salzburg at 9.30 a.m. and travelled by way of Vöcklabruck, Lambach (28th, a.m.) and Ebelsberg (29th) to Linz, where they stayed for three weeks as the guests of " old " Count Thun on the Minoritenplatz (now Altstadt 17 and Klostergasse 20).

Johann Joseph Anton, Count Thun, the father of Count Franz Joseph in Vienna, was the senior member of the Thun-Hohenstein family ; he lived alternately at Linz and Prague. The Mozarts had known him for a long time.

FROM CRAMER'S " MAGAZIN DER MUSIK ", HAMBURG, 30 OCTOBER 1783

Extracts from Letters, News, Deaths.

Prague, August 1783. . . . The operas performed here since Easter at the Count's National Theatre are the following :

The younger Mozart's *Die Entführung aus dem Serail*, which received exceptional applause.

Vol. I, p. 999 f.—*Die Entführung* had been given in Prague since the autumn of 1782. Count Nostitz's theatre. later called the Estates Theatre and now known as the Tyl Theatre, was opened in 1783. Franz Anton, Count Nostiz-Rieneck, was supreme Burgrave, *i.e.* governor, of Bohemia.

On 4 November Mozart gave a concert in the theatre at Linz, performing his new symphony in C major (K. 425).

Mozart's introduction to a symphony by Michael Haydn (K. 444) was written at Linz for Count Thun, the dedicatee of the Linz symphony, but the programme of this concert in the theatre has not been established.

At Count Thun's house on 13 November Mozart drew an *Ecce homo* for Constanze.

Constanze mentioned this (a single sheet of paper) in a letter to Breitkopf & Härtel of 21 July 1800, but it has not survived.

On 25 November 1783 *Die Entführung* was performed in Polish in Warsaw.

Cf. 8 May 1783.

At the end of November Mozart returned to Vienna with his wife.

FROM THE POSTER OF A CONCERT AT THE BURGTHEATER
(in German and Italian)

Today, Monday, 22 December 1783,
at the I. & R. National Court Theatre,
will be held
for the benefit of the newly established Society of Musicians,
A GRAND MUSICAL CONCERT
consisting of the following items :

.   .   .   .   .

5) Concerto on the Fortepiano played by Herr *Mozart*.

.   .   .   .   .

7) A new Rondeaux composed by Herr *Mozart*,
sung by Herr *Adamberger*.

.   .   .   .   .

To begin at 7 o'clock.

Copy in the possession of the Gesellschaft der Musikfreunde, Vienna.—Although Mozart did not appear when the concert was repeated on the 23rd, Adamberger again sang the rondo. This was probably the recitative " Misero ! o sogno ! " and the aria " Aura, che intorno " (K. 431).

1784

FROM FORKEL'S " MUSIKALISCHER ALMANACH FÜR DEUTSCHLAND
AUF DAS JAHR 1784 ", LEIPZIG

List of Composers now living in Germany

Mozart (J. J. Wolfgang), son of the preceding, Concertmeister of the Archiepiscopal Chapel of Salzburg, which post he has now relinquished again, however, to be able to travel more freely : born at Augsburg, 1759. His father travelled with him in the years 1769–70, when he was but 9 years of age, together with a sister aged 11, through Germany, France and England, and thereby not only afforded him the best opportunity to develop his rare musical talents, but also to make himself known in the world at the same time. This family at that time earned so much applause and honour on this journey that in Paris the father and the children were engraved in copper in the actual performance of a concert. He is said to be now living in Vienna. *Six Sonatas pour le Clavecin, avec accomp. d'un Violon*, Paris, 1767. (These sonatas he composed in his ninth year.) *2 similar Sonatas*, London. *2 similar, 6 similar, 6 Trios*, Amsterdam. *Airs variès pour le Clavecin*. In the year 1782 he composed an opera in Vienna, *Die Entführung aus dem Serail*, which received general approbation.

> P. 104.—The dates given here are mostly wrong.—The group portrait is that by Carmontelle, engraved by Delafosse.—The printed works were already mentioned in the almanach for 1782, with the exception of the variations ; these were evidently K. 179, 180 and 354, which had been published by Heina of Paris in 1778.

FROM THE " WIENER ZEITUNG ", 14 JANUARY 1784

Music.

Johann Traeg again has the honour of announcing for connoisseurs and amateurs :

.   .   .   .   .   .

4)   Various Variations for clavier by Mozart.

> Probably manuscript copies of the variations K. 179, 180 and 354 published by Heina in Paris in 1778.

In January 1784 Mozart removed from the Judenplatz to the Trattnerhof, Am Graben, No. 591-596 in the Inner City (now Graben 29), 2nd staircase, 3rd floor.

> This large building, erected in 1776, belonged to the printer Johann Thomas von Trattner, whose wife was one of Mozart's pupils.

On 24 January *Die Entführung* was given at Mainz.

> Whether this was the first performance there is uncertain. The *Journal von und für Deutschland*, published in Ellrich by Leopold Friedrich Günther von Goeckingk, which lists this performance without any particulars (Part iii, p. 308), erroneously describes the Vienna *Entführung* of 25 January as performed " for the first time " (Part i, p. 190) ; however, it is true that the work had not been given in Vienna for nearly a year.

IBID., 24 JANUARY 1784

Plays.

. . . At the I. & R. Kärntnertor Theatre, to-morrow, 25 January, Mme Lange, member of the I. & R. National Court Theatre, will give for her benefit the German Singspiel : *Die Entführung aus dem Serail*, which is composed by Herr Mozart, Kapellmeister, and at which he will conduct in person.

IBID., 31 JANUARY 1784

Plays.

. . . At the Kärntnertor Theatre, to-morrow, 1 February, Mme Lange will give a repeat performance of the German Singspiel : *Die Entführung aus dem Serail*, given for the first time a week ago.

It is unlikely that Frau Lange was allowed a second benefit performance. Each principal singer was granted one per season by contract.

On 9 February Mozart began his thematic catalogue.

This catalogue, which he kept fairly accurately until his death, has become an important source for research into the period of Mozart's full maturity. The original is in the Stefan Zweig Collection in London (deposited on loan at the British Museum). A facsimile edition, edited by O. E. Deutsch, was published in Vienna in 1938 and in New York in 1956.

On 24 February Mozart paid 2 gulden as a deposit on 6 months' rent for the Trattnerhof lodgings.

The rent-books of the Trattnerhof were in the possession of Herr Franz Mayr-Melnhof in Vienna. The third book (1782–90) has been mislaid since it was used by Hermine Cloeter for her book on the Trattners (Vienna, 1952, pp. 99 ff.). The rent amounted to 75 gulden for the half-year from St. George's day (24 April) to Michaelmas (29 September), but the landlord remitted 10 gulden. On the other hand a contribution of one gulden was due for lighting. In the lost rent-book Mozart was described as " *fürstl. Salzb. Kapellmeister*, from Salzburg ".

On 26 February Mozart played at the house of Prince Galitsin, the Russian Ambassador (Krugerstrasse, No. 1046 in the Inner City).

Also on 4, 11, 18 and 25 March. These were five successive Thursdays.

On 1 March Mozart played at Count Johann Esterházy's.

Also on 5, 8, 12, 15, 19, 22, 26 and 29 March, *i.e.* every Monday and Friday of that month. The Count was one of the most active music-lovers in Viennese society. He was Master of the " Crowned Hope " masonic lodge in Vienna.

On 17, 24 and 31 March, three Wednesdays during Lent, Mozart held subscription concerts in the private hall of the Trattnerhof.

The hall was room No. 9 on the first floor, rebuilt in 1783 out of St. George's Chapel, released at the Emperor's command, and provided with anterooms. Before a casino was established there in 1785, the hall was let, at a rent of 550 gulden per half-year, to " Georg Friedrich Richter *et* Wolfgang Amadeus Mozart, *frstl. Salzburg. Kapellmeister* ". The pianist Richter, who came from Holland, does not seem to have used the hall more often than Mozart did, if indeed the Saturday concerts he planned with Mozart's collaboration for 20 and 27 March and 3 April even took place. An entry in the rent-book for an unspecified month (April 1784 rather than January, as suggested by Cloeter, p. 101) says : " 20th do., Wolfgang Amadeus Mozart, for 3 musical concerts likewise held during this Lent, 9 Austrian ducats, *id est* 38 florins, 42 *Kreuzer* ; the rent for the remaining period to be cancelled, 433 fl. 54 kr." At each of these concerts Mozart played a new pianoforte concerto : Eb major, K. 449, on 17 March ; Bb major, K. 450, on the 24th ; and D major, K. 451, on the 31st. The remainder of the programmes is unknown.

On 20 March Mozart sent his father the list of subscribers to his Trattnerhof Wednesday concerts.

See Appendix No. 1.—On 3 March Mozart had sent his father a calendar of all his Lenten concerts.

On 20 March, the same day, Mozart played at Count Karl Zichy's.

Cf. 16 July 1782.—If Richter's first concert took place on that evening, Mozart probably did not take part in it.

Mozart's concert at the Burgtheater, announced for 21 March, was postponed till 1 April.

> The reason was that on this day Prince Alois Liechtenstein had an opera performed at his palace, so that Mozart would have lost the best members of the orchestra, and the nobility from among his audience. He therefore had an announcement printed, the wording of which is not known.

FROM THE "WIENERBLÄTTCHEN", 23 MARCH 1784

Musical Concert.

Herr Stadler, senior, in actual service of His Majesty the Emperor, will hold a musical concert for his benefit at the I. & R. National Court Theatre, at which will be given, among other well-chosen pieces, a great wind piece of a very special kind composed by Herr Mozart.

> Anton Stadler, the elder of two brothers, was an outstanding clarinettist. The work played at Mozart's concert was no doubt the wind serenade in B♭ major (K. 361) with parts for two basset horns, which were probably taken by Anton and Johann Stadler. (Pohl, *Haydn*, Vol. II, p. 142, supposed it to have been one of the serenades K. 375 or 388.)

IBID., 1 APRIL 1784

Musical Concert.

Today, Thursday, 1 April, Herr Kapellmeister Mozart will have the honour to hold a great musical concert for his benefit at the I. & R. National Court Theatre. The pieces to occur in it are the following : 1) A grand Symphony with trumpets and drums. 2) An aria, sung by Herr Adamberger. 3) Herr Mozart, Kapellmeister, will play an entirely new Concerto on the Fortepiano. 4) A quite new grand Symphony. 5) An aria, sung by Mlle Cavalieri. 6) Herr Mozart, Kapellmeister, will play an entirely new grand Quintet. 7) An aria, sung by Herr Marchesi, senior. 8) Herr Kapellmeister Mozart will improvise entirely alone on the *Fortepiano*. 9) To conclude, a Symphony. Apart from the three arias, everything is composed by Kapellmeister Mozart.

> Although the programme mentions three symphonies, it is likely that only two were played, but one of them divided (*cf.* 23 March 1783). No. 4, the "quite new" symphony, was the Linz (K. 425) ; Nos. 1 and 9 perhaps the Haffner symphony (K. 385) (see Pohl, *Haydn*, Vol. II, p. 145). No. 3 was one of the two "quite new" pianoforte concertos, K. 450 and 451 (see 24 and 31 March 1784) ; No. 6 the pianoforte and wind quintet in E♭ major (K. 452).—Antonio Marchesi had been a member of the Italian Opera since 1783.

Musical Concerts

were given in the I. & R. National Court Theatre on the 1st inst. by Herr *Mozart* and on the 4th by Herr Ludwig *Fischer*, formerly singer at the German *Sinsgpiel* of the National Theatre.

> Fischer, Mozart's first Osmin, had been engaged from 1780 to 1783.

On 9 April Mozart played at a concert in the house of Count Leopold Pálffy.

> *Cf.* 16 October 1762. The Count may have been a nephew of the Hungarian Court Chancellor.

On 10 April Mozart played at Prince Kaunitz's.

On 18 April *Die Entführung* was performed at Mannheim.

> *Journal von und für Deutschland*, 1784, Part v, p. 581.—*Cf.* Anton Hasenhut's biography by F. J. Hadatsch, *Die Launen des Schicksals* (Vienna, 1834), p. 94 f.— Fischer later sang Osmin at Mannheim too.

On 29 April Mozart appeared at the concert given by the violinist Regina Strinasacchi at the Kärntnertor Theatre in the presence of the Emperor ; he played the violin and pianoforte sonata in B♭ major (K. 454) with her and also a piano concerto (K.453?).

> The sonata was written for the famous virtuosa from Ostiglia, near Mantua, who later married a Herr Schlick. She lived from 1761 to 1839.—Zinzendorf's diary mentions a theatre concert given by Strinasacchi as on 29 March.

FROM MOZART'S EXPENSES BOOK

1 May 1784 two mayflowers   1 kreuzer.

> Jahn (2nd ed.), Vol. I, p. 749.—Mozart kept such a book for a short period at this time.

On 8 May Mozart played at a private concert given by Therese von Trattner, his landlord's wife and his pupil.

FRIEDRICH LUDWIG SCHRÖDER TO WOLFGANG HERIBERT VON DALBERG, VIENNA, 22 MAY 1784

Mozart received 50 ducats for *Die Entführung aus dem Serail* ; below that price he will hardly compose one.

> Jahn, Vol. I, p. 736.—The famous German actor Schröder was engaged at the Burgtheater from April 1781 to February 1785 ; he translated *Don Giovanni* for Hamburg in 1789. Baron von Dalberg had been Intendant of the National Theatre at Mannheim since 1778 (see 18 April 1784).—Mozart had received the usual lump sum of 100 ducats for *Die Entführung* (see 16 July 1782).

FROM MOZART'S EXPENSES BOOK

27 May 1784   starling bird   34 kreuzer.

That was fine !

Jahn (2nd ed.), Vol. I, p. 749.—This starling was almost able to whistle the finale theme of the new piano concerto in G major (K. 453), but as given above. On 4 June 1787, when he had to bury the bird in the garden of his lodgings on the Landstrasse, Mozart wrote the serio-comic verse " Here lies a cherished fool, a starling bird . . . ", in its memory (G. Nottebohm, *Mozartiana* [Leipzig, 1880], p. 8 f.).—In Nissen's notes (Rudolf von Lewicki in *Mozarteums-Mitteilungen* [Salzburg], Year 2, Vol. I, November 1929) the story runs thus : " When a bird died, he arranged a funeral procession, in which everyone who could sing had to join in, heavily veiled—made a sort of requiem, epitaph in verse ".

Early in June Mozart visited Count Johann Thun at Baden near Vienna, where he had gone from Linz for a short cure ; on his return journey Mozart passed through Laxenburg.

On 13 June a private concert took place at Herr Ployer's lodgings in the suburb of Döbling, in the presence of Paisiello. Ployer's daughter Barbara played the D major sonata for two pianofortes (K. 448) with Mozart, who then took part in the Eb major quintet for piano and wind (K. 452) ; and Barbara Ployer finally played the G major pianoforte concerto (K. 453).

Gottfried Ignaz von Ployer (ennobled in 1773), was a representative on the Education Commission and at the High Court of Justice, and Exchequer representative for the Mint and Mines department ; he was also Salzburg Court Agent in Vienna. He lived on the Lugeck, and in summer at the out-lying village of Döbling. His musically gifted daughter Barbara was a pupil of Mozart's, who had written the concerto in Eb (K. 449) for her in February 1784.—For K. 448 see 23 November 1781, for K. 452 see 1 April 1784 ; the G major concerto, like that in Eb (K. 449) had been written for Barbara Ployer. —For Paisiello see 23 August 1784.

On 18 June Mozart paid the remainder of his six months' rent at the Trattnerhof : 63 gulden ; on the 23rd he gave notice to quit these lodgings.

A quarter's notice was required in order to move on the dates in April and September from which the lease could be renewed. The rent-book observes : " This party has given legal notice on 23 June 1784 to leave at Michaelmas 1784. Will lodge in future at No. 816, in the Kamesina House in the City, Grosse Schulerstrasse." *Cf.* 29 September 1784.

FROM THE " WIENER ZEITUNG ", 7 JULY 1784

New Music and Art Objects.

From the pen of the famous Herr Kapellmeister Mozart, will be published by subscription by the undermentioned firm 3 new *clavier Sonatas*, of

M.—8

which the first two are for the *clavier* alone, and the third is accompanied by a *violin*, as recently played at the theatre with general applause by the celebrated *Mlle Strinasachy* and Herr Mozart, and thus needs no further recommendation ; and care has been taken to satisfy the amateurs by issuing the *clavier solos* and the *accompaniment* all together. The subscription is 2 florins per copy and remains open to the end of July. . . .

Christoph Torricella,
Publisher of art, copper engravings and music in the Herrengasse.

The publishing-house of Torricella had been founded in 1775, but produced printed music only in its last years before it was taken over by Artaria in 1786. The sonatas in B♭, D and B♭ major announced here are K. 333, 284 and 454. (*Cf.* 29 April 1784.) The work appeared as Op. VII, engraved by Joseph Zahradniczek and dedicated to Countess Therese Cobenzl, the wife of Count Ludwig Cobenzl, who was a kinsman of the Chancellor of State Johann Philipp, Count Cobenzl, and ambassador in St. Petersburg. This handsome edition, advertised with the date of May 1784 in Cramer's *Magazin der Musik* for 17 November (p. 251), in fact appeared on 28 August, without list of subscribers. Torricella, like Trattner and Pasquale Artaria, was a freemason ; Zahradniczek, trumpeter in the Hungarian Lifeguards, belonged to the same lodge as Mozart in 1790. The work was reprinted by Artaria & Co. in 1787, without the border of masonic emblems on the title-page.

FROM THE " WIENER ZEITUNG ", 10 JULY 1784
(partly in Italian)

New Arias at the Pianoforte.

The opera *Wenn zwey sich zanken* may also be had for wind instruments, viz. for 2 oboes, 2 clarinets, 2 horns and 2 bassoons, arranged by *Went*, Court Musician.

do. do. *Die Pilgrime von Mecca*, by *Gluck*.
do. do. *Die Entführung aus dem Serail*, by *Mozart*.

Mozart, 6 Concertos for the Harpsichord.

Lorenz Lausch,
Music Publisher, in the Kärntnerstrasse
the 3 White Roses above No. 1085.

Like Traeg, Lausch was a dealer in manuscript copies of music. As with Sarti's opera (*cf.* 18 August 1784), these arrangements of *Die Entführung* and Gluck's singspiel *Die Pilgrime von Mecca* (*cf.* 14 September 1785) were made by the oboist Johann Went, for whom see under 7 August 1782. The advertisement for this arrangement (there is a copy in the Florence Conservatoire library) was repeated on 2 April 1785 and 27 August 1791.—The six concertos were probably K. 413, 414, 415, 449, 450 and 451, but perhaps K. 453 may already have been available in place of one of the earlier ones.

Music.

Johann Traeg . . . has the honour to announce the following new music in manuscript :

2) A new Double Concerto for Pianoforte by Mozart,   4 fl. 22 kr.

5) New Variations by Mozart and Sarti,   1 fl.

> The " double concerto " was that in E♭ K. 365 ; the pianoforte variations, K. 460, whose authenticity has been questioned by Professor Kurt von Fischer in the *Mozart-Jahrbuch 1958* (Salzburg, 1959), pp. 18 ff., were those written in June 1784 on the air " Come un' agnello " from Giuseppe Sarti's opera *Fra i due litiganti il terzo gode*, which had been given its first performance at the Burg-theater on 28 May.   Sarti had himself written variations on this theme, an-nounced by Lausch on 2 April 1785 at 45 kreuzer.—*Cf. Mozart-Jahrbuch 1959* (Salzburg, 1960), pp. 127 f. (Paul and Eva Badura-Skoda) and pp. 140 f. (Kurt von Fischer).

On 23 August Mozart's sister, Maria Anna, married Johann Baptist von Berchtold zu Sonnenburg, prefect at St. Gilgen.

> Marriage register of the parish of St. Gilgen.—*Cf.* 25 December 1720.   Nannerl married a successor of her maternal grandfather, in the official house in which her mother had grown up.   Berchtold, who had held the post there since 1769, had been widowed twice and brought five children to the new marriage. On 18 August Mozart had congratulated Nannerl in humorous verse.

On 23 August Mozart attended the first performance of Paisiello's opera *Il rè Teodoro in Venezia* at the Burgtheater.

> The composer, who was staying in Vienna at the time, received the exceptional sum of 300 ducats for this opera, which was very successful.—Mozart was attacked during this performance by a chill on the kidneys and was ill until the middle of September.

Announcement.

At the art establishment of *Artaria Comp.* . . . . the following novelties are to be had :

. . . Three Pianoforte Sonatas, *Opus 6*, by Herr Kapellmeister Mozart, 2 fl. 30 kr.

> The sonatas were those in C, A and F major, K. 330-32.

At *Christoph Torricella's,*

art and music publisher . . . the following novelties are to be had :
The 3 *pianoforte Sonatas* by the celebrated Herr *A. W. Mozart*, I. & R. Kapell-meister, announced some time ago, of which the first two are for the

pianoforte alone and the last is accompanied by a *violin obbligato*, which he played at the theatre with *Mlle Strinasachi* to great applause, and which need no recommendation, have appeared especially finely engraved ; they cost 2 fl. 45 kr. . . .

Cf. 7 July 1784.

FROM THE " PROVINZIALNACHRICHTEN AUS DEN KAISERL. KÖNIGL.
STAATEN UND ERBLÄNDERN ", VIENNA, 18 SEPTEMBER 1784

Music at Artaria and comp.'s

By Herr *Mozart*, Kapellmeister, 3 Sonatas for the pianoforte.

The advertisements and reports appearing in this periodical published by Trattner were discovered by Mr. Christopher Raeburn.—The sonatas are K. 330-2. (*Cf.* 25 August 1784.)

On 21 September Mozart's second child, Karl Thomas, was born.

The christening took place in St. Peter's. Johann Thomas von Trattner was the godfather. Karl was to survive the whole family and died unmarried at Milan on 31 October 1858, as an official in the Austrian finance department.

On 29 September, Michaelmas, Mozart removed from the Trattnerhof to the Grosse Schulerstrasse, No. 846 in the Inner City (now Schulerstrasse 8 and Domgasse 5), 1st floor.

The house belonged to two brothers, Joseph and Albert Camesina, whose father, Joseph, had been a stucco worker and had decorated the smaller of the two front rooms as a showroom. This room, presumably Mozart's study, and the larger one adjoining it, have been turned into a memorial by the Museum of the City of Vienna. The lodging, which had several additional courtyard and back rooms, cost 240 gulden per half-year, as against the 75 (in reality 65) for the admittedly smaller and higher apartment on the Graben.

On 16 October *Die Entführung* was performed at Carlsruhe.

FROM THE TRAVEL DIARY OF COUNT LUDWIG VON BENTHEIM-
STEINFURT, COLOGNE, 24 OCTOBER 1784

Herr Boem's company, which played at Hanau this summer, gave *Die Entführung aus dem Serail*, a nice operetta with beautiful music by *Motzart* of Vienna. I marked the best of the arias, but the actors had to be so loudly prompted that it gave me the horrors, the scenery, too, went right against all the dresses, being European instead of Turkish, which repelled me very much. The orchestra also is quite miserable, and the first violinist, a rough fellow, was so eager that he sweated all over and cursed and railed over the multifarious mistakes, especially in the wind instruments. Among the actors none is outstanding and none above mediocrity—*how different is the Mannheim stage and the orchestra there.*

Eigel Kruttge in the *Zeitschrift für Musikwissenschaft* (Leipzig) October 1923 (Year VI, No. 1), p. 21.—The company was again that of Johann Böhm.—

The "first violinist" was in fact the Konzertmeister who directed the performance.—It is uncertain whether this was the first performance of the
singspiel at Cologne.

FROM THE "WIENER ZEITUNG", 27 OCTOBER 1784

At Johann Traeg's . . . the following new manuscript music is likewise
to be had :

.   .   .   .   .   .

1 Double Concerto by Mozart.
Pianoforte Concertos by Hayden, Mozart, Bach . . .

Cf. 10 July and 18 August 1784. Which of Mozart's pianoforte concertos
were distributed by Traeg is not known.

On 31 October, Mozart's name-day, there was a small domestic concert at his
lodgings, at which some of his lady pupils performed.

It is to be supposed that Fräulein Auernhammer and Fräulein Ployer were
among them ; perhaps Frau Trattner too.

On 5 November the Schikaneder-Kumpf company began its season at the Kärntnertor Theatre with Die Entführung in the presence of the Emperor.

The company led by Emanuel Schikaneder and Hubert Kumpf performed
plays and operas in German. The visit lasted until 6 February 1785. How
often Die Entführung was given during these three months, if at all, is unknown.

IBID., 13 NOVEMBER 1784
Plays.

. . . The company of actors under the management of Messrs Schikaneder
and Kumpf plays in the theatre next to the Kärntnertor, and on Friday, the
5th inst., began by performing the opera Die Entführung aus dem Serail.

FROM CRAMER'S "MAGAZIN DER MUSIK", HAMBURG, 17 NOVEMBER
1784

. . . The following works will be published by me by subscription, neatly
engraved on copper, which I herewith announce to our respected amateurs
of music, viz. :

1) Mozart, opera, Die Entführung
   aus dem Serail:
   in Pianoforte Score   =   4 mks. 8 sch. or 2 fl. 30 kr.
2) The same, 3 new Pianoforte
   Sonatas, with accom-
   paniment of a Violin   =   3 mks. — sch. or 2 fl. – kr.

.   .   .   .   .

Provided a sufficient number of subscribers be found, delivery will take place here in October this year. Letters and remittances to be sent post free, so far as that is possible.

Vienna, May 1784.
Christoph Torricella,
Music Publisher.

(At Hamburg subscriptions are accepted by the Musical Depot.)

Vol. II, p. 251 f.—*Cf.* 7 July and 28 August 1784.—The pianoforte score of *Die Entführung* announced here was that begun by Mozart himself. He gave up work on it before the third act when another score was published by Schott in 1785. Of Mozart's arrangement the only autograph fragments to have survived are Nos. 11 and 12 (Constanze's and Blonde's arias) from the second act. Of Torricella's pianoforte score the overture, dedicated by the publisher to the young Count Franz Dietrichstein, has been found. (Müller von Asow in *Die Musikforschung* (Cassel) Year 8, January 1955, p. 78.) His successors, Artaria & Co., who reissued this overture, offered the first act as well on 7 December 1785, perhaps in Torricella's edition with a new title-page, but no copy has come to light so far.—*Cf.* 16 April and 17 September 1785.

On 17 November Ludwig Schmidt's company performed *Die Entführung* at Salzburg.

In the letter in which Leopold Mozart gave his daughter an account of this performance he also mentions one each at Mainz (*see* 24 January 1784) and Berlin ; but *Die Entführung* was not in fact performed in Berlin until 16 October 1788.

COMMUNICATION FROM THE "BENEFICENCE" TO THE VIENNESE SISTER LODGES, 5 DECEMBER 1784

Proposed : Kapellmeister Mozart.—Our departed Secretary, Brother Hoffmann, forgot to circulate this nominee among the most honourable sister ▭ ▭ ; his name was already submitted 4 weeks ago to the highly honoured District ▭, and we should therefore wish to proceed to his admittance next week, if the most honourable sister ▭ ▭ have no objection to him.

W.i. O. [Vienna in the Orient]

57 $\frac{5}{\text{XII}}$ 84   Schwanckhardt : Sec.

Vienna, State Archives, Vertrauliche Akten, fasc. 108.—O. E. Deutsch, *Mozart und die Wiener Logen* (Vienna, 1932), p. 23.—The small freemasons' lodge " Zur Wohlthätigkeit [Beneficence] " was one of the eight Viennese "Johannis lodges". Its Master was Otto, Baron von Gemmingen-Hornberg (see early 1779), who had moved from Mannheim to Vienna in 1782.—Leopold Anton Hoffmann had gone to Pest as Professor of German Language and Literature ; he made an attack on the Viennese freemasons in 1786.—The principal lodge of the district was called " Zur wohlthätigen Eintracht " [Beneficent Concord].—Johann Daniel Schwanckhardt was a teacher at the Theresian Ritter-Akademie.—The rectangle signifies a lodge ; two such figures for lodges in the plural. In the masonic calendar 5784 meant the year 1784.

IBID., 14 DECEMBER 1784

57 $\frac{14}{XII}$ 84   At 6.30 o'clock, in the first Grade.
Wenzel Summer, Chaplain at Erdberg, and
Mozart, Kapellmeister.
Proposed: Franz Wolf, Calculator at the Municipal Court Accountancy.
w. i. O. [Vienna in the Orient]
57 – $\frac{11}{XII}$ – – 84   Schwanckhardt : Sec.

> *Ibid.*—Summer, later "almoner" of the lodge, had already been proposed
> for admission on 1 November 1784. Mozart was given the number 20 in the
> list of the lodge. The first grade was that of apprentice, the next that of
> journeyman, the highest that of master.

On 15 December Torricella again announced Mozart's "Opus VII" in the *Wiener
Zeitung.*

> *Cf.* 7 July and 28 August 1784.

FROM THE ATTENDANCE RECORD OF THE "TRUE CONCORD" LODGE, 24 DECEMBER 1784

CCCXL. [Session] Vienna $\frac{24}{12}$ 5784 the "True Concord" [＿＿＿]
was opened, the undersigned Brother being present :
. . . . . . Visiting Brothers
. . . . . . Mozart . . . . . .

> Vienna, State Archives, *loc. cit.*, fasc. 134.—Deutsch, *op. cit.*, p. 23.—The
> lodge "Zur wahren Eintracht [True Concord]", under the leadership of
> the naturalist Ignaz von Born, secretary of the Austrian Grand Lodge, was the
> largest and most aristocratic in Vienna.—Mozart, as the best of the musical
> "Brothers", was welcome in all the lodges.

FROM THE "LITTERATUR- UND THEATER-ZEITUNG", BERLIN, 1784

To Mamsell Sophie Niclas,
on her having admirably well played the part of
Constanze in the opera *Die Entführung aus dem Serail,**
at the Court Theatre of Schwedt.

Belovéd singer, long ago
My heart, like many another, fell
To the enchantment of thy voice,
More sweet than that of Philomel.
How oft did I not see thy art,
Of artfulness so innocent,
Strive but to copy nature's truth
And show us skill with candour blent !

* With Mozart's excellent music.

> But, friend, when Constance is thy part
> In radiance thy own beauty shines,
> Adorning with thyself our stage
> And with oriental pomp combines ;
> When thou disdainest rank and wealth,
> By love and troth alone inspired,
> Striving to find and rescue him
> Whom thy chaste heart had long desired ;
> By neither threats nor perils shaken
> The resolution thou hast taken :
> Who then could fail to form the hope
> With thee as Belmont to elope ?

v. Br.

Part 3, No. 36, p. 160.—Schwedt near Angermünde belonged to the Prussian government district of Potsdam. The singspiel had been performed in the Margrave of Brandenburg-Schwedt's court theatre, but the date is unknown. Frau Niclas was formerly Fräulein Semler.

1785

FROM THE "THEATER-KALENDER", GOTHA, 1785

Mozard . . . Kapellmeister at Salzburg :
Seminarius, musical drama by Baron von Gemmingen. *Die Entführung aus dem Serail. Die verstellte Gärtnerin*, operetta.

> *Cf. Theater-Kalender* for 1779.—*Seminarius* should, of course, read *Semiramis. Die verstellte Gärtnerin* is *La finta giardiniera*.

FROM SCHINK'S "LITTERARISCHE FRAGMENTE", GRAZ, 1785
Gabriel Wilhelm Steinfeld's Wanderings.

·   ·   ·   ·   ·

Musical concert held by Stadler, Clarinet Virtuoso.

My thanks to three, brave Virtuoso ! I have never heard the like of what thou contrivest with thy instrument. Never should I have thought that a clarinet could be capable of imitating a human voice so deceptively as it was imitated by thee. Verily, thy instrument has so soft and so lovely a tone that nobody can resist it who has a heart, and I have one, dear Virtuoso ; let me thank thee !

I heard music for wind instruments to-day, too, by Herr Mozart, in four movements—glorious and sublime ! It consisted of thirteen instruments, viz. four *corni*, two *oboi*, two *fagotti*, two *clarinetti*, two *basset-corni*, a *contre-violon*, and at each instrument sat a master—oh, what an effect it made—glorious and grand, excellent and sublime !—

.   .   .   .   .

Mozart.

What a life we lead here, as in the land of the blessed, the land of music. I have heard Mozart, too ; great and original in his compositions, and a master when seated at the keyboard. His Concerto on the *Piano-Forte*, how excellent that was ! And his improvisations, what a wealth of ideas ! what variety ! what contrasts in passionate sounds ! One swims away with him unresistingly on the stream of his emotions.

> Vol. II, pp. 286-8.—Jahn, Vol. I, p. 684.—For Schink see end of 1782.—Stadler's concert had taken place at the Burgtheater on 23 March 1784, with Mozart's wind serenade (K. 361) in the programme. Mozart's concert had followed on 1 April.—" Steinfeld " was a pseudonym of Schink's, who stayed in Vienna in the spring of 1784.

FROM THE ATTENDANCE RECORD OF THE " TRUE CONCORD " LODGE, 7 JANUARY 1785

CCCXLIII. [Session] Vienna $\frac{7}{1}$ 5785....
....Visiting Brothers.
....Mozart....

> Vienna, State Archives, *loc. cit.*, fasc. 134.—Deutsch, *op. cit.*, p. 24.—*Cf.* the following document.

FROM THE EVENTS RECORD OF THE " TRUE CONCORD " LODGE, 7 JANUARY 1785

CCCXLIII. [Session] Vienna, the $\frac{7}{1}$ 5785 the ☐☐☐ of " The True Concord " was opened, those brothers being present whose signatures are to be found in the *Protocollum Praesentium.*

1) After the opening of the Apprentices' and Journeymen's ☐☐☐ the Apprentice Brothers Vincenz, Marquis Canarisi, son of Joseph, 34 years of age, born at Como in Austrian Lombardy, Captain of the I. & R. Infantry Regiment Belgio[jo]so, at the request of the hon. ☐☐☐ of " The Rising Sun " at Brno, and further Brother Wolfgang Mozard, at the request of the hon. ☐☐☐ " Beneficence ", were promoted to the second Grade with the accustomed ceremonies.

> *Ibid.*, fasc. 133.—*Ibid.*—Canaresi, as a Brother staying only temporarily in Vienna, was promoted to the grade of Master on 14 January, without having had to pass through the grade of journeyman. Mozart's promotion to the second grade, too, was unusually rapid for a local " Brother ". His own lodge, which had perhaps been obliged to interrupt its " sessions ", had requested the " Concord " to deputize (*cf.* 16 and 22 April 1785).

M.—8 *a*

On 12 January 1785 Artaria & Co. announced, *inter alia*, the orchestral parts of the pianoforte concertos in A, F and C (K. 414, 413, 415) in a publisher's supplement to the *Wiener Zeitung*.

> No copy of this supplement referred to by Köchel is to be found in the Viennese collections.—*Cf.* 15 January 1783 and 29 March 1785.

FROM THE "MAGAZIN DER SÄCHSISCHEN GESCHICHTE", DRESDEN, 1785

Miscellaneous News from Dresden.

The local theatre company [under Bondini's management] performed in January : . . . On the 12th an operetta, by *Bretzner*, *Die Entführung aus dem Serail*, composed by *Mozart*, pleased generally, although it is somewhat heavily set, and was very entertaining thanks to *Günther's* caricature (as Osmin) and Mme *Günther's* mischievous acting. Herr *Hurka* as Belmont delivered well, with feeling and often brilliantly, which made one readily forget his somewhat unpractised acting.

> Part 2, p. 57 f.—For Bondini *cf.* September 1783.—Friedrich Günther and his wife Sophie, *née* Huber, had been engaged at the Vienna Court Theatre until 1783, he at the German Opera (see 31 March 1781) and she in drama.

FROM THE ATTENDANCE RECORD OF THE "TRUE CONCORD" LODGE, 14 JANUARY 1785

CCCXLVI. [Session] Vienna $\frac{14}{1}$ 5785 . . .

. . . . . . Visiting Brothers.

. . . . . . Mozart, of the ⬚⬚⬚ "Beneficence".

> Vienna, State Archives, *loc. cit.*, fasc. 133.—Deutsch, *op. cit.*, p. 24.

FROM THE "WIENER ZEITUNG", 15 JANUARY 1785

At Lausch's music establishment is to be had :

.   .   .

Mozart, Variations on the aria *Salve tu Domine*   32 kr.

> The theme of the variations (K. 398) came from Paisiello's opera *I filosofi immaginarii*, which had been performed at the Burgtheater in German on 22 May 1781 and in Italian on 8 October 1783. *Cf.* 23 March 1783. Lausch's offer again refers to MS. copies.

On 15 January Mozart and friends of his played the six string quartets later dedicated to Haydn, who was present.

> In fact probably only the first three were played.—*Cf.* 12 February 1785.

In the morning of 28 January Leopold Mozart journeyed from Salzburg to Munich.

> Leopold Mozart stayed there with the theatre manager Theobald Marchand from 29 January to 6 February.

FROM THE ATTENDANCE RECORD OF THE "TRUE CONCORD" LODGE,
28 JANUARY, 1785

CCCLI. [Session] Vienna $\frac{28}{1}$ 5785....

...... Visiting Brothers.

...... Mozart of the [⬜] "Beneficence"....

<small>Vienna, State Archives, *loc. cit.*, fasc. 133.—Deutsch, *op. cit.*, p. 24.</small>

THE EMPEROR JOSEPH II TO COUNT JOHANN ANTON PERGEN,
31 JANUARY 1785

I hear that the well-known comedy *Le Mariage de Figaro* is said to have been proposed for the Kärntnertor Theatre in a German translation ; since this piece contains much that is objectionable, I therefore expect that the Censor shall either reject it altogether, or at any rate have such alterations made in it that he shall be responsible for the performance of this play and for the impression it may make.

<small>Vienna, State Archives, Billeten-Protokolle.—Rudolf Payer von Thurn, *Joseph II. als Theaterdirektor* (Vienna, 1920), p. 60.—Count Pergen was President of the Lower Austrian Government.—In Paris too it was only after great difficulties that Beaumarchais's comedy reached the stage in 1784. *Cf.* the following two documents.</small>

FROM THE "WIENERBLÄTTCHEN", 2 FEBRUARY 1785

Herr Rautenstrauch has recently translated into German the comedy *Les Noces de Figaro*, received with such extraordinary applause in Paris. This will be performed for the first time to-morrow by the company of Messrs Schikaneder and Kumpf.

<small>The translation was by Johann Rautenstrauch.</small>

IBID., 4 FEBRUARY 1785

The comedy promised by Herr Schikaneder, *Die Hochzeit des Figaro*, was not performed yesterday, and according to the news imparted to the public by yesterday's poster, the Censorship has authorized it to be printed but not performed.

<small>The performance announced for 3 February, with Heinrich Wilhelm von Kronstein as Figaro, was prohibited on the same day. The newspaper, on 28 February, 1 and 2 March, published extracts from the book, which appeared before the end of 1785. Rautenstrauch mentioned the prohibition in his foreword to the book, which he dedicated to the memory of the two hundred ducats he had lost thereby.—The Schikaneder-Kumpf company played at the Kärntnertor Theatre only till 6 February, but Schikaneder belonged to the drama ensemble at the Burgtheater from April 1785 to February 1786.</small>

On 7 February, Carnival Monday, Mozart's father left Munich for a visit to Vienna.

> He brought the violinist Heinrich Marchand with him. Heinrich and Margarethe, the children of the theatre manager, had been pupils of Leopold Mozart's at Salzburg.

On 11 February Mozart petitioned the Society of Musicians for membership.

> See 3 April 1781.—C. F. Pohl, *Denkschrift* . . . *der Tonkünstler-Societät* (Vienna, 1871), p. 17 f.—In this petition, which is otherwise unknown, Mozart regretted his inability to produce his birth certificate at the moment, but promised to forward it. His request remained in abeyance, partly for this reason and partly because it was hoped that the differences within the society would be settled. After the performances of his cantata *Davidde penitente* on 13 and 15 March 1785 Mozart renewed his petition, " since he had rendered frequent useful services to the society and offered to do so again in the future "; the birth certificate required for his admission he would hand in " as soon as he received it ". On 24 August the society resolved to send the following reply : " When the birth certificate has been submitted, further information will follow ". Works by Mozart were also performed at the society's concerts on 23 December 1785, 22 December 1789 and 16–17 April 1791, and on the first of these occasions he played himself. The birth certificate, however, was never submitted, and the petition was never granted. *Cf.* 20 January 1792.—The society that was later to bear Joseph Haydn's name also postponed its acceptance of him from 1778 to 1797, though for different reasons.

On the same day, 11 February, at 1 p.m., Leopold Mozart arrived in Vienna and put up at his son's.

> He remained until 25 April and was able to take a part in arranging his son' activities.

In the evening of 11 February Mozart gave the first of six Friday concerts at the " Mehlgrube " casino in the Neuer Markt.

> Mozart played the new pianoforte concerto in D minor, K. 466. The rest of the programme is not precisely known.—On the same evening Haydn was admitted to the " Concord " lodge ; but as he never again appeared there, he never passed the apprentice stage. Mozart was probably prevented from attending the ceremony by his concert.

On 12 February Haydn visited Mozart, and three of the six string quartets later dedicated to him (K. 458, 464 and 465) were played to him again.

> The dedication is dated 1 September 1785. Haydn had already heard the first three of these quartets (K. 387, 421 and 428) at Mozart's on 15 January. The remainder were now probably played to him by the Mozarts, father and son, and the Barons Anton and Bartholomäus Tinti, two members of the " Concord " lodge. It was on this occasion that Haydn made his famous remark about Mozart to his father, which Leopold reported to his daughter on 16 February.

On 13 February Mozart played a pianoforte concerto in the presence of the Emperor at the concert given by the singer Luisa Laschi in the Burgtheater.

> Abert (Vol. I, p. 1015) and Einstein (Köchel, 1937, p. 578) wrongly give 12 February as the date.—Luisa Laschi (*cf.* 21 September 1768) had belonged to the Italian Opera ensemble since 1784 ; her visit to Italy after this concert was probably only a brief one.—Mozart had written the concerto in 1784 for a

visit to Paris of the blind pianist Maria Theresia Paradies ; it was most likely that in B♭ major (K. 456).

On 15 February Mozart again played the D minor pianoforte concerto (K. 466) at the concert given in the Burgtheater by the singer Elisabeth Distler.

> Fräulein Distler (or Diestler), now aged 16, was the sister of Johann Georg Distler, a pupil of Haydn's who later became director of the chapel at Stuttgart, and of the former Burgtheater actor Joseph Anton Thomas Distler. She became a member of the German Opera ensemble in 1785. *Cf.* 13 March 1785.

FROM THE " WIENER ZEITUNG ", 16 FEBRUARY 1785

Johann Traeg . . . has the honour to announce the following music to musical amateurs :
. . . 3 Symphonies by A. W. Mozart . . .

> Perhaps the symphonies in B♭, C and D major, K. 319, 338 and 385 (Haffner).

In the evening of 16 February father and son were present at a concert given by Herr Ployer at Döbling.

> Mozart probably also played there. *Cf.* 13 June 1784 and 23 March 1784 1785.

On 17 February the Mozarts visited the Webers. In the evening a concert was held at the Burgtheater by the actress Josepha Hortensia Müller, who played a pianoforte concerto.

> Fräulein Müller, at the Burgtheater since 1782, married the painter Heinrich Friedrich Füger in 1791.

On 18 February, in the company of Ludwig August and Franziska Lebrun, and Karl Cannabich, the Mozarts visited the producer Gottlieb Stephanie. That evening Mozart's second Friday concert at the " Mehlgrube " took place.

> The oboist Lebrun (Le Brun) and his wife (*née* Danzi), a singer, who were on their way from Munich to Russia, arrived in Vienna after Leopold Mozart ; Christian Cannabich's son, a violinist and composer, seems to have been there since the autumn of 1784.

On 20 February the Mozarts attended a grand luncheon at the house of the Burgtheater actor Johann Heinrich Friedrich Müller.

> *Cf.* 3 March 1783.—Müller, Josepha's father, was an actor and producer at the Burgtheater ; in 1778–79 he had directed the German singspiel there.

On 21 February Mozart and the Lebruns played at a concert in Count Zichy's house.

> *Cf.* 20 July 1782 and 20 March 1784.

On 23 February the Lebruns' first concert took place at the Burgtheater.

On 24 February Fräulein Auernhammer held a concert there.

> Mozart probably took part.

On 25 February Mozart's third concert at the " Mehlgrube " took place.

On 28 February the Lebruns' second concert took place at the Burgtheater.

> It seems that Mozart took part in this one too.

On 1 March *Die Entführung* was given at Riga.

On 2 March Heinrich Marchand's first concert took place at the Burgtheater.

On 4 March Mozart's fourth concert at the " Mehlgrube " took place.

★ FROM THE " PROVINZIALNACHRICHTEN ", VIENNA, 5 MARCH 1785
Music.

At the art establishment of Artaria Comp. . . . are newly to be had : . . .
Also, three Pianoforte Concertos by Herr Kapellmeister Mozart, in A
maj., F maj. and C, have been engraved, and each is to be had at 2 fl. 30 kr.

> The concertos were K. 414, 413 and 415 ; *cf.* 15 January 1783 and 29 March
> 1785.

On 7 March the Lebruns gave their third concert at the Burgtheater.

★ FROM " THE PUBLIC ADVERTISER ", LONDON, 9 MARCH 1785
(in English)

Miss Paradis, with various abatements, how many prodigies of the musical
world have appeared—allowing this and that deficience, how wonderful. So
it has been with every infantine exertion of late—the Mozart, the Thomasino,
little Parke etc. But what is all this to positive excellence ? To Charles
Burney, Miss Guest, and yet more to Clemente ?—Very well it may be for
a poor blind girl—But—why is the auditor at an half-guinea concert to be
fobb'd off with buts.

> Discovered by C. B. Oldman.—Hermann Ullrich in *Music & Letters*, January
> 1962, p. 23.—Maria Theresia Paradies from Vienna took part in three concerts
> in London in February and March 1785 ; this notice appeared after the third
> of them.—" Thomasino " is Thomas Linley ; " Little Parke " is Maria Hester
> Parke ; " Charles Burney " probably Charles Rousseau Burney, nephew and
> son-in-law of the great Charles ; " Miss Guest " clearly Jane Guest, and
> " Clemente " of course is Muzio Clementi.

FROM THE " WIENER ZEITUNG ", 9 MARCH 1785
New Music.

Haydn, Gius., 3 Symphonies copied from the original.

> .   .   .   .

Mozart, 3 ditto . . .
7 kr. per sheet each.

                                          Laurent Lausch, . . .

> *Cf.* 16 February 1785.—Lausch probably handled the same Mozart symphonies
> as Traeg.—The price of music was usually reckoned by the number of sheets
> (each comprising four pages).

FROM THE " WIENERBLÄTTCHEN ", 10 MARCH 1785
Concert.

Today there is to be a grand concert given by Herr *Mozart* at the I. & R. National Court Theatre, to which all amateurs and connoisseurs are respectfully invited.

Müller von Asow, Vol. III, p. 328.

ANNOUNCEMENT OF MOZART'S CONCERT AT THE BURGTHEATER,
10 MARCH 1785
Information.

On Thursday, 10th March 1785
Herr Kapellmeister *Mozart*
will have the honour of giving at the
I. & R. National Court Theatre
a Grand Musical Concert
for his benefit, at which not only a
new, just *finished Forte piano Concerto*
will be played by him, but also an
especially *large Forte piano pedale* will
be used by him in *improvising*. The
remaining pieces will be announced
by the large poster on the day itself.

Salzburg, Mozarteum.—E. W. Engel, *Mozart-Kalender* (Vienna, 1914), p. 83. —Only this handbill has been preserved, and no poster. Mozart played the new C major pianoforte concerto (K. 467) ; the rest of the programme is not known. This concert is also mentioned in the list of performances at the two Court Theatres for 1785, published by the prompter Joseph Krauss (Appendix, p. 42). 12 March, given in Köchel-Einstein, p. 589, is incorrect. The receipts amounted to 559 gulden.—Mozart's " wing-shaped fortepiano " had, according to Leopold's report to his daughter of 12 March 1785, been " carried from the house to the theatre or into another house at least 12 times since I have been here " (it was probably the instrument by Anton Walter now in the Mozart Museum at Salzburg). The " grand fortepiano pedale " Mozart caused to be made for himself appears to have been transported no less frequently. The physician Dr. Joseph Frank later (1852) wrote about Mozart's fortepiano : " He had augmented it with a second keyboard, which served him as pedal ". This auxiliary instrument, a pedal-board, was in Mozart's effects after his death, but has not survived (*cf.* Eva and Paul Badura-Skoda, *Mozart-Interpretation* [Vienna, 1957], pp. 26 ff.).—In Leopold Mozart's figure of at least twelve concerts is included one at Prince Kaunitz's, which cannot be precisely dated.—During this Lent, indeed, there were almost daily concerts at the Burgtheater.

On 11 March Mozart gave his fifth concert at the " Mehlgrube ".

ANNOUNCEMENT OF THE CONCERT TO BE HELD BY THE SOCIETY OF
MUSICIANS AT THE BURGTHEATER ON 13 MARCH 1785
(in Italian)

Notice.

On Sunday the 13th March 1785
at the National Theatre of the Imperial Court
will be held
for the benefit of the Society of Musicians
the usual
Concert of Music
in two parts . . .

.   .   .

Part the Second.

A new Cantata adapted to this occasion by *Sig. Amadeo Mozart*, for three
voices with choruses, performed by *Sigra Cavallieri, Sigra Distler* and
by *Sig. Adamberger.*

British Museum, London (Hirsch Library).—Köchel-Einstein, p. 593.—The
cantata, *Davidde penitente* (K. 469), the words of which are by Lorenzo da
Ponte, was put together from the C minor Mass (K. 427, see 26 October 1783),
with two new arias. The Society had asked Mozart and Righini in January for
a new vocal work for this concert, and in February Mozart had written to them
that he had been unable to finish the Psalm he had promised them in the meantime, but offered them another Psalm which would be quite new to Vienna
(Pohl, *op. cit.*, p. 48). The cost of the copying was 93 florins 55 kreutzer
(Vienna City Archives). The first part of the concert contained a new Symphony by Joseph Haydn (*see* 29 March 1785).

FROM THE PROGRAMME OF THE CONCERT OF 13 MARCH 1785
(in German and Italian)

Grand
Musical Concert
Today, Sunday, 13 March 1785, at the
I. & R. National Court Theatre,
for the Benefit of the Society of Musicians,
will be held
the usual
Grand Musical Concert
in two parts.

.   .   .

Part the Second.

An entirely new Cantata, adapted to this occasion, by Herr Amad.
Mozart, for three voices with choruses, in which Dlle *Kavallieri,* Dlle *Dister*
and Herr *Adamberger* will sing the principal arias. . . .

.   .   .

To begin at 7 o'clock.

Gesellschaft der Musikfreunde, Vienna.—Otto Schneider, *Mozart in Wirklich-keit* (Vienna, 1955), p. 96.—The attendance was poor, the receipts being only 733 fl. 13 kr., of which 50 ducats (216 fl. 40 kr.) came from the Emperor (documents in Vienna City Archives).

On 14 March Heinrich Marchand's second concert took place at the Burgtheater.

Mozart probably did not play on this occasion.

On 15 March the Society of Musicians' concert was repeated.

The date of 17 March given in Köchel-Einstein (p. 593) is wrong.—The worst attended of the Tonkünstler concerts ; about 200 people ; the receipts were only 163 fl. 42 kr.

On 18 March Mozart gave his sixth and last concert at the " Mehlgrube ".

The programmes of these concerts have remained unknown, but at one of them was played one of the first six symphonies of Adalbert Gyrowetz (*cf.* 1848).

On 20 March the singer Ann Storace held a concert at the Burgtheater.

This London-born soprano was engaged at the Italian Opera in Vienna from 1784 to 1787.—Mozart may have performed on this evening.

FROM ZINZENDORF'S DIARY, 23 MARCH 1785
(in French)

. . . then to the agent *Ployer's* concert, where I heard his daughter play the harpsichord to admiration . . .

Barbara von Ployer may have played the E♭ concerto (K. 449) on this occasion. —*Cf.* 13 June 1784.

On 25 March the Mozarts visited the Langes, who on the 19th had returned to Vienna from Munich, where they had been on leave.

Lange made a drawing of Leopold Mozart, but this portrait seems to be lost.

On Easter Sunday, 27 March, the Mozarts dined at Wetzlar's.

On 28 March they were the guests of the barrister Dr. Ignaz Raab.

The attorney was a kinsman of Leopold Mozart's Salzburg landlady, Fräulein Maria Anna Raab.

ANNOUNCEMENT OF THE " BENEFICENCE " LODGE, 28 MARCH 1785

Proposed : Kapellmeister [Leopold] Mozart and Joseph Bashy ; as both will be leaving here shortly, we have applied for dispensation on their behalf.

W. i. O. [Vienna in the Orient]
the 57 $\frac{28}{3}$ 85 Schwankhardt, Sec.

Vienna, State Archives, *loc. cit.*, fasc. 133.—Deutsch, *op. cit.*, p. 24. Leopold Mozart thus sought admission to the lodge to which his son belonged, and the procedure was specially hastened for him.

At the art establishment of Artaria Comp. . . . are newly to be had :
Haydn's three new Symphonies in *G maj.*, *F maj*, and *D min*. . . .

At the same art establishment three Pianoforte Concertos by Herr Kapellmeister Mozart, in *A maj.*, *F maj.* and *C*, have been engraved, and each
is to be had at 2 fl. 30 kr.

> *Cf.* 5 March 1785.—K. 414, 413, 415.

On 29 March the Mozarts dined at Adamberger's, on the 30th at the Langes' once
more, and on the 31st at Ployer's.

ANNOUNCEMENT OF THE " BENEFICENCE " LODGE, I APRIL 1785

Wednesday the $\frac{6}{4}$ 85, at 6.30 o'clock, in I Gr. [1st grade]
Leopold Mozart, Kapellmeister—
we have applied for dispensation on behalf of this visiting applicant, as he
will be leaving in a few days, and have received the same also from the
Grand District [＿＿＿]

W. i. O. [Vienna in the Orient]
57 $\frac{1}{4}$ 85   Schwankhardt, Sec.

> Vienna, State Archives, *loc. cit.*, fasc. 133.—Deutsch, *op. cit.*, p. 24.—The
> District Lodge of Vienna was, after the Grand Lodge of Austria, the highest
> masonic authority in the realm.

On 1 April *Die Entführung* was performed in Munich at the Salvatorplatz Theatre.
The singspiel was to have been given there already during Lent.

FROM THE " WIENER ZEITUNG ", 2 APRIL 1785
(partly in French)
Announcement of Music.

. . . at Lorenz Lausch's, music dealer . . . Operas set for wind instruments . . . Mozart, *Die Entführung aus dem Serail*, 8 do. 5 fl. . . . Variations
for the Fortepiano : . . . Mozart, 12 *do.* in E flat, 1 fl. The same, 9 *do.* in C,
" Lison dormait ", 1 fl. The same, 5 *do.* in F, 24 kr. The same, 12 *do.* in C,
the Minuet by Fischer, 1 fl. The same, 6 *do.* in A from a Sonata, 36 kr. The
same 6, *do.* in D from a Concerto, 30 kr. The same, *do.* in F, " Salve tu
Domine ", 32 kr.

> On the arrangement of *Die Entführung* for 8 wind instruments see July 1784.
> According to Professor Kurt von Fischer the pianoforte variations were those
> on " La Belle Françoise " (K. 353) or on " Je suis Lindor " (K. 354), those on
> " Lison dormait " (K. 264), those on the march from *Les mariages samnites*
> (K. 352, Nos. 1-4 and 6), and those on a minuet by Johann Christian Fischer
> (K. 179) ; in addition there were the third movement of the sonata in A
> (K. 331) and probably a piano arrangement of the concerto-rondo in D (K. 382).

On 2 April the Mozarts went to Wetzlar's for a quartet evening.
Both Mozart and his father may have played there.

On 3 April the Langes dined at the Mozarts'.

On 6 April Leopold Mozart was admitted as an apprentice to the " Charity " lodge.

On 7 April the elder Mozart visited Mlle Villersi.

> She was governess in Prince Fürstenberg's household and had made the Mozarts' acquaintance at Donaueschingen in October 1766. The Fürstenbergs must at that time have been on a visit to Vienna.

On 15 April the Mozarts visited the commandant Philipp Lehmann at Laxenburg.

> *Cf.* 12 August 1773 and 20 July 1782.

IBID., 16 APRIL 1785

Music.

which is to be had of Wenzel Sukowaty, Court Theatre copyist, on the Petersplatz in Matz's house, No. 554, 3rd floor in the courtyard :
. . . *Die Entführung aus dem Serail* by Herr Mozart, 15 fl. . . .

> *Cf.* 17 November 1784 and 14 September 1785.—Sukowaty took advantage of his post to distribute MS copies of opera scores.

FROM THE ATTENDANCE RECORD OF THE " TRUE CONCORD " LODGE, 16 APRIL 1785

CCCLXXIV. [Session] Vienna the $\frac{16}{4}$ 5785 . . .
. . . . Visiting Brothers.
Leopold Mozart ⎫ of the " Beneficence " . . .
Wolfgang Mozart ⎭

> Vienna, State Archives, *loc. cit.*, fasc. 133.—Deutsch, *op. cit.*, p. 25.—The entries are holograph.

FROM THE EVENTS RECORD OF THE " TRUE CONCORD " LODGE, 16 APRIL 1785

CCCLXXIV. [Session] Vienna the $\frac{16}{4}$ 5785 . . .

1) After the opening of the Apprentices' and Journeymen's ⬚⬚⬚ the Apprentice Brothers . . . . . . and the Apprentice Brother and member of the hon. " Beneficence " ⬚⬚⬚ Leopold Mozart was, at the request of his ⬚⬚⬚, promoted to the second Grade of Our Royal Order with the usual ceremonies.

> Vienna, State Archives, *loc. cit.*, fasc. 133.—Deutsch, *op. cit.*, p. 25.—Leopold Mozart thus became a "journeyman".—He had first taken leave of Mlle Villersi.—*Cf.* 6 and 7 April.—Mozart had written the song " Gesellenreise " (K. 468) for this occasion.

On 19 April the Mozarts visited Baroness Waldstätten at Klosterneuburg.

> The Baroness had retired from Vienna.

FROM THE ATTENDANCE RECORD OF THE " TRUE CONCORD " LODGE,
22 APRIL 1785

CCCLXXVI. [Session] Vienna the $\frac{22}{4}$ 5875 . . .

. . . Visiting Brothers.
Leopold Mozart ⎫
Wolfgang Mozart⎭ of the " Beneficence " . . .

> Vienna, State Archives, *loc. cit.*, fasc. 133.—Deutsch, *op. cit.*, p. 25.—Leopold
> Mozart's signature is crossed out because, as a "journeyman", he was not at
> first allowed to attend the Master Lodge.

FROM THE EVENTS RECORD OF THE " TRUE CONCORD " LODGE,
22 APRIL 1785

CCCLXXVI. [Session] Vienna the $\frac{22}{4}$ 5785 . . .
1) After the opening of the Apprentices', Journeymen's and Masters'
☐☐☐☐the hon. Master indicated that at the request of the hon. " Beneficence" ☐☐☐☐ of this city the Brother Journeyman Leopold Mozard . . .
was to be promoted to the third Grade.
2) the Journeymen Brothers Leopold Mozard, son of Johann Georg, and
member of the hon. " Beneficence " ☐☐☐☐ of this city . . . were promoted to the third Grade of Our Royal Order, with the usual ceremonies.

> Vienna, State Archives, *loc. cit.*, fasc. 133.—Deutsch, *op. cit.*, p. 25.—Mozarts
> father had now also become a " master ".—Ignaz von Born presided at th'
> meeting.

FROM THE " PROVINZIALNACHRICHTEN ", VIENNA, 23 APRIL 1785

Arias.

From *Operas*, to be sung at the pianoforte : to be had at Lausch's music
establishment . . .

Mozart. Die Entführung aus dem Serail. L'overtura	36 kr.
" Ach gehe doch, ich rathe Dir ". *Duetto*	1 fl.
" Wenn der Freude thränen fliessen ". *Aria*	25 kr.
" O ! wie will ich *triumphiren* ". *do.*	45 kr.
" *Vivat Bachus, Bachus* lebe ". *Duetto*	35 kr.
" Konstanze ! dich wieder zu sehen ". *Aria*	35 kr.
" Wer ein Liebchen hat gefunden ". *do.*	15 kr.
" Nie werd ich deine Huld verkennen ". *do.*	20 kr.
" Durch Zärtlichkeit und Schmeicheln ". *do.*	20 kr.
" Hier soll ich dich dann sehen. Konstanze ! " *do.*	15 kr.
" Ich baue ganz an deine Stärke ". *do.*	40 kr.

Cf. 16 April 1785.

On 24 April, at the "Crowned Hope" lodge, a festivity was held in honour of
Ignaz von Born, master of the "Concord" lodge, in the presence of Leopold and
Wolfgang Mozart, and the latter's cantata *Die Maurerfreude* (K. 471) was performed.

> The occasion was Born's discovery of a new method of smelting which meant
> a saving of both labour and wood in the mines. On 14 April the Emperor
> decreed the introduction of the new method throughout the realm ; Born
> was given a share in the profits and created a Knight of the Realm on the 24th.
> —For Mozart's cantata see 17 August 1785.

On 25 April, at noon, Leopold Mozart left Vienna with Heinrich Marchand ; his
son and Constanze accompanied them as far as Purkersdorf, where they ate a snack
together before parting.

> About 7 p.m. on the 26th Leopold Mozart reached Linz, alighted at the Black
> Buck and on the 29th attended a party at Count Johann Thun's house. On
> 1 May he was in time to witness the entry of the first Bishop of Linz, Ernst
> Johann, Count Herberstein (see 20 September 1762). On the 4th he arrived
> with Marchand at Munich, where he remained for about a week before
> returning to Salzburg.

FROM THE "WIENER ZEITUNG", 30 APRIL 1785
New Music.

> .   .   .   .   .

Variations *per il Clavicemb.* by Bach, . . . Haydn, Mozart, . . . 1 fl. each
2 new Symphonies in C and D by Mozart,   7 kr. per sheet.
Johann Traeg . . . He announces at the same time that at the usual removal
term he will remove to the house No. 423 on the Hohe Markt, corner
house at the Wipplingerstrasse, where the glass shop is, 4th floor. He requests his patrons and friends to visit him there from 10 May onward.

> The symphonies were presumably the Linz (K. 425) and the Haffner (K. 385).

DECREE OF ARCHBISHOP HIERONYMUS TO THE SALZBURG EXCHEQUER,
1 MAY 1785

At the humble request of our Vice-Kapellmeister Leopold Mozart we
have granted him permission to betake himself hence to Vienna for 6 weeks :
Since however, without obtaining an extension of his leave, he is still
protracting his residence in Vienna, we therefore command that unless he
returns here by the middle of the current month he shall receive no
pay until further orders, and we also command that our intention in this
matter shall in the future be put punctually into practice with all those who
fail to report for the fulfilment of their duty within the prescribed time.
Hieronymus   Salzburg, the 1st of May 1785

> Salzburg, Provincial Archives.—Communicated by Dr. Herbert Klein.—The
> Archbishop himself advanced the final date from the end to the middle of the
> month.

DECREE OF THE SALZBURG EXCHEQUER TO THE PRINCELY COURT
PAY OFFICE

His Serene Highness has ordered by a most gracious *Decretum proprium de hesterno* that the *Vice* Kapellmeister Leopold Mozart, who has gone to Vienna for 6 weeks with the most gracious permission, is no longer to receive any pay until further notice, unless he returns here by the middle of this month ; the which is herewith imparted to the Princely Court Pay Office for obedient notice.

Decretum in Consilio Camerae Salisburgensis
Die 2da Maji 1785.

> Salzburg, Provincial Archives (Catenichel 1785, p. 60).—Pirkmayer, *op. cit.*, p. 22.—Leopold Mozart had left Salzburg on 28 January and did not return until mid-May ; he was thus absent for about 14 weeks.

On 26 May *Die Entführung* was given at Cassel.

On 13 June *Die Entführung* was given at Bratislava by Count Ladislaus Erdödy's opera company, conducted by Kapellmeister Joseph Chudy.

> Erwin Major, *Mozart in Ungarn* (Budapest, 1956), p. 25. The singspiel was repeated five times there. "Arias" from it were printed at the time by Franz August Patzko in Bratislava.

FROM A PROSPECTUS OF TORRICELLA'S, VIENNA 1785

Newest Fantasy-variations by Kappellmeister A. W. Mozart. The eagerness with which the works of this famous master are on all sides especially awaited (these works which win the attention of the connoisseur with their exceptional art and freshness, and so gently move our hearts with their melodies) persuaded me to make these very beautiful variations my own, and thereby to be once more of service to the most esteemed lovers of music ; for I offer them a work which will bring fresh honour to its creator.

These variations, finely engraved, may already be had for 36 kr. at my music shop.

I shall spare no effort to provide the public with engraved copies of all the remaining variations of this outstanding master.

C. T.

> Berlin, German State Library ; box 4 of the Mozart Correspondence, removed to the University Library at Tübingen.—Found by Dr. Ernst Fritz Schmid. —Broadsheet, on the front of which is announced a work by Silvere Müller that Torricella published in 1785, marked 1785 in red ink. Without advertising them in the *Wiener Zeitung*, Torricella published the following variations by Mozart : K. 265 (" Ah, vous dirai-je maman ") without publisher's number, probably K. 398 (" Salve tu, Domine ") with the number 28, and K. 455 (" Unser dummer Pöbel meint ") without number ; all three appeared in 1785, or at least were engraved then and published soon after by Artaria from already engraved plates. Since no copy of Torricella's K. 398 or 455 has yet come to light, it is impossible to state which of the three volumes is referred to

in this prospectus. Prof. Kurt von Fischer believes that it can only be K. 398, but it should be noted that Artaria & Co. in 1786 also published K. 352, 353, 359 and 360, and these may have been acquired from Torricella.

In the summer *Die Entführung* was performed at Aachen.

The first performance at Augsburg, which also took place in 1785, cannot be dated more precisely.

On 27 July Nannerl's son Leopold was born in Leopold Mozart's lodgings on the Hannibalplatz at Salzburg.

The grandfather kept the child with him while he lived, *i.e.* for nearly two years.

FROM THE ATTENDANCE RECORD OF THE "TRUE CONCORD" LODGE, 12 AUGUST 1785

CCCV. [Session] Vienna the $\frac{12}{8}$ 5785 . . .
. . . . . . Visiting Brothers.
. . . . . . Mozart . . . . . .

Vienna, State Archives, *loc. cit.*, fasc. 133.—Deutsch, *op. cit.*, p. 26.

FROM THE "WIENER ZEITUNG", 17 AUGUST 1785

Announcement.

At the art establishment *Artaria & Comp.* . . . . is to be had :
. . . "Die Maurer-Freude" ["Masonic Joy"]. A cantata for tenor voice, and lastly a short chorus. By the celebrated Kapellmeister W. A. Mozart. This cantata is engraved in score and at the same time furnished with a supplementary pianoforte part, price thereof 2 fl.

Cf. 24 April 1785 and the two following documents.—Announced also in the *Realzeitung* of 18 October 1785.

WENZEL TOBIAS EPSTEIN'S PREFACE TO THE SCORE OF "DIE MAURERFREUDE"

Touched by the kindness which the wisest and most just of Monarchs, Joseph II, has bestowed on one of its Brothers, and full of sympathy with the impending happiness of this noble man, this profound scholar, this meritorious mason, the assembly of Brothers known as "The Crowned Hope", of Vienna, resolved to express its sentiments in fraternal concord at a friendly and joyous repast, and to give vent to them in conviviality through the arts of poetry and of music. The present cantata is a distinguished item of the songs of joy sung at the feast. The Brothers of the said lodge believe that they fitly interpret the views of their Monarch, the opinions of their honoured guest and the feelings of their own hearts by making this cantata generally known and by dedicating its proceeds to the benefit of their needy fellow-men.

> Deutsch, *op. cit.*, p. 10.—Epstein, still a merchant at that time but later a civil servant, collected minerals and books. He was " Second Overseer " of the " Crowned Hope " lodge.

INFORMATION

When not long ago our gracious Monarch rewarded with his well-known great generosity the invention of a new amalgam for the separation of metals made by the hon. Brother *Born*, Master of the very hon. sister ⬛️⬛️ of *The True Concord*, the very hon. ⬛️⬛️of *The Crowned Hope* resolved, in order to show pleasurable participation in the hon. Brother *Born's* good fortune, as well as its especial affection and so justly deserved respect for his person in particular, and in general for his very hon. ⬛️⬛️ issued from the womb of the very hon. ⬛️⬛️ of *The Crowned Hope*, to mark the occasion with a feast of joy. Various songs written and set to music by Brothers of our very hon. ⬛️⬛️ appeared on this occasion, including a cantata written by our Brother *Petran* and set to music by the celebrated Brother *Mozart* of the very hon. *Beneficence* ⬛️⬛️ , sung by our Brother *Adamberger* and now committed to print by our Brother *Artaria*, with an engraved title-page from the drawing of our Brother *Unterberger* with a preface by our Brother *Epstein*. The proceeds of the sale having been devoted to the benefit of the poor by our worthy Brother *Artaria*, we give you information thereof, so that you too may find a market for this cantata, in so far as that may be feasible in your region.

At the very hon. ⬛️⬛️ of *The*
Crowned Hope   C. D. Bartsch
In the Orient of *Vienna*.   Secretary.

> A copy of this printed sheet (the secretary's name alone is in handwriting), once in the archives of the firm of Artaria & Co. was later acquired by the Vienna City Library.—Deutsch, *op. cit.*, p. 9 (facsimile).—The words of the cantata are by Franz Petran, chaplain to Count Franz Joseph Thun, who was also a freemason.—Pasquale Artaria was one of the partners in the publishing house.—The handsome title-page was engraved by Sebastian Mansfeld after Ignaz Unterberger—Mozart's name appears on several copies as Mxxxxt, but is fully written out on others. The publisher is not named.

On 20 August Franz Anton Weber married Genoveva Brenner in the Schottenkirche in Vienna ; the witnesses were Joseph Lange and Vincenzo Righini.

> This couple, Constanze's uncle and aunt, were to be the parents of Carl Maria von Weber (*cf.* 8 January 1787).—Righini was the director of the opera buffa and Genoveva's teacher.

MOZART'S NOTE FOR THOMAS ATTWOOD ON THE MS OF A MUSIC
LESSON, AFTER 23 AUGUST 1785
(in English)

This after noon I am not at home, therefore I pray you to come to morrow
at three & a half.

Mozart.

Mozart collection of C. B. Oldman, London.—Facsimile in *The Musical Times*
(London), 1 December 1900 (F. G. Edwards).—On p. 8 of the first volume of
the young Englishman's exercises in composition supervised by Mozart, we
read in the former's hand (in English): "Thos. Attwood's comp[ts] to M[r]
Mozardt, hoping this example will meet his approbation, as he has taken
all possible Care to leave no room for Correction. Tuesday 23[d] August in
the year of our Lord 1785." Mozart's note is undated. Attwood stayed in
Vienna as Mozart's pupil from the middle of 1785 to at least the end of 1786.
Cf. Oldman in *Gedenkboek aan Dr. D. F. Scheurleer* (The Hague, 1925), p. 227.
—Mozart used sometimes to write in English between 1785 and 1787.

On 24 August the Society of Musicians resolved to send Mozart a preliminary
intimation concerning his petition for admission.

Cf. 11 February 1785.

On 25 August *Die Entführung* was given at Nuremberg.

FROM THE " WIENER ZEITUNG ", 31 AUGUST 1785
(In French and Italian)

. . . Mozart : Cassation [*Cassazio*] in F. for 2 violins, 2 horns, viola
and bass,   2 fl. 30 kr.
—— Concerto for the harpsichord, in G.   4 fl. 30 kr.
—— 12 Variations in G, with accompaniment for a violin   40 kr.
—— 6 Do. in G minor, do.   35 kr.

Lorenz Lausch,
Music Publishers. . . .

The "Cassazio" is the divertimento (K. 247), which was first printed under that
title by Artaria in 1799. The pianoforte concerto is K. 453. The Variations
are those on "La Bergère Célimène" (K. 359), and those on "Hélas, j'ai perdu
mon amant" (K. 360).—*Cf.* 14 September 1785.

FROM THE " MAINZER WOCHENBLATT ", 31 AUGUST 1785

The very excellent and generally well-received opera, entitled *Die
Entführung aus dem Serail*, by Herr Mozart, at last appears after numerous
requests in a pianoforte score by Herr Abbé Stark, done by the Electoral
Court music engraver Schott of this place. 14 sheets, 3 assimilated thalers.

Communicated by Dr. Adam Gottron, Mainz.—The singspiel had been first
given at Mainz in January 1784.—Johann Franz Xaver Stark was a canon of

St. Mary's and a vicar of the cathedral, but also organist and later musical director there. (*Cf.* Gottron, *Mozart und Mainz* [Mainz, 1951], p. 67.) Leopold Mozart mentions in a letter to his daughter of 16 December 1785 that this pianoforte score was issued "by the Augspurg bookseller Stage . . . and moreover engraved at Mayntz". Conrad Heinrich Stage had evidently advertised in the Augsburg papers the pianoforte score engraved and published by Bernhard Schott, "with many high encomiums of the famous Herr von Mozart". It was this score which induced Mozart and Torricella to give up their own project (see 17 November 1784).

TITLE-PAGE AND DEDICATION OF THE STRING QUARTETS
DEDICATED TO HAYDN
(in Italian)

Sei Quartetti
per due Violini, Viola e Violoncello.
Composti e dedicati al Signor Giuseppe Haydn
Maestro di Cappella di S.A. il Principe d'Esterhazy &c &c
dal suo amico
W. A. Mozart.
Opera X

To my dear friend Haydn,

A father who had resolved to send his children out into the great world took it to be his duty to confide them to the protection and guidance of a very celebrated Man, especially when the latter by good fortune was at the same time his best Friend. Here they are then, O great Man and my dearest Friend, these six children of mine. They are, it is true, the fruit of long and laborious endeavour, yet the hope inspired in me by several Friends that it may be at least partly compensated encourages me, and I flatter myself that this offspring will serve to afford me some solace one day. You yourself, dearest friend, told me of your satisfaction with them during your last Visit to this Capital. It is this indulgence above all which urges me to commend them to you and encourages me to hope that they will not seem to you altogether unworthy of your favour. May it therefore please you to receive them kindly and to be their Father, Guide and Friend ! From this moment I resign to you all my rights in them, begging you however to look indulgently upon the defects which the partiality of a Father's eye may have concealed from me, and in spite of them to continue in your generous Friendship for him who so greatly values it, in expectation of which I am, with all my Heart, my dearest Friend, your most Sincere Friend

W. A. Mozart.

Vienna, 1 September 1785.

Jahn, Vol. II, p. 371.—K. 387, 421, 458, 428, 464 and 465. *Cf.* 12 February and 17 September 1785.—Only the first edition contains the dedicatory epistle (facsimile in Robert Haas, *Mozart*, p. 113).

Mozard

6 Quartets for 2 violins, viola and violoncello, are to be had from my art establishment in the Kohlmarkt, next door to the Milano, at the cheapest price.

Christoph Torricella.

This advertisement, referring to six early string quartets (K. 168-73), must have been very inconvenient to Artaria and Mozart at this particular time.

IBID., 14 SEPTEMBER 1785
Music

to be had of Wenzel *Sukowaty*, Court Theatre copyist, viz.
. . . *Entführung aus dem Serail, del Sign. Mozart*, complete,   16 fl.

Cf. 16 April 1785.—By way of exception, this advertisement is printed here a second time because the word "complete" has been added and the price increased from 15 to 16 gulden. Perhaps the overture was not originally included.

IBID., 14 SEPTEMBER 1785
New Music.

Johann Traeg, at the Glazier's house, No. 423, 4th floor, in the Hohe Markt, has the honour of announcing :

Further the following new music, neatly and correctly written, at 7 kr. per sheet.
A Double Concerto for two harpsichords in D by Schuster.
2 do. in A and F by Mozart.
1 Concerto for harpsichord in G by Mozart,
    N.B. quite new.
1 *Cassatio* in F for 2 violins, 2 horns, viola & bass by Mozart.
1 Trio for harpsichord, violin and violoncello by Mozart.

Various new Symphonies by Pleyel, Mozart and Mich. Haydn.

10 Variations for harpsichord ("unser dummer Pöbel") by Mozart   1 fl.
12 do. in G. ("La Bergere Selimene")   1 fl.
6 do. in G min. by Mozart   40 kr.

Joseph Schuster was a native of Dresden and lived there.—The two "double concertos" may have been K. 414 and 413, though they are not for two pianofortes but, like the following one, K. 453, for only one. The "Cassatio" is K. 247, the pianoforte trio that in B♭ major (K. 254) (published by Heina of Paris about 1782). The variations are K. 455, 359 and 360, the two last-named being pianoforte and violin.—Of these works Lausch had offered K. 453, 247, 359 and 360 on 31 August, *i.e.* a fortnight earlier, also in MS. copies.

FROM THE " WIENER ZEITUNG ", 17 SEPTEMBER 1785

Announcement.

At the art establishment *Artaria Comp.* . . . are to be had : By Herr Kapellmeister W. A. Mozart, 6 entirely new Quartets for 2 violins, viola and violoncello, *Opus* X, engraved, for 6 fl. 30 kr.—Mozart's works call for no special praise, so that it should be quite superfluous to go into details ; it need only be affirmed that here is a masterpiece. This may be taken as the more certain since the author has dedicated this work to his friend Joseph Haydn, Kapellmeister to Prince Esterházy, who has honoured it with all the approval of which a man of great genius is alone worthy. In view thereof the publishers have not spared any costs either to present amateurs and connoisseurs with this work beautifully and clearly engraved as regards both paper and print, relying upon it that the price fixed for it, which could not have been less than 12 fl. for manuscript, will not be regarded as excessive, since the Quartets cover 150 pages.

As the art dealer Herr *Torricella* also announced 6 Quartets by Mozart at a low price in the recent newspapers, without saying whether they were in manuscript or engraved, old or new, Herr Mozart regards it as his duty to inform the estimable public that the said 6 Quartets are by no means new, but an old work written by him as long as 15 years ago, so that amateurs who had been expecting the new ones should not be wrongly served.

> No. 75, p. 2191. (These references are given because the same page has been wrongly cited for Torricella's reply.)—*Cf.* 10 September 1785, and the following document.—Artaria's advertisement also appeared in the *Realzeitung* for 18 September.

TORRICELLA'S REPLY TO ARTARIA, AUTUMN 1785

At the art establishment of Christoph Torricella . . . are to be had :
By Herr Kapellmeister W. A. Mozart, 6 Quartets for 2 violins, viola and violoncello, fairly and correctly copied, at 5 fl.

Since in the announcement of Herr Artaria Comp. concerning the publication of the latest and newest Quartets, it has been quite superfluously asserted that those which I made known to the public had been written 15 years ago, and the public thus seemed to be warned against a kind of deliberate exploitation, I find myself under the necessity of explaining that my not saying whether they were engraved or in manuscript, old or new, should in fact prove that I had no intention of misleading the public—supposing that proven honesty should fail to speak for me.

As regards the 15-year-old Quartets, then, I believe that they too stand in need of no other recommendation than their master's name—indeed I am convinced that they too may be a novelty for many an admirer of the latest, thanks to their quite peculiar quality ; and that therefore amateurs could never be wrongly served, since these too are assuredly Mozart's children.

> Jahn, Vol. II, p. 355 ; Köchel-Einstein, p. 233 ; Müller von Asow, Vol. III, p. 401 f.—*Cf.* 10 and 17 September 1785.—The source of this reply has been given as *Wiener Zeitung*, p. 2191, where, however, only Artaria's rejoinder is found. Though this document is undated it is unquestionably authentic, but the place of its original publication has eluded discovery.—The string quartets K. 168-73, which are clearly the ones in question, were written in Vienna in August and September 1773, and were thus no more than twelve years old.

FROM THE " WIENERBLÄTTCHEN ", 26 SEPTEMBER 1785

For the happy recovery of the favourite virtuosa Mme. Storace the I. & R. Court Theatre poet Herr *Abbate da Ponte* has produced an Italian song of joy : " Per la ricuperata salute di Ophelia ".

This has been set to music, to be sung at the pianoforte, by the three famous Kapellmeister Salieri, Mozart and Cornetti, and is for sale at the art establishment of Artaria Compagnie on the Michaelsplatz at 17 kr.

> Köchel-Einstein, p. 599.—Ann Storace lost her voice entirely for a time at the first performance of her brother Stephen's opera *Gli sposi malcontenti*, which took place at the Burgtheater on 1 June 1785. *Cf.* Michael Kelly, *Reminiscences* (London, 1826), Vol. I, 234, and Da Ponte, *Denkwürdigkeiten*, ed. by Gustav Gugitz (Dresden, 1925), Vol. II, p. 322, and Vol. III, p. 356.—*Cornetti* may perhaps be Alessandro Cornet, but he was in any case scarcely a " famous Kapellmeister ". No copy of this cantata (K. App. 11a) is known, nor has the libretto been preserved ; the allusion to Ophelia is thus hardly comprehensible.—See 18 October 1785.

In September *Die Entführung* was performed by Joseph Bellomo's company at Weimar.

> The *Ephemeriden der Litteratur und des Theaters* (Berlin, 1786), Vol. III, p. 406 (see 4 October 1780), where this performance is mentioned without a precise date, says no more than that it " pleased ".—In 1785 this periodical published Daniel Berger's engraving of Joseph Lange's double portrait of himself and his wife.

FROM THE " WIENER ZEITUNG ", 5 OCTOBER 1785
(partly in Italian)

Lausch's music establishment . . .
Mozart, 6 Quartets for 2 violins, viola and violoncello, Op. X, quite new, and handsomely engraved   6 fl. 30 kr.
" Mio caro Adone " with 6 variations, for the harpsichord, by the same, 24 kr.

> Contrary to his custom Lausch here offered a printed volume ; these are the quartets published by Artaria on 17 September. However, the variations on a theme from Salieri's opera *La fiera di Venezia* (K. 180, written in Vienna in the

autumn of 1773 and published by Heina of Paris about 1778) were to be had in manuscript.

On 11 October the Paris publisher Boyer announced the six sonatas for pianoforte and violin (K. 376, 296, 377-380) as Œuvre 2ᵉ in the *Gazette de France*.

Mozart en France (Paris, 1956), p. 69.—This was a reprint.

INVITATION OF THE UNITED LODGES " THE THREE EAGLES " AND " THE PALMTREE " TO THE VIENNESE SISTER LODGES, 15 OCTOBER 1785

To support two visiting Brothers—both of them virtuosi on the basset horn—who some time ago came to Vienna with the intention of finding shelter here, but have meanwhile fallen into difficult circumstances through their fruitless expectations, and are at the moment unable to undertake the return journey home on which they have decided, the two very honourable lodges of " The Three Eagles " and " The Palmtree " have decided to give a concert in the evening of next Thursday, $\frac{20}{x}$, at 6.30 o'clock in the ☐ quarters, at which the honourable Brothers Mozart and Stadler will also be heard.

A brotherly request is therefore made to the very honourable sister lodges to allow this to circulate among their honoured and esteemed members and to be good enough to request that they may appear in as large numbers as possible, and on entering contribute something according to their own discretion for the benefit of these visiting Brothers.

From the two very hon. ☐ ☐
" The Three Eagles " and " The Palm-   *Puthon.*
tree " I.O.z.W. [in the Orient of Vienna]   Master of the 3 E. ☐
57 $\frac{15}{x}$ 85.   *Loibel,* Mstr. of " The Palm-
                                                                    tree ".

P.S. Brother Mozart will entertain the Brothers with his much-loved extemporizations.   *Kette.*
                                                                Sec. of the 3 E. ☐

Vienna, State Archives, *loc. cit.,* fasc. 103.—Deutsch, *op. cit.,* p. 26.—The two lodges that issued the invitation were among the smallest of the eight Viennese lodges. The wholesale merchant Johann Baptist, Baron von Puthon, Treasurer of the Austrian Grand Lodge, was head of the one ; the other was directed by Johann Martin Loibel (Loibl), a Councillor of the Hungarian-Transylvanian Exchequer and Master of Ceremonies to the Grand Lodge, who was Mozart's neighbour in the Schulerstrasse. The postscript is in Loibel's hand. Johann Kette was also secretary of the Financial Directorate of Tobacco Taxes. —Anton Stadler, the clarinettist, had been admitted to the " Palm-Tree " [*Palmbaum*] lodge only three weeks before.—The two virtuosi on the basset horn, a type of clarinet whose low register is extended downwards from the normal E to C, were Anton David of Offenburg in the Ortenau, near Strasbourg, and Vinzent Springer of Mladá Boleslav (Jungbunzlau) near Prague ; they were thus far from " compatriots ". In Johann Friedrich Reichardt's *Musikalische Monatsschrift,* Berlin, August 1792 (p. 41) Springer is described as

David's pupil.—After his meeting with these two, Mozart often made use of the instrument in his scores.—*Cf.* 9 December 1785.

FROM THE " WIENER REALZEITUNG ", VIENNA, 18 OCTOBER 1785

Fine Arts and Sciences.

316. By Herr Kapellmeister W. A. Mozart, 6 new Quartets for 2 violins, viola and violoncello, *Opus X.* 6 fl. 30 kr. At Artaria's on the Kohlmarkt, No. 132 [133].

317. " Die Maurer-Freude ". The music by Herr W. A. Mozart, 2 fl. At Artaria's.

319. " Per la ricuperata salute da Ophelia " [" For Ophelia's Recovered Health "]. By Abbate da Ponte. Set to music by the Kapellmeister Salieri, Mozart and *Cornetti.* 17 kr. At Artaria's.

> From a list of new publications.—See 17 September, 17 August and 26 September 1785.—The fact that the name Cornetti is here printed in italics may indicate that it is a pseudonym.

In October the Paris publisher Pierre Le Duc announced Mozart's " first " pianoforte concerto in the *Mercure de France.*

> Cari Johansson, *French Music Publishers' Catalogues of the Second Half of the Eighteenth Century* (Stockholm, 1955), pp. 95 and 100.—This was the F major concerto (K. 413), published by Artaria & Co. on 29 March 1785.

On 17 November a funeral celebration was held at the " Crowned Hope " lodge in honour of two deceased brothers, Georg August, Duke of Mecklenburg-Strelitz and Count Franz Esterházy von Galántha ; Mozart's *Maurerische Trauermusik* (K. 477), written for the occasion, was performed.

> Vienna, State Archives, *loc. cit.*, fasc. 108—The invitation of the lodge is dated 11 November. The Duke, a Major-General, had died on 6 November at Nagyszombat (Trnava) in Hungary ; as an absent Brother he was an honorary member of the " Three Eagles " [*Zu den drei Adlern*] lodge, which was not able to hold his commemoration until 7 December. The Count, who was Hungarian-Transylvanian Court Chancellor, had died in Vienna on 7 November ; he belonged to the " Hope " [*Hoffnung*] lodge (whose Master was Count Johann Esterházy). *Cf.* Deutsch, *op. cit.*, pp. 12 and 30 f.—The funeral oration on the Count which Wenzel Epstein delivered on 17 November was printed and the proceeds given for the benefit of the poor.—*Cf. Realzeitung,* 20 December 1785, p. 882 f.

On 28 November, at the first performance of Francesco Bianchi's opera *La villanella rapita* at the Burgtheater, two interpolated numbers by Mozart were sung.

> The additional items were the quartet " Dite almeno, in che mancai " (K. 479), sung by Celesta Coltellini, Vincenzio Calvesi, Stefano Mandini and Francesco Bussani, and the trio " Mandina amabile " (K. 480), sung by Coltellini, Calvesi and Mandini. Signora Coltellini was the daughter of the librettist of *La finta semplice* and the wife of Mozart's friend from Lyons, the merchant Johann Georg Meurikofer (who later spelt his name Meuricoffre).—Sukowaty sold manuscript scores of these numbers (a copy of the trio was at the Gymnasium at Zittau).—The poster gives 25 November as the date of first performance,

but it must have been postponed from the Friday to the Monday, since the *Wiener Zeitung* of 3 December gives it as 28 November.

FROM ZINZENDORF'S DIARY, 30 NOVEMBER 1785
(in French)

. . . At the theatre. *La villanella rapita*. The spectacle is gay, the music contains some pieces by Moshart, the words much that is equivocal. The *souflet* [? *couplet*] repeated.

FROM THE " WIENER ZEITUNG ", 3 DECEMBER 1785

At the I. & R. Court Theatre next the Kärntnertor a German *Singspiel* after Herr Bretzner, with music by Herr Mozart, was performed on Friday 25 November, *Die Entführung aus dem Serail*, at which Mme Lange reappeared for the first time after her grave illness and was deservedly welcomed most favourably.

> Frau Lange had been seriously ill. *Cf.* Leopold Mozart's letter to his daughter of 22 September 1785 (Deutsch-Paumgartner edition of these letters [Salzburg, 1936], p. 121).

IBID., 7 DECEMBER 1785
New Music.

. . . *Mozart*, a Fantasy and Sonata for the *forte-piano opera* II. 1 fl. 30 kr. ——the first act of the opera *Die Entführung aus dem Serail* finely engraved for the pianoforte 2 fl.

At *Artaria & Company*
Art Establishment on the Michaelsplatz.

> Jahn, Vol. I, p. 738.—These are the works in C minor dedicated to Frau Trattner (K. 475 and 457) and the lost fragment of the original pianoforte score of *Die Entführung*, probably taken over from Torricella (*cf.* 17 November 1784).

INVITATION FROM " THE CROWNED HOPE " LODGE TO THE VIENNESE
SISTER LODGES, 9 DECEMBER 1785

Highly honoured Master !
Highly honoured Deputy Master .
  Much honoured Brother Supervisors and Officials !
  Highly honoured and honourable Brothers all !
  At the request of the two hon. Brothers David and Sprenger the very

hon. [____] of " The Crowned Hope " has resolved to hold an assembly on 15 December, at which, with several other honoured and honourable Brothers they will endeavour to delight the society with harmony and the art of music.

1stly a Symphony will be performed which the hon. Brother Wranizky has specially composed for the very hon. [____].

2ndly a Concerto which the two hon. Brothers David and Sprenger will play on the basset horn.

3rdly the Cantata in honour of the very hon. Brother Born with music by the hon. Brother Mozard, sung by the hon. Brother Adamberger.

4thly a Concerto on the pianoforte played by the hon. Brother Mozard.

5thly the Partitas drafted by Brother Stadler for 6 wind instruments, at which the hon. Brother Locz will play the great 8ve bassoon.

6thly a second Symphony by the hon. Brother Wranizky, also written for the very hon. [____]

7thly Fantasias by the hon. Brother Mozard.

Assured that your very hon. [____] will gladly participate in an entertainment which with the pleasure of hearing select pieces by artists and Brothers combines that of supporting visiting Brothers, the undersigned has the honour of inviting you to this assembly and to announce at the same time that the very hon. Brother Treasurer will receive and collect at the door of the [____] that with which the benevolence of hon. and honourable Brothers may wish to benefit the travellers.

In the Orient of Vienna
9. XII. 5875

In the name and at the behest of
the very hon. [____] of " The
Crowned Hope "
C. D. *Bartsch*
Secretary

Vienna, State Archives, *loc. cit.*, fasc. 103.—Deutsch, *op. cit.*, p. 27.—For the masonic terms conventional abbreviations are used in the original.—*Cf.* 15 October 1785.—Paul Wranitzky, Musical Director to Count Johann Esterházy, also belonged to the " Hope " lodge.—The cantata was *Die Maurerfreude* (see 24 April 1785).—" Partita " (*Parthie* in the original) here means a suite.—Theodor Lotz, viola-player and first clarinettist in Prince Joseph Batthyány's orchestra at Bratislava, had improved the basset horn in 1782 ; it was probably he who played the double bassoon on this evening. The Stadler brothers, however, soon learnt to play the basset horn themselves.—The treasurer of the lodge was Count Joseph Stockhammer, the Imperial Cupbearer.

On 15 December Mozart took part in a concert held at the " Crowned Hope " lodge for the benefit of the basset-horn players David and Springer.

—*Cf.* 30 November 1785.

---

*   FROM ZINZENDORF'S DIARY, 16 DECEMBER 1785

. . . to the opera . . . la *Villanella rapita*. The quartetto is fine.
    M.—9

FROM THE ATTENDANCE REGISTER OF THE "TRUE CONCORD" LODGE,
19 DECEMBER 1785

CCCCXXXVII. [Session] Vienna the $\frac{19}{12}$ 5785 . . .

...... Visiting Brothers.

...... Mozart of the "Beneficence".

> Vienna, State Archives, *loc. cit.*, fasc. 133.—Deutsch, *op. cit.*, p. 26.—The surviving Viennese masonic documents become reticent at about this time. On 11 December the Emperor Joseph decreed that the eight lodges should be amalgamated into two or three, presumably to make them easier to supervise. This was carried into effect on 28 December. The "Concord" lodge, together with the "Palm-Tree" and the "Three Eagles", formed the new "Truth" [*Zur Wahrheit*] lodge, which opened on 6 January 1786. The "Crowned Hope", with the "Beneficence" (Mozart's lodge) and the "Three Fires" formed the principal Viennese lodge, "The New-crowned Hope" [*Zur neugekrönten Hoffnung*] on 14 January 1786. The two remaining lodges, "St. Joseph" [*Zum heiligen Joseph*] and "Steadfastness" [*Zur Beständigkeit*] disappeared.—In the manuscript register of the "New-crowned Hope" Mozart appears in 1786 as a Master, but it is not known when he reached the third grade.

FROM THE "WIENER ZEITUNG", 21 DECEMBER 1785

Information.

At Johann Traeg's . . . the following music is to be had :

1 Concerto in B♭ *per il clavicembalo &c, &c*, by W. A. Mozart, 7 kr. per sheet.

New Symphonies by the same, at 7 kr.

> The pianoforte concerto was probably K. 456 (see 13 February 1785). On the symphonies *cf.* 30 April 1785.

★ GOETHE TO PHILIPP CHRISTOPH KAYSER, WEIMAR, 22 DECEMBER 1785

Die Entführung aus dem Serail, composed by Mozart, was given recently. Everyone declared himself for the music. The first time they played it tolerably, the text itself is very bad and the music too did not appeal to me. The second time it was badly played and I even went out. But the piece survived and everyone praised the music. When they gave it for the fifth time I went to it again. They acted and sang better than before. I ignored the text, and now understand the difference between my judgement and the work's impact on the public, and know where I am.

> The Weimar Sophien-Ausgabe of Goethe's works, section IV, vol. 7, p. 143.—Kayser (1755–1823), a composer and piano virtuoso, was a friend of Goethe's. *Die Entführung* had been performed in Weimar from September 1785. *Cf.* November 1787.

On 23 December Karl Ditters von Dittersdorf's oratorio *Esther* was performed at the Burgtheater. Between the two parts of the oratorio Mozart played the piano.

This oratorio had already been performed on 22 December at the first Advent concert of the Society of Musicians, in which the violinist Joseph Otter took part. (At the first performance of the oratorio, on 19 December 1773 at the Kärntnertor Theatre, Dittersdorf had himself played a violin concerto.) The announcement of the second concert promised " as an entr'acte, a pianoforte Concerto newly composed and played by W. A. Mozart ". (Köchel-Einstein, p. 605.) In the Society's proceedings we read : " Herr W. A. Mozart will play on the forte-piano a new Concerto of his own composition ". (Pohl, *op. cit.*, p. 61.)—The oratorio was conducted by Salieri.—On 28 December Mozart wrote to Salzburg (as we know from Leopold's letter to Nannerl of 13 January 1786) that he had " hastily given 3 subscription concerts, with 120 subscribers ". Where these took place and what he played we do not know— only that he had to repeat the Andante of the new concerto in E flat (K. 482).

FROM THE " WIENER ZEITUNG ", 24 DECEMBER 1785
Musical Concert.

On 22 and 23 inst. the local Society of Musicians held the concert usual each year for the benefit of its widows and orphans, and on that occasion performed the oratorio entitled *Esther* by the celebrated Herr Ditters von Dittersdorf, with great success. His Majesty the Emperor as well as H.H. the Archduke Franz and the Princess Elisabeth were present, together with the high nobility and a numerous public. Between the two parts . . . Herr Joseph Otter . . . was to be heard with a concerto on the violin . . . On the second day Herr Wolfgang Amade Mozart made a change with a concerto of his own composition on the fortepiano, the favourable reception of which we forbear to mention, since our praise is superfluous in view of the deserved fame of this master, as well known as he is universally valued.

Reprinted on 28 December in the *Provinzialnachrichten*.

On 24 December Hieronymus Löschenkohl advertised in the *Wiener Zeitung* two new calendars with engraved silhouettes of Viennese notabilities, among whom was Mozart.

Löschenkohl was an engraver and publisher of topical prints, and occasionally of music too.—The " calendars " for 1786 were the *Gelehrten-Almanach von Wien*, containing 36 silhouettes, and the *Österreichischer National-Kalender*, containing 53. The latter contains the following sections : " Nature and Art " (drama), " Spirit and Harmony " (composers), " Song and Artistic Acting " (opera). Mozart's silhouette is in the small second section, after Gluck's and Haydn's, and before Salieri's.—Both calendars were brought out again in the following years, somewhat augmented and altered.

FROM THE " PRESSBURGER ZEITUNG ", 24 DECEMBER 1785
(partly in Italian)

At Schauff's art establishment in the Schneeweissgassel are to be had : Mozart, 6 Quartets for two violins, viola and violoncello : Op. 10. 6 fl. 30 kr.

Ervin Major, *op. cit.*, p. 43.—These were the quartets dedicated to Haydn and published by Artaria.

FROM THE "WIENERBLÄTTCHEN", 31 DECEMBER 1785

In Edler von Schönfeld's book-shop at the Kärntnertor, and at the printing-office in the great Jakoberhof, No. 837, is to be had :

" Wiener Musik- und Theater-Allmanach " for the year 1786. It contains, as promised . . . 4) Six of the most favoured operatic arias. 5) six of the best and most favoured Italian operatic arias. The 12 arias are by Ritter Gluck, Paisiell, Mozart, Salieri, Umlauff and Gretry. . . . The price is 1 fl. 30 kr. . . .

> The almanach, which is now rare, contains on pp. 20-23 the duet " Vivat Bacchus " from *Die Entführung* (No. 14), but set for a single voice.—Johann Ferdinand von Schönfeld probably printed the almanach for his colleague Johann Georg Weigand (see 4 January 1786) and sold it in his capacity as a bookseller.

1786

FROM THE " WIENER ZEITUNG ", 4 JANUARY 1786

At Weingand's book-shop in the Graben, No. 1174, are . . . to be had :
" Wiener Musik- und Theateralmanach " for the year 1786 in 4to. Containing : . . . 4) Six of the best and most favoured German operatic arias by the most celebrated masters, viz. Herr Gluck, Mozart, Paisiello, Saliery and Gretry. 5) Six of the best and most favoured Italian operatic arias. . . .

> Cf. the preceding advertisement.

On 14 January 1786, at the " New-Crowned Hope " lodge, the two choruses " On the Opening of the Lodge " (K. 483) and " At the Closing of the Lodge " (K. 484) were sung.

> This took place at the first meeting of the new lodge (*cf.* 19 December 1785). Both consist of solos with three-part chorus and organ accompaniment. The words, which were printed, were by Augustin Veith, Edler von Schittlersberg, an officer of the Supreme Treasury. See Deutsch, *op. cit.*, p. 14.

FROM THE " ALLGEMEINE WIENER BÜCHER-NACHRICHTEN ", 18 JANUARY 1786

" Wiener Musenalmanach auf das Jahr 1786 ", edited by J. F. Ratschky and Blumauer. 8. Vienna, Gr. Phil. Wucherer. 45 kr.

> No. III, p. 44.—Joseph Franz Ratschky was the author of the words of " Gesellenreise " (K. 468) and, like Alois Blumauer, had been a member of the

" Concord " lodge, now amalgamated with the " Truth ". Mozart must also have set Blumauer's " Lied der Freiheit " (K. 506) as early as 1785, though it appeared in the *Wiener Musenalmanach* for 1786. Johann Holzer, one of the outstanding Viennese song composers of this time, had set " Gesellenreise " before Mozart, but for two voices.

In January Le Duc of Paris announced in the *Mercure de France* the pianoforte variations on Nicolas Dezède's ariette " Lison dormait " (K. 264) and the string quartets dedicated to Haydn, " Opus X " (K. 387, &c.).

Johansson, *op. cit.*, pp. 95 and 100.—The variations, written in Paris in 1778, were first advertised by Artaria on 26 April 1786, and again by Le Duc in the *Affiches* on 28 April. The string quartets had been published in Vienna in September 1785.

FROM THE " PROTOCOLLUM AULICUM IN CEREMONIALIBUS ", 1786

Tuesday the 7th February. Whereas his Majesty the Emperor, on account of the presence of the Archduchess Marie-Christine, Governor-General of the Austrian Netherlands, and of Duke Albert of Sachsen-Teschen, decided to entertain their Royal Highnesses with a fête in the Orangerie at Schönbrunn after the manner of last year's, and was graciously pleased to name 41 Cavaliers and an equal number of ladies and personally to invite them to take part ;

These, then, some with barouches, some with coaches drawn by 4 or 6 horses, met on the Burgplatz beside the Black Eagle at 2 o'clock, and until their departure assembled in those rooms on the first floor of the Amalische Hof where the draw for the order of departure took place ; the which took place at a half past three o'clock in the following order, proceeding from the Hofburg towards Schönbrunn :

In barouches, before each of which rode two grooms. . . .

Then followed in coaches and six. . . .

Immediately upon their arrival at 4 o'clock in the Orangerie a banquet of 82 covers was served at a table prepared in the middle ; the Imperial and Royal pages serving.

During the banquet the I. & R. Chamber Music performed near by with wind instruments.

At the end of the banquet, and during the time that his Majesty with all the guests repaired to one of the theatres set up at the end of the Orangerie, the entire table was removed from the building ; and at once the whole length of the Parterre on both sides was brilliantly illuminated. Whereupon his Majesty with his guests repaired to the theatre erected at the other end of the Orangerie, where a German play with arias intermingled was performed.

When this was finished the entire company repaired to the theatre at the other end, where an Italian *singspiel* was at once performed.

After which, about 9 o'clock, the company rode back to the city in the

order in which they came, in barouches and carriages, each preceded by two
outriders with lanterns.

Vienna, National Archives.   Folios 7-10 of the Minutes of Court Ceremonies
for 1786.—Discovered by Frau Erna Felmayer.

FROM ZINZENDORF'S DIARY, 7 FEBRUARY 1786
(in French)

Arrived at Schoenbrunn [.] This Orangerie which makes such a lovely
vase was much better decorated than last year . . . We went to hear a German comedy entitled *Der Schauspiel Director*, in which la Sacco and Lang
played a piece from *Bianca Capello*, la Adam Berger and Weidmann a
piece from *Die galante Bäurin*. La Cavalieri and la Lang sang. The whole
was very mediocre. Passed to the other end of the hall afterwards, where
Benucci, Mandini, la Storace and la Coltellini sang a little piece, *Prima la
musica e poi le parole*, in which la Storace gave a perfect imitation of Marchesi
in singing arias from *Giulio Sabino* . . .

> The Emperor Joseph had held a similar reception a year before (6 February
> 1785) in the long orangery at Schönbrunn, the only hall in the palace that could
> be satisfactorily heated. As on the earlier occasion, the long table for the
> guests occupied the centre, while at the ends, facing each other, were two stages,
> in front of which the chairs were placed by turns. This time the "Spring
> Festival on a Winter's Day"—as Löschenkohl's engraving of the scene
> in 1785 is entitled—was held in honour of the Governors-General of the
> Austrian Netherlands, *i.e.* Duke Albert of Sachsen-Teschen and his wife, the
> Archduchess Marie Christine, a sister of the Emperor's. There was also a
> foreign prince among the noble guests, Stanislas Poniatowski, nephew of the
> Polish King of the same name. The two one-act parodies given were a German
> comedy, *Der Schauspieldirektor* by Gottlieb Stephanie, with music by Mozart,
> and (opposite) an opera buffa, *Prima la musica, e poi le parole*, with libretto by
> Giovanni Battista Casti and music by Salieri. The artists in the comedy, from
> the Burgtheater, were Johanna Sacco, Maria Anna Adamberger, Anna Maria
> Stephanie, Franz Karl Brockmann, Joseph Lange and Joseph Weidmann, with
> the author in the title-part. The other six actors appeared two by two in
> interpolated scenes from various plays : *Der aufgehetzte Ehemann, Bianka Capello*
> (by August Gottlieb Meissner) and *Die galante Bäuerin*. Mozart's vocal
> numbers were sung by Aloisia Lange, Caterina Cavalieri and Valentin Joseph
> Adamberger. Salieri's singspiel, in which Storace and Coltellini appeared with
> Francesco Benucci and Stefano Mandini, made fun of Da Ponte in Kelly's role,
> and also quoted from Sarti's *Giulio Sabino* in which Ann Storace parodied the
> castrato Luigi Marchesi, who had appeared as a guest in Vienna in 1785.—At
> dinner the Imperial chamber music played arrangements for wind band of
> melodies from Salieri's opera *La grotta di Trofonio*, which had been given at the
> Burgtheater in 1785.—*Cf.* O. E. Deutsch in the *Österreichische Musikzeitschrift*
> (Vienna), February 1954, and Christopher Raeburn in *The Music Review*
> (Cambridge), May 1955 and the *Österreichische Musikzeitschrift*, January 1958 ;
> also Gerhard Croll in the Preface to the *Neue Mozart-Ausgabe* II/5/15, *Der
> Schauspieldirector*, with facsimiles of the libretto.

JOSEPH II TO COUNT ORSINI-ROSENBERG, 7 FEBRUARY 1786

I here send you enclosed 1,000#, which you are to distribute as follows among the individuals made use of at the festivity at Schönbrunn to-day : viz.

to Salieri	100 # [ducats]
. . . . Mozart	50.
to 10 German actors, at 50 # each .	500.
. . . . 4 Italian opera singers, at 50 # each	200.
to Bussani	50.
to the orchestra, &c.	100.
	1000#

Vienna, State Archives. Kabinetts-Protokolle der Kabinetts-Kanzlei, Vol. XL, p. 80.—Payer von Thurn, *op. cit.*, p. 65 f.—Count Rosenberg was Lord Chamberlain and Director-in-Chief of the Court Theatres (*cf.* 23 April 1775 and 23 January 1778).—The fact that Mozart received only 50 ducats is explained by his having provided only incidental music (an overture and four vocal numbers), while Salieri had written a small opera.—The three singers from the German Opera were counted among the German actors. (Cavalieri, later engaged at the Italian Opera, actually bore the name of Cavalier.) The production was by Francesco Bussani, who belonged to the Italian Opera.—This instruction must evidently have been written before the banquet took place.

FROM THE "WIENER ZEITUNG", 8 FEBRUARY 1786

Home News.
Vienna.

On Tuesday H.M. the Emperor gave a festivity at Schönbrunn for the exalted Governors-General of the I. & R. Netherlands and a gathering of the local nobility. 40 Cavaliers, as well as the above-mentioned Prince Poniatowsky, being invited, they made their choice of ladies, left the Hofburg at 3 o'clock in pairs for Schönbrunn in barouches and closed carriages, with His Imp. Maj., who conducted Her Serene Highness the Archduchess Christina, and there alighted at the orangery. This had been prepared most lavishly and prettily for luncheon with which to receive these guests. The table, below the orange trees, was most agreeably decorated with local and exotic flowers, blossoms and fruit. While His Maj. partook of the meal with the exalted visitors and the guests, the Imperial and Royal Chamber Music was to be heard on wind instruments. The repast concluded, there was a performance on the stage erected at one end of the orangery of a play with arias especially composed for this festivity, entitled *Der Schauspiel-Director*, by the actors of the I. & R. National Theatre. At the conclusion of this, on the Italian stage erected at the other end of the orangery, was given by the company of Court Opera singers an *opera buffa* likewise quite newly written for this occasion, under the title of *Prima la musica e poi le parole*. All this time the orangery was most gloriously illuminated with numerous lights from candelabra and brackets. After 9 o'clock the whole company returned to town in the same order, with each coach accompanied by two grooms with links.

> Müller von Asow, Vol. III, p. 242.—Reprinted on 11 February in the *Provinzial-nachrichten.*—This account agrees with that given in the official chronicle of ceremonies (*cf.* 7 February).

*   FROM THE "WIENER ZEITUNG", 8 FEBRUARY 1786

At Johann Traeg's . . . may be had the following new Music, cleanly and correctly copied and at a cheap price :

The Quartetto by Mozart from the opera *la Villanella rapita.*
The Terzetto from the same.

> These are K. 479 and 480.

IBID., 8 FEBRUARY 1786

. . . at Lausch's music establishment are to be had, viz. :

Mozart, " Mandina amabile, questo danaro ', *terzetto*, 48 kr.
—   " Dite almeno in che maniera ", *quartetto*, 1 fl. 8 kr.

Mozart, 10 Variations, " Unser dumme Pöbel meint ", for the harpsichord, 51 kr.

> K. 480, 479 and 455.—For " maniera " read " mancai ".

POSTER OF 11 FEBRUARY 1786

At the Theatre next to the Kärntnertor, by the National Court actors (for the first time) : *Der Schauspiel-Director*, an occasional piece in one act. The music for it by Herr Kapellmeister Mozart. Afterwards, by the Italian Court opera singers, *Prima la musica, poi le parole* (*Erst die Musik, dann die Worte*), a comic Singspiel in one act. The music for it is by Herr Salieri, Kapellmeister in actual service of His Majesty the Emperor.

> Oskar Teuber, *Die Theater Wiens* (Vienna, 1903), Vol. II/ii, Part i, p. 76.—Repeated on 18 and 25 February.—It has been wrongly supposed that the performance fixed for the 11th was cancelled ; but it is true that the performance of Gluck's *Die Pilgrime von Mekka* was replaced on the 10th by Umlauf's *Irrlicht*, owing to the indisposition of the singer Dauer (information supplied by Christopher Raeburn).

FROM THE " WIENER ZEITUNG ", 15 FEBRUARY 1786

Theatre News.

On Saturday, the 11th inst., at the I. & R. Court Theatre next to the Kärntnertor, appeared for the first time the two novelties which had been written for the garden festivity at Schönbrunn : *Der Schauspieldirektor*, an occasional piece in one act, the music for which is by Herr Kapellmeister Mozart. To this succeeded the Italian Court opera singers with the comic Singspiel : *Prima la musica, poi le parolle* ; the music is by Herr Kapellmeister Salieri.

On Sunday 19 February, Mozart went to the masked ball at the Hofburg Assembly Room dressed as an Indian philosopher and distributed a printed sheet with eight riddles and fourteen " Selections from Zoroaster's Fragments ", all invented by himself.

> No copy of this broadsheet is known ; but see 23 March 1786.—The Carnival did not end until 28 February.—*Cf.* 3 March 1783 and 23 March 1786.

FROM THE " WIENER REALZEITUNG ", 21 FEBRUARY 1786

Two New Pieces.*

On the 11th inst., at the theatre next to the Kärntnertor, was performed (for the first time) by the National Court actors *Der Schauspieldirektor*. An occasional piece in one act. The music for it is by Herr Kapellmeister Mozart.

For an occasional piece, for which the author (Herr *Stephani junior*) had both the plot and the number and names of the actors engaged in it prescribed for him, it doubtless contains much that is good. Only the scene from *Der aufgehetzte Ehemann* did not seem appropriate here : it was fatiguing. A more favourable choice could also easily have been made instead of the tragic scene from *Bianka Capello* ; but if the author was tied to that piece, he could even there have found situations that would have made a better effect. The more happily chosen, however, was the scene from *Die galante Bäuerinn*, in which Mme *Adamberger* and Herr *Weidmann* received general applause.

The music by Herr *Mozart* was also distinguished by some especial beauties.

[Here follows a short description of Salieri's Singspiel.]

                                                    ——r.

* These two pieces were written for a festivity at Schönbrunn, given by H. Majesty the Emperor on the 7th inst. for the exalted Governors-General of the I. & R. Netherlands and a gathering of the local nobility.

Part viii, p. 126 f.

M.—9 *a*

FROM "ALLGEMEINE WIENER BÜCHER-NACHRICHTEN ODER VERZEICHNIS
NEUER UND ALTER BÜCHER FÜR DAS JAHR 1786," 22 FEBRUARY 1786

I. & R. National Court Theatre.

Der Schauspieldirektor, play with arias. *Prima la musica, e poi le parole,* a comic *Singspiel*—both performed at the festivity at Schönbrunn held on the 7th inst. at the instigation of H. Majesty the Emperor for the exalted Governors-General of the Netherlands. *Occasional plays,* given at a feast by an idolized monarch for a beloved sister : who would examine them by the torchlight of criticism, where sympathetic participation in pleasure stifles any cold-blooded examination ? But it is most certainly not due to national partiality, nor to base flattery, if we say that the German piece infinitely surpassed the Italian one in intrinsic value—that this time Cottelini, with all the graces of her art, had to yield to the excellent acting of Adamsberger—that without the splendid and tasteful arrangement of the whole, and all the magic that went with it, neither words nor music would have found indulgence.

No. VIII, p. 119.—This paper was published by Trattner.

FROM "EPHEMERIDEN DER LITTERATUR UND DES THEATERS",
BERLIN, 1786

Miscellaneous News.

.   .   .   .

His Majesty the Emperor is this year for the first time allowing the national actors to appear four times a week at the Kärntnertor Theatre during Lent up to Palm Sunday. The same is, however, not allowed either in the Austrian provinces or to another company in Vienna itself. His Maj. also held a festivity at Schönbrunn again on 7 Feb., of the same kind as last year, having plays specially written for it performed by the German actors as well as the Italian opera singers. The Germans were : Herr Stephanie junior, Mme Stephanie, Herr Brockmann, Herr and Mme Lange, Herr and Mme Adamberger, Herr Weinann, Mlle Cavalieri and Mme Sacco. The Italians : Mme Storacci, Mlle Coltalini, Herr Benuci and Herr Mandini. The German piece was written by Herr Stephanie jun. and the Italian one by Herr Casti. Each of the acting persons received 50 ducats, while the preceding year they had received only 25. Both pieces were afterwards performed three times in Vienna at the Kärntnertor Theatre with extraordinary success and attendance.

Vol. III, p. 189.—These three performances could clearly be given only during Lent, when the Burgtheater was closed.—"Weinann" should read "Weidmann".

FROM THE " WIENER ZEITUNG ", 4 MARCH 1786

New Music.

At Wenzel *Sukowaty's*, Court Theatre copyist, . . . are to be had :
Der Schauspieldirektor, by Herr *Mozart*, in score, 6 fl. 30 kr.
Prima la musica, poi le parole, by Herr *Salieri*, in score, 3 ducats.

> Sukowaty's pianoforte scores were also listed on 15 March in Trattner's
> *Bücher-Nachrichten* (No. XI, p. 175).—The manuscript of *Der Schauspiel-
> direktor* in the Vienna National Library (M. 16, 144) probably came from
> Lausch's copyists ; see 25 March.

FROM ZINZENDORF'S DIARY, 13 MARCH 1786
(in French)

. . . at 10 o'clock I called upon *Louise*, who returned from the opera
Idomenée at Prince Auersperg's.

> Frau Louise von Dieden was Zinzendorf's friend.—Prince Johann Adam
> Auersperg's Palace on the Glacis, beyond the Hofburg, had its own private
> theatre. It was not only used for plays and concerts : from the middle of 1781
> operas were also staged there. This theatre, which no longer exists, was behind
> the palace at what is now Lerchenfelderstrasse 6 ; it was used from 1776 to 1781
> by Franz Scherzer's company and then taken over by the Prince.—Mozart, who
> conducted this performance himself, had adapted his Munich opera of 1781 and
> added two new numbers : a scena and rondo for soprano (or tenor) with a
> violin solo (K. 490) and a duet for soprano and tenor (K. 489). The soloists
> were : Ilia—Frau Anna von Pufendorf (see 25 December 1762) ; Elettra—
> Countess Hortense Hatzfeld ; Idomeneo—Dr. Antonio Giacomo Bridi of
> Rovereto ; Idamante (tenor)—Pulini ; solo violin—Count August Hatzfeld,
> Mozart's exact contemporary and close friend, who predeceased him in 1787.
> (*Cf.* 26 July 1787 and Ernst Fritz Schmid in *Mozart-Jahrbuch 1954* [Salzburg,
> 1955].) At Auersperg's Countess Hatzfeld, born Countess Zierotin, the wife of
> August's half-brother Clemens, had sung the title-roles in Righini's *Armida* on
> 23 July 1782 and Gluck's *Alceste* on 12 February 1786, the latter under the
> composer's own direction ; in January 1788 she sang Aspasia in Salieri's *Axur*
> there. However, professional singers also appeared at this private theatre.—
> " Pulini " sang the tenor part in K. 489, but also the part in K. 490 written in
> the soprano clef.

FROM THE " WIENER ZEITUNG ", 18 MARCH 1786
At Christoph Torricella's

art, copper engraving and music establishment . . . are to be had :

. . . . .

Mozart, a Sonata for pianoforte, written for four hands, 1 fl.
— Two Sonatas for the pianoforte, together with a third, which is
accompanied by a violin, Op. 7. 2 fl. 45 kr.

No sonata for four hands published by Torricella is known, nor yet one printed from his plates by Artaria & Co. Perhaps the reference is to a manuscript copy.—The other sonatas are those already advertised by Torricella on 28 August 1784 : K. 333, 284 and 454.

FROM THE "OBERDEUTSCHE STAATSZEITUNG", SALZBURG, 23 MARCH 1786

Anecdote : At the last *Carnival in Vienna* (on 19 February) a masquerader distributed *Portions from Zoroaster's Fragments*, printed *for the edification of the rout* : at the head 8 very good conundrums were to be read, below which the *solution* was shown by displaced letters : *e.g. No. V* :
  " I may be possessed without being seen."
  " I may be carried without being felt."
  " I may be given without being possessed."
      S. H. N. O. R.   [Horns.]
Best of all, however, were the *Fragments*, of which, being short of more important matters, we single out a few :

1) Talk much—and talk badly ; but this last will follow of itself : all eyes and ears will be directed towards you.

4) I prefer an open vice to an equivocal virtue ; it shows me at least where I am.

5) A hypocrite anxious to pretend to virtue can imitate it only with water-colours.

10) It is not seemly for everybody to be modest ; only great men are able to be so.

11) If you are poor but clever, arm yourself with patience, and work. If you do not grow rich, you will at least remain a clever man.—If you are an ass, but wealthy, take advantage of your good fortune and be lazy. If you do not become poor, you will at least remain an ass.

12) A woman is praised in the surest and most tender fashion by abuse of her rivals. But how many men are not women in this respect ?

14) If you are a poor dunce—become a K——r [? *Kleriker*..cleric]. If you are a rich dunce, become a tenant. If you are a noble but poor dunce—become what you can, for bread. If you are a wealthy noble dunce, become what you like ; only—pray—not a man of sense.

P. 233 f.—Rudolf von Lewicki in *Mozarteums Mitteilungen* (Salzburg), November 1919, Vol. II, No. 1, p. 29 f. ; Ernst von Frisch, in *Das Mozart-Museum in Salzburg* (Salzburg, 1925), p. 28 f.—*Cf.* 19 February 1785.—The editor of this paper was Lorenz Hübner, at whose disposal Leopold Mozart had placed the broadsheet, but who suppressed the author's name. We know from Leopold's letter to his daughter of the same day that in the last fragment the word " K - - - r " was a euphemism for consumption at Salzburg ; according to the notes left by Nissen (Salzburg, Mozarteum), which Lewicki used, while Frisch quoted from the paper, the word should read " Canonikus "—perhaps as remembered by Constanze.—It may here be remarked that the name of the Iranian prophet Zoroaster, who died in 563 B.C., was the origin not only of Zarathustra, but also of Sarastro.

* FROM ZINZENDORF'S DIARY, 23 MARCH 1786
(in French)

. . . I went to dine with the Prince de Paar. There were there the Thuns mother and daughter, M. and Mme Duschek 2 virtuosos, the Diedes . . . Mme Duschek sang us la Storace's lovely air of king Theodore, " Come lasciar potrei il mio primiero amor ". And " Non vi turbate, no ".

> Wenzel Johann Joseph, Prince Paar, whom the Mozarts had known for a long time, was Imperial Postmaster.—The singer Josepha Dušek and her husband, the composer František Xaver Dušek, close friends of the Mozarts since 1777, had been " summoned " to Vienna from Prague on 14 March (cf. 12 April 1786). They soon afterwards gave a concert at the Burgtheater ; Josepha also appeared at an unknown date at the Hofburg with Mozart and the Munich violinist Johann Friedrich Eck.—On 24 March she sang at the house of Count Johann Buquoy, the President of the Court Commission for Secular Foundations ; on 27 March and 6 April Zinzendorf heard her again at Prince Paar's.

FROM THE " WIENER ZEITUNG ", 25 MARCH 1786

New Music.

Der Schauspieldirektor, an occasional piece ; the music is by Herr *Mozart* ; in Pianoforte Score.

L' overtura, 28 kr.
" Da schlägt die Abschiedsstunde ", *aria,* 20 kr.
" Bester Jüngling mit Entzücken ", do., 20 kr.
" Ich bin die erste Sängerin ", *terzetto,* 56 kr.
" Jeder Künstler strebt nach Ehre ", final number, 44 kr.
The whole *pièce* in score, with the libretto, 6 fl. 30 kr.
Mozart, " Mandina amabile questo danaro ", *terzetto,* 52 kr.
—   " Dite almeno in che maniera [i.e. mancai]", *quartetto,* 1 fl. 8 kr.
—   Quartet for harpsichord, violin, viola and violoncello, 2 fl. 30 kr.
To be had of Lausch's music establishment . . .

> *Cf.* 4 March 1786.—Single copies of both the piano score and the full score of *Der Schauspieldirektor* are preserved in Prince Fürstenberg's Library at Donaueschingen (Mus. MS. 1391). With the manuscript full score was included the printed libretto, evidently that published by Joseph von Kurzbeck, of which the National Library in Vienna possesses two copies. This libretto is complete and contains the vocal numbers, contrary to the statement in Köchel-Einstein, p. 610.—For the other two vocal pieces see 8 February 1786.—The pianoforte quartet was that in G minor (K. 478), which had probably been published already by Franz Anton Hoffmeister in Vienna the previous winter.

FROM ZINZENDORF'S DIARY, 27 MARCH 1786
(in French)

. . . In the evening after 7 o'clock to *Prince de* Paar's. Mme Duschek sang to perfection.

> *Cf.* 23 March 1786.

FROM THE PERIODICAL "PFEFFER UND SALZ", SALZBURG (VIENNA) 1786

5 April.

The plays take turns with musical concerts, given by various virtuosi on their account and for their own profit. Among these Herr Mozart is particularly distinguished. He is uncommonly liked, and his expression has to be marvelled at. He is also so agreeable as to give frequent public performances. His harvest is not confined to Lent, for he also appears during Advent or, if the public so desires, in the summer. His opera, too much filled up with accompaniments, which was given by the nobility at Prince Auersberg's, did not receive the approbation that is usually vouchsafed to his art when he is heard on the fortepiano.

Countess Hatzfeld, who sings excellently, and indeed (without in any way belittling the merits of Baroness Buffendorf, who also sang at Prince Auersberg's) almost excels our Mme Storaze, has given Herr Mozart a handsome present. Were Herr Mozart richer than the Countess, it would have been for him to distribute presents ; for his opera profited in the eyes of connoisseurs through the art of the Countess, not the Countess through the opera.

Do not interpret this verdict wrongly, dear friend ! I do not here speak of Mozart's art in general, but solely of his opera.

It is no secret that Herr Leopold Kozeluch competes with Mozart. His art on the pianoforte is not to be judged, for he is perhaps the only virtuoso in Vienna who never plays in public. His compositions, on the other hand, bespeak an excellent mind, and no other fault is to be found with them than that they are too difficult. Herr Kozeluch also has cause for pride in Fräulein von Buton, who at the age of twelve may challenge many a virtuoso.

In general, there are amateur ladies here who play such concertos as they have learnt almost as well as Mozart himself.

One looks forward to an opera which Herr Mozart is said to have written for the theatre ; it may well surpass the Italian operas that have lately been given. Herr Kozeluch too was asked to write one ; he wrote it for M. Coldolini, and they wanted to give it only after Coldelini should have left Vienna. Kozeluch saw through the Italian plot of Ro+g's favourites and backed out. If the same is going to happen to Herr Mozart, ha ! what support for indigenous artists ! Long live Salieri and Casti !

Fasc. I, pp. 15-17. Copies in the City Library, Vienna, and the Studienbibliothek, Salzburg.—Quoted (only the last paragraph) in Gustav Gugitz's edition of the *Denkwürdigkeiten des Venezianers Lorenzo da Ponte* (Dresden, 1924), Vol. I, p. 389 f.—The periodical, which was probably prohibited after only the second number, was written by Franz Xaver Huber and Karl Franz Guolfinger von Steinsberg (information kindly supplied by Gustav Gugitz).—The first of the two Mozart operas is *Idomeneo*, the second *Figaro*.—Buffendorf is a mistake for Puf(f)endorf, Buton for Puthon. The latter was probably a daughter of the Johann Baptist von Puthon who in 1784 appeared among the subscribers to Mozart's concerts (see Appendix I).—"M. Coldelini" was Celesta

Coltellini, who however, remained with the Italian Opera in Vienna until 1788.—" Ro + g " is Count Rosenberg.—None of Leopold Kozeluch's operas was performed in Vienna ; the reference here is presumbaly to his *Deborah und Sisera* (Müller von Asow).

On 7 April Mozart held a concert at the Burgtheater and probably played, *inter alia*, the new C minor pianoforte concerto (K. 491).

Nothing else is known of this programme.—There is no proof that Mozart gave two other concerts at the theatre that season, as has been stated (Abert, Vol. I, p. 1015), or that at one of them—perhaps this one—*La Betulia liberata* was performed (Köchel-Einstein, p. 147), although there exists a Viennese libretto of the oratorio dated 1786.—The concert of 7 April was Mozart's last at the Burgtheater.

FROM THE " WIENER ZEITUNG ", 8 APRIL 1786

Theatrical News.

On Friday, 7th inst., Herr Mozart held a grand musical concert, which is the last before Easter at this theatre, after performances given there by various foreign and local virtuosi during this Lent, on the days on which no plays were given.

The theatre was the Burgtheater.

JOHANN THOMAS KLEINHARDT TO COUNT FRANZ STERNBERG IN PRAGUE

Vienna, 12–18 April 1786.

Herr Duschek and Madame were called to Vienna this past 14 March. She gave a public performance at the Royal Theatre, which owing to the presence of the monarch, the whole court, all the nobility and the whole public was so full that people had to be turned away. The monarch remained from beginning to end, himself often clapped bravo and betokened his entire satisfaction. A few days later Mme Duschak was granted a special audience. She was accompanied by the famous pianist Mozart and the virtuoso Herr Eck. After the holidays they will leave Vienna. The accompaniment by the other musici cost Mme Duschek 100 thalers. Expensive Austrian musicians ! And that when with our indubitably polite countrymen it would have cost her about 12 ducats. From hence they will make their return journey to Salzburg, where she is to collect her legacy from her late grandfather : then by a stage to Dresden to visit all the savants and good friends, and then full of yearning to Prague and her little country place.

I am curious already to hear from her by word of mouth what has happened everywhere during her absence, and anxious also to visit her little country place again to breathe fresh air there and to arrange her collection of engravings.

Prague, Archives of the National Museum.—Paul Nettl, *Mozart in Böhmen* (Prague, 1938), p. 37 f.—Kleinhardt (jun.) was a painter and copper engraver in Prague, who was at that time on a visit to Vienna.—František and Josepha

Dušek had already arrived at Salzburg on 12 April, before Easter. Burgo-master Weiser (see January 1770), whom the Dušeks had visited at Salzburg in 1777 (see 15 August), left his granddaughter Josepha a legacy, but this was partly awarded to his Salzburg grandchildren.—The Dušek's country house had been since April 1784 the Villa Bertramka near Prague, later dis-tinguished by Mozart's visits there.—Count Franz Joseph Sternberg was an important art collector.

FROM THE " WIENER ZEITUNG ", 26 APRIL 1786
(partly in French)

Information.

At the art establishment of *Artaria Comp.* . . . . are newly to be had :
. . . *Mozart*, Fantasy and Sonata for the Forte piano, 1 fl. 30 kr.
— Arietta ' Lison dormoit' with variations for the harpsichord, 40 kr.

K. 475 and 457 (*cf.* 7 December 1785) ; K. 264 (see January 1786) : both original editions.

BURGTHEATER POSTER, I MAY 1786

New *Singspiel*.
At the I. & R. National Court Theatre
will be performed to-day, Monday, 1 May 1786
(for the first time)
LE NOZZE DI FIGARO
Die Hochzeit des Figaro.
An Italian Singspiel in four acts.
The Music is by Herr Kapellmeister Mozart.

The librettos, Italian and German, are to be had at 20 kr. each
of the Keeper of the Boxes.
The performance will begin at 6.30 o'clock.

Vienna, National Library.—Facsimile in Teuber, *op. cit.*, p. 77.—The date of production was to have been 28 April, but it had to be postponed for three days. Da Ponte, the librettist, is not named here, but appears on the libretto. For the text *cf.* 4 February 1785.—Mozart directed the first two performances, and Joseph Weigl, then aged twenty, took over from the third onwards ; both conducted from the harpsichord. At the second performance five numbers had to be repeated, at the third seven, including a second encore of a short duet. The opera was given nine times in 1786 : 1, 3, 8 and 24 May, 4 July, 28 August, 22 (? 23) September, 15 November and 18 December. In 1787–88 it was not performed. In 1789, with two new arias, it was performed on 29 and 31 August, 2, 11 and 19 September, 3, 9 and 24 October, 5, 13 and 27 November ; in 1790 on 8 January, 1 February, 1, 7, 9, 19 and 30 May, 22 June, 24 and 26 July, 22 August, 3 and 25 September and 11 October ; in 1791 on 4 and 20 January, and 9 February. Thereafter, until 10 July 1798, when *Figaro* was revived at the Kärntnertor Theatre, no opera by Mozart was performed at either of the Court Theatres.—The cast of 1786 was : La Contessa—Luisa Laschi ; Susanna—Ann Storace ; Cherubino—Dorotea Bussani ; Marcellina—Maria Mandini ; Barbarina—Anna Gottlieb (born 1774) ; Il Conte—Stefano Mandini ; Figaro—Francesco Benucci ; Bartolo and Antonio —Francesco Bussani ; Don Basilio and Don Curzio—Michael Kelly.

TITLE-PAGE OF THE ITALIAN LIBRETTO

LE NOZZE / DI FIGARO. / Comedia per musica / tratta dal francese / in quattro atti. / Da rappresentarsi / nel teatro di corte / l' anno 1786. / In Vienna, presso Giuseppe Nob. de Kurzbek, / Stampatore di S. M. I. R.

La Poesia è dell' Ab. da Ponte, Poe- / ta del Teatro Imp. / La Musica è del Signor Volfgango / Mozart, Maestro di Cappella, / Tedesco.

> Copies in the Library of Congress, Washington, and in the Istituto musicale, Florence.

TITLE-PAGE OF THE GERMAN LIBRETTO

DIE HOCHZEIT DES FIGARO. / A / play with music / in 4 acts / adapted from the French. / Performed / at the I. & R. National Court Theatre. / In the year 1786. / Vienna, / at Joseph, Edler von Kurzbeck's, I. & R. / Court Printer, Wholesale and Book Merchant.

The poetry is by the Abbé da Ponte, / Poet to the I. & R. Theatre.
The music is by Herr Wolfgang Mozart, / German Kapellmeister.

> Two copies in the City Library, Vienna.—Title-page reproduced in Teuber, *op. cit.*, p. 78.—The German libretto is entirely in prose.

DA PONTE'S PREFACE TO THE LIBRETTO
[2 editions, German and Italian]

The duration prescribed as being usual for dramatic performances, a certain number of characters generally introduced into the same, and some other prudent considerations and exigencies imposed by morality, place and spectators, were the reasons why I did not make a translation of this excellent comedy [by Beaumarchais], but rather an adaptation or, let us say, an extract.

To this end I was obliged to reduce the sixteen characters of which it consists to eleven, two of which may be performed by a single person, and to omit, apart from an entire act, many a very charming scene and a number of good jests and sallies with which it is strewn, in place of which I had to substitute canzonettas, arias, choruses and other forms, and words susceptible to music, things which can be supplied only by verse, but never by prose. In spite, however, of every effort, and of all the diligence and care taken by the composer and by myself to be brief, the opera will not be one of the shortest to have appeared on our stage, for which we hope sufficient excuse will be found in the variety of the threads from which the action of this play is woven, the vastness and grandeur of the same, the multiplicity of the musical numbers that had to be made in order not to leave the actors too long unemployed, to diminish the vexation and monotony of long recitatives, and to express with varied colours the various emotions that occur, but above all in our desire to offer as it were a new kind of spectacle to a public of so refined a taste and such just understanding.

The Poet.

Oscar Sonneck, *Catalogue of Opera Librettos printed before 1800* (Washington, 1914) Vol. I, p. 807.   For the German version, see Teuber, *op. cit.*, pp. 78 f. (The German edition differs from the above in points of detail.)

FROM THE ACCOUNTS OF THE COURT THEATRES, 1786/7

Salaries of the Italian opera company from 1 March 1786 to the last day of February 1787

Poet
To Abbate da Ponte, per annum   600 [fl.]
To Da Ponte, Lorenzo, for three Italian operas written over and above the obligations imposed by his contract.   As per receipt *ut* No. 153.   600.—
To Mozart, Wolfgang Amade, for composition of the *musique* for the opera *Le Nozze di Figaro ut* No. 179.   450.—

Vienna, State Archives, Vol. XXI, pp. 30, 56 and 60.—O. E. Deutsch in *Music & Letters* (London) April 1944, p. 97.—During this season Da Ponte also furnished the librettos for Anfossi's *Il trionfo delle donne* (after Giovanni Bertati) and for Vicente Martín y Soler's *Il burbero di buon cuore* (after Goldoni).   He thus received 200 gulden for each of these three books.

FROM ZINZENDORF'S DIARY, 1 MAY 1786

. . . at 7 o'clock to the opera *le Nozze di Figaro*, the poetry by da Ponte, the music by Mozhardt.   Louise in our box, the opera bored me . . .

FROM THE "WIENER ZEITUNG", 3 MAY 1786

I. & R. Court Theatre.

Monday, 1 May, a new Italian singspiel in four acts, entitled *le Nozze di Figaro*, after the French comedy by Herr von Beaumarchais, adapted by Herr Ab. da Ponte, the theatre poet ; the music for it is by Herr Kapellmeister Mozart.   La Signora Laschi, who returned hither not long ago, and la Signora Bussani, a new singer, made their first appearances on this occasion, as the Countess and the Page.

IBID., 3 MAY 1786

Le Nozze di Figaro, Die Hochzeit des Figaro.

Since I am so fortunate as to be able already to supply the highly estimable public with this beautiful as well as ingenious work by the celebrated Herr Kapellmeister Mozart, I did not wish any longer to withhold the news from the respected lovers of music that the score of the whole of this opera is to be had to order from my establishment at the cheapest price.

Acquainted with the hon. public's excellent taste, I have entrusted experienced musicians with the making of a pianoforte score as well as of quartets for 2 violins, viola and bass, and amateurs will be able to be served to order with these likewise within a short time ; those who wish to possess this opera in one form or another are therefore requested to enter their names in good time, so that they may be most punctiliously served with this opera, which is already much in demand in the neighbouring I. & R. States as well as abroad.

Christoph Torricella

Purveyor and publisher of Art, Engravings and Music in the Kohlmarkt next to Milani's Coffee House.

> The full score was, of course, to be distributed in MS. copies.—The two arrangements planned by Torricella did not appear.

EMPEROR JOSEPH TO COUNT ROSENBERG, 9 MAY 1786

To prevent the excessive duration of the operas, without however prejudicing the fame often sought by opera singers from the repetition of vocal pieces, I deem the enclosed notice to the public (that no piece for more than a single voice is to be repeated) to be the most reasonable expedient. You will therefore cause some posters to this effect to be printed. The same ruling is to be observed henceforth by the German Singspiel Company, and notice to this effect to be given.

> Vienna, State Archives, *loc. cit.*—Payer von Thurn, *op. cit.*, p. 69.—It seems likely that this decree was occasioned by *Figaro.*—On 3 May five items were encored, on the 8th seven, including a duet twice.

FROM THE BURGTHEATER POSTER, 12 MAY 1786

N.B. It is hereby publicly intimated that from now on, in order not to exceed the duration fixed for Singspiele, no piece for more than a single voice will be repeated.

> Teuber, *op. cit.*, p. 80.—Domenico Cimarosa's *L' Italiana in Londra* was given that evening.

FROM FRANZ KAZINCZY'S AUTOBIOGRAPHY
(in Hungarian)

[Vienna, May 1786]

Storace, the beautiful singer, enchanted eye, ear and soul.—Mozart directed the orchestra, playing his fortepiano ; but the joy which this music causes is so far removed from all sensuality that one cannot speak of it. Where could words be found that are worthy to describe such a joy ?

> First printed in Széphalom in 1828, though without Mozart's name ; a new, complete edition was published by Lajos Abafi (Budapest, 1879), pp. 86 f. ; a new edition by Ladislaus Orosz (Budapest, 1956).—*Mozart in Ungarn*, a bibliography by Lidia F. Wendelin (Budapest, 1958), p. 151.—Kazinczy was a distinguished Hungarian poet, from 1790 a protégé of Van Swieten in Vienna.

In June *Figaro* was also performed in the palace theatre at Laxenburg, by the singers of the Vienna cast.

Teuber, *op. cit.*, p. 79.

FROM THE " WIENER ZEITUNG ", I JULY 1786

LE NOZZE DI FIGARO

the *opera* by the celebrated Kapellmeister, Herr *W. A. Mozart*, received with general applause, carefully arranged to be sung at the pianoforte, 7 kr. per sheet.

Atto I

	fl.	kr.
L' overtura .	—	28
No. 1. Cinque . . . dieci . . . venti . . . trenta, Duetto .	—	25
2. Se a casa Madama, do. (Din din, Don don) .	—	35
3. Se vuol ballare, Signor Contino, Aria (le suonero, si)	—	18
4. Non so più cosa son, cosa faccio, do. .	—	21
5. Cosa sento ! tosto andate, Terz[etto] .	—	53
6. Giovanni liete, fiore spargete, Coro .	—	14
7. Non più andrai farfallone amoroso, Aria .	—	25

Atto II

	fl.	kr.
No. 1. Porgi amor qualche ristoro, Ar[ia] .	—	11
2. Voi che sapete che cosa è amor, do. (with guitar) .	—	18
3. Venite inginocchiatevi : restate fermo li, do. .	—	21
4. Susanna or via sortite, Terzetto .	—	35
5. Aprite presto aprite, Duetto .	—	18
6. Esci omai, garzon mal nato, Fin[ale] .	—	35
7. Signore, cos' equel Stupore ? Terz[etto] .	—	14
8. Susanna, son morta : il fiato mi manca, do. .	—	39

Cf. 3 May 1786.—Like Torricella, Lausch offered, also by subscription, a score, a pianoforte score, again in separate numbers only, and an arrangement for string quartet. In the pianoforte score the original Nos. 4 (Bartolo's aria), 5 (duet for Susanna and Marcellina) and 24 (Marcellina's aria) are missing. The finales of the second and fourth acts are split up into six and five numbers respectively.—The MS. full score copies in Florence (Istituto musicale, A. 262) and in London (British Museum, Add. MSS 16055-6) are possibly by Lausch. Nos. 7 of Act I and 4 of Act IV of Lausch's vocal score are in the " Emperor's Collection " of the Music Section of the National Library, Vienna, Nos. 5 to 9 of Act IV are in the Schwarzenberg Music Archives, Český Krumlov [Krumau].

FROM ZINZENDORF'S DIARY, 4 JULY 1786

. . . At the opera, *Le nozze di Figaro*. Mozart's music singular, hands without head . . .

> Teuber, *op. cit.*, p. 79, and Gustav Gugitz in *Wiener Geschichtsblätter*, 1956, No. 1, p. 18.

On 5 July *Die Entführung* was given at Rostock, on the 17th at Altona and in July or August by Böhm's company at Bad Pyrmont.

> The performance at Pyrmont is attested by *Ephemeriden der Litteratur und des Theaters* (Berlin, 1787), Vol. V, p. 271.

FROM THE "WIENER REALZEITUNG", 11 JULY 1786

On Monday, 1 May, was performed at the I. & R. National Court Theatre (for the first time) *La Nozze di Figaro*. *Die Hochzeit des Figaro*. An Italian Singspiel in four acts. The music is by Herr Kapellmeister Mozart.

"What is *not allowed* to be said these days, is sung" one may say with *Figaro*.* This piece, which was prohibited in Paris and not allowed to be performed here as a *comedy* either in a bad or in a good translation, we have at last had the felicity to see represented as an *opera*. It will be seen that we are doing better than the French.

Herr Mozart's music was generally admired by connoisseurs already at the first performance, if I except only those whose self-love and conceit will not allow them to find merit in anything not written by themselves.

The *public*, however (and this often happens to the public) did not really know on the first day where it stood. It heard many a *bravo* from unbiassed connoisseurs, but obstreperous louts in the uppermost storey exerted their hired lungs with all their might to deafen singers and audience alike with their *St!* and *Pst!*; and consequently opinions were divided at the end of the piece.

Apart from that, it is true that the first performance was none of the best, owing to the difficulty of the composition.

But now, after several performances, one would be subscribing either to the *cabal* or to *tastelessness* if one were to maintain that Herr *Mozart's* music is anything but a masterpiece of art.

It contains so many beauties, and such a wealth of ideas, as can be drawn only from the source of innate genius.

Some journalists liked to tell that Herr Mozart's opera had not pleased at all. It may be guessed what sort of correspondents they must be who recklessly publish such obvious lies. I believe it to be sufficiently well known that it was precisely the third performance and the frequent demand for encores to which it gave rise that led to the *Imperial Decree* which a few days

---

* In *The Barber of Seville*.

later publicly announced *that it would in future be forbidden to repeat in an opera any piece written for more than a single voice.*

Fr.

> No. 28, p. 447.—Christopher Raeburn in the *Österreichische Musikzeitschrift*, (Vienna) July–August 1957.—The quotation from Beaumarchais's *Le Barbier de Séville* is from Act I, scene 2.

On 16 July the Paris publisher M. Wenck announced a duet sonata (K. 381) in *Affiches, Annonces et Avis divers* (the title of the magazine had been changed in 1783).

FROM THE "WIENER ZEITUNG", 5 AUGUST 1786

From Artaria Compagnie, art dealers . . . the following maps and pieces of music are to be had :

Mozart, Ariette. La Belle Francoise, quite new variations for the pianoforte		40 kr.
– – Lison dormoit, with variations for the pianoforte	.	40 kr.
– – Salve tu Domine, ditto	.	36 kr.
– – Unser dummer Pöbel meint, ditto .	.	40 kr.
– – March from the *Mariages Samnites*, ditto	.	30 kr.
– – Variat[ions] for piano with violin .	.	40 kr.
– – La Bergere Silimene, variations for pianoforte and violin .		40 kr.

> K. 353, 264, 398, 455, 352, 360 and 359.—The unnamed variations for pianoforte and violin were those on the Andantino "Hélas, j'ai perdu mon amant" (K. 360), which Lausch and Torricella had already offered in MS. copies in 1785 (31 August and 14 September), together with K. 359. The theme, like that of "La Bergère Célimène" (K. 359) is by M. Albanèse.—The variations on "Salve tu, Domine" (K. 398) had also been obtainable from Lausch in MS. copies since 15 January 1785, and those on "Unser dummer Pöbel meint" (K. 455) had already been published by Torricella in 1785, according to Jahn. Artaria's edition of K. 398 may have been printed from plates prepared by Torricella, and Artaria's edition of K. 455 was perhaps only a reprint of Torricella's missing one. See the following advertisement.

IBID., 9 AUGUST 1786

Sale of Music Plates.

The I. & R. Lower Austrian Mercantile and Exchange Tribunal announces hereby that on 18 August and further on 1 and 15 September of this year will be offered for sale by auction, at 9 o'clock a.m. in the City on the Graben, at The White Rose, No. 1150, 1st floor, various music plates, to wit :

Mozart, 3 Sonatas, with 59 plates engraved in pewter, . . . Hayden, 3 Symphonies, with 111 do. . . . Haydn, "La Chasse", with 38 do. . . ., and that, in case these music plates should not be disposed of either at the first or the second term at or above the reserve placed on them, they may be sold at the third term even below the reserve.

The only work by Mozart named here, Op. VII, contained the Sonatas K. 333,
284 and (for pianoforte and violin) 454 ; see 28 August 1784.—Artaria & Co.
acquired Torricella's plates and with them the right of publication.

FROM THE "PROVINZIALNACHRICHTEN", VIENNA, 9 AUGUST 1786

New Music.

At Lausch's music establishment . . . is to be had : . . .
Mozart : *Le Nozze di Figaro*, do. do. [Opera, for violins, viola and violon-
cello] 6 fl. 30 kr.

On 18 October the Mozarts' third child, Johann Thomas Leopold, was born.

> Blümml, *op. cit.*, p. 6.—At the christening in St. Stephen's Johann Thomas von
> Trattner stood godfather. The name Leopold was chosen in honour of the
> grandfather, as with Nannerl's child.

On 9 November Thekla Podleska appeared at the Kärntnertor Theatre as Constanze
in *Die Entführung*.

> *Ephemeriden der Litteratur und des Theaters* (Berlin, 1787), Vol. V, p. 208.—
> Fräulein Podleska, who later married a Herr Batka, was engaged at the German
> Opera only from 1 November 1786 to 31 August 1787, when she went to
> Prague. Zinzendorf noted on 22 December 1786 that he had heard her
> "miaow" at a concert ; this was in Anton Teyber's oratorio *Gioas* at the
> Burgtheater, in which Storace, Benucci and Kelly also took part.

On 15 November the Mozarts' third child died of suffocation ("*Stickfrais*") and on
17th was buried in the cemetery of the St. Marx suburb.

> This cemetery, then new, was the appropriate one for the cathedral quarter,
> in which both the Schulerstrasse and the Rauhensteingasse were situated, where
> Mozart lived in 1786 and 1791 respectively.

On 5 December, at one of his four Advent concerts in the Trattner casino, Mozart
is said to have played his new C major pianoforte concerto (K. 503).

> There is no documentary evidence for this statement (Abert, Vol. I, p. 1015),
> nor that these four concerts were actually held. That they were at least
> planned is clear from Leopold Mozart's letter to his daughter of 8 December
> 1786.—That autumn Mozart intended to go to England with his wife for some
> considerable time, but this project was frustrated by his father's refusal to take
> care of the child Karl at Salzburg, where he was already in charge of Nannerl's
> son Leopold.

FROM THE "PRAGER OBERPOSTAMTSZEITUNG", 12 DECEMBER 1786

Prague, 11 December.

No piece (so every one here asserts) has ever caused such a sensation as
the Italian opera *Die Hochzeit des Figaro*, which has already been given
several times here with unlimited applause by Bondini's resident company
of opera virtuosi, among whom Mme. Bondini and Herr Ponziani in the
comic roles especially distinguished themselves. The music is by our cele-

brated Herr Mozart. Connoisseurs who have seen this opera in Vienna are anxious to declare that it was done much better here ; and this is very likely, since the wind instruments, on which the Bohemians are well known to be decided masters, have a great deal to do in the whole piece ; the duets for trumpets and for horns please especially. Our great Mozart must have heard about this himself, for there has been a rumour since that he will come here in person to see the piece, to the happy performance of which the well-manned orchestra and Herr Strobach's musical direction contribute so much.

A not quite complete copy of this newspaper is in the University Library, Prague.—Oskar Teuber, *Geschichte des Prager Theaters* (Prague, 1885), Vol. II, p. 207.—The precise date of the first performance in Prague is unknown.— For Bondini see 25 September 1783 and p. 207, bottom. His wife, Caterina, sang Susanna, Felice Ponziani was Figaro and Luigi Bassi the Count. Johann Joseph Strobach conducted. On 14 December *Figaro* was given for the benefit of Signora Bondini, on 4 January for that of Ponziani.—The Prague libretto, printed in 1786 by Joseph Emanuel Diesbach (copy in the City Library, Vienna) is entitled *Le nozze di Figaro, o sia La folle giornata*, but the entry on the composer inside is identical with that of the Italian libretto published in Vienna.

Cramer's *Magazin der Musik* (Hamburg) for 17 December 1786 (Vol. II, pp. 1056-61) (1079) has a criticism of *Die Entführung* which was taken almost verbatim from the passage in Schink's *Dramaturgische Fragmente* (Graz, 1782). See above, end of 1782.

IBID., 19 DECEMBER 1786

Prague, 16 December.

On Thursday last, at our National Theatre, the masterpiece by Herr Mozart already mentioned recently was given for the benefit of Madame Bondini. It has not yet been heard enough, for the theatre was again filled with spectators, although it was not a subscribers' day. This time it positively rained German poems, thrown down from the gallery, a manuscript one of which we caught and will quote here :

> Bondini sings
> And pleasure brings
> To th' melancholy heart ;
> Sorrows at least depart
> The while Bondini sings,
> The while her roguish art
> Its vocal changes rings.

It will be possible to give this opera many times yet, before—to the honour of Prague's taste, be it said—a new one will be asked for in its stead.

Teuber, *op. cit.*, Vol. II, p. 208.—The benefit performance had taken place on the 14th.—The scattering of poetic tributes, printed or in manuscript, was customary about 1800 ; at first performances they were addressed to authors, and on their benefit nights to famous performers. The word " German " was used in Prague at that time in contrast to " Italian ".

The celebrated composer Herr Mozart is preparing to travel to London
in the coming spring, having the most advantageous offers there. He will
go by way of Paris.

> Nettl, *op. cit.*, p. 81.—This report was connected with Mozart's plans for the
> autumn, which had not yet been abandoned by the New Year, according to
> Leopold's letter to Nannerl of 12 January 1787. In Munich too this journey
> was discussed at that time. A formal invitation to London, however, was
> delayed until December 1790, when Johann Peter Salomon visited Vienna
> from London ; he had already performed a Mozart symphony as No. 1 at his
> first Subscription Concert in the Hanover Square Rooms (C. F. Pohl, *Haydn
> in London* [Vienna, 1867], p. 80, where a London criticism is quoted in German
> without indication of its source : " a large composition, and performed with
> much spirit and effect "). Mozart's English friends in Vienna, Attwood,
> Kelly and the Storaces, on the point of returning home, had suggested a journey
> to London in the winter of 1786–87.

ANTON DANIEL BREICHA'S POETIC TRIBUTE, PRAGUE, END OF 1786

To Mozart on the Occasion of the Performance of the Opera Le nozze di Figaro.

Enchanted by thee I incline to refuse
The Muses' assistance.   Be thou then my Muse !
Be thou Pindus' clear and intoxicant source !
I heard thee, melodious thinker, and lo !
The pow'r of thy genius soon did I know,
Drawn on by its strong, irresistible course.

'Tis true, by thy music thou dost not move trees
And rocks, nor ever wild beasts does it please,
As Orpheus' did ; but thou breakest the barriers,
With more ease than he ; for the souls of us mortals
To heavenly bliss dost thou open the portals,
For children, for maidens, for men and for warriors.

When love of thy heart-melting strains is the theme
The youth seeks his maid, and more passionate seem
The beats of his heart in his love-laden breast.
She beckons him on to the heavenly bliss
Which they seal with a long and a rapturous kiss
By the youth on the maiden's lips ardently pressed.

When feverish anguish inspires thy strain
We freeze with compassion and horror ; again
When it's playful and gay we revive with delight ;
When plaintive and gloomy, like sounds of the tomb,

Thy mournfullest music enwraps us in gloom ;
The cords of our hearts with thy music unite.

Thy fatherland, cordially grasping thy hand,
As Germans are wont, now shall sever the band
Of Friendship with strangers, and honour in thee
The German Apollo.   Germania's Muses
Rejoice, and fell rivalry's furtive abuses
Destroy their own plots and are vanquished by thee.

(Sung by B – – – a on behalf of a Numerous Society of Friends of Music.)

Nissen, Appendix, pp. 184 f., printed the poem in two parts and erroneously dated it 1785.—*Cf.* Nottebohm, *Mozartiana*, p. 115, and Rudolf von Procházka, *Mozart in Prag* (Prague, 1892), p. 27 f.—The poem was first distributed as a pamphlet, in which form Mozart sent a copy from Vienna to Salzburg early in January.   It is also reprinted in the Prague anthology *Blumen, Blümchen und Blätter*, edited in 1787 by Johann Dionis John.—Breicha was a doctor ; he had shortly before played Hamlet on (Count Franz) Trauttmansdorff's amateur stage in Prague.—Mozart had received the poem from Prague at the same time as invitations to go there, which came " from the orchestra and a society of great connoisseurs and amateurs " (Leopold Mozart to his daughter, 12 January 1787) : probably Kapellmeister Strobach, Count Johann Thun and the Dušeks who, however, were not in Prague in January 1787.

1787

MOZART'S ENTRY IN EDMUND WEBER'S ALBUM

Be industrious—shun idleness—and never forget your cousin, who loves you with all his heart,

Wolfgang Amadè Mozart △∴

Vienna, 8 January 1787
5 o'clock in the morning, before departure.

The album was in the possession of Frau Sophie Lichtenberger (by birth a Heckel of Mannheim) at Speyer, but was auctioned by J. A. Stargardt of Marburg in 1962.—Jahn, Vol. I, p. 471.—Edmund, like his elder brother Fritz (Fridolin), was a pupil of Joseph Haydn's, who inscribed the album on 22 May 1788, when the brothers left Vienna (Pohl, *Haydn*, Vol. II, p. 204). On 3 April 1788 Maximilian Stadler had already made an entry in it at Esterháza : " May you soon rival your master Haydn and your friend Mozart ". Their father, Franz Anton Weber, Fridolin's brother, had come to Vienna with these two grown-up sons in 1784 and in 1785 had married the twenty-one year old singer Genoveva von Brenner ; Carl Maria von Weber was their child (*cf.* O. E. Deutsch in *Music & Letters* [London] April 1944).   See 20 August 1785.—In 1787 Mozart kept an album himself (see 1 April 1787).

In the morning of 8 January 1787 Mozart went to Prague with Constanze.

In their company was the violinist Franz Hofer (who in 1788 married Constanze's eldest sister Josepha) and also his little colleague, the thirteen-year-old Marianne Crux of Mannheim.

FROM THE " PRAGER OBERPOSTAMTSZEITUNG ", 9 JANUARY 1787

Prague, 7 January.

... The pity is only that this very fine [theatre] company is about to depart, and we truly congratulate those who engage Herr Ponziani for their theatre, a man who here, and wherever he has appeared, has been the favourite of connoisseurs and of all who have heard him.

Nettl, *op. cit.*, p. 75.—On 4 January *Figaro* had been given for Ponziani's benefit : " The theatre was so crowded that people could hardly move."— *Cf.* 12 December 1786.—Bondini's company in fact stayed on in Prague.

At noon on 11 January Mozart arrived in Prague and put up at the Three Lions inn ; he soon removed to Count Johann Thun's palace in the Small Side (Mala Strana).

In the evening of the same day Mozart, with Count Joseph Emanuel Canal, visited the ball which was held at the Seminary hall every Thursday at the instigation of Professor Johann (Baron) Bretfeld ; he there heard the *Figaro* dances that had been arranged in Prague.

On 12 January Mozart performed his comic trio " Das Bandel " (K. 441), as well as one of the pianoforte quartets (probably that in E♭ major, K. 493), at the Thun palace.

The music was performed in Mozart's room.

IBID., 13 JANUARY 1787

Prague, 12 January.

Last night our great and beloved composer Herr Mozard arrived here from Vienna. We do not doubt that in honour of this man Herr Bondini will have *Die Hochzeit des Figaro* performed, this well-loved work of his musical genius ; our famous orchestra will then not fail to give new proofs of its art, and the discerning inhabitants of Prague will surely assemble in large numbers, notwithstanding that they have already heard the piece frequently. We would dearly like to be able to admire Herr Mozard's playing for ourselves.

Teuber, *op. cit.*, Vol. II, p. 209.—The theatre was built between 1781 and 1783 by the Burgrave (Governor) Franz Anton Count Nostitz and Rieneck, at his own expense. (For Nostitz see the subscription list in the Appendix, p. 578.)

In the morning of 13 January Mozart visited the library and the theological seminary at the Clementinum, at midday he went to Count Canal and in the evening to Paisiello's opera *Le gare generose*.

For the Seminary *cf.* 12 November 1787.—Count Canal, who also had an orchestra of his own, was a freemason.—Paisiello's opera had been first performed at Naples in the spring of 1786 ; it was given in Vienna on 1 September of that year.

On 17 January *Figaro* was revived in Mozart's presence.

> Teuber, *op. cit.*, Vol. II, p. 212.

PERMIT FROM THE GOVERNOR OF BOHEMIA'S OFFICE

Mozart's application for permission to hold a musical concert is granted. 18 January 1787. Heimbacher.

> Teuber, *op. cit.*, Vo. II, p. 212.—Nettl, *op. cit.*, p. 96.

On 19 January Mozart held a concert at the Prague theatre ; he performed the D major symphony (K. 504) and played three improvisations on the pianoforte, the third being on " Non più andrai " from *Figaro.*

> The symphony was later called the Prague symphony. *Cf.* Niemetschek's memoirs, 1808.—Whether there was a second concert at the theatre is uncertain, in spite of Nissen's assertion (p. 517).

On 22 January Mozart conducted *Figaro.*

> On the same day Marianne Crux played at Count Thun's. Mozart, then, may not have taken part.

FROM THE " PRAGER OBERPOSTAMTSZEITUNG ", 25 JANUARY 1787

On Friday the 19th Herr Mozard gave a concert on the fortepiano in our National Theatre. Everything that was to be expected of this great artist he fulfilled to perfection. Yesterday he himself conducted the opera *Figaro,* this work of his genius.

> Rudolf von Freisauff (*Mozart's Don Juan 1787–1887* [Salzburg, 1887], p. 14), Teuber, Vol. II, p. 226, and Nettl (p. 95) date this report 21 January (a Sunday) and deduce from this that Mozart must have conducted *Figaro* on the 20th. Abert, Vol. II, p. 412. Teuber, Vol. II, p. 212, supposes that he did so on the 18th.

Mozart left Prague about 8 February and arrived in Vienna some four days later.

> Mozart brought back with him Bondini's commission to write an opera for the next Prague season.

Mozart's father left for Munich on 10 February and arrived back in Salzburg in the evening of the 23rd. He went for the Carnival.

On 23 February Ann Storace gave a farewell concert at the Kärntnertor Theatre.

> On this occasion she probably sang the scena and rondo " Ch' io mi scordi di te—Non temer, amato bene " (K. 505), perhaps accompanied by Mozart.

The *Wiener Zeitung* of 24 February announced a *Wochenblatt für Kinder zur angenehmen und lehrreichen Beschäftigung in ihren Freystunden* [Weekly Paper for Children for Agreeable and Instructive Occupation in their Leisure-Hours], edited by Joseph May and Johann Strommer, teachers at the Deaf and Dumb Institute, to be published from 5 April onward at the rate of one sheet per week.

> Among the subscribers for these four little volumes, which appeared in 1787 and 1788 (Monastery library, Klosterneuburg), were " Mozart, I. and R.

Chamber Musician ", Ignaz von Born, Franz Georg, Edler von Keess (one of the sons of the well-known music-lover, Franz Bernhard von Keess), Karl Schubert (a teacher in the Leopoldstadt, and uncle of Franz Schubert) and Baron Wetzlar. As Mozart was not appointed Chamber Musician until 7 December 1787, the subscription list was probably not printed before 1788. This journal issued a music supplement twice a year, the first one for 1787 including " Die kleine Spinnerin " (K. 531) and the second one for the following year " Beim Auszug in das Feld " (K. 552). " Des kleinen Friedrichs Geburtstag " (K. 529) seems to have appeared in the *Neue Kinderbibliothek* (later entitled *Bibliothek für Kinder und Kinderfreunde*), published by Joseph May and F. A. Gaheis from 1788. This journal is even rarer than the *Wochenblatt für Kinder* . . . (Six small volumes, printed by the Deaf and Dumb Institute, Vienna.)

In the evening of 26 February Attwood, Kelly, Ann Storace and her mother and brother reached Salzburg from Vienna on their homeward journey to London. During the morning of the 27th they were shown the town by Leopold Mozart. Ann Storace having sung at the archbishop's in the evening, they continued their journey to Munich, leaving at midnight.

An opera by Stephen Storace had been performed in Vienna in 1785, and another one in 1786. The party arrived in London in March 1787, but they had been unable to follow their intention of taking Mozart with them.

On 3 March the Paris publishers Boyer et Le Menu advertised the pianoforte sonata in D major (K. 284) in the *Mercure de France*.

Mozart en France (Paris, 1956), p. 69.—This was a reprint.

On 7 March Walburga Willmann, with her brother and sister, held a concert at the Kärntnertor Theatre and played a pianoforte concerto by Mozart (? K. 503).

The Willmanns were a large family of musicians. Three of them had given concerts in the Burgtheater in 1784 and 1785, and they held another in 1787. They were Maximilian, the cellist, Walburga, the pianist, and Magdalena, the singer. Walburga is said to have been a pupil of Mozart's, which would explain the performance of one of his pianoforte concertos, an unusual occurrence.

On 12 March Friedrich Zöllner, director of Count Batthyány's theatrical company at Hainburg (Lower Austria), approached the administration of the province in Krain with the proposal that his company should give a guest season in Ljubljana during the winter of 1787-88. Their repertoire included *Die Entführung*.

Ljubljana, Slovene State Archives : Ständearchiv, fasc. F. 49.—Information supplied by Professor Dragotin Cvetko, Ljubljana. *Cf. Laibacher Zeitung*, 1787, No. 46. It is not known whether Mozart's opera was actually performed at Ljubljana at this time. *Cf.* 13 June 1785 for a performance in Bratislava.

On 14 March the oboist Friedrich Ramm gave a concert at the Kärntnertor Theatre. It began with a symphony by Mozart and also included one of his arias, sung by Aloisia Lange.

For Ramm see 13 February 1778.

On 21 March a concert given by the bass Ludwig Karl Fischer took place at the Kärntnertor Theatre ; it began with a Mozart symphony and ended with the bass aria "Alcandro, lo confesso—Non so, d' onde viene " (K. 512), written for this concert.

Fischer, the first Osmin in *Die Entführung*, was only on a visit to Vienna.

MOZART'S ENTRY IN JOHANN GEORG KRONAUER'S ALBUM
(text in English)

Patience and tranquillity of mind contribute more to cure our distempers as the whole art of medecine.—

Vienna, 30 March *1787*.   Your true, sincere friend and Brother
Wolfgang Amadè Mozart
Member of the very hon. ⬚ of The New-crowned Hope
in the Orient of Vienna.

Vienna, National Library.—George Grove's article on Schubert in his *Dictionary of Music and Musicians* (London, 1882), Vol. III, p. 332.—Grove, to whom C. F. Pohl had communicated the text, thought that an English freemason was concerned. Kronauer, a teacher of languages in Vienna, was born at Winterthur in Switzerland. His album, started in 1783 and rich in content, was reproduced in facsimile about 1935 for an American lodge. (*Cf.* Edwin Zellweker in the *Österreichische Musikzeitschrift*, February 1951 ; Paul Nettl in the *Neue Zürcher Zeitung*, 22 January 1956, and in *Acta Mozartiana* [Augsburg], April 1956, Vol. II, No. 2 ; Frank Bernhart in *Ars Quatuor Coronatorum* [London], 5 October 1956, English translation of the entire album.)—Whether this sentence is Mozart's own or a quotation is undecided. Mozart seems at this time to have practised English, perhaps in view of his projected journey to London. *Cf.* 23 August 1785 and 24 April 1787.

ANNOUNCEMENT OF A PIANOFORTE SCORE OF "FIGARO", ARRANGED BY
VINCENZ MASCHEK (MAŠEK), PRAGUE 1787

Information.

Prompted by the desire of various exalted and most gracious patrons, as well as some of my friends, I have made a pianoforte score of the very justly favoured opera entitled *Le nozze di Figaro*, with which the high and gracious nobility, as well as the much-honoured public, will be promptly served daily, by application at my house in the Brennten Gasse, No. 84, second floor.

The complete opera, with all the recitatives, neatly bound, costs . . . 6 ducats.

Do. the complete work, without recitatives   4 ducats.

Should anyone order but single acts of this opera, then the 1st act costs 4 fl., the 2nd 6 fl., the 3rd 4 fl. and the 4th 6 fl.—Single numbers may also be obtained at all times, each number, without distinction, at 1 fl.

N.B. In recommendation of my transcription I add that I have taken all imaginable pains to set this masterpiece simply, without however omitting to retain all the beauties of the music ; I can also guarantee the copying, since I personally examine every copy in order to give satisfaction. In each act will also be found an index, by means of which each number may be found without trouble.

Winzens Maschek
Composer.

Prague, Library of the National Museum (where there is also a copy of this MS pianoforte score).—Nettl. *op. cit.*, plate facing p. 125.—The sheet is undated and is tentatively placed here.—*Cf.* 3 May and 1 July 1786, and 6 June 1787.

LUDWIG KARL FISCHER IN MOZART'S ALBUM

The gentle goddess harmony,
The art of sound and soul,
I deem that it should ev'rywhere
The Muses' sons control.
But oft are lips and hearts untuned
Where envy's fires burn,
And song becomes a mockery
When friends against us turn.
For friends who show the stamp of truth
Are scarce, and faith is rare,
Then let me tell thee, I for one
Can friendship's trials bear.
Wilt thou my devotion know ?
This my recompense shall be :
Be my friend, for long ago
Hast thou had a friend in me.   Vienna, 1 April 1787
                                                Louis Fischer.

Mozart's album of the years 1787–89 (which his son Karl made further use of from 1795 to 1836) belonged from 1856 to the Mozarteum at Salzburg, but has been missing since 1945. Its Archivist, Johann Evangelist Engl, in 1911 reprinted the eleven entries written for Mozart : in the 31st *Jahresbericht der Internationalen Stiftung Mozarteum* and in the Viennese periodical *Ton und Wort* (November and December) ; the two publications do not entirely tally.— Fischer's entry (Jahn, Vol. II, p. 345) was the earliest.—Nine of the eleven leaves date from 1787, one is undated and one dates from 1789.—The present editor made copies of the entries in 1937, of which the first (Fischer's) and the undated one (Bauernfeld's) have unfortunately not been preserved.—For Fischer see 21 March 1787.—The Novellos saw the album when they visited Constanze in Salzburg in 1829.—Mozart himself lost his " biggest album " on a journey (*cf.* Constanze's letter to Breitkopf & Härtel, 30 July 1799).

On 4 April Mozart wrote to his father for the last time.

Leopold Mozart was taken seriously ill in the middle of March ; Nannerl stayed with him until the beginning of May.—In the last letter but one, which is lost, Mozart had already mentioned the death of Count Hatzfeld (30 January), calling him his " dearest, best friend " (*cf.* 3 September 1787).

On 7 April Beethoven, aged sixteen, came to Vienna from Bonn to have lessons from Mozart.

He remained only until 20 April, being recalled home by the mortal illness of his mother.—Opinions about the precise time and duration of Beethoven's first sojourn in Vienna vary between March and June 1787. His mother died in July.

GOTTFRIED VON JACQUIN IN MOZART'S ALBUM

True genius without heart is a thing of naught—for not great under-
standing alone, not imagination alone, nor both together, make genius—
Love ! Love ! Love ! that is the soul of genius.
Vienna, 11 April 1787.

> Your friend Emilian Gottfried Edler von
> Jacquin.

The famous botanist Nikolaus Joseph von Jacquin (1727–1817) had three
children : Gottfried (1763–92), Joseph Franz (1766–1839) and Franziska,
later Frau Lagusius (1769–1853). Gottfried and Franziska were very musical,
and the elder brother also composed. The younger brother became his father's
successor. The family lived on the Rennweg, near the Botanical Gardens.
Mozart was a close friend of theirs ; he wrote several complimentary compositions for Gottfried, which were performed or published under the latter's
name.

On 12 April *Die Entführung* was performed by Grossmann's company at Hanover.

The conductor was Bernhard Anselm Weber.—See 3 October 1788.

SIGMUND BARISANI IN MOZART'S ALBUM

Vienna, the 14th day of the month of April, 1787.

> Though Britons, great in spirit as they are,
> Know how to pay their tribute to thy art,
> And rapt in admiration hear thee play
> With mastery thy keyboard instrument ;
> Though Latins envy thy composer's skill
> And try to follow it as best they may ;
> Though long thy art has won thee fame and bliss,
> By Bach and Joseph Hayden only match'd ;
>
> Do not forget thy friend, whose happiness
> And pride it is to know he served thee twice
> To save thee for the world's delight. This boast
> Is yet surpassed by joy and pride to know
> Thou art his friend, as he is ever thine.

> Thy Friend Sigmund Barisani
> *Physicus Primarius* at the general
> Hospital.

Facsimiles in F. X. Jelinek's *Salzburger Mozart-Album*, 1871, and in Schiedermair's *Mozart-Ikonographie*, plate 63.—Jahn, Vol. I, p. 839—Sigmund Barisani
was a son of the Salzburg physician-in-ordinary (see 20 January 1781) ; he
died in 1787, aged twenty-nine. He had treated Mozart in the late summer of
1784 (see 23 August) and probably also for a recurrence of his kidney complaint.
Cf. 3 September 1787 and 5 December 1791.

M.—10

FROM CRAMER'S "MAGAZIN DER MUSIK", HAMBURG, 23 APRIL 1787

Vienna, 29 January 1787. . . . Mozart started a few weeks ago a musical tour to Prague, Berlin and, it is said, even London. I hope it will turn out to his advantage and pleasure. He is the most skilful and best keyboard scholar I have ever heard; the pity is only that he aims too high in his artful and truly beautiful compositions, in order to become a new creator, whereby it must be said that feeling and heart profit little; his new Quartets for 2 violins, viola and bass, which he has dedicated to Haydn, may well be called too highly seasoned—and whose palate can endure this for long? Forgive this simile from the cookery book. . . . Mme. Aurenhammer is an excellent mistress of the clavier, on which she also gives lessons. I have not heard her for a long time. She it was who supervised and corrected the engraving of many sonatas and ariettas with variations by Mozart at Messrs. Artaria's.

A ⋆ ⋆ .

> Vol. II, pp. 1273 f.—Jahn, Vol. I, pp. 779 and 806.—Abert, Vol. I, pp. 977 and 1003 ; Vol. II, p. 171.—Mozart's journey in January took him only as far as Prague.

MOZART'S ENTRY IN JOSEPH FRANZ VON JACQUIN'S ALBUM
(in English)

Don't never forget your true and faithfull friend

Wolfgang Amadè Mozart

Vienna. the 24 April. *1787.*

> Salzburg, Mozarteum.—Facsimile in Roland Tenschert's Mozart book (Amsterdam, 1931) Plate 51.—For Jacquin see 11 April, for Mozart's knowledge of English see 30 March 1787.—He wrote this sentence under the double canon K. 228.

JOSEPH FRANZ VON JACQUIN IN MOZART'S ALBUM
(in Latin)

To thee who canst " gently move the attentive oaks with thy melodious strings ".

In token of friendship.

Vienna, 24 April 1787.   Josephus Franciscus à Jacquin.

> The quotation is an adaptation of Horace, *Carmina*, I. 12. 11, where the text actually reads : "Blandum et auritas . . ."—Jahn, Vol. II, p. 53.—On 24 April, then, the two albums were exchanged.—In his pamphlet *Die Säkularfeier der Geburt Mozart's in Salzburg* 1856, p. 19, Ludwig Mielichhofer mentions a further entry by Nikolaus Joseph von Jacquin, the father, but this must have been lost.

On 24 April Mozart removed from the Schulerstrasse to the high street of the Landstrasse suburb, No. 224 (the site is now occupied by a new building, Nos. 75 and 77) ; his lodgings faced the garden.

Mozart was ill again at this time.

On 25 April (or a little earlier) *Die Entführung* was performed by Schikaneder's company at Ratisbon (?).

> The date seems questionable for two reasons : Egon Komorzynski says in his book on Schikaneder, (Vienna, 1951), p. 110, that the latter did not take over the management there until 29 May ; and Schikaneder acknowledged the receipt of a manuscript score from Artaria & Co. (ordered on 11 June) only on 3 July. (The letter is in the archives of the Gesellschaft der Musik-freunde, Vienna ; the receipt, not in his own hand, was formerly in the collection of Fritz Donebaur, Prague, and was auctioned by J. A. Stargardt of Marburg in 1963.)

IGNAZ VON BORN IN MOZART'S ALBUM
(in Latin)

O gentle Apollo ! who gavest thine arts and thy gifts to our Mozart, so that at his request the string yields whatever sounds his hand and mind desire ; be they shrill, solemn, fast, slow, tuneful, plaintive, great or small, sounding together without offence ; decree that the number of his happy days may accord with the agreeable music of his lyre and that such may be the harmony of his fate.

27 April 1787.   Ignatius a Born

> Jahn, Vol. III, p. 310.—Facsimile in Robert Haas's Mozart book, p. 152.—For Born see 24 April 1785.

In the *Wiener Zeitung* of 2 May the creditors of Franz Anton Gilowsky, "absconded", are exhorted to report their claims to the Lower Austrian Law Court before 21 July.

> This Franz Anton Gilowsky von Urazowa was a cousin of the witness at Mozart's wedding, Franz Wenzel Gilowsky. He had run the "Kleine Post" (local letter post) in Vienna about 1784 and lost his money in it. It is probable that he was the "Franz Gilowsky" to whom Mozart had lent 300 gulden on 23 August 1786, a sum designated in Mozart's estate as irrecoverable. Gilowsky, whose bankruptcy was annulled in 1788, was again declared insolvent in 1790 and 1800 ; there is no further trace of him.

FROM THE "NEUE LITTERATUR UND VÖLKERKUNDE", DESSAU, MAY 1787
(partly in Italian and French)

Artaria & Co., art dealers in Vienna, have published the following music at their own expense.

Symphonies
. . . Mozart, 1 Symph. Op. 8. 3 fl. do. 1 Symph. Op. 9. 3 fl.

Quartets
. . . Mozart, 6 do. [Quartets for 2 violins, viola and violoncello]. Op. 10.
6 fl. 30 kr.

.   .   .   .   .

Pianoforte Concertos
. . . Mozart, Conc. for the same [harpsichord or pianoforte with accompaniment for several instruments]. Op. No. 1. 2 fl. 30 kr. do. Conc. for
the same. Op. No. 2. 2 fl. 30 kr. do. Conc. for the same. Op. No. 3.
2 fl. 30 kr.

.   .   .   .   .

Pianoforte Sonatas with Accompaniment
. . . Mozart, 6 Sonatas for harpsichord with violin. Op. 2. 5 fl. do.
Arietta with variations for harpsichord & violin. Op. No. 6. 40 kr. do—
" La Bergere Silimene ", varied for clav. & V. Op. No. 7. 40 kr.

.   .   .   .   .

Sonatas for Pianoforte alone
. . . Mozart, 3 Sonatas for the harpsichord or fortepiano. Op. 6. 2 fl. do.
Fantasy and a Sonata for the fortepiano. Op. 11. 1 fl. 30 kr. do. Arietta,
" Lison dormoit ", with variations for clav. Op. No. 1. 40 fl. [kr.] do.—
" La belle Francoise ", with variations do. Op. No. 2. 40 kr. do—" Unser
dummer Pöbel meint" with variations. Op. No. 3. 40 fl. [kr.] do.—
" Salve tu Domine" with variations do.—Op. No. 4. 40 kr. do.—March
from Mariages samnites with Vars. Op. No. 5. 40 kr.

.   .   .   .   .

Sonatas for 2 Persons at one Clavier
. . . Mozart, 2 Sonatas for the same. Op. 3. 2 fl.

.   .   .   .   .

Vol. I (Vol. X of the whole series), App., pp. 40-43.—Edited by Johann
Wilhelm von Archenholz.—Discovered by Christopher Raeburn.—The advertisement dates from March or April 1787. It stands between the second and
the fourth catalogue of the publishers Artaria & Co., issued in 1782 and 1788
(Gesellschaft der Musikfreunde, Vienna), and replaces the third catalogue of
December 1787, which, like the first of 1781, is lost.—The works by Mozart
are : symphonies—K. 319 and 385 ; string quartets—K. 387, 421, 458, 428,
464 and 465 ; pianoforte concertos—K. 414, 413 and 415 ; pianoforte and
violin sonatas, &c.—K. 376, 296, 377-80, 360 and 359 ; pianoforte sonatas, &c.
—K. 330-32, 475, 457, 264, 353, 455, 398 and 352 ; sonatas for four hands—
K. 381 and 358.—Mozart's variations formed a special series at Artaria's : thus
" Op. No. 1 " meant No. 1 of that series.—Among the prices " 40 fl." appears
twice instead of " 40 kr." as indicated.

FROM DOMINIKUS HAGENAUER'S DIARY, 28 MAY 1787

On Whit Monday the 28th, in the year 1787, early, died our Vice Kapell-meister Leopold Mozart, who did especial honour to Salzburg with his two children some 20 years ago, by taking his boy Wolfgang and his daughter Anna, the former aged 7 and the latter 10, all over Germany, France, Holland, England, Switzerland and Italy as far as Rome, as great virtuosi on the clavier, finding applause and praise everywhere, and also bringing back an abundance of presents. The son is now one of the most famous composers in Vienna and the daughter is married to Herr von Sonnenburg, Prefect at St. Gilgen in the Province of Salzburg. The mother died in Paris during her second visit there with her son. The father who died to-day was a man of much wit and sagacity, who would have been capable of rendering good service to the State even apart from music. He was the most correct violinist of his time, to which his twice-published Violin School bears witness. He was born at Augsburg and spent most of the days of his life in the service of the Court here, but had the misfortune of being always persecuted here and was not as much favoured by a long way as in other, larger places in Europe. [He] reached the age of 68 years.

> Vol. I, pp. 246 f.—Salzburg, Archives of St. Peter's monastery.—Pater Domini-kus had become Abbot of this monastery in 1786.—According to the *Salz-burger Intelligenzblatt* of 2 June Leopold Mozart died " of consumption ", according to his doctor, Joseph Barisani, of " congestion of the spleen ". The Court Councillor of War, Franz D'Yppold (Ipold) an old friend of the family, informed Mozart of his father's death.

         ★   [*See* Addenda, p. 605]

On 4 June Mozart buried his pet starling.

Cf. 27 May 1784.

FROM THE " WIENER ZEITUNG ", 6 JUNE 1787

Announcement

to the high and gracious nobility and most esteemed public.

The unanimous loud applause with which Mozart's masterpiece, *Die Hochzeit des Figaro*, was received in Prague, occasions the surmise that not a few will wish to possess a pianoforte score of this singspiel, unique in its kind and surpassing all praise. To fulfil this noble wish, I have decided to cause this to be effected, and to give myself the honour of offering it to the high and gracious nobility and the highly honoured public ; but so that each may estimate the value of this pianoforte score, I add that this work has been transcribed with the utmost diligence by the meritorious and great musician and pianoforte master, Herr Kucharz. Owing to the costliness of the piece I hereby propose the expedient of subscription, and shall deliver one act each month, each act to cost 4 fl. 30 kr. ; the whole piece, con-sisting of 4 acts, to be furnished act by act on clean paper, correctly written.

In addition, subscriptions will also be received for the same work transcribed into quintets by Herr Abbee Vogel, to appear in 2 large sections, each section to cost 6 fl., 12 fl. altogether, to be begun at the end of next month. The same work is moreover to be had of me for wind instruments, written in 6 as well as in 8 parts, of which that in 6 parts costs 20 fl. and that in 8 parts, 27 fl. This work may be subscribed for each day at the art establishment of Balzer & Co., in Trattner's Freyhof, second court, shop No. 20.

> *Cf.* the advertisement of Mašek's Prague pianoforte score (inserted before 1 April 1787).—Johann Baptist Kucharz, organist in Prague and from 1791 to 1800 conductor at the Opera there, also made pianoforte scores of Mozart's next four operas. The National Library in Vienna has a copy of this manuscript pianoforte score of *Figaro*, with the address of the Prague dealer Anton Grams. (Other copies in the possession of the National Museum in Prague and of Professor Paul Nettl, Bloomington, Indiana, U.S.A.) Balzer & Co. may have been agents for Vienna only : they were a family of copper engravers from Bohemia (Anton and Joseph Balzer lived in Vienna, others in Prague).—The arrangement for string quintet was by the former Jesuit, Abbé Cajetan Vogel, of Prague ; there was a copy in Mozart's estate (see Appendix II, No. 60, p. 603), and another from the music archives of Osek Monastery is now in the National Museum, Prague (as revealed by E. F. Schmid). Of the arrangements for wind instruments no details are known.

On 18 June *Die Entführung* was given at Hamburg.

FRANZ KAJETAN VON PLOYER IN MOZART'S ALBUM
(in Latin)

> To thee who, surpassing every one in the
> art of heavenly Apollo, hast thereby brought
> glory to his [*i.e.* von Ployer's] daughter, as
> a perpetual token of gratitude and friendship.

28 June 1787.   Franc. Cajetan a Ployer.

> For Ployer see 13 June 1784. Franz Kajetan may have been a near relation of Gottfried Ignaz von Ployer. Engl, *op. cit.*, read " Franc. Cajetana " ; Tenschert in the 39th *Jahresbericht des Mozarteums in Salzburg für 1926* (published 1927), p. 12, has " Franc. Cajetan. a Ployer ".—Babette's album in the Mozarteum at Salzburg was also lost in 1945 ; it contained a " little funeral march " for pianoforte (KE. 453a), written by Mozart about 1784.

In June *Figaro* was given in German at the Rosenthal Theatre in Prague.

> Teuber, *op. cit.*, Vol. II, p. 244.

FROM JOHANN GEORG MEUSEL'S " MUSEUM FÜR KÜNSTLER UND KUNST-LIEBHABER ", MANNHEIM, 1787

Young Musical Artists of our Time.

. . . . It is well known that in our own days *Mozart* was to be heard even as a child. Everywhere on his travels, undertaken in his father's company, he received unfeigned approbation. And the agility and expression of his playing surpassed the highest expectations.

> No. 3, p. 29.—This journal, which only occasionally concerned itself with music, was the sequel to *Miscellaneen artistischen Inhalts*.

JOHANN NEPOMUK VON GREZMÜLLER IN MOZART'S ALBUM

As truly only those
Who in their art possess a master's hand
Enrapture those who know
As well as those who barely understand,
So Mozart weaves his spell,
Worthy the name of master, surely he
Enchants us, ev'ry one,
Judges of art, as simple hearers : me.

13 July 1787.   Johann Nep. v. Grezmüller.

> Grezmüller (jun.) was Councillor of the Saltworks Department. He and the Aulic Council agent Erasmus von Grezmüller (? his father) were among the subscribers to Mozart's concerts in 1784.

On 13 July the score of *Figaro* which Haydn had ordered arrived at Esterháza.

> Budapest, Esterházy Archives.—Probably a Lausch copy. It was not performed in Eisenstadt till 1789.

FROM THE " WIENER ZEITUNG ", 21 JULY 1787

From *Artaria Compagnie*, Art Dealers . . . are to be had :

Music.

. . . Mozart, 1 Quartet for harpsichord with violin, viola and violoncello. 1 fl. 30 kr.

> The E♭ major pianoforte quartet (K. 493), published as Op. 13.

FROM CRAMER'S " MAGAZIN DER MUSIK ", HAMBURG, 26 JULY 1787

Bonn, 14 February 1787.—The too early death of Count *August von Hatzfeld*, Canon of Eichstädt, deserves to be announced in your pages. . . . In Vienna he became acquainted and friendly with *Mozart*. He studied there and played his famous *quadros* under the author's guidance, and became so intimate with their composer's spirit that the latter became almost disinclined to hear his masterpiece from anyone else. Some two months before his death I heard him deliver them with an accuracy and fervour which excited the admiration of every connoisseur and enchanted the hearts of all. . . .

S. N.

Vol. II, pp. 1380 ff.—Ernst Fritz Schmid in the *Mozart-Jahrbuch 1954* (Salzburg, 1955), pp. 25 f.—For Hatzfeld see 13 March 1786. He had died at Düsseldorf on 30 January 1787.—The " Quadros " were no doubt the six string quartets dedicated to Haydn.—In the same number of this journal there is mention of Clementi being influenced by the style of Haydn, Mozart and Kozeluch during his time in Vienna.

FROM THE MINUTES OF THE PRINCELY COUNCIL, SALZBURG, 21 AUGUST 1787

The heirs in tail of Leopold Motzart present to this exalted office, *sub dato et praesentato* 20 August *anni curr.* their humble petition for gracious authorization of a legally valid auction of effects during the first week of the coming Michaelmas Fair.

The auction is to be permitted in the requested term, with the proviso that no disadvantage shall thereby accrue to the Princely Pledge Office.

Salzburg Provincial Archives.—Discovered by Franz Martin in 1937 and published by Walter Senn in the *Neues Augsburger Mozart-Buch* (1962), p. 392— Michaelmas is 29 September. See 15 September 1787.

On 24 August *Die Entführung* was performed at Wrocław [Breslau].

MOZART'S NOTE BELOW SIGMUND BARISANI'S ENTRY IN HIS ALBUM

To-day, 3 September of this same year, I was so unfortunate as quite unexpectedly to lose by death this noble man, dearest, best of friends and preserver of my life.—He is at rest !—but I, we, all that knew him well— we shall *never* be at rest again—until we have the felicity of seeing him again—in a better world—and *never more to part.*—Mozart.

Facsimile in Jelinek's *Salzburger Mozart-Album*, 1871, and in Schiedermair's *Mozart-Ikonographie*, Pl. 63. *Cf.* 14 April 1787 and Mozart's tribute to Hatzfeld, 4 April 1787.

FROM THE " SALZBURGER INTELLIGENZBLATT ", 15 SEPTEMBER 1787

Auction. It is herewith made known to all and sundry that on the 25th inst. and on the days following, from 9 to 11 in the forenoon, and also from 2 to 5 in the afternoon, at the so-called Tanzmeisterhaus, beyond the bridge, will be sold by public action and assigned to the highest bidders, various valuables, fancy goods and silver ware, personal and other linen, men's clothing, pewter, brass, porcelain and domestic utensils, together with some books and musical instruments. Among the goods to be sold are : *Firstly* a composite microscope with all appurtenances, made by Dollond of London, still in prime condition and deficient in no particular. *Secondly* an excellent solar microscope with all appurtenances, likewise made by Dollond. *Thirdly* an achromatic *tubus* of *three* feet in length with

double objective glass made by the same *Dollond* and in first-rate condition :
as also *fourthly* a harpsichord by the celebrated *Friderizi* of *Gera* with two
manuals of ebony and ivory throughout five whole octaves, with moreover a special cornett and lute stop.   *Salzburg*, 14 September 1787.

The Chancellery of His Serene Highness's Council.

Appendix to the *Oberdeutsche Staatszeitung*.—Erich Valentin in the *Neues
Mozart-Jahrbuch* (Regensburg, 1943), Vol. III, pp. 93 f.—On 18 September the
Salzburg Councillor Ernst von Gilowsky brought about a settlement between
Mozart and his sister on the inheritance, according to which Mozart was to
receive a lump sum of 1,000 gulden. (See 21 and 25–28 September and 10
October 1787.) Nannerl sent copies of church music by her father and her
brother from her father's estate to the Holy Cross Monastery at Augsburg,
and at the end of 1787 she returned her brother's manuscripts to him. But in
the resulting confusion many compositions by Leopold and by W. A. Mozart
seem to have been lost. (Nannerl to Breitkopf & Härtel, 6 April 1803.) The
family letters she kept for herself.—The firm of opticians founded by John
Dollond, who had invented the telescope named here, still exists in London.—
" Friderizi " is Christian Gottlob Friederici.

FROM THE MINUTES OF THE PRINCELY COUNCIL, SALZBURG,
21 SEPTEMBER 1787

Herr Josef Ernst von Gilowsky, Princely Councillor, here resident, as
representative of Wolfgang Amade Mozart in Vienna, and Herr Johann
Bapt. Berchtold von Sonnenburg, Princely Councillor and Prefect of St.
Gilgen, here supplicate *sub praes. 21 huius*, for most gracious ratification,
according to its full contents, of the submitted agreement arrived at by
Herr von Sonnenburg with Wolfgang Mozart, and with respect to the
latter's assignment with Herr von Gilowsky, Princely Councillor, as representative, concerning one half of the paternal inheritance apportioned to
him under date of the 18th inst, which agreement is to the effect that Mozart
is to resign to his brother-in-law Herr von Sonnenburg the goods specified
in the inventory as his legitimate property against payment of a purchase
sum of 1,000 fl., Viennese currency, in consideration of which the purchaser
promises

a) to have the purchase sum paid at once by a bill of exchange on Vienna ;

b) to discharge all legal and other expenses, howsoever named and so
far as they would have fallen upon the vendor ; and

c) to pay the duty money on the 1,000 fl. going abroad to the Government of the Province.

Conclusum : fiat decretum to Herr von Gilowsky, Princely Councillor, as
Wolfgang Mozart's representative and Herr von Sonnenburg as assignee of
Wolfgang Mozart's share in the paternal heritage, that the submitted pur-
chase contract is to be ratified by proper authority, and that Herr von
Sonnenburg and his spouse shall with the assistance of a third party so

M.—10 a

formulate their guarantee that they will be and shall be fully responsible and liable in case sooner or later claims should be made on Leopold Mozart's heritage.

Concerning the minute, however, from Herr Hofer, Hereditary Commissioner of Foreclosure, that at the making of the inventory of Mozart's goods for probate a few ducats and silver pieces amounting to some 30 fl. were found, and since Herr von Sonnenburg, having taken over everything, makes a claim thereto, Herr von Gilowsky, Princely Councillor, is to be informed of this, more especially because this sum of money is not included in the inventory to which this contract refers.

> Salzburg Provincial Archives.—Discovered by Franz Martin, published by Walter Senn in the *Neues Augsburger Mozart-Buch* (1962), pp. 393 f.

On 23 September *Figaro* was given in German at Donaueschingen.

> This performance did not take place in the private theatre of Prince Johann Friedrich von Hohenlohe. (Alfred Loewenberg, *Annals of Opera* [Cambridge, 1943], p. 212.) The translation ("for the Prince of Fürstenberg's Court Theatre") was by the secretary Michael Held and the court chamber singer Walter ; the libretto appeared anonymously, however.

From 25 to 28 September the goods and chattels of Leopold Mozart were sold by auction in the Dancing-Master's Hall on the Hannibalplatz (now Makartplatz 8) at Salzburg.

> J. E. Engl published in the *11. Jahresbericht des Mozarteums 1891* (p. 76) an extract from the Licitation Records, now lost, drawn up by the Court Council Secretary Johann Nepomuk Hofer. According to this the 579 numbers of this auction were valued at 999 florins, 42 kreuzer, but 314 were sold for 1507 fl. 56 kr. There were court dresses, hunting-gear, linen, kitchen utensils, furniture, jewellery and musical instruments, among these the large harpsichord, valued at 100 gulden.—If Mozart really did receive 1,000 gulden as his share, Nannerl had probably already helped herself to a number of things before the auction. Mozart wrote to his brother-in-law Berchtold at St. Gilgen on 29 September, asking him to send the agreed sum, which he does not name, to Michael Puchberg by a bill of exchange, as he was to leave the day after next. (This letter, discovered by Emily Anderson, was published by O. E. Deutsch in the *Österreichische Musikzeitschrift* [Vienna], September 1956.)

In the autumn of 1787 *Figaro* was given at Monza.

> The third and fourth acts had been newly composed by Angelo Tarchi. See Alfred Einstein in *Monthly Musical Record* (London) July–August 1935.

On 1 October Mozart went to Prague with Constanze.

> *Cf.* Mozart's letter of 29 September to his brother-in-law Berchtold zu Sonnenburg.—They may on this occasion, as in 1791, have asked the pedagogue Wenzel Bernhard Heeger, rather than Frau Weber, to take care of their small son Karl, now aged three. Heeger opened an educational establishment at Perchtoldsdorf, near Vienna, in 1782.

FROM THE " PRAGER OBERPOSTAMTSZEITUNG ", 6 OCTOBER 1787

Prague, 4 October.

Our celebrated Herr Mozart has again arrived in Prague, and the news has spread here since that the opera newly written by him, *Das steinene Gastmahl*, will be given for the first time at the National Theatre.

> Nettl, *op. cit.*, p. 117.—The journey had thus taken three days. Mozart alighted at the Three Lions inn (then Kohlmarkt 20), but also stayed intermittently with the Dušeks at the Villa Bertramka, their country seat at Smíchov (a Prague suburb) since 1784.

IBID., 9 OCTOBER 1787

Prague, 8 October.

The I. & R. poet, Herr Abbee Laurenz da Ponte, a Venetian by birth, has arrived here from Vienna and will remain here for a few days.

> Nettl, *op. cit.*, p. 129.—Da Ponte, Mozart's librettist, stayed opposite the Three Lions at the Glatteis inn. He remained in Prague for only a week, however, ostensibly because he had to return to Vienna to attend the rehearsals of Salieri's opera *Axur* (his libretto), which, however, was not performed at the Burgtheater until 8 January 1788.

TAX DECREE OF THE GOVERNMENT OF THE PROVINCE OF SALZBURG,
10 OCTOBER 1787

Intimation to the Provincial Government of this place.

The Princely Councillor and Prefect of St. Gilgen, Herr Johann von Sonnenburg, and Wolfgang Motzart in Vienna, have come to an agreement in respect of the heritage of Leopold Motzart, late Princely Vice Kapellmeister here, by the terms of which the latter has assigned to the former his share in the paternal heritage against payment of 1,000 fl., Viennese currency.

Since on the occasion of this payment the Commissioner of Foreclosure has duly taken into consideration the usual export duty of 10 fl. per cent., this amount of 120 fl. shall without fail be handed over against the proper receipt.

Enacted at Salzburg in the Princely Council this 10 Oct. 1787.

Pres. 20 Oct. 1787.

In re dues from Leopold Mozart's estate.

Franz Thad[dä] v. Kleinmayrn m.p.   Joh. Martin Sauter m.p.

Actum St[eue]r [Tax] : Stuben, 12 Nov. 1787.

To be filed after payment of 120 fl. duty.

> Salzburg Provincial Archives.—Discovered by Franz Martin and published by Walter Senn in the *Neues Augsburger Mozart-Buch* (1962), p. 364.—In Austria the 20 gulden standard was current, in Salzburg the 24 gulden standard. 1,000 Viennese gulden was therefore the equivalent of 1,200 Salzburg gulden.

On 14 October *Figaro* was revived in Prague under Mozart's direction.

On the previous day Bondini's request for permission to perform Beaumarchais's comedy had been refused by a court decree with the words : " that this piece may not be performed in Prague as a play, but it may be given as an Italian opera, as staged at the Vienna Court Theatre " (Teuber, *op. cit.*, pp. 190 f.). *Cf.* 4 February 1785.—The première of *Don Giovanni* had originally been planned for 14 October in celebration of the marriage of Archduchess Maria Theresia, a niece of the emperor, and Prince Anton Clemens of Saxony. The couple had actually been married in Florence on 8 September with their uncle, the Archduke Ferdinand, as proxy. Vicente Martín y Soler's *L' arbore di Diana* (libretto by Da Ponte) had been performed in Vienna on 1 October, also in honour of the bridal couple. The archduchess had left Vienna on 10 October with her brother, Archduke Franz, and they arrived in Prague on the 13th. (They were the children of Grand Duke Leopold of Tuscany, who succeeded Joseph as emperor, followed in turn by his son Franz, while his daughter became Queen of Saxony.)

FROM THE " PRAGER OBERPOSTAMTSZEITUNG ", 16 OCTOBER 1787

Prague, 15 October.

. . . At half-past six o'clock they [Their Highnesses] betook themselves to Nostitz's National Theatre, which was for this occasion embellished and illuminated in a very distinguished manner. The auditorium was so much glorified by the finery of the numerous guests that one has to admit never having beheld such a magnificent scene. At the entry of Their Highnesses they were greeted with the most evident marks of joy by the whole public, which they acknowledged with gracious gratitude. At their request the well-known opera *Die Hochzeit des Figaro*, generally admitted to be so well performed here, was given. The zeal of the musicians and the presence of Mozart, the Master, awakened a general approbation and satisfaction in Their Highnesses. After the first act a sonnet, ordered by several Bohemian patriots for this festivity, was publicly distributed. By reason of their early departure, Their Highnesses returned to the royal castle before the conclusion of the opera.

Jahn, Vol. II, p. 350.—Teuber, *op. cit.*, p. 228 f.—The bride left Prague on 15 October, without having heard the opera intended for her. The marriage ceremony with both parties present actually took place in Dresden on 18 October. Archduke Franz returned to Vienna on the same day.

FROM THE " WIENER ZEITUNG ", 17 OCTOBER 1787
New Music.

Johann Traeg announces . . . that the following new music may be had of him :

.   .   .   .   .

3 Quartets for flute, violin, viola and violoncello by Pleyel . . . 1 do. by Mozart. 1 fl.

Probably the A major quartet (K. 298), which first appeared in print in 1808, also from Traeg.

(in French)

. . . in the evening to the opera *L' arbore di Diana* . . . It was not at all appropriate for fêting a newly-married woman.   At Prague they gave her *le Nozze di Figaro*, also not at all appropriate.

For Martín y Soler's opera, and likewise for Mozart's, see 14 October.

FROM THE " WIENER ZEITUNG ", 20 OCTOBER 1787

Bohemia.   The following report is dated Prague, 15 October :
" In the afternoon of the day before yesterday, H.R.H. the Archduchess *Mar*[ia] *Theresia*, accompanied by her exalted Brother, the Archduke *Franz*, arrived at the Royal Castle here.   The next day they attended High Mass at the Metropolitan Church.   They lunched alone in the company of their High Stewards.   At 5 o'clock there was a *cercle*, at which all the local nobility as well as the Generals, the Staff and other Officers, were present.   The presentation was performed by the Consort of the High Steward for Bohemia, Count Wieschnick.   In the evening their Royal Highnesses betook themselves to Count Nostitz's National Theatre, which was illuminated in a very pretty way for the occasion.   At their entry, their Highnesses were greeted with the most evident marks of joy by the whole public.   The well-known opera *Die Hochzeit des Figaro* was given.   After the first act a poem written for this festivity was publicly distributed.   Early this morning H.R.H. departed for Dresden accompanied by blessings and good wishes."

> Franz Xaver, Count Wieschnick (Věžnik), had since 1783 been High Steward of Bohemia.—Archduchess Maria Theresia and Archduke Franz left on 15 October.   He accompanied her as far as Lobošitz and then returned via Prague to Vienna, where he arrived on the 18th.   She reached Dresden on the same day ; the marriage took place there.   In celebration of this occasion a cantata by Johann Gottlieb Naumann, with text by Giovanni Ambrogio Migliavacca, was performed on the 21st.

On 25 October (or a little earlier) Giacomo Casanova visited Prague from Dux.

> Nettl, *op. cit.*, p. 145.   On 4 November 1787 Count Max Lamberg wrote from Brno to the author Johann Ferdinand Opitz at Časlav : " Casanova is in Prague ; his letter to me is dated 25 October ".—Casanova had since 1785 been living at Dux as librarian to Count Joseph Karl Emanuel Waldstein.   He had gone to Prague for negotiations with a publisher, and may have been present at the première of *Don Giovanni*, which had been once more postponed from the 24th on account of the indisposition of a singer.   Nettl found in the Bohemian Casanova Archives a fragmentary alteration of the text of the sextet in the second act of the opera (*op. cit.*, pp. 146-8).

DOMENICO GUARDASONI TO LORENZO DA PONTE
(in Italian)

. . . Long live da Ponte, long live Mozart ! Every impresario, every virtuoso must bless them ! As long as they live, it shall never be known what theatrical misery means. . . .

> Abert, Vol. II, p. 422.—The letter is said to have been sent from Prague to Vienna before the first performance.—*Cf.* Da Ponte's Memoirs, 1829-30, p. 469.
> —Guardasoni was a singer ; between 1785 and 1788 he was producer for, and then as Bondini's successor, impresario of this company ; it played at Leipzig in the summer.

FROM THE " PRAGER OBERPOSTAMTSZEITUNG ", 30 OCTOBER 1787

Prague, 29 October.

The director of the Italian company here yesterday issued news of the opera *Don Jouan, oder die bestrafte Ausschweifung,* appointed for performance during the sojourn of the exalted Tuscan guests. It has the Court Theatre Poet, the Abbé da Ponte, for its author, and is to be performed for the first time to-day, the 29th. All look forward with pleasure to the excellent composition of our great master, Mozart. More of this anon.

> Freisauff, *op. cit.,* pp. 38 f.—Teuber, *op. cit.,* Vol. II, p. 236.—Nettl, *op. cit.,* p. 159.—This report should have appeared on 29 October, a Monday, and seems to have been delayed by mistake.—The playbill (often reprinted and in 1887 even reconstructed by a typographical process) is spurious; it is in Italian and names a cast in which Teresina instead of Caterina Bondini is the Zerlina. An idea of the appearance of the original poster may be obtained from the German copies announcing the Prague performances of 30 November 1787 (in the Czech National Theatre, Prague, *c.* 1890 ; reproduced by Procházka, pp. 119 f.) and 23 September 1788 (formerly in the Strahov Monastery and reproduced by Nettl, facing p. 152). The title is, of course, *Il dissoluto punito osia Il D. Giovanni,* but the German title below it differs from the versions in the *Prager Zeitung* of (29) 30 October and 3 November (*cf.* 6 October) : *Der gestrafte Ausschweifende, oder : Don Jean.* It then continues :
>
> A grand singspiel in two acts. The poetry is by the Imperial Royal theatre poet the Herr Abbé da Ponte, written expressly for the purpose. And the completely new, excellent music is by the famous *Kapellmeister* Herr Mozart, also especially composed for the occasion. . . . N.B. The libretto, in Italian only, is to be had at the box-office, bound in gold paper, price 40 kr. a copy, and ordinary, price 20 kr. The arias and other pieces of the music in score are to be had of the Impresario Herr Guardasoni, domiciled opposite the National Theatre in Bergmand's house, No. 285, on the first floor. . . . The curtain rises at 7 o'clock and falls at 9.30 o'clock.
>
> The fact that Mozart's court title (see 6–7 December 1787) is not yet shown suggests that the text of September 1788 was identical with that of October 1787. The same company's handbill for the first Leipzig performance on 15 June 1788, reproduced in facsimile by Freisauff (*op. cit.,* facing p. 152), has the same titles, but adds to "A grand singspiel " the words " with choruses, many stage-sets and double orchestra ", which is followed by the remark : " With

regard to repetition of the arias, the well-disposed public is requested kindly to be indulgent ". The Leipzig bill also shows the cast, which is added in brackets to that of the Prague production ; the cast-list is derived mainly from Mozart's own notes in his catalogue of his works : Don Giovanni—Luigi Bassi (Kosta) ; Donna Anna—Teresa Saporiti (Mme Prospero Crespi) ; Don Ottavio—Antonio Baglioni (ditto) ; Commendatore—Giuseppe Lolli (ditto) ; Donna Elvira—Caterina Micelli (the younger Micelli) ; Leporello—Felice Ponziani (ditto) ; Zerlina—Caterina Bondini (the elder Micelli) ; Masetto— Lolli (ditto). For the libretto see the following document.—Guardasoni sold scores of this and other operas to other theatres ; but Anton Grams as well (*cf.* 6 June 1787) again had one in stock. Kucharz again made a pianoforte score. All three of these MS versions are preserved (see Köchel-Einstein, pp. 675 f.).—Da Ponte is said to have received 50 ducats outright in Prague, Mozart 100 ducats ; they received an additional honorarium in Vienna (*cf.* p. 314).

TITLE-PAGE AND PREFATORY NOTE OF THE PRAGUE LIBRETTO

Il/D I S S O L U T O/P U N I T O./O sia/Il D. Giovanni./

Dramma giocoso/in due atti./Da rappresentarsi/nel Teatro di Praga l' anno 1787./In Praga./di Schoenfeld. . . La Poesia è dell' Ab. Da Ponte Poeta/de' Teatri Imperiali di Vienna./La Musica è del Sig. Wolfgango Mozzart,/Maestro di Cap. tedesco.

Copies in the University Library, Prague, and the Library of Congress, Washington.—Prior to this a libretto had already been printed in Vienna, but not sold. Da Ponte had evidently produced a version for the Court Censors, the first act of which finished in the middle of the quartet " Non ti fidar ". The title-page of this libretto (Gesellschaft der Musikfreunde, Vienna), without a printer's name, bears the addendum : " per l' arrivo di Sua Altezza Reale / Maria Teresa / Arciduchessa d' Austria : sposa del / Ser. Principe Antonio di Sassonia ".—Facsimile of both title-pages in Paul Stefan's *Don Giovanni* (Vienna, 1938), p. 75.

FROM THE " PRAGER OBERPOSTAMTSZEITUNG ", 3 NOVEMBER 1787

Prague, 1 November.

On Monday the 29th the Italian opera company gave the ardently awaited opera by Maestro Mozard, *Don Giovani*, or *das steinerne Gastmahl*. Connoisseurs and musicians say that Prague had never yet heard the like. Herr Mozard conducted in person ; when he entered the orchestra he was received with threefold cheers, which again happened when he left it. The opera is, moreover, extremely difficult to perform, and every one admired the good performance given in spite of this after such a short period of study. Everybody, on the stage and in the orchestra, strained every nerve to thank Mozard by rewarding him with a good performance. There were also heavy additional costs, caused by several choruses and changes of scenery, all of which Herr Guardasoni had brilliantly attended to. The unusually large attendance testifies to a unanimous approbation.

> Teuber, *op. cit.*, Vol. II, pp. 236 f.—Facsimile in Stefan, *op. cit.*, p. 81.—This report also appeared in the *Wiener Zeitung* of 14 November.

On 3 November *Don Giovanni* was repeated for Mozart's benefit.

> This was the fourth performance of the opera, probably, like the others, under Mozart's direction; the performance on 30 November was certainly conducted by Strobach.

FROM THE " PROVINZIALNACHRICHTEN ", VIENNA, 10 NOVEMBER 1787

Prague Theatre.

On Monday, 29 October, the Italian opera *Don Giovani*, or *der steinerne Gast*, music by Herr Mozard, was performed for the first time with general applause. Herr Mozard conducted in person and was welcomed joyously and jubilantly by the numerous gathering.

ADELHEID WEBER IN MOZART'S ALBUM

He who knows not genuine, heartfelt, unselfish friendship does not know the best that men can give each other. This, dear Mozart, is offered you with a full heart by

Your true friend

Prague, 11 November 1787. and aunt Weber.

> According to Karl Maria Pisarowitz the writer was not Genoveva Weber (see 8 January 1787) but her sister-in-law Adelheid Weber (*c.* 1729–1807), the elder sister of Fridolin and Franz Anton Weber. From 1754 till 1758 she had been married to a Herr Krebs.

JOSEPH HURDALEK IN MOZART'S ALBUM

> When Orpheus' magic lute out-rings,
> Amphion to his lyre sings,
> The lions tame, the rivers quiet grow,
> The tigers listen, rocks a-walking go.
>
> When Mozart masterly music plays
> And gathers undivided praise,
> The quire of Muses stays to hear,
> Apollo is himself all ear.

Prague, 12 November 1787 Your admirer and friend

Joseph Hurdalek,
Rector of the General Seminary.

See 13 January 1787.—The Prague Clementinum at this time housed the Archiepiscopal Seminary, which the Emperor Joseph had transformed into a general seminary for the training of priests. Bishop Hurdálek was rector of this seminary from 1785 to 1790.

Mozart left Prague on 13 November and arrived back in Vienna on the 16th (?). These dates are not quite certain.

Gluck died on 15 November.

On 23 November *Die Entführung* was given at Coblenz.

FROM GOETHE'S "ITALIENISCHE REISE", ROME, NOVEMBER 1787

All our endeavour . . . to confine ourselves to what is simple and limited was lost when Mozart appeared. *Die Entführung aus dem Serail* conquered all, and our own carefully written piece has never been so much as mentioned in theatre circles.

Abert, Vol. I, p. 973.—Goethe's "piece" was *Scherz, List und Rache,* a one-act singspiel written in 1784, and his first libretto ; it was printed in 1790 ; it was first set to music by Christoph Kayser and later by Peter von Winter. Goethe had repeatedly heard *Die Entführung* at Weimar since the autumn of 1785.

Early in December Mozart moved from the Landstrasse suburb back to the Inner City, No. 281, "unter den Tuchlauben" (now No. 27), corner of Schultergasse.

REQUEST OF THE HIGH CHAMBERLAIN, COUNT FRANZ ROSENBERG, FOR THE EMPEROR'S CONSENT TO WOLFGANG MOZART'S ENGAGEMENT AS CHAMBER MUSICIAN

Since Your Majesty has been most graciously pleased to command me verbally to see to it that Wolfgang Mozart be engaged as Kammermusikus with an annual salary of 800 fl., I am emboldened to beg Your Majesty with the most profound humility to signify in writing your most gracious consent to the enactment both of his engagement and of the assignment of his salary.

Placet.

Vienna, 6 December 1787.   Rosenberg.

Vienna, State Archives.—Ludwig von Köchel in the *Jahrbuch für Landeskunde von Nieder-Oesterreich* (Vienna) 1868, p. 357.—For Rosenberg, *cf.* 23 April 1775 and 23 January 1778.

NOTE FROM THE HIGH CHAMBERLAIN, COUNT ROSENBERG, TO THE HIGH STEWARD'S OFFICE

His Majesty the Emperor, in response to a most humbly submitted proposal, has most graciously consented to command that Wolfgang *Mozart* be appointed Kammermusicus with a salary of eight hundred gulden per annum, as from 1 December of this year.

The I. & R. High Steward's Office is therefore kindly requested to have the goodness to issue the necessary instruction for his payment to the I. & R. General Purposes Treasury.

Vienna, 7 December 1787.   Rosenberg.

> Vienna, State Archives.—Köchel, *op. cit.*, p. 357.

FROM THE MINUTES OF THE IMPERIAL CHANCELLERY, 6–7 DECEMBER 1787

[*datum Exhibitionis* :] 6 Dec. [Exhibiting authority :] Rosenberg [Contents of the Exhibit :] N. 5949. Proposal of 6 December concerning the engagement of Wolfgang Mozart as Kammer-Musicus with a salary of 800 fl. [Discharged and dispatched :] Res : *Placet.* [Date :] *eod. dato* [7 Dec.].

> Vienna, State Archives : Kabinetts-Protokolle, Vol. 44, p. 1167.—Karl Glossy, *Das Burgtheater unter seinem Gründer Joseph II* (Vienna, 1926), p. 67.

DECREE OF MOZART'S APPOINTMENT

From His Apostolic Majesty, Emperor of the Holy Roman Empire, King of Hungary and Bohemia, Archduke of Austria, &c. Our most gracious sovereign, concerning Wolfgang Mozart, graciously subjoins : that it has been H. I. & R. Apost. Maj.'s pleasure to do him the most signal honour of appointing him H.M. Kammermusikus, in view of his knowledge and capacity in music and the approbation he has earned thereby, and to condescend to command the I. & R. Treasury to assign him a salary of eight hundred gulden per annum from 1 December of this year.

In pursuance of which this Imperial resolution is herewith imparted to the said Wolfgang Mozart and the present decree of the High Chamberlain's Office drawn up at Imperial command as his guarantee.

Rosenberg.

Pres. I. & R. High Chamberlain's Office.

Vienna, 7 December 1787.

Johann Thorwart.

> Salzburg, Mozarteum.—Köchel, *op. cit.*, pp. 357 f.—Jahn, Vol. I, pp. 806 f., 355, 700.—Facsimile in Bory, *op. cit.*, p. 159.—Two circumstances may have supported this preferment : the Prague festival opera for the Emperor's niece and the death of Gluck, who had received 2000 gulden a year for the same sinecure. (Leopold Kozeluch, who did not succeed Mozart in this office, received 1500 gulden a year as " composer " to the Court Chapel from 1792.) The only duty informally imposed on Mozart was an obligation to write some dances—minuets and German dances—each year for the court masked balls held in the Grand and the Small Assembly Hall. In the four following winters Mozart wrote 36 minuets and at least 31 German dances for the orchestras

in the assembly halls.—In the Court and State records for 1789 and 1791 Mozart was entered as " Composer " among the " Imperial and Royal Court Chamber Musicians " or simply the " Chamber Musicians " ; he was thus " I. & R. Chamber Composer ", but not " Kapellmeister in the actual service of His I. & R. Majesty ", as he himself believed and as he was frequently called during those years. On 19 December 1787 he wrote to his sister that he had been " taken into the Emperor's service " ; and on 2 August 1788 he explained to her after the performance of *Don Giovanni* at the Burgtheater, when the poster (*cf.* 26 January 1790), " which surely does not state too much, since it is issued by the I. & R. Theatre Directorate ", had called him " Kapellmeister in actual Imperial service " (the libretto has, in Italian, " in actual service of the Imperial Court ", and the *Wiener Zeitung* of 10 May has the same words, but in German) : " the Emperor has taken me into his household, and I am thus formally appointed ; but for the present with only 800 florins—however, there is no one else in the household who has as much ". Mozart himself, soon after his appointment, signed himself " I. & R. Chamber Musician " (see 24 February 1787) ; on the occasion of another subscription (1788), he appeared as " Musician in the service of His I. & R. Apost. Majesty " ; in the *Wiener Zeitung* of 2 April 1788 as " Kapellmeister in actual service of His Majesty " ; in his testimonial for Joseph Eybler on 30 May 1790 as " Kapellmeister in Imperial service " ; but in April 1791, in his petition to the Vienna Magistracy, he signed himself " I. & R. Court Composer ". In her petition for a pension on 11 December 1791 Constanze described him as " I. & R. Chamber Composer ". At the baptism of his children he was called Kapellmeister in 1783, which meant nothing in particular in the case of a composer, but later (1784, 1786 and 1789) " I. & R. Kapellmeister ", and in 1787 and 1791 " I. & R. Court Kapellmeister ". The death certificates have " I. & R. Kapellmeister and Chamber Composer ". Among his Viennese publishers, Artaria & Co. give him no title ; Hoffmeister, about 1790, describes him on Italian title-pages as being " in actual service of His I. and R. Majesty " (K. 426) or as " *Maestro di Capella* in actual service of His I. & R. Majesty " (K. 546) ; a French title-page has " au Service de sa Majeste I. et R." (K. 533 with 494) ; Lausch calls him " Kapellmeister in actual I. & R. service " (K. 527) or " Kapell-Meister in actual service of His Majesty the Emperor " (K. 539, 577 and 599-605). On the poster for *Così fan tutte* in 1790 he is similarly described, also in the libretto of *La clemenza di Tito* (Prague, 1791), though here in Italian. Finally, the playbill for *Die Zauberflöte* in 1791 calls him " Kapellmeister and I. & R. Chamber Composer ", though the libretto has " Kapellmeister and actual I. & R. Chamber Composer ".—Giuseppe Bonno (died 1788), and then Antonio Salieri, were officially entitled to call themselves court Kapellmeister.

FROM THE " PRAGER OBERPOSTAMTSZEITUNG ", (?8) DECEMBER 1787

On 6 December, at the Church of St. Nicolas, a musical Mass written by Herr Mozart, the composer so greatly favoured here, was performed, and every one admitted that in this kind of composition too he is a complete master.

Teuber, *op. cit.*, Vol. II, p. 240 ; Jahn, Vol. II, p. 355.—6 December is the Feast of St. Nicolas. The church is in the Small Side in Prague (*cf.* 14 Dec. 1791). The mass may have been that in C minor, K.427.

On 15 December the German Opera in Vienna was disbanded ; Aloisia Lange went over to the Italian company.

FROM THE " WIENER ZEITUNG ", 19 DECEMBER 1787

At the art establishment of Artaria Compagnie are to be had :

By *Mozart* 1 new Quartet for pianoforte with violin, viola and violoncello. Op. 13   .   .   .   . 1 fl. 40 kr.
By do. 1 new Sonata for 2 persons on one pianoforte, Op. 12   2 fl.

> The price of the E♭ major pianoforte quartet (K. 493) had been raised 10 kreuzer by mistake (*cf.* 21 July 1787). The F major sonata for pianoforte duet (K. 497) was here advertised for the first time.—The same page also contains an advertisement by Lausch for the same works, evidently in Artaria's edition, with opus numbers and at the original prices.

On 27 December Mozart's fourth child, Theresia, was born.

> The christening took place in St. Peter's Church. Frau Theresia von Trattner stood godmother. This child too lived for only six months.

JOSEPH HAYDN TO FRANZ ROTT, CHIEF OF COMMISSARIAT IN PRAGUE, DECEMBER 1787

You ask an *opera buffa* of me. With the greatest pleasure, if you have the desire to possess some vocal composition of mine all for yourself. But if it is to be performed on the stage in Prague, I cannot oblige you in that case, since all my operas are too closely bound up with our personnel, and moreover would never produce the effect which I calculated according to local conditions. It would be quite another matter if I had the incalculable felicity of composing an entirely new libretto for the theatre there. But even in that event I should be taking a great risk, since the *great Mozart* can scarcely have his equal.

For if I were able to impress the soul of every music-lover, and more especially the great ones, with my own understanding of and feeling for Mozart's incomparable works, *so profound* and so full of *musical intelligence*, as my own *strong sentiment* dictates, then the nations would vie with each other to possess such a jewel within their encircling walls. Let Prague hold fast to the precious man—but also reward him ; for without that the story of great genius is a sad one and gives posterity little encouragement for further effort ; for which reason, alas, so many hopeful spirits suffer defeat. It makes me angry to think that this *unique* Mozart has not yet found an appointment at some imperial or royal court ! Forgive me if I stray from my path. I love the man too much . . .

> Franz Xaver Niemetschek's Mozart book (Prague, 1798), pp. 51 f.—*Allgemeine musikalische Zeitung*, (Leipzig) 19 December 1798, Vol. I, pp. 182 f.—Nissen, *op. cit.*, pp. 643 f.—*Wiener allgemeine Musik-Zeitung*, 4 December 1847, No.

VII, p. 581.—Rott was an active music-lover (*cf.* Gottfried Johann Dlabacz, *Allgemeines historisches Künstlerlexikon für Böhmen* [Prague, 1815], Vol. II, p. 597).—" Our personnel " refers to the company of Prince Esterházy's theatres at Eisenstadt and Esterháza.

FROM FRANZ KRATTER'S " PHILOSOPHISCHE UND STATISTISCHE BEOBACHTUNGEN VORZÜGLICH DIE ÖSTERREICHISCHEN STAATEN BETREFFEND ", FRANKFURT AND LEIPZIG, 1787

. . . But, artistic Talent, what canst thou expect of thy fatherland, where people fight to hear a few arias negligently sung at a bad concert by the arrogant foreigner Storace,* whose talent for art equals that for impertinence, while thy Mozart, so excellent an artist, is not even paid as much for a good concert as will cover his costs for it.

    * Mme. Storace's receipt from this concert amounted to over 4,000 gulden.

Vol. I, pp. 48 f.—The preface to this volume is dated Vienna, 17 September 1787. (A second part, published at Brno in 1791, with a preface dated Lwów, 22 March 1791, bears the sub-title " Remarks . . . on . . . my journey through some provinces of Upper Germany ".) Kratter had published a book on Galicia and a pamphlet against freemasonry in 1786.—Ann Storace's concert had taken place on 23 February 1787. Mozart had more subscribers for his concerts in 1784 than his rivals Richter (see 17 March 1784) and the violinist John Abraham Fisher (1784/85), Storace's husband, combined.

1788

In 1788 two books were published in Vienna in the subscribers' lists of which Mozart's name figures : Gottlieb Leon's *Gedichte* (" Mozart, Kapellmeister ") and [Anton Stein's] *Österreichische und türkische Kriegslieder* (" Hr. Mozart, Tonkünstler in Diensten Sr. k. k. apost. Majestät ").

Cf. 24 February 1787.—Leon, the author of the texts of two lost masonic songs by Mozart (*cf.* Deutsch, *op. cit.*, p. 15, and Köchel-Einstein, p. 605) was a secretary at the Court Library.—Anton Joseph Stein was professor of poetics at the Academic Gymnasium, later professor of classical literature at Vienna University. Franz Grillparzer was one of his pupils, and through another, Eduard von Bauernfeld, Schubert made his acquaintance. The printer of the anonymously published collection, Joseph Hraschansky, also printed Mozart's *Kleine Freimaurer-Kantate* (K. 623) in 1792.—The second Turkish war (1787-1792), waged by Austria in alliance with Russia, went against Austria, until General Gedeon von Laudon captured Belgrade in 1789 ; Austria made peace with Turkey in 1791. Mozart's interest in this war is attested by " Ein deutsches Kriegslied " (K. 539) and another song, " Beim Auszug in das Feld " (K. 552), as also by the country dance (K. 535), entitled " La Bataille " or " The Siege of Belgrade " (see 19 March 1788).

On 6 January 1788 Archduke Franz, nephew of the emperor, married Princess Elisabeth of Württemberg (see 16 November 1781).

On this occasion the Burgtheater on 8 January performed Salieri's opera *Axur, rè d' Ormus*, libretto by Da Ponte, an adaptation of *Tarare*, given in Paris six months earlier.

On 4 February the German singspiel venture at the Kärntnertor Theatre came to an end with *Die Entführung*.

Singspiele had been cultivated there since 16 October 1785, sometimes in rotation with the Burgtheater.

The Kärntnertor Theatre remained closed from 5 February 1788 till 16 November 1791.

Performances were given on only three days during this period : Cimarosa's opera *Pimmalione* on 17 and 25 July 1791, and a concert given by Marianne Kirchgessner on 19 August 1791.

FROM ZINZENDORF'S DIARY, 10 FEBRUARY 1788
(in French)

Thence to the Venetian Ambassador's, where there was a great gathering. A concert at which Mandini and la Morichelli sang, Mozart and a certain Muller, a shoemaker's daughter, played, one the pianoforte, the other the harp. I was afflicted with spleen.

Pohl, *Haydn*, Vol. II, p. 146.—Gugitz in *Wiener Geschichtsblätter*, 1956, No. 1, p. 18.—The envoy Andrea Dolfin lived in the Dorotheergasse (the present No. 9).—Stefano Mandini and Anna Morichelli were members of the Italian Opera in Vienna. Josepha Müllner, later Frau Gollenhofer, at this time aged eighteen and from 1811 to 1823 court harpist, gave an annual concert at the Burgtheater from 1788 onwards.

On 15 February Stefano Mandini held an academy at the Burgtheater, at which a symphony by Mozart was played.

FROM FORKEL'S " MUSIKALISCHER ALMANACH FÜR DEUTSCHLAND AUF DAS JAHR 1789 ", LEIPZIG

Vienna 26 February 1788. On this day and on 4 March Ramler's cantata *Die Auferstehung und Himmelfahrt Christi*, in the excellent composition of the incomparable Hamburg *Bach*, was performed at Count *Johann Esterhazy's*, with the unanimous approbation of all the nobility present, by an orchestra of 86 persons in the presence and under the direction of that great connoisseur of the art of music, Baron *von Swieten*. The I. & R. Capellmeister Herr *Mozart* beat time and had the score, and the I. & R. Capellmeister Herr *Umlauff* was at the keyboard. The performance was the more excellent because it had been preceded by two general rehearsals. At the performance of 4 March the Count caused the portrait of Herr Capellmeister *Bach*, engraved in copper, to circulate in the hall. The Princesses and Countesses present and the whole of the brilliant nobility admired the great composer, and there occurred a hearty *vivat* and a threefold, loud round of applause. Among the singers were Mme. *Lange*, the tenor *Adamberger*, the bass *Saale*, 30 choristers, &c.   On the 7th the same piece was performed at the I. & R. National Court Theatre.

> According to E. F. Schmid Mozart at this time re-orchestrated one of the arias of the cantata ; *cf.* K. App. 109ᵍ, No. 19, and KE., p. 984.—The "Hamburg Bach" was Carl Philipp Emanuel, Johann Sebastian Bach's second son.   Karl Wilhelm Ramler's *Geistliche Kantaten* had been published in Berlin in 1760, Bach's setting at Leipzig in 1787.—Count Esterházy seems to have lived in the other Palais Pálffy (*cf.* 16 October 1762) in the Hintere Schenkenstrasse (City No. 50, now No. 17, a new building).—Ignaz Umlauf, who had started his career as a viola player in the Burgtheater orchestra and been first Kapellmeister of the German Opera at the National Court Theatre (1778–83), became Salieri's deputy as Court Kapellmeister in 1789.—Ignaz Saal had been a member of the German Opera from 1782.—Gottfried van Swieten had founded a Society of Noblemen for the cultivation of classical music (see November 1788).

In February *Die Entführung* was given at Brunswick.

The first performance may have taken place a little earlier.

On 7 March C. P. E. Bach's Resurrection Cantata was publicly performed at the Burgtheater.

> *Cf.* 26 February 1788.—Mozart probably conducted the work again.

On the same day, 7 March, Friedrich Baumann sang at his concert in the Leopold-stadt Theatre "Ein deutsches Kriegslied" with orchestral accompaniment (K. 539).

> Baumann was a popular comedian at the theatre in the Leopoldstadt suburb, later a Court opera singer.   His wife Therese was a daughter of the first Bassa Selim in *Die Entführung*, Dominik Jautz (see 16 July 1782).   Mozart had written the song for Baumann's concert.   The words ("Ich möchte wohl der Kayser sein") had been published by Johann Wilhelm Ludwig Gleim as long as twelve years before, but had achieved a topical significance through the Turkish war.   Gleim had entitled the poem "Meine Wünsche.   An unsern deutschgesinnten grossen Kaiser" (Joseph II), and Johann Holzer's setting of it (see 18 January 1786), published as early as 1779, was called "Der Kaiser".—Baumann may have repeated Mozart's song on 12 March, at his elder brother Anton's concert.   See the following advertisement.

FROM THE "WIENER ZEITUNG", 19 MARCH 1788

New Battle-Song

of a German soldier, by Herr Mozart, Kapellmeister in actual service of His Majesty the Emperor.
>   "Ich möchte wohl der Kaiser seyn", with all the parts, 1 fl.
>   *ditto* in pianoforte score,   12 kr.
>   – – "Die Belagerung Belgrads", with all the parts, 1 fl.
>   *ditto* in pianoforte score,   12 kr.

To be had at Lausch's music establishment . . .

> For the "Kriegslied" see 1 August 1789 ; for the country dance "Die Bela-gerung Belgrads" (or "La Bataille") (K. 535) see 17 January 1789 and February 1790.

Mozart, a star of the first magnitude in the present musical firmament, has become Kapellmeister to the Archduke Franz. The captious declare that he has transplanted the magic of his genius entirely to the pianoforte and that in more extended compositions he fails to make an effect with this all-transfiguring fire.

> 1st Half-Year, p. 30.—Copy in the Württemberg State Library, Stuttgart.— This is, of course, a confusion with Mozart's appointment as Imperial chamber musician (see 7 December 1787). This false rumour is of some interest in connection with Mozart's attempts to secure the post of music master to the Archduke's betrothed (see 16 November 1781) and, through his intervention in May 1790, that of second Court Kapellmeister.

Musical News

Three new Quintets *a 2 violini, 2 viole, e violoncello*, which I offer by subscription, finely and correctly written. The subscription price is 4 ducats, at 18 fl. Viennese currency.—The subscription tickets are to be had daily from Herr *Puchberg*, at Sallinz's warehouse in the Hohe Markt, where from 1 July onwards the work itself may also be had. Amateurs abroad are requested to frank their orders. Vienna, 1 April 1788.

Kapellmeister Mozart
in actual service of His Majesty.

> Jahn, Vol. I, p. 826.—This notice was also published in the Weimar *Journal des Luxus und der Moden* (*Intelligenz-Blatt* No. 6) in June. The works in question are the string quintets in C minor, C major and G minor (K. 406, 515 and 516), all dating from the spring of 1787. *Cf.* 25 June 1788. None of these MS. copies is known or has been recognized, if indeed they were ever made.—The three quintets appeared separately with Artaria & Co. : K. 406 in 1792, K. 515 in 1789 and K. 516 in 1790.—" 4 ducats, at 18 fl. Viennese currency " means 4 ducats or 18 gulden in Austrian assimilated coinage, as the repetitions of the advertisement make clear (" or 18 fl."exp).—This is the second piece of evidence of the friendly business relationship between Mozart and his " Brother " Puchberg (see 25–28 September 1787), the proprietor of the textile firm of Michael Salliet at Hoher Markt 522, in the house of Count Franz Walsegg-Stuppach (who commissioned the Requiem in 1791). As is shown by Mozart's letter to Puchberg of 17 June 1788, this subscription was to help in clearing a debt to Puchberg.—For the second and third reprint of Mozart's announcement, 5 and 9 April, Puchberg's business address was replaced by that of his dwelling at the same place : " in Count Walsegg's house, Hoher Markt No. 522 ".

On 9 April *Die Entführung* was given at Hildesheim.

The first performance there may have been a little earlier.

FROM THE " MAGAZIN DER SÄCHSISCHEN GESCHICHTE ", DRESDEN, 1788

Dresden Curiosities

On the 17th [April] Mme. *Duscheck*, the famous singer, and on the 22nd the former Electoral Court Singer *Hurka*, held concerts on their own account at the Hôtel de Pologne. The former sang 2 scenas by Mozart and some fragments from Naumann's opera *Orpheus*.

Vol. V, p. 252.—Richard Engländer, *J. G. Naumann als Opernkomponist* (Berlin, 1916).—In the spring of 1789 Mozart himself stayed at this hotel.—Friedrich Franz Hurka was a tenor and song composer.—Johann Gottlieb Naumann, whose acquaintance Mozart made at Dresden, was Chief Kapellmeister at the Saxon Electoral Court. His opera *Orpheus og Euridice* had been performed in Copenhagen in 1786.

POSTER FOR THE FIRST VIENNA PERFORMANCE OF " DON GIOVANNI ", 7 MAY 1788

New Singspiel. / At the I. & R. National Court Theatre / will be performed today, Wednesday, 7 May 1788 : / (for the first time)

IL DISSOLUTO PUNITO,
osia :
IL DON GIOVANNI.
Don Juan, oder : der bestrafte Bösewicht.
A Singspiel in two Acts,

The poetry is by Herr Abbate da Ponte, Poet of the Italian Opera at the I. & R. Theatre. / The music is by Herr Wolfgang Mozzart, Kapellmeister in actual imperial service. / The librettos, Italian only, are to be had of the Box Master at 20 kr. / To begin at 7 o'clock.

Vienna, National Library.—Teuber, *Die Theater Wiens* (Vienna, 1903), Vol. II, Part ii, pp. 80 f.—The performance was given at the Emperor's command (*cf.* 16 May and 15 December 1788).—The cast was : Donna Anna—Aloisia Lange ; Zerlina—Luisa Mombelli (*née* Laschi) ; Donna Elvira—Caterina Cavalieri ; Don Giovanni—Francesco Albertarelli ; Leporello—Francesco Benucci ; Don Ottavio—Francesco Morella ; Commendatore and Masetto—Francesco Bussani. (Albertarelli and Morella had been newly engaged.)—The opera was not again heard in Mozart's lifetime after 1788, when it was given on 7, 9, 12, 16, 23 and 30 May, 16 and 23 June, 5, 11 and 21 July, 2 August, 24 October, 3 November and 15 December.—There is a copy of the libretto in the National Library, Vienna.

FROM ZINZENDORF'S DIARY, 7 MAY 1788
(In French)

. . to the Opera. *Don Giovanni*. Mozart's music is agreeable and very varied.

FROM THE ACCOUNTS OF THE COURT THEATRES, 1788–89

To Da Ponte Lorenz for composition of the poetry for the opera *il Don Giovanni*	100.–
To Hoffmann Johann for extra services in place of Woborzill, indisposed	2.–
item	3.–
item for the musical personnel required by the Italian *opera il Don Giovanni*	240.–
Together, according to 3rd receipt, as No. 139	245.–
To Mozart Wolfgang for composition of the music for the opera *Il Don Giovanni*, as No. 138	225.–

Vienna, State Archives, Half-Years 25 and 26, pp. 45-47.—Teuber, *op. cit.*, p. 81.—Facsimile in Paul Stefan, *Don Giovanni* (Vienna, 1938), p. 85.—O. E. Deutsch in *Music & Letters*, London, April 1944, p. 97.—The honorarium was calculated as for a revival of the opera already paid for in Prague.— Johann Hoffmann was the choirmaster ; Thomas Woborzill (Vobořil) was a violinist in the Hofkapelle and played at Joseph II's afternoon concerts ; earlier he had also been conductor of the German Opera. The " musical personnel required " were the stage band.

FROM THE " WIENER ZEITUNG ", 10 MAY 1788

At the I. & R. National Court Theatre

was performed for the first time on Wednesday, 7 May : *il Dissoluto punito, osia : il Don Giovanni*. A Singspiel in two acts, by Herr Abbate da Ponte, opera poet of the I. & R. Theatre. The music is by Herr Wolfgang Mozzart, Kapellmeister in actual service of the Imperial Court.

Teuber, *op. cit.*, pp. 80 f.

FROM ZINZENDORF'S DIARY, 12 MAY 1788
(in French)

To the Opera. *Don Giovanni*. Mme. de la Lippe finds the music learned, little suited to the voice.

Gugitz, *op. cit.*, p. 18.—The lady was the wife of Count Karl Christian zur Lippe, Chamberlain and Councillor of the Realm.

ARCHDUCHESS ELISABETH WILHELMINE TO HER HUSBAND, ARCHDUKE FRANZ
(in French)

[Vienna,] 15 May [1788.]

In the last few days a new opera composed by Mozart has been given, but I was told that it did not have much success. La Coltellini can hardly have made an advantageous début at the première, which was given immediately upon her arrival.

> *Briefe an Erzherzog Franz von seiner ersten Gemählin Elisabeth, 1785-1789*, edited by H. Weyda (Vienna, 1870) p. 91.—Supplied by Frau Erna Felmayer, Vienna. —The archduchess was by birth a Princess of Württemberg. The archduke was taking part in the campaign against the Turks.—Anna Coltellini, Celesta's sister, had probably made her début in Paisiello's *La modista raggiratrice* in the Burgtheater on 23 April 1788. As far as is known she sang in *Don Giovanni* neither on 7, 9 nor 12 May. Aloisia Lange was Donna Anna, Caterina Cavalieri was Donna Elvira and Luisa Laschi-Mombelli, Zerlina. The last named was relieved by Therese Teyber after seven performances because she was pregnant.

EMPEROR JOSEPH II TO COUNT ROSENBERG, SEMLIN, 16 MAY 1788
(in French)

Mozart's music is certainly too difficult for the singers.

> Vienna, State Archives : Protokolle der Kabinettskanzlei, Vol. XLVII, p. 366. —Payer von Thurn, *op. cit.*, p. 75.—The Emperor, who had been at the front since 29 February, had not yet heard the opera. See 15 December 1788.

On 18 May *Figaro* was performed in German at Lübeck by Grossmann's company.

> *Annalen des Theaters* (continuation of the *Ephemeriden*) (Berlin, 1790) No. 5, pp. 29 f., where " Fräulein von Knigge" is named as translator. It appears from Baron Adolf Knigge's *Dramaturgische Blätter* of 23 May 1789, which deals with the performance at Hanover on the 19th, that his daughter Philippine Eregine von Knigge had translated the dialogue with reference to the French original, and that he had done the arias. (Alfred Loewenberg, *Annals of Opera* [Cambridge, 1943], p. 212, where, however, the first performance at Lübeck is not mentioned.)

FROM THE "WIENER ZEITUNG", 24 MAY 1788

Il Don Giovanni, o sia il Dissoluto punito.

New opera by Herr Mozart, Kapellmeister in actual I. & R. service, to be sung at the pianoforte ; transcribed by Herr Haydenreich.

L'Overtura 32 kr.

Atto I⁰

1. " Notte e giorno faticar ". *Introduzione Terzetto* 48 kr.
2. " Ma qual mai ", *Recitativo*, " Fuggi crudele ", *Duetto. S. e T.* (" Che giuramento o Dei ! ") 40 kr.
3. " Ah chi mi dice mai, quel barbaro dove ", *Aria. S.* 20 kr.
4. " Madamina, il catalogo é questo ", *do. B.* (" Ma in Spagna son giá mille e tre ") 32 kr.
5. " Giovinette che fate all' amore ", *Coro* 16 kr.
6. " Ho capito Signor si ", *Aria. B.* (" Cavaliera ancora te ") 16 kr.

7. "Lá ci darem la mano", *Duettino. S. e B.* ("Andiam mio bene")
    16 kr.
8. "Ah fuggi il traditor", *Aria. S.*   12 kr.
9. "Non ti fidar o misera", *Quartetto*   32 kr.
10. "Don Ottavio son morta!", *Recit.*, "Or sai Chi l' onore", *Aria, S.*
    32 kr.
11. "Dalla sua pace la mia dipende", *do. T.* ("Morte mi da")   12 kr.
12. "Fin ch' han dal vino, Calda la Testa", *do. B.*   24 kr.
13. "Batti batti, o bel Masetto", *do. S.*   20 kr.
14. "Presto presto pria ch' ei venga", *Finale*   1 fl. 4 kr.
15. "Proteggo il giusto cielo", *Terzetto*   8 kr.
16. "Risposate vezzose ragazze" ("Viva la libertá")   36 kr.
17. "Da bravi via ballare" (*The Ball*)   1 fl. 4 kr.

Atto II^do

1. "Eh via buffone non mi seccar", *Duetto. B.*   12 kr.
2. "Ah taci ingiusto Core" *Terzetto* (Donna Elvira at the Window)
    28 kr.
3. "Deh vieni alla finestra", *Aria, B. con mandolino* (The Serenade)   12 kr.
4. "Metà di voi quà vadone", *do. B.* ("Fe' or vedrai cos'è")   16 kr.
5. "Vedrai carino se sei buonino", *do. S.*   16 kr.
6. "Sola in bujo loco, palpitar il cor mi sento", *Sestetto*   1 fl. 12 kr.
7. "Per queste tue manine", *Duetto. S. e B.* (At the tying up)   24 kr.
8. "In quali eccessi", *Recit.*, "Mi tradi quell' alma ingrata", *Aria. S.*
    32 kr.
9. "O Statua gentilissima", *Duetto. B.*   24 kr.
10. "Crudele! Ah non mio bene", *Recit.*, "Non mi dir bell' Idol mio",
    Rondeau   24 kr.
11. "Già la Menza è preparata", *Finale*   3 fl. 24 kr.

    The whole opera in score, with the libretto   34 fl.

    In pianoforte score, bound   16 fl.

    For quartet, to be subscribed for until 30 June at 5 fl.

In Vienna, at Lausch's Music Establishment in the Kärntnerstrasse No. 1085
over The Three White Roses.

Joseph Heidenreich was a modest composer and prolific arranger of operas
for wind ensemble ; he offered in the *Wiener Zeitung* (1796, p. 1038) a MS.
copy of a *Fundament zur Erlernung des Generalbasses* alleged to be by Mozart.—
Nos. 14-17 constitute the finale of the first act.—No. 7 (of Act II), the duet for
Zerlina and Leporello, had been written to take the place of Don Ottavio's "Il
mio tesoro" for the Vienna production ; but the preceding aria for Leporello
"Ah, pietà, signori miei!", had also been omitted in Vienna.—A copy
of the MS. score is preserved in the Istituto musicale at Florence (P 265).
—E. F. Schmid found many numbers from the piano score and parts for
the quartet arrangement in the Schwarzenberg Archives, Český Krumlov
[Krumau] (*cf.* 16 July 1788).

In May Le Duc of Paris announced the G minor pianoforte quartet (K. 478) in the *Mercure de France* as " Opus 14 ".

> Johansson, *op. cit.*, p. 99.—The advertisement was repeated in the *Affiches* on 13 July 1788.—The quartet had been published by Hoffmeister in Vienna in the winter of 1785–86 without opus number.

On 2 June, at the Burgtheater, the bass Albertarelli sang the arietta " Un bacio di mano " (K. 541) interpolated into Anfossi's *Le gelosie fortunate*.

> The libretto of the opera, which was first performed at Venice in 1786, is by Filippo Livigni. The words for the extra number may have been written by Da Ponte. Its text is found in the Vienna libretto, which was printed at the Deaf and Dumb Institute (copy in the Biblioteca del Conservatorio S. Pietro a Majella, Naples). Haydn cut this arietta when the opera was performed at Esterháza in 1789.

FROM THE " GAZZETTA TOSCANA ", FLORENCE, 14 JUNE 1788
(in Italian)

On the evening of the 11th inst. there was staged in the Regio Teatro degl'Intrepidi known as della Palla a Corda an opera seria with the title : *L' Idalide, o sia : La Vergine del Sole*. The bravura of the actors, and in particular of the prima Donna Signora Caterina Lusini, and the music of the celebrated Signor Giuseppe Sarti, met with the approval of the spectators. On the following evening in the Regio Teatro di via della Pergola were performed the first two acts of an Opera buffa entitled : *Il Matrimonio di Figaro*, and on Monday evening the other two acts were staged.

> Supplied by Christopher Raeburn (*cf.* Michael and Christopher Raeburn in *Music & Letters* [London], October 1959, p. 336.)—*Figaro* was therefore performed in the Teatro della Pergola in two parts, on 12 and 16 June. The libretto (German State Library, Berlin) contains the statement : " La Musica è del Signor Volfgango Mozart/Maestro di Cappella Tedesco ".

On 15 June (?) *Die Entführung* was given at Graz ; on the same day Guardasoni's company performed *Don Giovanni* at Leipzig (?).

> For the performance of *Don Giovanni* see 30 October 1787.

FROM THE " JOURNAL DES LUXUS UND DER MODEN ", WEIMAR,
JUNE 1788

Concerning the Latest Favourite Music at Grand Concerts, especially in regard to Ladies' Predilections in Pianoforte Dilettantism.

. . . *Mozart* has now gone to Vienna as Imperial Kapellmeister. Any philosophical lover of music will regard him as a remarkable man. He was an extremely precocious genius, composing and playing from his ninth year onwards (indeed, even earlier) like a true virtuoso, to every one's astonishment. But what is very rare is that he was not only a skilled musician at an unusually early age : he matured in the happiest manner and on reaching man's estate continued to show steady development. We know the flashes of ephemeral genius from bitter experience ! Where is its fruit when the right time comes ? Where its solid durability ? Not so in Mozart's case ! A few words now on an odd phenomenon occasioned by him (or by his fame). Some time ago a single *Quadro* by him (for pianoforte, 1 violin, 1 viola and violoncello) was engraved and published, which is very cunningly set and in performance needs the utmost precision in all the four parts, but even when well played, or so it seems, is able and intended to delight only connoisseurs of music in a *musica di camera*. The cry soon made itself heard : " Mozart has written a very special new *Quadro*, and such and such a Princess or Countess possesses and plays it ! ", and this excited curiosity and led to the rash resolve to produce this original composition at grand and noisy concerts and to make a parade with it *invita Minerva*. Many another piece keeps some countenance even when indifferently performed ; but this product of Mozart's can in truth hardly bear listening to when it falls into mediocre amateurish hands and is negligently played.—Now this is what happened innumerable times last winter ; at nearly every place to which my travels led me and where I was taken to a concert, some young lady or pretentious middle-class *demoiselle*, or some other pert dilettante in a noisy gathering, came up with this printed *Quadro* and fancied that it would be enjoyed. But it *could* not please : everybody yawned with boredom over the incomprehensible *tintamarre* of 4 instruments which did not keep together for four bars on end, and whose senseless *concentus* never allowed any unity of feeling ; but it *had to* to please, it *had to* be praised ! It is difficult for me to describe to you the persistence with which attempts were nearly everywhere made to enforce this. It were too little merely to rail at an ephemeral *manie du jour*, for it went on almost throughout a whole winter and (according to what I have additionally learned from hearsay) showed itself far too frequently. It deserves a public rebuke in your pages, where so many another fashionable idiocy, so many a misguided ostentation has already been justly exposed. For indeed, such clumsy forwardness is not only unseemly, not only useless and purposeless, but it does harm to Art and to the spread of true taste. " Is that all it is ? " (thinks the half-instructed hearer of this music) " This is supposed to verge on the extreme of excellence in art, and yet I feel tempted to block my ears to it frequently as I listen. What sense does that make ? How am I to know in the end what I may honestly praise or find fault with in music ? " —In this way is a true love of music spoiled, sound human reason and sound natural impulses misled, and that directness and thoroughness of culture obstructed without which no art can ever rise to and maintain itself on the heights. What a difference when this much-advertised work of art is performed with the highest degree of accuracy by four skilled musicians who have studied it carefully, in a quiet room where the suspension of every note cannot escape the listening ear, and in the presence of only two or three attentive persons ! But, of course, in that case no *éclat*, no brilliant, modish success is to be thought of, nor is conventional praise to be obtained ! Political ambition can here have no part to play, nothing to gain, nothing

to bestow, nothing to give and nothing to take—in contrast to *public* concerts of the modern kind, where such factors exert an almost constant
influence.

Pp. 231 ff.—The book dealer Friedrich Justin Bertuch and the painter Georg
Melchior Kraus had edited this paper since 1786.—The piano quartet may
have been that in G minor (K. 478) but seems more likely to have been the
one in E♭ major (K. 493) which appeared in 1787.

FROM ZINZENDORF'S DIARY, 16 JUNE 1788
(in French)

. . . Thence to the opera *Don Giovanni*. He was informally dressed,
Taeuber took Monbelli's part.

This may have been Elisabeth Teyber, the eldest sister of Therese, who had
been the first Blonde in *Die Entführung*. Elisabeth appeared as a guest artist at
the Vienna Court Opera in 1788. She took over the part of Zerlina from
Mombelli (see 24 October 1788).

On 17 June Mozart removed from the Tuchlauben to the Alsergrund suburb, No.
135, the "Three Stars" in the Währingerstrasse (now No. 16), facing the garden.

FROM THE "WIENER ZEITUNG", 18 JUNE 1788
Information.

At Joh. Traeg's . . . the following music is to be had at the price indicated :

.   .   .   .   .

1 Concerto in G for harpsichord, by W. A. Mozart.   2 fl. 40 kr.

.   .   .   .   .

6 *detti* [*Duetti*] for violin and viola. The first 4 are by M. Haydenreich,
the 5th and 6th by Mozart.   5 fl. 30 kr.

For the pianoforte concerto cf. 14 September 1785.—The duos K. 423 and 424
did not appear in print until 1792, with Artaria & Co.—For Heidenreich (see
24 May 1788), read Haydn ; see 2 July 1788.

FROM ZINZENDORF'S DIARY, 23 JUNE 1788
(in French)

. . . In the evening I was very much bored at the opera *Don Giovanni*.

FROM THE "WIENER ZEITUNG", 25 JUNE 1788
Musical News.

As the number of subscribers is still very small, I find myself obliged to
postpone the publication of my 3 Quintets until 1 January 1789. Subscription tickets are still to be had on payment of 4 ducats or 18 fl. Viennese

currency, of Herr Puchberg at Salietz's warehouse in the Hohe Markt. Vienna, 23 June 1788.

Kapellmeister Mozart,
in actual service of His Majesty.

Cf. 2 April 1788.—The subscription was insufficiently patronised.

FROM THE " PROVINZIALNACHRICHTEN ", VIENNA, 25 JUNE 1788

New Music.

. . . . .

Mozart, Menuetto from *Don Giovanni,* in the first *Finale, per il Clavi Cembalo.* 4 kr.

. . . .

Vienna, at Lausch's Music Establishment. . . .

> This advertisement did not appear in the *Wiener Zeitung* till 2 July. *Cf.* 24 May 1788.

On 29 June Mozart's fourth child, Theresia, died of intestinal cramp (*Gedärmfrais*) and was buried in the Währing General Cemetery outside the Nussdorf Line.

Cf. 27 December 1787.—Blümml, *op. cit.*, p. 7.

In June 1788 Mozart planned to hold "Concerts in the Casino ".

> This transpires from one of two undated letters to Puchberg, the first to have been preserved. According to this letter, these concerts were to begin (in the Trattnerhof, or in Philipp Otto's new Casino in the Spiegelgasse) in the week following one of the letters, and the two tickets enclosed by Mozart were doubtless valid for this series. But what is said about subscriptions in these two letters (the second of which may be dated in mid June) refers not to these concerts but to copies of the string quintets (see 2 April and 25 June). The concerts do not seem to have materialized, although the last three symphonies (K. 543, 550 and 551, finished 26 June, 25 July and 10 August 1788) were perhaps connected with this project. Mozart was not to hold any more public concerts, neither did he write further symphonies or pianoforte concertos, save that in B♭ major (K. 595), which he played on 4 March 1791 at the concert of the clarinettist Joseph Bähr.

FROM THE " WIENER ZEITUNG ", 2 JULY 1788

Information.

At Joh. Traeg's . . . the following new music is to be had at the prices indicated :

1 Concerto in D for solo violin by Ignaz Pleyel   2 fl. 45 kr.

. . . . .

1 *do.* in G for harpsichord, by W. A. Mozart   2 fl. 40 kr.

. . . .

6 Duets for violin and viola by Devienne   2 fl. 30 kr.

6 do. for violin and viola.   The first 4 are by M. Haydn, the 5th and
6th by Mozart.   5 fl. 30 kr.

Cf. 18 June 1788.

IBID., 16 JULY 1788

Music

From the new opera *Le gelosie fortunate* by Herr Anfossi the following
pieces, to be sung at the pianoforte, are to be had at Lausch's music establishment . . .

.   .   .   .   .

" Un baccio di mano vi fa maraviglia ", do. do. [*Aria. B.*]   20 kr.

.   .   .   .

Mozart, Singing Tutor [*Singfundament*] for soprano   2 fl.
   do. Don Giovanni, opera, for 2 violins, viola and violoncello   6 fl. 30 kr.

> For the interpolation (K. 541) in Anfossi's opera *cf.* 2 June 1788 ; for the
> quartet arrangement of *Don Giovanni cf.* 24 May 1788.—The " Singfundament"
> (" Foundation of Singing ") is unknown ; according to Köchel-Einstein, p.
> 492, the solfeggi (K. 393), written for Constanze in 1782, may perhaps have
> been used in it.

On 21 July Josepha Weber, Constanze's eldest sister, married the violinist Franz
Hofer in St. Stephen's Cathedral.

> For Hofer see 8 January 1787.   He became a violinist in the Hofmusik-
> Kapelle in 1789.

FROM ZINZENDORF'S DIARY, 21 JULY 1788
(in French)

. . . In the evening to the Prater, then to the opera *Don Giovanni*.

On 22 July the Stadttheater at Carlsbad opened with a performance of *Figaro*.

On 24 July Schikaneder gave an open-air performance of *Die Entführung* at Regensburg (*cf.* 25 April 1787).

FROM HEINRICH PHILIPP BOSSLER'S " MUSIKALISCHE REAL-ZEITUNG ",
SPEYER, 30 JULY 1788

At Councillor *Bossler's* publishing house at Speyer, straight from the
press . . . Mozart, Flute Quartet, Op. 14   1 fl.

> The first edition of the C major quartet for flute, violin, viola and cello (K.
> App. 171 = KE 285 f.)

On 9 August *Figaro* was given in German in Graz.

> Cf. Hellmut Federhofer in the *Mozart-Jahrbuch* for 1957, p. 142, and for 1958,
> p. 109.

M.—11

Reviews.

VIII. Variations d'un Thema de M. Mozart pour le Clavecin / par M. Em. Alois Foerster. Et VI Variations pour le Clavecin / avec un Violon par M. W. Amad. Mozart. Speier, at Councillor Bossler's. 4. / (Price 42 Rhenish kr. Or 10 Saxon groschen.)

The variations by these two composers make up the third and fourth piece of the Musical Archives. Herr *F.'s* theme is a Tempo di Menuetto in F major, and *Mozart's* an Andantino in G minor in $\frac{6}{8}$ time. In the matter of execution the two works are rather alike, that is to say, the modifications affect only the melismatic aspect ; difficulties are piled on difficulties, and quick, winged passages for the right hand alternate with similar ones for the left. This is apt to give such products a certain uniformity, so that when one has been heard, they have nearly all been heard. One could thus very much wish that for this kind of music too the two *Bachs* and other older masters of music might be taken as models. It is true that it will always be pleasant to hear variations by *F.* and *M.*, and they will be valued as good exercises ; but one nevertheless misses in them, as in most of the recent musical pieces of this kind, the ingenious inversions and imitations, and the variety of treatment in a sustained manner of writing, whereby alone such compositions achieve a true value.

Zx.

Sonate pour le Clavecin avec accompagnement d'un Violon / par M. W. A. Mozart. Archives No. 11. Speier, at Councillor Bossler's. 4. / (Price 1 fl.)

This Sonata by Herr *M.*, thanks to the pleasing manner in which it is written, will also be popular with lovers of art. It were to be wished, though, that Herr *M.* did not allow himself to be captivated so much by the modish taste of our time. His works would thereby gain an even more general, and at the same time more durable, value. And this work as well as several others we know, assures us that Herr *M.* is not so lacking in sound principles of harmony, nor in wealth of imagination, as to be unable to serve us with stronger meat.—The first movement of this Sonata in E♭ is a very gay, fluent Allegro. Only, the reviewer feels the divided broken chords on the fourth page to be partly too hackneyed, partly too extended, and the second part much too long in comparison with the first. It is true that in the system of musical science there is no definite rule for such cases ; but it is clear that a difference of $3\frac{1}{2}$ pages is no reasonable proportion. The Adagio is full of gentle emotions, the true expression of languishing love, I would say, and the change of tonality which Herr *M.* twice permits himself in this movement, though not without hardness, is also of good effect. The conclusion is an Allegro with 6 variations.

Zx.

Column 49 f.—A. Hyatt King, *Mozart in Retrospect* (London, 1955), p. 176.—
Bossler had founded a music-publishing firm in 1781, which published, *inter
alia*, the *Musikalische Real-Zeitung* (1788–90 ; continued under the title of
Musikalische Korrespondenz, 1790–92), the *Archiv der auserlesensten Musikalien*
(1788), the *Bibliothek der Grazien* (1789–91) and, as supplement to the *Real-
Zeitung*, the *Musikalische Anthologie für Kenner und Liebhaber* (1790). On the
whole he was content to confine his publications to reprints.—Förster came
from Prussian Silesia, but had lived in Vienna as a respected music teacher
since 1776. His ten variations on an Allegretto from Sarti's opera *I finti eredi*,
composed in 1788, were ascribed to Mozart about 1800 (K. App. 289).—By
the " two Bachs " Carl Philipp Emanuel and Johann Christian are probably
meant.—The variations on the Andantino " Hélas, j'ai perdu mon amant "
(K. 360) had been published by Artaria in 1786, and the E♭ major violin
sonata (K. 481) by Hoffmeister about 1785.

IBID., 13 AUGUST 1788

From the same place [*Dresden*], 28 July.

The famous organist from Erfurt, Herr *Hässler*, is now here, . . . And
it is taken as certain that he wishes to go from here to Vienna in order to
show the Viennese musical public in a competition on the clavier with the
great *Mozart*, that the latter, powerful as he is on the fortepiano, cannot play
the clavier.

Abert, Vol. II, p. 626.—Johann Wilhelm Hässler did not go to Vienna, but
Mozart competed with him on the organ at Dresden on 15 April 1789, and
afterwards on the fortepiano, Mozart apparently being successful ; but there
was no competition on the clavichord, which Hässler may indeed have played
better. He played a pianoforte concerto by Mozart in London on 30 May
1792 (King, *op. cit.*, p. 14).

FROM JOACHIM DANIEL PREISLER'S " JOURNAL OVER EN REJSE IGIENNEN
FRANKERIGE OG TYDSKLAND I AARET 1788 ", COPENHAGEN, 1789
(in Danish)

Wednesday, 20 August [1788]. Between 10 and 11 [a.m.] the actor
Lange came to fetch us, to see his collection of pictures by himself and to
hear his wife sing.—A melancholy ecstasy was to be read at once in her
eyes. She was great with child and could not perform in that condition.
Too bad for us ! for she was, although a *German*, the *prima donna* of the
Italian Opera. The well-known *Mozardt* is her brother-in-law, and has
taught her so well that she accompanies from a score and plays interludes
like a Kapellmeister. Thus she sang and played a grand *aria di bravura*
for us, a *scena* by *Paisiello* and a *rondo* from the opera *Creso*. The voice is
something exceptional ! but (to speak as a music-lover, not as a *Dane*)
not by a long way as good as that of our *Müller* ; yet her high range and
her delicacy, her execution, taste and theoretical knowledge cannot fail to
be admired by any impartial critic. Nevertheless, hers will be the *same fate*

as that for which so many good subjects of foreign nations are destined.—
Whatever is *outlandish must* be admired, be it extraordinarily good or extraordinarily bad. She receives scarcely half the salary given to the *Italians*,
and yet she is made to and can sing the longest and most difficult parts
incomparably better than the songstresses who are here pampered by the
Viennese nobility. The *Italian Opera* was given notice today and will only
continue to play until *Lent*.—I am now eager to hear the *Emperor's* decision
whether this delightful *Madame Lange* is also to be got rid of with the others.
—We saw some excellent portraits, among them most of the actors from
the *Theatre Gallery* in *miniature*, and Lange deserves the credit for having
often improved on the *originals* with his *copies*. Actually, for some *reason* or
another, he has given up painting, for which he was exceptionally gifted,
not in my opinion but in that of *Schmutzer* and the whole *Academy*.—In
the evening we went to the *Opera buffa* and heard good music by *Anfossi*.
This performance was the more fatiguing because we had already heard
something really good in the forenoon. I knew the *better numbers* of the opera
well, from concerts in Copenhagen, but only the *tenor* sang decently. The
others did not even know their parts. What is more, these artists permitted
themselves liberties on the stage for which the Emperor should have them
put in the stocks. The tenor, for instance, quite familiarly greeted a good
friend in the stalls—it was a wonder he did not offer him a *pinch of snuff* !
—and the *bass*, who squatted under a table so as not to be seen by his partners,
made *faces* at them, as who should say : " *You are not to see me until we
reach the right bar in the music !* " Which shows that *illusion* is a word
unknown among these *well-paid* bunglers !

Pp. 228-31.—Supplied by Hans Jörgen Hurum, Oslo.—In May 1788 the
Theatre Royal in Copenhagen had sent three of its members to study at the
principal theatres on the continent of Europe : Joachim Daniel Preisler,
Michael Rosing and Peter Rasmus Saabye. Vienna had not originally been on
the programme. Two of these three actors left records of their impressions.
Preisler, who published his diary himself, was very musical and described himself as being also an accompanist in the orchestra. For Rosing, the other diarist,
see 24 August.—The Langes, who lived in the Mariahilferstrasse, already had
a small son ; the expected child, as well as three earlier and two later children,
died at an early age.—The aria by Paisiello may have been from the opera *La
grotta di Trofonio*, which had been given at the Burgtheater in Italian in 1785
and in German in 1787. *Creso* may have been Anfossi's setting (Rome, 1787).
—Catarine Möller was the prima donna of the Copenhagen theatre ; she was
the first Donna Anna there in 1807.—The singers of the Italian Opera had first
been given notice on 3 August ; the only exceptions were Cavalieri, Ferdinand
and Therese Arnold (*née* Teyber) and Saal. In the end, however, the Italian
Opera was kept on, and Aloisia Lange was not dismissed.—The Burgtheater
has since 1786 had a gallery with portraits of its best members, mainly actors ;
the first were painted by Joseph Hickel (see 15 October 1781). Lange's small
copies do not appear to have been preserved. If he really gave up painting
before 1789, this may explain why he never finished his well-known portrait
of Mozart (Mozarteum, Salzburg).—The copper engraver Jakob Schmutzer,
who belonged to a well-known Austrian family of artists, was director of one

of the schools of the Academy of Fine Arts, and Lange's teacher.—Anfossi's opera was *Gli amanti canuti*, given at the Burgtheater from 15 July, soon after *Le gelosie fortunate* (see 2 June 1788). The tenor was perhaps Francesco Morella and the bass Francesco Albertarelli (see 7 May 1788).

FROM THE "DRAMATURGISCHE BLÄTTER", FRANKFURT ON MAIN, 1788

On the 21st day in August : *Die Entführung aus dem Serail*. Operetta in 3 acts, by Brezner. The music by Mozart.

Considered as an operetta, this piece has the merit that it brings in the songs fairly naturally ; that they give the music the opportunity of revealing its full range : now to express the quiet sorrow of deserted love, its faint hopes, mixed with fear and anxious foreboding ; then the delight of reunion, the festive jubilation of the Janissaries, the merry transports of the drunken Osmin, &c. Apart from that there is little to be found of oriental costumery ; little of anything to produce a dramatic effect. Mozart's otherwise beautiful music has the fault—to my ears, at any rate—of unduly distorting individual expressions, and thereby becoming empty note-spinning . . .

> Year I, 1st Quarter, No. 10, pp. 159 f.—The singspiel had been performed for the first time at Frankfurt on 2 August 1783.—Of the revival on 9 September 1788 the same journal (No. 13, p. 230) wrote that it was " worthy of the poet and the composer ".

FROM PREISLER'S "JOURNAL", COPENHAGEN, 1789
(in Danish)

Sunday, 24 August [1788]. . . . In the afternoon *Jünger*, *Lange* and *Werner* came to fetch us to go to Kapellmeister *Mozardt's*. There I had the happiest hour of music that has ever fallen to my lot. This small man and great master twice *extemporized* on a *pedal pianoforte*, so wonderfully ! so wonderfully ! that I quite lost myself. He intertwined the most difficult passages with the most lovely *themes*.—His wife cut quill-pens for the copyist, a pupil composed, a little boy aged four walked about in the garden and sang recitatives—in short, everything that surrounded this splendid man was *musical !* I thought with pleasure of his *Entführung aus dem Serail*, which I had heard at Hamburg in 1787, and which I know almost by heart, but he called this *operetta* a " trifle " ; but it were unworthy of a man like *Mozardt* to be praised in the presence of people who themselves amount to nothing, and so I kept silent. He [now] writes church music in Vienna, and as the *Operetta* has closed down, he has nothing to do with the theatre [any longer].

> Pp. 251 f.—H. J. Hurum, *I Mozart verden*, Oslo, 1955, p. 107.—Johann Friedrich Jünger was a successful author at the Burgtheater.—Dr. Karl Werner (if

it was he) was the Medical Superintendent for Lower Austria.—For Mozart's pedal pianoforte *cf.* 10 March 1785.—The boy was Karl, then nearly four years of age.—At Hamburg *Die Entführung* had been given since June 1787.— " Operetta " here means firstly singspiel, and then opera company, perhaps that of the German Opera, which was discontinued in 1783.—What Preisler describes as church music may be work done by Mozart for van Swieten.

FROM MICHAEL ROSING'S DIARY, 24 AUGUST 1788
(in Danish)

At 4 o'clock [p.m.] Jünger, Lange and Dr. Werner came to take us to Kapellmeister Mozart's ; he played free improvisations for us in such a manner that I wished that I could improvise like this ; his pedal in the second improvisation in particular made the most agreeable impression. Happy and quite overcome at having heard Mozart, we went [back] into the town.

Frederik Schyberg, *Den store teaterrejse* (Copenhagen, 1943), pp. 285 f.—Rosing, whose diary and letters were first published in this book, was born in Norway. He was an actor and had shortly before become producer at the Copenhagen theatre.

FROM THE " NEUES THEATER-JOURNAL FÜR DEUTSCHLAND ", LEIPZIG, 1788

Short Account of the Theatre in Breslau at present.

. . . 24 August : *Bellmont und Konstanze, oder Die Entführung aus dem Serail*, S. 3.A. [*Singspiel* in 3 acts] by Bretzner with music by Mozart. It is a veritable feast for the ear to hear a performance of such glorious music, made for the ear and the heart. Not a single sentiment remains unsatisfied when Herr Mozart is seen to paint and present passion after passion, and immediately afterwards the most droll humour. The following arias pleased us most particularly : "Ach ich liebte, &c ", " Martern aller Arten, &c ", " Wenn der Freude Thränen fliessen, &c ". And the last duet : " Welch [ein] Geschick ! &c " . . . Notwithstanding this, the *Singspiel* did not produce the same sensation here at Breslau as it has done in other places. Perhaps there was a scarcity of musical connoisseurs.

No. 1, p. 51.—At Wrocław this singspiel had first been given on 24 August 1787.

In August the song " Beim Auszug in das Feld " (" Dem hohen Kaiser-Worte treu " [K. 552]) appeared in the *Wochenblatt für Kinder.*

Copies at Klosterneuburg Monastery, in the Gesellschaft der Musikfreunde, Vienna, and in the British Museum (Hirsch Library), London.—For the *Wochenblatt* see 24 February 1787 ; for the Turkish war see early 1788 and 7 March 1788.

FROM THE " WIENER ZEITUNG ", 27 SEPTEMBER 1788

New Music.

From Artaria Comp., art dealers, are to be had : . . . Mozart 1 new Sonata for pianoforte with violin and viola or clarinet—Opera 14, 1 fl. 20 kr.

> The E♭ major trio (K. 498) was actually written for pianoforte, clarinet and viola, for Franziska von Jacquin (see 11 April 1787), supposedly during a skittle party, and it is therefore nicknamed the " skittle-alley trio ". The violin part was thus intended as an alternative to the clarinet part.

FROM KNIGGE'S " DRAMATURGISCHE BLÄTTER ", HANOVER, 1788

The third of October : *Belmonte und Konstanza, oder: die Entführung aus dem Serail*—One of those garrulous titles concerning which I quoted a passage from the *Theater-Kalender* in the last issue !—A Singspiel in three acts, by Bretzner, set to music by Mozart.

About the play itself there is not much to be said. The invention of the plot and the manner of the adaptation do not possess the value of novelty, nor are poetic felicities to be met with here ; one is, however, always glad to find that the favourable impression made by the music is not weakened by haphazard, ineffectual rubbish and buffoonery, as in the Italian *opere buffe*. And, indeed, it is the music about which I wish to speak in some detail.

I had often asked myself how it was that Mozart's glorious composition, which one reads and plays from the score with a veritable enchantment, and the incidental beauties of which also carry one away in performance, yet on the whole fails to make the general favourable impression one would expect of it. It is true that this work of art surprised and greatly pleased on its first appearance. The brilliant overture ; the unusual quality of the Turkish music, even in the accompaniment to arias ; all this did not fail of its purpose ; yet once again ! I was hard put to it to explain to myself why this splendid music, with its many fine details, left empty the hearts of many people who are not so much connoisseurs of art as sensitive lovers of melody. I discussed this with a man whose theoretical and practical knowledge of music, whose diligence in daily making still further progress therein, and whose modesty, are deserving of equal praise—in a word, with our *Weber*, who, since he conducts the music of the Singspiele here, with no small credit in their good performance, is most particularly acquainted with the incidental beauties and faults of every composition, and I will here set down part of that whereby he has set to rights my ideas on Mozart's theatrical style.

In the first place, the music of *Die Entführung aus dem Serail* is here and there too serious for the subject of a comic opera ; in many passages, which for the rest are worked with great mastery, it approaches too near to the style of serious opera, and since other truly comic pieces make too great a contrast with them, there is a want of unity in the style. Next, the composer has been too loquacious with the wind instruments. Instead of only reinforcing the melody where that is required, and supporting the harmony as a whole, they often darken the former and confuse the latter, prevent simple, beautiful singing and disturb the singer's delivery. I noticed this particularly in an aria sung by Konstanze.—This is a fault into which the best Italian composers never fall, but which is now growing the more common among us in proportion as we formerly neglected the role of the wind instruments. No less does too artful a texture obscure the fluency of song in many places. The expert knows the value of such passages, but for popular delivery this kind of thing is of no use. The same is true of the frequent modulations and the many enharmonic progressions, which, beautiful as they sound on the pianoforte, have no effect in the orchestra, partly because the intonation is never pure enough either on the singers' or the players' part, and especially is this true of the wind instruments ; and partly because the resolutions alternate too quickly with the discords, so that only a practised ear can follow the course of the harmony. This awkwardness is especially noticeable in the numerous arias in minor keys which, because of their numerous chromatic passages, are difficult to perform for the singer, difficult to grasp for the hearer, and are altogether somewhat disquieting. Such strange harmonies betray the great master, but they are not suitable for the theatre. Herr Weber has frequently remarked in the theatre that, if the fourth in a minor key is unexpectedly heard with the minor third and seventh, or inverted with the augmented sixth, this harmony excited a great sensation, but failed to please most of the listeners on being often repeated, and lost all its effect. For many of the reasons just mentioned, half the beauties of the admirably worked quartet at the end of the second act, for example, go for nothing. This quartet is a veritable masterpiece for the connoisseur ; but how few will feel the value of the art that went to its making ! Lastly, the vocal line in this opera is too much syncopated in many places, especially in duets, quartets, &c. The singer is not given time to breathe, to give new strength to his voice, and it becomes dull and lame. One fine idea jostles the next and removes it from the listener's admiration.

But oh, would that all composers were capable of committing such faults ! And what glorious individual numbers there are in this opera ! Most rich in beauty is the second act. The first duet occurring in it is entrancing ; Blonde's aria, which Mme. Grossman sang so incomparably, quite excellent ; the rondeau : " Welche Wonne, welche Lust ! " most charming of all ; the vaudeville at the end of the third act written in a delicious style—but who is to enumerate all the individual beauties of this opera ? . . .

No. 2, pp. 21 ff., published on 11 October.—Jahn, 1st ed., Vol. III, pp. 470 ff.— This periodical, published at Hanover in 1788–89 and found among Mozart's papers, must not be confused with the one of the same name published at

Frankfurt.—The first performance of the singspiel at Hanover had taken place on 12 April 1787.—The article seems to have been written by the editor, Adolf von Knigge (see 18 May 1788). His adviser was Bernhard Anselm Weber (see 12 April 1787).—At the end of 1788 the same periodical (Part 11, p. 171) published a report by the theatre manager Grossmann concerning the success of his performances ; we read there " Very good : *Die Räuber, Die Entführung aus dem Serail.*" (Schiller's drama had appeared in 1781.)

FROM THE " DRAMATURGISCHE BLÄTTER ", FRANKFURT ON MAIN, 1788

On the 11th day in October : *Figaro*—operetta in four acts. With music by Herr Mozart.

The comedy by Beaumarchais, from which this operetta is taken, was written for Paris alone. The satire which is strewn about it everywhere, was largely lost to us Germans. Hence among us the divergent judgments on this piece which, regarded as a dramatic product, is hardly of great value. The whole intrigue, too, is more proper to an opera, where one does not look for so apt a linking-up of the scenes, nor for so much truth in the situations, nor yet such accurately drawn characters, as in an actual play. Mozart's music has fine passages, but also familiar ideas and turns . . .

Year I, 2nd Quarter, No. 4, pp. 88 f.—The new translation was by Christian August Vulpius, Goethe's brother-in-law.—See the following document.

IBID., 1788

On the 13th day in October : *Figaro*—Operetta.

This piece has already outlived its term here. Does the fault lie in the piece itself ? Does it lie in the music—or in the presentation by the actors ? Perhaps in all three in equal share . . .

No. 5, pp. 97 f.—Writing on the performance of 21 October, this periodical (No. 7, pp. 131 f.) still found fault with the production.

FROM THE " MUSIKALISCHE REAL-ZEITUNG ", SPEYER, 15 OCTOBER 1788

At this music establishment are to be had : . . .
Mozart Ouverture dell' Opera *Il Don Giov.* Pianoforte Score   24 kr.

Vol. I, No. 16, col. 128.

On 16 October *Die Entführung* was given in Berlin.

In a letter from Leopold Mozart to his daughter of November 1784 (*Schweizer-ische Musikzeitung* [Zürich] April 1953, p. 152) he writes that he had heard from two Barons Fechenbach that they had seen the singspiel in Berlin, Mainz and Mannheim. However, it was not performed in Berlin till October 1788 ; it was given seven times before the end of the year.—Friedrich Karl Lippert, who had already sung Belmonte in Vienna on 7 May 1786, took the same part in Berlin. (In 1798 he made a new German translation for Vienna of *Don*

M.—11 *a*

Giovanni, in Schröder's version of which he had sung in Berlin in 1790.)—On the occasion of this performance a vocal score of *Arien und Gesänge* was published in Berlin.

. . . Thence to the theatre. *Don Giovanni*, informally dressed, la Laschi was not playing.

Cf. 16 June 1788.—Signora Mombelli's maiden name was Laschi.

From Artaria Comp., art dealers . . . are to be had :
By Herr Mozart 3 quite new Sonatas for the pianoforte, with the accompaniment of a violin and violoncello, *Opera* 15, 3 fl.

The three pianoforte trios in B♭, E and C major (K. 502, 542 and 548).

Agreeable and instructive occupation for children in their leisure hours . . . Songs with music by the celebrated Mozart . . .

No. 18, p. 276.—In this notice from the *Wochenblatt* (see 24 February 1787), published in the *Rapport*, the two songs K. 531 and 552 were briefly mentioned. —The copy of the *Rapport* in the Vienna University Library was unfortunately burnt ; the wording could therefore not be checked.

In November (?) Handel's pastorale *Acis and Galatea* was performed for Mozart's benefit at Jahn's Rooms in the Himmelpfortgasse (No. 991 in the Inner City, now Himmelpfortgasse 6), with the orchestration amplified by him (K. 566) and under his direction. The soloists were Signora Cavalieri, Valentin Adamberger and Tobias Gsur.

Jahn, Vol. II, p. 461.—This was the first of the four Handel arrangements which Mozart made for Gottfried van Swieten, who in 1780 undertook the direction of the Society of Noblemen for the cultivation of classical music, especially Handel's. Among the members of this society were Prince Johann Karl Dietrichstein, Prince Ferdinand Philipp Joseph Lobkowitz (died 1784), Prince Johann Nepomuk Schwarzenberg, Count Anton Georg Apponyi, Count Anton Batthyány and Count Johann Esterházy. The rehearsals probably took place at Swieten's official residence in the Court Library, of which he was director. (It was not till 1795 that he acquired the house in the Renngasse [City No. 146, now No. 3] and moved into it.) *Acis and Galatea* too may have been rehearsed in Swieten's residence. See 30 December 1788.— The bass Gsur was a member of the Court Chapel.—The hall belonging to the restaurateur Ignaz Jahn was frequently used for concerts about 1790 (*cf.* 4 March 1791) ; it seated 400 at the most.

On 13 December Le Duc of Paris announced in the *Affiches, Annonces et Avis divers* (supplement) a pianoforte trio by Mozart as " Opus XVI ".

> The title (*Trio pour le clavecin ou le forte-piano avec accompagnement de violon ou [clarinette] & d'alto*) shows that the work in question is K. 498, which had been published by Artaria & Co. as Op. 14 on 27 September 1788.

On 15 December C. P. E. Bach died in Hamburg.

On 15 December Emperor Joseph was present at a performance of *Don Giovanni* in the Burgtheater.

> The Emperor had returned on 5 December, ill after more than nine months in the field ; *cf.* 16 May 1788.—This performance was the last in Vienna in Mozart's lifetime.

FROM THE " MUSIKALISCHE REAL-ZEITUNG ", SPEYER, 24 DECEMBER 1788
(partly in Italian)

Catalogue of the material contained in the " Musikalische Anthologie für Kenner und Liebhaber ", in its proper order.
Arias from the opera : *Il Don Giov.* by Signore A. Mozart   25.

> Vol. I, No. 26, col. 203.

FROM ZINZENDORF'S DIARY, 30 DECEMBER 1788
(in French)

. . . In the evening to a concert at Jean Esztherh[ázy]'s, conducted by the Baron, *Acis et Galatée* by Hendel.

> See 26 February and November 1788.—The " Baron " is Gottfried van Swieten.

In 1788 two symphonies by Mozart, " Opp. 8 and 9 " (K. 385 and 319), a pianoforte quartet (K. 478 or 493) and the six string quartets dedicated to Haydn (K. 387 &c.), were performed in London.

> C. F. Pohl, *Mozart in London* (Vienna, 1867), p. 142.—Pohl regrettably omitted to mention his source, and it has not yet been rediscovered.—*Cf.* 26 December 1786.

FROM PAUL VON STETTEN'S " KUNST-, GEWERB- UND HANDWERKS-
GESCHICHTE DER REICHSSTADT AUGSBURG ", VOL. II, 1788

On young Mozart, who is now Kapellmeister in Vienna, there is an entertaining report by Herr Daines Barrington in the Philos. Transact. Vol. 60, p. 54 &c.

> P. 318.—*Cf.* end of 1779.—For Barrington see 28 November 1769.

1789

List of Composers now living in Germany.

Mozart (J. J. Wolfgang) since 1787 Capellmeister in Vienna. s. *Die
Entführung aus dem Serail*, printed in 1785. Since 1784 various *Symphonies,
Quartets* and *Sets of Sonatas*, as well as *Concertos* for the pianoforte, have
become publicly known.

P. 84 f.—See end of 1781, 1782 and 1783.

I. & R. Court Chamber Musicians.
Composer.
Herr Wolfgang Mozart, living at Währingergasse 135.

P. 400.—This entry was still unchanged in 1791, even as regards the address,
which was correct only for 1788 ; but " Hofkammermusici " had become
simply " Kammermusici ".—In 1788 Salieri was named as " composer "
among the I. & R. Court and Chamber Musicians.—The directory did no.
appear in 1790.

Herr Wolfgang Mozart has been taken into the actual service of His
Majesty the Emperor with a handsome salary. All lovers of music will
doubtless feel the most lively satisfaction at this promotion, this excellent
musician having for so long been misjudged and not valued according to
his true merits.

P. 115.

Early in 1789 Mozart moved from the Währingerstrasse back to the Inner City
to the house called the " Mother of God " (No. 245) on the Judenplatz (now No. 4)

The house was next to that inhabited by Mozart in 1783. Nos. 3 and 4 were
joined as part of a new building in 1895.

A Correspondent's Account of the Grossmann Company [in Lübeck].

According to local tradition no performances may be given before Twelfth
Night. The theatre thus opened on 7 January, with *Die Entführung aus dem
Serail*.

How truly speaks Reichard in his *Musikalisches Kunst-Magazin* when he

says : " The musician is much less fortunate than the painter and the
sculptor. For them their own eye and their own hand suffice to allow them
to make their greatest creations ; the musicians needs the ears, hands and
throats of hundreds for his work.—Without singers, without an orchestra,
the composer can do nothing ", and so on. The truth of these words,
especially as regards the orchestra, was confirmed by the performance of
this *Singspiel* today : *Die Entführung aus dem Serail* by Mozart is an opera
which in any case is difficult, very difficult to perform, even for an orchestra
of uniformly good men, on account of the considerable demands it imposes
on all sorts of wind instruments, and the concertante arias and passages
which it contains. Now when this task is approached by an orchestra that
has not worked together, and indeed mediocre and often less than mediocre
wind players, then there is bound now and again to be a lamentable howling,
enough to make one grind one's teeth. Arias written perhaps for a single
place, designed for the vocal compass of specific singers and, in the concertante parts, for the instruments of great artists, have then to be performed everywhere by people not made for art by nature, but only for
whistling and fiddling, who either on their string instruments always give
a foretaste of the following bar while perhaps the greater part of the orchestra
is still half a bar behind, or on their wind instruments will perhaps add
a little trill to a sustained note which the composer has purposely written
so. Thus the poor singer, who at home exercises diligence and care to sing
his part beautifully, is crucified, and what is still sadder, the finest works of
art are cruelly murdered. Not otherwise did *Die Entführung* by our German
master Mozart fare here. If it did not please altogether, the reason may
easily be gathered from what has been said above. Herr Bilow, who distinguishes himself as a true artist of genius and talent by his skill on the
violin as regards his tone and his tasteful execution, and not less by his
politeness and modesty—a gift so seldom bestowed on an executive musician—has been so kind, as has Herr Kunze, an accomplished clavier player,
to play with the orchestra at the performance of operas, from sheer love of
art, *i.e.* the former on the violin and the latter on the violoncello, whereby
the performance gains a good deal.

In addition, the two horns distinguish themselves especially by their firm,
round tone, their punctilious accuracy in observing rests, and the purity of
their intonation. Would that the rest were to take trouble to emulate the
two Messrs. Hernberg in application and attention. They would then
deserve the same praise and oblige the public, which possesses taste and
knowledge . . .

> No. 15, pp. 226 ff.—The report concerns the first performance of the singspiel
> at Lübeck.—Johann Friedrich Reichardt published the *Musikalisches Kunst-*
> *magazin* in Berlin from 1782 to 1791.—For the German performance of An-
> fossi's *Il geloso in cimento* on 9 January the same journal (p. 230) commented :
> " The execution by the orchestra was incomparably better to-day than at the
> performance of *Die Entführung aus dem Serail*."

FROM ZINZENDORF'S DIARY, 15 JANUARY 1789
(in French)

. . . At the High Chamberlain's. The abbé da Ponte talked to him of a plan to open a subscription to keep the Italian Opera here, to which all the foreign ministers wish to subscribe.

> The High Chamberlain was Count Rosenberg.—On 29 July 1788 the Emperor, then at Semlin, had ordered him to suspend the Italian Opera until further notice, owing to a deficit of 80,000 gulden. (Payer von Thurn, *op. cit.*, p. 81). It continued nevertheless, apparently through Da Ponte's intervention.

FROM THE " WIENER ZEITUNG ", 17 JANUARY 1789
Music.

From Artaria *Comp.* in the Kohlmarkt the following dance music is to be had :

. . . . .

Mozart, 6 Country Dances. 1 fl. 3 kr.

> The dances were K. 462 (No. 3), 534, 535 and 535a in pianoforte score.—For K. 535 *cf.* 19 March 1788 and February 1790.

FROM THE " MUSIKALISCHE REAL-ZEITUNG ", SPEYER, 18 FEBRUARY 1789

Dresden, 25 January.

At a private concert here *Mozart's* excellent opera *Il Don Giovanni* was performed in an arrangement for 8 wind instruments ; the effect it had on the listeners is not to be described.—Since as a rule one hears nothing but suites and marches on these instruments, the impression made by this masterpiece was all the stronger. But it is true that much was contributed by the great virtuosi who performed it, only a few of whom I will name : Herr *Richter* on the oboe, Herr *Schmidt* on the bassoon and Herr *Rothe* on the clarinet.

> Vol. I, No. 7, col. 62 f. (see also cols. 86 and 188).—This arrangement does not seem to have been preserved. *Cf.* 24 June 1789.

FROM THE " DRAMATURGISCHE BLÄTTER ", FRANKFURT ON MAIN, 1789
National Theatre, Mainz.

On 31 January : *Das verstellte Gärtnermädchen*, comic opera in 3 acts, from the Italian. Music by W. Mozart. A new piece, in which everybody's expectation was aroused beforehand by the composer's name, and which yet thoroughly failed to please. But then the piece is in the highest degree jejune and tedious ; and Mozart's writing, nearly always difficult and ingeniously wrought, seems particularly in this opera to defeat the power of assimilation of ordinary dilettanti, majestic or humorous though it be in individual passages, and full of strong harmony as a whole.

> Year II, 3rd Quarter, No. 8, p. 116. (Communicated by Christopher Rae-burn.)—This first performance in the Electoral National Theatre has so far been overlooked in the relevant literature (Loewenberg, *op. cit.*, p. 170 ; Gottron, *op. cit.*, p. 35). At Frankfurt the opera (produced at Munich on 13 January 1775) had already been given in German under another title on 2 April 1782. The Mainz company again brought it to Frankfurt on 30 April 1789, having started their visit there with *Die Entführung* on the 13th.

* FROM ZINZENDORF'S DIARY, 27 FEBRUARY 1789

. . . To the theatre in the evening. *L' ape musicale*. Formed from various operas. La Ferraresi sang in it marvellously.

> Libretto in the National Library, Vienna.—This pasticcio, with text by Da Ponte, was performed at the Burgtheater. It contained (Act I, Sc. 7) a parody of the Zerlina-Don Giovanni " Là ci darem la mano " from *Don Giovanni*, sung by Signora Mombelli (the first Zerlina in Vienna) and Signor Benucci (the first Leporello in Vienna). This " musical comedy " in two acts was given six times up to 13 March, and it was done again at Trieste (where Da Ponte was then living) on 24 January 1792, with the subtitle *Il poeta impresario*. —See 21 March 1789 and 23 March 1791.

On 6 March Handel's *Messiah* was performed for the first time in Mozart's orchestration (K. 572) at Count Johann Esterházy's (*cf.* 7 April 1789).

> Dr. Andreas Holschneider of Freiburg/Breisgau in 1958 discovered in the library of Klosterneuburg Monastery a copy of the text (printed in Vienna in 1789 by Christian Friedrich Wappler), containing a handwritten note with further information about this performance.

HANDWRITTEN NOTE ON THE TITLE-PAGE OF A TEXTBOOK OF " MESSIAH ", 6 MARCH 1789

Excellently performed on 6 March 1789 at Count Johann Esterhazy's.— Mozart directed the orchestra, Umlauf the vocalists. Madam Lange, Mad^elle Altamonte, Herr Saal and Herr Adamberger sang in it, with 12 choristers. Herr Hausmann of Hanover was invited to this concert with me and my eldest daughter.

> The identity of the writer is unknown.—For Fräulein von Altamonte (Alto-monte) *cf.* 26 March 1791.

FROM THE " DRAMATURGISCHE BLÄTTER ", FRANKFURT ON MAIN, 1789

[Mainz] On the 13th [March] : *Don Juan*—Singspiel in 2 acts, freely adapted from the Italian ; music by Mozart. Another opera that has turned the heads of our public. They were within an inch of storming the theatre because the doors had not been opened three hours before the beginning.— Much pomp and noise for the general public ; insipid and jejune stuff for the educated section ! The music too, although great and harmonious, is difficult and artificial rather than pleasing and popular . . .

> Year II, 3rd Quarter, No. 9, pp. 131 f.—The translation was by Heinrich Gottlieb Schmieder.

FROM THE " WIENER ZEITUNG ", 21 MARCH 1789

Music.

From Artaria *Comp.*, art dealers on the Kohlmarkt, are to be had :

. . . . .

Mozart, 12 German Dances, which were performed in the I. & R. Small Assembly Hall, transcribed for the pianoforte   40 kr.
Do. 12 Minuets   40 kr.

. . . . .

Mozart, 2 very fine new German arias, to be sung at the pianoforte.   40 kr.

> The German dances were K. 536 and 567, the minuets K. 568 (both groups were later designated as " 1st Part "). The two songs (similarly designated) were K. 523 and 524 : "Abendempfindung" and "An Chloe". The pretty title-page of the set of songs was engraved by Sebastian Mansfeld.

IBID., 21 MARCH 1789

L' ape musicale, *Opera* by some of the most famous composers, assembled and to be sung at the pianoforte, to be had in Vienna at Lausch's music establishment . . .

Atto I°

		fl.	kr.
L' overtura from *L' inganno amoroso*		–	20
No. 1. " Sedete amici mei ", *l' Introduz*[ione]		–	36
2. " Com ape ingegnosa ", Cav[atina] Basso		–	8
3. " Permettete o Madamina ", Terz[etto]		–	40
4. " Donne mie voi siete quelle ", Ar[ia]. B.		–	20
5. " Ch' é una petegolla senza creanza ", Q[uartette]		–	52
6. " Que vos yeux sont touchants ", Recitativo		–	12
" Votre coeur aimable flore ", Cavatina Soprano			
7. " Amour nous parle sans cesse ", do. / Soprano con Mandolino		–	12
" Amor schenkt uns die Schönen " do. (with German words)		–	12
8. " Je suis né natif de ferrare ", Romance, Tenor / (" Ahi povero Calpigi ")		–	28

9. " Un vate Signora ", do. B. (" Non posso parlare lascia-   – 20
   remi star ")
10. " Da questi Liniamenti, intendo chlaramente ", Cavatina   – 12
    Soprano
11. " Vi presento amico caro ".   Finale.   1 44

Atto II°

1. " Dunque per un infido ", Recitativo   – 40
   " Il mio cor gli affetti miei ", Rond[o] S.
2. " Voi che sapete che cosa é amor ", A[ria] T. [from *Figaro*]   – 16
3. " Le Donzellette che sono amanti ", do. S.   – 16
4. " Care piante fortunate ", Due[to] S. e. T.   – 20
5. " Ah chi fa questo suo male ", T[e]rz[etto]   – 12
6. " Non piu andrai farfallone amoroso ", Aria Basso [from   – 24
   Figaro]
7. " Sento che in seno mi batte il core ", Cavatina Soprano   – 20
8. " Ah se tu m' ami ", Recit " Ah sol bramo o mia speranza ",   – 32
   Rond[o] S.
9. " Sposa ! Consorte ! " Recit. " Cari ogetti del mio core ",   – 40
   Rondeau. S. (" Compati e i casi miei, Compiangete il   –
   mio dolor ")
10. " Guarda bene so chi sono ", Finale   2 20

See 27 February.—No copy of this hand-written pianoforte score has yet come
to light. The overture was taken from an opera by Pietro Guglielmi, which
had been given in Vienna since 9 April 1787. Curiously enough, the duet " Là
ci darem la mano " is missing in this score, while in the libretto Mozart's name
is not given at either of the arias taken from *Figaro*. In other respects, too,
the libretto differs from the pianoforte score ; the pasticcio seems to have been
frequently varied.

GOTTFRIED VAN SWIETEN TO MOZART

21 March 1789.

Your idea of setting the text of the cold aria as a recitative is excellent,
and not being sure whether you retained the words, I am sending you a
copy herewith. He who can clothe Händel so solemnly and so tastefully
that he pleases the modish fop on the one hand and on the other still shows
himself in his sublimity, has felt his worth, has understood him, has pene-
trated to the well-spring of his expression, from which he can and will
draw confidently. That is how I view what you have accomplished, and
I need now say no more of my confidence, but only of my desire to receive
the recitative soon.

Swieten.

Niemetschek, *op. cit.*, p. 31. The authenticity of this letter is open to doubt.—
The " cold " aria is No. 48 from Handel's *Messiah* (" If God be for us "), the

text of which Mozart shaped into a recitative. Reinhold Bernhardt in 1929 republished this recitative in the Berlin periodical *Die Musik*, Year XXII, No. 1, pp. 434 f.—See 7 April 1789.

On 22 March Nannerl's second child, Johanna, was born.

The girl died on 1 September 1805 at Salzburg, where Frau von Berchtold zu Sonnenburg retired after her husband's death in 1801 with her two children and four stepchildren. Her third child, Marie Babette, was born in 1790 and died in the following year.

JOSEPH HAYDN TO JOSEPH EYBLER

Estoras, 22 March 1789.

. . . Embrace for me those 2 great men Mozart and Albrechtsberger.

Original in the possession of Professor Robert Keldorfer, Klagenfurt.—Supplied by H. C. Robbins Landon.—Estoras is an old form of Esterháza, one of the castles of the Princes Esterházy, where Haydn was employed as Kapellmeister.

MOZART'S BILL OF EXCHANGE IN FAVOUR OF FRANZ HOFDEMEL

Vienna, 2 April 1789.

100 fl. Viennese currency in cash.

A Dato 4 months I, the undersigned, shall pay the sum of 100 fl., in words *One Hundred Gulden*, to Herr von Hofdemel or upon order ; having received value in cash, I shall duly pay on expiration and submit myself to the I. & R. Mercantile and Exchange Court.

Sola to me.   Wolfgang Amadè Mozart
                                        Kapellmeister in actual I. & R. service.

Original in the Louis Koch collection at Basle (Switzerland).—Georg Kinsky's catalogue of the collection (Stuttgart, 1953), p. 36, No. 32.—Hofdemel was a clerk of the Supreme Judiciary and about to enter Mozart's lodge. Mozart had requested this loan of him in an undated letter, but only for a month. It appears that he needed the money for his impending journey to Berlin. Hofdemel cashed the bill only three months later (see 2 July 1789). Hofdemel's wife, Maria Magdalena (*née* Pokorny, born in 1766), is said to have been a pianoforte pupil of Mozart's (see 6 December 1791).—*Cf.* 1 October 1790.

FROM ZINZENDORF'S DIARY, 7 APRIL 1789
(in French)

. . . Before 7 o'clock to the concert at Jean Eszterhasy's. *Der Messias*, music by Haendel. I found it a little tedious, although the music was quite beautiful.

Cf. 6 and 21 March 1789. No. 44 of *Messiah*, the aria "The trumpet shall sound", was heavily cut, probably not by Mozart himself, though with his agreement. The new instrumentation is K. 572.—As Zinzendorf's diary offers us no information on this point, we do not know when Mozart's instrumentations of Handel's *Alexander's Feast* and St Cecilia Ode (July 1790, K. 591 and 592) were first performed.

In the morning of 8 April Mozart left Vienna with Prince Karl Lichnowsky and travelled by way of Znojmo, Moravskí Budějovice, Jihlava and Časlav to Prague, where they arrived on the 10th, Good Friday, and rested at the Unicorn inn from 1.30 to 9 p.m.

It is worthy of note that their departure, which probably took place early in the morning, was on the day after the *Messiah* performance.—Mährisch-Budwitz (Moravskí Budějovice) is north-west of Znaim (Znojmo). They probably spent the second night in Časlav.—Mozart was expected in Dresden and Berlin. The music-loving prince, himself going to Berlin, offered him a free passage. Lichnowsky was a freemason and married to Christine, one of the beautiful daughters of Countess Wilhelmine Thun; in 1796 he took Beethoven with him as far as Prague, when the composer was on his way to Berlin.

On 12 April Mozart and Lichnowsky arrived at Dresden, where they lodged at the " Hôtel de Pologne " at the corner of Schloss-strasse and Grosse Brüderstrasse.

On 13 April Mozart gave a private concert at the " Hôtel de Pologne ".

Mozart performed quartets with the organist Anton Teyber and the cellist Anton Kraft, who had come from Eisenstadt ; they also played the string trio in E♭ major (K. 563) ; Mozart also accompanied Josepha Dušek, who was staying at Dresden, in arias from *Figaro* and *Don Giovanni*.—During the morning of that same day Mozart had heard a mass by Naumann in the chapel of the palace.

FROM THE " JOURNAL DES DRESDENER HOFMARSCHALLAMTES ",
14 APRIL 1789

In the evening there was a concert in H.S.H. the Electress's chamber, at which the Viennese Capellmeister Herr Mozzard was heard on the pianoforte, Herr Prinz on the flute, and a little boy of 9, Kraft, on the violoncello ; they were much applauded.

Dresden, Central State Archives.—Müller von Asow, *op. cit.*, Vol. III, p. 258. —The Elector was Frederick Augustus III of Saxony ; his consort was Amalie of Pfalz-Zweibrücken.—The concert began at 5.30 p.m. Mozart played, *inter alia*, his new D major pianoforte concerto (K. 537). Apart from Johann Friedrich Prinz and young Nikolaus Kraft, a son of the cellist, Josepha Dušek also took part again. Mozart was on the following day presented with 100 ducats in a handsome snuff box.—See 17 June 1789.

On 14 April a concert performance of *Die Entführung* was given at Bamberg.

On 15 April, after lunch with the Russian Ambassador, the music-loving Prince Alexander Belovselsky-Beloserky, Mozart engaged in a trial of skill with the organist Hässler in the Court Church, and then they competed on the pianoforte at the Ambassador's residence.—In the evening Mozart went to the opera (Cimarosa's *Le trame deluse*) with Prince Lichnowsky.

Cf. 13 August 1788 and 15 April 1789.

On 16 or 17 April Mozart visited the consistorial councillor Christian Gottfried Körner, whose sister-in-law Doris Stock did a drawing of Mozart.

Körner was a friend of Schiller's and the father of the poet Theodor Körner. The silverpoint drawing on ivory board, rapidly sketched by Doris Stock, was one of the last portraits of Mozart.

On 18 April Mozart travelled by way of Meissen, Oschatz and Wurzen to Leipzig where he arrived on the 20th and remained three days.

On 22 April Mozart improvised on the organ of St. Thomas's Church, the Cantor, Johann Friedrich Doles and the organist, Karl Friedrich Görner, manipulating the stops for him.

Doles was a pupil of J. S. Bach and the organist was a son of Johann Gottlieb Görner, who had been organist of the church when Bach was cantor. (Reichardt in the *Berlinische Musikalische Zeitung*, 1805, Year I, No. 33, p. 132.)— Mozart had played the fortepiano in Körner's house at Dresden, and when at Leipzig he played in the house of the rector of the university, Dr Ernst Platner.

On 23 April Mozart left Leipzig for Potsdam, where he arrived on the 25th.

Neither date is precise.—Mozart is said to have lodged at Potsdam with the horn player Karl Türrschmiedt. (See *Neue Berliner Musikzeitung*, 30 January 1856, Year X, No. 5, pp. 34 ff., where Mozart's arrival is given too early.)

PROPOSAL FROM THE CABINET TO KING FREDERICK WILLIAM II, POTSDAM, 26 APRIL 1789

One named Motzart (who at his ingress declared himself to be a Capellmeister from Vienna) reports here that he was brought hither in the company of Prince Lichnowsky, that he desired to lay his talents before Your Sovereign Majesty's feet and awaited the command whether he may hope that Your Sovereign Majesty will receive him.

Ernst Friedlaender in *Mitteilungen der Berliner Mozart-Gemeinde*, No. 4, April 1897.—The King of Prussia was at that time at Potsdam. At this point in the document he wrote in the margin : " Directeur du Port ", which means that Mozart was to get into touch with the director of chamber music, Jean Pierre Duport, with whom he was not on good terms. On 29 April he nevertheless wrote nine pianoforte variations (K. 573) on a favourite piece of the king's, a minuet by Duport, which was published in No. 6 of his " Op. 4 " (*Six Sonates pour le Violoncelle*) by J. J. Imbault, Paris (*cf.* F. Peters-Marquard in the *Zeitschrift für Musik* [Regensburg, 1951], p. 469).—Little else is known of Mozart's visit to Potsdam.

FROM THE " DRAMATURGISCHE BLÄTTER ", FRANKFURT ON MAIN, 1789

On 30th April : *Das verstellte Gärtnermädchen*—Singspiel in 3 acts, after the Italian ; the music by Mozart.

A gaudy, tasteless thing, like most of the operettas of the Italian stage. Nor did Mozart's music make much sensation among our public. It is for the connoisseur who knows how to unravel its refinements rather than for the dilettante who lets himself be guided only by his natural feeling and judges only according to the first, immediate impression.

> Year II, 1st Quarter, No. 7, p. 100.—See 31 January 1789.

IBID., 1789

On the 3rd [May] : *Don Juan*—Singspiel in 2 acts, after the Italian ; the music by Mozart.

A legend in Father Kochem's vein, to which the glorious—if here and there too artful—music by Mozart is about as well suited as Raphael's manner to the ideas of a Teniers or a Calot. But although the whole is a monkish farce, I must admit that the scene in the churchyard filled me with horror. Mozart seems to have learnt the language of ghosts from Shakespear.—A hollow, sepulchral tone seemed to rise from the earth ; it was as though the shades of the departed were seen to issue from their resting-places.

> *Ibid.*, No. 8, p. 116.—See 13 March 1789.—The Mainz company also wished to perform *Don Giovanni* at Frankfurt on 5 October 1790, while Mozart was there, but the plan came to nothing.—Martin von Kochem (1634–1712), a Capuchin, was an itinerant preacher.

IBID., 1789

On the 4th [May] : *Don Juan.*

The piece will soon be past its term here. The music is not popular enough to arouse general interest.

> *Ibid.*

On 8 May Mozart and Prince Lichnowsky reached Leipzig from Potsdam.

> The *Berlinische Zeitungen* (Spener and Voss) report that the prince remained in Berlin from 30 April till 2 May and thence travelled to Leipzig.

On 9 May Giuseppe Gazzaniga's opera *La vendemmia* was given for the first time in London, at the King's Theatre in the Haymarket ; the duet " Crudel ! perchè finora " from *Figaro* was interpolated and sung by Benucci and Ann Storace.

> Loewenberg, *op. cit.*, p. 181.—The opera, performed at Florence in 1778, was given in London furnished with arias by Paisiello, Angelo Tarchi and Carlo Pozzi.—Benucci that evening made his second appearance in London. The duet is for the Count and Susanna in the original ; in Vienna Benucci had sung the part of Figaro, with Ann Storace as Susanna. The performance, in which music from a Mozart opera was probably heard for the first time in London (*cf.* 1 March 1790), was repeated on 12 May by order of the King.

FROM THE " LEIPZIGER ZEITUNGEN ", 12 MAY 1789

Today, being 12 May, Herr Mozart, Capellmeister in actual service of His I. & R. Majesty, will hold a concert for his benefit in the great Concert

Hall of Leipzig.   Tickets are to be had for 1 gulden of Herr Rost in Auer-
bach's Court and at the entrance to the hall.   To begin at 6 o'clock.

> Jahn, Vol. II, p. 477.—Copy in the University Library, Leipzig.—The hall was
> that of the old Gewandhaus, where concerts had been held since 1781.

PROGRAMME OF THE LEIPZIG CONCERT, 12 MAY 1789

Concert
of
Herr Mozart, Kapellmeister
in I. & R. Service.
At the Hall of the Gewandhaus.
Tuesday, 12 May 1789

Part I.
Symphony.
Scena.   Mme. Duscheck.
Concerto, on the Pianoforte.
Symphony.

Part II.
Concerto, on the Pianoforte.
Scena.   Mme. Duscheck.
Fantasy, on the Pianoforte.
Symphony.

All these musical pieces are of Herr Kapellmeister Mozart's composition.
Tickets of admission are to be had of Rost's Art Establishment, and of the
Library Attendant, Herr Meyer, at 16 Groschen.
To begin at 6 o'clock.

> Facsimile reproduction in the volume *Die Gewandhaus-Konzerte zu Leipzig
> 1781–1931* (Leipzig), 1931, p. 37.—It happened that Mozart again met Josepha
> Dušek at Leipzig, as a month earlier at Dresden.   She sang the scena and rondo
> K. 505 (" Ch' io mi scordi di te—Non temer, amato bene ") and probably the
> soprano scena written for her in Prague, K. 528 (" Bella mia fiamma—Resta, oh
> cara ").   He played two pianoforte concertos, the ones in B♭ major (K. 456)
> and C major (K. 503), followed by the C minor fantasy (K. 475) and a set of
> variations (K. 353 or 354).   The two symphonies, two movements from each
> of which began and ended the first half, cannot be identified with any cer-
> tainty.   (*Cf.* Johann Friedrich Rochlitz in the *Allgemeine musikalische Zeitung*
> [Leipzig, 1798], Vol. I, cols. 20–22, 85 f., 179 ; and 1820, Vol. XXII, p. 297 ;
> also his work *Für Freunde der Tonkunst*, 3rd ed., 1868, Vol. II, p. 181.)

Announcement.

Johann Traeg has the honour of acquainting Connoisseurs and Amateurs of music that he has opened a music shop in the Singerstrasse, No. 863, opposite to the apothecary's. He hopes to merit much custom by means of diligent service. He will always endeavour to procure not only new but also old and good pieces by the best masters. From among his stock he meanwhile announces the following things :

1 Violin Concerto by Mozart   3 fl.

The violin concerto cannot be identified.

Mozart left Leipzig on 17 May and arrived in Berlin on the 19th, where he stayed with the stucco worker Sartory on the Gendarmen-Markt and in the evening attended *Die Entführung*.

Sartory was a friend of Türrschmiedt's, Mozart's host at Potsdam. According to other information he stayed with a Herr Moser in Berlin.—*Die Entführung* had been given in Berlin since 16 October 1788 under the title *Belmonte und Constanze*. The *Chronik von Berlin* (Vol. IV, Nos. 79-80, p. 1222) and the Weimar *Journal des Luxus und der Moden* (p. 394) announced that the performance on 19 May 1789 took place " at loud request ", but failed to mention Mozart's presence, which Rochlitz reported as an anecdote in the *Allgemeine musikalische Zeitung* in 1798, and which is depicted in an engraving published at Zürich in 1833. (*Cf.* Tieck's Memoirs, 1855.)—The cast seen by Mozart in Berlin was as follows : Constanze—Marianne Hellmuth ; Blonde—Henriette Baranius ; Belmonte—Friedrich Karl Lippert ; Pedrillo—Greibe ; Osmin— Franz Frankenberg ; Bassa Selim—Karl Czechtitzky.—Fräulein Hellmuth (later Frau Müller) may have been the daughter of the Josepha Hellmuth who sang Constanze at Mainz on 19 November 1789 ; Marianne was then only just seventeen years of age. In 1790 she sang Cherubino and Donna Elvira, and in 1794 the Queen of Night, in Berlin.—Frankenberg had been at the German Opera in Vienna from 1779 to 1783.

Continuing our Account of the Grossmann Company.

18 May : *Die Hochzeit des Figaro* ; a Singspiel in four acts, after the Italian ; music by Mozart.

The Italian piece, based on Beaumarchais's comedy and turned into a Singspiel, is very pleasing, and its many good situations and embroilments are very well suited to a comic opera. But since the piece itself has to be played very well and with great liveliness, if the subtleties of each situation are to be perceived, I doubt very much whether Italian singers, few of whom take much trouble to develop their dramatic gifts, are able to perform this piece as perfectly as it deserves, so far as acting is concerned.

What is more, the finest strokes must needs appear in the finales, where it is impossible for every singer to sing so distinctly and also to act so well, that many a *pointe* is not lost ; and that is certainly a pity in the case of a piece written with so much wit.

The dialogue is by my daughter. She made use of the French play for it and thus restored a number of amusing passages omitted in the Italian. The words for the arias are by myself. Those who know the difficulties of the thankless task of substituting German verses for Italian for music already written, and music which is moreover so very difficult, will not expect beautiful poetry in these arias. Great attention has to be paid to the agreement of the musical accents with the grammatical and oratorical, or else the result will be a schoolboy's work ; metres must be found to correspond with the Italian ones ; the composer sometimes draws together the vowels, in which the Italian language is so rich, making a single syllable out of more than one, only to separate them again in some other passage of the same aria. And where in a language so blessed with consonants as is ours are there words to be found with which this can be done ? Then it will not do to use narrow vowels in German where florid passages use A or O. Translation almost line by line is called for if that which has been painted by the music is not to coincide with different words that do not fit the picture—and so the vexations continue ! For a sample, here is the translation of three arias together with the Italian text :

Voi, che sapete,	Ihr, die Ihr Triebe
Che cosa e amor,	Des Herzens kennt ;

.   .   .   .   .   .

It is Cherubino who sings this and the following song :

Non so piu cosa son', cosa faccio,	Neue Freuden, neue Schmerzen
Or di foco, ora sono di ghiaccio	Toben jetzt in meinem Herzen ;

.   .   .   .

And finally a song sung by the Countess :

Dove sono i bei momenti	Nur zu flüchtig bist Du verschwunden,
Di dolcezza e di piacer ?	Freudenvolle, frohe Zeit !

.   .   .   .

[Knigge.]

Concerning the Music of this Opera.

It is what was to be expected of Mozart : great and beautiful, full of new ideas and unexpected turns, full of art, fire and genius. Now we are enchanted by beautiful, charming song ; now we are made to smile at subtle, comic wit and fancy ; now we admire the naturally conceived and superbly executed planning ; now the magnificence and greatness of Art takes us by surprise. Where all this is united, it is bound to make its effect and to satisfy the sensitive hearer as well as the experienced and practised expert. Mozart is gifted with the happy genius that can blend art with nature and song with grace. Again he ventures on impetuous and fiery sallies, and how bold are his harmonies ! In this opera, too, he shows that he possesses a true talent for the comic-dramatic style, just as his piano-forte things, because they suit the instrument, are acknowledged and admired as masterpieces by the German public and by foreign nations.

Figaro's arias finely portray his character, especially the last in the first act : " Dort vergiss leises Flehen, süsses Wimmern ! " The Page's two songs are delicious, with their romantic ardour. Those of the Countess, again, contain beauties of their own, which are well suited to her person. How sweet and melting is the *andantino* in the third act : " Nur zu flüchtig bist Du verschwunden, freudenreiche, frohe Zeit ". The duet for her and Susanna that follows :

> " Wenn die sanften Abendlüfte
> Über unsre Fluren wehn,
> Wollen wir durch süsse Düfte
> In den stillen Garten gehn."

with oboe and bassoon *obbligato*, is nature itself. The charming choruses, and especially the conclusion of the third act, adorn the whole with variety and grace. The pretty little cavatina at the opening of the fourth act, Basilio's aria and the one for Figaro that follows it, are differentiated by characteristic features. The two trios in the first and second act are full of art and expression. Basilio's interpolated strain in the first trio of the first act, " Ja so machens alle Schönen " is a veritable stroke of genius. But it is the finale of the second act which in many respects must be regarded as the masterpiece of the whole opera. Magnificent and rich in art, it re-gales our soul with sweet, melodious song. Every incident is represented picturesquely and beautifully. The very opening is full of fire and force. The entry of Susanna, the moment when the gardener appears, and then the scene with the letter, [and then] with Figaro, are masterly, full of wit, and originally and truly depicted. The conclusion is grand and splendid. It is true that, according to the verdict of the tasteful section of the public, there are passages that do not make the effect one would desire ; thus, for example, the sextet of the third act, although here too original traits pierce through, remains a little obscure and elusive ; but one should be prepared to sacrifice a little for the great beauties and masterstrokes contained in this work by a German artist.

W.

The performance went very well, notwithstanding that the music of this opera is among the most difficult that we have . . .

No. 31, pp. 492-94 ; No. 32, pp. 495-501.—*Cf.* 18 May 1788.—The literary part of this article is by Knigge himself, the musical part probably by Bernhard Anselm Weber (*see* 3 October 1788).—The specimens of his translation of the arias show how strongly Knigge's version influenced later German trans-lations.

Dresden, 16 April.

On 10 March Herr *Hummel*, a young pianof[orte] player aged 9, native of *Vienna* and Mozart's pupil, was heard in public here to the admiration of every listener, with *Mozart's* variations on " Lison dormoit " and his grand concerto in C major.   He is to go to *Berlin* from here.

> Col. 156.—Johann Nepomuk Hummel was born at Bratislava in 1778 and had been Mozart's pupil in Vienna in 1786 and 1787.   He and his father Johannes Hummel (who is said to have been director of music at the Vienna Freihaus-Theater) were at this time on a three year long concert tour.   *Cf.* Karl Benyovszky, *J. N. Hummel*, Bratislava, 1934, pp. 30-32.—Maximilian Johann Seidel's *Biographische Notizen* (MS., 1837) and the entry in Waldo Selden Pratt's *The New Encyclopedia of Music and Musicians*, New York, 1929, p. 460, have not been taken into consideration here as being unreliable.—The variations referred to are K. 264, the concerto was probably K. 503.

On Saturday, 23 May, a virtuoso aged ten, Mons. Hummel from Vienna, will be heard on the fortepiano in a finely wrought concerto in the Corsika Hall.   He is a pupil of the famous Herr Mozart and exceeds all expectation in agility, sureness and delicacy.   Each person pays 16 groschen.   Tickets are to be had of Herr Corsika, of Herr Toussaint in the Poststrasse at the Golden Eagle, and at the entrance.   To begin at 4 o'clock.

> Ernst Friedlaender, *op. cit.*—At this concert Hummel met his former teacher again.

On 26 May Mozart played before the king and queen at the Berlin royal palace.

> It may have been on this occasion that Mozart received the commission from Frederick William II to write six easy pianoforte sonatas for Princess Friederike and six string quartets for the king himself.   For the first quartet, in D major (K. 575), which he composed in Vienna in June, he is said to have received 100 *Friedrichsd'or* in a gold snuff-box.   Only two more of the planned quartets, in B♭ major and in F major (K. 589 and 590), were completed (1790), and the three were published as Op. 18 by Artaria & Co., on 28 December 1791, shortly after Mozart's death, but without a dedication to the king.

On 27 May *Die Entführung* was performed at Buda by Hubert Kumpf's company (see 5 November 1784 and 4 February 1785) ;   the composer was not named.

> The title there was *Der Wettstreit der Grossmuth* [The Contest of Magnanimity]. —The opera was repeated at Pest on 30 May.   A libretto had been published (in Pest ?) in 1788.   *Cf.* 13 June 1785 (Bratislava) and 19 June 1791 (Pest).

On 28 May Mozart left Berlin and went by way of Dresden to Prague, where he stayed from 31 May to 2 June, so that he was back in Vienna at midday on the 4th.

> Prince Lichnowsky had left Mozart at Leipzig in the middle of May.

Extract from a Report from Dresden of 28 May.

On 14 April the famous composer Herr *W. A. Mozart* of *Vienna* was heard at the fortepiano by *His Elect. Highness*—furthermore he also played here at *Dresden* in many noble and private houses with boundless success ; his agility on the clavier and on the fortepiano is inexpressible—and to this is added an extraordinary ability to read at sight, which truly borders on the incredible :—for he himself is hardly able to play a thing better after practice than he does the very first time. On the organ too he showed his great skill in the strict style.—He goes to *Berlin* from here.

> Year I, No. 24, col. 191.—Jahn, Vol. II, p. 471.—This report had twice been delayed.

New Music.

At the Musikalisches Magazin, opposite the Holy Trinity Column in the Graben, Untere Breunerstrasse, No. 1152, the following music is to be had :

.   .   .   .

Mozard Variations for the pianoforte   a 45 kr.

.   .   .   .

> The proprietor of this publishing firm, founded in 1785, with whom Mozart intended to publish his string quartets written for the King of Prussia (see 26 May 1789), was the composer Leopold Kozeluch.—The variations on " Je suis Lindor " (K. 354), engraved for Torricella, were actually published by Kozeluch without a publisher's mark, though with the original publisher's number 17 (established by Professor Kurt von Fischer).

Dresden, 20 May.

On 30 March, at the instigation of a music-lover, a concert of wind instruments was given in the large music-room of the Hotel de Bologne, namely, in the first part the symphony and the finest arias from Mozart's *Don Juan,* and in the second, the symphony and the finest pieces from *Una Cosa rara* by Martin ; the extraordinarily numerous audience, which included almost all the high nobility and many other music lovers, departed in unanimous satisfaction.

The excellence of a Richter, a Schmidt, a Hummel, a Haudeck and the brothers Rothe, as well as the good selection from operas that are in any case excellent, would alone have elicited almost unanimous applause.

> Year I, No. 25, col. 198 f.—This report, like that of 17 June, appeared only after being twice delayed.—The " Hôtel de Bologne " was properly the " Hôtel de Pologne ".—Martín y Soler's *Una cosa rara* was given for the first time at

the Burgtheater in 1786 and was then given at Prague in 1787 and at Dresden in 1788. Mozart quoted the conclusion of the first finale of this opera (" O quanto un si bel giubilo ") in the wind music which accompanies Don Giovanni's supper.—For the musicians *cf.* 18 February 1789.

During the summer *Figaro* was performed at Baden near Vienna by Georg Wilhelm's company.

Theaterkalender, Gotha, 1790, pp. 116 ff. Discovered by Gustav Gugitz.

HOFDEMEL CASHES MOZART'S BILL OF EXCHANGE

Myself, to the order of Herr Mathias Anzenberger, with my further *obligo*, amount received in cash.

Vienna, 2 July 1789 :
Franz Hofdemel

See 2 April 1789.—Anzenberger was the proprietor of the fashion establishment " Zum Meerfräule [The Mermaid] " on the Kohlmarkt (information supplied by Dr. Ernst Weizmann).—*Cf.* Mozart's letter to Puchberg, early May 1790, where there is mention of a debt of 100 gulden in favour of a fashion-dealer in the Stock-im-Eisen-Platz.

On 7, 10 and 24 July Aloisia Lange sang the part of Constanze in *Die Entführung* at Hamburg. *Cf.* Johann Friedrich Schütze, *Hamburgische Theater-Geschichte* (Hamburg, 1794), p. 627. *Cf.* also *Annalen des Theaters* (Berlin, 1790), No. 6, p. 78.

MOZART WITNESSES A RECEIPT

madame Elisab : Rothmann's receipt for July 1789, No. 2.

Of my much-loved brother-in-law Herr Martin Rothmann I have this day received in the Presence of the Executors Messrs. Ignaz von Kunnersdorff, R. Exchequer Councillor, Amadeus Mozart, R. Hoffkapell Director, and Jost. von Spaug, R. Councillor, a sum of two Thousand Florins in Hard Cash. Given Vienna, 10 July 1789.

Elisabeth Rothmann
J. A. Born's widow.

Witnesses present

Ignatz v. Kunnersdorf   Mozart   v. Spaug

Original in the Kungl. Musikaliska Akademiens Bibliotek, Stockholm.—Erich H. Müller von Asow in the *Österreichische Musikzeitschrift*, Vienna, April 1956, Year 11, No. 4, p. 146.—Nothing is known of Mozart's relations with these persons ; nor that he was executor of the late Herr Rothmann's will.—It is unlikely that this testimomy had anything to do with Hofdemel's bill of exchange, since this did not fall due until 2 August 1789.

FROM THE " MUSIKALISCHE REAL-ZEITUNG ", SPEYER, 22 JULY 1789

Mozart's 4 arias from *Belmonte und Constanze*, Op. 50. Berlin, at J. C. F. Rellstab's.

Year II, No. 29, col. 231.—The four favourite arias were Nos. 8, 12, 13 and 19 of the singspiel. (Second edition in the Hirsch Library, British Museum, London.)—Rellstab numbered his publications consecutively as " opera ".

FROM CRAMER'S " MAGAZIN DER MUSIK ", COPENHAGEN, 1789

July 1789. (Letter from A. to his friend.)

. . . The works of this composer [Kozeluch] maintain themselves and [in Vienna] find access everywhere, whereas Mozart's works do not in general please quite so much. It is true, too, and his six quartets for violins, viola and bass dedicated to Haydn confirm it once again, that he has a decided leaning towards the difficult and the unusual. But then, what great and elevated ideas he has too, testifying to a bold spirit !

This unnamed correspondent had stayed in Vienna on his return journey from Italy, perhaps as early as 1787 or 1788.—For Kozeluch see 7 December 1787 and 24 June 1789.—Cramer's magazine had previously been published in Hamburg.

FROM THE " WIENER ZEITUNG ", 1 AUGUST 1789

Of Johann Traeg . . . the following new music may be had :

2 Quint. for 2 violins, 2 violas and violoncello by Mozart   4 fl.

Duets for do. [2 violins] from *Figaro*   3 fl.
" Freyheitslied " by Mozart   10 kr.
" Kriegslied " by Mozart   15 kr.
1 Sonata for 2 harpsichords by Mozart   2 fl.
1 Concerto in E♭ for harpsichord by Mozart   4 fl. 30 kr.

The quintets were probably those in C major and G minor (K. 515 and 516), which Artaria & Co. published in 1789. The " Freiheitslied " was evidently the " Lied der Freiheit " (K. 506), which had already appeared in print in the *Wiener Musenalmanach* for 1786, and the " Kriegslied " was " Ein deutsches Kriegslied " (K. 539), which Lausch had in 1788 offered in manuscript copies of the parts, and in a pianoforte score. The sonata for two pianofortes was that in D major (K. 448) and the pianoforte concerto that in E♭ major (K. 482). The price of the concerto was announced on 8 September 1790 as being 3 fl. 30 kr.

On 11 August *Figaro* was given in German at Brunswick.

FROM THE " CHRONIK VON BERLIN ", 1789

Diary of the Royal National Theatre in Berlin, August 1789.

The 13th. At urgent request : *Belmonte und Constanze.* (*Der Zauber-Spiegel* and *Die beiden Billette* had previously been advertised in the public press.) Madame Lange from Vienna appeared as Constanze. When an artist is heralded by the fanfares of a good reputation, it is only to be expected that they shall resound very widely indeed. Needless to say, the attendance was very numerous. Madame Lange received the loudest applause. When at first it showed signs of not becoming general, some whispered to others : " Do applaud, good people. The woman deserves it ! There are not many singers like her. In Hamburg, at Schröder's theatre, the greatest honour was done her ! What a disgrace if we Berliners did not show that we feel as deeply towards great singers." After that the clapping really did grow more general. About Lippert we are bound to say that he took particularly great pains as Belmont to-day.

> Vol. IV, Nos. 87-88, p. 1355.—On pp. 1354 f. of this journal it is reported that on 11 and 12 August the public at the theatre had called for " Madame Lange as Constanze ! ". For her appearance at Hamburg, where Friedrich Ludwig Schröder (cf. 22 May 1784) was director of the theatre, see 10 July 1789.—Der Zauberspiegel was the Berlin version (first staged in 1781) of A. E. M. Grétry's La fausse magie, libretto by J. F. Marmontel, translated by C. F. von Bonin. Die beiden Billets was a one-act comedy by J. P. C. de Florian, translated by Anton Wall.—Frau Lange (now pregnant) and her husband were staying in Berlin.

From 15 (?) to 18 August Mozart stayed with his wife at Baden near Vienna.

> Constanze, who was suffering from a foot complaint, had been recommended a cure at the sulphur springs there by the Mozarts' physician, Dr. Thomas Franz Closset.

FROM THE " MUSIKALISCHE REAL-ZEITUNG ", SPEYER, 19 AUGUST 1789

[About an unnamed organist at Hechingen, a pupil of Abbé Vogler's.]
. . . But I am told that his playing on the fortepiano and the clavier is detestable. This he has in common with most professional organists. Refined connoisseurs of music at Strasbourg, such as the famous Silbermann, who have heard Vogler, tell me he has the very same fault to a considerable degree, and that in the matter of refinement and expression in playing they by far preferred Becke, Mozart, nay even their organist at the New Church, named Heppe (a very delicate and agreeable player, in fact).

> Col. 262.—Members of the well-known Silbermann family of organ builders and pianoforte makers living at that time at Strasbourg were Johann Heinrich, who made pianofortes, and Johann Friedrich, who built organs.

On 19 August the first rehearsal for the revival of Figaro was held.

On 29 August Figaro was revived at the Burgtheater.

> The last performance had taken place on 18 December 1786.—Mozart had written two new soprano numbers for Adriana Ferrarese del Bene, who sang Susanna : the rondo " Al desio di chi t' adora " (K. 577) and the aria " Un moto di gioia " (K. 579). The words, probably by Da Ponte, were reprinted in the new libretto (cf. Leopold von Sonnleithner in Recensionen und Mittheilungen über Theater und Musik [Vienna, 1865], No. 46). Ferrarese's real name was Francesca Gabrielli ; she came from Ferrara and had been engaged at the

Italian Opera in Vienna since 1788. Caterina Cavalieri sang the Countess. Joseph Weigl conducted (*see* 1 May 1786).

FROM ZINZENDORF'S DIARY, 31 AUGUST 1789
(in French)

. . . To the Opera. Le *nozze di Figaro*. A charming duet for la Cavalieri and la Ferraresi.

The *duettino* for Susanna and the Countess is No. 20 in the original score : " Sull' aria . . . Che soave zefiretto ".

FROM THE " WIENER ZEITUNG ", 5 SEPTEMBER 1789
New Music.

From Artaria Comp., art dealers in the Kohlmarkt, are to be had, finely engraved and printed on good paper :

Mozart, 2 German arias for the clavier, Part II, 30 kr.

Mozart, 3 Sonatas for pianoforte, violin and basso, Op. 15, 3 fl.

The " German arias " were " Das Veilchen " (Goethe, K. 476) and " Das Lied der Trennung " (K. 519) ; the " sonatas " were the pianoforte trios in B♭, E and C major (K. 502, 542 and 548).

FROM ZINZENDORF'S DIARY, 6 SEPTEMBER 1789
(in French)

. . . On my return to town to the Opera. I *due Baroni*. A bad opera. La Bussani is pretty. . . .

Cimarosa's opera I *due baroni di Rocca Azzurra*, produced in Rome in 1783, was given in Vienna on 6 and 13 September with an additional aria by Mozart, " Alma grande e nobil core " (K. 578), written for Dlle. Louise Villeneuve. This beautiful sister (?) of Signora Ferrarese (Pohl, *Haydn*, Vol. II, p. 124) joined the opera company in 1789.—For Dorotea Bussani, *née* Sardi, see 1 May 1786.

FROM THE " WIENER ZEITUNG ", 23 SEPTEMBER 1789
New Rondeau

sung by Mme. Ferarese, from the opera Le *Nozze di Figaro* by Herr Kapellmeister Mozart, in actual service of H.M. the Emperor, in pianoforte score. " Giunse alfin ", Recitativo : " Al desio di chi t' adora ", Rondeau [for] Soprano 28 kr.

To be had in Vienna at Lausch's music establishment . . .

See 29 August 1789.—Copy in the British Museum, London (Add. MSS. 14, 316).

On 27 September *Don Giovanni* was given in German at Mannheim.

The translation was by Christian Gottlieb Neefe (see 4 October 1780 and 2 March 1783).

FROM THE " ANALYTICAL REVIEW ", LONDON, SEPTEMBER 1789
(in English)

Art. LXXV.   *A Duet for two Performers on one Piano-Forte or Harpsichord. By A. Moyart. Pr. 2s.   Andrews.*

This is a pleasing, familiar composition, and the parts are so adjusted as to move together with very good effect. It comprises three movements : the first in common time of four crochets in a bar, the second a *minuetto* 3/4 with a trio, and the third a rondo 2/4 *allegretto*. In the first movement we discover a pleasing train of ideas, well connected, and somewhat novel. The minuetto is also conceived with taste and ingenuity, while the rondo, or concluding movement, possesses a spirited subject, successfully relieved by its several digressions.   This piece, we apprehend, by the ease of its style, not to be designed for proficients on the pianoforte or harpsichord, but for the use of practitioners, for whose improvement it certainly is well calculated, and will be found by them as pleasing as it is profitable.

> P. 111.—King, *op. cit.*, pp. 108 f. Alan Tyson in *Music Review* (Cambridge), August 1961, p. 222—This sonata (KE. 19d) had been written in London early in May 1765. F. de Roullede had published it in Paris in 1788 (but see end of 1789). Hugh Andrews's edition was reprinted about 1795 by Robert Birchall as Op. 16, with a new title-page.

On 4 October *Don Giovanni* was given at Passau in German, with the title *Don Juan, oder das steinerne Nachtmahl*.

On 13 October *Don Giovanni* was given in German at Bonn.

The translation was Neefe's (see 27 September). *Cf.* early 1791.

On 14 October *Don Giovanni* was given in Italian in Warsaw.

Guardasoni's company was there in 1789/91.

FROM THE " DRAMATURGISCHE BLÄTTER ", FRANKFURT ON MAIN, 1789

On the 17th [October] : *Figaro*—operetta in 4 acts.

This operetta is given here in a translation by Herr Vulpius : to judge of its poetical worth one need only hear the following passage from an aria for the Countess :

> Woe, the precious stones love brought me
> Are transformed to bitter tears ;
> What is it that I have bought me ?
> Grief and pain my bosom sears !

Such a passage should call for no further criticism. Herr von Knigge has
also put this opera into German, and his name is a guarantee of the value
of his work. I could wish that in future we might be given this translation
instead of that by Herr Vulpius . . .

> Year II, 3rd Quarter, No. 7, pp. 100 f.—The translation by Vulpius, Goethe's
> brother-in-law, had been in use at Frankfurt since 11 October 1788 ; that by
> Knigge had been in use at Lübeck since 18 May 1788 and at Hanover since 18
> May 1789.

IBID., 1789

On the 22nd [October] : *Die Entführung aus dem Serail.*

Herr von Knigge says of Mozart's music for this opera that it fails in
general to make the impression one expects of it as a true work of art.—
With us, at least, this is not the case ; the piece is seen with ever-renewed
pleasure at oft-repeated performances. It may be that the orchestra at
Brunswick does not know how to deal properly with Mozart's difficult
writing, or that the required number of instruments is not available, or
that the public there differs from ours in regard to music. Here and there
fault is found with this composition for the combination of serious with
comic elements ; but I cannot understand why a composer should be
denied an advantage which is granted to the poet. Deviations from the
fundamental tone make for variety and liveliness, so long as they do not
occur too often and do not make too great a contrast.

> *Ibid.*, pp. 102 f.—For Knigge see 3 October 1788. His essay related to Han-
> over ; the work had been given there since 12 April 1787, and at Brunswick
> since February 1788 at the latest. (At Frankfurt it was first performed on 2
> August 1783.)

On 27 October *Don Giovanni* was given in German in Hamburg.

> This third translation was by Friedrich Ludwig Schröder, the director of the
> theatre.

FROM SCHINK'S " DRAMATURGISCHE MONATE ", SCHWERIN, 1790
[Hamburg, 1789]

On the twenty-seventh of October : *Don Juan, oder der steinerne Gast,*
Singspiel in 4 acts, from the Italian, the music by Mozart.

According to the operatic ideal which the Italian poets have given us in
their musical works, and according to the impression which these products
of the Italian mind have made on our public, a more fit and proper subject
for a Singspiel could hardly have been found than this originally Spanish
absurdity which Herr Mozart has endeavoured to glorify with his excellent
composition. *Don Juan* combines all the nonsensical, extravagant, contra-
dictory and unnatural features that ever qualified a poetic absurdity of a
human being for the role of an operatic hero. He is the stupidest, most

M.—12

senseless creature imaginable, the misbegotten product of a crazed Spanish imagination. The most dissolute, base and profligate fellow, whose life is an uninterrupted series of infamies, seductions of the innocent and murders. A hypocrite and atheist, a dissipated voluptuary and crafty betrayer, a double-dealer and a fop ; the most treacherous and malicious beast, a scoundrel without conscience and without honour. He commits the greatest abominations with a coldness and equanimity as though he were drinking a glass of water, fells a man as though he were going to a ball, and seduces and betrays female virtue as though he were taking a pinch of snuff. And all these horrors amuse him, all these bestialities are great sport for him. At any spoken play such a caricature would be chased off the stage with oranges and nutshells and hissed into the wings ; but in an opera he is found uncommonly entertaining, and as he is a personality on the musical stage, his infamies are considered delightful things, and provoke laughter and pleasure. Well, that is no more than just and right, for is not this an opera ? How should music, one of the fairest and loveliest gifts of Heaven, come to imitate nature and truth ? How should reason in song delight people who only wish to hear singing, to have their ear-drums tickled, to digest a meal of oysters in comfort, and to spend a few hours thinking about nothing ? What, then, could be more welcome in such circumstances than the kind of nonsense that goes on here and the absurdities that are here enacted ? A stone statue sings, receives an invitation to dinner, which it accepts, dismounts from its horse and duly arrives at the right moment. Delicious ! A pity it does not eat as well, for only then would the fun be complete ! Some honest man among the spectators thought this singing statue without rhyme or reason, but probably owing to his sheer lack of operatic theory. Those acquainted with that theory will hardly find it so. I for one would hardly have been surprised even if the stone guest's stone *horse* had sung, or indeed shown itself off in an *aria di bravura*. That would be no wonder in an opera ; for do I not remember an Italian sing-song, entitled *Judith*, in which the severed head of *Holofernes* and his trunk sang a most touching duet together over their forcible separation ? The more unnatural the better : this is the watchword, known the world over, which every opera should bear on its front—if it is to please.

Now, if *Don Juan*, for all these praiseworthy characteristics of a true operatic hero, did not after all make the universal fortune which his qualities had led one to expect, the fault is hardly to be found in the subject but— may the artist forgive my frankness !—in Herr *Mozart's* composition. What induced him to write such unoperatic, beautiful, great and noble music for such a truly Italian operatic theme ? Is such magnificent, majestic and powerful song really stuff for ordinary opera-lovers, who only bring their *ears* to the Singspiel and leave their *hearts* at home ? But then, what should the heart be doing at a play which depends only on being seen and heard, the first requirement for which is, if it is to be successful, that the author's heart should take a holiday as well as his head during the making of it ?

Herr *Mozart* may thus be never so excellent a composer, but he will never become one for our real opera-lovers, unless he first endows them with a property of which they know as little as a blind man does of colour—feeling. And I fear he would sooner succeed, like Orpheus, in setting fields and woods in motion with his art than in imparting an understanding of his music to these amateurs of opera, with their hearts of stone.

This assertion does not by any means concern any particular public ; it applies to the German opera public altogether. The beauty, greatness and nobility of the music for *Don Juan* will never appeal anywhere to more than a handful of the elect. It is not music to every one's taste, merely tickling the ear and letting the heart starve. To appreciate its whole excellence one must possess a true musical sense and have the right, educated notions of what is music's first and highest purpose ; one must know what end is served by song and how it is to make its effect.

Mozart is no ordinary composer. He is not content with light, pleasing melodies written down at random. His music is carefully planned, profoundly felt work, suited to the personalities, situations and sentiments of his characters. It shows study of the language, which he treats musically, and just knowledge of prosody. He carefully observes in the length and shortness of the syllables, and in the mode of expression, the interrelation that comes nearest to their natural proportion, as well as the nearest possible correspondence of the musical tones with those which sensibility would cause to be uttered in declamation. With a few exceptions his modulations correspond perfectly with the rules of proper declamation ; his punctuations are natural and his pauses used with wise judgment. He never applies runs and trills to syllables which are unable to bear them, and altogether never ornaments his song with needless and soulless flourishes. For that is to banish expression from music, and expression never lies in single words but in the wise, natural combination of notes, through which speaks true feeling. This kind of expression *Mozart* has entirely in his power. With him every note proceeds from feeling and generates feeling. His expression is glowing, vivid and picturesque, yet without becoming fulsome and excessive. He has the richest and yet the most restrained imagination. He is the true virtuoso who never lets his imagination run away with intelligence. Reason guides his enthusiasm and calm judgment his presentation.

The application of these characteristics of *Mozart's* talent to his admirable works themselves I beg leave to pass over. I am no musician, not even a dilettante. I judge this music solely according to the general purpose of the fine arts : to imitate nature, and through that imitation to touch our hearts and our sentiments. *Mozart's* works affect these infallibly, provided one does possess a heart and sentiments. To acknowledge this power and to draw attention to the how and the why thereof, according to my own lights, is all I can do. Closer application and critical examination of this fine product of art, is a matter for experts, to whom I delegate it.

Now, as regards the theatrical representation of *Don Juan* by the singers, it can surely turn out to the composer's satisfaction only extremely seldom in our theatres. Vocal music is a kind of language agreed upon by mankind, and as a language it must therefore be made articulate to the human ear with clearness and decision. A pure and intelligible pronunciation of the words written down by the poet to convey the character's sentiments and reinforced with musical expression by the composer, is the singer's first care, and the more so, the more force and vigour the composer and poet have imparted to those words. Without this clear and comprehensible language the finest voice of a singer is nothing but an instrument giving forth notes, but no words, an agreeable nightingale's throat at best, not a human voice ; and human song is a very different thing from that of a nightingale. The former has articulated sounds to express feeling—words ; the latter only inarticulate sounds. Human song must therefore make itself understood by words, or it is a mere nothing, and no one is entitled to be called a singer who is not aware of this. Nightingales' runs and larks' trills, an unnatural emphasis on and biting off of notes and syllables, rope-dancer's leaps with the voice, wondrously odd conglomerations of sound, *con naso obligato*, and musical somersaults are not singing ; the truthful and emphatic expression of feeling is.

Without this outpouring of true, generous sentiment all song is dead jingling, soulless clanging, and without it music like Mozart's cannot be interpreted and made to penetrate the hearer's soul at all. It is, as I said, born of feeling, and feeling alone can reproduce it. His notes are not just to be trilled ; they have to be expressed and made sensuous with precision, spirit and animation. They must be thought out and felt deeply. The rules of declamation have to be understood if one is to put one's whole soul into the composer's meaning. The voice must float gently along on the stream of the accompaniment, without being submerged and drowned ; it must not scream away above the accompanying instruments and, instead of delighting our ear, hack and tear it with squeaking and cracked sounds.

With these remarks on the power and expression of singing I have no wish to offend anybody who sang in the performance of *Don Juan* on the Hamburg stage. They are remarks about the general state of singing in Germany. That which is called expression in song and penetration into the spirit and personality of the characters, as represented by the composer, is extremely rare in all our opera houses. Nearly everywhere singers make such a wintry approach towards song as though they had been brought up at Spitzbergen and had had their hearts chilled and their feelings turned to a rigid January frost in Nova Zembla's eternal ice. To be fair to the local singers, they at least did everything in their power to do justice to *Mozart's* glorious achievement. And if something of my remarks on singing and song interpretation has gone home, of which they may say with Lessing's Lisidor in *Der Freigeist* " That was aimed at me ", well, all the better ! My recollections will then not have been entirely scattered to the winds, and I shall enjoy the pleasure of having done a good deed.

Vol. II, pp. 320-30.—Freisauff. *Op. cit.*, p. 51. Jahn Vol. II, p. 360 (excerpts).
—For Schink *cf.* end of 1782 and beginning of 1785. He seems to forget that
Mozart had set an Italian libretto.—Novaya Zemlya is a pair of islands in the
Arctic Ocean.—Lessing's play *Der Freigeist* had appeared in 1755.

ANTON SCHMITH IN MOZART'S ALBUM

(all in Latin)

PALLAS IN LOVDON IN MOZART REGNAT APOLLO, VIVET VTERQVE INGENS ARTE PER AEVA SVA.

[Pallas reigns in Laudon, Apollo in Mozart.
Each shall live, great in his art throughout his life.]

[Vienna,] 31 October 1789.   Your sincere friend
                                                     Ant. Schmith, Med. Dr.

Engl, *op. cit.*—The chronogram yields the year 1789, which is in accordance
with the conquest of Belgrade by Laudon on 9 October 1789 (see beginning
of 1788). This and perhaps the undated entry inserted at the end of 1789
were the only ones in Mozart's album not dating from 1787.—Dr. Anton
Schmith was an enthusiastic violinist, who in 1815 joined the committee
of the new Gesellschaft der Musikfreunde in Vienna ; he was one of the
first to recognize Schubert's gifts. He later settled at Kiev. Further details
about him are to be found in the English edition of O. E. Deutsch's Schubert
biography, London, 1946, New York, 1947. Also in the same writer's lecture,
" Ein vergessener Freund Mozarts ", printed in the *Mozart-Jahrbuch 1960*, Salzburg, 1961.

On 9 November Martín y Soler's opera *Il burbero di buon cuore* was revived at the
Burgtheater, with the addition of two new soprano arias by Mozart.

The first performance of this opera took place at the same theatre on 4 January
1786.—The two arias, " Chi sà, chi sà, qual sia " (K. 582) and " Vado, ma
dove ? " (K. 583) were again written for Dlle. Villeneuve (*cf.* 6 September
1789).

On 16 November Mozart's fifth child, Anna Maria, was born ; she died an hour
later of cramp.

Blümml, *op. cit.*, p. 8.—The clergy of the Church Am Hof was only able to
administer an emergency baptism. The child was buried on 17 November,
probably in the cemetery outside the Matzleinsdorf Line.

FROM THE " MUSIKALISCHE REAL-ZEITUNG ", SPEYER, 25 NOVEMBER 1789

Cassel, 14 October.

Our usual winter concert was resumed on the 6th of this month . . . It
is held each Tuesday, begins at 6 o'clock and goes on till half-past 8 . . .
The symphonies are by *Haydn, Pleyl, Wranizky, Mozart* . . .

Vol. II, No. 47, col. 374 f.—The symphonies were played at the beginning
and end of these concerts, each probably being divided into two parts.

On 25 November *Figaro* was given in German at Mainz.

Annalen des Theaters (Berlin, 1790,) No. 5, p. 70 : "pleased very much". The translation was probably that by Vulpius, which had been in use at Frankfurt since 11 October 1788.

FROM THE " MUSIKALISCHE REAL-ZEITUNG ", SPEYER, 25 NOVEMBER 1789

Continuation of the " Philosophical Fragments on Practical Music " published in Vienna.

. . . The sixth essay concedes only that it is possible to become a good particular composer, and denies that there are good universal composers. Why did the man not think of *Joseph Haydn*, who after all daily walks about in *Vienna* in front of his very eyes ? Why did not *Gassemann*, *Vogler*, the younger *Mozart* occur to him, and a hundred others, who so surely may claim the title of universal composer, and indeed of a good one ?

. . . . .

The eighth and ninth essays deal with the name of a virtuoso and with young, premature virtuosi . . . What is more, the V. [*Verfasser*=author] has not considered the fact that not all premature virtuosi are immature virtuosi, else what would have become of *Hendel*, and what of *Wolfgang Mozart* ?

Vol. II, No. 48, col. 378.—These extracts from the book published in Vienna in 1787 began on 25 November and continued until 9 December. The preface to the book, published at the expense of the Deaf-and-Dumb Institute, is signed " A. W. S.", *i.e.*, Amand Wilhelm Smith, who was presumably the author referred to in the extracts. Although Mozart's name is not among those of the subscribers, a copy of the book was found among his estate (No. 17 in the list of his books).

On 30 November *Don Giovanni* was given in German at Graz.

POSTER OF A CONCERT GIVEN BY THE SOCIETY OF MUSICIANS
(in German and Italian)

Musical Concert. / Today, Tuesday, 22 December 1789. / will be held at the I. & R. National Court Theatre / by the / Established Society of Musicians / for the / Benefit of its Widows and Orphans / a / *Grand Musical Concert*, / at which a Cantata composed by Herr Vinzenz / *Righini*, Hofkapellmeister of his Electoral Highness / at Mainz, will be sung, entitled : / *Das Geburtsfest des Apoll.*

The singers will be : Mademoiselle Kavalieri. Herr Kalvesi. / Madame Hofer. Herr Saal.

Between the two Parts of the Cantata a Quintet by Herr / *Mozart* will be given, in which the principal players will be Herr *Stadler*, / I. & R. Court Musician, and Herr *Zistler*, in actual service of / Prince Krasalkowitz.

The music, counting both instruments and voices, will be / performed by more than 180 persons.

. . . . .

To begin at 7 o'clock.

Copy in possession of the Gesellschaft der Musikfreunde, Vienna.—Otto Schneider, *Mozart in Wirklichkeit* (Vienna, 1955), p. 334 (facsimile).—The announcement is in Italian and German. (When the cantata *Il natale d' Apollo* was repeated on 23 December, a trio for clarinet, flute and bassoon by François Devienne was performed, Anton Stadler again playing the clarinet ; see Pohl, *Tonkünstler-Societät*, p. 63.)—The last Elector of Mainz was Friedrich Karl Joseph, Baron Erthal, in whose palace Mozart gave a concert on 20 October 1790.—Josepha Hofer, *née* Weber, Mozart's sister-in-law, had been a member of the Theater auf der Wieden, in the Starhemberg Freihaus, since early 1789 ; she had been engaged by Johann Friedel, who had in the meantime been succeeded by Schikaneder. Righini, of whose cantata (first performed in 1781) Mozart had a poor opinion, had taught her from 1783 to 1785.—Mozart had written the clarinet quintet in A major (K. 581) for Stadler.—Joseph Zistler, formerly in the service of Joseph, Prince Batthyány, Cardinal and Primate of Hungary, was a violinist in the orchestra of Prince Anton Grassalkovics at Bratislava.

FROM THE "WIENER ZEITUNG", 27 DECEMBER 1789

New Music.

At Hofmeister's music, art and book establishment Am Hof are to be had, along with numerous other musical publications, the following quite new works in particular :

.   .   .   .   .

12 Minuets from the I. & R. Assembly Room, by Herr Mozart, quite newly arranged for 7 instruments. 1 fl. 30 kr.
The same for the pianoforte   40 kr.

Franz Anton Hoffmeister, like Leopold Kozeluch a publisher as well as a composer, had founded his own publishing-house five years before ; it issued mainly chamber music.—The minuets by Mozart, which were probably distributed only in manuscript parts and in pianoforte score, may have been those of December 1789 (K. 585), originally written for two violins and bass only, but to which were later added parts for timpani and the wind instruments usually employed in the Assembly Hall dances.

On 30 December a domestic concert at Mozart's was cancelled.

In this chamber concert the violinist Zistler (see 22 December) was to take part, and Puchberg was to be in the audience.

On 31 December there was a "little opera rehearsal" for *Così fan tutte* at Mozart's.

Haydn and Puchberg were invited, and probably also came.

Don Giovanni was given in German at Brno during December.

About New Year 1790 *Figaro* was given in German at Bonn ; see Reichard's *Theater-Kalender* for 1791, p. 199. (The translation by Vulpius had already been printed at Cologne in 1787.) According to that calendar (1790, p. 131) a German performance of *Don Giovanni* had also been planned at Pest by that time, but it did not materialize until 1797, or even 1801 (Loewenberg, *op. cit.*, p. 224).

FROM THE " CALENDRIER MUSICAL UNIVERSEL ", PARIS, 1789
(in French)

Sonata for four hands for the pianoforte by Monsieur A. Mozart : 14th work, Price 3 liv[res] 12 s[ols]. at de Roullede's.

P. 239.—Eduard Reeser, *De klaviersonate met vioolbegeleiding* (Rotterdam, 1939), p. 32. William S. Newman in *Notes*, Washington, March 1954, p. 204. King, *op. cit.*, pp. 109 ff.—Wolfgang Rehm in the Critical Commentary to the *Neue Mozart-Ausgabe*, IX/24/Section 2, pp. 62 ff.—*Cf.* September 1789. King dates the series of the *Calendrier* collected in 1789, which includes p. 239, between 20 November 1787 and 15 December 1788. He doubts whether Roullede's " œuv. 14ᵉ " is KE. 19d and suspects that it was rather the C major sonata (K. 521).

JOSEPH VON BAUERNFELD IN MOZART'S ALBUM [? 1789]

The album's purpose is adornment !
Thou needest none above thine own.
For he who ever does his duty
And wraps his life in naught but beauty,
Who virtue seeks and vice eschews
And who, like thee, what's good pursues :
True joy in life has he alone
And he's the album's fair adornment.

Joseph Edler von Bauernfeld

This leaf was undated.—Bauernfeld, a fellow-mason of Mozart's, was the sleeping partner who financed Emanuel and Eleonore Schikaneder when they took over the Freihaus Theatre (*cf.* 22 December 1789) after Johann Friedel's death in the spring of 1789.

1790

FROM THE " MUSIKALISCHE REAL-ZEITUNG ", SPEYER, 6 JANUARY 1790

Review

Two German Arias to be sung at the Pianoforte, set to music by Herr Kapellmeister W. A. Mozart. Part II. Vienna, Artaria. (Price 30 kr.)

The songs are the following : " Ein Veilchen auf der Wiese stand " and the Song of Farewell, entitled : " Die Engel Gottes weinen ". Both are set to music throughout, and treated with insight, taste and fine feeling. From among the mass of settings with which the former song has already been honoured and dishonoured, the reviewer is unacquainted with any but that by the late Kapellmeister *Schweizer* which could be set side by side with the present one. Very surprising and uncommonly fine is the treatment of the text at the end, where Herr *M.* at the close of the third verse once more repeats the words :

Poor violet !

It was a darling violet.

and then ends with them. Would that such songs were studied by many a rising song composer as models for good vocal writing and pure harmony.*

Z.

* Fine things of this kind are especially suited to our anthology, and we shall therefore include one of these songs, " Das Veilchen ", in our next issue. D. H.

Col. 1.—K. 476 and 519 had appeared on 5 September 1789.—Goethe's " Veilchen " had so far been set to music, among others, by Johann André, the Duchess Anna Amalia of Saxe-Weimar, Philipp Christoph Kayser, Karl David Stegman, Joseph Anton Steffan, Karl Friberth, J. F. Reichardt and Anton Schweitzer ; but not all these settings had yet been printed. (*Cf.* Max Friedlaender in the *Jahrbuch*, Vol. XVII, p. 181, and in the *Schriften der Goethe-Gesellschaft*, Weimar, Vol. XI, pp. 133 ff., Vol. XXXI, p. 228.) Mozart's estate included Part iii of the *Sammlung deutscher Lieder für das Klavier* (Vienna, 1780), containing Friberth's setting ; that by Steffan had already appeared in 1778 in Part i, where the poem was erroneously ascribed to Gleim, who had written another entitled " Veilchen im Hornung ", also composed by Steffan. (Mozart was not deceived by this, as has often been asserted.)—According to the announcement of Bossler, the editor (" D.H."), " Das Veilchen " was reprinted on 13 January 1790 in the *Musikalische Anthologie für Kenner und Liebhaber*, the " practical section " of the *Real-Zeitung*, also called *Anthologie zur musikalischen Realzeitung* (Vol. I, No. vii, p. 5).

On 21 January 1790 the first orchestral rehearsal for *Così fan tutte* was held at the Burgtheater.

Haydn and Puchberg were to call for Mozart at 10 a.m. to go to this rehearsal, and they probably did so.

BURGTHEATER POSTER, 26 JANUARY 1790

New Singspiel.

At the I. & R. National Court Theatre
is to be performed today, Tuesday, 26 January 1790 :
(for the first time)

COSI FAN TUTTE,

o sia :

LA SCUOLA DEGLI AMANTI.

So machen sie's, oder : die Schule der Liebhaber.

A comic Singspiel in two Acts.

The poetry is by Herr Abbé da Ponte, Poet to the Italian Singspiel at the I. & R. Court Theatre. The music is by Herr Wolfgang Mozart, Kapellmeister in actual service of His Majesty the Emperor.

———

The librettos, Italian only, are to be had of the Box Master at 24 kr.

M.—12 *a*

Vienna, National Library.—The cast was : Fiordiligi—Adriana Ferrarese del
Bene ; Dorabella—Louise Villeneuve ; Despina—Dorotea Bussani ; Ferrando
—Vincenzio Calvesi ; Guglielmo—Francesco Benucci ; Don Alfonso—Francesco Bussani.—The opera was performed on 26, 28 and 30 January, 7 and 11
February, 6 and 12 June, 6 and 16 July and 7 (not 17) August 1790 ; then no
more in Mozart's lifetime (and not again in Italian until 1850, in the Kärntnertor
Theatre).—As we lack the account books of the Court Theatres for 1789-90,
it is not possible to tell precisely how much Mozart and Da Ponte were paid
outright. According to Mozart's letter to Puchberg of 29 December 1789, he
appears to have received 200 ducats, which would have been twice the usual
amount.

TITLE-PAGE OF THE LIBRETTO OF " COSÌ FAN TUTTE "

COSI FAN TUTTE,
O SIA
LA SCUOLA DEGLI AMANTI.

DRAMMA GIOCOSO
IN DUE ATTI
DA RAPPRESENTARSI
NEL TEATRO DI CORTE L' ANNO 1790.
VIENNA
PRESSO LA SOCIETÀ TIPOGRAFICA

[On page 2 :]
La poesia è dell' Abbate Da Ponte, Poeta del Teatro Imperiale. / La musica
è del Signor Wolfgango Mozzart Maestro di / Cappella in / actual servigio
di S. Maestà Cesarea.

Two copies in the City Library, Vienna.—Teuber, *op. cit.*, p. 83.

FROM ZINZENDORF'S DIARY, 26 JANUARY 1790
(in French)

. . . Before 7 o'clock to the new Opera. *Cosi fan tutte*, osia *la Scuola degli
Amanti.* The music by Mozart is charming, and the subject rather amusing.

This was the first and last time that the Count deigned to praise Mozart unreservedly.

FROM THE " WIENER ZEITUNG ", 30 JANUARY 1790

At the I. & R. National Court Theatre a new comic Singspiel in two acts
was performed for the first time last Wednesday, the 16th inst., entitled :
Cosi fan tutte, o sia : la Scuola degli Amanti. The poetry is by the Herr
Abbé da Ponte, poet to the Italian Singspiel at the I. & R. Court Theatre,
and the music by Herr Wolfgang Mozart, Kapellmeister in actual service
of H. Maj. the Emperor.

" Wednesday the 16th " should read " Tuesday the 26th ".

Vienna, 17 [*recte* 27] January 1790. I can again announce an excellent work by Mozart to you, which has been taken up by our theatre. Yesterday, that is, it was given for the first time at the I. & R. National Theatre. It is entitled *Cosi fan tutte, o sia, la Scuola degli Amanti*. The libretto is by the Herr Abbé Da Ponte, poet to the Italian Singspiel at the I. & R. Court Theatre. That the music is by Mozart says, I believe, everything.

P. 148.

JOSEPH HAYDN TO MARIA ANNA VON GENZINGER

Estoras, 9 February 1790

. . . I could sleep little, even my dreams pursued me; then just as I dreamed I was hearing the opera *le Nozze di Figaro* most splendidly, the horrid North wind woke me up and nearly blew my nightcap off my head. . . .

> Original in the National Library, Vienna.—Theodor von Karajan, *J. Haydn in London 1791 und 1792* (Vienna, 1861).—Frau Genzinger, Haydn's Vienna friend, was the wife of the doctor Peter Leopold, Edler von Genzinger; Mozart too is said to have played occasionally in their salon in the Schottenhof.—*Figaro* had probably not then been performed in Esterháza (Estoras). The score and vocal parts had, it is true, been purchased on 7 January 1789, and Pietro Travaglia's account for the sets is dated 8 August 1789 (Esterházy Archives in the National Museum, Budapest). For Travaglia cf. 6 September 1791 (*La clemenza di Tito*).

FROM THE "MUSIKALISCHE REAL-ZEITUNG", SPEYER, 17 FEBRUARY 1790

Life Story of Herr Justin Heinrich Knecht . . . Musical Director of the Free City of Biberach.

. . . For the stage at Biberach *Knecht* wrote several operettas, which however were not printed. *Die treuen Köhler, der Erndtekranz, die Entführung aus dem Serail* deserve mention above the others because of the happy rivalry of *Wolf, Hiller* and *Mozart*. It may be assumed that most readers of these news are well aware that the works by these three composers bearing these titles distinguish themselves particularly among the rest of the works of their genius . . . By means of his treatment of the meagre text of the *Entführung* Mozart provided the informed public with evidence of the worthiness of his aspirations to the post of Kapellmeister . . .

> Vol. I, No. 7, col. 52.—Ernst Wilhelm Wolf composed his singspiel *Die treuen Köhler* in 1773, Johann Adam Hiller his popular *Ärndtekranz* in 1771.

Thalia, a monthly for lovers of the violin, furnishes a tasteful selection of especially fine arias and overtures from our latest and most favoured operas, for 2 violins, viola and bass . . . The first number contains the following arias from the excellent Mozart opera *Belmont und Konstanze* : 1. " O wie will ich triumphiren ". 2. " Durch Zärtlichkeit und Schmeicheln." 3. Minuet. 4. " Frisch zum Kampfe, frisch zum Streite." . . . Speyer, 10 February 1790.

> *Ibid.*, col. 65.—*Cf.* 2 June 1790.

New Music.

From Artaria Comp., art dealers in the Kohlmarkt, the following best arias . . ., well transcribed for the pianoforte and clearly engraved, are to be had :

.   .   .   .   .

From the new Opera : *Cosi fan tutte*, by Herr Mozart, that most beautiful Duetto : " Il Core vi dono bel Idolo mio ". 20 kr.

> The duet (No. 23) for Dorabella and Guglielmo appeared as No. 73 in Artaria's *Raccolta d' arie*. Apart from this the only extract printed in Mozart's lifetime was the pianoforte score of the overture (No. 58 of the same collection).

On 20 February Joseph II died.

> His brother Leopold, Grand Duke of Tuscany, became his successor as Roman Emperor and ruler of Austria.

In February a reprint of a pianoforte score of the country dance " La Bataille " (K. 535) appeared in Bossler's *Bibliothek der Grazien. Eine Monatsschrift für Gesang und Klavier* at Speyer.

> Vol. II, No. 2, pp. 38 f.—See 19 March 1788 and 17 January 1789.

(in English)

A new comic opera was last night produced at this theatre . . . The music of it is evidently a melange though announced as the composition of Bianchi and Hogart. Martini has certainly contributed a share, and most of the airs given to the new tenor are from Painello. The general character of such music must be, of course, that it abounds in good passages but it must also prove extremely unequal.

> Communicated by Christopher Raeburn. At the King's Theatre, Haymarket, a pasticcio with the title of *La vilanella rapita* had been performed on 27 February (not Bianchi's opera of that name, which had been given at the Vienna Burgtheater on 25 November 1785 with two extra numbers by

Mozart). "Hogart" should read "Mozart" : Ann Storace sang Susanna's aria "Deh vieni non tardar" from *Figaro* and Zerlina's "Batti, batti" from *Don Giovanni*. Other musical numbers were evidently by Martín y Soler ("Martini") and Paisiello ("Painello").

On 8 March, at Covent Garden Theatre in London, William Shield's comic opera *The Czar Peter* was produced, in the second act of which John Bannister and Elizabeth Billington sang the duet for Don Giovanni and Zerlina, "Là ci darem la mano".

> Alfred Loewenberg in *Music & Letters*, London, July 1943.—The words fitted to the duet were "Should worldly cares oppressing / Encircle us with woes . . .".

On 13 March Leopold II arrived in Vienna.

On 9 April Mozart performed at Count Hadik's the divertimento in E♭ major for string trio (K. 563) and the clarinet quintet in A major (K. 581).

> The count was probably Johann Karl, Councillor to the Hungarian Exchequer, a gifted amateur painter, and the eldest son of Field-Marshal Andreas Hadik, who died on 12 March 1790. Johann Baptist von Häring (see end of 1782), a banker and an able violinist (who in 1807 founded the Amateur Concerts of the Nobility in Vienna), took part, as probably did also Anton Stadler, for whom the quintet was written. Mozart invited Puchberg to attend ; it was for him that he had written the trio.

FROM THE "MUSIKALISCHE REAL-ZEITUNG", SPEYER, 14 APRIL 1790

VI English Dances for the Clavier or Fortepiano by Herr Vanhal. Vienna, at Artaria's. Pp. 5, oblong fol. (Pr[ice] 24 kr.)

VI likewise by Herr Mozart. Also Pp. 5, oblong fol. (Pr[ice] 24 kr.)

Both authors have long been known by larger products, and even these small leaves do not diminish the fame they have won thereby. Among the set by M., characteristic dance music is also included, No. 3, *e.g.* being "La Tempete", and No. 6, "La Bataille". The pianoforte score is very meagre in places.

> Vol. I, No. 15, col. 118.—Johann Baptist Vanhal (Wanhall) came from Bohemia and lived in Vienna as a prolific composer.—Mozart's "English Dances" are the *VI Contretaenze*, which had been published by Artaria on 17 January 1789 (K. 462 No. 3, 534, 535 and 535a). K. 534, "Das Donnerwetter" is called "La Tempête" in this edition, and K. 535 "La Bataille".

On 19 April Genoveva Weber sang Constanze in *Die Entführung* at Meiningen.

> She sang the same rôle in Weimar on 16 June 1794. She died in Salzburg on 13 March 1798 and was buried there in Leopold Mozart's grave in the St. Sebastian cemetery. Nissen was placed in the same grave in 1826. *Cf.* 20 August 1785 and 8 January 1787.

FROM THE "MUSIKALISCHE REAL-ZEITUNG", SPEYER, 28 APRIL 1790

Catalogue raisonné.

. . . *Grand Quintetto per due Violini, due Viole & Violoncello del Signor Mozart.* Vienna, at Artaria's, in fol. (Pr[ice] 2 fl.).

Is worked with much diligence and taste, and, so far as may be judged by ear, according to the strict rules of composition. The theme is to be found in the Anth[ology], p. 70. . . .

> Vol. I, No. 15, col. 137.—The C major string quintet (K. 515) had been published by Artaria in 1789. The theme is in the first volume of the *Musikalische Anthologie* (p. 70).

* FROM ZINZENDORF'S DIARY, 1 MAY 1790
(in French)

. . . to the theatre. Source of melancholy. *Le nozze di Figaro.*

IBID., 7 MAY 1790
(in French)

. . . At the Opera *le Nozze di Figaro*. The duet for the two women and the rondo for la Ferraresi continue to please.

> The Letter Duet was sung by Cavalieri (the Countess) and Ferrarese (Susanna) ; the rondo is " Al desio di chi t'adora " (K. 577, see 29 August 1789).

Mozart visited Schwechat on a Sunday in mid-May (? 16th).

> For Schwechat cf. 22 September 1773. Mozart visited the parents of the young musician Joseph Eybler there (see 30 September 1790), who is said to have assisted him with the rehearsals for *Così fan tutte.*—Constanze, who was again undergoing a cure at Baden, was to come to Vienna for a short time and go to Schwechat with her husband. Eybler's father was a schoolmaster and choirmaster.

On 22 May the string quartets in D major (K. 575) and B flat major (K. 589) were performed at Mozart's lodgings.

> These were the first two of the quartets (Mozart's last) written for Frederick William II (K. 575, 589 and 590) ; cf. 26 May, 1789.—Puchberg and his wife were invited to this musical evening.

MOZART'S TESTIMONIAL FOR JOSEPH EYBLER

I, the undersigned, attest herewith that I have found the bearer of this, Herr Joseph Eybler, to be a worthy pupil of his famous master Albrechtsberger, a well-grounded composer, equally skilled in chamber music and the church style, fully experienced in the art of song, also an accomplished organ and clavier player, in short a young musician such, one can only regret, as so seldom has his equal.

Vienna, 30 May 1790.   Wolfgang Amadè Mozart
                                        Kapellmeister in Imperial Service.

> Vienna, National Library.—Jahn, Vol. II, p. 647.—A few days later, on 8 June, Haydn gave Eybler a similar testimonial ; but not until 24 January 1793 did his teacher, Albrechtsberger, do likewise. (These two testimonials are also in the National Library, Vienna.) In 1792 Eybler became choirmaster of

the Carmelite Church in the Leopoldstadt suburb, then Court Kapellmeister in succession to Salieri, and finally he was ennobled.

HAYDN TO MARIA ANNA VON GENZINGER

Estoras, 30 May 1790.

. . . this time too will pass, and that will return in which I shall have the inestimable pleasure of sitting at the clavier beside your gracious self, to hear you play Mozart's master pieces, and to kiss your hands for so many beautiful things . . .

Vienna, National Library.—Karajan, *op. cit.*

In May Mozart attended the opera *Der Fall ist noch weit seltner !* at the Freihaus Theatre.

The text of this German sequel to the Da Ponte-Martín opera *Una cosa rara* was by Schikaneder and the music by the tenor Benedikt Schack ; it was first performed on 10 May. Mozart reported to his wife at Baden that this work had not pleased him as much as " the Antons "—a reference to *Der dumme Gärtner aus dem Gebürge oder Die zween Anton*, a comic opera by Schikaneder with music by Schack and the bass Franz Xaver Gerl, which had entered the repertory there on 12 July 1789. A song from the first of the six sequels, *Die verdeckten Sachen*, inspired Mozart in March 1791 to write the pianoforte variations K. 613.

In the same month Mozart drafted a petition to Archduke Franz for a recommendation to the emperor, his father, for the post of second Kapellmeister to the court.

The undated draft, supposed to have been written early in May, is in the Mozarteum at Salzburg ; whether the petition was ever sent is uncertain, but at any rate nothing came of it. Mozart mentioned that Salieri was not as familiar with the church style as himself ; he also recommended himself for the post of music teacher to the Court on account of his virtuosity on the keyboard. Joseph II had appointed Salieri music teacher to Franz's first betrothed, Elisabeth of Württemberg.—Mozart's application reveals an awareness of the following points of etiquette : to call an Austrian archduke " Your Royal Highness " had been customary from the time of Maria Theresa. Since Leopold II was not elected Emperor until 30 September 1790, his highest title at this time was only that of King (of Bohemia and Hungary), nor did his family hold more than royal rank.

FROM THE " MUSIKALISCHE REAL-ZEITUNG ", SPEYER, 2 JUNE 1790

At Councillor Bossler's publishing-house at Speyer the 4th issue of *Thalie*, or the Monthly for Quartet Lovers, has appeared, and contains : (1) the *Ouverture* to the opera *Le Nozze di Figaro* . . .

Vol. I, No. 22, col. 176.—*Cf.* 17 February and 23 June 1790.

Early in June Mozart probably went to stay with Constanze at Baden.

On about 6 June he may have gone to stay there for a few weeks, returning to Vienna only for odd days.

FROM THE " WIENER ZEITUNG ", 9 JUNE 1790

Announcement.

At Lausch's music establishment, at present in the Weihburggasse, No. 959, opposite the Violin Maker's, is to be had :

Mozart, Sonata for 4 hands on one pianoforte   2 fl.

> This sonata cannot be identified with any certainty. Unless only a manuscript copy is meant, it may have been the F major sonata (K. 497), which had been published by Artaria on 19 December 1787 at 2 fl.

On 12 June Mozart conducted *Così fan tutte* at the Burgtheater.

> After five performances in January and February the opera was revived on 6 June and given three more times in July and August : ten performances in all.

On Sunday 13 June a mass by Mozart was sung in the parish church at Baden.

> The choirmaster there was Anton Stoll, with whom Mozart (and later Haydn) entered into friendly relations.—The mass was presumably that in C major, the so-called Coronation Mass (K. 317).—Mozart may not have returned from Vienna in time.

FROM THE " MUSIKALISCHE REAL-ZEITUNG ", SPEYER, 23 JUNE 1790

The June issue of the *Grazienbibliothek* contains . . . the overture to *Le Nozze di Figaro* by Herr *A. Mozart.*

> Vol. I, No. 25, col. 200.—*Cf.* 2 June 1790.—The monthly series was actually entitled *Bibliothek der Grazien.*

FROM A CATALOGUE OF THE LONDON PUBLISHER JOHN BLAND,
25 JUNE 1790
(in English)

The Public will be pleased to take notice . . . that in a Journey of more than 4000 Miles in Germany, &c, (last Year) he personally settled a Connexion with Haydn, Hoffmeister, Mozart, Kozeluch, Paradies, Vanhall, and many others, whose Works will come out with all possible Expedition. And they may be assured all the new Works will be original, and published for such Instruments, &c. as first written for.

> Copy at the Royal College of Music, London.—Communicated by Dr. Edith Schnapper, Cambridge.—Bland, who had published music since about 1776 and was in the habit of precisely dating his catalogues (which were sometimes thematic), had already paid a four months' visit to the Continent in the autumn of 1788 and a second visit in the autumn of 1789, each time in order to negotiate with composers. Haydn, whom he visited at Esterháza early in November 1789, with the additional purpose of inviting him to London, stayed with him for the first day of his London visit in 1791 and gave him his *Stabat Mater* and the cantata *Arianna a Naxos* to publish. He published no original work by Mozart, whom he may also have visited in the autumn of 1789.

On 26 June the Toscani-Müller company performed *Don Giovanni* in German at Soest.

On the same day *Figaro* had to be cancelled at the Burgtheater owing to the illness of Benucci (the Figaro).

In the summer of 1790 Mozart was among those present when Johann Georg Albrechtsberger, the court organist, tried out the new organ by Franz Xaver Chrismann at St. Laurence's Church in the Schottenfeld suburb.

> King, *op. cit.*, p. 235.—C. F. Pohl wrote on this event in his articles on Chrismann in the *Allgemeine Deutsche Biographie* (Leipzig, 1876), Vol. IV, pp. 139 f., and in George Grove's *Dictionary of Music and Musicians* (London, 1879), Vol. I, p. 355. He reported in 1876 from a printed programme, the " only copy " of which then existing seems to have been lost, that the court organist played " pieces by Bach, Albrechtsberger, Haydn and Gassmann as well as a free fantasy ". Albrechtsberger and Mozart appear to have described the organ verbally as the best then in Vienna. (Pastor Honorius Ludwig Kraus in the *Denkbuch der Pfarre und Kirche* [Vienna, 1839], p. 9.)—Chrismann, priest and organ builder, also constructed the famous instrument in the St. Florian monastery in Upper Austria. For the Vienna organ he received 4200 gulden (information supplied by the Schottenstift, Vienna).

On 5 July *Don Giovanni* was given in German at Schwerin.

FROM SCHUBART'S " SCHWÄBISCHER MERKUR ", STUTTGART, 12 JULY 1790

Stuttgart. Theatre amusements this week. . . . Friday, 16 July : For the first time, the Singspiel received with so much sensation within and outside Germany : *Die Hochzeit des Figaro*, in four acts. Translated from the Italian into German by the theatre poet Vulpius, with poetic licence. The music is by Mozart, whose name is celebrated all over Germany. He has shown in this piece that his Muse is capable of greater things than working merely for the pianoforte.

> No. 83, p. 178.—Copy in the Württemberg State Library, Stuttgart.—Ernst Holzer, *Schubart als Musiker* (Stuttgart, 1905).—*Cf.* 27 April 1775 and spring 1788.—The first performance had to be postponed from 16 to 23 July.—The preliminary notice was Schubart's own.

IBID., 19 JULY 1790

Stuttgart. Theatre amusements this week. . . . Friday, 23 July. For the first time : *Die Hochzeit des Figaro*, a play in 4 acts. Also a Dance and a Ballet connected with it.

                                            The Theatre Directorate.

> No. 86, p. 188.

FROM THE " MUSIKALISCHE KORRESPONDENZ DER TEUTSCHEN FILARMONISCHEN GESELLSCHAFT " (SPEYER, BOSSLER), 28 JULY 1790

Extract from a Letter from Vienna of 5 July 1790.

[Concerning Joseph II's domestic music, as organized by his valet Johann Kilian Strack and his first violinist Franz Kreibich.]

. . . But why these gentlemen kept the door shut upon a *Haydn*, a *Mozart*, a *Kozeluch*, a *Pleyel* and other worthy men, and upon their artistic products, I shall not try to decide. Suffice it to say that Joseph never heard a note by these meritorious composers ; but all the more by such as are not worthy to unloose their shoe's latchets.

> No. 4, cols. 27-31.—The *Korrespondenz* was the continuation of the *Real-Zeitung*.—The Director of Chamber Music, Franz Kreibich (who played first violin), and J. K. Strack are said to have kept Haydn's string quartets out of the Emperor's music-room, as well as Mozart's chamber music, and Salieri did nothing to obstruct them (Pohl, *Haydn*, Vol. II, pp. 25 and 111 f.).—Mozart had met Strack at Hickel's in 1781 (see 15 October 1781) and thought he had made a friend of him. He lived in the Graben, No. 585, where Mozart repeatedly visited him in 1782.—Ignaz Pleyel, a very successful Austrian composer and a pupil of Haydn, was at that time Kapellmeister at Strasbourg Cathedral.

In July 1790 Mozart finished the new orchestration of Handel's *Alexander's Feast* (K. 591) and *Ode for St. Cecilia's Day* (K. 592).

> It is to be supposed that both works were soon afterwards privately performed in van Swieten's Society of Noblemen, under Mozart's direction ; but where and when is not known. Zinzendorf mentions performances of *Alexander's Feast* on 10 March 1771 and 15 March 1772 ; Gluck told Burney in Vienna in 1772 that the St. Cecilia Ode had already been performed there once in Italian.

FROM THE " WIENER ZEITUNG ", 21 AUGUST 1790
(partly in Italian)

At the art establishment of Artaria & Co., in the Kohlmarkt, the following pieces are to be had, quite new :

.   .   .   .   .

Mozart, Grand Quintet for 2 violins, 2 violas and violoncello. No. 2   2 fl.

> The string quintet in G minor (K. 516) was the second of the three of which Mozart had offered copies to subscribers on 2 April 1788.

On 29 August a daughter, Josepha, was born to the Hofers.

> Joseph von Bauernfeld was her godfather. She became a singer and, although married to the Stock Exchange Commissary Karl Hönig, was a member of the Kärntnertor Theatre from 1814 to 1824.

On 11 September Schikaneder's opera *Der Stein der Weisen, oder Die Zauberinsel* [" The Philosophers' Stone, or The Magic Island "] was performed at the Freihaus Theatre, with the duet " Nun, liebes Weibchen " (K. 625), which is attributed to Mozart.

> The music of this " heroic-comic " opera was by Schack, Gerl and the Kapellmeister of the theatre, Johann Baptist Henneberg. It seems probable that Mozart merely orchestrated this duet (Act II, Sc. 4), sung by Schikaneder and Gerl's wife Barbara.

On 14 September *Figaro* was performed in German in Berlin.

> The Italian and German libretto shows that the translation by Vulpius was used (see 11 October 1788).—The work was praised by the critics, but the

public preferred the operas of Martín y Soler and Dittersdorf (see 2 October 1790).

On 23 September Mozart and his brother-in-law Hofer set out for Frankfurt on Main for the coronation of Leopold II.

> In their own carriage, and changing post horses, they travelled by way of Eferding, Regensburg, Nuremberg, Würzburg and Aschaffenburg.

FROM THE " REGENSBURGISCHES DIARIUM ODER WÖCHENTLICHE FRAG- UND ANZEIGE NACHRICHTEN ", END OF SEPTEMBER 1790

The 25th [Sept. : Entered by the East Gate :] *per posta* Herr Mozart, Roy. Hung. Kapellmeister, with 2, lodg. at The White Lamb.

> Erich Valentin in the *Neues Mozart-Jahrbuch* (Regensburg, 1942), Vol. II, pp. 162 f.—" With 2 " means with two persons : Mozart had also taken a servant with him.

At 1 p.m. on 28 September they arrived at Frankfurt, where they at first put up at an inn ; two days later they moved into private lodgings.

FROM THE 20TH LIST OF VISITORS, EDITED BY THE BOOKSELLER FRIEDRICH EHSLINGER, FRANKFURT ON MAIN, 29 SEPTEMBER 1790

Herr Mozart, Royal Capellmeister of Vienna, Steinweg, E. N. 221, The White Swan.

> P. 80.—Copy in the Prince Waldburg-Zeil Archives, Schloss Zeil.—Supplied by Ernst Fritz Schmid.—The inn was in the Steinweg (now No. 12, a new building), on the corner of the Theaterplatz. According to one tradition Mozart spent his first night in the Three Oxen inn (in what is now the Brückenstrasse), Sachsenhausen, on the left bank of the Main. This may be correct for the night of 29/30. On 30 September Mozart and Hofer moved to the house of theatre director Böhm in the Kalbächer Gasse (No. 167, now No. 10, a new building), where they paid 30 gulden a month. This house is sometimes erroneously described as being on the corner of Töngesgasse and Hasengasse.

At the end of September Mozart saw the play *Lanassa* (see p. 185) performed by Böhm's company, with his symphony in E flat major (K. 184) played as overture.

On 30 September Constanze and Karl removed to the Rauhensteingasse, No. 970 in the Inner City (now Rauhensteingasse 8), 1st floor.

> The house was called the " Little Kaiserhaus ", after the first owners, named Kayser. *Cf.* O. E. Deutsch in the *Österreichische Musikzeitschrift*, Vienna, April 1956.

In the autumn of 1790 *Figaro* was given in Italian at Potsdam.

> Loewenberg, *op. cit.*, p. 211.—The first Berlin performance, on 14 September 1790, was in German.

PROMISSORY NOTE

I, the undersigned, Wolfg. A. Mozart, Court Composer of this place, herewith declare and acknowledge for myself and for my heirs and assigns officially and in due legal form, that Herr Heinrich Lackenbacher, licensed merchant of this place, has lent me at my request and my then need, and paid to me in cash without any deduction whatsoever, a capital of 1,000 fl. (in words one thousand gulden) in assimilated coinage, that is in Imper. Austr. twenty-kreutzer pieces in silver circulated at the twenty-gulden standard at 3 pieces to one Cologne mark in silver. I therefore not only acknowledge herewith due receipt of this loan, but also bind myself and my heirs and assigns to repay this capital to the above-named lender or his heirs and assigns at the end of two years *a dato*, without preliminary notice and in the same coinage described above, without exception of any kind, and in the meantime to pay interest at five per cent in the same currency, which interest to be punctually paid here in Vienna in half-yearly instalments, failing which I am to forfeit the term of repayment of the capital and the lender may at once redemand the same with full interest and costs.

As security for both the capital and the interest I pledge the lender all my goods and chattels.

In witness whereof my and the invited witnesses' own hands. Enacted in Vienna on 1 October 1790.

Mathias Brünner   Anton Heindl   W. A. Mozart.
    as witness   witness

Salzburg, Mozarteum.—Ludwig Karpath in *Der Merker* (Vienna, 1916), pp. 832 f. ; Müller von Asow, *op. cit.*, Vol. III, p. 276.—This promissory note may have been signed only after Mozart's return home, *i.e.* postdated. He wrote to Constanze from Frankfurt on 28 and 30 September 1790 about the unnamed endorser (Hoffmeister ?) and an intermediary whom Anton Stadler was to send to her. Lackenbacher did not appear among the creditors at the end of 1791. No particulars are known about him and the two witnesses. The promissory note is not in Mozart's hand.—*Cf.* 2 April 1789.

On 2 October Mozart dined with the Frankfurt banker Franz Maria Schweitzer.

FROM THE " CHRONIK VON BERLIN ", 2 OCTOBER 1790

National Theatre.

14 Sept. for the first time : *Die Hochzeit des Figaro.* A Singspiel in 4 acts. The music by Mozart. The piece is too well known for its contents to be set forth in detail ; nor has it lost much of the original in its form as an operetta. Mozart is among those extraordinary men whose reputation will endure for centuries. His great genius embraces, so to speak, the whole extent of the art of music : it is rich in ideas ; his works are a river in spate which carries along with it every stream that approaches it. None before him has surpassed him, and posterity will never deny this great man its profound reverence and admiration. To judge him one must be more than a mere connoisseur. What a masterpiece is the music of today ! How interesting for those who understand ; how grand, how overwhelming, how enchanting the harmony ! For the general public too ? That is another question. The only thing one missed was a manly tenor among the principal voices, and it is a great loss that Mozart composed his *Figaro* for a Court at a time when it had good basses but no good tenor . . .

> Vol. VIII, No. 175, pp. 1229-32.—Calvesi was one good tenor active in Vienna in 1786.

On 4 October Leopold II made his ceremonial entry into Frankfurt.

On 5 October the Mainz theatre company performed Dittersdorf's *Die Liebe im Narrenhause* in place of the projected *Don Giovanni* in German.

> *Don Giovanni* was to have been given in Mozart's honour.

On 9 October Leopold II was crowned in the cathedral.

> The music for the Coronation Mass was furnished by the Court Chapel of the Elector of Mainz (see 22 December 1789), who administered the sacraments. It was Righini's *Missa solemnis*, with the soprano solo sung by Margareta Louise Schick, *née* Hamel, of Mainz. She sang the Countess in *Figaro* there, and Righini was the Mainz Court Kapellmeister.—The Emperor had Salieri in his retinue, as at Prague in 1791, while Mozart was merely an onlooker at the coronation.

IBID., 9 OCTOBER 1790

The 16th. [September] *Die Hochzeit des Figaro*, opera, repeated for the first time. The house was not as full as on the day of the first performance, a proof that this grand, heavenly music lies quite beyond the confines of the local public's perceptive faculty ; for it cannot sing this through to itself afterwards, as it can with *Der Baum der Diana* and *Lilla*. The finales, which are a masterpiece of musical art, were excellently performed, and it is astonishing that so many unmusical people fare so well with them.

> Vol. VIII, No. 176, pp. 1244 f.—Martín's *L'arbore di Diana* had been given in Berlin in German since 1789 and his *Cosa rara* (under the title *Lilla*) since 1788. —" Unmusical people " here refers to actors called upon to sing, like Unzelmann as Figaro.

On 12 October Johann Böhm, the director of the company of the electoral theatre at Trier, performed *Die Entführung* at Frankfurt.

> See 29 September 1790.

FROM THE " RATS- UND SCHÖFFENPROTOKOLL DER REICHSSTADT FRANKFURT ZUR WAHL UND KRÖNUNG DES KAISERS LEOPOLD "

Wednesday, 13 October 1790. It being requested that the Imperial Concert-Meister Mozart be given permission to hold a concert to-morrow morning at the Municipal Playhouse : this is to be granted without establishing a precedent for other such cases.

> P. 400.—Jahn, Vol. II, p. 535.—The concert did not take place till 15 October, although it had been planned for the 13th or 14th.

PROGRAMME OF THE FRANKFURT CONCERT

With gracious Permission / Herr Kapellmeister Mozart / will give a
Great / Musical Concert / for his Benefit / today, Friday, 15 October
1790 / in the Great Municipal Playhouse.

Part I

A New Grand Symphony by Herr Mozart. / An Aria, sung by Madame
Schick. / A Concerto on the Forte-piano, played by Herr Kapellmeister /
Mozart, of his own composition. / An Aria, sung by Herr Cecarelli.

Part II

A Concerto by Herr Kapellmeister Mozart of his own com- / position. /
A Duet, sung by Madame Schick and Herr Cecarelli. / A Fantasy impro-
vised by Herr Mozart. / A Symphony.
Each person pays 2 fl. 45 kr. for boxes and stalls. / In the gallery 24 kr.
Tickets are to be had of Herr Mozart, living in the Kahlbechergasse,
No. 167, from Thurs- / day afternoon onwards, and early on Friday of
Herr Scheidweiler, Cashier, at the / Box Office.
To begin at 11 o'clock a.m.

> Salzburg, Mozarteum.—Engel, *op. cit.*, p. 143.—The two pianoforte concertos,
> only the second of which is usually known as the "Coronation Concerto",
> were those in F Major (K. 459) and D major (K. 537). Johann André of
> Offenbach published them both in 1794 with the same notice regarding this
> performance.—For Frau Schick see 9 October 1790, for Ceccarelli see 21
> December 1777. Her vocal pieces cannot with certainty be identified;
> Ceccarelli's aria was perhaps K. 374, but the duet does not appear to have been
> by Mozart.—The symphony, probably performed in two parts at the opening
> and conclusion (*cf.* the following document), was probably one of the three
> published ones, K. 297, 319 or 385. In Wolfgang Rehm's opinion two sym-
> phonies were planned—K. 550 and perhaps K. 551.—The material yield was
> poor.—The second concert at Frankfurt, planned for 17 October, came to
> nothing.

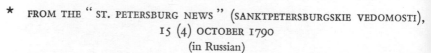

* FROM THE "ST. PETERSBURG NEWS" (SANKTPETERSBURGSKIE VEDOMOSTI),
15 (4) OCTOBER 1790
(in Russian)

Frau Schulz, pupil of Herr Mozart, will have the honour to give a grand
concert on the piano on Wednesday, i.e. 20 (9) October, at the Anichkov
house, wherein she will play one of her own concertos and one of Herr
Mozart's.

> Communicated by Boris Steinpress, Moscow.—About Frau Schulz and her
> relations with Mozart nothing is known. On 19 (8) January 1793 she an-
> nounced in the *Moskauer Nachrichten* a concert on the 23rd (12th), and here
> again she is called a pupil of Mozart's. (The bracketed dates are these of the
> Old Style.)

FROM THE TRAVEL DIARY OF COUNT LUDWIG VON BENTHEIM-STEINFURT,
FRANKFURT, 15 OCTOBER 1790
(in French)

Friday the 15th.   At 11 o'clock in the morning there was a grand *concert*
by Mozart in the auditorium of the National Playhouse.   It began with
that fine (1) *Symphony* by Mozart which I have long possessed.   (2) Then
came a superb Italian scena, " Non so di chi ", which Madame *Schick* sang
with infinite expressiveness.   (3) *Mozart* played *a Concerto* composed by
him which was of an *extraordinary prettiness and charm*, he had a forte Piano
by Stein of Augsburg which must be supreme of its kind and costs from
90 to 100# [;] this instrument belonged to the Baroness de Frentz. Mozart's
Playing is a little like that of the late *Klöffler* but infinitely more perfect[.]
Monsieur Mozart is a small man of rather a pleasant appearance [;] he had
a coat of Brown marine satin nicely embroidered, he is engaged at the
Imperial Court.   (4) The soprano *Cecarelli* sang a beautiful scena and
rondeau, for bravura airs do not appear to be his forte ; he has grace and a
perfect method, an excellent singer but his tone is a little on the decline, that
and his ugly Physiognomy, for the rest his passages, ornaments and trills are
admirable, I shall have to see if I can engage him for the summer months
to give lessons to Henriette. He could perhaps come with Edom or
some other : for he could have permission, not belonging to the Comedy
like Madame Schick who in the summer are at Frankfort.

In the second Act, No. 5, another concerto by Mozart, which however
did not please me like the first.   (6) A duet which we possess and I recognized by the passage " Per te, per te " with the ascending notes . . . it was
a real pleasure to hear these two people although la *Chicke* lost by comparison with the soprano in the matter of voice and ornaments, but she
scored in the passages at least.   (7) *A Fantasy* without the music by *Mozart*
very charming *in which he shone infinitely exhibiting all the power of his talent.*
(8) The last Symphony was not given for it was almost two o'clock and
everybody was sighing for dinner.   The music thus lasted three hours which
was due to the fact that between all the Pieces there were very long pauses.
The orchestra was no more than rather weak with 5 or six violins but
apart from that very accurate : there was only one accursed thing that
displeased me very much.   There were not many people and I sat next to
a young songstress named Succarini a German and quite good, Monsieur
Westerholt that great music-lover was behind me.

> Eigel Kruttge in *Zeitschrift für Musikwissenschaft* VI (Leipzig, October 1923),
> p. 29.—The double cross was the symbol for ducats.—Johann Friedrich
> Klöffler, who died in February 1790, had been the count's director of music.—
> Henriette was the count's daughter.—The old castle of Steinfurt belongs to
> the estate of Schloss Bentheim, on the Dutch border.

On 16 October Mozart sailed by market-boat to Mainz, where he put up at the
Arnsberger Hof (Schusterstrasse 45) opposite the casino.

Gottron, *op. cit.*, pp. 43-48.—Mozart had written to Constanze on 15 October, after the concert, that he intended to leave on the 18th ; but his next, and lost, letter of the 17th seems to have been sent from Mainz.—During his stay at Mainz, Mozart, according to reports from Xaver Schnyder von Wartensee, appears to have played in private the violin sonata in A major (K. 526) with the violinist Heinrich Anton Hoffmann, and with his brother, the pianist Karl Philipp Hoffmann, the pianoforte duet sonata in F major (K. 497). Mozart met Ignaz von Beecke (see 27 April 1775 and 25-27 October 1777) again at Mainz, or perhaps even at Frankfurt on 2 or 3 October ; they seem to have played a pianoforte concerto together, arranged for four hands (King, *op. cit.*, p. 258).

FROM THE " WIENER ZEITUNG ", 20 OCTOBER 1790
(partly in Italian)

New Music.

Artaria & Comp., in the Kohlmarkt, have published the following new music, cleanly, clearly and correctly engraved :

.   .   .   .   .

Mozart, 1 Trio for the harpsichord, violin and bass, Op. 16.   1 fl. 30 kr.

.   .   .   .   .

The G major pianoforte trio (K. 564) had already appeared in London in 1789 as No. 5 of Vol. II of Stephen Storace's *Collection of Original Harpsichord Music* ; the Andante with the first two variations had been published in a pianoforte arrangement as early as 1786 (by Thonus, Leipzig, as No. 3 of *XII petites pièces*) ; Hoffmeister and Kühnel took it over in 1801.

On 20 October Mozart gave a concert in the concert hall of the electoral palace at Mainz.

Gottron, *op. cit.*, p. 48, surmises that the programme was the same as that at Frankfurt on 15 October. What seems probable is that Mozart repeated the instrumental pieces in it.

FROM THE COURT MUSIC ACCOUNTS, MAINZ, 1790

Virtuoso Mozard   165 fl.

Gottron, *ibid.*—Mozart mentions in his letter to Constanze, of 23 October, " a meagre 15 Carolins " as the Elector's present. A Carolin was actually equivalent to 11 gulden in the 24-gulden standard.

FROM THE " PRIVILEGIERTE MAINZER ZEITUNG ", 22 OCTOBER 1790

Mainz, 21 Octob. Among several exalted personages on a visit here are His Serene Highness Prince Colloredo, Vice Chancellor of the Realm, with his Consort and children. Yesterday there was a grand dinner at Court, to which all the exalted visitors were invited, and in the evening a concert, at which the celebrated musician Herr Mozart, Kapellmeister to H.R.H. the Archduke Franz, was heard on the pianoforte to the satisfaction of his Serene and Noble hearers.

Copy in the Municipal Library, Mainz.—Gottron, *ibid.*—Franz de Paula Gundaccar, Prince Colloredo, the eldest son of Prince Rudolf Joseph (see 11 October 1762), had succeeded his father as Vice Chancellor of the Realm in 1788. His wife was Maria Isabella, *née* Countess Mansfeld ; the sons' names were Rudolf Joseph and Hieronymus.—As once before (see spring 1788) and again later (pp. 383, 434), Mozart was erroneously described as being in the service of Archduke Franz.

On 21 October Mozart travelled from Mainz to Mannheim, where he arrived on the 23rd.

Gottron, *op. cit.*, p. 50, supposes that Mozart left Mainz on 21 October.

On 23 October Mozart was present at the dress rehearsal of *Figaro* at Mannheim.

The Mannheim actor Wilhelm Backhaus related how he wished to refuse entrance to Mozart until the latter identified himself. (Ludwig Nohl, *Musikalisches Skizzenbuch* [Leipzig, 1866], p. 190.)

On Sunday, 24 October, Mozart made an excursion to Schwetzingen ; in the evening he attended the first performance of *Figaro* at Mannheim ; it was given in German.

FROM THE " ANNALEN DES THEATERS ", BERLIN, 1791

Survey of the most notable events of the Mannheim Stage. For the year 1790.

. . . . .

On 24 October, for the first time : *Die Hochzeit des Figaro*. An Operetta in four acts. The music by Mozart. It is Mozart's music alone that can make this caponized [*kombabisirten*] Figaro tolerable, so much has he suffered from this mutilation ; it suits the characters and the sentiments of the singing personages, and for ear and heart alike is full of expression and truth. These qualities are characteristic of Mozart's works, and of him himself as a thoughtful artist . . .

No. 7, p. 47.

On 25 October Mozart travelled from Mannheim by way of Bruchsal, Cannstatt, Göppingen, Ulm and Günzburg to Augsburg, where he arrived on the 28th or 29th and lodged at the White Lamb.

Cf. 1 November 1790.

ROBERT MAY O'REILLY TO MOZART
(in French)

To *Monsieur / Monsieur / Mozart* Celebrated Composer of Music in / Vienna.
London, 26 October 1790.

Sir,

Through a person attached to H.R.H. the Prince of Wales I learn of your design to undertake a journey to England, and as I desire to know people of talent personally and am at present in a position to contribute to their advantage, I offer you, Sir, such a position as [? few] Composers have had in England. If you are thus able to be in London towards the end of the month of December next, 1790, and to stay until the end of June 1791, and within that space of time to compose at least two Operas, serious or comic, according to the choice of the Directorate, I offer you three hundred pounds Sterling, with the advantage to write for the professional concerts or any other concert-hall with the exception only of other Theatres. If this proposal seems agreeable to you and you are in a position to accept it, do me the favour of letting me have a reply by return, and this letter shall serve you in place of a Contract.

I have the honour to be,

Sir,

Your very humble Servant

Rob. May O'Reilly.

Kindly address your reply to
the Pantheon in London.

> Nottebohm, *Mozartiana*, p. 67. (Something seems to be missing from line 4.) —This letter reached Mozart only after his return to Vienna. Whether he answered it, and how, is not known.—O'Reilly was manager of an Italian opera season in London. Coming after the persuasions of the English musicians in Vienna and the visit of the publisher Bland, and before that of Salomon in December, this was one of several invitations to go to London which Mozart did not follow up, or was unable to consider.—The Prince of Wales was later King George IV of England.—The Pantheon, a concert-hall, was in Oxford Street.

On 29 October Mozart reached Munich and again stayed at the Black Eagle.

FROM THE " AUGSBURGISCHES INTELLIGENZ-BLATT ", I NOVEMBER 1790

Newly-arrived personages and travellers . . . At The White Lamb . . . on the 29th [October] . . . Herr von Mozart, Imp. Court Musician, with companions and servants, from Frankfurt.

> E. F. Schmid in the *Augsburger Mozartbuch* (Augsburg, 1943), p. 182.—The 29th should read the 28th. The "companion" was, of course, Franz Hofer.

FROM THE " KURFÜRSTL. GNÄDIGST PRIVILEGIERTES MÜNCHNER WOCHEN-ODER ANZEIGSBLATT ", 3 NOVEMBER 1790

Announcement of visitors arrived here . . . At Herr Albert's, landlord of The Black Eagle in the Kaufingergasse . . . the 29th [October] . . . Herr Mozart, Imp. & Roy. Court Musician and Kapellmeister, of Vienna.

> E. F. Schmid, *Ibid.*—Copy in the Municipal Library, Munich.

On 4 or 5 November Mozart took part in a court concert held in honour of King Ferdinand IV of Naples and Sicily in the Imperial Hall of the electoral palace in Munich.

The King of the two Sicilies, married to the Archduchess Maria Karolina, a daughter of Maria Theresa, was a music-lover (*cf.* 23 October 1767 and end of March 1768). Mozart had arrived at Munich in good time for this visit to Karl Theodor's court. The newspaper gave no details of the participants in this concert.

On 6 or 7 November Mozart left Munich for Vienna, where he arrived about the 10th and joined his family at their new lodgings in the Rauhensteingasse.

On 17 November Nannerl's third child, Marie Babette, was born.

She died on 29 April 1791.—Mozart does not appear to have stopped at Salzburg on his homeward journey, nor to have visited his sister at St. Gilgen.

FROM BOSSLER'S " MUSIKALISCHE KORRESPONDENZ DER TEUTSCHEN FILARMONISCHEN GESELLSCHAFT ", SPEYER, 24 NOVEMBER 1790

(Letter from Herr Pastor Christmann, containing some brief intelligence of the circumstances of Father [Sixt] Bachmann.)

. . . A fortunate circumstance for the youthful virtuoso was the Count's love of music : he . . . sought . . . to stimulate his ardour even more and to spur on his ambition to ever greater perfection in this art. To this end the Count took particular advantage of the occasion when Herr Kapellmeister Mozart, then a young virtuoso travelling with his father, gave proofs of his skill in music at the Count's castle. Young *Bachmann* was encouraged to enter into a contest with *Mozart* on the organ. Each did his utmost to dispute the other's advantage, and the competition ended very honourably for both.

No. 21, col. 163 f.—Jahn, Vol. I, p. 52.—For Father Sixtus Bachmann see 19 October 1766. He was born in 1754 at Kettershausen in Count Fugger's domain of Babenhausen and had become prior at Obermarchtal Monastery on the Danube. The Württemberg priest Johann Friedrich Christmann was a writer on music and a composer.—Bachmann's patron was Count Christoph Moritz Bernhard Fugger of Kirchheim and Weissenborn (E. F. Schmid in the *Schwäbisches Mozartbuch*).

On 14 December a farewell dinner was given for Haydn in Vienna on the eve of his departure for London.

The concert promoter Johann Peter Salomon, who had successfully invited Haydn to London, is on this occasion supposed to have made a similar offer to Mozart for the following winter season (Pohl, *Haydn*, Vol. II, p. 250). *Cf.* 26 December 1786 and 26 October 1790.

On 20 December *Don Giovanni* was given in German in Berlin.

The translation was that by Schröder made for Hamburg (27 October 1789). For the Berlin performance, which King Frederick William II attended on the first night, a libretto without dialogue had been printed.—The cast was : Donna Anna—Frau Friederike Unzelmann (later Frau Bethmann) ; Donna Elvira—Fräulein Marianne Hellmuth ; Zerlina—Frau Henriette Baranius (later Frau Rietz) ; Don Juan—Friedrich Karl Lippert ; the Commendatore—Herr

Kaselitz ; Don Ottavio—Christian Benda ; Leporello—Karl Wilhelm Ferdinand Unzelmann ; Masetto—Christian Brandl.

FROM THE " CHRONIK VON BERLIN ", 5 FEBRUARY 1791

National Theatre.

The 20th December, for the first time : *Don Juan,* or *der steinerne Gast. A Singspiel in four acts.* The music is by Herr Kapellmeister *Mozart.* If ever an opera was awaited with eagerness, if ever a Mozartian composition was trumpeted to the clouds even before it was performed,—it was this same *Don Juan.* Indeed, people went so far as to say that, from the time when Adam bit into the apple, to the *Congress of Reichenbach,* there had never been anything so great, anything so excellent, anything so directly inspired by *Euterpe,* as this same *Don Juan.* Nor was there any lack, among *Mozart's warm friends,* of declarations that " since Mozart had been working at his *Don Juan, Hippocrene* and *Aganippe* had dried up so completely that for all the composers still to come Helicon can provide not one single further drop of inspiration ! " Whether he who chatters away in this manner be a connoisseur or a wit or a blockhead is soon decided, and the blockhead then stands exposed.—That Mozart is an *excellent,* a *great* composer, all the world will admit ; but whether nothing *greater* had ever been written before him, or would ever be written after him, than this opera under review, we beg leave to doubt. Pedants and pettifoggers may go on measuring, bar by bar, the progressions of notes and the harmonies necessarily resulting therefrom, precisely and according to the rules, determining their limits and their relationships ; this we are prepared to admit in the case of the Danish chorale and of Bach's church music, so that this kind of thing should not be entirely lost ; but theatrical music knows no other rule, no other judge, than our hearts, and *whether* and *how* it works upon them is what determines its whole value. Not the art of overloading the instruments, but the heart, the feelings and the passions must be allowed to speak by the composer, for then he writes great music, then his name goes down to posterity, and an evergreen laurel blooms for him in the Temple of Immortality. *Gretry, Monsigny,* and Phylidor serve and will continue to serve as proof. *Mozart* in his *Don Juan* wanted to write something extraordinary, something *inimitably great,* that much is certain, and the extraordinary quality is there, but not the *inimitable greatness* ! Whim, caprice, pride, but not the heart created *Don Juan,* and we would rather admire his great musical potentialities in an *oratorio* or some other solemn piece of church music, than in his *Don Juan,* the end of which is tolerably analogous to a depiction of the *Last Judgment* in which the graves burst open like soap-bubbles, the mountains split and the Lord's Avenging Angel blows the awakening on his dread trumpet. With all that, this opera has brought the directorate good receipts, and the gallery, the boxes and the stalls will hardly be empty in the future; for a ghost in armour and Furies breathing fire are a very strong magnet.—*Ah, Reason of the Abderites!*

> Vol. IX, No. 201, pp. 132 f.—Rudolf von Freisauff, *Mozart's Don Juan 1787–1887* (Salzburg, 1887), pp. 51f. Jahn, Vol. II, p. 361 (both incomplete).—Conferences had taken place at Reichenbach in 1790 whereby a war between Austria and Prussia had been averted.—On the Helicon in Bocotia, the seat of the Muses, were the sources of Aganippe and Hippocrene; the latter was supposed to inspire poetry.—The "Danish chorale" is probably a psalm tune. —The Abderites became known as the "men of Gotham" of ancient Greece through a novel by Wieland (1776).—The continuation of this report, published on 12 February in No. 202, pp. 145 ff., deals with the singers in the Berlin performance (see 9 April 1791).—Freisauff, pp. 52 f., gives two further criticisms without indicating his sources.

FROM THE "JOURNAL DES LUXUS UND DER MODEN", WEIMAR,
FEBRUARY 1791

Berlin.

Pieces performed in December 1790.

. . . 20th. For the first time *Don Juan, oder; der steinerne Gast*, O. 4A. [opera in 4 acts] with music by Mozart. The composition of this Singspiel is fine, but very artificial here and there, difficult and overloaded with instruments. The contents of the play are the old, well-known subject, which pleases the general public only because of the burlesque jests of Leporello, whilom Jack Pudding, and of the stone Commendatore on horseback . . .

P. 76.

In 1790 *Don Giovanni* was given in German at Augsburg, and a production in German was also planned for Pest.

> Loewenberg, *op. cit.*, pp. 223 f.—According to the *Gothaer Theaterkalender* for 1790, p. 131, the company of Count Ladislaus Erdödy (see 13 June 1785) was preparing a performance at Pest in 1790, probably in Franz Xaver Girzik's translation; however, the opera was not given there until 28 December 1797.

In 1790 the Leipzig Cantor Johann Friedrich Doles dedicated his cantata *Ich komme vor Dein Angesicht* to Mozart and Naumann.

> For Doles see 22 April 1789, for Naumann see 17 April 1788.—The *Kantate über das Lied des seel. Gellert . . . Herrn Mozart . . . und Herrn Naumann zugeeignet* was printed with a preface which, however, does not mention Mozart. There was a copy in Mozart's estate (No. 70 in the list of books).

FROM F. F. S. A. VON BOEKLIN'S "BEYTRÄGE ZUR GESCHICHTE DER MUSIK, BESONDERS IN DEUTSCHLAND . . .", FREIBURG IM BREISGAU, 1790

Vienna.

. . . Gluck, Salieri, Mozard, what excellent artists are they not?—I could wish that you might hear their like.—For when one is absent, nothing can be properly judged, nor said.

Salieri and Mozart are happier in the expression of the tender than the strong passions.—

Salzburg.

While in this pretty and lively town the church music is good, tasteful and entirely suited to sacred subjects, and several fine wind players are also to be heard here, the concert orchestra on the other hand is by no means particularly brilliant ; although there are nevertheless a few excellent and well-known musicians to be found, who in sonatas and concert pieces mitigate these shadows by their charming playing ; and indeed, shed a light over their weak accompanists which to a visitor often conveys a most favourable impression of the whole . . .

Pp. 19 and 28 f.—Boeklin's impressions date from the mid 1780s.

FROM ERNST LUDWIG GERBER'S " HISTORISCH-BIOGRAPHISCHES LEXICON DER TONKÜNSTLER ", LEIPZIG, 1790

Mozart (Leopold). Vice-Kapellmeister, violinist and leader of the orchestra of the Prince Archbishop of Salzburg, b. at Augsburg on 14 December 1719 ; entered on this post in 1743 after studying law. Since then he has deserved well of music in every direction ; firstly as author, then as composer, and lastly through the admirable and creditable musical education of his son and his daughter.

In the year 1764 he undertook with these two young virtuosi, of whom the daughter was nine and the son seven years of age, a musical tour to France, England and Italy. We still clearly recollect how much honour he acquired in all these countries with his two children. In Paris he at once caused such great astonishment with his young family that all three were immortalized in a copper engraving : on which the son plays the harpsichord, the father, standing behind him, the violin, while the daughter, standing beside them, sings. Some details of their honourable reception in other countries will be found in the following article.

In the year 1756 he had printed at Augsburg at his own expense : A Thorough Violin School Essay'd, devised and furnished with four Copper-Plates and a Tabulation, &c. The work shows its author to be a thorough and skilled virtuoso, a reasonable and methodical teacher, and a learned musician alike. Of his many practical works only 6 violin trios have been published, engraved in copper by himself in 1740.

In MS, on the other hand, he has written 12 oratorios and other church music, a quantity of works for the stage, among which *Semiramis* and *die verstellte Gärtnerin* are well-known, also pantomimes, and lastly a great number of symphonies, over 30 grand serenades, many concertos for wind instruments, and even more trios, etc. As recently as 1759 he published 12 clavier pieces at Augsburg under the title of " Morning and Evening, proclaim'd in melody and harmony to the Inhabitants of Salzburg ". These

are the pieces played morning and evening from the fortress of Hohensalzburg on the so-called horn-work, or rather organ-work.

Mozart (Wolfgang Amadei, according to others J. G. Wolfg.). Knight of
the Golden Spur, Kapellmeister to the Archduke Franz in Vienna, born
at Salzburg in 1757, already advanced so far in his tender childhood under
the guidance of his father that, on reaching Paris with his father and his
sister in his 7th year, he won universal admiration for his skill on the clavier ;
what is more, his compositions at that age were appreciated there and were
made known in 1767 by being engraved, as the little boy of 7 had previously, in 1764, been engraved in copper. He enjoyed similar admiration
on going to London with his father a few years later. In the year 1769
his father took him to Rome, where again he was so much admired that
His Papal Holiness honoured him with the *sprone d' oro*. From there they
went to Naples and thence to Milan, where this young artist was even
commissioned to compose the opera for the Archduke's nuptials. This
composition was so well received, that he was commissioned to compose
the opera for the following Carnival also. After their return to Salzburg
the Archbishop nominated him his Conzertmeister.

How much promise for Music in so early and so admirably developed
a talent ! It seems, too, as if his sphere of activity at Salzburg had become
too narrow for this young man ; for he again left his birthplace about
1780 and betook himself to Vienna. In this great city, where the arts, and
music in particular, are so much loved by every one, he had no difficulty
in making a comfortable living by giving keyboard lessons to the foremost
music-lovers, male and female. His compositions for the stage and the
music-room, and the musical concerts, which were entrusted to him as
composer to the National Theatre, and of which one alone in 1783 brought
him in 1,600 gulden, contributed not a little thereto. In this way his fame
grew there with his success day by day, until at the marriage of the Archduke Franz in January 1788 he was nominated by the Emperor to be his
Kapellmeister, at an annual salary of 6,000 fl.

This great master, through his early acquaintance with harmony, had
become so profoundly intimate with it that an unpractised ear finds it difficult to follow his works. Even more experienced ones have to hear his
things several times. It is fortunate for him that he attained to perfection
when still young, and among the pleasing and playful Viennese Muses ;
he might otherwise easily have met with the fate of the great Friedemann
Bach, whose flight the eyes of but few other mortals were able to behold.
That he is still among the best and most skilful of our clavier players now
living will be believed without any reminder from me.

His first opera in Vienna is *Die Entführung aus dem Serail*, of 1782, received
with incredible approbation, which indeed it deserves in every respect. A
pianoforte score of it was engraved at Mayence in 1785. (2) *Le Nozze di
Figaro*, in 4 acts, in Vienna, and (3) *der Schauspieldirektor*, 1786, *ibid. Il Don
Giovanni*, 1787, *ibid.* Further, *Die Maurerfreude*, engraved in 1786. Of

pianoforte sonatas, pianoforte trios with a violin, and violin quartets, some 10 works were engraved up to 1788, which, apart from his youthful works, engraved in Paris in 1767, contain much that is excellent. A fair number of varied Ariettas for the pianoforte are especially liked by amateurs, the engraving of which is said to be the responsibility of a certain Madam Aurenhammer in Vienna.

> Part I, cols. 976-79.—The Paris engraving is the plate engraved by Delafosse after Carmontelle. For Leopold Mozart's " violin trios " see 14 November 1719 (he was not born on 14 December). The ascription of the lost fragment of the melodrama *Semiramis* (K. App. 11) and of the opera *La finta giardiniera* (K. 196) to Leopold Mozart is, of course, an error. For the " 12 Clavier Pieces " see end of 1759.—Other errors are the assertion repeated here that Mozart was Kapellmeister to the Archduke Franz, the year 1757 given as that of his birth, and 1767 as that of the publication of the first sonatas. The Archduke at Milan was not Franz but Ferdinand. Mozart's honorarium for *Die Entführung* and his salary as Chamber Composer are greatly over-estimated.—For Josepha Auernhammer *cf.* 23 April 1787.—The articles on the Mozarts may have been written some years before 1790. In the second edition of the *Lexikon* (1813) Gerber expressed himself somewhat differently on Mozart.

1791

FROM THE " ANNALEN DES THEATERS ", BERLIN, 1791

Concerning Faller's Company of Actors.
Erlangen, 1790.

On 19 June, *Die Entführung aus dem Serail*. On 26 June *Figaro* . . . On 8 July, *Die Entführung aus dem Serail*.

From here the company went to Hildburghausen, being engaged by the Court there. Now, however, since December 1790, it has been playing at Bayreuth.

> No. 7, p. 58.—Neither of the first two performances of *Die Entführung* and *Figaro* mentioned above appears to have been the first at Erlangen. Faller's company may also have given both operas at Hildburghausen in July and at Bayreuth in December.

FROM THE " THEATER-KALENDER FÜR 1791 ", GOTHA

Bonn . . . 13 Oct. 1789. . . . *Don Giovanni*, op. by Mozart. The music greatly pleased the connoisseurs. The action was not liked. . . . [Early 1790.] *Die Hochzeit des Figaro*, op. by Mozart, pleased uncommonly. Singers and orchestra vied with each other to do justice to this beautiful opera.

> P. 199.—Thayer, *Beethoven*, 3rd ed. (Leipzig, 1917), Vol. I, p. 252.—The supposition that these notices were written by Neefe is questionable.

On 1 January 1791 Stephen Storace's pasticcio opera *The Siege of Belgrade* was performed at the Drury Lane Theatre in London, with one or two numbers by Mozart.

Loewenberg, *op. cit.*, p. 242 ; additional information from Mr. Harry R. Beard.—The libretto of this successful opera was by James Cobb. The music came for the most part from Martín's *Una cosa rara* ; to this were added a minuet by Salieri, the "Rondo alla turca" from Mozart's A major pianoforte sonata (K. 331), used as an introductory chorus, and possibly also the duet for Susanna and the Countess (No. 20) from his *Figaro*. Storace had, of course, also contributed music of his own. He is said to have earned £1000 with this opera.—Belgrade, as already mentioned, had been taken by the Austrians under General Laudon on 9 October 1789.

FROM THE "WIENER ZEITUNG", 15 JANUARY 1791

New Music.

At Franz Anton Hoffmeister's, music, art and book dealer in the Woll-zeile, No. 803, next the Schwebbogen, the following new music is to be had, finely and correctly copied :

Dance Music.

Mozart, 6 German Dances from the I. & R. Assembly Room, full parts. 1 fl. 40 kr.

. . . . .

Cavatina del Sig. Salieri, varied alla Bach, Mozart, Haydn, Kozeluch, Clementi, &c. with accompaniment of a violin 1fl.

The German dances may have been K. 571, composed in February 1789 for the Small Assembly Hall. The Gesellschaft der Musikfreunde in Vienna possesses manuscript parts of these dances, dated 1790.

In January *Die Entführung* was performed in Amsterdam.

Loewenberg, *op. cit.*, p. 196.—The singspiel is said to have been performed there privately as early as 1789.

ABRAHAM NICLAS EDELCRANTZ TO KING GUSTAVUS III OF SWEDEN
(in French)

Copenhagen, 25 January 1791

. . . In the French provinces the talents, the standard and the ensemble of the theatres are definitely inferior to those in Paris ; but when one gets as far as Mannheim, Hanover, Hamburg and Copenhagen one finds oneself by successive degrees plunged into the darkness and the bad taste of the barbarous 14th century . . . But this judgment would be yet too flattering for Hamburg. Never have I felt so complete a sense of boredom. There has been much talk of ideal beauty ; if ideal wretchedness were to be the object of our attentions, it is to the amateurs of this latter genre that one could here turn. *Le Festin de pierre* of Molière, turned into an opera, is a favourite piece of the inhabitants of Hamburg, who seem to have less tact

M.—13

in dramas than in bills of exchange. The author of this German piece has come to the conclusion that the French was too true to life. That is why he wanted to improve upon the original, and in the first act one sees the Commendatore in nightcap, dressing-gown and slippers fighting Dom Juan with his sword. The death of the former concludes the act. The set for the second represents a very dense forest, in which the mounted statue of the Commendatore, killed two minutes before, is discovered exposed to the regard of spectators amazed at the sculptor's address. The piece drags on in this way for five mortal acts, where the comic scenes of the original are always replaced by episodes foreign to the subject. Finally, in the last scene, Dom Juan finds himself surrounded by devils armed with torches, brandishing which they pursue him ; but the flames unfortunately having gone out, the powder which these torches scattered had the effect of hair-dressers' powder-puffs, and Dom Juan in hell seemed to be pursued by a swarm of wig-makers' assistants, although their costumes in other respects caused them to look more like chimney-sweeps.

> *Bref rörande teatern under Gustav III, 1788–1792.* Edited by Eugène Lewenhaupt (Upsala, 1894).—Edelcrantz was originally called Clewberg ; he was ennobled in 1789. He was one of the directors of the Royal Theatre in Stockholm. There is a reference to this passage, which was abstracted by Cari Johansson, in Maxim Stempel, " Mozart in Schweden ", a paper read at the Prague Mozart Congress in 1956 ; it is printed in the report, p. 190.—The opera had been given in Hamburg in German from 27 October 1789, in the translation of Friedrich Ludwig Schröder.

* FROM THE " JOURNAL DES LUXUS UND DER MODEN ", WEIMAR, FEBRUARY 1791

Critique of Don Juan, Berlin, 20 December 1790.

The music of this Singspiel is beautiful, but here and there very artificial, difficult and overloaded with instrumental detail.

P. 76.—K. G. Fellerer in the *Mozart-Jahrbuch 1959* (Salzburg, 1960), p. 84.

HANDBILL ANNOUNCING THE VIENNA CONCERT OF THE CLARINET VIRTUOSO JOSEPH BÄHR ON 4 MARCH 1791

Notice.

Herr *Bähr*, Chamber Musician in actual service of H. Russian Imp Majesty, will have the honour on Friday next, 4 March, to hold a grand musical concert at Herr Jahn's hall, letting himself be heard several times on the clarinet ; at which Mme. Lange will sing and Herr Kapellmeister Mozart will play a Concerto on the fortepiano. Those who are still desirous of subscribing can be provided with tickets each day at Herr Jahn's.

To begin at 7 o'clock p.m.

Salzburg, Mozarteum.—Facsimile in Bory, *op. cit.*, p. 177 (see 12 March).—
Josef Bähr (1770–1819), whom Mozart met in Paris and who had dealings with
Beethoven about 1800 (he was in Prince Johann Liechtenstein's service) is
not to be confused with the clarinettist Joseph Beer (1744 ?–1811 ?).—Mozart,
who could see the house of the restaurateur Jahn from his study, played his
new pianoforte concerto in B♭ major (K. 595), his last. This was also his
last appearance at a concert.

On the same evening, 4 March, *Don Giovanni* was given in German at Hanover.

The translation was Neefe's ; *cf.* 27 September and 13 October 1789. Three
scenes from Molière's *Don Juan* were interpolated.

On 5 March Johann Christian Lorenz published, in the Erfurt periodical *Nicht zu*
wenig, Nicht zu viel, a poem on Josepha Beck, who had sung the part of Constanze
at Weimar.

Pp. 73 f.—*Die Entführung* had again been performed by Joseph Bellomo's
company at Weimar on 22 January. The singspiel was celebrated in the poem
as " Mozart's masterpiece ".—The editor of the journal was Gottlieb Friedrich
Lorenz, probably a near relative of the poet.—Frau Beck was a pupil of
Dorothea Wendling at Mannheim (see 29 January 1781), was engaged there
in 1790 and in 1799 sang Constanze at Munich also.

FROM THE " WIENER ZEITUNG ", 12 MARCH 1791

Herr Bähr, Chamber Musician in actual service of H. Imperial Russian
Maj., held a grand musical concert on 4 March in the hall at Herr Jahn's,
and won the unanimous approbation of an audience consisting for the most
part of connoisseurs, by his extraordinary skill on the clarinet.—Herr
Kapellmeister Mozart played a Concerto on the *forte piano*, and every one
admired his art, in composition as well as in performance, while Madame
Lange also completed the perfection of the proceedings with some arias.

IBID., 12 MARCH 1791

New Music.

At Lausch's music establishment . . . may now be had :

.   .   .   .   .

By Herr Mozart, Kapellmeister in actual service of H.M. the Emperor,
12 Minuets and 12 Trios of 1791, from the I. & R. Small Assembly Room,
with all the parts   2 fl. 30 kr.
– – in Pianoforte Score   48 kr.
– – 12 German Dances, 12 Trios and Coda, with all the parts   2 fl. 30 kr.
– – in Pianoforte Score   48 kr.
– – " The Sleigh-Ride ", German Dance and Trio, with all the parts   20 kr.
– – in Pianoforte Score   8 kr.

The minuets are K. 599, 601 and 604 ; the German dances (actually 13) K. 600,
602 and 605 ; the " Sleigh-Ride " dance is No. 3 from K. 605.—MS. copies.
See 16 and 23 March, 1 June and 30 November 1791.

FROM THE "WIENER ZEITUNG", 16 MARCH 1791

From Artaria & Comp., art dealers in the Kohlmarkt, are quite newly
to be had :

.   .   .   .   .

Mozart, 12 German Dances from the Small Assembly Room for the Pianoforte   45 kr.
– – 12 Minuetti for the Pianoforte   45 kr.
K. 600, 602 and 605 ; K. 599, 601 and 604. First prints in pianoforte score.

IBID., 23 MARCH 1791

At Johann Träg's . . . the following new music is to be had :

.   .   .   .   .

Rout Minuets and German Dances. Part II by Mozart, 1791, for the
pianoforte   1 fl. 30 kr.
K. 599, 601 and 604, K. 600, 602 and 605. See 16 March.—MS. copies ;
cf. 12 March.

On 23 March, at the Burgtheater, the pasticcio *L' ape musicale rinnuovata* (" The
Renovated Musical Bee ") was performed.

> *Cf.* 4 and 21 March 1789.—The text was again by Da Ponte, who soon after-
> wards moved out of Vienna to Mödling. The " musical comedy " in three
> acts, with " almost entirely new music", was given on 23 March for Da
> Ponte's benefit, on 30 March for Benucci's and on 6 April, " altered ", for
> Gasparo Bellentani's (a new opera singer) : six times in all.

IBID., 26 MARCH 1791

Notice.

Herr Müller, who has become generally known through his art collection on the Stockameisenplatz, No. 610, first floor, opened on the 23rd of
March the Mausoleum erected by him, which he has at great expense built
in memory of the unforgettable and world-famous Field Marshal Baron
von Loudon, in the Himmelpfortgasse over against the Mint, in the house
of Herr Gerl, master-builder (No. 1355). Here this remarkable monument
may be seen in a setting especially designed for it on the ground floor,
splendidly illuminated from 8 o'clock in the morning till 10 o'clock at
night ; access to which is by the large door at the top of the third flight
of the main staircase. The distributed advertisements as well as the posters
have given some description of it, but since it is impossible to describe the
whole with sufficient vividness, the sight of it will not fail to surprise every
one who visits this Mausoleum and thereby renews the memory of this
great and meritorious man. Herr Müller has caused it to be engraved in
copper, and illuminated prints will shortly be available at the entrance. The

seats are arranged in the best possible way, and each person pays 1 fl. for a first place and 30 kr. for a second ; upon the stroke of each hour a Funeral Musique will be heard, and will be different every week. This week the composition is by Herr Kapellmeister Mozart.

Discovered by Frau Erna Felmayer, Vienna.—Joseph Count Deym von Stritetz, an Austrian officer, had left the country after a duel and changed his name to Müller. He returned *ca.* 1780, bringing with him a collection of plaster-cast copies of ancient sculptures and opening " Müller's Art-Gallery " on the Stock-im-Eisen-Platz. It gradually turned into a panopticon, complete with mechanical toys ; it was moved to the Kohlmarkt *ca.* 1795 and three years later to a specially constructed building near the Red Tower on the Danube canal. After the death of the count in 1804 it passed into the possession of his widow Josephine (*née* Countess Brunsvik). In 1819 it closed down, and its contents vanished without trace.—Mozart wrote several pieces for the count's mechanical instruments, including the Adagio and Allegro (K. 594) referred to here. Laudon died on 14 July 1790, and Mozart completed the work which Deym had commissioned in December. From 1797 there stood by Laudon's wax monument a wax figure of Joseph II, in conversation with him. At Laudon's feet sat a little Turkish girl (exactly as in the mausoleum), a foster-child whom the field marshal had brought back from Belgrade.—*Cf.* O. E. Deutsch in *Music & Letters* (London, April 1948), and in the *Konzertblatt der Gesellschaft der Musikfreunde* (Vienna, 1 December 1948).—Deym is said to have made a life-size likeness of Laudon in wax *ca.* 1789.—The house of the architect, Joseph Gerl (the present No. 9), is still standing opposite Prince Eugen's winter palace, where the Mint was then housed—not far from Jahn's restaurant and Mozart's last dwelling.—There seems to be no extant description of the mausoleum. A copy of the anonymous engraving, probably unique, was found in the Albertina, Vienna, and is reproduced in the pictorial volume, *Mozart und seine Welt in zeitgenössischen Bildern*, of the *Neue Mozart-Ausgabe* (Series X, category 32) : Laudon is shown lying in a coffin of glass.— As the first of the three other announcements appeared on a Saturday, some two or three days after the opening of the mausoleum, it seems probable that Mozart's was the music heard during the first week. There is some doubt as to whether Deym actually did use other music in the mausoleum.—See 27 April, 23 July and particularly 17 August, 1791.

On 26 March Lausch announced in the *Wiener Zeitung* " Des Herrn von Jacquin 6 deutsche Lieder beym Klavier zu singen " (" Six German Songs by Herr von Jacquin, to be sung at the Pianoforte ").

Among these songs were two which Mozart had written in 1787 for Gottfried von Jacquin, the first in the latter's room, the second in Prague : " Als Luise die Briefe ihres ungetreuen Liebhabers verbrannte " (K. 520) and " Das Traumbild " (K. 530). The second song, first printed in Cahier V of Mozart's *Œuvres* (Breitkopf & Härtel) in 1799, appeared in 1803 in an engraved book of six songs by Jacquin brought out by Jean Cappi in Vienna. Jacquin dedicated the first of these songs to Fräulein Katharina von Altomonte, the second, under the title of " An eine Unbekannte " to Fräulein Marianne von Natorp (his sister-in-law's sister). Jacquin died in 1792 and was thus guilty of these plagiarisms, although Mozart had tolerated them.—*Cf.* Hedwig Kraus in the *Zeitschrift für Musikwissenschaft* (Leipzig, January 1933), and Alfred Einstein in *The Music Review* (Cambridge, May 1941), pp. 151 f.

List of the Pieces performed at the National Theatre, Mannheim, from
November 1790 to April 1791, with some Remarks.

.   .   .   .

On 26 March we at last saw again, after a long time, the Singspiel *Don
Juan*, which gives such extraordinary pleasure owing to Mozart's glorious
music. My musical knowledge is too restricted for me to venture on an
extensive criticism of this music. It carries me away, it gives me the liveliest
pleasure ; whenever I hear it I discover some new beauty in it—why then
should I allow pedantic carping to spoil this pleasure for me ? . . .

> No. 8, pp. 72 f.—*Don Giovanni* had been given at Mannheim since 27 Sep-
> tember 1789.

In March *Die Entführung* was probably given at Erfurt.

> It is not certain that this performance took place.

In the spring the section *Frühlingslieder* (" Spring Songs ") of the *Liedersammlung
für Kinder und Kinderfreunde am Clavier* (" Collection of songs at the Pianoforte for
Children and Child-Lovers "), which included three songs by Mozart, was published
in Vienna.

> These songs were " Sehnsucht nach dem Frühlinge ", " In Frühlings Anfang "
> and " Das Kinderspiel " (K. 596-598).—This rare book, printed by Ignaz
> Alberti, was dedicated by the editor of the collection, Placidus Partsch, to
> the Archduke Franz and his second wife, his cousin Maria Theresia of Sicily.
> *Cf.* O. E. Deutsch's epilogue to the facsimile of the *Drei Frühlingslieder von
> Mozart* (Vienna, 1937).

On 4 April *Figaro* was given in German in Hamburg.

> The translation was that by Knigge, first used on 18 May 1788 at Lübeck
> and then on 18 May 1789 at Hanover.

FROM THE " CHRONIK VON BERLIN ", 9 & 16 APRIL AND 14 MAY 1791
Concerning the Singspiel Don Juan
A Letter.

Dear Friend,

You asked me in your last letter to give you some intelligence of the
Singspiel *Don Juan*, now performed six times in Berlin ; but my belief
that it is a duty to fulfil as far as possible a friend's request, is equalled only
by my inclination to satisfy your desire, and much as I dare to hope that
your indulgence will be adequate to my shortcomings, it is with reluctance
that I take up my pen.

Even for gods and goddesses, it is no small thing to deliver judgment
on a work of taste : for since the word *to please* is a concept which has gained
citizenship throughout the realm of thinking beings, it would be very
arbitrary on anyone's part to try to restrict its rights and liberties ; not to
mention what an inexhaustible source of physical advantage to mankind is
provided by the variety of taste.

Rumours of the great inward worth of this singspiel—which, be it noted, is the second adaptation of Molière's *Don Juan*—had long before the first performance awakened a desire for enjoyment in many who are friends of the drama ; and it seemed indeed as though this time Thalia had taken Fama into her pay, so that the magic sound of her trumpet should stir the attention of those who wished to hear. In this she succeeded. At every gathering *Don Juan* formed part of the talk ; in no public place did *Don Juan* fail to be the subject of conversation, whether it was fashionable to go to it or not ; and even where one would have thought that Vulcan's faithless spouse ruled alone, she was unable to refuse admission to the name of this worker of miracles.

As soon as they had acquainted themselves somewhat with the contents of this longed-for drama, the ladies of fashion secretly busied themselves with inventing excuses of which to make use in case of need ; while the male adherents of the great world in their hearts envied him whom they regarded as the fortunate Don.

After protracted expectation the longed-for morning appeared at last, when a Mercury armed with a paste-pot adorned the corners of the town with a poster proclaiming to the hopeful ones that the day had arrived on which they were to reach the goal of their desire. With blissful avidity their glances devoured the two words *Don Juan*, and so great was their joy therein that many did not so much as notice what was written above them. A pity that those who like to impart pleasurable news to their fellow-men this time failed of their object with many ; for they were too late in the case of those who had been at the play the night before or who had read the newspapers.

For many now the winter's day, short in itself, seemed inordinately long. At long last grey-shadowed Evening rose on the eastern horizon ; its glance spread darkness over the sphere ; and now to Thalia's open temple the sons and daughters of Borussia's royal city began to wend their way. My time and affairs prevented my being among these pilgrims, and my eager curiosity was compelled to await its satisfaction until the fifth performance. Then, full of the highest anticipations I went, to see and hear a musical drama in which, to my mind, *the eye was feasted, the ear enchanted, reason offended, modesty outraged, and virtue and sensibility trampled upon by vice.*

How, I seem to hear, could the like have appeared on the public stage of Berlin ? Berlin, the favoured seat of the German Muses ! Where Frederick the Second for half a century taught taste and truth to his people ! Where Frederick William, the philanthropist, the devotee of the arts and sciences, lent his helping hand to give Thalia's temple that lustre which has already put darkness to flight in so many cities of Europe by means of its penetrating rays ! Where to an *Engel*, to a *Ramler* is entrusted the task of preventing this temple's desecration ! And should such an abortion of human invention creep in there ? No, impossible ! You are right, for I too should say the same, were I in your place. But understand : I spoke only of my own notions. Yet I feel nevertheless bound to justify my bold pronouncement to you, and I will try to do so, as far as I may succeed.

. . . There is little speaking : the greater part of the text is ruled by song ; and if ever a nation were entitled to take pride in a compatriot, it would be Germany in regard to *Mozart*, the composer of this Singspiel. Never, certainly never, has the greatness of a human spirit been more palpable, and never has the art of music reached to a higher degree ! Melodies which seem to have been invented by an angel are here accompanied by heavenly harmonies, and any one whose soul is even a little receptive to true beauty will surely forgive me for saying that *the ear is enchanted*. . . . It has already been given six times, and each time the box office has testified eloquently to the management's profitable choice . . . but the foremost reason for the constantly crowded houses is undoubtedly the music, which is of a greatness not to be expressed. True, many may regret that the excellent *Mozart* was not more careful in his choice. I myself could not refrain from secretly wishing, " Oh, hadst thou not thus squandered the power of thy spirit ! had thy sentiments been more in harmony with thine imagination and not led thee to take such unclean steps to greatness ! How much more deeply would thy song and thy harmony penetrate into the souls of thy hearers, were they not constantly arrested by the thought of the ignoble text ! No, beloved man ! Be less cruel in future towards thine amiable Muse ! Seek to extend the halls of thy fame upon pillars before which the upright man is pleased to tarry and which the honest maiden may pass without a blush ! What could it avail thee if thy name were to be inscribed in letters of diamond upon a golden tablet—and this tablet were to hang on a pillory of shame ? . . .

Your friend,

N. N.

Berlin, 20 January
   1791.

> Vol. IX, No. 212, pp. 316-20 ; Nos. 213-214, p. 327 ; Nos. 221-222 pp. 452-454. (The letter appeared in five instalments.).—See 20 December 1790 (report in the *Chronik* of 5 February 1791).—" The second adaptation of Molière's *Don Juan* " may mean that Goldoni's *Don Giovanni Tenorio* is reckoned as the first ; but it is also possible that Giuseppe Gazzaniga's opera *Don Giovanni Tenorio*, to a libretto by Giovanni Bertati (Venice, 5 February 1787), a forerunner of Da Ponte's and Mozart's *Don Giovanni*, is meant.— Johann Jakob Engel and Karl Wilhelm Ramler, both authors, were directors of the Berlin National Theatre.

FROM THE POSTER OF A CONCERT AT THE BURGTHEATER

(in German and Italian)

On Saturday, the 16th, and Sunday, the 17th April 1791 will be held at the I. & R. National Court Theatre by the established Society of Musicians for the benefit of its widows and orphans, *a Grand Musical Concert* consisting of the following pieces :

      (1) A Grand Symphony composed by Herr *Mozart*.
      (2) An extract from the opera *Phedra*.

            In which will sing :

The part of Arizia .	.	. Madame Lange.
The part of Ippolit .	.	. Herr Kalvesi.
The part of Teseus .	.	. Herr Nenzini.

                Chorus.

The music is by Herr Johann *Paisello*, with the exception of the aria sung by Madame Lange, which is by Herr *Mozart*.

To begin at 7 o'clock.

> Copies in the possession of the Gesellschaft der Musikfreunde, and in the Theatre Collection of the National Library, Vienna.—This concert, in which more than 180 musicians took part, was as usual conducted by Salieri.—The symphony may have been the one in G minor (K. 550) in its second version, which includes clarinets. The brothers Anton and Johann Stadler, who were both clarinettists, took part (according to the list [Verzeichnüss] of the Musicians' Society in the City Archives, Vienna, discovered by H. C. Robbins Landon).—The aria was one of the two extra numbers written for Aloisia Lange in 1783 (see 30 June), " No, no, che non sei capace " (K. 419).— Pohl, *op. cit.*, p. 63, erroneously mentions Righini as the composer of the opera *Fedra*. The Gesellschaft der Musikfreunde, Vienna, also possesses the special poster for the repeat performance on 17 April.

On 16 April Grossmann's company performed *Don Giovanni* in German at Cassel.

About 25 April Mozart submitted to the City Council of Vienna his (undated) petition for the post of assistant to the cathedral Kapellmeister.

> Louis Koch Collection, Basle (Switzerland).—*Allgemeine musikalische Zeitung* (Leipzig, 9 March 1836). Georg Kinsky, Koch Catalogue (Stuttgart, 1953), p. 39. The version of the petition published by Ernst Weizmann in the Vienna *Weltpresse* for 7 April 1956 is a signed fair copy in an unknown hand. —The Cathedral Kapellmeister Leopold Hofmann had been ailing for some time, but he did not die until 17 March 1793, *i.e.* after Mozart. The City Council's favourable decision (see 28 April and 9 May 1791) thus did not take effect.

FROM THE PROGRAMME OF A CONCERT GIVEN BY JOSEPHA DUŠEK IN THE ROYAL NATIONAL THEATRE, PRAGUE, 26 APRIL 1791

    4thly. A quite newly written grand scena by Herr Mozart.
    5thly. A Concerto on the forte piano by Herr Mozart, played by Herr Witassek.
    6thly. A Rondo by Herr Mozart with basset-horn *obbligato*.

> Prague, National Museum.—Reproduced in *Mozart und Prag*, 1957.—The scena was probably K. 583 and the concerto K. 595. The rondo may perhaps

have been Vitellia's aria from *La clemenza di Tito* (K. 621, No. 23 ; *cf.* 9 (?)
February 1794 and 29 March 1798), although Mozart did not receive the
libretto until the middle of July 1791. If Anton Stadler was in Prague at this
time, he presumably played the basset-horn. Johann Wittassek (Jan Vitásek)
was a pupil of František Dušek.

FROM THE " WIENER ZEITUNG ", 27 APRIL 1791

(Announcement by Joseph Müller concerning the Laudon Mausoleum)
. . . Every hour a splendid funeral musique specially composed for it
will be heard, and as there will be a different composition each week, the
composer's name will be announced on the posters . . .

(see 26 March).—24 March is here named as the opening day. The prices of
the engravings (now ready for sale) are announced as 20 kreuzer coloured
and 10 kreuzer black and white. None of the posters seems to have survived.

DRAFT FOR THE DISCHARGE OF MOZART'S PETITION

This is to be rejected, and particularly since the Herr Kapellmeister at
St. Stephen's has not so far asked for an assistant, this application cannot
be granted.

Ex Cons. Mag. Vien.
28 April 1791
Hübner, Sec.

Weizmann, *op. cit.*, 14 April 1956.—This discharge was written on the reverse
of the fair copy of the petition, but crossed out again (see *ca.* 25 April and
9 May 1791).—Johann Hübner was secretary to the City Council.

FROM FRIEDRICH LUDWIG SCHRÖDER'S DIARY, 28 APRIL 1791

So machen sie's Alle [" That's What They All Do "], Singspiel composed
by Mozart, is a miserable thing, which lowers all women, cannot possibly
please female spectators, and will therefore not make its fortune.

F. L. W. Meyer, *Fr. L. Schröder* (Hamburg, 1819), Vol. II, Part i, pp. 63 and
68.—This entry was written after a reading of the translated libretto. Three
days later Schröder attended the first performance of the opera at Frankfurt.

On 1 May the Mainz company performed *Così fan tutte* at Frankfurt on Main in
German under the title *Liebe und Versuchung* [" Love and Temptation "].

The translation was by Heinrich Gottlieb Schmieder and by David Stegmann,
the composer, who was then director of the Opera at Mainz.—According to
Meyer, *op. cit.*, p. 68, Schröder is said to have exclaimed after the first performance : " Miserable ! Even of Mozart's music only the second act pleases
me ! "

FROM THE "ANNALEN DES THEATERS", BERLIN, 1791

1 May. *Liebe und Versuchung* ["Love and Temptation"], a miserable Italian piece of work with the forceful, elevated music of a Mozart.

No. 5, p. 46.—At Mainz the opera was not given till 11 June.

DECREE OF THE CITY COUNCIL

The City Council of the I. & R. Capital City of Vienna declares that Herr Wolfgang Amadeus Mozart shall in consequence of his petition be assigned as assistant to Herr Leopold Hofmann, Kapellmeister at St. Stephen's Cathedral Church, in such wise that he shall make himself liable by a legal agreement, to be deposited here, to assist the said Herr Kapellmeister in his service without remuneration, to deputize for him when he cannot appear in person, and in case this post of Kapellmeister shall fall vacant, to be satisfied with the salary and with all that which the City Council may decree and deem advisable.

Which is herewith imparted to the above for his information.

Jos. Georg Hörl, I. & R. Councillor and Burgomaster.

Ex Cons. Magis. Vien.

9 May 1781.

Johann Hübner,   *Secret.*

Louis Koch Collection, Basle.—Jahn, Vol. II, pp. 701 f. ; Kinsky, *op. cit.*, p. 40 (see 25 and 28 April and 12 December 1791).

FROM THE "PRESSBURGER ZEITUNG", 22 MAY 1791

Vienna. The Court Composer Mozart has received from the City Council here the reversion of the post of Kapellmeister at St. Stephen's, which brings in 2,000 gulden.

Weizmann, *op. cit.*, 14 April 1956.

FROM THE "WIENER ZEITUNG", 1 JUNE 1791

Announcement of Music.

At Lausch's music establishment . . . are to be had :

.   .   .   .   .

By Herr Kapellmeister Mozart, 12 Minuets and 12 Trios of 1791 from the I. & R. Small Assembly Room. Part I, No. 1, in D, with all the parts 2 fl. 30 kr.

– – in Pianoforte Score   48 kr.

– – 12 German Dances, 12 Trios and Coda. Part I, No. 1, in C, with all the parts   2 fl. 30 kr.

– – in Pianoforte Score   48 kr.
– – 12 Minuets and 12 Trios. Part II, No. 1, in C, with all the parts   3 fl.
– – in Pianoforte Score   48 kr.
The " Sleigh-Ride " German Dance with Trio may also be had separately,
with all the parts   20 kr.
– – in Pianoforte Score   8 kr.
    N.B. The pianoforte score is genuine, arranged by Herr Haydenreich
and, as usual, written in the discant and violin clef, to be obtained on request.

> What Lausch calls the first part, and in the case of the minuets the second,
> does not correspond to the numbering of Artaria's engraved editions.   The
> first 12 minuets, in D major, may correspond to K. 585, which were, however,
> written at the end of 1789 and had probably been performed by the beginning
> of 1790 ; the second set of 12 minuets and the 12 German Dances Lausch had
> already announced on 12 March, also " Die Schlittenfahrt ".—For Heidenreich
> *cf.* 24 May 1788.

FROM THE " WIENER ZEITUNG ", 4 JUNE 1791

New Music.

From Artaria & Comp., art dealers in the Kohlmarkt, are newly to be
had : By Herr Mozart, 12 Variations for the pianoforte, on the aria " Ein
Weib ist das herrlichste Ding auf der Welt", from the opera *Der dumme
Gärtner.*   40 kr.

> For *Der dumme Gärtner* see May 1790.—The variations (K. 613) number eight,
> not twelve ; *cf.* 27 August 1791.

On the same day, 4 June, Constanze, with her small son Karl, again went to Baden
near Vienna to take the waters.

> The choirmaster Stoll (see 13 June 1790) had rented for them a room at
> Renngasse 29 (now No. 4), the house of Johann Georg Grundgeyer, the town
> syndic.

On 6 June Mozart went to the Freihaus Theatre with Frau Anna von Schwingen-
schuh to see Schikaneder's comic opera *Anton bei Hofe, oder Das Namensfest* (" Anton
at Court, or The Name-Day ").

> This was the fifth part, *i.e.* the fourth sequel, of the successful opera *Die zween
> Anton* (*cf.* May 1790).   The first performance had taken place on 4 June.
> Mozart's companion was the wife of an assistant at the Mint.

At 5 a.m. on 8 June Mozart went to Baden.

> On the following day Mozart stayed with his wife.   Constanze had met at
> Baden Mozart's pupil Franz Xaver Süssmayer (Süssmayr), who was much
> with him during these last months.

On 10 June Guardasoni and his opera company returned from Warsaw to Prague.

On 11 June Mozart went to the Leopoldstadt Theatre to see Joachim Perinet's
singspiel : *Der Fagottist, oder Die Zauberzither* (" The Bassoonist, or The Magic
Zither "), with music by Wenzel Müller.

> The first performance took place on 8 June.   This successful piece, usually
> called *Kaspar der Fagottist*, had the same literary source as *Die Zauberflöte* :

Wieland's *Dschinnistan, oder auserlesene Feen- und Geister-Mährchen*, published in 1785–89.

On the same evening, 11 June, *Così fan tutte* was given in German at Mainz. *Cf.* 1 May 1791.

On 14 June Mozart's uncle, Franz Alois Mozart, died at Augsburg.

> *Augsburger Mozartbuch*, 1943, p. 183.—*Cf.* 12 and 16 October 1777.

On 15 June Mozart again went to Baden.

On 18 June the motet *Ave verum corpus* (K. 618) was composed at Baden.

> The motet was no doubt intended for Stoll, perhaps for Corpus Christi Day, which fell on 23 June. Stoll, who later on also took care of Haydn's wife at Baden, before her death there in 1800, repeatedly performed music by Mozart in the parish church.

On 19 June *Die Entführung* was given at Pest again.

> *Cf.* 30 May 1789.

IBID., 22 JUNE 1791
(partly in French)

New Music.

At Johann Träg's . . . the following new music is to be had :

.   .   .   .   .   .

6 Country Dances for Pianoforte by Mozart   40 kr.

> The works concerned were perhaps K. 534, K. 535a (3 dances), K. 462, No. 3 and K. 535, which, however, had already been published by Artaria in engraved pianoforte score on 16 January 1789 (K. 535 had been brought out by Lausch in MS. copy as early as 19 March 1788). The new MS. copy by Traeg could also have been K. 607 and 609 (5 dances).

On 26 June Mozart walked in the Corpus Christi procession which set out from and returned to the Piarists' Church in the Josefstadt suburb.

> Corpus Christi Day was on the 23rd, but in the suburbs the procession was often deferred to the following Sunday, in this case the 26th.

FROM SCHUBART'S "CHRONIK", STUTTGART, 1791

Music.

Clavier Sonata with nine Variations in Mozart's manner by Abeille, engraved by Amon of Heilbronn . . . Price 48 kr.

> 1st half-year, p. 344.—Copy in the Württemberg State Library, Stuttgart.—Johann Christian Abeille was Konzertmeister and court organist there.

FROM THE ANONYMOUS BOOK "ANTI-DA PONTE . . . VON EINEM COSMOPOLITEN", VIENNA, 1791

. . . The conversation now turned to *Beaumarchais*. . . . He maintained that da Ponte had not at all understood his play *La folle journée ou le mariage de Figaro*, else he could not have made such a changeling of it . . .

Salieri and Mozart complained loudly about the tasteless, jolting and disjointed opera texts he had several times submitted to them to set to music. They had often to exert all their art to make something harmonious of them for the public, they declared, and had now firmly resolved never again to write a single note to a " da Ponte*ish* " text, adding that if they were to receive well-written operas, they would ever make it their first concern in their work to please the public for whose unanimous approval they wished to sue. . . .

[Da Ponte :] . . . *Salieri* and *Mozart* offer me . . . a great insult by wishing never to set another text by me to music . . . But I shall certainly not leave this insult unavenged.

> Pp. 49, 51 and 62.—Copy in the City Library, Vienna.—Printed by Joseph Hraschansky.—Da Ponte left Vienna in March 1791 and Mödling in July to remove to Trieste, returning briefly to Vienna in 1792. The pamphlet (based on London models) deals with an imaginary court-case, with accusations against Da Ponte and his defence. He had also written librettos for Salieri, *e.g. Axur* (8 January 1788).

In 1791 (?) Mozart subscribed to Karl Zulehner's piano arrangement of *Don Giovanni*, which was published, with the Italian text, by Schott of Mainz about 1792.

In the summer of 1791 *Così fan tutte* was probably performed at Leipzig in Italian.

> Loewenberg, *op. cit.*, p. 237.—It looks as though the Guardasoni company had first performed the opera in Prague earlier in the year, to judge from an undated libretto which still describes " Mozzart " as " maestro di Capella in attual servizio di S. Maestà Cesarea ". *Cf.* 5 October 1791.—Guardasoni left Prague for Vienna in mid-July, perhaps in order to hand the libretto of *La clemenza di Tito* to Mozart, and then left for Bologna, to engage leading singers of both sexes.

On 8 July *Don Giovanni* was given in German at Bad Pyrmont.

Mozart stayed at Baden from 9 to 11 July ; on Sunday the 10th, Michael Haydn's " Pax vobiscum " and Mozart's *Missa brevis* in B♭ major (K. 275) were sung in the parish church.

> The eleven-year-old Antonie Huber (later Frau Haradauer), a sister-in-law of the choirmaster, Stoll, sang the soprano solo in the mass. (*Cf. Der Aufmerksame*, Graz, 18 January 1856.)

In the middle of July Mozart took his wife and child back to Vienna.

FROM THE " WIENER ZEITUNG ", 23 JULY 1791
[Announcement by Joseph Müller]

. . . The Mausoleum likewise erected by me in memory of Field Marshal Loudon in the Himmelpfortgasse, No. 1355, is to be seen there only a few days longer . . .

> See 26 March and 27 April.—This notice also mentions the Art Collection on the Stock-im-Eisen-Platz, Müller's headquarters, which he had advertised again on 1 June.

On 26 July Mozart's sixth child, Franz Xaver Wolfgang, was born.

> Blümml, *op. cit.*, pp. 8 f.—The baptism took place in St. Stephen's Cathedral. Trattner, as godfather, was represented by the bookseller Michael Klorf.—Wolfgang became a musician and died at Carlsbad in 1844.

IBID., 27 JULY 1791

New Music.

At Johann Träg's . . . the following new music is to be had :

.   .   .

Masses, Oratorios and Motets by Mozart, Haydn, . . . all at cheap prices.

FROM THE " ALLGEMEINES THEATERJOURNAL ", FRANKFURT AND MAINZ, 1792

[Munich.]

Don Juan, 7 & 23 Aug., 27 Sept. [1791.]

(The performance was prohibited by the censor, but allowed by special gracious permission of the Elector. The music pleased extraordinarily ; the libretto was found tasteless.)

> Vol. I, No. 1, p. 62.—Freisauff, *op. cit.*, p. 151.—The editor of this journal was Heinrich Gottlieb Schmieder (see 13 March 1789 and 1 May 1791). The performance took place in the theatre on the Salvatorplatz (*cf.* 1 April 1785). —The Elector was Karl Theodor of Bavaria and the Palatinate.

FROM THE " WIENER ZEITUNG ", 10 AUGUST 1791

New Music.

From Artaria & Comp., art dealers in the Kohlmarkt, are to be had :

.   .   .   .   .

Mozart, a new Pianoforte Concerto, Opera 17.   3 fl.
- – –   12 new Rout German Dances for the Pianoforte, 2nd Part.   45 kr.
- – –   12 *do.*, 3rd Part.   45 kr.
- – –   12 Rout Minuets, 2nd Part.   45 kr.
- – –   12 *do.*, 3rd Part.   45 kr.

> The B♭ major pianoforte concerto (K. 595), had been published in parts, as usual ; the price was announced on 31 August as only 2 fl. 45 kr. The two series of German dances (K. 600, 602 and 605) and minuets (K. 599, 601 and 604) had been announced in pianoforte score on 16 March 1791. The third series of German dances is K. 586, that of minuets K. 585.

IBID., 13 AUGUST 1791

Musical Notice.

Filled with feelings of the warmest gratitude for the happy applause with which I was honoured at the musical concert held by me on 10 June of this year at the I. & R. National Court Theatre, I deem it my duty to respond with all that lies in my power to the exhortation, so flattering to me, to allow myself to be heard on the armonica once more. I shall therefore, by most gracious I. & R. permission already obtained, hold another grand musical concert next week, before my departure hence to Berlin, at the I. & R. Kärntnertor Theatre, and play on the armonica an entirely new and surpassingly beautiful concert quintet accompanied by wind instruments by Herr Kapellmeister Mozart, as well as new variations on the favourite duet from the *Molinaria*, " Nel cor piu non mi sento ", by Herr Kapellmeister Wanhal, and altogether such pleasing pieces as to persuade every connoisseur of music entirely that the armonica is the noblest of all musical instruments, exciting not sad and melancholy, but rather glad, gentle and elevated feelings. The forthcoming poster will give further details.

Marianne Kirchgessner.

The blind virtuosa from the State of Baden, then twenty-one years of age, played on a glass harmonica made by the Carlsruhe Kapellmeister Joseph Alois Schmittbauer. An enthusiastic report of her concert at Linz on 24 April 1791 appeared in the *Wiener Zeitung* for 7 May. On 10 June she had given a concert at the Burgtheater (as her rival Karl Leopold Röllig had already done on 2 April). Mozart may have heard her then. At the concert she gave in the Kärntnertor Theatre on 19 August she performed the Adagio and Rondo (K. 617) for armonica, flute, oboe, viola and violoncello written for her. The repetition of this announcement on 17 August gave the " coming Friday ", the 19th, as the date of the concert. Mozart seems to have used the work for the mechanical toy in the so-called " Bedroom of the Graces ", in Müller's art collection (see 17 August). On 8 September Marianne Kirchgessner gave her last concert in Vienna, at Jahn's hall. The publisher Bossler of Speyer accompanied her on her journeys.—Paisiello's singspiel *La molinara* was first given at the Burgtheater on 13 November 1790. The duet for variations by Vanhal was again used for pianoforte variations by Beethoven in 1795.

FROM THE " WIENER ZEITUNG ", 17 AUGUST 1791

Announcement.

The Müller Art Collection on the Stockameisenplatz, which has hitherto been appraised and visited with unanimous approbation by all connoisseurs and friends of art, local as well as from without the city, has now been almost wholly rearranged and considerably augmented. The artist, not content to satisfy the visitor's eye alone by works so nearly approaching nature, has at great cost procured the most excellent mechanical works of art in order to delight the spectator's ear also ; to this end various musical clocks are to be heard, of which one deceptively imitates the *piano Forte*, another the *Flaut travers*, and the third a canary. Yet other new pieces of his own making have accrued to the collection . . . When the first two rooms have been viewed, there will be found in the third the magnificent Mausoleum erected to the great Field Marshal Baron von Loudon ; on which certainly neither cost nor pains have been spared, and which has so far been applauded by all ; and during the contemplation of the whole occurs the surprise of choice funeral music composed by the famous Herr Capellmeister Mozart, which is wholly appropriate to the purpose for which it has been written . . .

March *Cf.* 26 1791.

At the end of August (? the 25th) Mozart set out for Prague with Constanze and Süssmayer.

> The boy Karl had probably been taken to Heeger's at Perchtoldsdorf again (see 1 October 1787).—Süssmayer wrote the *secco* recitatives for *La clemenza di Tito.*

IBID., 27 AUGUST 1791

Musical Announcement.

At Lausch's music establishment . . . are to be had :
Operas for wind or military instruments, in 8 parts, *a* 2 oboes, 2 clarinets, 2 horns and 2 bassoons. Transcription by Herr Vent, I. & R. Chamber Musician, *i.e.* :
> Le Nozze di Figaro . . ., 6 fl. 40 kr. each.
N.B. These are especially recommended to Regimental Commandants . . . Herr Kapellmeister Mozart's 6 Variazione on the Minuet, per il clavicembalo 30 kr.
– – – 8 *ditto* on the aria " ein Weib ist das herrlichste Ding auf der Welt " for the same 1 fl.
From Part II of *die zween Anton.*

> For Went see 10 July 1784.—The variations on the minuet by Duport (K. 573) had been written at Potsdam (*cf.* 26 April 1789). The autograph is lost. The printed copies contain nine variations, but Mozart's own catalogue of works lists only six, as does Lausch in this advertisement.—The variations on a tune from the second part of *Der dumme Gärtner . . . oder die zween Anton* (K. 613) had been published by Artaria on 4 June. While Artaria mistakenly advertised twelve variations for 40 kreuzer, Lausch correctly mentions only eight for his more expensive MS copy.

On 28 August Mozart and his companions arrived in Prague for the coronation of Leopold II.

> The *Prager Oberpostamtszeitung* announced on 30 August that " Herr Mozart, I. & R. Kapellmeister [had] passed through the New Gate " two days before. The *Prager Interessante Nachrichten* of 3 September makes the same announcement (Christopher Raeburn).—Salieri, who stayed in the castle, had arrived in Prague at the end of August with seven court musicians.—Mozart probably stayed in the town again, though spending much time with the Dušeks at the Villa Bertramka.—*Cf.* Johann Debrois's *Urkunde über die vollzogene Krönung . . . Leopold des Zweiten* (Prague, 1818).

Leopold II arrived in Prague on 29 August and the Empress Maria Louisa on the 30th.

(in French)

. . . With M[arsh]el Lascy and Christian Sternberg to P[rin]ce Rosenberg's . . . The music from *Don Juan*. . . .

> The Count had gone to Prague for the coronation. "Lascy" is Field-Marshal Moriz, Count Lacy. Count Philipp Christian Sternberg was a Privy Councillor. The Minister of State and Minister without Portfolio, Count Rosenberg, who had also accompanied the emperor to the coronation at Frankfurt in 1790, had there been elevated to the rank of Prince of the Realm.

On 2 September a festival performance of *Don Giovanni* was given in Prague.

> Mozart probably conducted this performance, which the emperor attended.— Of the singers from the première (see 29 October 1787) all remained except Saporiti (Donna Anna) and Bondini (Zerlina). Anton Stadler played in the orchestra.

FROM THE "TAGEBUCH DER BÖHMISCHEN KÖNIGSKRÖNUNG", PRAGUE, 1791

The 2nd September.

Today will be performed in the National Theatre in the Old Town : *Il dissoluto Punito ossia : Il D. Jiovanni. Der gestrafte Ausschweifende oder : Don Jeann.* A comic Singspiel in 2 acts. The music is by Herr Mozart.

> P. 156.—Freisauff, *op. cit.*, p. 122. Nettl, *op. cit.*, pp. 190 f.

IBID., 3 SEPTEMBER, 1791

[On the 2nd] In the evening their I. & R. Majesties, with the Royal Princes and Princesses, honoured our National Theatre in the Old Town with their most gracious presence, where at their exalted request the Italian opera *Il dissoluto punito, oder Il Don Iovanni* was given. The theatre was brightly lit with candelabra and the Imperial boxes decorated.

> P. 157.—Freisauff and Nettl, *op. cit.*

FROM THE "ANNALEN DES THEATERS", BERLIN, 1791

Announcement.

With an uncalled-for readiness I too have been anticipated on a surreptitious path by one of the species of certain people who have found their Linnaeus in Herr Müller at Itzehoe, by committing to print something which I did not wish to have published (at any rate not by *him*). This is *Die Hochzeit des Figaro*, an operetta, freely adapted from the Italian, which

I sold to the Frankfort theatre in *manuscript* a few years ago. How it thence came into the hands of that honourable pirate, *Lange* of Cologne on the Rhine, I do not know, but what I do know is that he has presumed to take unlawful possession of my property. This immaculate edition not only bristles with misprints, but there has also been attributed to me an elegance of diction from which may God in His mercy preserve me !—Many passages show no sense at all, and seem to have been taken down only aurally, and the metre of the songs, like the rhyme, has frequently been cruelly tortured. I warn every one to beware of buying this immaculate reprint and of spending his money on stolen goods, which have been so grossly falsified into the bargain.—The fear of having to experience more blows of a similar nature has induced me to offer the public a reprint of my adaptations of operettas from the Italian myself, so as not again to expose myself to the cupidity of such pirates, who do not even hand over their prey in an unadulterated shape and form. For the rest, *Lange's* speculation remains an illegal undertaking, and his name may be exposed to view with those of his fellow-robbers of Neuwied, Reutlingen, Carlsruhe, &c.—Weimar, 5 September 1791.

C. A. Vulpius.

> No. 8, pp. 126 f.—The translation by Vulpius had first been used at Frankfurt on 11 October 1788. The Cologne libretto appeared in 1789 ; it was probably printed for the performance at Bonn given early in 1790. It appears that Vulpius did not make a collected edition of his translations of Italian librettos. He later became involved in open controversies with Schikaneder on account of his bad adaptations of Viennese singspiele. (The allusion to Linnaeus's nomenclature is now hardly intelligible.)

FROM THE " PRAGER OBERPOSTAMTSZEITUNG ", 6 SEPTEMBER 1791

Prague, 4 September.

The day before yesterday . . . their gracious Majesties honoured the National Theatre in the Old Town with their presence, where the Italian opera *Il dissoluto punito* was performed. The spacious theatre, which can hold more than a thousand persons, was crammed full, and the route which their gracious Majesties took was quite filled with people.

Prague, Municipal Archives.—Discovered by Christopher Raeburn.

On 6 September *La clemenza di Tito* was performed in Prague as part of the coronation celebrations.

> Mozart, who had received the commission for this opera from the Bohemian Estates through Guardasoni, conducted it himself. It was given only a few times, the last being on 30 September, the day of the first performance of *Die Zauberflöte* in Vienna. (The letter alleged to have been written by Schikaneder to Mozart, dated 5 September 1790 and referring to details in *Die Zauberflöte*, has here been deliberately disregarded.)

LA CLEMENZA DI TITO,

Dramma Serio per Musica / in due Atti / da rappresentarsi /
NEL TEATRO NAZIONALE DI PRAGA
nel Settembre 1791. / In occasione di sollenizzare /
il giorno dell' incoronazione / di sua /
MAESTA L' IMPERATORE LEOPOLDO II.

Nella Stamperia di Nob. De Schönfeld.

Copy in the Saxon State Library, Dresden.—Facsimile in the monthly *Città di Milano*, December 1955, p. 715.—Metastasio's text, first set by Antonio Caldara in 1734, had been abridged and altered for Prague by the Saxon Court Poet Caterino Mazzolà, who was also staying in Prague.

DRAMATIS PERSONAE FROM THE SAME
(in Italian)

Titus Vespasian,	Emperor of Rome.
Vitellia,	Daughter of the Emperor Vitellius.
Servilia,	Sister of Sextus, in love with Annius.
Sextus,	Friend of Titus, in love with Vitellia.
Annius,	Friend of Sextus, in love with Servilia.
Publius,	Prefect of the Praetorium.

The Scene is laid in Rome.

The music is entirely new, composed by the celebrated Signor Wolfgang Amadeus Mozart, maestro di capella in actual service of His Imperial Majesty.

The first three stage-sets are of the invention of Signor Pietro Travaglia, in actual service of H.H. Prince Esterházy.

The fourth stage-set is by Signor Preisig of Coblenz. The entirely new dresses are of the rich and handsome invention of Signor Cherubino Babbini of Mantua.

From the libretto (as above).—The cast, according to Christopher Raeburn (*Musica* [Kassel] 1959, pp. 158 f.) and J. A. Westrup (*Music & Letters* [London] October 1958), was as follows : Tito—Antonio Baglioni (the first Don Ottavio in 1787) ; Vitellia—Maria Marchetti-Fantozzi ; Servilia—Signorina Antonini ; Sesto—Domenico Bedini ; Annio—Carolina Perini ; Publio—Gaetano Campi. (Bedini was a castrato.)—The clarinettist Anton Stadler, who played in the orchestra, remained in Prague for some time and gave a concert of his own in the theatre there on 16 October.

FROM ZINZENDORF'S DIARY, PRAGUE, 6 SEPTEMBER 1791
(in French)

. . . At 5 o'c. to the *Theatre* in the Old Town. . . . The Court did not arrive until past 7.30 and we were regaled with the most tedious spectacle,

La clemenza di Tito . . . La Marchetti sings very well, the Emperor is in raptures about her.

" 5 o'clock " should probably be 7 o'clock and " 7.30 " perhaps 8 o'clock.

FROM THE " TAGEBUCH DER BÖHMISCHEN KÖNIGSKRÖNUNG ", PRAGUE, 1791

The 7th September

In the evening [of the 6th] there was given a free opera, to attend which His Majesty, the Imperial Family and the Court shortly after 8 o'clock entered the boxes prepared for Their Highnesses. They were accompanied thither through all the streets by unanimous and joyous huzzahs, and Their Highnesses were also received in the theatre with similar manifestations.

P. 225.—Freisauff, *op. cit.*, p. 122.—See also Debrois's *Urkunde*, 1818.

FROM THE " KRÖNUNGSJOURNAL FÜR PRAG ", PUBLISHED BY ALBRECHT,
PRAGUE, 1791

Festivities of the Estates.

On the 6th., that is the day of the Coronation, the Estates gave a quite newly composed opera (the text of which, however, had been arranged from the Italian of Metastasio, though by Herr Mazzola, theatre poet in Dresden) to glorify His Majesty's day. The composition is by the famous Mozart, and does him honour, though he did not have much time for it and was also the victim of an illness, during which he had to complete the last part of the same.

The Estates had spared no pains over the performance of the same ; they had sent the manager to Italy, who brought back with him a *prima donna* and a *primo uomo*. The title of the opera itself was *la Clemenza di Tito*. The entry was free, and many tickets were distributed. The house holds a great number of persons, and yet, as one may well imagine, the demand for tickets was on such an occasion so great, that the supply came to an end, because of which many natives and visitors, among them persons of quality, had to go away again as they had not provided themselves with tickets.

His Majesty appeared at half past seven o'clock and was received with the loud applause of those present. The Members of the Estates themselves took in the tickets and were responsible for the necessary arrangements, so that no one having a ticket was refused admission, and no one without one was able to force his way in.

Of the dramatic entertainments

The Court paid one visit to the National Theatre and saw a performance of the opera *Don Juan oder der bestrafte Verschwender*, the text of which is by da Ponte, and the music by Mozart. It cannot be denied that Herr Guardasoni's company performs this piece excellently, and that many individuals excel themselves particularly . . .

Meanwhile the dramatic performances are not very well attended. Are the other entertainments responsible for this, or is it the high price which frightens away connoisseurs ? Neither the second opera performance given by the Estates, nor the theatre in the Small Side had large audiences.

> Pp. 382-4.—Prague, University Library.—Discovered by Christopher Raeburn.
> —The *Krönungsjournal* was brought out in book form by Johann Friedrich Ernst Albrecht or, more probably, by Sophie Albrecht, an actress at the Prague Theatre.—The *prima donna* was Maria Marchetti-Fantozzi, the first Vitellia in *La clemenza di Tito*, the *primo uomo* the castrato Domenico Bedini, the first Sextus. However, " the famous Italian " singer Anchulina (Carolina) Perini, the first Annius, and a Herr Anton Attenberg had sung during the emperor's luncheon on the day of the coronation.—*La clemenza di Tito* was given for the second time on 7 or 8 September.—A German and a Bohemian troupe were playing in the former Irish Monastery in the Small Side, and Haydn's opera *Der Ritter Roland* (*Orlando Palatino*) was even then being rehearsed there.

On 10 September Mozart visited the " Truth and Unity " lodge in Prague, where his cantata *Die Maurerfreude* (K. 471) was performed.

> Nettl, *op. cit.*, p. 209.—For the cantata see 24 April 1785.—Mozart seems to have visited the lodge several times ; he was honoured in this way on the occasion of his last visit.

FROM THE " PRAGER OBERPOSTAMTSZEITUNG ", 10 SEPTEMBER 1791

Prague, 8 September

The day before yesterday, in the evening, there was a free opera performance in the National Theatre in the Old Town, which was filled largely by the high nobility, who are at present here in great numbers. Their gracious Majesties also arrived at 8 o'clock, and were accompanied on their drive there and back by many thousand joyously cheering people.

> Prague, Municipal Archives.—Discovered by Christopher Raeburn.

On 12 September a folk festival and invitation ball was held at the National Theatre in Prague ; during supper Leopold Kozeluch's Homage Cantata, with text by August Gottlieb Meissner, was sung by Josepha Dušek in the presence of Their Majesties.

> The cantata, too, had been commissioned by the Bohemian Estates. It was repeated at a concert in the National Theatre on 23 September (see 31 December 1791).

In mid-September Mozart and his two companions returned to Vienna.

COUNT ANDREY KYRILLOVICH RASUMOVSKY TO PRINCE GRIGORY
ALEXANDROVICH POTEMKIN, VIENNA, 15 SEPTEMBER 1791
(in French)

. . . It was not for me, Sir, to send you the first keyboard player and one of the most gifted composers in Germany, named Mozart, who, being somewhat discontented here, might be disposed to undertake such a journey. He is in Bohemia at the moment, but will be back soon. If Your Highness will authorize me to engage him then, not for a long term, but simply to present himself to you for you to hear him and to attach him to your service, should you think fit. . . .

> A. Wassiltschikow, *Les Razoumowski* (Halle on the Saale, 1893), Vol. II, Part i, pp. 133 f.—*Acta Mozartiana* (Augsburg, 1955), Vol. II, Parts iii–iv, p. 45 (German translation by Dieter Lehmann).—Rasumovsky, later a prince and Russian Ambassador in Vienna, was on a diplomatic mission there in 1790–92, where he married Elisabeth, the daughter of Countess Wilhelmine Thun. He probably became acquainted with Mozart through her. Prince Potemkin, the Russian Field-Marshal, died in Bessarabia on 16 October that year.

On 30 September, at the theatre on the Wieden, the so-called Freihaus Theatre, the first performance of *Die Zauberflöte* took place.

> The libretto was by Schikaneder, the director of the theatre. Mozart conducted the first two performances from the pianoforte, with Süssmayer turning over for him ; the second performance was on the next day. The later performances were conducted by Henneberg, the Kapellmeister of the theatre.

TITLE-PAGE OF THE LIBRETTO OF " DIE ZAUBERFLÖTE "

DIE ZAUBERFLÖTE.
A / grand Opera in 2 acts. / By /
Emmanuel Schikaneder. / — /
The Music is by Herr Wolfgang Amade /
Mozart, Kapellmeister, and Kammer-Compositeur /
actually in Royal and Imperial Service. /
Vienna,
printed by Ignaz Alberti, 1791.

> Copy in the possession of the Gesellschaft der Musikfreunde, Vienna.—A facsimile was published by the Wiener Bibliophilen-Gesellschaft in 1942.—The libretto has a frontispiece with masonic symbols and contains a picture of Schikaneder in the costume of Papageno, both engraved by Ignaz Alberti, the masonic printer.

PLAYBILL

I. & R. priv. Wieden Theatre
Today, Friday, 30 September 1791.
The Actors of the Imperial and Royal privileged Theatre
on the Wieden will have the honour to perform
For the First Time :
DIE ZAUBERFLÖTE.
A Grand Opera in 2 Acts, by Emanuel Schikaneder.

Characters

Sarastro	Herr Gerl.
Tamino	Herr Schack.
Speaker	Herr Winter.
First ⎫	⎧Herr Schikaneder, sen.
Second ⎬ Priest	⎨Herr Kistler.
Third ⎭	⎩Herr Moll.
Queen of Night	Mme. Hofer.
Pamina, her Daughter . . .	Mlle. Gottlieb.
First ⎫	⎧Mlle. Klöpfer.
Second ⎬ Lady	⎨Mlle. Hofmann.
Third ⎭	⎩Mme. Schack.
Papageno	Herr Schikaneder, jun.
An Old Woman	Mme. Gerl.
Monostatos, a Moor . . .	Herr Nouseul.
First ⎫	⎧Herr Gieseke.
Second ⎬ Slave	⎨Herr Frasel.
Third ⎭	⎩Herr Starke.

Priests, Slaves, Retinue.

The music is by Herr Wolfgang Amade Mozart, Kapellmeister, and actual I. & R. Chamber Composer. Herr Mozard, out of respect for a gracious and honourable public, and from friendship for the author of this piece, will today direct the orchestra in person.

The book of the opera, furnished with two copper-plates, on which is engraved Herr Schikaneder in the costume he wears for the role of Papageno, may be had at the box office for 30 kr.

Herr Gayl, theatre painter, and Herr Nesslthaler as designer, flatter themselves that they have worked with the utmost artistic zeal according to the prescribed plan of the piece.

Prices of admission are as usual.

––––––––––

To begin at 7 o'clock.

Copy in the Mozart Museum at Salzburg.—Urban Schikaneder was Emanuel's elder brother. Josepha Hofer was Mozart's sister-in-law. Anna Gottlieb, now aged seventeen, had been the first Barbarina in *Figaro* in 1786. Johann Joseph Nouseul, engaged at the Burgtheater before and after, was really an actor, but was made use of in singspiele as well as in spoken plays, like most members of the company. Karl Ludwig Gieseke (properly Metzler), to whom the libretto of *Die Zauberflöte* has from time to time been ascribed, later became professor of mineralogy at Dublin. The other artists in the cast were Franz Xaver and Barbara Gerl (*née* Reisinger), Benedikt Schack and his wife (*née* Weinhold), the stage manager Winter, the tenor Kistler, the bass Moll, the soubrette Klöpfer, the ingénue Hofmann, Wilhelm Frasel and the supernumerary Starke. The theatre painter was Joseph Gayl, the stage designer was Nesslthaler ; he seems to have been the uncle of the painter Andreas Nesselthaler, who had been living in Salzburg since 1789.—The opera must have been given about twenty times in October, that is almost daily, which was remarkable even for this theatre (*cf.* 6 November 1791).—It is not known what honorarium Mozart received.—Pamina actually appears as Pramina, a printing error.

On 5 October Guardasoni's company performed *Così fan tutte* in Italian at Dresden.

A special libretto was published there in Italian and German. The opera is said to have been also performed in Prague by this company during the autumn.

On 7 October Constanze again went to Baden to take the waters.

This time the boy Karl was certainly sent to Perchtoldsdorf (*cf.* mid-August 1791), but little Wolfgang was with his mother and her sister Sophie at Baden.

On 7 October Mozart again attended *Die Zauberflöte* ; on the same evening *Don Giovanni* was given in German at Cologne.

On 8 October Mozart himself played Papageno's glockenspiel behind the scenes in *Die Zauberflöte*.

Apart from this diversion he sat in the box of a Bavarian that evening, and afterwards in that of the City Council official Franz Xaver Flamm.

On 9 October Mozart lunched with the Piarists in the Josefstadt suburb (see 26 June) and in the evening he took his mother-in-law, Frau Weber, to *Die Zauberflöte*.

The Piarists' seminary dissolved by the Emperor Joseph in 1782 was to be reopened. Mozart evidently intended to place his son Karl there. He went to Mass at the Piarist Church in order to speak to the rector before dinner.

[10 October : *see* Addenda, p. 605.]

FROM THE " MUSIKALISCHES WOCHENBLATT ", BERLIN, [? 10 DECEMBER]
1791

Vienna, the 9th October. The new comedy with machines, *Die Zauberflöte*, with music by our Kapellmeister *Mozard*, which is given at great cost and with much magnificence in the scenery, fails to have the hoped-for success, the contents and the language of the piece being altogether too bad.

We now daily await the arrival here of the new Imperial Kapellmeister *Cimarosa*, who is said to be bringing some excellent singers with him from St. Petersburg. It looks as though no very advantageous epoch were in sight here for German composers and musicians.

No. X, p. 79, not published till early December.—Abert, Vol. II, p. 754.— This periodical, published in 24 numbers between October 1791 and March 1792, was edited by Friedrich Ludwig Ämilius Kunzen and Karl Spazier. The numbers are undated.—Domenico Cimarosa had been active in St. Petersburg in 1789–91 after the departure of Paisiello, and was now to become Salieri's successor in Vienna. He brought five female and six male singers with him, all Italians, and wrote the opera *Il matrimonio segreto* for Vienna ; it was first performed at the Burgtheater on 7 February 1792. After the death of Leopold II (1 March 1792) Cimarosa was obliged to make way for Salieri again, and he returned home to Naples in 1793.

On 10 October Giuseppe Gazzaniga's opera *Don Giovanni Tenorio* was performed at the Théâtre Feydeau in Paris ; the conductor, Luigi Cherubini, inserted some numbers from Mozart's opera.

On 13 October Mozart went to Perchtoldsdorf with his brother-in-law, Hofer, to fetch Karl ; in the evening he took them both to *Die Zauberflöte* with Frau Weber ; Salieri and Caterina Cavalieri, for whom he called in a carriage, also came to the performance.

> Although the boy was to be absent from the institution for only three days, including a visit to his mother at Baden on the 15th, he does not seem to have returned to Heeger's.—Mozart's last letter to his wife, known only from an old copy, refers to Cavalieri as " he ", not " she ". There was a " Musical Director at the Assembly Hall " of that name ; he, Joseph Cavalier, a former schoolmaster, was Caterina Cavalieri's father ; however, as he died in 1787 and the singer was a friend of Salieri's, it seems likely that the copyist of the letter made a mistake.

HAYDN TO MARIA ANNA VON GENZINGER

London, 13th October 1791

. . . My good wife wrote to me, and yet I cannot believe it, that Mozart was said to disparage me very much. I forgive him for it ; . . . concerning the remuneration, Mozart should go to Count Fries for information, with whom I deposited 500 ducats, and with my Prince 1,000 gulden—in all, well nigh 6000 fl., I thank my Maker daily for this favour, and I flatter myself I shall bring home another thousand in cash. . . .

> Vienna, National Library.—Karajan, *op. cit.*—Haydn's wife, Anna, was much given to malicious gossip.—Mozart's doubts appear to refer to the material success of Haydn's journey and should perhaps be equated with his own plan to visit London.—Fries's bank had been founded by Count Johann Fries, who died in 1785, and now belonged to his wife, Anna, and her son Moritz, who was still a minor.—Haydn's prince was now Anton Esterházy.

On the morning of 15 October Mozart went to Baden with Karl to collect Constanze and take her home.

FROM THE " WIENER ZEITUNG ", 16 OCTOBER 1791

New Music.

From Johann Träg . . . the following new music is to be had from the 17th : *Duetti* for 2 violins from the opera (*Le Nozze di Figaro*) at 2 fl. 30 kr.

FROM THE " MUSIKALISCHES WOCHENBLATT ", BERLIN [? 22 OCTOBER], 1791

Amateur Concert.

Berlin. At a public amateur concert on 8 October the following distinguished themselves : Mme Bachmann, who made an excellent impression with her singing of a charming scena, and a young Herr Rück, who played a concerto by Mozart on the pianoforte with much lightness and precision, in which he threw well into relief the emotional passages as well as the peculiar traits of this rich artist, who—like all the greater geniuses who compel art to obey them even in the most bizarre effusions of the soul—occasionally delights in the strangest paradoxes. It is a great pleasure to see an artistic genius of this kind make light of a curious passage which, one suspects, would cost others the most enormous effort. This pleasure, however, turns into strenuous labour, which then has again to be turned to enjoyment by the circuitous route of study, if such an artist for once strives with all his might, which is especially true of Mozart's *Don Juan*, where he throws the whole store of his art at the hearer at once, whereby the excellent whole almost becomes lost to sight. Of which perhaps more another time.

C[arl] S[pazier]

> No. III, p. 19.—Jahn, Vol. III, p. 362.—Charlotte Bachmann, *née* Stöwe, was a member of the Berlin Singakademie under Karl Fasch.—The pianist Rück does not seem to have got very far.—The journal reverted to *Don Giovanni* in its very next issue.

---

*   COUNT HEINRICH ROTTENHAN ON GUARDASONI'S PETITION FOR COMPENSATION OF HIS LOSSES ON THE OPERA " LA CLEMENZA DI TITO ", PRAGUE, 29 OCTOBER 1791

It is generally known that by reason of the many court festivities, and the balls and parties given in private houses, both theatre managers had very small audiences ; and at court there was moreover a certain prejudice against Mozart's composition. Accordingly, as the opera drew scarcely any spectators after the first, gala performance, the manager's whole enterprise (apart from the agreed donation from the Estates), which relied on deriving a considerable sum from the sale of tickets, failed completely.

> Prague, National Central Archives (Fond Nationalausschuss, Abt. 84/12 Karton 1176).—Tomislav Volek in the *Mozart-Jahrbuch 1959* (Salzburg, 1960) pp. 284 f.—The other manager was Franz Seconda, who appeared during the summer with his Saxon theatre company in the Thun Theatre.—Guardasoni had addressed two appeals to the Bohemian Estates in September and October for reimbursement of his losses on the opera *La clemenza di Tito*. The members of the theatre commission gave their opinions on this matter individually between 29 October and 10 December 1791. Whereas Baron Johann Hennet proposed the sum of 150 ducats, Guardasoni finally received only 15 ducats compensation. Count Johann Prokop Hartmann mentions that despite the preparations for the ball (12 September) " the opera *La clemenza di Tito* was rehearsed on the stage ", and that the sets and costumes were not worthy of the festive occasion. A minute entry (Abt. 91/3, Karton 1481) intensifies Rottenhan's judgment on Mozart to "a strong prejudice", but this does not extend to Mozart as a person, for *Don Giovanni* was given on 2 September " by royal command ".

FROM THE " MUSIKALISCHES WOCHENBLATT ", BERLIN [? 29 OCTOBER] 1791

National Theatre, Berlin.

Wednesday, 12 October. *Don Juan, oder der steinerne Gast,* by Mozart.

Let us unite profound knowledge of the art with the happiest talent for inventing lovely melodies, and then link both with the greatest possible originality, in order to obtain the most faithful picture of Mozart's musical genius. Nowhere in his work does one ever find an idea one had heard before : even his accompaniments are always novel. One is, as it were, incessantly pulled along from one notion to another, without rest or repose, so that admiration of the latest constantly swallows up admiration for what has gone before, and even by straining all one's forces one is scarcely able to absorb all the beauties that present themselves to the soul. If any fault had to be found with Mozart, it could surely be only this : that such abundance of beauty almost tires the soul and the effect of the whole is sometimes obscured thereby. But happy the artist whose only fault lies in an *all too great* perfection ! — . . .

W.
[Bernhard Anselm Weber.]

No. IV, pp. 30 f.—Freisauff, *op. cit.*, p. 53.—The opera had been in the Berlin repertory since 20 December 1790.—In the further course of this article Weber gives an appreciation of the finest parts of the opera.

FROM THE " WIENER ZEITUNG ", 5 NOVEMBER 1791

Die Zauberflöte

Opera by Herr Mozart, Kapellmeister to His Majesty the Emperor, from which various pieces, to be sung at the pianoforte, may be had of Lausch's music establishment . . .

These fragments of a first pianoforte score were again the work of Joseph Heidenreich.—Copies in Kremsmünster Monastery and in the Schwarzenberg Archives, Krumau.

FROM ZINZENDORF'S DIARY, 6 NOVEMBER 1791

(in French)

. . . At half past 6 o'c. to Starhemberg's theatre in the Wien suburb, in the box of Monsieur and Mme. d'Auersperg, to hear the 24th performance of the *Zauberflöte*. The music and the stage-designs are pretty, the rest an incredible farce. A huge audience.

Christopher Raeburn in the programme book of the 1956 Glyndebourne Festival, p. 53.—The Freihaus in the Wieden suburb belonged to the Starhemberg family, whose head at that time was Prince Georg Adam Starhemberg.— In the box sat a Count Auersperg and his wife (? Franz Joseph and Johanna Elisabeth, *née* Engel).

FROM THE MS VIENNA NEWSPAPER " DER HEIMLICHE BOTSCHAFTER ",
18 NOVEMBER 1791

Herr Schikaneder will before long have an opera performed which is by far to surpass die *Zauberflöte*. Some rehearsals have already been held for this opera, entitled *Helena und Paris*.

Vienna, National Library.—O. E. Deutsch, *Das Wiener Freihaustheater* (Vienna, 1937), p. 20.—This journal, produced by Franz Staudinger, appeared twice weekly in numerous copies from 1 March 1791 to 19 December 1793. It contains some fantastic lies ; but Peter Winter's opera *Helena und Paris* really was performed at the Freihaus Theatre on 24 November.

On 18 November the new temple of the " New-Crowned Hope " lodge was inaugurated ; Mozart conducted his *Kleine Freimaurer-Kantate* (K. 623), written specially for the occasion.

The words are said to be by Schikaneder, who however, after a brief member-ship of a lodge at Regensburg (1788–89), does not appear to have belonged to any lodge in Vienna.—Whether the appendix to the first edition of the cantata (25 January 1792), "Anhang zum Schluss der ⬜ " (" Lasst uns mit geschlungen Händen . . ."), is also by the same authors, is uncertain. Gieseke is in fact the more likely author of the text.

On 20 November Mozart took to his bed.

About this time, " 14 days before his death ", he is supposed to have presented the musician Franz de Paula Roser with the MS. copies, supplemented with wind parts by Mozart, of the minuets Nos. 1, 2 and 4 from K. 585 (Gesell-schaft der Musikfreunde, Vienna). The copyist's score contained only the original version of these three minuets out of twelve, for two violins and bass. —Roser, then twelve years old, is said to have been a pupil of Mozart's for a time. Leopold and W. A. Mozart are reported to have stayed eleven days with his father, the Linz Cathedral Kapellmeister Johann Georg Roser von Reiter, who is named among the mourners at Mozart's burial (*cf. ca.* 1825).

FROM THE " WIENER ZEITUNG ", 23 NOVEMBER 1791

New Music.

From Artaria & Comp., art dealers in the Kohlmarkt, are quite newly to be had :

.   .   .

Mozart, Duet : " Bey Männern welche Liebe fühlen ", for the pianoforte, from the new opera *die Zauberflöte* 20 kr.
– – Aria ; " In diesen heil'gen Hallen ", for the pianoforte, from the same opera 20 kr.

This was the beginning of one of the two engraved Viennese pianoforte scores. See the next advertisement.

IBID., 26 NOVEMBER 1791

New Music.

At the Musikalisches Magazin . . . may be had the following new music, printed on paper of good quality and well and correctly engraved :

.   .   .

From the opera *Die Zauberflöte*, by Herr Mozard :
Aria (" In diesen heil'gen Mauern ") for the pianoforte. 10 kr.

– – *Duetto* ("Bei Männern, welche Liebe fühlen") for the pianoforte.
15 kr.

> Leopold Kozeluch in all haste brought out, as extracts from the pianoforte
> score prepared by him, the same two numbers as had been published by
> Artaria & Co. (see 3 December 1791).—It is the second verse of Sarastro's aria
> which begins with the words "In diesen heil'gen Mauern" (instead of
> "Hallen").—Both pianoforte scores were completed only in 1793. Only
> Kozeluch's was published complete ; Artaria's remained fragmentary as did
> a third by Hoffmeister (11 February to 19 May 1792).

On 28 November Mozart's doctors, Dr. Thomas Franz Closset and Dr. Matthia
von Sallaba, met to discuss his condition.

> Sallaba, too, was a distinguished doctor, finally becoming head physician of
> the General Hospital. He died in 1797, aged only thirty-one.

FROM THE "WIENER ZEITUNG", 30 NOVEMBER 1791

Announcement.

From Artaria & Comp. in the Kohlmarkt the following dance music is to
be had :
Mozart, 12 Minuets for the Rout with all the parts   1 fl. 30 kr.
– –   12 German Dances   1 fl. 30 kr.

.   .   .   .   .

Mozart 12 German Dances for the Rout for the pianoforte, 2nd part   45 kr.
– –   12 – – – 3rd part   45 kr.
– –   12 Minuets, 2nd part   45 kr.
– –   12 German Dances, 3rd part   45 kr.

> Minuets in (? all) parts and pianoforte score : K. 599, 601 and 604 ; in piano-
> forte score alone : K. 585. German dances in (? all) parts and pianoforte
> score : K. 600, 602 & 605 ; in piano score alone : K. 586.

FROM THE "MUSIKALISCHE KORRESPONDENZ DER TEUTSCHEN FILAR-
MONISCHEN GESELLSCHAFT", SPEYER, 30 NOVEMBER 1791
[the titles in French and Italian respectively]

Quartet for 2 Violins, Viola and Violoncello, composed by Monsieur
W. A. Mozart, *ibid.* [Vienna, Hoffmeister] in fol. (Pr. 1 fl. 20 kr.)
Quartet for the Harpsichord or Fortepiano with the accompaniment of
one violin, viola and violoncello. *Ibid.*, Artaria, oblong fol. (Pr. 1 fl. 40 kr.)
Op. 13.
Both these quartets are written with that fire of the imagination and
that correctness, which long since won for Herr M. the reputation of one
of the best composers in Germany. The first consists of four, the second
of only three movements, and even the Minuet in the former is composed
with an ingenuity (being interwoven with canonic imitations) that one not

infrequently finds wanting in other such compositions, even by famous masters.

> No. 48, col. 377 f.—The string quartet is that in D major (K. 499), published in 1786; the pianoforte quartet that in E♭ major (K. 493), advertised on 21 July 1787.

FROM THE " WIENER ZEITUNG ", 3 DECEMBER 1791

New Music.

At the Musikalisches Magazin . . . have appeared certain completely new works, fresh from the press, on the best paper, well and correctly engraved, viz. :

.   .   .   .   .

From the opera *die Zauberflöte* by Herr Mozart :
Terzetto : " Seid uns zum zweitenmal wilkommen " for the pianoforte, 15 kr.
Duetto : " Bei Männern, welche Liebe fühlen ", 15 kr.
Aria : " In diesen heilgen Mauern ", 10 kr.

> *Cf.* 26 November 1791.

On 3 December there was a slight improvement in Mozart's condition.

At 2 p.m. on 4 December a kind of rehearsal of the as yet unfinished Requiem was held at Mozart's sick-bed.

> Count Franz Walsegg-Stuppach (see 2 April 1788) had the Requiem commissioned from Mozart anonymously in Spring, 1791, wishing to perform it as his own composition in memory of his late wife. Mozart had already earlier tried out parts of the work with Constanze, Süssmayer and other friends at his home. On this occasion he sang the alto part to Schack's falsetto, Hofer's tenor and Gerl's bass.

On Monday 5 December 1791, at five minutes to 1 a.m., Mozart died.

> Dr. Closset had been called in during the evening of 4 December, but was unable to do anything more. The diagnosis at the time was " heated miliary fever " ; the supposition today is that the cause of death was " a uraemic coma following a lengthy kidney disease ". (Aloys Greither, *Wolfgang Amadé Mozart. Seine Leidensgeschichte an Briefen und Dokumenten dargestellt* [Heidelberg, 1958].)

POSTHUMOUS DOCUMENTS

ENTRY BY CONSTANZE IN MOZART'S ALBUM

What thou once wrote to thy friend on this page,
do I now in my affliction write to thee,
dearly beloved husband ; Mozart—never to be forgotten by me or by the
whole of Europe—now thou too art at peace—eternal peace ! ! . . .
About one o'clock in the morning of the 5th of December in this year
he left in his 36th year—alas ! all too soon !—
this good—but ungrateful world !—dear God !—
For 8 years we were joined together by the most tender bond,
never to be broken here below !—
O ! could I soon be joined with thee for ever,

Thy grievously afflicted wife
Constance Mozart <i>neè</i> Weber

Vienna the 5th December, 1791.

> Formerly in the Mozarteum, Salzburg.—Facsimile in Arthur Schurig's Mozart
> biography (Leipzig, 1913), Vol. II, p. 333 ; (1923), Vol. II, p. 416— Müller
> von Asow, III. 496.—Constanze wrote these words on the reverse of Dr.
> Barisani's entry (14 April 1787), below which Mozart himself had expressed
> his grief at the loss of this friend (3 September 1787).—It has been doubted
> whether Constanze really wrote these lines on the day of Mozart's death, when,
> almost beside herself, it is said that she had to be taken away from the house.

FROM THE REGISTER OF DEATHS OF ST. STEPHEN'S CATHEDRAL

1791
Xber
5th

(City) No. 970 Herr Wolfgang Amadeus Mozart, I. & R. Kapellmeister and Kammer Compositor (Catholic) 1 (Male) 1 (Age) 36
(Sickness and manner of death) Severe miliary fever (Place and
date of burial) The 6th ditto [Xber] ditto [the burial ground
outside St. Marx]

> Folio 173.—Words in parentheses are those printed as headings to the columns
> in the register of deaths ; those in square brackets contain words not repeated
> from the entries above.—The cemetery, laid out only a few years earlier
> outside the toll boundary of St. Marx, was the appropriate one for the dis-
> trict of the parish of St. Stephen in which Mozart died (see 15 November
> 1786).—The death certificate, which Jahn, Vol. II, p. 702, reprinted from
> the year 1847, is only an extract from the death register.

FROM ZINZENDORF'S DIARY, 5 DECEMBER 1791
(in French)

. . . Mild weather. Mist three or four times a day for some time.

> Zinzendorf recorded the weather in his diary each evening (see 6 December).

FROM THE "NECROLOGIUM PARTICULARE" OF ABBOT DOMINICUS HAGENAUER
(in Latin)

Dec. 5th 1791 died Master Wolfgang Motzart of Salzburg, director of music to the Emperors Joseph II and Leopold II, at the age of 35.

Salzburg, Archives of St. Peter's Monastery, Ms.A. 250.

At 3 p.m. on 6 December Mozart's body was blessed in front of the Crucifix Chapel (at the foot of the unfinished northern spire) of St. Stephen's Cathedral, then taken through the Stubentor and by way of the Landstrasse suburb to the St. Marx cemetery, and buried in a common grave.

> From 5 to 6 December the body was presumably laid out in the house where Mozart died. The consecration took place in the open, as was usual for plain funerals, in this case in front of the open Renaissance hall which formed the entry to the catacombs and was ornamented with a crucifix, near the so-called Capistrano pulpit. The priest stood aloft in this " Crucifix Chapel " (popularly and misleadingly called " Cross Chapel ") ; the coffin was placed by the steps. It was not a pauper's funeral, but the cheapest available.—That neither the widow nor close friends, nor yet any of the freemasons attended the procession is explicable only by the simplicity that became customary for funerals in Emperor Joseph's time. (On 5 December van Swieten lost his position as President of the Court Commission of Education, according to information in a minute of Leopold II made available by E. F. Schmid.)— Common graves were about 7½ ft. deep ; coffins were buried in three layers over a period of time. The persons of the same quarter who were buried ca. 6 December remained Mozart's neighbours and are to be found in the death register of St Stephen's. But the fact that common graves were not marked and that none of Mozart's intimates seems to have witnessed the burial made it impossible later on to identify with any certainty the place where he lay. (Hermine Cloeter, Die Grabstätte W. A. Mozarts, Vienna, 1956.) Nissen's notes in the Salzburg Mozarteum state that graves in these " general burial grounds " are said to have been " opened and cleared " every seven years. (Rudolf von Lewicki in Mozarteums-Mitteilungen [Salzburg], November 1919, p. 29.)

FROM THE REGISTER OF DEATHS OF ST. STEPHEN'S PARISH, 6 DECEMBER 1791

The 6th Xber

Mozart	Herr Wolfgang Amandeus
3rd class	Mozart, I. & R. Kapellmeister and
Parish	Kammer Compositeur, in the Rauchen-
St: Stephen	steingasse, in the small Kaiserhaus Nr.
	970, of severe miliary fever, ex-
	amined, 36 years old

In the burial ground outside St. Marx

8 fl. 56 kr. Paid   .   .   .   .   .   . 4.36.   4.20.

Hearse f 3 —

Jahn, Vol. II, p. 703.—Otto Schneider, Mozart in Wirklichkeit (Vienna, 1955), p. 320 (reproduction).—The cost was 4 fl. 36 kr. in parish charges and 4 fl. 20 kr. in church expenses.

M.—14

FROM ZINZENDORF'S DIARY, 6 DECEMBER 1791
[in French]

. . . Mild weather and frequent mist.

This seems to contradict the tradition (see Deiner's *Memoirs*, 1856) that th mourners were unable to follow the coffin to the grave on account of rain and snow. (*Cf.* Nicolas Slonimsky in *The Musical Quarterly* [New York, January 1960], Vol. 46, No. 1, pp. 12-21.)—N.B. Litigation dragged on into 1793 ; the relevant documents (Archives of the City of Vienna) are printed in Appendix II.

On the same day, 6 December, Hofdemel attempted to murder his wife and then committed suicide.

Ferdinand Bischoff in the *Mitteilungen für die Mozart-Gemeinde in Berlin*, October 1900.—Ernst Weizmann in the *Weltpresse* (Vienna, 4 February 1956 and eight Saturdays following).—Gustav Gugitz in the *Österreichische Musik-zeitschrift*, July 1956.—For Hofdemel see 2 April 1789.—To connect this affair with Mozart's death and to hold him responsible for the boy born to Frau Hofdemel on 10 May 1792, seems inadmissible.

FROM THE " WIENER ZEITUNG ", 7 DECEMBER 1791

In the night of the 4th and 5th of this month there died here the I. & R Hofkammerkompositor Wolfgang Mozart. Known from his childhood as the possessor of the finest musical talent in all *Europe*, through the fortunate development of his exceptional natural gifts and through persistent application he climbed the pinnacle of the greatest Masters ; his works, loved and admired by all, bear witness to this, and are the measure of the irreplaceable loss that the noble art of music has suffered by his death.

This was an editorial notice ; it was reproduced in the *Prager Oberpostamts-zeitung* on the 13th ; the first sentence also appeared in the *Pressburger Zeitung* of the 10th.—*Cf.* 10 and 31 December.

★ IBID., 7 DECEMBER 1791

Barometric readings

Date	8 a.m.		3 p.m.		10 p.m.	
	Zoll	Lin.	Zoll	Lin.	Zoll	Lin.
4	27	$6\frac{1}{2}$	27	$5\frac{2}{3}$	27	$5\frac{1}{2}$
5	27	$7\frac{1}{2}$	27	8	27	7

Réaumur thermometric readings

Date	Degrees	Degrees	Degrees
4	3 –	$4\frac{1}{2}$	$2\frac{1}{2}$
5	2 –	$3\frac{1}{2}$	3 –

Wind

Date			
4	–	Light north wind	–
5	–	Calm	–

No. 98, Appendix, p. 3129.—One Viennese "Zoll" (inch) contained 12 Viennese "Linien" (line) ; 1 Viennese Linie = 2·195 mm.

IBID., 7 DECEMBER 1791

New Music.

From Artaria & Comp., art dealers in the Kohlmarkt, are to be had the following arias from the new opera *Die Zauberflöte* by Mozart, arranged for pianoforte :

Aria, Der Vogelfänger bin ich ja,   8 kr.

Terzetto, Du feines Täubchen nur herein,   15 kr.

Terzetto of the 3 Boys, Zum Ziele führt dich diese Bahn,   10 kr.

Glockenspiel and Chorus, followed by Duetto between Pamina and Papageno, 10 kr.

Duetto, Bey Männern welche Liebe fühlen,

– –   Bewahret euch für Weiber Tücke,   6 kr.

Aria, Alles fühlt der Liebe Freuden,   10 kr.

– –   In diesen heilgen Hallen,

– –   Ach ich fühle es ist verschwunden,   10 kr.

Terzetto, Soll ich dich Theurer nicht mehr sehen,   24 kr.

Aria, Ein Mädchen oder Weibchen,   10 kr.

Terzetto of the 3 Boys, Seid uns zum zweytenmal willkommen,   10 kr.

     Cf. 23 November 1791.

TESTIMONIAL FOR EMANUEL ALOYS FÖRSTER, *ca.* 7 DECEMBER 1791

I, the undersigned, attest and declare in the interests of pure truth, pleasing to God, that for the last four years I have been very well acquainted with Herr Emanuel Aloys Förster, not only as to his great skill in the practice of the art of music and composition, but also as to his moral character. As regards his skill in keyboard-playing the late, great master Mozart has often publicly averred to the said Herr Förster, both in my presence and that of others, that the latter was certainly the strongest and most skilful master of the keyboard after himself. Further, all musicians grant that the said Herr Förster can, in the art of composition, justly be placed between Hayden and Mozart . . . Vienna, the 3rd Xber 1791.

Augustinus Erasmus Donath

I. & R. Bohemian and Austrian Hofagent

Vienna, State Archives, Akten der Hofmusikkapelle, 1791, fol. 100 f.—Karl Pfannhauser in *Acta Mozartiana* (Stuttgart, 1956), Year III, No. 3, p. 7 f.— Although this certificate is dated 3 December, it cannot have been written before the 5th, since Mozart is mentioned as already dead.—For Förster see 13 August 1788.—The phrase used here and in the following document for "keyboard-playing" is "Fliegschlagen" (Flieg = Flügel).—The object of this recommendation is made clear by the following document.

EMANUEL ALOYS FÖRSTER'S PETITION TO THE EMPEROR, *ca.* 8 DECEMBER 1791

Your Majesty,

The undersigned begs to be graciously admitted into the Hofkammer-kapelle in the place of the late musician and composer Wolfgang Mozart.

His most humble petition is supported 1° by the recommendations contained in the attached testimonial A. ; and if the petitioner must on the one hand admit that in keyboard-playing and composition he is not quite so perfect as the late Mozart was, on the other hand the certainty that no-one could be found to equal Mozart in this speciality, may be allowed to speak for him.

2° he wishes to undergo a demonstration of his keyboard-playing, and also to submit several examples of his skill in composition.

Emanuel Aloys Förster

Ibid., fol. 99-102.—Pfannhauser, as above.—On fol. 102 we read : " praes. den 9ten Xber 1791 " ; the undated petition may thus have been written *ca.* 8 December (see 12 January and 12 March 1792).

FROM THE MS. VIENNA NEWSPAPER " DER HEIMLICHE BOTSCHAFTER ", 9 DECEMBER 1791

A sad event for music and exceedingly distressing for all amateurs of the art is Mozart's death. A case of severe miliary fever carried away together with him the second part of Herr Schikaneder's *Zauberflötte*, for which he had already composed the first act.

Vienna, National Library. — Gustav Gugitz in *Mozarteums-Mitteilungen* (Salzburg, November 1920), year 3, vol. 1, p. 2.—*Cf.* 18 November 1791.

FROM " HADI ÉS MÁS NEVEZETES TÖRTÉNETEK ", VIENNA, 9 DECEMBER 1791
(in Hungarian)

On the fifth of this month, in the early morning, there died Wolfgang Mozart, the I. & R. Court Composer, famed throughout the whole of Europe, at the early age of 35. Even the greatest masters were astonished at the rare talent of this great musician. But what has this richly endowed man left behind him ? A name that will live for ever, but also a helpless widow with two orphan children, and many debts. The magnanimous Baron Swieten has already come to the assistance of the orphans. One of these children, though still very small, already plays the clavichord in such a way as to astound all hearers.

P. 739 f.—Ervin Major, *Mozart und Ungarn* (Budapest, 1956), p. 44, with facsimile of the original.—*Cf.* 13 and 16 December 1791.

FROM THE " WIENER ZEITUNG ", 10 DECEMBER 1791

Deaths in Vienna.

Herr Wolfg. Amadeus Mozart, I. & R. Kapellmeister and Kammer-kompositor, aged 36 years, in the Rauhensteingasse No. 970.

CONSTANZE MOZART'S PETITION FOR A PENSION

Your Majesty !

The undersigned has had the misfortune to suffer the irreparable loss of her husband, and to be left by him with two infant sons in circumstances which border upon indigence and want.

She knows, to her still greater distress, that because her deceased husband had not yet completed ten years' service, according to the existing quali-fication for a pension she has no claim whatsoever to any allowance, and that there is therefore no course left to her but to trust in Your Majesty's favour and well-known love of providing for the indigent of all kinds.

But lest she might perhaps appear unworthy of your most gracious benevolence, she ventures humbly to present a feeble description of her most unhappy plight and of its causes :

1° her late husband never had the good fortune here in Vienna to meet with the propitious opportunity that would have allowed him to reveal his talents sufficiently to begin to improve his prospects in the world—and it was for that reason that he was not in a position to leave any means. It would moreover in the

2nd place have gone very easily with him abroad to make his fortune and to place his family in more brilliant circumstances, had he given heed to frequent propositions, and not chosen to seek his greatest fame in the favour of this most illustrious court.

3rdly, granted that he was still in the prime of life and had the most likely prospect of being able to establish the well-being of his dependants in good time through his rare talent, it will be seen that there was no room in his thoughts for the possibility of the present situation.

Hence it came about that he never thought to ensure provision, however meagre, for his dependants by enrolling them in the Society for the Widows and Orphans of Musicians.

4thly. Finally this picture is the more pitiful in that he was snatched from the world at that very moment when his prospects for the future were beginning to grow brighter on all sides.

For besides the reversion which he recently obtained of the position of Kapellmeister at St. Stephen's Cathedral, he was assured shortly before his death of an annual subscription of 1000 florins from a number of the Hun-garian nobility ; while from Amsterdam he was advised of a still larger annual sum, for which he would have had to compose only a few works for the exclusive use of the subscribers.

The petitioner presumes to commend herself once more to your gracious favour and well-known paternal benevolence, especially towards cases of need of this kind, all the more completely in that only one thing still suffices to support her in her grievous situation, namely her confidence that Your Majesty will not exclude her and her *two infant sons* from your gracious liberality.

Vienna, the 11th December 1791

> Konstantia Mozart, *née*
> Weber, widow relict
> of the late Wolfgang Amadeus
> Mozart, I. & R. Kammerkom-
> positor

[on cover :]

To

His Majesty

Konstantia Mozart, *née* Weber, relict of the late Wolfgang Amadeus Mozart, I. & R. Kammer-Kompositor

> In consideration of her extremely wretched situation appeals for a pension for herself and her 2 infant sons, and in the absence of any justifiable claim makes bold to commit herself entirely to the mercy of His Majesty.

[Decision :]

The applicant is hereby advised at the behest of the Lord High Steward's office that in accordance with the existing royal ordinances she must accompany her request for a pension with the executors' certificate or with some other legally valid document, and must at the same time give evidence that she has no prospect of a pension from the Court Musical Society funds. Vienna, the 5th January 1792.

> For the Director of Court Music.
> von Caballini

Salzburg, Mozarteum.—Abert, Vol. II, pp. 912-14.—Fair copy in an unknown hand, probably written by a friend of the family.—Constanze is said to have handed this petition to Leopold II at an audience.—Nothing is known of proposals from abroad that might have offered Mozart a permanent post.—For the Musicians' Society see 11 February and 24 August 1785. At this time there was also a society fund for widows and orphans of the Imperial chamber musicians and the Hofkapelle.—For the reversion of the post of Cathedral Kapellmeister see 9 May and 12 December 1791.—No further details are known of revenues offered to Mozart for commissioned works by Hungarian nobles and Amsterdam music-lovers. Among the Hungarian nobility in Vienna the possible families were those of Apponyi, Bánffy, Batthyány, Esterházy, Pálffy and Zichy. The posthumous string quintets in D major (K. 593) and E♭ major (K. 614) were published in 1793 by Artaria with the indication " Composto per un Amatore Ongarese ". (Perhaps the Viennese music-lover Johann Tost, born at Uherské Hradiště, though this place was actually in Moravia.)—For the petition see 30 December 1791, and 20 January, 12 and 13 March 1792.

On the same day, 11 December, Anton Eberl finished his cantata *Bey Mozarts Grabe.*

The Viennese pianist and composer Eberl, some of whose works were to appear under Mozart's name, accompanied Constanze and her sister Aloisia Lange on a concert tour in the north in 1795–96 and often appeared at concerts for the widow's benefit.—The words of the cantata were by Eberl's brother Ferdinand. In it the Muses, Terpsichore, the Genius of Germany and the artists unite in a complaint against the Fates (Robert Haas in the *Mozart-Jahrbuch für 1951* [Salzburg, 1953], p. 126). The holograph score was in the Wilhelm Heyer Collection in Cologne (Georg Kinsky's Catalogue [Cologne, 1916], p. 109). Haas also mentions a pianoforte score of the cantata.

THE VIENNA CITY COUNCIL TO JOHANN GEORG ALBRECHTSBERGER, 12 DECEMBER 1791

The city council, etc., begs to inform him that he is granted his request for the post of deputy Kapellmeister in the Metropolitan Church of St Stephen rendered vacant by the death of Herr Mozart, provided that he pledge himself by means of a legal affidavit, and that he agree without payment to take the place of the official Kapellmeister when the latter is not able to appear personally for reasons of health or any other cause, and to accompany the order of service ; and provided also that, when the post of official Kapellmeister shall in due time fall vacant, he shall be satisfied with the salary which the city council shall in the future deem proper.

Which is imparted to Herr Albrechtsberger for his information and advantage.

Ex Cons. Mag. Vien.

Vienna, the 12th December 1791

Jahn, Vol. I, p. 809.—Ernst Weizmann in the *Weltpresse*, 28 April 1956 (with facsimile).—Albrechtsberger seems to have petitioned for the reversion directly after Mozart's death, as Förster did for the post of Court Chamber Composer. When Leopold Hofmann died on 17 March 1793, Albrechtsberger became his successor. Moreover, he remained organist of the Hofmusikkapelle until 1 April 1793, having been promoted in preference to the two regular organists on 1 December 1791.

FROM THE MS VIENNA NEWSPAPER " DER HEIMLICHE BOTSCHAFTER ", 13 DECEMBER 1791

Mozhart unfortunately had that indifference to his family circumstances which so often attaches to great minds. The widow of a man to whom so many crowned heads, to whom all Europe accorded unstinted admiration ; who, apart from his position as Hof-Kapells Meister, and deputy at St Stephen's, had pupils taken exclusively from the highest and richest nobility ; who could have, nay should have, earned riches for such famous works ;—

this man's widow sits sighing on a sack of straw amidst her needy children and under a sizeable burden of debt. An administrative official gave ten Gulden against Mozhart's watch, so that he could be buried. Who is not here reminded of Handel? Who would not wish it of the Viennese that they might, through generosity to Mozhart's widow, make good the ingratitude shown to Handel?

National Library, Vienna.—Gugitz, *op. cit.*, pp. 2 f.

FROM THE " EPHEMERIDES POLITICO-LITTERARIAE ", PEST,
13 DECEMBER 1791
(in Latin)

Vienna, 9 December.
Wolfgang Mozart, aulic musician and composer celebrated in Europe, died on the fifth day of December.

Ervin Major, *op. cit.*, p. 44.

INVITATION CARD FROM THE PRAGUE THEATRE ORCHESTRA

The orchestra of the Prague National Theatre begs to announce that on 14 December at 10 o'clock a Solemn Mass for Capellmeister and Kammer-componist *Wolfgang Gottlieb Mozart*, who fell peacefully asleep in the Lord on 5 December in Vienna, will be held in the Small Side Parish Church o St Niclas as a mark of its boundless veneration and esteem. To which a very respectful invitation is extended to the high nobility and the honoured public.

Procházka, *op. cit.*, p. 185 (after Dlabacs).—For St. Nicholas Church see 8 (?) December 1787.—For the requiem mass see 24 December and *cf.* 28 December 1791.

* FROM THE " WIENER ZEITUNG ", 14 DECEMBER 1791
Barometric readings

Date	8 a.m.		3 p.m.		10 p.m.	
	Zoll	Lin.	Zoll	Lin.	Zoll	Lin.
6	27	$7\frac{1}{2}$	27	7	27	8

Réaumur thermometric readings

	Degrees	Degrees	Degrees
6	$2\frac{1}{2}$ above zero	3 above zero	3 above zero

Wind

6	dead calm	dead calm	dead calm

No. 100, Appendix, p. 3193. The records of the Vienna Observatory give the temperature at 8 a.m. as 2·6 degrees and note a light east wind for the whole day.

FROM THE MS VIENNA NEWSPAPER " DER HEIMLICHE BOTSCHAFTER ",
16 DECEMBER 1791

All are concerned with Mozart's widow, trying to make good her loss
to some extent, and to comfort her. Thus the worthy Baron von Suitten
has adopted the boy, who already plays the clavier excellently, and the
Countess *Thun* the girl. Herr Schikaneder had obsequies performed for
the departed, at which the Requiem, which he composed in his last illness,
was executed. Herr *Schikaneder* will give a performance of the *Zauberflötte*
in the next few days for the benefit of the widow.

> Gugitz, *op. cit.*, p. 3.—Bossler's *Musikalische Korrespondenz* wrote similarly
> about van Swieten on 4 January 1792, and Niemetschek (p. 31) said in 1798 :
> " This excellent . . . man . . . is now a father to his [Mozart's] bereaved
> orphans ". Legally van Swieten became nothing of the kind, but he appears
> to have taken care of the two boys until he was relieved about 1800 by Georg
> Nikolaus Nissen, Constanze's second husband.—For the rest the *Botschafter*
> once again contains nothing but fantasies.

FROM THE " WIENER ZEITUNG ", 17 DECEMBER 1791

New music.

At the Musikalisches Magazin . . . may be had the following new music,
straight from the press, printed on paper of good quality and well and
accurately engraved, namely :

.   .   .   .   .

From the opera *die Zauberflöte*, by Hr. Mozart :
Aria, In diesen heil'gen Hallen, 8 kr.
 – – Alles fühlt der Liebe Freuden, 9 kr. which the Moor sings
 – – Der Vogelfänger bin ich ja, 7 kr.
 – – Ach ich fühle es ist verschwunden, 9 kr.
 – – Ein Mädchen oder Weibchen, 9 kr.
Duetto, Bey Männern welche Liebe fühlen, 10 kr.
 – – Bewahret euch für Weiber Tücke, 5 kr.
Terzetto, Du feines Taübchen nur herein, 14 kr.
 – – Zum Ziele führt dich diese Bahn, the 3 boys 9 kr.
 – – Seid uns zum zweytenmal willkommen, the 3 boys, 9 kr.
 – – Soll ich dich Theurer nicht mehr sehen, 22 kr.
Glockenspiel and Chorus, followed by Duetto, for Pamina and Papageno,
   9 kr.

> *Cf.* 26 November, 3 and 7 December 1791.

M.—14 *a*

* FROM THE MS VIENNA NEWSPAPER " DER HEIMLICHE BOTSCHAFTER ",
VIENNA, 18 DECEMBER 1791

In place of the late Kapellmeister and Kammerkompositeur Mozart
His Majesty has appointed Herr Kockzeluit with a salary of 2,000 gulden.
in consideration of his capabilities and good judgement.

> Discovered by Richard Smekal in an otherwise unknown copy of this MS
> newspaper (not preserved in the Austrian National Library) ; published by
> Albert Wilhelm in *Das kleine Volksblatt*, Vienna, 8 January 1961. The name
> Kozeluch appears in a corrupt form ; he was not appointed.

HAYDN TO FRAU VON GENZINGER, LONDON, 20 DECEMBER 1791

Like a child I long to be home again to embrace my good friends, only
regretting that I cannot do this to the great Mozart, if it is true—which I
do not wish—that he is dead. Posterity will not have such a talent again
in 100 years.

> Vienna, National Library.—Karajan, *op. cit.*

FROM THE " PRESSBURGER ZEITUNG ", 21 DECEMBER 1791

Vienna, 18 December.

The widow of the suicide (see No. 100) who, as is now known, took his
life from faint-heartedness rather than jealousy, is still alive, and not only
several ladies, but also Her Majesty the Empress herself, have promised
assistance to this woman, whose conduct is known to be unexceptionable.
Provision has also been made for the widow of the late Kapellmeister
Mozart. His Majesty the Emperor has granted her her husband's full
salary, and Baron van Swieten has provided for her son.

> Discovered by Frau Lidia F. Wendelin, Budapest.—The newspaper had
> reported Hofdemel's attempt at murder and his suicide on 7 December,
> though without naming him. Emperor Leopold's consort was Maria Louisa,
> Princess of Spain.—The reports about Constanze were current in Vienna at
> this time. *Cf.* 6 and 16 December 1791.

JOSEPH EYBLER'S STATEMENT CONCERNING THE REQUIEM

The undersigned hereby imparts that Frau Konstanzie Mozart, widow,
has entrusted him with the completion of the Requiem Mass begun by her
late husband ; the same undertakes to complete it by the middle of the
coming Lent, and at the same time guarantees that it shall neither be copied,
nor given into other hands than those of the aforementioned widow.
Vienna, 21 December 1791.

Wiener-Neustadt, Municipal Archives—Abert, Vol. II, p. 850.—For Eybler *cf.* 30 May 1790.—Constanze, who wished to have the Requiem completed for the client, who was unknown to her, at first entrusted the manuscript to Eybler, who completed the instrumentation up to the " Confutatis ", but then abandoned the work, which was in the end completed by Süssmayer.

FROM THE " WIENER ZEITUNG ", 24 DECEMBER 1791

The Friends of Music in *Prague*, on the 14th inst. and in the Small Side parish church of *St Niklas*, performed solemn obsequies for Wolfgang Gottlieb *Mozart*, Kapellmeister and Hofkomponist, who died here on the 5th. This ceremony had been arranged by the Prague Orchestra of the National Theatre, under the direction of Hr. Joseph *Strohbach*, and all Prague's well-known musicians took part in it. On the appointed day the bells of the parish church were rung for half an hour ; almost the entire city streamed thither, so that the Wälsche Platz could not hold the coaches, nor the church (which is, moreover, big enough to hold nearly 4,000 people) the admirers of the dead artist. The Requiem was by Kapellmeister *Rössler*, it was admirably performed by 120 of the leading musicians, first among whom was the well-loved singer Mad. *Duscheck*. In the middle of the church stood a finely illuminated catafalque ; 3 choirs of drums and trumpets sounded forth with muffled tones ; the parish priest, Herr Rudolph *Fischer*, read the Mass ; 12 boys from the Small Side Gymnasium carried torches, wore mourning-crapes draped diagonally across one shoulder, and bore white cloths in their hands ; solemn silence lay all about, and a thousand tears flowed in poignant memory of the artist who through [his] harmonies so often tuned all hearts to the liveliest feelings.

> Nissen, p. 577 f., made use of this report.—According to Procházka, *op. cit.*, pp. 186 f., an almost identical report appeared in the *Prager Oberpostamts-zeitung* on 17 December.—Franz Anton Rössler, who as a composer used the name Rosetti, was born in Bohemia and had been Court Capellmeister at Ludwigslust (Mecklenburg-Schwerin) since 1789 ; he died soon after.—A *Cantate auf Mozart's Tod* (text by Schmidt) which appeared in Prague in 1798 was by Joseph Johann Rösler.

FROM THE " WIENER ZEITUNG ", 28 DECEMBER 1791

New music.

From Artaria & Comp., art dealers in the Kohlmarkt, are to be had : Three entirely new concertante quartets for two violins, viola and violon-cello by Hr. Kapellmeister Mozart. Op. 18.

These quartets are one of the most estimable works of the composer *Mozart*, who was torn untimely from this world ; they flowed from the pen of this so great musical genius not long before his death, and they display all that musical interest in respect of art, beauty and taste which must awaken pleasure and admiration not only in the amateur, but in the true connoisseur also.   Care has therefore also been taken as to their outward appearance, and the edition of this masterpiece has been prepared and printed in a clear, clean and correct type on fine and good paper.—These 3 quartets cost 3 fl.

> The three quartets intended for the King of Prussia, in D, B♭ and F (K. 575, 589 and 590), were composed in 1789–90, but were Mozart's last.

FROM THE " MUSIKALISCHE KORRESPONDENZ DER TEUTSCHEN FILHARMO-
NISCHEN GESELLSCHAFT ", SPEYER, 28 DECEMBER 1791

Obituary.

It is our sad duty at the close of this year to impart to our readers an intelligence which will cause great sorrow in the world of music, namely that on the 5th day of this month the universally known, much sought-after and beloved Royal and Imperial Hofkammerkompositeur Hr. *Mozart* died of a dropsy of the heart in the 34th year of his age. All Vienna, and with the Imperial city the entire musical world, laments the early loss of this immortal man. His body has gone from us, his soul has soared upwards to higher harmonies, and for our comfort he leaves the beautiful products of his mind . . .

> No. 52, col. 411.—The journal published on 4 January 1792 a " Biographische Nachricht " on Mozart.

CONSTANZE MOZART TO LUIGI SIMONETTI

> Vienna
> à Monsieur Louigi Simonetti
> primo Tenore di Sua Altezza
> Elettorale di Cologna
> à Bonn.

Monsieur,

You can have both *la Clemenza di Tito* and *die Zauberflöte* from me very soon, as soon, that is, as the copyist can complete the copy. For one score I ask 100 Kremniz ducats, and await your speedy decision which you will take, if either, so that the copyist may begin at once. Be so kind as to arrange the order in such a way that the money may be drawn as soon as the required score is handed over, for it is all the property of my sons, who are not yet of age.   With respect,

> Monsieur,
> I am your humble servant
> Constanze Mozart
> *née* Weber

Vienna, the
28th December 1791

Paris, Roger de Garate Collection.—*Mozart en France* (Paris, 1956), Catalogue No. 176 (French translation).—Simonetti was concert tenor at the Court of Maximilian. *Die Zauberflöte* was performed in June 1793 in the great Assembly Hall at Godesberg.—The price asked for was doubtless much too high. A ducat was equivalent to 4½ gulden. The ducats coined at Kremnitz in Hungary were especially valued.

FROM THE INVITATION TO THE CONCERT IN THE PRAGUE NATIONAL THEATRE, 28 DECEMBER 1791, FOR THE BENEFIT OF MOZART'S WIDOW AND CHILDREN

Concert of music in memory of Wolfgang Gottlieb Mozart.

Mozart is no more ! In the annals of music his name will shine unforgettably among the most prominent musicians of all times and nations. As a child already a wonder in his art, in his maturity (still rarer occurrence) he even exceeded the expectations which he had aroused. Never did genius embrace a wider range of his art, nor shine in almost every sphere of the same with [more] exceptional merit, than he . . .

Niemetschek (1798), p. 38.—Nottebohm, *Mozartiana*, p. 3. The concert seems to have been postponed to 13 June (not January) 1792. See 9 (?) February 1794.—It is untrue that a benefit concert for Constanze was given in Vienna on 28 December 1791 (Abert, Vol. II, p. 849), although Nissen (p. 581) reports that Leopold II had advised Constanze to give such a concert when he received her in audience on 11 December, and that he had contributed enough to it to enable her to clear Mozart's debts of 3,000 gulden. (The unpaid bills hardly amounted to 1,000 gulden.) *Cf.* 31 December 1791. Benefit concerts for Constanze in Vienna did not actually take place until 29 December 1794 and 31 March 1795 : concert performances of *La clemenza di Tito* at the Kärntnertor Theatre and the Burgtheater respectively. But by that time Francis II was on the throne.

COUNT JOHANN WENZEL UGARTE TO PRINCE GEORG ADAM STARHEMBERG, 30 DECEMBER 1791

To
His Highness the Lord High Steward and Minister without Portfolio
Prince Starhemberg
Your Highness,

In the enclosure the widow of the Kammer Kompositor Mozart begs for a pension for herself and her 2 infant sons by reason of their extreme penury, and leaves the granting of her request solely to His Majesty's favour, the fact being that, her husband not having completed ten years service, she has no claim to a normal pension :

However, as the further enclosures show, Emanuel *Förster* and Joseph *Preindl* have, moreover, registered their requests for the position made vacant by Mozart's death ; these petitions I have considered it proper to place together before you, by reason of their relevance.

Mozart in fact received the title of Kammer Kompositor with a salary of 800 fl. per year from His Majesty the late Emperor, solely out of consideration that so rare a genius in the world of music should not be obliged to seek abroad for recognition and his daily bread ;

In my opinion his post is at present superfluous, and I think it should not be filled, in which case both the above-named applicants would for this reason be rejected, to which end I would ask you to return the enclosed petitions in the event of your agreement.

In the case of the widow, her fate depends entirely on the grace of His Majesty, as in the circumstances to which she herself admits, the grounds for a normal pension do not obtain.

But that her position is in fact sad, that she really is in need of royal favour, that the widow of a man who was so famous in his sphere might be worthy of some consideration—these circumstances I feel myself in duty bound to mention ;

And I therefore consider that, out of the consideration that an annual salary of 800 fl. returns to the Treasury through so unexpectedly premature a mortality, it would certainly be in accord with His Majesty's generosity and graciousness to grant Mozart's widow 200 fl. and each of her sons 50 fl., 300 fl. in toto, as an extraordinary pension.

Vienna, 30 December 1791   Ugarte
[*Endorsement*]
Report by H.M. Director of Music [Hof Music Graf]
    ddo. 30th December : 1791
Wherein the petition for a pension submitted by the Kammer Compositor Mozart's widow Constantia is recommended and the proposed rejection of the applications of Emanuel Förster and Joseph Preindl for this position expedited.   2 January 1791 [actually 1792]

> Vienna, State Archives.—Supplied by Dr. Walter Goldinger, Vienna ; like-wise the documents of 25 and 27 February, 5 and 13 March 1792.—Georg Adam, Prince Starhemberg was the Lord High Steward ; Johann Wenzel, Count Ugarte (see 24 April 1775, 25 and 27 February 1792) was Hofmusikgraf from 1791 (from 25 November 1791 to 10 November 1792 he was also Director of the Court Theatres).—For Förster *cf.* 13 August 1788 and *ca.* 7 and *ca.* 8 December 1791 ; for Preindl *cf.* 12 January 1792.

FROM THE " EPHEMERIDES POLITICO-LITTERARIAE ", PEST, 30 DECEMBER 1791
(in Latin)

Archduke Maximilian, Elector of Cologne, left Vienna on the 18th day of this month . . . he gave 24 gold coins to the widow of the celebrated musician Mozart.

In Prague a chorus of musicians recently performed, with memorable melodies, a solemn requiem music by the hand of the celebrated Mozart, in the principal church of the city.

Pp. 395 and 396.—Lidia F. Wendelin in *Mozart in Ungarn* (Budapest, 1958), pp. 101 and 170.—The gold pieces were naturally ducats.—Maximilian (see 15 October 1762, 23 April 1775, etc.) became Elector of Cologne in 1784.—The memorial service in Prague took place on 14 December.

FROM THE " WIENER ZEITUNG ", 31 DECEMBER 1791
(in Latin)

AN INSCRIPTION
FOR MOZART'S TOMB

He who lies here as a child added to the wonders of the world and as a man surpassed Orpheus with his playing.

Go on your way !

And pray for his soul !

K.

Jahn, Vol. II, p. 721.—It is a pity that no attempt was made at the time to place this epitaph on the spot where Mozart was buried, which might then still have been identifiable.—There is no proof that the draft signed " K." was written and published by Leopold Kozeluch, the owner of the Musikalisches Magazin.

IBID., 31 DECEMBER 1791

New dance music.

At the Musikalisches Magazin . . . may be had the following new dance music, arranged by H. Stanislaus Ossowsky for the present carnival season, namely : 12 German dances from the opera *die Zauberflöte* by the late Herr Mozart, with all parts, 1 fl. 30 kr., in piano score, 40 kr.

Kozeluch published several works by Ossowsky.

FROM THE " PRESSBURGER ZEITUNG ", 31 DECEMBER 1791

Vienna, the 29th December.

Mozart's widow was granted most gracious permission to hold a musical academy for her benefit in the National Theatre last Friday, at which not only the entire court, but also a large number of the public were present ; and she received 150 ducats from the court, and in all her receipts amounted to 1,500 gulden.

Discovered by Frau Lidia F. Wendelin, Budapest.—Friday was 23 December. There is no other evidence that such a concert took place in December. *Cf.* 28 December 1791.

FROM THE " MUSIKALISCHES WOCHENBLATT ", BERLIN, ?31 DECEMBER 1791

Intelligence from letters.

Prague, 12 December. At the coronation in this city two musical works were notable. One was a grand—or rather, semi-grand—serious opera, another setting of the *Clemenza di Tito*, which, however, although the music was by Mozart, did not find favour. This normally great composer seems to have forgotten Octavius's motto : *Festina lente !* Also, only the arias and choruses were from his hand, the recitatives were by another. The second [notable musical work] was a great cantata composed by Kozeluch. The text for it was written by Meisner at the request of the Estates. This composition met with applause despite the unpropitious time and place chosen for the performance. If you wish it, I will shortly write more to you about it ; and will also do my best to procure one or other aria from his score, although I rather fear that they are too extensive to be printed on the last sheet of your weekly journal. Just as I was finishing my letter I received a piece of news which is, alas, true, and which I will here at once impart to you.

Mozart is—dead. He returned home from Prague a sick man, and continued to get worse ; he was said to be dropsical, and he died in Vienna at the end of last week. Because his body swelled up after death, some people believe that he was poisoned. One of his last works is said to be a Requiem Mass, which was performed at his obsequies. Now that he is dead the Viennese will at last realize what they have lost in him. In his life he was constantly the object of cabals, which he at times may well have provoked by his *sans souci* manner. Neither his *Figaro* nor his *Don Juan* was successful in Vienna ; but by so much the more in Prague. Peace to his ashes !

> No. XII, p. 94.—Jahn, Vol. II, pp. 663 f. (third paragraph only).—The two performances in Prague were given on 6 September (*La clemenza di Tito*) and 12 (Cantata).—The motto is that of Caesar Octavius Augustus (31 B.C.–A.D. 14) —The recitatives of *La clemenza di Tito* had been written by Süssmayer.—The words of the cantata, by August Gottlieb Meissner, first appeared in the *Krönungstagebuch* and then separately in 1792. The cantata was probably performed in the open air, at a popular festivity. Kozeluch had arrived in Prague on 2 August. (*Cf. Der Bär* [Leipzig, 1928], p. 105.)—The rumour of the poisoning of Mozart did not circulate in Vienna until later.—The Requiem, still unfinished, was not performed for Mozart there.

FROM HAYDN'S LONDON DIARY, END OF 1791

Mozart died the 5th December 1791.

> Vienna, National Library.—C. F. Pohl, *Haydn in London* (Vienna, 1867), p. 172.

FROM FRANZ ALEXANDER VON KLEIST'S " PHANTASIEN AUF EINER REISE NACH PRAG ", DRESDEN, 1792

Never have I left an opera house so richly rewarded as today, when I saw so many people, notable in such different ways, in one place. The Emperor and his family were to come to the opera today, and the entire

route from the castle to the opera house swarmed with people anxious to
see an emperor on his way to the play. In the house all the boxes and the
stalls were filled with people, and when the Emperor finally arrived, he
was received with threefold hand-clapping and cries of Vivat ! . . . The
Emperor seemed pleased with his welcome and bowed to the spectators a
few times . . . " Away with these people ! "—with a gesture a little man
in a green coat, whose eye proclaims what his modest appearance would
conceal, bids me attend to more attractive matters. It is Mozart, whose
opera *Don Juan* is to be given today, whose joy it is to see for himself the
transports into which his glorious harmonies put the audience's hearts.
Who in the whole house can be more proud and glad than he ? Who can
derive more satisfaction from his own self than he ? In vain would monarchs exhaust their treasures, in vain ancestral pride its riches : these cannot
buy one little spark of the feeling with which Art rewards her darling !
. . . All men must fear Death, only the artist fears him not. His immortality is his hope, nay certainty . . . He will still move future generations
when the bones of kings have long since mouldered away. And secure in
these convictions Mozart could stand there, when a thousand ears were
listening for every quivering of a string, **every** whisper of a flute, and
swelling breasts and beating hearts betrayed the holy sensations which his
harmonies awakened . . . Be it fanatical enthusiasm, be it genuine human
feeling : enough, at that moment I would rather have been Mozart than
[the Emperor] Leopold. And even if our German audiences lack the high
receptivity to inspiration which characterizes the Englishman's admiration
for Handel or the Frenchman's for Gluck, the spontaneous utterances even
of a less sensitive people must be a fine and heavenly reward for the artist
who can take from the spheres their harmony and delight men's souls
with his tones . . .
In the evening a very beautiful opera, *La Clemenza di Tito*, was given gratis
by the Estates. The music is by Mozart, and entirely worthy of its master ;
here it is with his Andantes that he particularly pleases, where his melodies
are so beautiful as to entice the angels down to earth. To give a critical
opinion of it is impossible for I only heard the opera once, amid a great
throng.

> The book appeared under the cipher " K ".—Nettl, *op. cit.*, pp. 192 and 202
> —Kleist's nephew Heinrich, then fourteen years of age, the future famous
> poet, was with him and attended the festival performance of *Don Giovanni*
> on the 2nd and the première of *La clemenza di Tito* on 6 September 1791.—
> Among the audience at the festival performance Kleist noticed several promi-
> nent French émigrés.

FROM THE " ALLGEMEINES THEATERJOURNAL ", FRANKFURT AND MAINZ,
1792

. . . But one must give Hr. Schikaneder credit for sparing no expense
with his new productions of works, and, where necessary, for having new

sets and costumes made. The expenditure on Mozart's last opera, *die Zauberflöte*—Mozart's swansong—is said to have amounted to 5,000 fl., but he is in return well repaid, for only by satisfying the desire for beautiful sets and appropriately grand costumes of those who bring their eyes rather than their feelings into the theatre, and by sparing no expense, can one perform the works more often and, in this way, make good the outlay with advantage and by saving on so many other quite new pieces. . . .

> Vol. I, No. 2, pp. 149 f.—From a report on the Vienna Freihaus Theatre where *Die Zauberflöte* had been produced on 30 September 1791.

HANDWRITTEN NOTES ON PARTS OF THE GRADUALE AD FESTUM BEATAE MARIAE (K. 273), IN THE ESTERHÁZY ARCHIVES, EISENSTADT
(in Latin)

[Title-page :] Auth. Wolfgango Mozart / rest in peace / B : F : D : [Tenor part :] Mozart : / Rest in peace : / Behold how good / and how pleasant / it is for brethren to dwell together in unity ! 1791
[Second violin part :] Mozartt frantz / offer for him 1 rosary.

> Communicated by H. C. Robbins Landon.—Similar remarks are to be found on other parts of this MS., all in the hand of a copyist.—The words in the tenor part are Psalm 133, verse 1.

FROM MEUSEL'S " MUSEUM FÜR KÜNSTLER UND KUNSTLIEBHABER ", MANNHEIM, 1792

Herr *Wolfgang Amadeus Mozart*, Kapellmeister to Archduke Franz, died in Vienna on 5 December in the 34th year of his meritorious age.

> No. 16, p. 291.—For Meusel see mid 1787.—The error that Mozart belonged to the retinue of the Archduke Franz was here repeated once more.

JOSEPH HAYDN TO PUCHBERG

[London, January 1792.]

. . . I was beside myself for some considerable time because of his death and could not believe that Providence should so soon summon an irreplaceable man to the other world. Yet I regret only that he had not been able to convince the still unenlightened English [of the truth of] what I daily preached to them . . . Dear friend, you will have the kindness to send me a list of the works which are not yet known here : I will spare myself no trouble to make them known for the benefit of his widow. I wrote to the poor lady three weeks ago myself, to tell her that when her favourite son is old enough, I will instruct him in composition to the best of my ability and without fee, so as to some slight extent to take the place of his father.

Nottebohm, *Mozartiana*, p. 10.—Haydn's orthography has here evidently been corrected by Nottebohm.—The "favourite son" was Karl, who was sent to the pedagogue Franz Xaver Niemetschek of Prague in 1792 or 1794. —In Charles Burney's posthumous article on Mozart, published in Abraham Rees's *Cyclopedia* in 1819, we read :

> " When Haydn was asked in our hearing by Broderip, in his music-shop, whether Mozart had left any MS. compositions behind him that were worth purchasing, as his widow had offered his unedited papers at a high price to the principal publishers of music throughout Europe ; Haydn eagerly said : " Purchase them by all means. He was truly a great musician. I have been often flattered by my friends with having some genius ; but he was much superior."

Percy A. Scholes (*The Great Burney* [London], 1948, Vol. II, p. 116) adds :

> " This anecdote is confirmed in the manuscript notes of R. J. S. Stevens the glee composer. He says : ' He called on Broderip in the Haymarket, and urged him to purchase all Mozart's compositions. Such a genius he never knew. I saw Haydn leave Broderip's shop, after he had made this declaration. Mr. Broderip mentioned Haydn's words to me.' "

Francis Broderip was a partner in the music publishing firm of Longman & Broderip in London. Stevens was a well-known London composer.

THE LORD HIGH STEWARD TO THE IMPERIAL DIRECTOR OF MUSIC,
2 JANUARY 1792

Intimation to the I. & R. Director of Music, Vienna, the 2nd January 1792. [Endorsed :] The report and the application are entered with the statement for the 12th March 1792 Num 289.

Although we are certainly disposed to place before His Majesty the petition for an annual pension submitted by Konstantia Mozart, the entirely impoverished widow of the Kammer Musick Kompositor Mozart, which petition was recommended on the 30th day of December last, we are at present still not in a position to approach the Exchequer for their consent, because the existing regulations require that such petitions be suitably accompanied by the executors' certificate or some other legally valid document, and we must further be prepared for the possibility that the aforementioned widow has the expectation of a pension from the Court Musical Society's funds.

To which information the attention of Count von Ugarte is called, and to which end the above-mentioned application is annexed for his further action.

Pp Lord High Steward's office.

Vienna, the 2nd January 1792.

> Draft in the State Archives, Vienna.—*Cf.* 11 December 1791 (5 January 1792), 30 December 1791 and 25 February 1792.

FROM THE "WIENER ZEITUNG", 4 JANUARY 1792

Announcement.

From F. A. Hoffmeister, dealers in music, works of art and books . . .
the following pieces of dance-music may be had, with complete parts, and
also in piano score :

.   .   .   .   .

6 German dances by Mozart, with complete parts,   1 fl. 40 kr.
12 German dances for the Rout by the same, in piano score,   48 kr.
13 German dances, 13 trios and coda written for the Small Assembly Room,
     1791, by Hr. Mozart, with complete parts,   3 fl.
12 Minuets for the Rout, by the same, in piano score,   48 kr.

> K. 509 ; 586 ; 600, 602 and 605 (here counted correctly as 13 German dances)
> 585.

IBID., 7 JANUARY 1792

New music.

From Artaria & Comp., art dealers in the Kohlmarkt, are to be had.

.   .   .   .   .

At the same time let it be recalled that the Quartets by Hr. Mozart, recently
published from our press, and received with such general acclamation, may
still be had at 3 fl.—

> K. 575, 589 and 590, first advertised on 28 December 1791.

FROM JOSEPH PREINDL'S APPLICATION FOR THE POST OF DEPUTY
COURT ORGANIST, 12 JANUARY 1792

Your Majesty,

   The undersigned was desirous of submitting his humble application for
the post of Kammermusikus rendered vacant by Mozart's death ; but his
wishes were made vain by the discontinuance of the post . . .

                                                    Joseph Preindl.
Vienna, the 12th January 1792.

> Vienna, State Archives, Hofmusikkapelle 1792, fol. 3 f.—Pfannhauser in *Acta
> Mozartiana* (Augsburg, 1956), Vol. III, No. 3, p. 9.—Preindl, of an age with
> Mozart, was choirmaster at St. Peter's Church in Vienna and later became
> Cathedral Kapellmeister in succession to Albrechtsberger.—*Cf.* 12 March
> 1792.

FROM THE "WIENER ZEITUNG", 14 JANUARY 1792

New music.

   As many friends of music have expressed the wish to possess a wind
arrangement of that well-loved opera, *die Zauberflöte*, the last work of the

great Mozart, the undersigned flatters himself that he gives no unpleasant tidings when he announces that he has arranged the said opera for 8 parts, and will publish it on subscription at 6 fl. 40 kr, open until the end of January, and the subscribers may collect their copies by 16 February against return of their vouchers. Should some music-lovers, however, desire to have this opera for 6 parts, the undersigned will be equally at their service, provided that there is support from sufficient subscribers.

.   .   .   .   .

Amateurs may order these pieces in the Durchhaus called the " Schmeckender Wurm " in the Obere Bäckenstrasse, at the hairbag-maker's, or from the undersigned at his shop, No. 456 in the Leopoldstadt, in the Schmelzgasse behind the theatre, at the house called the "kleiner Ring."

Joseph Haydenreich, Publisher.

> For Haydenreich (Heidenreich, 1753–1821) see 24 May and 18 June 1788 and 1 June 1791. On 22 August 1791 Lausch announced a MS. vocal score of *Die Zauberflöte* made by Heidenreich.—A Durchhaus is a building with entrances in two streets.

IBID., 14 JANUARY 1792

New music.

From Johann Träg . . . the following new music is to be had :

.   .   .   .

Duetti for 2 violins. (From *die Zauberflöte*.) 3 fl.

.   .   .   .

7 new country dances with an overture and figures thereto, by W. A. Mozart   3 fl.
– – for the pianoforte   40 kr.

> The seven country dances, with an overture, were K. 106 (Overture und 3 dances), 609 No. 3, 587, 603 Nos. 1 and 2, written in 1789–91. A copy of this MS. is in the possession of the Gesellschaft der Musikfreunde, Vienna.

IBID., 14 JANUARY 1792

Die Zauberflöte

Opera by Hr. Kapellmeister Mozart, from which the following numbers, arranged for voice and pianoforte, may now be had of Hr. Lausch's music shop . . . namely :
Der Vogelfänger bin ich ja, Aria Basso, (Hey heya ! Pupaya !).   16 kr.
Du feines Täubchen nur herein, Terzetto (Hu ! das ist der Teufel sicherlich).   20 kr.
Bey Männern, welche Liebe fühlen, Duetto Soprano e B.   12 kr.
Zum Ziele führt dich diese Bahn, Terzetto the 3 boys.   12 kr.
Wie stark ist nicht dein Zauberton, Aria, Tenor.   Flauto solo 16 kr.

Das klinget so herrlich, the Glockenspiel, Coro. 12 kr.
Bewahret euch vor Weibertücken, Duetto, T. e B. 8 kr.
Alles fühlt der Liebe Freuden, Aria, T. 16 kr.
In diesen heil'gen Hallen, detta B. 12 kr.
Sey uns zum zweytenmal willkommen, Terzetto, the 3 boys. 12 kr.
Ach ich fühls, es ist verschwunden, A[ria]s. 12 kr.
Soll ich dich Theurer nicht mehr seh'n, Terzetto. (Die Stunde schlägt,
wir seh'n uns wieder !) 20 kr.
Ein Mädchen oder Weibchen, Aria, B. mit Variationen. 24 kr.
Subscriptions at 5 fl. 30 kr. are invited for quartet versions of the same for
2 violins, viola and violoncello ; vouchers will be issued until the last day
of January, and copies will assuredly be ready by 15 February against return
of the same. N.B. This is the last work of this world-famous composer ;
lovers of the art of music, shed a tear for him !—Wolfgang Amade Mozart,
the darling of the Muses, is no more.—

.　　　.　　　.　　　.　　　.

12 German dances and coda from *die Zauberflöte*, with all parts. 1 fl. 30 kr.
– – in piano score. 40 kr.
Both sets of Hr. Mozart's minuets and German dances for 1791 may also
be had :
Complete parts. 3 fl. each.
– – in piano score. 48 kr. each.

FROM THE " WIENER ZEITUNG ", 14 JANUARY 1792

Announcement.

　　From F. A. Hoffmeister, dealers in music, works of art and books . . .
the following pieces of dance-music may be had, with complete parts and
also in piano score :

.　　　.　　　.　　　.　　　.

Recently published and also available from this shop are :
Arias from the opera, *die Zauberflöte*, by Hr. Kapellmeister Mozart, with
piano accompaniment :
Aria, In diesen heil'gen Hallen, 8 kr.
– – Alles fühlt der Liebe Freuden, 9 kr.
　　which the Moor sings
– – Ach ich fühle es ist verschwunden, 9 kr.
– – Der Vogelfänger bin ich ja, 7 kr.
– – Ein Mädchen, oder Weibchen, 9 kr.
Duetto, Bey Männern welche Liebe fühlen, 10 kr.
– – Bewahret euch für Weiber Tücke, 5 kr.
Terzetto, Du feines Täubchen nur herein, 14 kr.
– – for the 3 boys, Zum Ziele führt dich diese Bahn, 9 kr.
– – for the 3 boys, Seid uns zum zweytenmal willkommen, 9 kr.

– –   Soll ich dich Theurer nicht mehr sehen, 22 kr.
Glockenspiel and Coro, followed by Duetto between Pamina and Papageno,
9 kr.
6 Minuets, with complete parts, from the opera *Die Zauberflöte*, 1 fl.
6 German dances – – – – – – – 1 fl.
6 ——————— in piano score ——————— 40 kr.

> Under "Dance Music" the pieces by Mozart of 4 January 1792 are listed
> again.

FROM THE " ZEITUNG FÜR DAMEN UND ANDERE FRAUENZIMMER ",
GRAZ, 18 JANUARY 1792

A few months before his death Mozart received a letter without a signature, requesting him to write a Requiem, and to ask for it what he wanted.
As this task did not appeal to him at all, he thought, " I will ask so much
that the amateur will be sure to give me up." On the next day a servant
came to collect an answer. Mozart wrote to the unknown man that he
could not write it for less than 60 ducats, and then not for 2 or 3 months.
The servant returned, brought 30 ducats at once, said he would call again
in 3 months, and if the Mass were ready, would hand over the other half
of the money directly. So Mozart had to write, which he often did with
tears in his eyes, constantly saying : " I fear that I am writing my own
Requiem " ; he completed it a few days before his death. When his death
was known, the servant called again and brought the remaining 30 ducats,
did *not* ask for the Requiem, and since then there has been no further request
for it. It will in fact be performed in St Michael's Church in his memory
when it has been copied.

> No. 3, p. 49.—This early report on the Requiem does not in detail accord with
> fact, but it is of historical interest.

ATTESTATION BY THE SOCIETY OF MUSICIANS

This is to certify that the late Herr Wolfgang Amadeus Mozart, I. & R.
Hof-Kompositor, was not a member of the Society for the Widows and
Orphans of Musicians and that in consequence his bereaved widow is neither
at present drawing a pension from the funds of the aforementioned Society,
nor has she any expectation of one in the future.

P.p. Society for the Widows and Orphans of Musicians.
Vienna, the 20th January 1792.
Joseph Scheidl
Secretary to the Society.

Pohl, *op. cit.*, p. 18. Nottebohm, *Mozartiana*, p. 16. Jahn, Vol. II, p. 705.—*Cf.*
3 April 1781, 11 February and 24 August 1785, 11 December 1791 and 12 March
1792.

Announcement of a Cantata by the late distinguished composer Mozart.

Reverence and gratitude towards our immortal Mozart occasion a Society of Philanthropists to announce the publication on a subscription basis of one of the works of this great artist in order to assist his distressed widow and orphans. It is a work which it is fitting to call his swan-song, fashioned with his usual artistry, and the first performance of which he himself directed among a circle of his best friends two days before his last illness. It is a Cantata for the inauguration of a Masonic Lodge in Vienna, and the text is the work of one of the members of the same. It would be superfluous to guarantee the authenticity of the work to connoisseurs and admirers ; it need only be remarked that the original score rests in the hands of this Society. Hr. Hraschanzky, by appointment printer and dealer in German and Hebrew books, will receive the subscription of 2 ducats at Prince Oettingen's house in the Strauchgässel, No. 206, from 15 January until 15 July 1792, and at the end of July the work may be had there in exchange for the subscription voucher. There is no need to remark that this Cantata will appear with complete parts, that the title-page will be decorated with a suitable engraving, and that extreme care will be paid to delicacy and accuracy in our edition of this excellent work. Those not resident in this country are requested to address themselves to Hr. Hraschanzky, post-paid.

The *Kleine Freimaurer-Kantate* (K. 623) had been finished on 15 November 1791 and first performed on the 18th at the " New-Crowned Hope " lodge. —The " Philanthropic Society " were freemasons.—The author of the words was most probably Gieseke (see 18 November 1791).—The autograph later went to the Gesellschaft der Musikfreunde in Vienna.—For Joseph Hraschansky *cf.* beginning of 1788 and middle of 1791.—The title-page of the score remained unadorned.—The authorship of the" Appendix. To conclude the [   ] " is not definitely known.—It is worth noting that Schikaneder had the cantata performed at a concert in the Freihaus Theatre on 13 March 1794 with a new text that has remained unknown, under the title of *Die Abreise des Fürsten* (The Prince's Departure).—Hraschansky announced in the *Wiener Zeitung* of 14 November 1792 that the edition had appeared. An undated broadsheet names Count Johann Esterházy as surety for the whereabouts of the score and the merchant Erzelt von Löwenfels as agent for the distribution of the printed edition. (Bernhard Beyer in *Quellen zur Geschichte der Freimaurerei* [Bayreuth, 1918], Vol. I., pp. 65 ff.)

KONSTANTIN PHILIPP WILHELM JACOBI, BARON KLÖST, TO KING FREDERICK WILLIAM II OF PRUSSIA
(in French)

Vienna, the 18th February 1792.

Sire,

In conformity with Your Majesty's very gracious orders of the 7th of this month I have firstly made arrangements with Mozart's widow to acquire for the price of 100 ducats each the eight pieces of music designated. I hope to be in possession of them during the first days of next week, so that I shall be able to have them dispatched to Berlin with the first post-chaise, leaving here on Friday next, the 24th day of this month.

I am with most profound respect

Sire, Your Majesty's

most humble, most obedient and

most loyal subject   Jacobi Klöst.

Ernst Friedlaender in *Mitteilungen für die Mozart-Gemeinde in Berlin*, April 1897, No. 4, pp. 119 f.—Jacobi von Klöst was Prussian ambassador in Vienna ; he had been among the subscribers to Mozart's concerts in 1784.—Among the eight works which the king acquired from the estate were the oratorio *La Betulia Liberata* (K. 118) and the two litanies K. 125 and K. 243. *Cf.* KE. p. xxvi.

COUNT UGARTE TO PRINCE STARHEMBERG, 25 FEBRUARY 1792

Your Highness,

With regard to the widow *Constantia Mozart's* application for a pension forwarded by me on the 30th December of last year with my recommendation, Your Highness honoured me on the 2nd January 1792 with the task of ensuring that the aforementioned widow give satisfactory evidence of her poverty, and also shew that she has no expectation of a *pension* from the Court Musical *Society's funds*.

She trusts that she meets these requirements by means of the Inventory and Valuation enclosed sub B, and also with the testimony of Joseph Scheidl, *Secretary* of the Court Musical *Society*.

I hereby entrust these documents to Your Highness, together with the request that, in accordance with the reasons stated in my report of 30 December last on behalf of the impoverished and bereaved widow and her 2 infant sons (whose father was most deserving in his profession), Your Highness may be pleased to effect a fitting pension from our most noble Sovereign.

Vienna, the 25th February 1792   Ugarte.

See 30 December 1791 and 2 January 1792. For Scheidl see 20 January 1792. —Appendix B is lost ; *cf.* Estate Documents, Appendix II.

FROM THE " MUSIKALISCHES WOCHENBLATT ", BERLIN, ?25 FEBRUARY 1792

[Carl Spazier in a critique of Wranitzky's *Oberon*, after the performance in Berlin on 15 February 1792 :]

. . . a certain affected, studied effusion which contrasts curiously with the genuine, original, natural wealth of ideas of a *Mozard*.

No. XX, p. 158.—Jahn, Vol. II, p. 362.—Paul Wranitzky's opera *Oberon*, libretto by Karl Ludwig Gieseke after Friederike Sophie Seyler, had been produced at the Freihaus Theatre for the first time on 7 November 1789.

PRINCE STARHEMBERG TO THE EXCHEQUER, 27 FEBRUARY 1792

Note.

By means of the enclosure, H.M. Director of Music, Count Ugarte, has favourably supported the application for a pension submitted by Konstantia *Mozart*, the entirely impoverished widow of the late Kammerkompositor. The Imperial and Royal Exchequer is therefore kindly requested to take receipt of the above-mentioned documents and to announce its decision so that the necessary further action may be taken.

Vienna, the 27th February 1792.   Starhemberg.

To

The Royal and Imperial Exchequer.

> See 30 December 1791 and 25 February 1792.—This note is preserved in the Exchequer Archives, Vienna, the draft in the State Archives, Vienna.

On 1 March 1792 Leopold II died. Archduke Franz, his son, became Emperor.

FROM THE " MUSIKALISCHES WOCHENBLATT ", BERLIN, ?3 MARCH 1792

From a letter from Cassel, February 1792.

. . . We celebrated the memory of Mozart on the 31st January. The entire concert consisted of music by Mozart, with the exception of the final chorus, which was a kind of apotheosis of the artist. Frau *von Jasmund* nd the Misses *d'Aubigny* greatly enhanced the concert through the rivalr y of their talents.—

v.A.

> No. XXI, p. 164 f.—Nina d'Aubigny von Engelbronner, born at Cassel in 1777, was, like her elder sister Susanna (Frau Horstig), an amateur singer. She published a successful singing-tutor at Leipzig in 1805 (*Briefe an Natalie über den Gesang*) and composed songs in several languages. She removed to Vienna later on, and Schubert played in her drawing-room in the spring of 1827.—Frau Henriette von Jasmund, *née* von Schlotheim, was a good pianist. (Information kindly given by Herr Franz Uhlendorff, Cassel.)

COUNT JOHANN RUDOLF CHOTEK TO THE LORD HIGH STEWARD'S OFFICE, 5 MARCH 1792

Note.

The widow of the late Hof-Kompositor Mozart, whose application of the 27th day of February together with the relevant documents is herewith accordingly returned with thanks, would not, in accordance with the strict pension statutes, be entitled to a pension, but only to a final payment of a quarter's stipend, because her husband had not been in Imperial service for 10 years.

However, the exceptional circumstances, confirmed moreover by the Director of Court Music, are of such a nature that, in the case of this widow, an exception to the general regulations can reasonably be made.

The late Hofkompositor Mozart was accepted into Court service expressly to prevent an artist of such outstanding genius from being obliged to seek his subsistence abroad. It would seem, therefore, considered in this light, that it would ill accord with the good reputation of the Court, if the widow of a man of such rare talents, who had been in the Court's service, were to be exposed to paupery.

In addition, circumstances worthy of consideration apply in the case of this widow, namely that she is left with 2 children, and without the slightest means, and has no hope of assistance from any quarter. She would, therefore, find herself in a most lamentable situation if she were to be excluded from the magnanimity of His Majesty.

A further ground for the granting of a pension to this widow arises from the fact that her late husband's position will not in future be filled, and that a yearly salary of 800 fl. accordingly reverts to the Imperial Treasury.

For these reasons this Court Department sees fit to disclose to the Lord High Steward's office its opinion that in this exceptional case, and without establishing a precedent, His Majesty may be recommended to grant a pension to the aforementioned widow and her 2 children of one third of her husband's salary of 800 fl. namely 266 fl. 40 kr. with effect from the 1st January 1792.

However, it would run counter to existing regulations to recommend a special allowance for the 2 children, as in the present case the requisite number of children, which has to be at least 4, does not obtain.

Vienna, the 5th March 1792   Joh. Chotek

To
the Lord High Steward's office
Information is hereby given that a pension of 266 fl. 40 k. may be recommended for the widow of the late Hof Kompositor Mozart.
Vienna, the 5th March 1792

> See 30 December 1791.—Johann Rudolf, Count Chotek was head of the new Court Finance department from 1792.—The Director of Court Music was Johann Wenzel, Count Ugarte.

FROM THE "WIENER ZEITUNG", 7 MARCH 1792

Convocation of Mozart's creditors.

The City Council of the Royal and Imperial capital city of Vienna hereby gives notice that, in respect of the death of Herr Wolfgang Andre Mozart, I. & R. Kapellmeister and Kammerkompositeur, and in order to proceed with the settlement of the estate, it has been deemed necessary to summon, and to hear the claims of, all those who either by right of inheritance or *jure crediti*, or for any other cause, can substantiate their claims on this estate. To this intent all those who consider themselves entitled to put forward a claim are requested to appear before this City Council in the forenoon of 19 March of this year at 9 a.m., either in person or adequately represented ; since at the expiry of this term the settlement shall take place and be made over to Frau Mozart.

> The notification also appeared on the same day in No. 19 of the *Posttägliche Anzeigen aus dem k. k. Frag- und Kundschaftsamt in Wien*, a supplement to the *Wiener Zeitung*. (Copy in the possession of Consul Fritz Hunziker, Berne.)—*Cf.* Estate Documents, Appendix II.

PROFESSOR JOHANN JAKOB ENGEL TO KING FREDERICK WILLIAM II OF PRUSSIA, BERLIN, 8 MARCH 1792

The Singspiel *Die Zauberflöte* which Your Majesty was pleased to send to me yesterday for examination, was already known to me from information received from Vienna and Prague as a piece with the most beautiful and various sets and transformation effects, the performance of which demands a theatre of very great size, and is thus unsuitable for the narrow space of our National Theatre here. On a closer examination I find this confirmed beyond my expectations. It seems to have been the author's intention to crowd together every conceivable difficulty for the stage designer and machinists, and a work has thus been created whose sole merit is visual splendour. At least, it is impossible for an audience which is ignorant of certain mysteries and incapable of seeing through the dark and heavy veil of allegory, to find the slightest interest in it. I regret moreover that the great composer Mozart has had to squander his talent on such unrewarding, mystical and untheatrical material.

> Götz Friedrich, *Die Zauberflöte* (Dresden, 1954), p. 101.—Engel was joint director with Ramler of the Berlin National Theatre. The king again recommended *Die Zauberflöte* to him in May 1792, and once more in vain. The work was not performed there until 12 May 1794.

REPORT OF THE LORD HIGH STEWARD, PRINCE GEORG ADAM VON STARHEMBERG, CONCERNING CONSTANZE MOZART'S APPLICATION FOR A PENSION, VIENNA, 12 MARCH 1792.

Most gracious Sovereign,

Immediately after the occurrence of the death of Kammercompositor Wolfgang Mozart the Director of Music, Count Ugarte, forwarded to me the very humble application of the said composer's widow, in which she pleads for an annual pension in consideration of her two infant children and her entire lack of means.

As this application was not accompanied by the prescribed evidence of her penury, I deemed it proper to inform Count Ugarte that the widow be requested to prove her poverty, and also demonstrate that she has no expectation of a pension from the Court Musical Society's funds.

Accordingly Your Majesty's Director of Music has included in his subsequent report the requisite documents, and these fully confirm that the late Mozart has in fact left his widow and two children in an impoverished state, and with no claim on the Society's funds.

In order to dispense with the usual formalities prescribed before an application for a pension is presented, the documents have been forwarded to the Exchequer for its approval.

Upon which matter this Department has expressed its opinion as subjoined : The widow is not entitled to a pension in accordance with the pension statutes, but only to the payment of one quarter's stipend, because her husband had not been in Imperial service for 10 years.

However, reason demands that an exception be made for the widow on account of the extraordinary circumstances of the case.

The late Kammerkompositor was taken into Court service so that an artist of such rare genius should not be obliged to earn his bread in a foreign land. It would therefore be contrary to the reputation of the Imperial Court if the widow of this man were to be exposed to paupery.

For these notable reasons the Exchequer approves that in this exceptional case, and without establishing a precedent, the widow and her 2 children should be recommended for the award of a pension of one third of her husband's salary of 800 fl., that is 266 fl. 40 kr., commencing from the 1st January of this year, but that there shall be no special allowance for the 2 children, as the number of children required for such a claim must be at least 4.

Most gracious Sovereign, in this widow's case circumstances obtain of a kind which to a certain extent entitle her to appeal to Your Majesty's magnanimity. In view of these circumstances Your Majesty may have the greater pleasure in consenting to the pension of 266 fl. 40 kr. recommended by the Exchequer, for, as in the opinion of the Director of Music there is no necessity to fill the position of Compositor, an economy of 800 fl. is thus effected.

For this same reason it will be proper if Your Majesty decides that the 2 competitors who have applied for this post be informed that their services are not required.

Placet.   Franz m.p.   Starhemberg.

Vienna, State Archives.—Köchel in the *Jahrbuch für Landeskunde von Nieder-Österreich* (Vienna, 1868), Vol. I, pp. 357 f.—Jahn, Vol. II, pp. 705 f.—Cf. 11 December 1791.—For Starhemberg see 15 January 1789 ; for the Musik-graf, Ugarte, see 24 April 1775 ; for the Musician's Society (Tonkünstler-Societät) see 25 February 1792 ; for the two competitors for the post of

Chamber Composer see *ca.* 7 December 1791 and 12 January 1792.—Francis II
wrote his consent on the manuscript of the petition.

FROM THE MINUTES OF THE IMPERIAL CHANCELLERY, 12 MARCH 1792

12 March (Appropriate authority :) Starhemberg
Report No. 72 of the 12th March the application for a pension of the impoverished Kammerkompositor's widow Konstantia Mozart. Further the
rejection of the 2 applicants Förster and Preindl.
Placet. / 266 f. 40 xr. from the 1st January.

> Vienna, State Archives : Kabinettsprotokolle, Vol. 119, No. 526.

DECISION [UPON CONSTANZE'S APPLICATION]

His Majesty is pleased to grant to the applicant and her two children a
pension of 266 fl. 40 xr, being one third of her husband's salary of 800 fl ;
which pension, effective from the 1st January of this year, is granted from
the Court General Funds as a special favour and does not establish a precedent.
Pr. the 13th March 1792.

> Vienna, State Archives.—Köchel, *loc. cit.* Jahn, *loc. cit.* (He misinterpreted the
> " Pr." (= presented) as " Prague ".)

THE LORD HIGH STEWARD'S OFFICE TO THE EXCHEQUER AND THE
DIRECTOR OF COURT MUSIC, 13 MARCH 1792

Court ordinance / to the Royal Exchequer. / given this 13th day of
March 1792.
His Majesty the King has been pleased to grant to the entirely impoverished Konstanzia Mozart, widow of the late Kammerkompositor, and to
her 2 children, an annual pension of 266 fl 40 kr, with effect from 1 January
of this year ; this is a special favour, and does not establish a precedent.
Which Royal decision is referred to the Exchequer for implementation.
            Intimatum
to the Director of Court Music
Count Ugarte.
13 March 1792.
Although the bereaved Kammerkompositor's widow Konstanzia Mozart is
not entitled to a pension according to the existing regulations, as her husband had not spent 10 years in the service of the Court, His Majesty has
nevertheless been pleased to grant her and her two children an annual
pension of 266 fl 40 kr, being one third of her husband's salary of 800 fl.;
which pension, effective from the 1st January of this year, is a special favour
and does not establish a precedent ; nor does it include a special allowance

for the aforementioned children, as according to statute there must be at least 4. His Majesty has deemed the filling of the vacant position of Kompositor to be unnecessary, and the two applicants for this position, whose papers are enclosed herewith, are accordingly to be rejected.

The Director of Music is requested to remark these decisions for information and necessary action.

See 30 December 1791.—Förster's and Preindl's applications were turned down.

FROM THE " MUSIKALISCHES WOCHENBLATT ", BERLIN, ?24 MARCH 1792

Public musical performances in Berlin.

Mozard's memory was celebrated on 18 March for the benefit of the poor in Herr D. Fliess's concert, in a Cantata by Herr Burmann, " Mozard's Urne ", composed by Herr Musikdirektor Wessely, and in instrumental and vocal pieces by Mozard . . .

C. S.

No. XXIV, p. 191.—" D. Fliess ", who at that time financed a monthly amateur concert in Berlin, is perhaps identical with Dr. Bernhard Flies, the composer of the " Wiegenlied " ascribed to Mozart (K. 350). Gottlob Wilhelm Burmann, a private teacher in Berlin, was himself a composer. Bernhard Wessely was musical director of the Berlin National Theatre. The cantata was to be printed by subscription in July 1792.—The *Musikalisches Wochenblatt* (see 10 [?] December 1791), in the last number of which this report by Carl Spazier appeared, was soon afterwards replaced by the *Musikalische Monatsschrift*.

On 20 April the " New-Crowned Hope " lodge distributed a circular letter on the subject of Mozart's death.

The letter's text and whereabouts are at present unknown.—Deutsch, *op. cit.*, p. 18.—Soon afterwards the " Mourning Lodge " took place at which the " Masonic Oration on Mozart's Death " was read.

MASONIC ORATION ON MOZART'S DEATH. DELIVERED ON THE OCCASION OF THE ADMISSION OF A MASTER TO THE MOST WORTHY LODGE OF ST. JOHN CALLED THE CROWNED HOPE IN THE ORIENT, VIENNA, BY BR. H . . . R. Vienna, printed by Br. Ignaz Alberti. 1792.

MOST REVERED
MASTER OF THE LODGE,
MOST REVERED
DEPUTY MASTER,
REVERED AND ESTEEMED BRETHREN !

. . . . .

Allow me, my honoured and most worthy Brethren, to take advantage of the present state of your minds and bring you back to an event very sorrowful and humiliating for us all. It has pleased the Eternal Architect of the world, to tear one of our most beloved, one of our most meritorious members from our brotherly chain. Who did not know him? who did not esteem him? who did not love him?—our worthy Brother Mozart. Scarcely a few weeks have passed since he was standing here in our midst, glorifying the inauguration of our Masonic Temple with his magical harmonies.

Which of us, my Brethren, would then have suspected the thread of his life to be so short? Which of us would have thought that we would be mourning him three weeks later? It is true—it is the sad lot of mankind to have to leave behind an often already distinguished career just as it is coming to fruition; kings die in the midst of their plans, which they bequeath to posterity unrealized—plans which often only centuries afterwards served to further the good of their fellow-men; artists die after they have used the lease of life allotted to them to perfect their art to the highest degree—universal admiration follows them to the grave, entire nations mourn them, and the common destiny of these great men is—to be forgotten by their admirers. But it is not true of us, my Brethren! Mozart's premature death remains an irreplaceable loss for Art—his talents, already expressed in earliest boyhood, made him even then the rarest phenomenon of his generation; half Europe revered him, the great called him their darling, and we—we called him our Brother. However much propriety demands that we recall to mind his artistic talents, by so much the less should we forget to offer a fitting sacrifice to his excellent heart.

He was a diligent member * of our Order: brotherly love, a peaceable disposition, advocacy of a good cause, beneficence, a true, sincere sense of pleasure whenever he could help one of his Brethren with his talents: these were the chief characteristics of his nature. He was a husband, a father, a friend to his friends, a Brother to his Brethren; he lacked only the riches which would have enabled him to make hundreds as happy as he would have wished.

Most honoured and worthy Brethren! Can we celebrate the memory of our now transfigured Brother in a more noble, or for us a more beneficial manner, than by renewing our vow of inviolable loyalty to virtue at the grave of A...? Would not he himself be looking down upon this mourning sacrifice with blessing gaze, if he had not been taken beyond our sphere, if he were hovering among us, and attending our act as an invisible witness?

My Brethren! an awesome thought for us: this was the spot whereon he stood, the spot which perhaps in a short time will claim the second from among our midst.

Decay!—I do not believe that human nature can conceive anything more terrifying, more awesome than this!

* The original has Anfänger (novice) in place of Anhänger (adherent, member).—Ed.

Accustomed as we are to looking upon our body as a vital part of our being, unacquainted with the nature, the condition and the particular occupations of our mind divorced from it—and then the thought : soon this body will disintegrate into dust or, according to circumstance, will become the habitat and the food for vile insects. The ability courageously to conquer such repugnant thoughts and to take the great and important step into the unknown fields of eternity with a calm smile, can only be attained by him who has learned in this very place the great art of living in virtue that he may die as a Mason, as a Christian.

Death, indeed, because of its natural consequences is the most terrifying thing that human nature can envisage ; often and all too soon he severs the holy bond between husband and wife, severs us from our friends and relations, robs children of their parents, and tears from our arms those whom we so tenderly loved.

Not one of all the changes awaiting man is in its consequences more irrevocable, none is in respect of its hour less certain, none more grave and solemn by nature of its cause and the circumstances thereof, none of more important influence on our future blessedness, than—Death.

Each day that we live, each hour that we number, night itself and sleep : all is either an image or a summons of Death for us.

How many a child withers at its mother's breast where it sought strength and life, how many youths die away like flowers in the springtime of their life, how many who have just begun to live for the good of Humanity, become the prey of Death in the summer of their days.

Ought we, however, because Death is for us so very certain, to thrust so important a thought from us ? or would it profit us if we even wanted to thrust it from us ?

Would not every separation from our friends, every corpse taken from our midst, serve to remind us of it ?

No, my Brethren ! Wisdom and prudence require that we learn to know our enemy : but to know him is not enough, we must also know how to conquer him.

And where can we find the means to conquer this enemy of Nature ? Where else than in our Masonic Temple which we have constructed in order to form good Men. Here, here at the grave of A . . ., who teaches us the wise art of living in happiness and of facing the day of our departure from this life with gladness.

We are blessed, my Brethren, if we are deemed worthy to be the tools of our great Master Builder for the furtherance of human happiness. We are blessed if we could show the profane world what manner of Men are formed within our halls, what principles the Masons' God roots in the hearts of his disciples.

May the ashes of our eternally dear brother rest in peace, may his early death be for us the most powerful encouragement to virtue ; may our

M.—15

remembrances be united with him in those supernatural halls, where full light from Jehovah's eternal spring will stream into all who dwell in heaven into all true Masons.

Rise ! mourn for him as Masons,
Whom Fate for Brother gave ;
Too soon from us he hastens,
Down to a sombre grave.

With gentleness and patience,
A Mason heart and soul,
He lifts our aspirations
Towards a higher goal.

The bond is snapped !   We give him
Our blessings and our love,
Our brother-love shall guide him
To harmony above.

Oft in his footsteps treading
We sought out the bereaved,
The widow in her steading
His rarest gifts received ;

He heard the orphans' blessing,
Clothes to the naked gave,
God's recompense confessing,
He takes it to the grave.

Midst flattery's siren voices
He shared his Brothers' lot,
In poor men's smiles rejoices,
His manhood not forgot.

Sleep softly 'neath the silent pall
That peace alone can bring,
Till Adoniram's nine-fold call
Summons thee to our ring,

Where re-united solely
Through God's eternal word,
We hear the thrice-sung Holy :
Jehovah is our Lord !

The only known copy is in the music collection of the National Library in Vienna.—First (inaccurate) reprint in the *Allgemeine Österreichische Freimaurer-Zeitung* (Vienna, 23 May 1875), Vol. II, Part 9, pp. 68-70. Facsimile and new reprint in *Schweizerische Musikzeitung* (Zürich, February 1956) by O. E. Deutsch.—The author of the speech and the poem at the end was the playwright Karl Friedrich Hensler and the printer of the booklet (17 pp. octavo) Ignaz Alberti, whose name also appears on the first libretto of *Die Zauberflöte* ; both were freemasons.—The contents of the speech are for the most part of a general nature, since this session of the lodge served for the promotion of three journeymen to the rank of master and only incidentally for a commemoration of Mozart. The beginning of the speech, nearly half of it, is therefore omitted here.—The Adoniram named in it, usually referred to here as " A... ", was King Solomon's treasurer ; for the freemasons his name signified the highest grade of the Scottish rite.

JOHANN ANDREAS SCHACHTNER TO MARIA ANNA VON BERCHTOLD ZU
SONNENBURG

To Madame
Marie Anne
De Sonnenburg.
To be delivered
at the Prefecture, *St. Gilgen*
No. 4
Most gracious lady !

Your kind letter was forwarded to me from Salzburg to the Hammerau, where I was on a visit to my son, an official at the Prefecture there ; from my desire always to be of service to everyone, and particularly to the Mozart family, you can judge how painful it was for me to be prevented from complying with your request at once. But to the point, and to your first question : what your late brother's favourite pastimes were in his childhood, NB apart from his preoccupation with music.

This question can have no answer ; for no sooner had he begun to busy himself with music than his interest in every other occupation was as dead, and even children's games had to have a musical accompaniment if they were to interest him ; if we, he and I, were carrying his playthings from one room to another, the one of us who went empty-handed always had to sing or fiddle a march the while. But before he had begun music, he was so ready for any prank spiced with a little humour that he could quite forget food, drink and all things else. He became so fond of me—for, as you know, we saw much of each other—that he would often ask me ten times in one day if I loved him, and when I sometimes said no, just for fun, bright tears welled up in his eyes, so tender and kind was his good heart.

2*nd* question, how he behaved as a child when the great admired his musical talent and art ?

In truth, he showed nothing less than pride or ambition : for he could in no wise better have satisfied these, than by playing to people who had little or no understanding of music ; but he did not want to play, except his audience were great amateurs of music, or he had to be deluded into thinking them such.

3rd question. What branch of learning did he like best ? Answer : in this respect he was easily led, it was of small matter to him what he was given to learn ; he simply wanted to learn, and he left the choice to his dearly loved father as to what field he was to work in—it seemed as if he understood that nowhere in the world could he have found a tutor, much less a guide, to equal his unforgettable father.

4th question. What characteristics, maxims, time-table, peculiarities and inclinations towards good and evil he had ?

Answer. He was of a fiery disposition, no object held his attention by more than a thread. I think that if he had not had the advantageously good education which he enjoyed, he might have become the most wicked villain, so susceptible was he to every attraction, the goodness or badness of which he was not yet able to examine.

> Some particular points worthy of admiration,
> concerning the fourth and fifth year of his age,
> the veracity of which I could swear to.

I once went with your father to the house, after Thursday service ; we found the 4-year old Wolfgängerl busy with his pen :

Papa : What are you writing ?

Wolfgang : A clavier concerto, the first part is nearly finished.

Papa : Show me. Wolfg. It's not ready yet.

Papa : Show me, it's sure to be interesting.

His father took it from him and showed me a smudge of notes, most of which were written over ink-blots which he had rubbed out. (NB : Little Wolfgangerl, knowing no better, plunged the pen to the bottom of the inkwell each time, and so, when he put it to the paper, a drop of ink was bound to fall off each time, but he was equal to it, and drawing the palm of his hand across it, wiped it away, and wrote on.)

At first we laughed at what seemed such a galimatias, but his father then began to observe the most important matter, the notes and music ; he stared long at the sheet, and then tears, tears of joy and wonder, fell from his eyes. Look, Herr Schachtner, [he] said, see how correctly and properly it is all written, only it can't be used, for it is so very difficult that no one could play it. Wolfgangerl said : That's why it's a concerto, you must practise it till you can get it right, look, that's how it goes. He played, and managed to get just enough out of it for us to see what he intended. At that time he had the notion that to play a concerto and work a miracle must be one and the same.

One further thing :

Madame, you will remember that I had a very good violin which the late Wolfgangerl called the " butter violin " because of its soft and full tone. One day shortly after your return from Vienna he played on it and could not find words to praise it highly enough ; one or two days later I came to see him again and found him amusing himself with his own violin. He at once said : How's your butter violin ? and went on fiddling away at his fantasia. Finally he thought a moment and said to me : Herr Schachtner, your violin is tuned half a quarter-tone lower than mine, if you left it tuned as it was last time I played it. I laughed at this, but Papa, knowing the extraordinary sense of pitch and memory of the child, asked me to fetch my violin and see if he was right. I did so, and he was right.

Shortly before this, in the days after your return from Vienna, Wolfgang having a little violin that he got as a present in Vienna, our former very good violinist, the late Herr Wenzl, came to us. He was a beginner in composition, and brought 6 trios with him, which he had written while your father was away and asked your father for an opinion on them. We played the trios, Papa playing the bass with his viola, Wenzl the first violin, and I was to play the 2nd violin. Wolfgang had asked to be allowed to play the 2nd violin, but Papa refused him this foolish request, because he had not yet had the least instruction in the violin, and Papa thought that he could not possibly play anything. Wolfgang said : You don't need to have studied in order to play 2nd violin, and when Papa insisted that he should go away and not bother us any more, Wolfgang began to weep bitterly and stamped off with his little violin. I asked them to let him play with me ; Papa eventually said : Play with Herr Schachtner, but so softly that we can't hear you, or you will have to go ; and so it was. Wolfgang played with me ; I soon noticed with astonishment that I was quite superfluous, I quietly put my violin down, and looked at your Papa ; tears of wonder and comfort ran down his cheeks at this scene, and so he played all 6 trios. When we had finished, Wolfgang was emboldened by our applause to maintain that he could play the 1st violin too. For a joke we made the experiment, and we almost died for laughter when he played this [part] too, though with nothing but wrong and irregular positioning, in such a way that he never actually broke down.

In conclusion. About the delicacy and fineness of his ear.

Until he was almost 9 he was terribly afraid of the trumpet when it was played alone, without other music. Merely to hold a trumpet in front of him was like aiming a loaded pistol at his heart. Papa wanted to cure him of this childish fear and once told me to blow [my trumpet] at him despite his reluctance, but my God ! I should not have been persuaded to do it ; Wolfgangerl scarcely heard the blaring sound, than he grew pale and began to collapse, and if I had continued, he would surely have had a fit.

This is the best I can do with the questions you ask ; forgive my dreadful scrawl, I am punished enough that I can do no better. With all esteem and due respect I am

Madame

Salzburg   Your most humble servant
the 24th April   Andre Schachtner
1792   Trumpeter to the Prince-Bishop

My humble respects to His Excellency your honoured husband.

To the third question.

Whatever he was given to learn occupied him so completely that he put all else, even music, on one side ; *e.g.* when he was doing sums, the table, chairs, walls, even the floor was covered with chalked figures.

> Original in the possession of Mr Albi Rosenthal, Oxford.—Ludwig Nohl, *Mozart nach den Schilderungen seiner Zeitgenossen* (Leipzig, 1880), pp. 4-7.—Jahn, Vol. I, pp. 21-24.—These were the first written recollections of Mozart, the last of which did not appear until about 1891.—Schachtner (1731-95) was one of the poets who wrote for the stage of the Salzburg University Hall. He translated librettos into German, including Varesco's *Idomeneo*, he wrote the text of the unfinished *Zaide* (K. 344) and published poems which Johann Christoph Gottsched honoured with a preface. He was, however, court and field trumpeter to the Archbishop of Salzburg by profession, and also played the violin and the violoncello. The office of Spielgraf which he eventually occupied made him the leading figure in civic music at Salzburg. He had been a friend of the Mozart family from the first. Mozart's sister, who lived at St. Gilgen with her family, had sent him a list of questions in time for Schlichtegroll's *Nekrolog*, published in 1793, asking him to write down his recollections of Mozart's childhood which she had been at the time too young to remember herself. In her efforts to collect material for Mozart's biography she followed the intentions of her father, who had carefully kept and bequeathed the family letters.—"Wenzl" was the nickname of Wenzel Hebelt (*cf.* 3 January 1765 and 10 March 1769).

MARIANNE VON BERCHTOLD'S REMINISCENCES, SPRING 1792

Data

For a biography of the late composer Wolfgang Mozart.

(1) Johannes Chrisostomus Wolfgang Gottlieb Mozart was born in Salzburg on the 27th January 1756.

(2) His father, Leopold Mozart, a book-binder's son from Augsburg, was born there on the 14th of November 1719. He came to study at the high school in Salzburg, then became valet to Count Thurn, a canon there, and entered the princely service as a chamber musician in 1743. (At the beginning of 1762 the father became vice-Capellmeister at the court of the Prince-Archbishop of Salzburg.) In 1743 on the 21st November he married Maria Anna Pertl, the daughter of the Prince-Bishop of Salzburg's late prefect at Hüttenstein. She was born in 1720 on the 25th December in the market-town of St. Gilgen in the Province of Salzburg. Apart from his duties at court and in the Metropolitan Church he was constantly busy with violin-instruction and composition. In 1756 he brought out a printed book, *Versuch einer gründlichen Violin Schulle*, which was reprinted in 1770.

A daughter, Maria Anna, and this son Wolfgang Gottlieb alone surviving of 7 children, he entirely gave up his violin-instruction and his composing so as to devote all the time remaining to him after his princely duties, to the education of his two children.

The son was three years old when the father began to instruct his seven year old daughter in the clavier.

The boy at once showed his God-given [and] extraordinary talent. He often spent much time at the clavier, picking out thirds, which he was always striking, and his pleasure showed that it sounded good.

In the fourth year of his age his father, for a game as it were, began to teach him a few minuets and pieces at the clavier. It was so easy for this child and for his father that he learned a piece in an hour and a minuet in half an hour, so that he could play it faultlessly and with the greatest delicacy, and keeping exactly in time. He made such progress that at the age of five he was already composing little pieces, which he played to his father who wrote them down.

(3) In the sixth year of his age his father and he made their first journey (4) to Munich, where both children played before the Elector (the Mozart family consisted of father, mother, son and daughter). After they had passed three weeks there they returned to Salzburg.

As the children were becoming ever better clavier players, the Mozart family journeyed on the 18th September 1762 via Passau [and] Linz to Vienna, where the children appeared at the imperial court a few days after their arrival. They also made a short journey to Pressburg, and returned to Salzburg in January 1763. (They were in the presence of Their Majesties for more than three hours, and only the grown-up archdukes and arch-duchesses were there. Emperor Francis said among other things to the son that there was no art in playing with all one's fingers, it would only be clever if the clavier were covered. The child thereupon played with one finger with the greatest ease, and then also let the keys be covered and played as if he had often practised it.)

On the 9th June 1763 the Mozart family made a journey to Munich, Augsburg, Ulm, Ludwigsburg, Bruchsal, Schwetzingen, Heidelberg, Mann-heim, Worms, Mainz, Frankfurt on Main, Mainz, Coblenz, Bonn, Brühl, Cologne, Aix-la-Chapelle, Liège, Tillemonde, Louvain, Brussels, Mons, Paris, where they arrived on the 18th November 1763.

(In *Munich* the children again performed in the presence of the Elector. The boy played a violin concerto there too, and extemporized. They also played at Duke Clement's. In *Augsburg* they gave two concerts. In Heidelberg the son played the organ in the Church of the Holy Ghost. In *Mannheim* they played for the Elector Palatine. [In] Frankfurt they gave 4 concerts. [In] Mainz they gave 2 concerts. The elector was ill, so they could not play for him. [In] Coblenz they played at the Elector's. Cologne. The Elector was in Westphalia, so they could not play for him. [In] Aix they gave a concert. [In] Brussels they gave a concert. In the other places they only stayed long enough to see all the sights.)

They performed for the royal family at Versailles. The son also played the organ in the Versailles court chapel in the presence of the whole court and won much applause.

They also gave two grand concerts in a private hall. After they [had] stayed 21 weeks in Paris,

(*Paris*. The son here wrote his first two keyboard works. The *first* he dedicated to Madame Victoire, the king's second daughter, and the *second* he dedicated to Md : La comtesse de Tessé. He was then seven years old. Both works were engraved in Paris.

Immediately after their arrival in Paris the children and their father were portrayed in an engraving.)

the Mozart family set out on the 10th April 1764 via Calais for England, where they arrived in London on the 22nd April. On the 27th April the children performed for both Their Majesties. On the 19th May they appeared before the King and Queen again. The son also played the King's organ, and everyone thought his organ playing far superior to his clavier playing. On the 5th June they gave a Benefit, or grand concert for their own profit. On the 5th August they had to rent a country house in Chelsea, outside the city of London, so that the father could recover from a dangerous throat ailment, which almost brought him to the doors of death. (If the father had not fallen ill, they would have travelled to Tunbridge, where the highest aristocracy assembled to take the waters.) As the father had at last completely recovered after two months, they returned to London.

(The son here composed 6 clavier sonatas, had them engraved and dedicated them to the Queen ; he was eight years old.

In Paris and in London they placed various difficult works by Bach, Handel, Paradies and other masters in front of the boy, and he not only played it all at sight, but with the appropriate tempo, and with delicacy.

London. When he was playing before the King he took a bare bass line and played the most beautiful melody above it. The son also sang arias with the greatest feeling.

The children now also played concertos on two pianos everywhere.

At this concert all the symphonies were of the son's composition.

On the 29th June was the benefit concert for the lying-in hospital. The father let his son play a concerto on the organ, gratis.

Herr Johann Christian Bach, the Queen's teacher, took the son between his legs, the former played a few bars, and then the other continued, and in this way they played a whole sonata, and someone not seeing it would have thought that only one man was playing it.)

On the 25th October they again played before the King and Queen.

On the 21st February 1765 they again gave a benefit concert for their own profit. After they had been heard by the highest aristocracy they departed from London on the 24th July 1765, to Canterbury and *Dover*, where they had such a favourable wind, that they made the crossing to Calais in

3½ hours. From there they went to *Dunkirk*, (In *Dunkirk* they saw everything of note.) *Lille* (They had to stay [in] *Lille* because father and son
were unwell.) *Ghent*, (The son played the organ at the Bernardines in *Ghent*.)
Antwerp. (In *Antwerp* the son played the great organ in the cathedral church.)
Mordyk. There [they] crossed a little inlet of the sea. From the other
side they travelled to Rotterdam by coach, and from there by ship to The
Hague, where they arrived in September 1765. As the daughter fell ill
immediately after their arrival, father and son twice went alone to the
Prince of Orange and once to his sister the Princess. When the daughter
had finally recovered a little from her very grave illness, the son fell sick
of a quite grave illness on the 15th November and had to remain in bed for
four weeks. (When the son was better again he composed 6 clavier sonatas,
had them engraved, and dedicated them to the Princess of Nassau-
Weilburg ; he was then 9 years old.)

After the children had finally fully recovered, after 4 months, they travelled
to Amsterdam at the end of January 1766, stayed there a month, [and]
returned to The Hague for the celebrations for the installation of the Prince
of Orange, held on the 11th of March.

(The Hague. For this festivity the son composed a *quotlibet* for all the
instruments. Two sets of variations for the clavier, a few arias for the
Princess.) [They] often played before the Prince. After they had stayed a
further 5 weeks at The Hague, they travelled via Harlem again (*Harlem*.
The son played the great organ.) to Amsterdam, Utrecht, Rotterdam,
Mordeck, Antwerp, Mecheln, Brussels, Valenciennes to Paris where they
arrived at the end of April 1766.

(During their stay in Paris they were twice at Versailles.) They stayed two
months in Paris. On the 9th July they left Paris, went to Dijon (in *Dijon*
they stayed 14 days.), Lyons (Lyons 4 weeks.) Geneva (Geneva 3 weeks.)
Lausanne (In Lausanne they stopped 8 days because of Prince Louis of
Württemberg.) Berne, Zürich (In Zürich they stayed 14 days.) via Winterthur to Schaffhausen. Donaueschingen. (In Donaueschingen for 14 days,
they daily made music before the Prince of Fürstenberg.) Mosskirch, Ulm,
Dillingen. (Dillingen. The children played for the Prince.) Augsburg,
Munich, where the children played for the Elector again. (Munich : The son
had to copy down, and perform, a theme at the Elector's which the Elector
sang for him. He did it in the presence of the Elector without using a clavier
or violin. When he had finished it he played it so that not only the Elector
but also the others who heard it were full of astonishment.) [They] returned
safe and sound to Salzburg at the end of the month of November 1766 after
a three and a half year journey.

On the 11th September 1767 the Mozart family travelled to Vienna for the
festivities which were arranged in Vienna for the marriage of the Archduchess Josepha with the King of Naples. Scarcely had they arrived when
the Archduchess died. As all were in mourning because of this death, they

intended to set off again at once, but as the Emperor often spoke of them, they were not permitted to depart because it was not certain that he would not summon them. But as the Archduchess Elisabeth also fell ill, they would no longer be delayed, and travelled to Brunn and Olmutz. (The father hurried away from Vienna because small-pox was raging in Vienna so fiercely, and his children had not yet [had] it.) As the son was unwell on their arrival in Olmutz, the father visited Count Podstatsky alone, the dean of the cathedral, who was also a canon at Salzburg. Now the son developed small-pox, and then the daughter likewise. (As Count Podstatsky learnt from the father that he was afraid his son might get small-pox, he gave excellent board and lodging to the whole family in the deanery, where he himself lived. There the children recovered safely from small-pox.) After they were quite recovered, they travelled to Brunn on the 23rd December 1767 and then on to Vienna again, where they arrived on the 10th January 1768. On the 19th of January the children performed before Emperor Joseph ; there was no one present but the Empress Maria Theresa, Prince Albert of Saxony, and the Archduchesses. Because of the children there was also a grand concert in the house of Prince Gallitzin, the Russian ambassador.

(Vienna. In the houses of Capellmeister Bono, Capellmeister Hasse, the poet Metestasio, the Duke of Braganza and Prince Kaunitz the father in each place bade someone open the first book of Italian arias to come to hand, and the son composed the music and instrumented it in the presence of these persons.

Vienna. The Emperor told the son he should write an opera buffa. The Emperor informed the Impresario who leased the theatre. The Impresario arranged everything with the father. The son composed the opera. But it was not performed . . . although Capellmeister Hasse [and] the poet Metastasio praised it uncommonly. The opera was called : *La finta Semplice*.)

At the consecration of the Orphanage Church on the Landstrasse this 12 year old boy conducted the service in the presence of the imperial court. (The son set the service, the offertory and a trumpet concerto for it.) In December 1768 they returned to Salzburg.

On the 12th December 1769 father and son went alone to Italy, via Innsbruck, Bolzano, Rovereto, Verona, Mantua, Milan, where they arrived on the 25th January 1770. (Before they made their journey to Italy in 1769 the son became Concert meister to the court orchestra of the Prince-Bishop of Salzburg.

Innsbruck. A concert was given at Count Königl's where the son played a concerto at sight. [In] Rovereto the son played the organ in the principal church, where a remarkable number of people were gathered. *Verona*. A concert was arranged. The son also played the organ in St Thomas's Church, where they could not reach the organ through the church because

of the crowd, and had to go through the monastery cloisters. *Mantua.*
They were invited to the weekly concert in the hall of the Academie Filarmonica. Milan. He wrote two Latin motets for two castrati. He also
composed several Italian arias and symphonies.) Here the son displayed
his talents to particular advantage in various tests of his knowledge in the
presence of the Maestro Samm Martino and an assemblage of the cleverest
people. There were many concerts in the house of Count Firmian where
the Duke and Princess of Modena were also present. After the son had
received the commission for the first opera for the carnival of 1771, they
travelled on the 15th March 1770 to Parma, Bologna, Florence, [on] to
Rome, where they arrived during Holy Week. On Wednesday afternoon
they accordingly went at once to the Sistine Chapel, to hear the famous
Miserere. And as according to tradition it was forbidden under ban of
excommunication to make a copy of it from the papal music, the son undertook to hear it and then copy it out. And so it came about that when he
came home, he wrote it out, the next day he went back again, holding his
copy in his hat, to see whether he had got it right or not. But a different
Miserere was sung. However, on Good Friday the first was repeated again.
After he had returned home he made a correction here and there, then it was
ready. It soon became known in Rome, [and] he had to sing it at the clavier
at a concert. The castrato Christofori, who sang it in the chapel, was present.
(Bologna. [Here] the fuss was greatest, for Father Maestro Martini, that
great contrapuntist, was, with all the other Capellmeisters, quite beside
himself when the son provided the correct counter-subject, according to the
rules of the mode, to the fugue theme which Padre Martini wrote down
for him, and at once performed the fugue on the clavier.

Florence. They were summoned at once to the Grand Duke, with whom
they spent 5 hours.

The astonishment here was all the greater as the Marchese Ligneville, the
music director and a great contrapuntist, placed the most difficult fugues
before the son, and gave him the most difficult themes, which he played
and developed at sight.

Florence. The son made friends with an Englishman, Tommaso Linley,
a boy of 14 years and the same age as young Mozart. A pupil of the famous
violinist Nardini. This boy played the violin quite enchantingly. This
Englishman and the young Mozart performed in turn, not like boys but
like men. Linley came to them on the day of their departure, amid many
embraces and tears gave young Mozart a poem which he had had written
by Sigra Corilla, and accompanied their coach as far as the town gateway.

Naples. When the son was playing in the Conservatorio alla Pieta, everyone
thought that the magic was due to his ring, [so] he took the ring off and
only then was everyone filled with astonishment.

Naples, a grand concert at the house of the Imperial Ambassador Count
Kaunitz.

Bologna. On the 9th October 1770 the son was elected member and maestro of the Academie Filarmonica, by unanimous vote. He was locked up quite alone, [and] had to set a given antiphon for four voices.

With which he was ready in a good half hour. Then the diploma was presented to him.

If the son had not had the commission for the first carnival opera for Milan in 1771, he would have been commissioned to write one for *Bologna*, Rome or Naples.)

From Rome they journeyed to Naples, and then back to Rome again.

The Pope wanted to see the son, and gave him the cross and the brief of a militiae auratae eques.

On the 10th July they travelled to Civita Castellana, where the son played the organ in the cathedral church. Loreto, Sinigaglia. Bologna. Here they had to remain longer, because they had been overturned on the journey and the father had injured his foot. They then went with Field Marshal Count Pallavicini to an estate until the foot was fully healed. Were it not for this mishap they would have gone back to Florence, Pisa [and] Livorno again, and via Genoa to Milan, but they had to go direct to Milan, where they arrived at the end of October. Here the son composed the opera seria *Mitridate*, which was given on the 26th December 1770 for the first time. (This opera was performed more than 20 times consecutively. That the opera was applauded can be deduced from the fact that the management at once gave him a written commission for the year 1773. When he wrote the opera he was 14 years old.)

After the son had conducted the first three performances of his opera from the clavier, as is the custom in Italy, they travelled to Turin to see the opera, came back to Milan to see the second opera : then straight on to Venice to spend the last days of the carnival there. They remained there until the 12th March 1771, and then went via Padua, Vicenza, Verona, (*Verona.* Here he also received the diploma of a member and Maestro di capella of the *Academia Filarmonica.* For Padua he had to write an oratorio *Betulia liberata.*) Rovereto, Trent, Innsbruck back to Salzburg. (The son was accorded the name *il cavaliere filarmonico* in Italy.)

On their arrival they found a letter from Count Firmian, Minister in Milan, [to the effect] that the son was commissioned by H.M. the Empress to write the great stage Serenata for the coming celebrations of the marriage of the Archduke Ferdinand in the October of this year. As H: Majesty had appointed Hr: Hasse, the oldest Capellmeister, to write the opera, he had chosen the youngest to write the Serenata. (The Serenata was called *Ascanio in Alba.*) On the 13th August 1771 they travelled back to Milan, where they arrived on the 21st August. The Serenata was performed for the first time on the 17th October. (The opera and the Serenata were given alternately as long as the festivities lasted.) On the 13th December 1771 they came back to Salzburg again.

(In the year 1772 the son made a serenata for the election of the Archbishop of Salzburg, *Il sogno di Scipione*.)

On the 24th October 1772 the father journeyed to Italy with his son for the third time, where the son wrote the opera seria : *Lucio Silla* for the carnival of 1773 in Milan. (The opera was performed 26 times.) On the 13th March 1773 they came back again.

In July 1773 the father made a short visit with the son to Vienna, in October they came back.

On the 9th December 1774 the father made a journey to Munich with the son.

(*Munich*. The son here composed an opera buffa. *La finta giardiniera*. 2 big Masses composed by the son were also performed in the Court Chapel.) On the 7th March 1775 they came back again.

In the month of April 1775, the son composed a Serenata, *il Re Pastore*, during the visit of Archduke Maximilian to Salzburg.

On the 23rd September 1777 the son travelled with his mother to Paris. It would have been to his advantage to have stayed in Paris, but he found French music so little to his taste that he joyfully returned to Germany. (*Paris*. He composed a symphony for the concert Spirituell, a Sinfonie concertante, a concerto for the Flute, a Concerto for the Harp ; [he] also had 6 Sonatas engraved in Paris, which he dedicated to the Electress of the Palatinate.

On the 3rd July 1778 his mother died in Paris, in the 58th year of her age.) In the month of January 1779 he returned to his father in Salzburg.

On the 8th November 1780 the son travelled to Munich, where he wrote an opera seria *Idomeneo* for the Carnival of 1781. As his Princely Grace the Archbishop of Salzburg travelled to Vienna for the carnival, he [Mozart] was summoned to him in Vienna, he therefore travelled direct from Munich to Vienna.

(The father died in Salzburg on the 28th May 1787.)

(5) For the events of his later life, you must make enquiries in Vienna, as I can find nothing from which I could write anything thorough.

(6) From information received from Vienna he died on 5 December (55 minutes after midnight) 1791 of a heated miliary fever. In the year 1788 I received the news from Vienna, that he had officially entered imperial service, what remains you must likewise learn in Vienna. (as also who his wife was, how many children they had of their union, how many of them are still alive etc.)

(7) He came to Vienna in his 24th year, and he was just ten years there. He will certainly have greatly improved in composition in this time, as in 1785 the famous Hr: Joseph Haydn said to his father, who was at that time in Vienna, " I tell you before God, and as an honest man, your son

is the greatest composer known to me by person and repute, he has taste and what is more the greatest skill in composition ".

(As soon as he sat down at the clavier he was absolutely the master, he could notice the slightest mistake even in fully orchestrated music, and said at once on which instrument the mistake had occurred, indeed, even what note it ought to have been. He was irritated by the slightest sound during a piece of music. In short, as long as the piece of music lasted, he was all music himself ; as soon as it was over, one saw the child again.)

(8) He was never forced to compose nor to play, on the contrary he always needed to be restrained, he would otherwise have remained sitting over his clavier or his compositions day and night.

(9) Is answered in No. 2.

(10) (Taken from a letter from London.) Hr. Baron von Grim's proposals to the father about Russia, and about the Hereditary Prince of Brunswick. (We were respectively engaged for Hamburg, we could travel to Copenhagen, as both the Danish Ambassador in Paris and the Danish Ambassador here were prepared to guarantee a certain sum in advance. Prince Gallazin also wanted to persuade me to go to Russia.)

(11) Even as a child he was desirous of learning everything he set eyes on ; in drawing [and] adding he showed much skill but, as he was too busy with music, he could not show his talents in any other direction.

Postscript.

The daughter Maria Anna Mozart has for some years been married to a [Salzburg] councillor and prefect, who brought her children from two previous marriages, and with whom she has also produced some children. So she lives at this time in the same place in which her late mother was born, in modest and peaceful retirement, given over entirely to the noble duties of a wife and mother. In the last years of her spinsterhood, which she passed at home with her father, she gave instruction in the clavier to a few young ladies of the capital city of Salzburg ; and even nowadays one can tell the Nannètte Mozart pupils from all others by their delicacy, precision and true application when playing.

Further

The two Mozart parents were in their day the handsomest couple in Salzburg ; and in her young years the daughter too was considered a regular beauty, but the son Wolfgang was small, thin, pale in colour, and entirely lacking in any pretensions as to physiognomy and bodily appearance. Apart from his music he was almost always a child, and thus he remained : and this is a main feature of his character on the dark side ; he always needed a father's, a mother's or some other guardian's care ; he could not manage his financial affairs. [He] married a girl quite unsuited to him, and against the will of his father, and thus the great domestic chaos at and after his death.

> Salzburg, Mozarteum.—Nannerl's handwriting, supplemented by an unknown person (especially the sections printed in italics), who tried to make the last sentence illegible.—Nottebohm, *Mozartiana*, pp. 95-111, where there are

some corrections.—Written for Schlichtegroll before June 1792, based on Leopold Mozart's letters. These recollections, in the form of answers to set questions, came to Schlichtegroll through the offices of a third person (Albert von Mölk), but he made greater use of Schachtner's (1792) than of Nannerl's notes. Whether these were also at Niemetschek's disposal (in 1798) is uncertain. On 24 November 1799 Nannerl sent a copy to the publishing-house of Breitkopf & Härtel, which intended to bring out a Mozart biography of its own. Nissen made use of them in his book, published in 1828, but he understandably omitted the final words disparaging Constanze.—*Cf.* also Nannerl's recollections printed in Breitkopf's journal in 1800.

On 15 May, in Franz Deyerkauf's garden in Graz, the first Mozart monument, a temple with a bust, was erected.

Deyerkauf, a freemason, was an art and music dealer, and a friend of Puchberg's. The temple still stands (now Schubertstrasse 35); it was restored in 1956. The frescoes on the inside have been destroyed, as have also the busts of Haydn and Mozart, which Herr Kargl had erected at Mariagrün, near Graz, in 1819. —The monument by Gottlieb Klauer, which was only of terracotta and which the music-loving Duchess Anna Amalie of Weimar caused to be set up in the park at Tiefurt in 1799, has not been preserved (picture in the Weimar *Journal des Luxus und der Modern* (1799) Plate 33). Not until 1824 and 1831 did the music-loving banker Giuseppe Antonio Bridi (son of the doctor mentioned under 13 March 1786) set up in his garden at Rovereto two monuments in Mozart's honour, with inscriptions in Latin and German, and the Temple of Harmony for Mozart and other composers, which still survives. *Cf.* the *Allgemeine musikalizche Zeitung* (Leipzig) 1824, col. 92, and [Antonio Rosaro's] *Mozart a Rovereto* (1935).

On 5 June the "New-Crowned Hope" opened, by means of a circular letter, a collection in aid of Mozart's impoverished widow and children.

The text and whereabouts are at present unknown.—Deutsch, *op. cit.*, p. 18.—Nothing is known about the result of this collection.

On 13 June a concert in memory of Mozart was held at the National Theatre in Prague, the proceeds of which went to his family.

Teuber, *op. cit.*, Vol. II, p. 274.—Nettl, *op. cit.*, pp. 145, 210 and 220. —Teuber followed Dlabacs's *Künstlerlexikon* in giving 13 January 1792 as the date; Nettl cites both dates, thereby implying that there were two different commemorations.—The concert had been organized by Count Franz Sternberg (see 12-18 April 1786) and Dr. Johann Nepomuk Vignet. The performers were Josepha Dušek, Fräulein de Vignet, Fräulein Mariani and Herr Ramisch; Johann Wittasek (Jan Vitášek), a pupil of Dušek's, was at the pianoforte. Vocal numbers from *Idomeneo* and a pianoforte concerto by Mozart were performed.

FROM SCHINK'S "HAMBURGISCHE THEATERZEITUNG", 7 JULY 1792

Performances in our theatre.

. . . on the twenty-fifth of June : *Figaro's Heyrat*, Singspiel in two acts, from the Italian, the music by Mozart.

A reminder from us that Beaumarchais's *folle journée* is the basis of this Singspiel would be superfluous. If one does not know the French original, or at least forgets one's former acquaintance with it, one unquestionably finds oneself very well entertained by it, even if one considers it as a play, particularly as it has fallen into the hands of such a good and tasteful translator as Baron *Knigge*. The music to it would make *Mozart's* name famous, if it were not so already. It is more theatrical than any other of his compositions for the stage. Faithful depiction of character, beautiful, spirited melodies, choruses that form an integral part of the action, above all a spirit of complaisance and lightness, give it a worth by means of which it will always maintain its place on our lyric stage. The death of this excellent composer is a real loss to music. How much was he already, and what more might he yet have become, because he was beginning to compose not merely at the dictate of his *genius*, but also at that of his *mind* ;—that is, he was beginning to subject his imagination to his intellect. May his ashes rest in peace ! . . .

        No. 27, pp. 433-7.—*Figaro* had been in the German repertoire at Hamburg since 4 April 1791.

FROM THE " WIENER ZEITUNG ", 11 AUGUST 1792

New Music.

From Johann Träg . . . the following works by *Mozart* are to be had :
6 *Masses by W. A. Mozart.*
2 Pianoforte concertos à 2 *Clavicemb.*
2 *Concerti à Corno Princ.*
1 *Concerto à Violino Princ.*
15 *Sinfon.*
1 *Cassatio à 2 Viol. 2 Cor. Viola è Basso.*
4 *Parthien à 2 Obe 2 Clarinetti 2 Cor. 2 Fag.*
1 *Quintetto à Corno 2 Viol. Viola è Basso.*
2 *Duetti à Violino è Viola.*
24 *Contredanses* with all parts.
7 – – – – – – with an *Overture.*
1 Sonata in D *à* 2 Clavicemb.
3 *Sonates per il Clav.*
Various *Arias* with Italian text in *Partitura.*
3 *Sinfon.* arranged as Quintets for 2 *Viol. 2 Viole è Basso.*
1 *Quintetto in G min.* arranged for *Clav. Viol. Viola è Basso.*
In addition to the above, various further *Quart.* and *Trios* arranged for violin and for flute.

        The masses were probably K. 257-9, 317, 337 and 427 ; the pianoforte concertos K. 242 (reduced from three pianofortes to two) and 365 ; the horn concertos perhaps K. 447 and 495 ; the violin concerto possibly K. 271a ; 15 of the symphonies ranging between K. 181 and 551 ; the *Cassatio* K. 247 or 287 ; the *Parthien* K. 375, 388 and two arrangements ; the quintet probably an arrangement of K. 407 ; the *Duetti* K. 423 and 424 ; the 24 country

dances probably K. 462, 510 (spurious), 535a, 565 and 609 Nos. 1, 2, 4 & 5 :
the 7 country dances as on 14 January 1792 ; the sonata for two pianofortes
K. 448 ; the three pianoforte sonatas perhaps K. 545, 570 and 576.

On 8 September Mozart's *Kleine Freimaurer-Kantate* was performed in the " New-
Crowned Hope " lodge as a " thank-offering " for Emperor Francis II. The new
text was by Karl Ludwig Gieseke.

> *Cf.* 18 November 1791.—A copy of the printed text is in the Vienna City
> Library.—See O. E. Deutsch in the *Österreichische Musikzeitschrift* (Vienna,
> July-August 1957).

IBID., 14 SEPTEMBER 1792

New music.

From Artaria & Comp., art dealers in the Kohlmarkt, are to be had :

.   .   .   .   .

Mozart, Trio per Clavicembalo Violino e Violoncello, Opera 27, 1 fl. 30 kr
– –   *die Zauberflöte*, arranged as Quartets for 2 violins, viola and bass, 3 fl.
– –   *detto* as Duets for 2 violins or 2 flutes, 1 fl. 30 kr.
– –   *die Zauberflöte* in piano score, 4 fl. 30 kr.

.   .   .   .   .

Mozart, 12 minuets for the Rout arranged for 2 violins and basso, 40 kr.
12 –   German dances for 2 violins and basso, 40 kr.

> The pianoforte trio K. App. 148 was an arrangement of the D major string
> quartet (K. 575).—Artaria's pianoforte score of *Die Zauberflöte* had been
> appearing since November 1791 in separate numbers, as had the one published
> by the *Musikalisches Magazin,* but neither had been completed by 1793.—The
> last of Mozart's dances for the Assembly Hall had been published by Artaria
> in pianoforte score and parts in 1791, but these arrangements were new.

FROM THE MS VIENNA NEWSPAPER " DER HEIMLICHE BOTSCHAFTER ", 25 SEPTEMBER 1792

The Theater auf der Wieden is to close in the near future, in as much
as the owner of the same, Prince Stahremberg, intends to have dwelling
houses built in its place.

> Vienna, National Library.—Deutsch, *op. cit.,* p. 20.—Notice was not given
> until 1 April 1800.

IBID., 2 OCTOBER 1792

Kapellmeister Hayden, who has [recently] arrived here, is working on
the 2nd part of the well-loved Opera of the late Mozart, *die Zauberflötte* ;
on the 15th of this month, however, being the Name-Day of Her Majesty

the Empress, a new opera of his composition will be given in the Court Theatre.

> Vienna, National Library.—Gugitz, *op. cit.*, p. 2.—It was only on 12 June 1798 that the Freihaus Theatre produced Peter Winter's opera *Das Labyrinth* (libretto by Schikaneder) as a sequel to *Die Zauberflöte.*—On 15 October 1792 Joseph Weigl's new singspiel *Der Strazzensammler* was produced at the Burgtheater.

FERDINAND COUNT WALDSTEIN IN BEETHOVEN'S ALBUM

Dear Beethoven,

You are now about to travel to Vienna to fulfil your wishes, so long opposed. Mozart's genius still mourns and laments the death of his charge. With the indefatigable Hayden he found refuge but not employment; through him he now wishes once more to be united with someone. By means of your ceaseless diligence you shall receive : *Mozart's spirit from Hayden's hands.*

Bonn, the 29th October 1792.

Your true friend Waldstein.

> Vienna, National Library.—Anton Schindler, *Beethoven* (Münster, 1840), Vol. I, p. 18.—Beethoven left his native town on 2 November 1792 to settle in Vienna.

FROM THE " MUSIKALISCHE MONATSSCHRIFT ", BERLIN, NOVEMBER 1792
Paris.
Théatre de la rue Feydeau.

On Monday the 24th [September] an Italian opera, *il confictato il Pietro,* or *le festin de Pierre,* was given. At the end of this piece there is a brilliant spectacle : but it was easy to foresee that this type of play would no longer have the success that it had in former times. There are fine passages in the music*, yet it did not excite the enthusiasm which the works of Paisiello and other great Italian masters † call forth. Various numbers were applauded, among others an aria by Mengazzi had to be encored.

* The journalist does not say who wrote it ; let us hope meanwhile that it was not Mozart's *Dom Juan,* of which single arias have more inner worth than whole operas by Paisiello.

† The translator of this article is entirely ignorant in which corner of Italy they may be living.

> No. 5, p. 122.—Jahn, Vol. II, p. 362.—This monthly, edited by Reichardt and others, was the continuation of the *Musikalisches Wochenblatt.*—François Lesure (Paris) has endeavoured in vain to trace this performance. It is probably a case of one of the many operas entitled *Il convitato di pietra.*—The editorial remarks are perhaps by Carl Spazier.—" Mengazzi " is in fact (Bernardo) Mengozzi.

IBID., BERLIN, NOVEMBER 1792

Candid thoughts on the first and fourth numbers of
the " Musikalisches Wochenblatt ".

His [Hr. W's] judgment on Mozart's *Don Juan* is extremely exaggerated
and one-sided.   No one will fail to recognize in Mozart the man of great
talents and the experienced, prolific and genial composer.   But I have yet
to see him considered a correct, much less a perfect artist, by any thorough-
going scholar of the art of music, and by so much the less will the critic
endowed with taste hold him to be a correct and sensitive composer in his
attitude towards poetry.

> No. 5, p. 139.—Jahn, Vol. II, p. 363 (inaccurate).—The *Gedanken*, perhaps
> also written by Spazier, relate to B. A. Weber's article in No. IV of the
> *Wochenblatt* (? 29 October) 1791.

FROM ZINZENDORF'S DIARY, 2 JANUARY 1793
(in French)

. . . In the evening to ᴾᵉˢˢᵉ *Schwarzenberg*, thence to old Princesse *Col-*
loredo, which caused me to miss Mozart's requiem.

> Köchel/Einstein, p. 811.—The Princess Schwarzenberg was probably Maria
> Eleonora, the widow of Prince Johann Nepomuk (see November 1788) ;
> Princess Colloredo was Marie Gabriele, the widow of Prince Rudolph (see
> 11 October 1762 and later).   See also below.

FROM THE NEWSPAPER " MAGYAR HÍRMONDÓ ", VIENNA, 4 JANUARY 1793
(in Hungarian)

Mozart, who made for himself an immortal name in music, left a widow
and two orphans in poverty.   Many noble benefactors are helping this
unhappy woman.   The day before yesterday Baron Swieten promoted a
concert with sung funeral-music in a public place in memory of Mozart.
His widow relict received the proceeds of more than 300 golden ducats.

> Supplied by Frau Lidia F. Wendelin, Budapest.—The Requiem was therefore
> given its first performance in Vienna, in memory of Mozart and for the
> benefit of Constanze, before the man who had commissioned it could use
> it (see 14 December 1793).   The performance evidently took place not in
> the Court Library, but in Jahn's Room, as Maximilian Stadler reports in his
> statement on the Requiem written in 1826.   Constanze, and following her
> Jahn, Vol. II, p. 652, erroneously placed the concert in the year 1792 (letter
> to Breitkopf, 17 November 1799) ; Salieri is said to have attended the
> rehearsals.

★   FROM ZINZENDORF'S DIARY, 19 FEBRUARY 1793
(in French)

. . . Dined . . . at Prince Schwarzenberg's . . . after dinner charming music
by Mozart. *Die Zauberflöte.*

Prince Joseph Johann Nepomuk was the eldest son of Prince Johann Nepomuk Schwarzenberg.

It is said that the immortal Mozart's universally popular opera, *die Zauberflöte*, is to be performed at the Italian Court Theatre here in an Italian translation. Herr Pertati is said to have received the commission to supply the translation.

> Vienna, National Library.—Deutsch, *op. cit.*, p. 20.—The libretto of *Die Zauberflöte* was not translated by Giovanni Bertati but (according to Willi Schuh) by Scipione Piattoli, and the work was performed in Italian, not in Vienna but in Prague during the Carnival of 1794. (It was there that the first performance of the original outside Vienna was given on 25 October 1792 ; the first performance in Czech probably also took place in Prague, in 1794.)

FRAU KATHARINA ELISABETH GOETHE TO HER SON, FRANKFURT ON MAIN,
9 NOVEMBER 1793

There is no news here but that *die Zauberflöte* has been given 18 times, and that the house was always packed full ; no person will have it said of him that he has not seen it, all the jobbing gardeners, indeed, even the inhabitants of Sachsenhausen, whose children play the apes and lions, go to see it. A spectacle like this has never been known here before ; the house has to be opened before 4 o'clock each time, and in spite of that some hundreds always have to go away again because they cannot get a seat—it has certainly brought the money in !

> *Die Briefe der Frau Rath Goethe* (Leipzig, 1923), Vol. I, pp. 240 f. (Albert Köster).—*Die Zauberflöte* had been given at Frankfurt since 16 August 1793. —Sachsenhausen was a suburb of Frankfurt (see 6 February 1794).

On 14 December 1793 Count Walsegg performed Mozart's Requiem, the authorship of which he claimed for himself.

> Alfred Schnerich's preface to the facsimile of the Requiem (Vienna, 1913) states that this performance took place in the church of the Cistercian monastery of Neukloster at Wiener-Neustadt after a rehearsal on 12 December in this church. The wife of Count Franz Walsegg-Stuppach (see 4 December 1791), Anna, *née* von Flammberg, in whose memory the Requiem was ordered and performed, had died on 14 February 1791. The copy used by the Count carried the title *Requiem composto del Conte Walsegg*. *Cf.* 2 and 4 January 1793, 20 April 1796, late 1798 and 1839.

★ FROM ZINZENDORF'S DIARY, 29 DECEMBER 1793
(in French)

. . . At the Baroness [Reischach]'s. Chotek arrived. He had his Dryden in his pocket with the *Ode on St. Cecilia* that was performed yesterday in Hendel's setting.

Simon Thaddäus, Baron Reischach, was a Minister in the Council of State for internal affairs.—For Johann Rudolf Count Chotek *cf.* 5 March 1792 and Appendix I.—The ode referred to is probably not *Alexander's Feast* but the *Ode for St. Cecilia's Day*, in Mozart's arrangement (*cf.* 7 April 1789 and July 1790).

FROM FRIEDRICH SCHLICHTEGROLL'S "NEKROLOG AUF DAS JAHR 1791", GOTHA, 1793

In Vienna he married Constanza Weber and found in her a good mother of the two children of their union, and a worthy wife who, moreover, sought to restrain him from many foolishnesses and excesses. Despite a considerable income, he yet, in consequence of his exceptional sensuality and domestic disorder, left his family nothing beyond the glory of his name, and the attention of a large public fixed upon them . . .

Year II, pp. 82 ff.—Jahn, Vol. II, p. 835. As this Necrology is based on Schachtner's and Nannerl's memoirs, only that part is here quoted which corrects the last paragraph of Nannerl's memoirs.

FRAU GOETHE TO HER SON, 7 FEBRUARY 1794

Just think ! *Die Zauberflöthe* was last week given for the 24th time with a tightly packed house, and has already brought in 22,000 f. ! How was your performance of it ? are your monkeys as good as our little people from Sachsenhaussen ?

Op. cit., p. 252.—Cf. 9 November 1793.—*Die Zauberflöte* was first given at Weimar on 16 January 1794.

FROM THE "PRAGER NEUE ZEITUNG", (?9) FEBRUARY 1794
(On the Mozart concert of 7 February)

The Akademiesaal was brightly illuminated. At the back and above the orchestra Mozart's name flamed in a sort of temple, on both sides of which stood two pyramids with the illuminated legend " Gratitude and Pleasure " in transparent letters. For this evening Mozart's best works had been chosen. A symphony in C formed the introduction, then Herr Wittassek, a very promising young musician from Bohemia, played Mozart's most splendid concerto, [the one] in D minor, on the fortepiano with as much precision as feeling. Next, Bohemia's popular singer Frau Duschek sang Vitellia's heavenly rondo from Mozart's opera seria *la clemenza di Tito*. Her artistry is known everywhere ; here her love for the great departed, and his widow, whose warm friend she ever was, inspired her. The concluding item was one of the best symphonies there is, one in D major by Mozart. The music went very well, although the works were difficult and mainly in concertante style—for the Prague Orchestra was playing, and they are entirely devoted to Mozart. It is easy to imagine how full the hall was, if one knows Prague's artistic sense and its love for Mozart's music. Mozart's widow and son both wept tears of grief at their loss, and of gratitude towards a noble nation. Thus this evening was fittingly and admirably devoted to an act of homage to merit and genius ; it was a rewarding feast for sensitive hearts—and a small tribute to the unspeakable delight that Mozart's divine tones often drew from us. From many a noble eye there flowed a silent tear for this well-loved man ! It is as though Mozart had composed especially for Bohemia ; nowhere was his music better understood and executed than in Prague, and even in the country districts it is universally popular . . . so many were the hearts that Mozart's great genius won for itself.

> No. 12.—Procházka, *op. cit.*, pp. 189 *ff.*—Constanze had gone to Prague on account of her son Karl, to lodge him at Franz Niemetschek's or to visit him there. (According to Karl Mozart's later recollections he spent the years 1792–97 there ; according to a letter from Niemetschek to Breitkopf & Härtel of 21 May 1800 only " more than 3 years "; see 9 April 1794).—The concert (according to Dlabacs, *op. cit.*, Vol. II, p. 34) was organized by the law students of the University and held in the hall of the Seminary.—The first of the symphonies is said to have been K. 425, the second K. 297 (? 504) ; the pianoforte concerto was K. 466.—For Wittasek see 13 June 1792.—The rondo from *La clemenza di Tito* is No. 23, " Non più di fiori ". (It had been used on 14 October 1793 at the Freihaus Theatre as an interpolation in Schikaneder's and Henneberg's opera *Die Waldmänner*, with the words " Schön ist der Abend ".)—According to Dlabacs a funeral ode was also performed, and according to Niemetschek, pp. 66 f., a poem by the young Joseph Georg Meinert was delivered. It is to be found in Nissen, pp. 697 f., and in Procházka, pp. 190 f.

* FROM ZINZENDORF'S DIARY, 16 FEBRUARY 1794
(in French)

. . . Dined at Princess Schwarzenberg's . . . Pretty music from the *Zauberflöte.*

Cf. 19 February 1793.

FROM THE MINUTES OF THE IMPERIAL CHANCELLERY, 31 MARCH 1794

526 (Protocol of the same) 26 March . . .

148 the request of the widow Mozart for permission to perform a cantata for her own benefit . . .

Ad Num : 148. Grant to the widow Mozart a day after Easter.

> Vienna, State Archives : Kabinettsprotokolle, Vol. 119, No. 526.—Gustav Gugitz, *Wiener Geschichtsblätter*, 1956, No. 1, p. 19.—The imperial sanction evidently came too late. The concert performances of *La clemenza di Tito* did not take place till 29 December 1794 at the Kärntnertor Theatre, and 31 March 1795 at the Burgtheater.

The esteemed Prague public, which well knows how to honour the name of Mozart, is deserving of an explanation, which has been rendered necessary by the last 2 opera notices. The boy Mozart, the son of the immortal man whose divine harmonies will continue to delight us to the end of our days, is to be sent to Prague for the benefit of his education and upbringing ; this being at the instigation of his noble patron, His Excellency the Baron van Swieten, who places full confidence in the spirit of the Bohemian nation. According to the wish of certain admirers of the name of Mozart, this 9 year old boy, full of ardour and vivacity, was to have appeared publicly on the stage in the opera *Axur* in the role of the boy who is offered up for sacrifice. What detrimental effect this might have had on the development of the young person's mind can be comprehended fully only by those to whose supervision and care the boy has been entrusted. The children of great men belong to the public to a certain extent ; and the boy's guardians have too high a respect for the latter and too much love for the boy's well-being to have permitted it. As these are also the opinions of his noble benefactor and of his mother, there was the less hesitation in preventing the boy's appearance. Had the opera announcements not revealed the matter to the public prematurely, this explanation would not have been necessary ; but in the present circumstances a person informed according to the latest opera bill might accuse the widow Mozart, who is full of respect and gratitude towards the Prague public, of a capriciousness of which she is entirely innocent.

> Nottebohm, *Mozartiana*, pp. 5 f.—For van Swieten *cf.* 9 and 16 December 1791.—*Axur, rè d' Ormus* was Da Ponte's Italian version of Salieri's opera *Tarare*, which had been performed with Beaumarchais's text in Paris in 1787. *Axur* was first performed at the Burgtheater on 8 January 1788, and later the same year in Prague and Leipzig.—Apart from Niemetschek, Franz Dušek had also taken care of the boy Karl's education ; according to Niemetschek's letter to Breitkopf & Härtel, quoted above, van Swieten had not made him any payment. Constanze may at this time still have been in Prague.

Notice.

The Supreme Court Theatre Management has graciously permitted the undersigned to give a concert for her own benefit during the present season of Advent. She has designated for this concert one of the best and last works of her late husband, Wolfgang Amade Mozart, Hofkammerkompositor, whose death came too soon both for herself and for Art, namely his music to Metastasio's opera *La Clemenza di Tito*, which hitherto has not been performed here. The general applause, with which Mozart's musical products have always been received, makes her hope that the esteemed public will also honour with its presence this performance of one of his last masterpieces. The date of the performance of this work, and the names of the singers participating, will be announced in due course by means of the usual bills.

Mozart, née Weber.

The poster has not been preserved.

FROM THE "WIENER ZEITUNG", 24 DECEMBER 1794

Notice.

The concert announced by the widow Mozart in the last three editions of this paper will take place next Monday, being the 29th day of this month of December, and further details will be published by means of the usual bills. The keys of the boxes are to be had either of the widow Mozart, residing in the Krugerstrasse at the sign of the Blue Sabre, on the second floor, or from the keeper of the boxes.

> The concert was held in the Kärntnertor Theatre on 29 December. (There is a reference to this concert in the minutes for 24 December 1794 in the archives of the former Ministry of the Interior, preserved in fragmentary form in the Vienna City Library.) Aloisia Lange sang the part of Sextus. Eberl (see 11 December 1791) played a pianoforte concerto by Mozart between the two parts.—Constanze's lodging in the Krugerstrasse (No. 10), City No. 1046 (later 1074), was in the house where Prince Galitsin had lived in 1784 (see 26 February 1784) and in which Joseph Haydn kept a *pied-à-terre* about 1798. This is the only identifiable residence of Constanze between 1791 and 1798.

FROM "TEUTSCHLANDS ANNALEN DES JAHRES 1794", CHEMNITZ, 1795

In this year 1794 nothing can or may be sung or played, and nothing heard with approbation, but that it bears on its brow the all-powerful and magic name of Mozart. Operas, Symphonies, Quartets, Trios, Duets, Piano pieces, Songs, even Dances—all must be by Mozart, if they are to lay claim to general approbation. Nor have the music publishers, for their part, in any way failed to satisfy these whims of the dilettantes. By means of the great art of arrangement we already have this composer's *die Zauberflöte*, printed and engraved in all the above-named forms. Heaven alone knows how strangely many of these attempts have worked out, were indeed bound to work out, on account of the nature of the piece. Sufficient to say that what is played or sung is by Mozart, and more particularly from his *Zauberflöte*.

That Mozart to a large extent deserves this applause will be disputed by no one. But that he was still in his years of ferment, and that his ideas were still frequently in a state of flux, as it were—of this there are only too many instances in his works. If we pause only to consider his symphonies: for all their fire, for all their pomp and brilliance they yet lack that sense of unity, that clarity and directness of presentation, which we rightly admire in Jos. Haydn's symphonies. He who has the opportunity to instigate similar comparisons between Mozart's works for voice and the works of other good masters, will find several other faults besides. More-over, one is often tempted, in hearing Mozart's works, to exclaim with the maid-servant in the comedy, " There's nothing natural about me, thank God ! ". An almost unadulteratedly spicy diet, which spoils the palate if one's taste for it continues ; and in the hands of the wretched imitators, who think they need only to Mozartize in order to please, every trace of noble simplicity will finally be banished from music. Such could easily prove to be the final result of this general idolization.

Mozart's *Zauberflöte* in piano score published in Mainz, Mannheim, Offenbach, Leipsig, Berlin and Brunswick : that is, six times in one and the same year : an hitherto unexampled occurrence in the history of music literature, and one which sufficiently justifies what was said above about the general enthusiasm for Mozart's works.

Edited by Friedrich Julius Heinrich, Count Soden, Book 7, *Geschichte der Musik*, p. 315 f.—Erich Valentin, *Wege zu Mozart* (Regensburg, 1941), pp. 168-170.

FROM THE " WIENER ZEITUNG ", 18 MARCH 1795

Musical Concert.

The undersigned permits herself the honour of announcing to the high nobility and the esteemed public that she has been granted permission by the Supreme Court Theatre Management to give a concert for her benefit in the present season of Lent. Very deeply moved by the unanimous approbation accorded to the performance of her late husband's last master-piece, *La clemenza di Tito*, instigated by her during the season of Advent last year, she finds herself in duty bound to express her warmest thanks therefor. The wish—so flattering for her, so often since expressed by lovers of Art—to hear again this Opera, the masterly performance of which she must with grateful recognition attribute to the orchestra, but more especially to the kind and freely given services of the singers, imposes upon her the duty to designate this last work of her late husband for performance. She promises herself a response the more gratifying as Vienna's noble citizens have always followed their favourite inclination : to do good, whenever it was a question of supporting widows and orphaned children. The day of the performance of this musical work and the names of the singers participating will be announced in due course by means of the usual bills.

Konstanza, Widow Mozart.

The poster has not been preserved ; the performance was held on 31 March. Aloisia Lange again sang Sextus. The rest of the cast, according to Eduard Wlassack's *Chronik des k.k. Hof-Burgtheaters* (Vienna, 1876), p. 98, was as

follows : Tito—Giuseppe Viganoni ; Vitellia—Marianne Sessi ; Servilia—
—Signora Marescalchi ; Publio—Johann Michael Vogl (later Schubert's
friend). Wlassack quotes from the (lost) programme : " After the first part
Herr Ludwig van Beethoven will perform on the pianoforte a concerto of
Mozart's composition." Probably K. 466.

FROM THE " WIENER ZEITUNG ", 21 MARCH 1795

Forte Piano and Clavicourt for sale.

A large Forte piano and a Clavicourt of the late Mozart's are for sale each
day. Prospective purchasers are invited to inquire at the sign of the Black
Elephant in the Rothe Thurmgasse, where the coffee-house is, on the first
floor, right hand side, before 1 o'clock p.m.

While Constanze's concert announcement appeared on 18, 21 and 25 March,
this curious offer was printed on the 21st, 25th and 28th ; but it is not to be
supposed that it emanated from her. She was living in the Krugerstrasse at
the end of 1794, and had probably been there for some time already. She
may have sold or pawned the two instruments about 1793, from necessity
or for lack of room. Her circumstances having improved in the meantime,
she may have been in a position to buy them back or to redeem them. They
are now in the Salzburg Mozart Museum, whither they passed after the death
of Mozart's sons.—The advertiser is unknown. His address, then City No. 677,
corresponds to the present No. 31 Rotenturmstrasse. The house belonged to
Michael Dutzinger's heirs, the coffee-house in it to Frau Barbara Holl.

* FROM ZINZENDORF'S DIARY, 30 MARCH 1795
(in French)

. . . Mme. Mozart called on me to ask me to come to her concert to-
morrow.

Cf. the following item.

* FROM ZINZENDORF'S DIARY, 31 MARCH 1795
(in French)

. . . In the evening to a concert for the widow Mozart, they gave an
oratorio *La Clemenza di Tito*. The chandelier makes a fine effect in the
theatre.

Cf. the advertisement of 18 March.

* FROM ZINZENDORF'S DIARY, 5 APRIL 1795
(in French)

. . . To the Haendel concert, *Der Messias*, at the Prince de Paar's house.

For *Messiah cf.* 6 March and 7 April 1789. Prince Wenzel Paar was the son
of Prince Wenzel Johann Joseph Paar.

★   IBID., 9 APRIL 1795
(in French)

. . . Before half past six to Stockhammer's house to hear a German comedy by a certain Steinsberger . . ., entitled *Menschen und Menschen Situationen*. There are 14 actors . . . Mme. Mozart . . .

> Countess Maria Theresia Stockhammer, *née* Countess Hartig, maintained a distinguished private theatre, where amateur actors appeared, including, on this occasion, Constanze Mozart.—Karl Franz Guolfinger, Ritter von Steinsberg, was a playwright. His play, unpublished, was given about 1788 in the Freihaustheater.

FROM THE "JOURNAL DES LUXUS UND DER MODEN",
WEIMAR, JULY 1795

ANNOUNCEMENT
of an Opera by Mozart.

Posterity does justice to the merits and genius of Mozart ; his heavenly harmonies resound everywhere, on the stages of public theatres and in the salons of music-lovers. Almost all of his greater and lesser works are already known either engraved, or printed, or in manuscript copies, and are to be found in the hands of everyone. Even the publication of the Opera *La Clemenza di Tito* in pianoforte score has been announced in Hamburg ; but the serious opera *Idomeneo* which Mozart wrote for the Electoral Court of Bavaria in Munich, is less well-known.—The undersigned considers that she owes a debt of gratitude to the world from which Mozart has departed, a world which pays homage to his great genius in such estimable fashion, by publishing this Opera, still practically unknown outside Munich, in an arrangement for the pianoforte. Lovers and connoisseurs of Mozart's music will find in it all the beauties and excellences of his art, which distinguish every work of Mozart above all others, combined perhaps in an even higher degree, because the material is heroic and Mozart's spirit shone most brilliantly in the treatment of great and sublime subjects[.]

The arrangement for pianoforte is being undertaken by the skilled Organist of the Metropolitan Church in Prague, Herr Wenzel, who through his arrangement of the *Zauberflöte* and other works of Mozart has won fame for himself both at home and abroad. He has taken commendable precautions to ensure that his version may be of equal value to artists and amateurs alike, that is to say simple, and yet not inadequate or devoid of harmony, which unfortunately is the case with the majority of the arrangements which appear.

It shall be clearly and attractively engraved in copper on fine large sheets in oblong folio. As the work necessitates a considerable initial outlay, it has been decided, as a measure of security, to publish it on a subscription basis. The subscription list will remain open until the end of August of this year. A golden half-sovereign or 6 Rhenish gulden, 40 kreuzer will be the cost of subscription for the whole Opera ; after publication it will only be obtainable at 2 Imperial ducats or 9 Rhenish florins. The Opera will be supplied in its entirety together with the necessary accompanied recitatives, for it will be adapted from the original score which Mozart himself wrote out. It consists of 34 numbers and is thus larger than all his other operas.

The undersigned, moreover, does not wish to promise too much, but rather to achieve more ; she trusts that she will gain considerable support from the German public, which so worthily appreciates the spirit of Mozart ; for it is a masterpiece of his genius and the only one of his larger works the use of which adverse circumstance has not yet denied to her and her orphaned children.

In Prague subscriptions will be received by Frau Duschek in the Welscher Platz in the house of Prince Lichtenstein ; by the Organist Herr Wenzel in the Rossmarkt at the Golden Lamb ; by the Bookseller Herr Kalve in the Jesuitengasse. In Vienna they will be received by the undersigned Widow Mozart in the Krugerstrasse at the Blue Sabre, No. 174 ; and in Hamburg at the Register Office [Address-Comtoir]. In other countries all reputable music-shops will accept subscriptions. Whoever purchases ten copies will receive the 11th gratis. The Opera will be ready in November of this year.

The 1st May, 1795   Constanze Mozart.

> Vol. 10, pp. 314-16.—The piano score of *La clemenza di Tito* was arranged by A. E. Müller and published by J. A. Böhme.—Johann Wenzel also arranged the Linz Symphony (K. 425) and the one in E flat major (K. 543) for the piano ; the piano score of *Die Zauberflöte* seems to have appeared only in MS. copies ; that of *Idomeneo*, engraved by Johann Berka, was published by Schmid & Rauh of Leipzig in 1796-97.—For " Kalve " read " Calve ", for 174 in the Inner City read 1074.—This announcement also appeared in the *Gratzer Frauen-Journal* (a supplement of the *Gratzer Zeitung*) for 9 September 1795, No. 36, p. 564.

FROM THE " GRATZER ZEITUNG ", 26 AUGUST 1795

A grand concert is to be given in the theatre here for the benefit of Mozart's widow and son. During the past few years it has become clearly evident that the taste of our esteemed public has declared itself more and more in favour of Mozart's music, and we have accordingly striven to obtain his last work, the serious opera *La clemenza di Tito*, written in Prague for the Coronation of the late Emperor Leopold II, in order to surprise our esteemed friends of music at this concert with a masterpiece still quite unknown outside Vienna and Prague.

Erika Kaufmann in *Mozart und Graz* (Graz, 1956), p. 13.

On 4 September 1795 *La clemenza di Tito* was given a concert performance in the Graz Theatre " for the benefit of Mozart's widow and son ".

Mozart-Jahrbuch 1959 (Salzburg, 1960), p. 293.

On 9 September the *Gratzer Frauen-Journal* published Constanze's " Announcement " of July 1795 (see above).

Mozart-Jahrbuch 1959 (Salzburg, 1960), pp. 287 f.

FROM THE " GEHEIME GESCHICHTE DES VERSCHWÖRUNGSSYSTEMS DER JAKO-
BINER IN DEN ÖSTERREICHISCHEN STAATEN. FÜR WAHRHEITSFREUNDE ",
LONDON, 1795

. . . The applause which it [*die Zauberflöte*] received in Vienna . . . was exceptionally great. It was performed sixty-two times in succession, and the attendance showed no sign of diminishing. In Vienna the curtain rises at 7 o'clock, yet for the first fortnight of *die Zauberflöte* one had to claim one's seat as early as 5 o'clock, for a little later people were turned away in hundreds because the house was full. Only in the third week was it possible to struggle for, and succeed in obtaining, a seat as late as 6 o'clock.

P. 47 f.—Egon Komorzynski, *Schikaneder* (Vienna, 1951), p. 232.—London was not the actual place of printing.—The judicial inquiry against the Austrian Jacobins, which also led to the prohibition of freemasonry, had begun in 1794.—Pp. 47-54 of the book deal with *Die Zauberflöte*, the text of which is interpreted allegorically, *e.g.* the Queen of Night representing the despotic reign of Louis XVI, Pamina Liberty, and Tamino the People.

FROM ANDRÉ ERNEST MODESTE GRÉTRY'S " MÉMOIRES OU ESSAIS SUR
LA MUSIQUE ", PARIS, 1795
(in French)

. . . Once in Geneva I met a child who could play everything at sight. His father said to me before the assembled company : So that no doubt shall remain as to my son's talent, write for him, for to-morrow, a very difficult Sonata movement. I wrote him an Allegro in E flat ; difficult, but unpretentious ; he played it, and everyone, except myself, believed that it was a miracle. The boy had not stopped ; but following the modulations, he had substituted a quantity of passages for those which I had written . . .

Vol. I, pp. 84 f.—Henri Kling, *Mozart et Grétry à Genève 1766-1767* in the *Journal de Genève*, 28 July 1886. Professor Willy Tappolet of Geneva also supposes that Grétry met Mozart in Geneva in the late summer of 1766.

In the autumn of 1795 Constanze undertook a concert tour in Germany with Aloisia Lange.

The sisters, at first accompanied by Eberl (see 25 December 1794), may have visited Prague on their outward and their return journey, where the boy

Karl was living with Niemetschek, and where Constanze now left young Wolfgang ; but nothing is known of a concert given there by the two. The concert said to have been given in Prague by Constanze early in 1796 did not take place until 15 November 1797. Constanze stayed for five weeks in the Hôtel de Saxe in Leipzig ; the landlord, one Ernst, would not accept any payment from her.

PROGRAMME OF A MOZART CONCERT IN THE LEIPZIG GEWANDHAUS, 11 NOVEMBER 1795

Concert of the two sisters Madame Lange and Madame Mozart.
At which Herr Capellmeister Eberl will be heard at the pianoforte.
Symphony.
Aria " No che non sei capace " (Mad. Lange).
Concerto for Pianoforte (Capellmeister Eberl).
Trio from *Clemenza di Tito* " Vengo, aspettate " (Mad. Mozart, Mad. Lange and Hr. Richter).
March from the same Opera.
An Allegro movement.
Recitative and Rondo " Mia speranza adorata " (Mad. Lange).
Quartet for the Pianoforte (Eberl).
Duet from *Clemenza di Tito* " Come ti piace, imponi " (Mad Lange and Mad. Mozart).
Recitative, Quintet and Chorus from *Clemenza di Tito* " Oh Dei, che smania è questa ".

> Alfred Dörffel, *Geschichte der Gewandhauskonzerte* (Leipzig, 1884), p. 195.—
> Aloisia Lange sang the arias K. 419 and 416, which had been written for her.
> —In mid-December Aloisia Lange, Constanze and Eberl were in Hamburg.

MINUTE IN THE HAND OF FREDERICK WILLIAM II

His Majesty the King of Prussia, etc. etc. is truly pleased to demonstrate, by acceding to the wish of Mozart's widow, how deeply He esteemed the talent of her late husband, and how much He regrets the unfavourable circumstances which prevented the latter from reaping the fruits of his works. His Majesty therefore grants to Mozart's widow [permission to use] the great Opera House, as well as the Royal Orchestra, for the performance of his last composition, *la Clemenza di Tito*, and He has also issued the necessary instructions therefor to the Chamberlain, Baron von der Reck, to whom she has henceforth to apply in order to discuss with him the proposed date therefor and any other details.
Berlin, the 14th February 1796.

> Niemetschek, *Mozart* (Prague, 1798), p. 43. Nissen, *Mozart*, p. 615.—Constanze, after her arrival in Berlin, had addressed herself to the king, who had already been very helpful to her four years before (see 18 February 1792).

ANNOUNCEMENT BY THE MANAGEMENT OF THE BERLIN OPERA

For the concert, which by most gracious permission of his Sovereign Majesty will be given in the Opera House on Sunday the 28th of this month for the benefit of Madame Mozart, private ownership of all and every box will be suspended, except by arrangement with her, which transaction may be effected daily in the Opera House at the advertised time. If any such agreement be reached, the keys to the boxes must be delivered over to the Steward of the Opera House.

Berlin, the 22nd February 1796.

Management of the Royal Opera.

Nottebohm, *Mozartiana*, p. 15.

PROGRAMME OF CONSTANZE'S BERLIN CONCERT

Today, Sunday the 28th February 1796.

and

by special favour of His Majesty the King
the widow of the deceased Kapellmeister Mozart,
in the Royal Opera House,
and assisted by the Royal Singers and the Royal
Orchestra, will have the honour to perform
the last work of her deceased husband :
LA CLEMENZA DI TITO.

First Part.

Overture from *die Zauberflöte*.
Aria, sung by Madame Righini, composed by Mozart.

Aria, sung by Demoiselle Schmalz, composed by Mozart.

Second Part.

A Selection, being the most considerable parts of the Opera :
La Clemenza di Tito, by Mozart ;
in which Madame Schick, Madame Righini, Demoiselle Schmalz, Her Fischer, Herr Hurka, and Madame Mozart will sing.

The words of the music will be on sale at the entrance for 4 groschen.

Prices of seats.

Tickets for whole boxes in the First Circle may be obtained from Mozart's widow in Schielen's house, Neue Friedrichsstrasse, by the Garrison Church.

The performance will commence at 5.30 o'clock.

Mitteilungen für die Mozart-Gemeinde in Berlin, No. 17 (March 1904), p. 227 (with facsimile of the programme).—Henriette Righini, *née* Kneisel, was the wife of the composer Vincenzo Righini, conductor of the Berlin Opera (*cf.* 22 December 1789 and 9 October 1790).—For Frau Schick see 9 October 1790 also ; she had gone to Berlin from Hamburg not long before.—Auguste Amalie Schmalz, in Berlin from 1790, became her successor there.—Ludwig Karl Fischer, the first Osmin in *Die Entführung,* had been engaged in Berlin since 1788 ; Friedrich Franz Hurka, a tenor (see 17 April 1788), since 1789.— Nottebohm, *Mozartiana,* p. 4, quotes a report on this concert from the *Camera obscura von Berlin,* Part 10, 29 February 1796, entitled *Mozarts Todtenfeier.*

FROM " MAGYAR HÍRMONDÓ ", VIENNA, 11 MARCH 1796
(in Hungarian)

The unhappy widow of the Imperial Court Kapellmeister and Composer Mozart is the recipient of divers favours from the Court in Vienna. She is now gone to pass some time in Berlin, where she has discovered in the King another great benefactor. She has experienced several proofs of his favour, and has also been granted permission to perform *La Clemenza di Tito* (*Titus kegyelmessége*) in the great Opera House and with the co-operation of the Court musicians. [There follows the King's decree of 14 February.]
Supplied by Frau Lidia F. Wendelin, Budapest.—*Cf.* 28 February 1796.

FROM THE " WIENER ZEITUNG ", 13 APRIL 1796
Music.

The following pieces are to be had of Joseph Haydenreich in his shop at the sign of the Little Ring in the Schmelzgasse, No. 414 in the Leopoldstadt, behind the theatre, namely :

.   .   .   .   .

A hitherto unknown manuscript Tutor for the learning of Thorough-bass, by Mozart, 4 fl. 30 kr.

.   .   .   .   .

Presumably the text of the *Generalbass-Schule,* which appeared under Mozart's name in Vienna (1818) and Berlin (1822) (KE. p. 833).—For Haydenreich see 24 May 1788, etc.

ANNOUNCEMENT OF THE SECOND LEIPZIG CONCERT, (?16) APRIL 1796
Musical Announcement.

Madame Mozart, after being received with the greatest honour in Berlin, is now [staying] in Leipsic, prior to journeying on to Dresden, and wishes to perform here her late husband's last work, his great Requiem, surely the most diligent and masterly work of his extraordinary genius ; and all friends of music, all admirers of Mozart join her in this wish. Permission has been graciously granted to use the concert hall in the Gewandhaus for the performance ; and Madame Mozart flatters herself that on the coming Wednesday, the 20th April, she will once more be able to commend the memory of her deceased husband to a large audience. The piece to be performed lasts a good hour ; at its conclusion Madame Mozart will sing and Herr Müller, Organist, will perform a Concerto by her husband. The concert will begin, as usual, at 5 o'clock. Tickets at 16 gr. are to be had of Madame Mozart at the Hôtel de Saxe, and of Herr Meyer, Librarian ; from whom, as also at the entrance, printed texts may be obtained for 2 gr.

> Nottebohm, *op. cit.*, pp. 16 f.—Dörffel, *op. cit.*, p. 44.—A pianoforte concerto was played by the organist August Eberhard Müller, the composer of several songs attributed to Mozart (K. App. 248, 249) and arranger of four published vocal scores of Mozart operas.

PROGRAMME OF THE MOZART CONCERT IN THE LEIPZIG GEWANDHAUS,
20 APRIL 1796

I. Missa pro defunctis (Opus posthumum Mozarti).
II. Aria from *Idomeneo* " Estinto è Idomeneo ".
Concerto for the Pianoforte.
Trio from *Idomeneo* " Pria di partir, oh Dio ".
Symphony.

> Dörffel, *op. cit.*, p. 195.—Constanze may have taken part.—The conductor of the concerts at that time was Johann Gottfried Schicht. His predecessor, Johann Adam Hiller, translated the words of the Requiem into German for this performance. The numbers from *Idomeneo* were the first aria for Electra (No. 4) and the trio No. 16.

FROM THE PROGRAMME OF THE THIRD CONCERT IN THE LEIPZIG
GEWANDHAUS, 25 APRIL 1796

Symphony by Mozart.
Sonata for four hands by Mozart (Herr and Mad. Müller).
Aria by Mozart " No che non sei capace " (Mad. Lange)

.   .   .   .   .

Hymn by Mozart " Preis dir, Gottheit ".

.   .   .   .   .

> Dörffel, *op. cit.*, p. 195.—A. E. Müller and his wife, *née* Rabert, played Mozart's pianoforte concertos particularly well. He wrote an *Anweisung* (Instruction) for their performance, and also left cadenzas for them.—The " Hymn " was the introductory chorus from *Thamos* (K. 345) with new words (K. App. 121).

ANNOUNCEMENT OF THE DRESDEN CONCERT, (?21) MAY 1796

The widow of the Royal and Imperial Kapellmeister Mozart is determined to perform some of her husband's compositions, which have not as yet

been publicly heard in Dresden. She herewith informs the esteemed public
that she will to this end give a concert next week on the 25th May of this
year in the main hall of the Hotel de Pologne at 6 o'clock, and that tickets
for it at 1 Thaler are to be had from the Hotel de Pologne and the Golden
Angel.

> Nottebohm, *op. cit.*, p. 15.—The programme is not known ; Loewenberg's
> *Annals of Opera* (26 May) records a performance of *La clemenza di Tito.*—For.
> the Hôtel de Pologne see 13 April 1789.—A Taler contained 24 Groschen.—
> Constanze remained in Dresden for at least a month.

On 2 October 1796 Josepha Dušek gave a Mozart concert at the Leipzig Gewandhaus

> Dörffel, *op. cit.*, p. 195.—Apart from a Haydn symphony all the items were
> by Mozart.—A. E. Müller again played a pianoforte concerto ; Josepha Dušek
> sang arias from *Idomeneo* and *La clemenza di Tito*, as well as the scena " Bella mia
> fiamma " (K. 528) written for her ; the orchestra and a chorus also performed
> pieces from *Idomeneo*.

PROGRAMME OF A CONCERT IN THE THEATRE AT LINZ, 22 NOVEMBER [1796]

Grand Concert. / Invitation to all noble Philanthropists and Patrons of
Music / to a grand / Vocal and Instrumental / CONCERT / which / this day,
Tuesday the 22nd November, being Music's own Festival Day, will be
given in the / Estates Theatre here for the better foundation of the newly
promoted / Music Fund ; and in two parts ; / at which / Madame Mozart,
Widow relict of the great and unforgettable / Artist will perform.

First part.

1. Overture from the Opera : *La* . . .
   Clemenza di / *Tito* by the late
   Herr Mozart.
2. Duet for 2 Soprani.
3. Soprano Aria.

5. Trio for 2 Soprani and Basso.
6. Tenor Aria.
7. Quintetto for 3 Soprani, Tenore
   e Basso.

Second part.

1. New Symphony by Herr Mozart.
2. Duet for Soprano and Tenore.
3. Soprano Aria.
4. Duet for 2 Tenori.

5. March. . . .
7. Trio for Soprano, Tenore, è Basso.
8. Chorus

All the vocal pieces are from the famous Opera : *La Clemenza di Titto.*

The performance will begin at half past 6 o'clock.

> Copy sold in the Dorotheum, Vienna, on 14 May 1959.—The concert had
> been announced in the *Linzer Zeitung* on 18 November 1796 (information
> kindly supplied by Prof. Othmar Wessely, who had earlier placed Constanze's

stay in Linz in the year 1795).—Here as elsewhere from the year 1793 onwards, Constanze put on a concert performance of the opera ; again it was given in an incomplete version. The march also seems to have been taken from *La clemenza di Tito*. The symphony cannot be defined any more exactly ; it might have been the Linz (K. 425). The orchestra consisted in part of amateurs. The singers (apart from Constanze) are not named.—Nothing further is known about this visit of Constanze's to Linz.—" Music's own Festival Day " was the Feast of St. Cecilia ; the " Music Fund " was, according to Wessely, the Musicians' Society of Linz, a benevolent fund founded in 1798.

FROM THE " GRÄTZER ZEITUNG ", 28 DECEMBER 1796

Mozart's widow hereby permits herself the honour to announce her arrival here to the esteemed inhabitants of this capital city, and thus above all to fulfil one of her most important duties by acknowledging publicly and with undying gratitude the support which she received two years ago at the concert given for her benefit. As she has just returned from a long and tiring journey to Vienna, she now intends with gracious permission to give a concert during her stay, in the Provincial Theatre and on Friday next, the 30th instant, for the benefit of herself and her infant children. The first part will consist of the opera seria, entirely new and unknown here, entitled : *Idomeneo*, and the second of the first act of the so well loved *Clemenza di Tito*. Mozart wrote the great work of *Idomeneo* for the Electoral Court at Munich and experienced connoisseurs of music accord it one of the highest places among his other works.

I may confidently trust, in a place where my husband, torn from me only too soon, has won such high esteem and affection, that this masterpiece, which harmonizes so well with the already familiar Opera *La Clemenza di Tito*, will be received with even greater approbation and delight, through the assurance of an accurate and successful performance due to the kind co-operation and support of the so talented and respected dilettantes, singers and other musicians. Noble and respected inhabitants of this capital city, be pleased graciously to accept my most humble invitation to this concert.

Constanze Mozart.

Mitteilungen für die Mozart-Gemeinde in Berlin, March 1901, No. 11, pp. 28 f. (Ferdinand Bischoff). *Mozart und Graz* (Graz, 1956), pp. 13 f. (Erika Kaufmann).—*Cf.* 4 September 1795.—Elsewhere Constanze also mentions Prague as a place where she will stop to give a concert ; whether her " etc." there includes Hamburg and Halle, which Niemetschek (p. 42) mentions as further stages of the tour, is doubtful. Constanze was in Hamburg in December 1795 and January 1796. Aloisia Lange may still have been there during Constanze's sojourn in Berlin ; she certainly sang Sextus there in *La clemenza di Tito* on 7 February, but not in Berlin on 28 February. That Constanze did visit Halle is shown by one of Reichardt's *Vertraute Briefe aus Wien*, 21 December 1808, in which her recollection of Giebichenstein is mentioned.—Whether she was really travelling until the end of 1796 is uncertain.

At the beginning of 1797 Constanze requested the Lower Austrian authorities for
permission to give a concert in the Burgtheater, but on 6 April was referred by the
police to the Emperor.

> Walter Goldinger in the *Neues Augsburger Mozartbuch* (1962), p. 84.

* FROM ZINZENDORF'S DIARY, 24 MARCH 1797
(in French)

. . . In the evening after 6 o'clock to Schwarzenberg's, where there was
the Haendel concert : *Acis et Galathée*. The music enchanting : Dryden's
text translated by Alxinger. Mlle Gerhardi, Spangler ; an unknown singer
took the part of Damon. Great press of people.

> For Prince Joseph Schwarzenberg *cf.* 19 February 1793.—For *Acis and Galatea*
> *cf.* 30 December 1788. Johann Baptist Alxinger had translated Gay's (not
> Dryden's) text for Swieten.—Christine Gerhardi (Gerardi), later Frank, was
> a favourite oratorio singer in Vienna. Ignaz Georg Spängler was a tenor in
> the Hofkapelle, as was later an Ignaz Spangler.

PROGRAMME OF THE MOZART CONCERT IN PRAGUE, 15 NOVEMBER 1797

With noble and gracious permission
Mozart's widow
will give
this day, Wednesday the 15th November 1797, in the National Theatre in
the Old Town,
a grand
Musical Concert
of her husband's posthumous compositions, still quite unknown here.

First Part.

Commencing with a Symphony by Mozart.

1. A Bravura Aria by Mozart, sung by Mad. Campi.

2. A grand and powerful Concerto by Mozart, played on the Pianoforte by Herr Witassek.

3. A Trio, one of the greatest posthumous works of Mozart, sung by Mad. Mozart, Herr Campi and Herr Benedetti.

4. Bass Aria by Mozart, sung by Herr Campi.

5. By special request, little Wolfgang, just 6 years old and the younger of Mozart's bereaved

Second Part.

1. An Overture with subsequent Quartet from an unfinished Opera by Mozart.

2. Aria by Mozart sung by Mad. Campi.

3. A Quartet Finale by Mozart, sung by Mad. Mozart, Herr Benedetti and Herr Zardi, and by Herr Campi.

4. Concluding with a German Scena and Final Chorus for the joyful Restoration of Peace. Its poetic text has been specially written by the famous Poet and Professor Herr A. Meissner.

The music of the recitative is by Hr. Witassek, and the Chorus is children, will give a small token of his respectful thanks to the worthy public of Prague for its affection towards his father, displayed here so many times ; he will demonstrate his growing desire to emulate his father's example by singing the Aria from the *Zauberflöte* : " der Vogelfänger bin ich ", accompanied at the pianoforte. Indulgence is pleaded for this first expression of his tender talent.

by Mozart from the Opera *la Clemenza di Tito* ; the latter has been chosen because it is to be hoped that the public will desire to join in the Chorus of Jubilation on such a happy occasion.

The printed text will be on sale at the box-office at 7 kr. and the proceeds will be donated to the Institute for the Poor.

N.B. All these pieces, with the exception of the Chorus, are new and have not yet been performed.

Prices of seats are throughout as for the Italian Operas.
The commencement at 7 o'clock precisely.
Concerning boxes, patrons are requested to apply to Widow Mozart at the Bertoni house on the Welsche Platz, or to the Lady in charge of Boxes at the Theatre.

Berlin, German State Library.—Eduard Crass, *W. A. Mozart. Sein Leben in Bildern* (Leipzig, 1956), Plate 148.—*Cf.* Teuber, *op. cit.*, Vol. II, p. 330, and Procházka, *op. cit.*, p. 192.—Constanze had in 1796 taken her second son to Prague, where he was first lodged at Frau Dušek's and then at Frau Niemetschek's. He may have returned to Vienna in 1797, together with Karl, who began his apprenticeship at Leghorn in 1798.—The Papageno aria is said to have been sung by Wolfgang standing on a table, with new words or with an additional verse.—Antonia Campi, *née* Miklaszewicz, who came from Poland, was the prima donna in Prague ; she had first sung the Countess in *Figaro* and the Queen of Night in *Die Zauberflöte* there in 1793. She and her husband, the bass Gaetano Campi, the first Publius in *La clemenza di Tito*, later went to the Kärntnertor Theatre in Vienna.—No. 1 of Part II was evidently the opening of the opera *Lo sposo deluso* (K. 430). The other numbers by Mozart are hardly identifiable.—For Meissner see 31 (?) December 1791.— France and Austria had signed the Peace of Campo Formio in October 1797.— About 1798 at a concert held by the Prague lawyers (*cf.* 7 February 1794) their musical director Anton Thomas Kunz, the inventor of an orchestrion, is said to have performed the cantata *Dir, Seele des Weltalls* (K. 429), orchestrated by himself (*Der Bär* [Leipzig, 1928], p. 106).

On 22 November 1797 a mortgage of 3,500 Florints on Dušek's Villa Bertramka, at 6% interest, was entered in favour of Constanze at the Prague Vintners' office.

Prague, Municipal Archives, Weinbergbuch (vineyard records), No. II de statu passivo, fol. 161 f.—After her husband's death Josepha Dušek in 1799 sold the villa ; the mortgage debt seems to have been cancelled.

At the end of 1797 Constanze made the acquaintance of Georg Nikolaus Nissen.

The Legation Secretary of the Danish Embassy had arrived in Vienna in February 1793 and since then had lived in various quarters ; however, neither in the Rauhensteingasse (1792) nor in the Krugerstrasse (1794) did he live in

Constanze's lodgings. Constanze took up her abode with Nissen on 1 September 1798 ; they lived first of all on the second floor in the Judengässchen, City No. 535, in 1799 they moved to the Franziskanerplatz, City No. 967, and finally they settled on the top floor of No. 5 Michaelerplatz. (These addresses of Nissen's are to be found in the annuals of the Court and State Records, where Constanze Mozart of course would not appear.) That Constanze and Nissen were already friends in 1797 is attested by the notes of Fredrik Samuel Silverstolpe, a Swedish diplomat, who was in touch with both of them in Vienna from 1798 onwards. (See C.-G. Stellan Mörner in *Svensk Tidskrift för Musikforskning* [Stockholm, 1948], p. 71, and his book *Johan Wikmanson und die Brüder Silverstolpe* [Stockholm, 1952], p. 335.)

GOETHE TO SCHILLER, WEIMAR, 30 DECEMBER 1797

The hope which you entertained for the opera you would have seen fulfilled to a high degree in *Don Juan* recently ; however, this piece too stands quite alone, and all prospect of something similar has been frustrated by Mozart's death.

Tenschert, *Mozart* (Amsterdam, 1931), p. 215.—*Don Giovanni* had been given at Weimar in German since 30 January 1792 ; it was not given in Italian till 4 September 1813.

On 29 March 1798 Frau Josepha Dušek gave a concert in Jahn's Rooms in Vienna, at which she performed a Mozart "rondo with obbligato basset-horn" (Anton Stadler), and Beethoven played one of his own violin sonatas with Ignaz Schuppanzigh.

Programme in the Archives of the Gesellschaft der Musikfreunde, Vienna.— Eduard Hanslick, *Geschichte des Concertwesens in Wien* (Vienna, 1869), p. 105. —For the rondo *cf.* 26 April 1791 ; it was probably No. 23 from *La clemenza di Tito*.

At the end of March 1798 Constanze petitioned the Supreme Directorate of Court Theatres for permission to hold a concert on 27 April.

Albert Josef Weltner, *Mozart's Werk und die Wiener Hof-Theater* (Vienna, 1896), p. 46.—The concert was sanctioned, but does not seem to have taken place. Weltner nevertheless reproduces the programme of a concert in the Kärntnertor Theatre on 28 April, but it contains nothing by Mozart, nor does it mention Constanze.—According to Silverstolpe's notes, Constanze appears to have arranged a concert in the Augarten in the autumn of 1798— an unusual season—but this is not attested either.—*Cf.* beginning of 1797.

In the summer of 1798 the Abbé Maximilian Stadler assisted Nissen in sorting out the music from Mozart's estate.

The occasion for this was clearly the letter from the Leipzig firm of Breitkopf & Härtel of 15 May 1798, in which Constanze was requested to support the publishing-house in its new undertaking, the *Oeuvres complettes de W. A. Mozart.* (Oskar von Hase, *Breitkopf & Härtel* [Leipzig, 1919], Vol. I, pp. 154 f.) The projected complete edition went as far as 50 fascicles (1798–1808) and remained unfinished.—Stadler had not removed from Linz to Vienna until 1796.

FROM THE "ALLGEMEINER LITTERARISCHER ANZEIGER", LEIPZIG,
28 AUGUST 1798
*Sum cuique.**

As 3 works composed by myself have already appeared in various music-shops under the name of the unforgettable Mozart, I find myself constrained publicly to warn the new publishers of all Mozart's works against being misled by the spurious designations of the works indicated below, and admitting the same to the complete Collection of Mozart's works ; for however flattering it may be for me that even connoisseurs were capable of judging these works to be the products of Mozart, I can in no wise allow the musical public to remain under this delusion. . . These 3 works, which I composed some considerable time before my summons to St Petersburg, appeared after Mozart's death and during my absence from Vienna, either inadvertently or for other reasons unknown to me, under the name of this eminent man. As I have been deprived in this manner of every advantage which these works might have afforded me, I am left with no other measure of consolation than the comforting knowledge of the approbation which these works were fortunate enough to win from the musical public.

St Petersburg.   Anton Eberl.

* We emphasize this intelligence . . . in the express hope that sundry persons may thereby be moved to pursue further these thefts, the more so as . . . Mozart's widow has so little respect for her husband's ashes that she not only willingly offers her support to all such unlawful dealings, but moreover was not ashamed to make similar proposals to a famous composer in Leipsic.   Ed.

No. 136, col. 1873-75.—Reprint from the Supplement to No. 118 of the *Hamburger unpartheiischer Correspondent* of 15 July 1798.—Three works by Eberl had so far appeared under Mozart's name : K. App. 284a (a sonata), 287 and 288 (2 sets of variations).—See 18 May 1805.—Constanze had warned Breitkopf & Härtel on 13 November 1799 not to include Eberl's variations Opp. 6 and 5 in Mozart's *Oeuvres* (*Mozart-Jahrbuch*, Leipzig, 1929), Vol. III, p. 187. In the first instance the warning came too late ; but the variations on Umlauf's " Zu Steffen sprach im Traume ", which Mozart is said to have liked, were not printed in his *Oeuvres*.—Eberl lived in St. Petersburg from 1796 to 1800. The " famous composer " of the footnote may be A. E. Müller (*cf.* 16 [?] April 1796).

On 8 September 1798 a concert performance of *La clemenza di Tito* was given in the Freihaus Theatre, Vienna.

Schikaneder wrote on the programme (City Library, Vienna) : " Mozart's work is beyond all praise. One feels only too keenly, on hearing this or any other of his music, what the Art has lost in him."—Constanze's sister Josepha, who had been widowed by Hofer in 1796 and remarried the following year, sang Servilia, and her second husband, Friedrich Sebastian Mayer was the Publius. (His repertory had included Sarastro since 1793 and Bassa Selim since 1794.)

On 14 November 1798 Marianne Kirchgessner played at Königsberg, *inter alia,* a " Concertante by Mozart, written by him for the harmonica with wind instruments shortly before his death ".

Hermann Güttler, *Königsbergs Musikkultur im 18. Jahrhundert* (Cassel, 1925), p. 177.—*Cf.* 13 August 1791.

In 1798 the first edition of Franz Xaver Niemetschek's biography of Mozart (see 1808), dedicated to Haydn, was published in Prague.

CONSTANZE'S DRAFT OF AN APPEAL TO THE PERSON WHO COMMISSIONED THE REQUIEM (?1798)

As the noble and anonymous gentleman who gave the late Mozart the commission to compose a Requiem a few months before his death, still after more than 7 years has not made this work publicly known, the widow gratefully acknowledges this attitude as an indication that this person wishes to grant her some advantage from its publication. In the meantime she considers it a measure of security for herself, and a matter of duty in view of the sentiments which he has occasioned in her, to invite this noble gentleman, through the columns of the Vienna, Hamburg and Frankfurt newspapers, kindly to acquaint her of his intentions within three months, after which time she will be bold enough to publish the Requiem in her late husband's Collected Works.

> Jahn, 1st ed., Vol. IV, p. 698, Note 41.—Constanze does not appear to have published this appeal. She sent the draft to Breitkopf & Härtel on 18 October 1799, after the publishers had announced the Requiem in their *Allgemeine musikalische Zeitung* in September of that year (*Intelligenzblatt* No. XIX, col. 97 f.), as issued "according to the manuscript communicated to us for this purpose by Mozart's widow". On 30 January 1800 she told the publishers : "You have performed a miracle, you have awakened the dead. The owner and commissioner of the work has come forward." And on 21 July of the same year : "In the meantime I have now myself received the true original from the anonym for perusal". (Nottebohm, *Mozartiana*, pp. 130-3.)—*Cf.* 14 December 1793 and 9 February 1800.

On 6 February and 11 September 1799 the Leipzig *Allgemeine musikalische Zeitung* published "Anecdotes from Mozart's Life, reported by his Widow".

> Vol. I, No. 19, col. 289, and No. 50, col. 854.—Albert Leitzmann, W. A. *Mozart. Berichte der Zeitgenossen und Briefe* (Leipzig, 1926), pp. 104 ff.—The periodical, edited by Rochlitz, was published by Breitkopf & Härtel.

★ FROM ZINZENDORF'S DIARY, 23 MARCH 1799
(in French)

. . . In the evening after 6 o'clock to Prince Schwarzenberg's for the Haendel concert, *Der Messias*.

Cf. 5 April 1795 and 24 March 1797.

On 25 March 1799 *La clemenza di Tito* was again given a concert performance at the Freihaus Theatre.

> Josepha Hofer, aged eight, Frau Mayer's child by her first husband, played a pianoforte concerto by Franz Anton Hoffmeister in the interval.

JOSEPH HAYDN TO BREITKOPF & HÄRTEL IN LEIPZIG, 12 JUNE 1799

. . . Yesterday I received from Herr Griesinger the 2nd, 3rd and 4th fascicles of [the works of] our immortal Mozart along with the musical journals.

. . . The publication of both works do you the greatest credit . . .

> Vienna, City Library.—Communicated by H. C. Robbins Landon.—Cahiers I and II of Mozart's *Oeuvres complettes* appeared in 1798, III and IV in 1799.— Georg August Griesinger, Secretary to the Saxon Legation in Vienna, a friend of Haydn and a confidant of Breitkopf, reported to Leipzig : " He looked at the volumes several times and said ' Very nice, very nice ; Mozart and I esteemed one another highly ; he even called me his Papa ' ". (Hermann von Hase, *Joseph Haydn und Breitkopf & Härtel* [Leipzig, 1909], p. 21.)

In the summer of 1799 the music from Mozart's estate was sifted once more.

> The work was again carried out by the Abbé Stadler, Constanze's musical assistant, and Nissen, her business adviser. After Breitkopf & Härtel, Johann Anton André, the young music publisher at Offenbach near Frankfurt o/M., now began to take an interest in Mozart's unpublished works.

On 4 August 1799 Marianne von Berchtold sent to Breitkopf & Härtel from St. Gilgen Leopold Mozart's list of his son's earliest works, amplified with dates in her own hand. *Cf.* 21 September 1768.

FROM WIELAND'S " NEUER TEUTSCHER MERKUR ", WEIMAR, SEPTEMBER 1799

The following is a literal translation of part of the letter of an Englishman residing in Vienna : " The Briton shows with happy awareness that he knows how to esteem every merit ; an example is the tomb of the German, Handel, in Westminster Abbey. Here the place in the cemetery where Mozart's mortal frame (extinguished, perhaps, by violence) lies buried, remains unknown."

This is a hurtful reproach, although one not new in the history of our " Worthies ". Might there not be ground for it ?

Good Mozart ! you erected a gravestone to a favourite bird in a garden which you rented, and you even wrote an epitaph for him. When will that be done for you which you did for your bird ?

> Vol. III, Part 9, p. 90 f.—The Englishman's name is unknown.—The paren- thesis " perhaps by violence " seems to have been an editorial gloss, occasioned by the following footnote to a poem on Mozart's death by Johann Isaak, Baron Gerning, published in February 1799 (Part 2, pp. 232 f.) : " For the sake of the honour of mankind and of the art of music, it is to be hoped that this Orpheus may after all have died a natural death ! "—For the starling, which Mozart had buried in the Landstrasse suburb on 4 June 1787, see 27 May 1784.—The Weimar notice was reprinted in 1808 in the Vienna *Vaterländische Blätter für den österreichischen Kaiserstaat* (p. 211), and this exhorta- tion caused Griesinger to go to the cemetery of St. Marx with Constanze and Nissen. The failure of their search for Mozart's grave was reported by

M.—16 a

Griesinger on 23 August 1808 in this same Viennese periodical (p. 252). *Cf.*
Rudolf von Lewicki in *Mozarteums-Mitteilungen* (Salzburg, August 1920),
year II, No. 4, pp. 97-101.

On 8 November 1799 an agreement for Mozart's manuscripts was signed in
Vienna by Constanze Mozart and Johann Anton André.

ARTICLE OF AGREEMENT BETWEEN CONSTANZE MOZART AND JOHANN ANTON
ANDRÉ, VIENNA, 8 NOVEMBER 1799

The following Contract has this day been concluded between the undersigned Frau Mozart, Widow, and Herr Johann André of Offenbach on the
Main, binding for them and their heirs, to the effect that

1. Frau Mozart, Widow, shall make over into the possession of Herr
   André those works of her deceased husband which are in her possession,
   and marked with my, André's, seal, consisting of 15 packets, together
   with the musical works specified *sub littera A* enclosed, for the sum of
   Three Thousand One Hundred and Fifty Gulden Vienna Currency.
2. Herr André pledges himself to have half of the above sum paid at the
   beginning of February 1800, and the remainder 6 weeks later, in cash,
   and here in Vienna ;
   in return for which the aforesaid sealed musical compositions are to
   be delivered over to Herr Paul Wranizky of this place before 9 January
   1800, against his, Wranizky's certificate of receipt, and against the
   transfer of a certificate of payment made out by me, André, as specified
   above and in the form as laid out in the appendix *sub Lit. B.*
3. Frau Mozart, Widow, promises in consequence of this Contract to
   deliver over into the sole possession of Herr André, without receiving
   any further payment, but at his expense, all those scores of her husband's which are hers to dispose of, but without involving her in any
   expenditure.
4. Herr André promises to deliver, carriage paid Vienna, Berlin or Hamburg, to Mozart's Widow or her Heirs, at his own expense, four copies
   of each work as soon as it appears at his establishment. However, if
   Herr André should entrust one or another of the works to any other
   music publisher for publication, the latter is bound to provide the
   aforementioned Widow with two copies, carriage paid as above, of
   the Mozart works published by that other publishing-house.
5. However, it shall remain open to Frau Mozart, Widow, to withdraw
   her consent to the points agreed above before 9 January 1800, but
   with the specific obligation that she present to Herr Paul Wranizky
   for forwarding, against his receipt, a statement addressed to me, André,
   by the aforementioned 9th day of January at the latest, confirming or
   annulling this Contract ; if no such Statement is received, the Contract
   will be held to have been accepted on her side.

6. In what concerns in particular the pieces of music specified *sub lit. A.*, in the event of all the remaining items not being made over to Herr André by Frau Mozart, Widow, the following has been agreed :

7. Frau Mozart, Widow, makes over from this day to Herr André for the sum of Six Hundred Gulden Vienna Currency all the musical compositions listed in *lit. A.* ; the half of this sum to be paid at once on exchange of this Contract and the remainder in 6 weeks from now, here in Vienna, to her or her heirs.

8. In the event that this last point alone should be agreed between the two signatories, Herr André is bound to return to Frau Mozart, Widow, before 1 September 1800 and at his cost, carriage paid Vienna, Berlin or Hamburg, the manuscript compositions listed *sub lit. A.* ; until which date he shall be permitted to make what use of them he will.

9. In respect of these same last-mentioned compositions listed *sub lit. A.* Herr ANDRÉ also promises to deliver to Frau Mozart, Widow, or to her heirs, gratis, to Vienna, Berlin or Hamburg, five copies of each work as soon as they shall be published.

10. Should Herr André not be in a position to return the original manuscripts listed *sub lit. A.* to Frau Mozart, Widow, or to her heirs, by 1 September 1800, which term may in any case be extended until the middle of September, he promises to pay to her at once and as an agreed indemnification the sum of Six Hundred Gulden Vienna Currency.

In witness thereof two identical copies of both parts of this Contract have been signed and sealed in the presence of the witnesses summoned for this purpose.

Vienna, this 8th day of November, 1799

Constance Mozart

Joh : André
DHG von Pilgram,
Court Official,
as Witness

Nissen
Secretary to the Royal Danish Legation, as Witness

Appendix to the Contract between Frau Mozart,
Widow, and Herr Johann André, of
8 November 1799.

Litt.A.
Original manuscripts.

Clavierconcert   N.3. *A major.*
for 2 Claviers N. 21. *E flat major.*
N. 5. *E flat major.*
N. 2. *C Minor.*
N. 6. *C major.*

N. 29. *C major.*
N. 17. *B flat major.*

Violin *Rondeau*   N. 44. *C major.*

Quintet   N. 24. *C minor.*
               N. 27. *E flat major.*
               N. 26. *D major.*
               N. 25. *C major.*

Quartet   N. 6. *D minor.*   bound with *Quintet in B flat major.*
               N. 36. *B flat major.*
               N. 35. *F major.*
               N. 34. *D major.*
               N. 17. *C major.*
               N. 33. *C major.*
               N. 32. *A major.*
               N. 31. *E flat major.*
               N. 30. *B flat major.*
               N. 29. *D minor.*
               N. 28. *G major.*
               N. 37. *D major.*
               N. 38. *C minor.*

Clavier Sonata (not entirely original) *C major.*

Also 211 engraved copies of Mozart's Clavier Concerto N. 1 in *C. major,*
which are to be obtained from *Breitkopf* and *Härtel.*   *Verte*

Lit. B.

Form of the certificate of payment agreed in the Contract

Against delivery of the 15 packets of Mozart compositions, sealed by me,
to Herr Paul Wranizky, who must give a receipt on delivery, I bind myself
to pay Frau Mozart, Widow, or her heirs, Two Thousand Five Hundred
and Fifty Gulden Vienna Currency in such a way that One Thousand Five
Hundred Gulden will be paid at the beginning of February 1800 and
the remainder in the middle of the month of March 1800, in cash, here in
Vienna.

One of the two originals is in the possession of Frau Friederike André in
Offenbach on the Main. Constanze's copy seems to be lost.—Appendix A,
the verso of which is not shown in the Deutsche Mozart-Gesellschaft's photo-
graph in Augsburg, contains works which André later published (*cf.* O. E.
Deutsch and C. B. Oldman in the *Zeitschrift für Musikwissenschaft* [Leipzig,
April 1932], pp. 348 ff.) ; the numbers here given refer to the numbers on the
autographs in André's 15 packets.—The witness David Heinrich Gottfried
von Pilgramm (*c.* 1743–1829) was at that time Aulic Council Agent ; until
1786 he had been secretary of the " True Concord " lodge.—Constanze
received 3,150 gulden in several instalments. André published about 55 works
by Mozart between 1800 and 1830 : 30 with and 25 without opus numbers.
(*Cf.* O. E. Deutsch in *Mozart-Jahrbuch 1953* [Salzburg, 1954].)

MARIANNE VON BERCHTOLD TO BREITKOPF & HÄRTEL

St. Gilgen, the 24th November 1799

I have great pleasure in sending you the essay which I have compiled from the letters sent to Salzburg by my father on his journeys, and which I forwarded to a friend of our family at his request, who then entrusted it to Professor Schlichtegroll . . .

I am also enclosing an engraving which was made during our stay in Paris. From this you can see how handsome my brother was as a child. It was only after the small-pox that he became so disfigured and, even worse, when he came back from Italy his complexion took on the sallow colour of the Italians, making him quite unrecognizable. He was a small but well-proportioned child.

> Nottebohm, *Mozartiana*, pp. 136 f.—Nannerl's recollections of 1792 now reached Breitkopf.—The copperplate was the group portrait by Carmontelle, engraved by Delafosse (see 18 November 1763). *Cf.* Nannerl's letter to Joseph Sonnleithner of 2 July 1819.

MEMOIRS OF MOZART'S SISTER, PUBLISHED IN THE " ALLGEMEINE
MUSIKALISCHE ZEITUNG ", LEIPZIG, 22 JANUARY 1800

(1) Mozart's over-rich imagination was so lively and so vivid, even in childhood, at a time when it still lies dormant in ordinary men, and perfected that which it had once taken hold of, to such an extent, that one cannot imagine anything more extraordinary and in some respects more moving than its enthusiastic creations ; which, because the little man still knew so little of the real world, were as far removed from it as the heavens themselves. Just one illustration : As the journeys which we used to make (he and I, his sister) took him to different lands, he would think out a kingdom for himself as we travelled from one place to another, and this he called the Kingdom of Back—why by this name, I can no longer recall. This kingdom and its inhabitants were endowed with everything that could make good and happy—children of them. He was the King of this land— and this notion became so rooted within him, and he carried it so far, that our servant, who could draw a little, had to make a chart of it, and he would dictate the names of the cities, market-towns and villages to him.

(2) He loved his parents, and especially his father, so dearly, that he composed a melody which he would sing out loud each day before going to sleep, to which end his father had to set him on a chair. Father always had to sing the second part, and when this ceremony, which might on no occasion be omitted, was over, he would kiss his father most tenderly and go to bed very peacefully and contentedly. He continued this game until he was in his tenth year.

(3) In London, where our father lay dangerously ill, we were forbidden to touch a piano. And so, in order to occupy himself, Mozart composed his first Symphony for all the instruments of the orchestra—but especially for trumpets and kettle-drums. I had to copy it out as I sat at his side. Whilst he composed and I copied he said to me : Remind me to give the horn something worthwhile to do !

(4) In Olmütz [November 1767], where he caught the small-pox, which made him so ill that he could see nothing for nine days and had to spare his eyes for several weeks after his recovery, time began to drag. He therefore sought some occupation. The Court Chaplain to the Bishop there, Herr Hay, later Bishop of Königsgrätz, visited us daily. He was highly skilled at card-tricks. My brother learned them from him with great rapidity, and as the local fencing-master also visited us, this gentleman had to teach him to fence. Even at this early age he showed a natural affection for all artists. Every composer, painter, engraver and the like, whose acquaintance we made on our journeys, had to give him some memento of his skill, and these he would carefully preserve.

> Year II, No. 17, col. 300 f.—Leitzmann, *op. cit.*, 1914, pp. 32 f. ; 1926, pp. 41 f.—*Cf.* Marianne's notes of 1792.—The servant was probably Sebastian Winter (see 9 June 1763). The nonsense words of Wolfgang's evening song, a variant of " Willem van Nassau " (*cf.* K. 25) ; were " oragnia figatafa ".— When Leopold Mozart was taken ill in London, the family moved to Five Fields Row.—Wolfgang's earliest symphonies, in E♭ and D major (K. 16 and 19) were written in London in the winter of 1764-65.—Johann Leopold Hay acquired when a bishop the sobriquet of an " Austrian Fénelon " (Wurzbach, *Lexikon* [Vienna, 1862], Vol. VIII, pp. 103-6).—Nissen (pp. 680 f.) reports an anecdote said to have been related by Nannerl, though not in the Leipzig periodical :
>
> > " When the family was back home again in 1766, and Wolfgang had already become famous by then, although he had not yet reached his ninth year, they had many visits paid them by grandees, among whom was a very haughty gentleman, who however did not know how he ought to address little Mozart. To say ' thou ' did not seem to him proper, yet he thought ' you ' or ' your ' too much ; and so he felt it best to say ' we '. So he began : ' We have been travelling, then, and gained much honour for ourselves ', on so on. In an instant little Mozart retorted : ' But I have never seen or met you anywhere except at Salzburg'."
>
> The Leipzig journal inaccurately described Nannerl's contribution as a kind of continuation of the Mozart anecdotes which they had published from information supplied by Constanze (see 6 February 1799).

CONSTANZE MOZART TO JOHANN ANTON ANDRÉ
[VIENNA, 9 FEBRUARY 1800]

Dear Herr André,
there is a possibility that I might be able to obtain the original score of my husband's famous Requiem from the anonymous gentleman who com-

missioned it ; his agent, however, mentioned to me the sum of fifty ducats. Do you wish to expend this amount on this work ? Or what is the highest price that you wish to expend on it ? Up till now I had believed my copy to be a good one ; but a connoisseur has assured me that it falls a long way short of the perfection of the original. I cannot as yet judge of the truth of this, but should it be so, it would of course be worth buying the original. As my husband did not entirely complete the work, because he died over it when it was nearly ready, I cannot be absolutely sure how much is actually written in his own hand. Meanwhile, whether it is more of it or less, this particular copy under discussion is obviously the most authentic of all. I have the honour to remain your most respectful and obedient servant

Constanze Mozart.

Manskopfsches Museum, deposited in the Town and University Library, Frankfurt on Main.—Supplied by Dr. Wolfgang Schmieder.—The letter is written by Nissen and signed by Constanze. The date is in André's hand.— Count Walsegg's commissioner was his Vienna lawyer, Dr. Johann Nepomuk Sortschan ; he demanded an explanation and an apology from Constanze. Constanze and the " connoisseur ", Abbé Maximilian Stadler, were permitted to inspect the autograph at his office and compare her copy against it, as she reported to Breitkopf & Härtel on 21 July 1800 and to André on 26 November of the same year. The autograph then returned to the Count, who therefore was not reimbursed for half of the fee paid. (However, the Vienna Court Library bought back the autograph for 50 ducats in 1839.) The first performance in Vienna (2 January 1793) and Breitkopf's first edition (1800) used the copy. Cf. end of 1798.—Fredrik Samuel Silverstolpe was present at Stadler's comparison of the copy of the Requiem with the original ; cf. Count C.-G. Stellan Mörner in Festschrift für Alfred Orel (Vienna, 1960), pp. 116 f.

CONSTANZE MOZART'S STATEMENT ABOUT MOZART'S MANUSCRIPTS
13 MARCH 1800

Statement
concerning the music of Mozart's estate

After I had passed on to Messrs. Breitkopf and Härtel in Leipsic against an honorarium some few original manuscripts of my late husband, consisting solely of songs, canons, fugues, a harmonica quintet, a march for the pianoforte, a pair of sonatas and one pianoforte concerto (apart from 6 sonatas and the Requiem in manuscript copies) for the betterment of their edition, and after I had sold them the plates of the pianoforte concerto published by me, I voluntarily offered them my entire large collection for sale in one lot. The aforementioned gentlemen, who believed they could not evaluate them at this remove, did not avail themselves of my offer. Herr André, who was enabled by his residence here to judge the worth and richness of this estate, has since purchased it from me and has thus become the sole legal possessor, not so much of a residue, as of an almost complete collection of absolutely accurate and absolutely authentic works in original manuscript from Mozart's earliest youth until his death. Herr

André requested this statement of me : he is entitled to it : it is in accordance with the strictest truth : I herewith make it to him.

Vienna, the 13th March 1800

Constance Mozart.

Offenbach on Main, Municipal Archives.—Supplied by the André family.—Written by Nissen, signed by Constanze.—This is the second version of Constanze's statement. The first, dated 12 March, is in the Manskopf Museum, Frankfurt on Main.—The final version appeared on 4 April in the *Frankfurter Staats-Ristretto*. An advertisement by André appeared in the same paper on 10 February, to which Breitkopf & Härtel replied in their journal in March. The publication of Constanze's statement led in April to a further reply in the *Allgemeine musikalische Zeitung* ; this ended the controversy.—*Cf.* 8 November 1799 ; and " Mozarts Nachlass ", by O. E. Deutsch, in the *Mozart-Jahrbuch 1953* (Salzburg, 1954).

FROM THE " GRÄTZER ZEITUNG ", 28 AUGUST 1800

The works of my late husband, both those previously published and those which are not yet known at all, are now about to appear in a new and elegant Collected Edition, which is largely based on his original manuscripts, and will thus be entirely correct and authentic. These new editions are all obtainable from me and will also remain so in the future. I can at present offer : 6 grand Pianoforte Concertos, 1 ditto for 2 pianofortes, among which are some unknown ones ; 1 unknown Rondo for 2 violins ; 4 Quartets, 5 Quintets, 1 Sonata with accompaniment, all engraved, 1 unknown Concerto, one detto Quintet for Harmonica or Pianoforte ; 6 volumes of Pianoforte Sonatas with and without accompaniment, for 2 and 4 hands, among them some unknown ones, one volume of songs, largely unknown, the great Requiem (Mozart's last work) in score, all printed. I have also a few copies of Quintets in manuscript parts.

Widow Mozart, Vienna, Michaelerplatz No. 5.

Erika Kaufmann in *Mozart und Graz* (Graz, 1956), p. 14.—Constanze had been in contact with Breitkopf & Härtel on the subject of their edition of the *Oeuvres complettes* before 1800, but had then sold Mozart's autographs to Johann Anton André, Offenbach on Main ; he published numerous works by Mozart.—The works listed by Constanze were probably the following, all of which, except for the last three, were in fact published by André : 6 grand pianoforte concertos (K. 503, 595, 491, 482, 488, 467) ; 1 concerto for two pianofortes (K. 365) ; rondo for two violins (K. 373 [?]) ; 4 string quartets (K. 499, 575, 589, 590) ; 5 string quintets (K. 174, 406, 593, 614 and one spurious) ; 1 sonata with accompaniment (K. 481 or 526) ; 1 Konzertstück (for violin ?)—(K. 268) ; harmonica quintet (K. 617—Breitkopf & Härtel) ; 6 pianoforte sonatas (Parts I, III, IV, VII and [?] VIII of the *Oeuvres complettes*—Breitkopf & Härtel) ; Requiem (K. 626—Breitkopf & Härtel). *Cf.* O. E. Deutsch, " Mozarts Verleger " in the *Mozart-Jahrbuch 1955* (Salzburg, 1956).—This announcement did not appear in the *Wiener Zeitung* at this time, but it did appear on 19 August in the Hungarian language newspaper *Magyar Hírmondó* which was printed in Vienna.

On 26 February 1801 Marianne's husband, Johann Baptist von Berchtold zu Sonnenburg, died at St. Gilgen.

On 29 October 1801 Marianne removed to Salzburg.

> From then until the end of her life she lived in the Barisani house in the Kirch-gasse (now Siegmund-Haffner-Gasse 12), on the third floor. The windows at the back, on the Universitätsplatz, overlook the back of the birthplace in the Getreidegasse.

In 1803 the booklet *Mozarts Geist* by Ignaz Ernst Ferdinand Karl Arnold was published at Erfurt.

> Schurig, *Konstanze Mozart*, pp. 142 f.—It should be noted that Arnold (1774–1812), who on pp. 64 ff. refers to Mozart's supposedly loose living, remarks : " No need for poison here . . . , his energies were worn out . . ."—Arnold's nine little biographies of musicians were published in 1816, collected into two volumes as *Gallerie der berühmtesten Tonkünstler des 18. und 19. Jahrhunderts* ; they also contain his *Versuch einer Parallele* between Mozart and Haydn, first published in 1810.

★ FROM ZINZENDORF'S DIARY, 20 APRIL 1804
(in French)

. . . At half past six to the theatre. *La Clemenza di Tito*. Some of Meta-stasio's airs left out, music by Mayer and Weigel mixed with Mozhart's.

> The work was first given a concert performance at the Burgtheater on 12 April, and then, on the 13th, staged at the Kärntnertor Theatre.—A Friedrich Sebastian Mayer had sung the role of Publio at the Freihaus Theatre in 1798, but the reference is probably to Simon Mayr, who had several works per-formed at the Vienna court theatres about this time ; Joseph Weigl wrote a new scena for one of the two Brizzis—the elder, Luigi, or the younger, Antonio.

JEAN-BAPTISTE-ANTOINE SUARD, " ANECDOTES SUR MOZART ", PARIS, 1804
(in French)

Mozart was one of those extraordinary children who astonish with their premature talent ; but, very different from almost all those little prodigies who, having reached maturer years, have turned out to be very ordinary men, his talent grew with his body and he became a man of genius.

Born the son of a musician, he was brought up for the same profession. Nature had endowed him for music. His instinct kept ahead of the instruc-tion he was given. The rapidity of his progress impressed all those who were witness of it. His father made him do the tour of Europe, 30 to 35 years ago. He was 6 to 7 years old. I heard him play the harpsichord at the Concert spirituel and in private houses. He astonished all amateurs by the facility and precision with which he executed the most difficult pieces. He could accompany from a full score at sight. He would impro-vise at his instrument, and in these extemporized capricci he revealed the happiest touches of melody, and already showed a deep feeling for harmony. In Italy and in England he excited the same admiration.

He realized the hopes that had been placed in his precocious talent. At 10 or 11 years he published some harpsichord pieces which were played everywhere. He long continued to compose instrumental music, and it was not until the last years of his life that he worked for the theatre.

It has constantly been observed that too prompt and too rapid a development of the moral faculties in children only operated at the expense of their physique. Mozart provided new proof of this. His body did not sustain normal growth as he grew older. All his life he remained weak and frail in health. His mind, limited to those ideas which concerned music, shed a bright light on all that interested his talent, but shewed little aptitude to occupy itself with other things. He was extremely irritable ; his affections were lively, but superficial and of short duration. He was melancholic and dominated by an active and mercurial imagination, which was only feebly kept in check by his reason.

He loved money ; but he was neither covetous nor mercenary. On the contrary, he was generous and beneficent ; a hundred examples of this can be found in his life. He often gave without discernment, and he yet more often spent money for no good reason. He had earned much money by his appointments, from the generosity of princes and by the product of his works ; he died poor, leaving his estimable wife, whom he loved greatly, no other resource than copies of the compositions which he had not yet published.

I have said that he loved his wife greatly ; she deserved it : she encouraged him in his work and sustained him in his fits of melancholy. Mozart was tenderly attached to her ; but that did not prevent him from conceiving a fancy for other women, and his fancies had such a hold over him that he could not resist them.

I have heard it said that he wrote *la Flûte Enchantée* only to please a woman of the theatre with whom he had fallen in love, and who had offered him her favours at this price. It is added that his triumph had very cruel consequences, and that he contracted from it an incurable disease of which he died shortly after. This fact seems to me to be very unlikely ; *la Flûte Enchantée* is not the last of his operas, and when he composed it, his health was already seriously impaired.

Mozart was all his life a sort of child. All his sentiments had more violence than depth. Light and inconstant in his affections, he was good and kind, but more from weakness than virtue. His strongest, or rather his sole passion, was for music ; he also loved a few women with a liveliness which at first gave the appearance of passion, but which promptly burnt itself out.

He judged his own works impartially, and often with a severity which he would not readily have tolerated from another. The Emperor Joseph loved Mozart, and had made him his maître de chapelle. He liked to think himself a dilettante. His tour in Italy had given him an inflated idea of the superiority of Italian music over all other kinds, and some Italians whom he had at his court carefully nurtured this prejudice, which was not without foundation. Foreign musicians who were in Vienna spoke of Mozart's first attempts with more jealousy than justice ; and the Emperor was easily swayed by the opinions of these professors. One day when he had just heard the rehearsal of a comic opera which he himself had commissioned from Mozart (*L'Enlèvement du sérail*), he said to the composer : " My dear Mozart, that is too beautiful for our ears ; there are many too many notes in it."—" I beg Your Majesty's pardon ", Mozart replied very drily, " there are precisely as many notes as are needed." The Emperor appeared somewhat embarrassed by this reply ; but when the opera was performed, he praised it very highly.

But Mozart himself was later less content with his work ; he made many corrections and cuts in it. Later, when playing at the clavier one of the arias which had been most applauded, he said : " That's all right for the music-room, but there's too much verbiage for the theatre. When I wrote it, I took pleasure in what I was doing, and found none of it too long."

He had been named Chamber Composer by the Emperor, and in respect of this position he had a salary of 800 florins per year ; but he never composed anything in this capacity. He was asked one day, in pursuance of a general order from the government, for a statement of the stipend that he received from the Court. He wrote in a sealed letter : " Too much for what I have done, too little for what I could have done." He was very irregular in his work. When he was seized by an idea, he could not be dragged away from his composition. He composed in the midst of his friends ; he passed whole nights in work. At other times he was sometimes only able to finish a work at the very moment when he had to perform it. It even came about one day that, having to do a piece for a court concert, he had no time to write out the part that he was to play. The Emperor Joseph, happening to glance at the music paper which Mozart appeared to be following, was astonished to see on it nothing but staves without any notes, and [he] said to him : " Where is your part ? "— " There ", said Mozart, putting his hand to his forehead.

I have said that he loved his wife tenderly, although he was sometimes unfaithful to her. She suffered from very bad health. During one long illness that she had, he formed the habit of walking in front of those who had come to see her, putting his finger to his lips and signing to them to make no sound. This habit became so much part of him that after his wife's recovery he would go up to people of his acquaintance and put his finger to his lips, signing to them in the same way to keep quiet, and not talking to them himself other than in a very low voice.

His health, by nature delicate, grew weaker from day to day. The nervous irritability which was part of his constitution, grew worse owing to the excesses of work and pleasure into which he alternately threw himself ; for he knew not how to be moderate in the one, nor in the other. The melancholy to which he was subject became habitual ; he sensed his approaching end, and it was with terror that he saw it draw near. A rather strange event occurred which accelerated in a distressing manner the effects of this mournful disposition.

One day when he was plunged in his melancholy reveries, he heard a carriage draw up at his door ; a stranger was announced who asked to speak to him. He was shown in ; it was a rather elderly man who gave every appearance of being a person of distinction. "I have been commissioned", said the stranger, "by a very illustrious gentleman, to seek you out."—"Who is this man ?", Mozart broke in.—"He wishes to remain anonymous."—"Well then, and what does he want ?"—"He has just lost a person who was very dear to him, and whose memory will be eternally precious to him. He wishes each year to celebrate the anniversary of the death of this person with a solemn service, and he asks you to compose a Requiem for this service." Mozart felt himself deeply stirred by this discourse, by the grave tone in which it was spoken, by the air of mystery which seemed to envelop this whole occurrence ; the state of his mind strengthened still further these impressions. He promised to do the Requiem. The stranger continued : "Put all your genius to this task ; you are working for a connoisseur of music."—"So much the better."—"How long will you require ?"—"Four weeks."—"Good, I will return in four weeks. What price do you put on your work ?"—"One hundred ducats."—The stranger counted them out on the table and disappeared.

Mozart remained for a few minutes plunged deep in thought ; then he suddenly called for a pen, ink and paper, and despite his wife's remonstrances, he began to write. This frenzy of work continued for several days ; he worked day and night, and with an ardour that seemed to grow as he continued. But his body could not keep pace with this effort. He fell down one day in a faint, and was obliged to suspend work. Shortly after, his wife seeking to distract him from the sombre thoughts that occupied him, Mozart said to her abruptly : "So much is certain : it is for myself that I am writing this Requiem. It will serve for my own funeral service." Nothing could distract him from this idea ; he continued to work at his Requiem, as Raphael worked at his painting of the Transfiguration, equally obsessed with the idea of his [approaching] death.

Mozart felt his strength grow less with each day, and his work made slow progress ; the four weeks he had asked for having passed, he saw the stranger coming into his house one day. "I have not been able to keep my word", said Mozart.—"Do not worry," said the stranger ; "how much longer do you need ?"—"Four weeks. The work has inspired me with more interest than I had expected, and I have made it much longer than I had intended." —"In that case it is fair to increase the honorarium. Here are a further

fifty ducats."—" Sir," said Mozart, ever more astonished, " who are you ? "
—" That does not concern us here. I shall return in four weeks." Mozart
at once sent one of his servants to follow this extraordinary man, and discover where he lived ; but the servant returned to report that he had not
been able to discover any trace of the stranger.

Poor Mozart became obsessed with the thought that this stranger was no
ordinary mortal being, that he for sure had dealings with the other world,
and that he had been sent to him to announce his approaching end. He
worked with still greater ardour at his Requiem, which he regarded as the
most lasting monument to his talent. During this work, he several times
fell prey to alarming fainting-fits. Finally, the work was completed before
the four weeks had expired. The stranger returned at the appointed time.
Mozart was no more.

All Germany regards this Requiem as this composer's masterpiece.   S.

> *Mélanges de Littérature* (Paris, 1804), Vol. V, pp. 337-47.—Suard (1734–1817),
> the permanent secretary of the Académie française, had appeared in Gluck's
> defence in Paris as " Anonym of Vaugirard ".—The story of the incurable
> disease is part of the malicious gossip concerning the last year of Mozart's
> life ; *cf.* Abert, Vol. I, p. 998.

On 8 April 1805 Wolfgang Gottlieb Mozart, aged thirteen, gave a musical concert
at the Theater an der Wien.

> Constanze had announced this concert in the *Wiener Zeitung* of 16 March ;
> the printed invitation is also in her name and gives the address : " Michaeler-
> platz No. 5, 3rd floor ". (Copy in the possession of the Gesellschaft der
> Musikfreunde ; facsimile in Erich W. Engel's *Mozart-Kalender* [Vienna, 1914],
> sheet 177.) The announcement in the *Wiener Zeitung* contains the following
> sentences : " May indulgent connoisseurs discover some traces of the father's
> talent in the son's endeavours ! It shall ever be my most earnest endeavour
> to keep Mozart's name in honoured memory through his descendants."—
> The concert included a cantata composed by little Mozart for Joseph Haydn's
> seventy-third birthday. The report in Joseph Richter's *Eipeldauer Briefe*
> (1805, No. 39, pp. 13 f.) shows that young Wolfgang improvised on the
> pianoforte.—The still existing Theater an der Wien had been opened in 1801,
> when Schikaneder was obliged to give up the Theater auf der Wieden.

FROM THE " WIENER ZEITUNG ", 18 MAY 1805
Statement.

Flattering as it must be for me, viewed from one aspect, that the public
so kindly received my early pianoforte works, which were published under
Mozart's name without my knowledge, I nevertheless consider that I owe
it to myself to lay claims to my own property. Besides a Sonata in C
minor and Variations on " Zu Stephan sprach im Traume " and on " Freundin sanfter Herzenstriebe", my Variations on " Marlborough s'en vat en guerre"
have been published by Herr Schott in Mainz, and [more] recently by Herr
Artaria & Comp. here, under Mozart's name as No. 22. Mozart, however,

never wrote variations on any of these themes. The last-mentioned are one of my earlier pieces, and I did not include them among my numbered works. Vienna, the 4th May 1805.

Anton Eberl, Composer.

> *Cf.* 28 August 1788.—After that first protest on Eberl's part K. App. 290 and 291 had been published under Mozart's name.

JOSEPH HAYDN TO BONIFAZIO ASIOLI IN MILAN
(in Italian)

My dear Colleague,

I should like Carlo Mozart to have the honour to be one of your pupils. I should congratulate him on having a master such as you, whose works and talents I prize highly.

Allow me to recommend this youth to you as the son of a friend of mine, now dead, and as the heir to a name which should be dear to all connoisseurs and friends of art. I am convinced that Carlo Mozart will show himself worthy of the pains which you, in your goodness, will doubtless take to form a subject who will do honour to his teacher and his father. I beg you to forgive me if, oppressed by the infirmities of old age, I limit myself to the honour of signing myself, with the utmost respect,

Sir,
Your most humble and obdt. servant,
Giuseppe Haydn.

Vienna, 23 April 1806.

> —Copy in the Biblioteca Musicale, Bologna.—Antonio Coli, *Vita di Bonifazio Asioli da Correggio* (Milan, 1835), p. 50.—Asioli was a composer, maestro di cappella and a director of studies at the new Conservatoire. Karl Mozart became his pupil, but after four years he gave up his studies ; in 1810 he became an Austrian civil servant in Milan.

FROM SCHUBART'S " IDEEN ZU EINER AESTHETIK DER TONKUNST ",
VIENNA, 1806 (WRITTEN 1784/5)

His [Leopold Mozart's] son has become even more famous than the father. His is one of the [truly] prodigious musical minds ; for as early as his eleventh year he composed an opera which was well received by all connoisseurs. This son is also one of our best keyboard players. He plays with magical dexterity and sight-reads so accurately that there can scarcely have been anyone to equal him in this respect.

> P. 158, in the section on Salzburg.—For Schubart, who died shortly before Mozart, *cf.* 27 April 1775 and spring 1788.—The book was published by his son Ludwig.

FROM THE "ZEITUNG FÜR THEATER, MUSIK UND POESIE", VIENNA,
13 APRIL 1808

How does Haydn hear and pronounce the name Mozart?

Curious question ! Like any other who possesses physiologically normal organs of hearing and speech (wretched answer !). Or does he rise from his seat, doff his hat, and even incline his head ?—God forbid ! Read here and feel the power of the immortal man's very own words, accompanied by a flood of tears * :

Forgive me—I cannot help—weeping—at the name of my Mozart—.

Note to this rubric.

A passionate worshipper of Mozart, who wanted to appear as such in all men's eyes, was not content to exaggerate merely in his recently published book with such distortions of the truth ; but he now even begins, in a manner that is already rather vexatious, to enrich these exaggerations with additions of his own making. Your critic believes that Haydn weeps like any other old man, and wishes that Herr —l may one day adopt a physiologically and psychologically normal attitude towards Mozart ! (The anti-criticism needs no comment.)

* To a few musician friends on the 30th December 1807 on the occasion of their offering him their new year congratulations, the subject turning to Mozart.

> Year III, No. 28, p. 217.—Abert, Vol. II, p. 59.—The "worshipper" of Mozart can unfortunately not be identified with any certainty. The visitors that day were Constanze Mozart, Johann Gänsbacher (see 1844) and an unnamed artist.

FROM JOSEPH LANGE'S REMINISCENCES, VIENNA, 1808

Never was Mozart less recognizably a great man in his conversation and actions, than when he was busied with an important work. At such times he not only spoke confusedly and disconnectedly, but occasionally made jests of a nature which one did not expect of him, indeed he even deliberately forgot himself in his behaviour. But he did not appear to be brooding and thinking about anything. Either he intentionally concealed his inner tension behind superficial frivolity, for reasons which could not be fathomed, or he took delight in throwing into sharp contrast the divine ideas of his music and these sudden outbursts of vulgar platitudes, and in giving himself pleasure by seeming to make fun of himself. I can understand that so exalted an artist can, out of a deep veneration for his Art, belittle and as it were expose to ridicule his own personality.

> P. 46 of the autobiography of Mozart's brother-in-law, who had since 1795 been living separated from Aloisia Lange.

FROM FRANZ XAVER NIEMETSCHEK'S MOZART BIOGRAPHY, PRAGUE, 1808

He was summoned from Munich by the archbishop's command ; and from this time, *i.e.* his twenty-fifth year, he lived in Vienna, that imperial city which as much through its inhabitants' decided propensity to music as through the number of excellent musicians could not but exert an important influence on Mozart's mind.

From here his astonishing compositions spread first to Bohemia and then to the rest of Germany, imparting to musical taste a mighty impetus and a new direction—which, however, his present imitators distort and destroy.

It was his pianoforte playing that first won admirers and devotees ; for although Vienna had many great masters of the instrument, the public's favourite, none of them could compare with our Mozart. A remarkable quickness, which particularly in consideration of his left hand or bass could be called unique, neatness and delicacy, the most beautiful, most eloquent expression, and a sensitivity that went straight to the heart—these were the qualities of his playing which, with the richness of his invention and his profound knowledge of composition technique, could not help captivating every hearer and raising Mozart to the greatest keyboard player of his age.

His keyboard compositions of all kinds, sonatas, variations and concertos, were soon widely known and loved. With every new work one was astonished by the newness of the style and of the ideas—one wondered at the heights to which music was raised so quickly through his works !

Mozart found a composer in Vienna whose genius was nearest to his own, I mean the famous creator of Alcestis and Iphigenia, the Ritter von Gluck, a Bohemian by birth. Intercourse with him and ceaseless study of his exalted works gave Mozart much sustenance and influenced his operas. Mozart also soon became the most devoted admirer of the great unforgettable Joseph Hayden, who was even then already the pride of music, and who now, after Mozart's death, remains our sole darling and our joy. Mozart often referred to him as his teacher.

Soon after Mozart had set up residence in Vienna, our unforgettable Emperor Joseph II formed the plan, so worthy of a German emperor, of alienating taste from Italian operas by supporting German Singspiele and singers, and of encouraging a more patriotic outlook. He accordingly assembled the best singers, and commissioned a German opera from Mozart. For these virtuosi he wrote the well-known and well-loved Singspiel *die Entführung aus dem Serail* in 1782.

It created a widespread sensation ; and the cunning Italians soon saw that such a mind could soon endanger their foreign tinklings. Envy now awoke with all the sharpness of Italian poison ! The monarch, at heart delighted with this new and deeply expressive music, nevertheless said to Mozart : " Very many notes, my dear Mozart ! "

" Exactly as many as are necessary, your Majesty ! ", replied the latter with that noble pride and candour so fitting in great minds. He realized that this was not a personal opinion, but gossip.

I should not here overlook to mention that, at the time when he was writing this opera, Mozart was in love with, and had just become engaged to, *Konstanza Weber*, later his wife, and sister of the famous singer *Lang*. The influence which his state of mind must have had on the composition of this opera will be recognized by everyone who has heard it ; for who is not aware how full it is of sweet feelings and yearning love ?

I cannot speak from my own experience of the applause and the sensation which it aroused in Vienna—but I was witness of the enthusiasm which it caused among cognoscenti and amateurs alike when it was performed in Prague ! It was as if all that we had previously heard and known had not been music ! All were captivated—all wondered at the new harmonies, the original, never before heard passages for the wind instruments. Now the Bohemians began to search out his compositions ; and in that same year all the better concerts contained pianoforte works and symphonies by Mozart. From this time forth Bohemia's preference for his works was decided ! The greatest cognoscenti and artists of our city were also the greatest admirers of Mozart and the most ardent prophets of his fame.

Until this time Mozart had lived without a permanent appointment, despite his great fame, and thus without a regular income. Instruction on the pianoforte and subscription concerts for a closed circle of the high aristocracy were still the most productive source of income to him, but in a city like Vienna he certainly could save nothing.

At this time he was writing very fine pianoforte works : sonatas with and without accompaniment, and concertos which are now in the hands of everyone.

In 1785 he published 6 masterly violin quartets, engraved, and with a dedication to his friend the Kapellmeister Joseph Hayden which is a beautiful expression of his esteem for this great man. And just as it increases Hayden's fame to be honoured by an artist like Mozart, so does it also do honour to the latter, and endear to us the kindness of heart of a man whose talent all men must admire.

To be sure, Mozart could not have honoured a Joseph Hayden better than with these quartets, which are a treasure-house of the finest thoughts, and a model and example of the art of composition. In the eyes of the connoisseur this work is as estimable as any of his operatic works. Everything in it is carefully considered and perfected !—We can see from these quartets that Mozart took pains to deserve Hayden's praise.

At this time, Beaumarchais's French comedy *Figaro* was establishing its fame and being performed on every stage. After it had been turned into a singspiel Mozart was encouraged by the Emperor Joseph to win a place for this comedy in the Italian opera theatre by means of his music. It was performed by the Italian opera company in Vienna. If there is truth in the report that is generally accepted to be true, and which with so many

reliable witnesses can scarcely be doubted, namely that at the first performance the singers made deliberate mistakes out of hatred, envy and low
cabals, in the intention of bringing about the opera's downfall : then
the reader may judge how much this faction of Italian singers and composers feared the supremacy of Mozart's genius, and how true is what
I have already reported above about the *Entführung aus dem Serail.* This
cowardly band of unworthy men remained fully active until the early
death of the immortal artist, full of hatred and slander, and denigrating his
art. Mozart's spirit indeed had to fight hard before he finally triumphed !

It is said that the singers had to be brought to their duty by a grave warning from our late Monarch when Mozart came, full of distress, to see him
in his box during the first act, and drew his attention to the matter.

Every one of his works was recognized and esteemed according to its
true worth in Bohemia ; thus it was with this opera too. It was performed
in Prague in 1787 [1786] by Bondini's company and received with an
enthusiasm at its first performance such as only *die Zauberflöte* later knew.
It is the strictest truth if I say that this opera was played almost uninter-
ruptedly that whole winter, and that it completely alleviated the wretched
circumstances of the entrepreneur. The enthusiasm it excited from the
public had no previous parallel ; people could not hear enough of it. It
soon came out in a good piano reduction by one of our best masters, Herr
Kucharž ; it appeared in wind parts, as a chamber quintet, as German
dances : in short, Figaro's songs rang out in the streets, in gardens—even
the harper inside the tavern had to play " Non piu andrai " if he wanted
a hearing. This phenomenon is of course mainly due to the excellence of
the work ; but only a public having such a feeling for the truly beautiful
in music, and so many thorough connoisseurs among its number, could
recognize the worth of such art at a first hearing ; the incomparable orchestra
of the Prague Opera did its part nobly, realizing with accuracy and zeal
all Mozart's ideas. For it was these worthy men, most of them not soloists,
but the more truly music-lovers and orchestral players for that, who
first and most deeply responded to the new harmonies and the fiery progress of the vocal parts ! The late and highly praised director of the orchestra,
Strobach, often maintained that he and his personnel were so fired by the
music at each performance, that despite the exhausting labours he would
gladly have started playing it all over again. Admiration for the composer
of this work went so far that one of our noblest aristocrats and musical
amateurs, Count Johann Joseph Thun, who himself had a fine orchestra,
invited him to Prague and offered him lodging, food and every comfort
in his own house. Mozart was too delighted with the effect which his
music had upon the Bohemians, and too desirous to become acquainted with
a nation which had such feeling for music, not to seize the opportunity with
joy. He came to Prague in January 1787 : *Figaro* was given on the day
of his arrival, and Mozart himself appeared in the theatre. At once the
word spread about that he was present in the stalls, and when the symphony

was over, the whole public applauded and welcomed him with their clapping.

By general request he then performed on the pianoforte at a great concert in the Opera House. Never had the theatre been so full of people as it was on this occasion ; never had there been greater or more unanimous delight than his playing aroused. Indeed, we did not know what to admire the more—the extraordinary composition, or the extraordinary playing ; both together made a total impression on our souls that could only be compared to a sweet enchantment ! But at the end of the concert, when Mozart extemporized alone for more than half an hour at the pianoforte, raising our delight to the highest degree, our enchantment dissolved into loud, overwhelming applause. And indeed, this extemporization exceeded anything normally understood by pianoforte playing, as the highest excellence in the art of composition was combined with the most perfect accomplishment in execution. For sure, just as this concert had no parallel for the citizens of Prague, so Mozart counted this day as one of the finest of his life.

The symphonies written for this occasion are true masterpieces of instrumental music, full of surprising transitions ; they have a rapid, fiery progression, and they attune the soul to expectation of something exalted. This is particularly true of the great symphony in D major and [the one in] E flat, which are still favourites of the Prague public, although they have been given at least a hundred times.

The opera director Bondini at once completed an agreement for a new opera from Mozart to be given on the Prague stage the next winter ; Mozart gladly accepted, having learnt how well the Bohemians appreciated and performed his music. He often repeated this to his Prague friends : he liked everything in Prague, where he was as it were carried along by an affectionate public and true friends—He expressed his very warm thanks to the opera orchestra in a letter to the then director Herr Strobach, attributing to its skilful performance the greater part of the success which his music had enjoyed in Prague. This trait of his heart is very fine, however unimportant it may seem ; it shows that pride, conceit or ingratitude were not his faults, as they so often are with much slighter virtuosi.

At the beginning of winter in the same year of 1787 Mozart returned to Prague according to his contract, and there completed the crown of all his masterpieces, the opera : *Il dissoluto punito*, or *Don Giovanni*.

The Bohemians are proud that he recognized and honoured their good taste with so noble a work, coming from the depths of his genius. " *Don Juan* was written for Prague "—one need say no more to demonstrate what a high regard Mozart had for the musical sense of the Bohemians. He succeeded completely in matching and touching this sense of theirs ; for no opera has here so long held the stage and enjoyed such favour as *Don Juan*. It is now 21 years since it was first given—and yet it is still heard with pleasure, it still entices a numerous audience into the stalls ! In short, *Don Juan* is the favourite opera of the cultivated public in Prague. When

Mozart appeared at the clavier in the orchestra for the first performance of it, the whole theatre, full to suffocation, received him with a general round of applause. On every occasion Mozart received in Prague great and unambiguous proofs of esteem and admiration, which were certainly sincere because not prejudice or fashion, but pure feeling for his art, were responsible for them. His beautiful works were loved and admired ; how could people remain indifferent to the person of their great creator?

In the month of December 1789 Mozart wrote the Italian comic singspiel *Così fan tutte*, or *The School for Lovers* ; everywhere people wonder how that great mind could lower itself to waste its heavenly melodies on so feeble a concoction of a text. It was not in his power to refuse the commission, and the text was expressly served on him.—His journey via Leipsic and Dresden to Berlin also falls into this period ; he undertook it in the spring of 1789. The great renown of his name went before him, and nowhere were the expectations disappointed which he had everywhere aroused. The then King of Prussia, a generous amateur and patron of music, was entirely captivated by him, and gave him excellent proofs of his esteem. The sincerity and permanence of his regard for Mozart were shown by his royal magnanimity in receiving and supporting Mozart's widow when she later came to Berlin.

Mozart was at this time still without an appointment and without a guaranteed income. Well known as was his talent, and sought-after as were his compositions, no one thought of rewarding and supporting him. It is true that he often had large receipts ; but with the uncertainty and irregularity of his income, the frequent lyings-in and illnesses of his wife, in a city like Vienna, Mozart could in fact hardly avoid starving. He therefore determined to leave the city where there was no employment for a man like Mozart. His plan was to go to England, where his expectations of a better fate were the more justified by the number of invitations and enticing offers he had received from there.

All was ready for his departure when Emperor Joseph offered him the title of Imperial Chamber Composer with an annual salary of 800 Gulden and the assurance that he would not be forgotten in the future. Mozart did not want to appear recalcitrant ; he gladly accepted, and stayed on. The decree of his appointment was made out on 7 December 1787.

I leave it to each reader to form his own conclusions about the causes for so long a neglect of so great an artist. It was certainly through no fault of his ; the blame must be laid at the door of his open, honest character, which would not permit him to bow and scrape.

However much his foes and those jealous of his fame tried to darken every one of his virtues through belittlement and slander, the triumph of his art was none the less complete among the unprejudiced and those whose souls were immune to the rust of fashion. All true amateurs of music paid homage to his genius. I will give an example.

Baron von Switten, equally deserving of praise as politician and scholar, a true amateur of music and full of feeling for the austere song of the exalted Händel, often had the works of this famous musician (too simple a food for the fashionable, trifling taste of our own day) performed at private concerts. To this end he employed the talents of our Mozart, who knew how to give new life to Händel's noble inspirations by means of the warmth of his own feeling, and through the magic of his own instrumental style to make them enjoyable for our age. Baron von Switten often corresponded with Mozart on this subject, and once wrote to him, among other matters :

[There follows the letter of 21 March 1789, printed under that date.]

The Turkish war and the death which it brought with it of our most noble unforgettable Monarch, Joseph, deprived Mozart too of a great support of his hopes ; he remained Kapellmeister with 800 florins and yet with no sphere of activity !

But his end too was now at hand ; he was not to outlive the great Monarch by long. The year 1791, dreadfully rich in notable deaths, was destined to tear from us the pride of music. But Mozart had already richly endowed posterity with his bounty. Thus this year is as remarkable for the creation of his finest works as it has become painful for us by reason of his unexpected death. In it, even at the very end of his life, he wrote the music for *die Zauberflöte*, for the serious opera *La Clemenza di Tito* and the awe-inspiring and noble Requiem (Mass for the Dead) which he was not even granted time to finish. So certain as it is that these three works alone would have assured him first place among the composers of his age, and immortal fame, they do but increase our longing for the man taken from us, through the thought which forces its way to the lips of the sensitive listener even as he enjoys his works : " Ah ! how much more would that man have accomplished, what new harmonies would he have created ? "

Die Zauberflöte he wrote for the theatre of the famous Schikaneder, who was an old friend of his. The music to the opera *La Clemenza di Tito* was commissioned by the Bohemian Estates for the Coronation of Emperor Leopold. He began this last-named work in the coach on his way from Vienna, and he completed it in Prague in the short time of 18 days.

The story of his last work, the above-mentioned Requiem for the Dead, is as full of mystery as it is remarkable.

Shortly before the Coronation of the Emperor Leopold, and before Mozart received the commission to go to Prague, an unsigned letter was handed to him by an unknown messenger which, with many flattering remarks, contained the question whether Mozart would like to undertake the composition of a Requiem, for what price, and how soon he would be able to deliver it.

Mozart, who was accustomed to take no step without consulting his wife, related to her this strange commission, and at the same time mentioned his desire to try his hand at this type of work too, the more so as the elevated and exalted style of church music was always close to his genius. She advised him to accept the commission. He therefore wrote to the unknown gentleman to say that he would write the Requiem for a certain sum ; he could not exactly state the time he would require to complete it ; but he would like to know the destination to which he was to deliver the work when it was finished. The same messenger shortly reappeared, bringing not only the agreed honorarium with him, but also the promise that, as he had been so reasonable in his price, he would receive a generous additional payment on handing over the work. He was moreover to write according to the mood and frame of his mind, but he was not to trouble to try and find out the name of his patron, for this search would certainly be vain.

In the meantime Mozart received the flattering and advantageous commission to write the opera *Titus* for the coronation of the Emperor Leopold n Prague. The chance of going to Prague and writing for his dear Bohemians was too attractive to be refused !

Even as Mozart and his wife were climbing into the coach, the messenger stood ghost-like before them, touched Mozart's wife on the coat, and asked : " What will happen to the Requiem now ? "—

Mozart apologized for the journey which he was obliged to make, and for the impossibility of informing his unknown patron about it ; moreover, it would be his first task on his return, and it was for the stranger to decide whether he was prepared to wait so long. The messenger was completely satisfied with this.

In Prague Mozart fell ill and dosed himself ceaselessly ; his colour was pale and his countenance sad, although his merry sense of humour often bubbled into jesting in the company of his friends. At the moment of departure from the circle of his friends he was so sad that he wept tears. A foreboding sense of his approaching death seemed to have produced this melancholy mood—for at this time he already had the seed of the disease which was so soon to carry him off.

On his return to Vienna he at once took up the Requiem, and worked at it with much effort and keen interest : but his illness visibly increased its hold on him and made him dark and melancholy. His wife noticed it with sadness. One day when she was driving with him in the Prater to divert and cheer him, and they both sat there alone, Mozart began to talk of death, and maintained that he was writing the Requiem for himself. Tears were in the eyes of this sensitive man. " I am only too conscious," he continued, " my end will not be long in coming : for sure, someone has poisoned me ! I cannot rid my mind of this thought.—"

This speech fell heavily on his wife's heart ; she was scarcely able to comfort him, and to show him the groundlessness of his heavy imaginings. As she was of the opinion that he was sickening for some illness, and the Requiem was over-straining his sensitive nerves, she called the doctor and took away the score of the Requiem.

His condition really did improve a little, and he was then able to write a small cantata which had been commissioned for a festival by a society.

The happy completion of this work, and the great applause with which it was received, revived his spirits. He became rather more gay, and constantly asked to be allowed to continue and finish his Requiem. His wife now had no objection to returning his music to him.

But this hopeful improvement was of short duration ; in a very few days he fell into a melancholy, grew feebler and weaker, until he at last collapsed completely on to his sickbed, from which, alas ! he was never to rise.

On the day of his death he had the score brought to his bed. " Did I not say that I was writing this Requiem for myself ? ", he said, and carefully looked through the whole score with moist eyes. It was the last painful, parting glance at his beloved art—a presentiment of his immortality !

Immediately after his death the messenger announced himself, asked for the work, unfinished as it was, and received it. From that moment the widow did not see him again, nor did she learn the least thing about the Requiem or the man who had commissioned it. Every reader can imagine for himself that they tried hard to seek out the mysterious messenger, but all means and attempts were fruitless.

During his illness Mozart maintained full consciousness right up to his end, and he died at peace, though very unwillingly. Everyone will find this understandable who considers that Mozart had shortly before received the decree appointing him Kapellmeister of St Stephen's Cathedral with all the emoluments which from time immemorial are connected with it, and now at last had the bright prospect of being able to live without the fear of starvation, and with a sufficient income. At almost the same time he also received from Hungary and Amsterdam considerable orders and commissions for the periodic delivery of certain compositions.

This strange coincidence of favourable omens for a better fate—his present sad financial plight—the picture of a comfortless widow—the thought of two young children : all this was not likely to sweeten the bitterness of death to an admired artist, who had never been a stoic, in his 35th year. " I must go ", he often lamented in his illness, " just at the very time when I could live in peace ! I must now leave my art when I, no longer the slave of fashion, no longer bound by speculators, would be free to follow the promptings of my sensitivity, could write freely and independently what my heart tells me ! I must leave my family and my poor children at the moment when I would be in a position to care better for their welfare ! " His death followed in the night of 5 December 1791. The doctors were not agreed about the cause of his death. It may be said that untold tears were shed for Mozart ; not only in Vienna, perhaps still more in Prague, where he was loved and admired. Every connoisseur and lover of music considered his loss to be irrepleaceable. . . .

Pp. 31 ff. of the *Lebensbeschreibung* of Mozart (1808), which represents a second edition of the *Leben* of 1798, where the part quoted (pp. 21 ff.) shows slight differences. (Reprint of the first edition, with variants of the second, edited by Ernst Rychnovsky [Prague, 1905].)—The "Symphony" from *Figaro* was of course the overture. Niemetschek made use of Schachtner's memoirs (see 24 April 1792) and Schlichtegroll's *Nekrolog* of 1793, perhaps also of Maria Anna von Berchtold's memoirs of the spring of 1792.—The symphony in E♭ major (K. 543), was not performed at Mozart's Prague concert : it was not composed till 1788.—The cantata was the *Kleine Freimaurer-Kantate.*— Walsegg, who commissioned the Requiem, later got into touch with Constanze.—Mozart did not live to be appointed Cathedral Kapellmeister.

FROM THE MEMOIRS OF PLACIDUS SCHARL, ANDECHS, 1808

. . . And I nearly forgot to mention young Wolfgang Mozart, a true musical prodigy. Even in the 6th year of his age he would play the most difficult pieces for the pianoforte, of his own invention. He skimmed the octave which his short little fingers could not span, at fascinating speed and with wonderful accuracy. One had only to give him the first subject which came to mind for a fugue or an invention : he would develop it with strange variations and constantly-changing passages as long as one wished ; he would improvise fugally on a subject for hours, and this fantasia-playing was his greatest passion. His sister was a great pianist but she only played the pieces of other masters : Wolfgang was at once author and performer ; he would extemporize with inexhaustible inspiration and it was in this that he shewed the creative genius which later brought him such great approbation in Vienna, The Hague and London. Out of him grew the great composer whose works are still admired : it is only to be regretted that this genius withered away so swiftly. It is none the less a subject for admiration that he was able to produce so many Operas, Masses, popular pieces and other musical works in the short span of his life. Everything he played was worthy to be written down, and he had an unusual facility in composition. His Requiem, which he left unfinished and which Joseph Haydn is said to have completed, was his last work : he often wept over its composition and would say : "That is my own Requiem . . ."

I quite often had the opportunity to admire the musical talent of the young Herr Mozart and to offer him small tokens of esteem in return for the entertainment he gave me. He promised to compose something especially for me. But I bear him no ill will for not keeping his word, because of the excessive preoccupations with which he was burdened every minute of the day. He was too much harassed to be able to be of service to everyone.

P. Placidus Scharl, *Meine, eines Mönches merkwürdige Lebensumstände . . . von mir im 77. Lebensjahre aufrichtigst beschrieben III* (3rd Part).—Andechs, Klosterarchiv, MS. No. 83, pp. 194-96.—See 6 January 1763.—Bauerreiss, *op. cit.,* pp. 85 f.—P. Magnus Sattler made use of the "Diary" in his biography of Scharl (Regensburg, 1868), p. 157, and after him Abert, Vol. I, pp. 30 f.

On 26 June 1809 Constanze and Nissen were married in Bratislava Cathedral.

The second of Napoleon's two sieges of Vienna (1805 and 1809) even caused diplomats to leave the city for a time. It was for this reason that Nissen and

Constanze went to Bratislava and were there finally married in anticipation of their removal to Copenhagen. (*Cf.* Ernst Weizmann in the *Arbeiter-Zeitung* [Vienna], 1 March 1959.) From the spring of 1808 they had lived for a year in the Landstrasse suburb, and when they returned from Bratislava in mid August 1809 they took lodgings Unter den Tuchlauben, where they remained until their departure for Copenhagen at the end of July 1810.

NIKOLAUS NISSEN TO KARL MOZART IN MILAN, VIENNA, 13 JUNE 1810

. . . You are aware that your great father left no fortune, only debts and an insignificant personal estate, which latter yielded far less than was promised to your mother in the marriage contract. Since then it has been taxed, and moreover it was left to your mother to determine and to place on deposit for her children a certain sum according to this settlement. This amount was 200 gulden each.

. . . By means of her tours, by means of the performance of concerts, as well as by means of the sale of the original scores of your late father (in whose autograph she now has only a number of most valuable fragments and sketches) your mother has been fortunate enough not only to settle the debts but also to amass a *small* capital. God willing, this sum will not be reduced, and you may expect a half-share at a juncture, which you and I desire may be as far distant as possible. She will continue to draw benefit from the interest or revenue of it ; but the deeds of this capital will remain here until further notice ; they are deposited with the merchant Johann Georg von Scheidlin.

Rudolf von Lewicki in *Mozarteums-Mitteilungen* (Salzburg, May 1919), Year I, No. 3, pp. 23 f.—Scheidlin was in Mozart's time cashier of the Imperial and Royal Privileged Warehouse Deputies.

On 27 July 1810 Nissen and Constanze left Vienna and settled in Copenhagen.

Nissen had already resigned his office of chargé d'affaires in Vienna on 15 February, for reasons of health, and was now appointed censor of political newspapers in Copenhagen, where he lived in the Lenadelsgade. On 13 October he was elected a Danish Councillor of State. The award of the Order of the Danebrog on 28 January 1809 did not ennoble him, but this did not prevent Constanze from calling him and herself " von Nissen " thereafter. (Erich Valentin in t he *Neues Mozart-Jahrbuch*, Year II [Regensburg, 1942].)

CONSTANZE NISSEN TO KARL MOZART, COPENHAGEN, 29 DECEMBER 1810

. . . All the money which I, your mother, have with toil and tenacity acquired, and which my present husband has helped to augment, has, after payment of the debts which your father left, been invested in Vienna. As the present rate of exchange here is so extraordinarily low, it would be unpardonable and unwise and disadvantageous to touch this capital. Otherwise I could even now (not just lend but) make over into your possession

M.—17

your half share. Your brother's half, however, would have to remain untouched. As things stand at present, we will leave the interest as it is, in the hope that one day it will amount to more than it does now, when one ducat is exchanged against 54 florins paper money.

> Lewicki, *op. cit.*, p. 28.—The depreciation of money in Austria led in 1811 to the introduction of the so-called Viennese currency.

FROM FELIX JOSEPH LIPOWSKY'S "BAIERISCHES MUSIK-LEXIKON", MUNICH, 1811

Schack composed the following operas in Vienna : (a) *Una cosa rara*, Part II ; (b) *Stein der Weisen* ; (c) *die Wiener Zeitung*.

These opera scores won for him the inestimable acquaintance of the immortal Mozart, and renewed the earlier benevolence of the great Joseph Hayden.

Mozart often came to take Schack for a walk, and while the latter was dressing, Kapellmeister Mozart would sit down at his desk and compose a piece here and there in his operas. Thus in Schack's operas several passages occur which reveal Mozart's hand and genius ; this great composer was so kind and well-disposed towards Schack that he also lent him several books to read about music, as well as scores to study by Händel, Emanuel and Sebastian Bach, etc. Mozart wrote Tamino in *die Zauberflöte* especially for Schack ; he sang and played this role 116 times in Vienna. Schack enjoyed this great artist's friendship until his [Mozart's] death.

> Pp. 300 f.—Of the three operas named, the music of the first is entirely by Schack (Freihaus Theatre, 10 May 1790), that of the second by Schack, Johann Baptist Henneberg and (K. 625) Mozart (11 September 1790), that of the third by Schack and Gerl (12 January 1791).—The " sang and played " probably refers not to Tamino's flute-playing, but merely to his singing and acting. —*Cf.* under 1827.

FROM THE "ALLGEMEINE MUSIKALISCHE ZEITUNG", LEIPZIG, 13 OCTOBER 1813

Fragments from [Johann Friedrich] Reichardt's Autobiography.

(4) His first visit to Vienna.

. . . Reichardt at that time saw in Vienna *Così fan tutte*, by Mozart, the *Barbier von Sevilla*, by Paesiello . . .

Joseph . . . knew the first numbers of Reichardt's *Kunstmagazin* . . . The Emperor and his brother each had his own full wind band, and as they heard that Reichardt was particularly taken by these, they promised him that he should one morning hear both groups playing together in the Small Assembly Hall. This duly took place, and afforded a wholly delightful pleasure. The atmosphere and the performances were alike pure and harmonious : some movements by Mozart were also exquisite. Unfortunately nothing by Haydn was performed . . .

Col. 665, 666 and 668.—Reichardt stayed in Vienna for some weeks during the summer of 1783. The first performance of the *Barbiere* there dates from this period, but *Die Entführung* was not given at this time, and *Così fan tutte* did not appear until 1790.—The *Musikalisches Kunst-Magazin* appeared from 1782 to 1791.—The Emperor Joseph's brother was Archduke Maximilian (see 15 October 1762 and 23 April 1775).

FROM SULPIZ BOISSERÉE'S DIARY, HEIDELBERG, NOVEMBER 1815

Detouche, Prince Wallerstein's Kapellmeister, is on a visit to us . . . He was with Mozart for seven years. The latter was a man of quite small stature, and very capricious. All his operas were a failure in Vienna except *Die Zauberflöte. Idomeneus,* his largest opera, he composed for Munich. At fourteen he wrote the little opera in one act, *Der Musikdirektor. Die Entführung,* written at the age of seventeen in Munich, made his name in Vienna. There he became third Kapellmeister with a salary of 600 florins. After *Die Entführung* he composed *Axur* for the wedding of Francis II and his first wife. Mozart used always to say of it : " It is a terrible opera." Then followed *Così fan tutte* and *Figaro.* Emperor Joseph was present at a rehearsal of *Figaro* ; the opera delighted him ; he asked Mozart why he did not write more operas for him. Mozart replied, pointing to the orchestra, " How on earth can I do anything with this collection of invalids ? You must go to Prague to hear real music ! " This of course doomed him to a complete failure, and he was even hissed : the Italian musicians united against him. Then came *Don Juan,* written for Prague, followed by *Die Zauberflöte, Titus* and lastly the Requiem. Detouche was with him when he wrote it ; usually the merriest of people, he now became melancholy and ailing and withdrew from life entirely ; he is said to have been given aqua toffana. He had already formed the desire to write a Requiem when along came a gentleman who wanted one for his friend, but for him alone, and paid 100 ducats at once. The man was never seen again.

The battle with the Italian musicians, particularly with Salieri, the first Kapellmeister, was a source of great pleasure to Mozart, and for this reason, although he was sure of a good reception in England, Spain, etc., he would not leave Vienna. He wanted to worry him to death. So when he had written a new work, he always used to say, " That will cost Salieri a pretty penny, that will make him pull at his purse strings " ; he meant, to have the work whistled off the boards. These intrigues cost Salieri a good 20,000 florins. His money came to him through his wife, a merchant's daughter. In the company of Paesiello, Martini, Salieri and Haydn etc. Mozart said to the last, with whom he was very friendly, " I will make an exception for you, but all other composers are veritable asses ! "

He was a passionate player of billiards, and played badly. Whenever a famous billiard-player arrived in Vienna, it was of more interest to him than the arrival of a famous musician. The latter, he opined, would come to him all right, the former he looked up himself; he played for high stakes, whole nights long. He was very thoughtless, but his wife excused him. She was a good pianist, and he loved her very dearly. He composed faster than the copyists could write it down, and all without playing or singing, etc., only now and then he struck a chord. He composed *Don Juan* in six weeks. He was always in need of money, and the many small pieces, sonatas and variations, were written for this reason. Artaria gave 25 ducats for every half-dozen variations. Manuscript paper was always lying there ready for him, so if he was passing and needed money, he had to write something. On one occasion he wanted to test whether the Viennese had any real love of art; he announced a concert for five o'clock in the morning in the Augarten; he sold a large number of tickets, but very few people were present.

Mozart bought six small Polish ponies which caused much comment; it was seemly only for princes, they said, to drive out with six horses. " Yes," he said, " if they *were* indeed horses; but these are only ponies, and there is no regulation about them." Joseph Haydn told him, " If you had only composed *Don Juan* it would be enough." For this Mozart dedicated his beautiful violin quartets to him. He wrote *Titus* for Prague; there was a male soprano there whom he could not tolerate, so he managed affairs in such a way that he could not help but be a failure, and he wrote the opera solely for Sextus and Vitellia, who paid him to place the emphasis on their roles alone; however, it was not his wont to act in this way. But he said then, " This time I will wrote an opera that is sure to fail ! "—

Sulpiz Boisserée, *Selbstbiographie, Tagebücher und Briefe*, ed. Mathilde Boisseré e (Stuttgart, 1862), Vol. I, pp. 292-4.—Schurig, *Mozart* (1923), Vol. II, pp. 484 f. (inaccurate and incomplete).—Franz Seraph von Destouches (Munich 1772-1844), composer and Kapellmeister, is said to have come to Vienna for a few years from 1787 to become a pupil of Haydn.—*Axur* was an opera by Salieri ; *Der Musikdirektor* is presumably *Der Schauspieldirektor*.—Aqua Tofana is a poison.—These reminiscences, which contain gross individual errors of fact, are also as a whole unreliable.—*Cf.* the following document.

KARL ANDREAS GÖPFERT TO THE DIRECTOR OF MUSIC TO PRINCE
OETTINGEN-WALLERSTEIN, 25 FEBRUARY 1817

(Offer of his arrangements of Haydn's *Creation*, Paer's *Sargino*, Mozart's *Zauberflöte* and Winter's *Unterbrochenes Opferfest* for wind band)

. . . As I have been studying music with the greatest fervour for some 20 years, and also enjoyed for $1\frac{1}{2}$ years the instruction of the immortal Mozart in the more advanced field of music theory, I always felt a preference for those instruments which are used in a wind ensemble, and for this reason my great teacher Mozart handed over to me the scores of all his operas, charging me to arrange them for wind band . .

Wallerstein, Prince Oettingen-Wallerstein Archives.—Ludwig Schiedermair, " Die Blütezeit der Oettingen-Wallerstein'schen Hofkapelle " in *Sammelbände der Internationalen Musikgesellschaft* (Leipzig, October–December 1907), pp. 115 f.—Göpfert (1768–1818) was a clarinet virtuoso and composer ; he eventually became a chamber musician in Sachsen-Meiningen. Nothing is otherwise known about his relations with Mozart.—Destouches was director of the Wallerstein Hofkapelle (see November 1815). The offer was declined.

NORBERT IGNAZ LOEHMANN TO FRANZ XAVER NIEMETSCHEK, PRAGUE, 1 MAY 1818

I herewith and at special request hand over the Mozzart theme together with its history. This virtuoso honoured the city of Prague with a visit in June 1787, in order to make the acquaintance of the musicians of this capital and to see the sights. He came to the Strahov Church one afternoon at 3 o'clock with Frau von Duschek, and expressed his desire to hear the organ. I, as assistant to the organist, was appointed by Prelate Wentzl Mayer to undertake this task. To be sure, I did not relish the task of playing before so great a master and composer ; yet I went to obey the order. Mozart sat *in navi ecclesiae* near to the pulpit. I let him hear the full power of the organ in the execution of a solemn theme. On its conclusion the virtuoso asked who had been playing the organ. Some of the priests who were with him replied, " A priest from our monastery ". Then he asked, " So there are organists among the priests ? "—" Yes ", answered Herr Matthias Ehrlich, then Patri . . . [the final syllable illegible] of the Gymnasium in the Small Side. Then he conceived the desire to play the organ himself. He mounted the console and played splendid chords, *pleno choro*, for approximately four minutes, and from these . . . [illegible word] every connoisseur could observe that he was no mean organist. After this he wanted to play the great without the swell and the choir. All 4 reed stops were too powerful for his liking. To the usual pedal without mixture he added the eight-foot trumpet. He now began a four-part fugue theme, which was the harder to perform in that it and its counter-subject consisted largely of mordents, which are exceptionally hard to perform on an organ with such a heavy action. But the 4th and 5th fingers of the right hand as well as of the left hand were as strong as the first [the thumb], second and third fingers, at which every one was much amazed. I concentrated my entire attention on the development of the theme, and would have been able to write it out to the end ; but the late Regens Chori, Father Lohelius, then came into the choir. He disturbed me so much with his questions that I lost the entire thread, just at the very moment when my attention was most necessary. Mozzart had soared up so high from G minor with the pedal and left hand, that he was able to continue in B minor. Lohelius of blessed memory interrupted me at that point, so that I could not tell how he modulated so swiftly into D sharp major. And now he wanted to conclude in this key, and therefore set about making a pedal-point. Holding a

B flat in the bass as his dominant, he attacked the two topmost octaves of the keyboard with both hands, gathering up so many notes and piling suspensions and resolutions on one another to such an extent that there he was playing in B major as beautifully as if it had been an F sharp that he was holding as his pedal. All his fingers were so fully employed, partly on account of the mordents, partly on account of the inner parts, that none of them was at rest for an instant. He did this with the intention that nothing should be heard of the pedals. Scarcely had I answered Lohelius's first questions, than a great many more had to be answered. He said, " My brother ".—" What is it ? "—" He is sustaining B flat on the pedal."—" Yes."—" He wants to modulate into D sharp major."—" Yes, of course."—" But he is playing in B major."—" Yes, I know."—" How can that harmonize ? "—" But it does." (Because in fact so many notes in the two upper octaves were making such a merciless din that one would not even have heard all four reeds. His 10 fingers skipped around in those 2 octaves as busily as when ants run about when their ant-hill has been destroyed.) Through these numerous questions I was deprived of the best and most artistic features whereby Mozzart revealed his strength in composition.

Then he developed the theme of a fugue from Brixi's Requiem in C minor in a quite different manner, it is true, but yet so artistically, that we stood there as if of stone. Each voice was given its due when it repeated the theme in another key, which was chiefly to be marvelled at with the tenor. When the bass lay too low and the tenor could not be managed by the left hand alone, the right hand had to help out with a few notes and fingers. If, Sir, you derive satisfaction from this trifling service, then I consider it a very great pleasure to oblige you in this way.

1 *May*
1818.

> From Niemetschek's posthumous papers ; published by Alfred Ebert in *Die Musik* (Berlin, November 1911), Year X, No. 2, pp. 106 ff., with the theme given in Köchel-Einstein at No. 528ª.—In 1787 Mozart was in Prague in the autumn, not in June.—The Strahov Monastery in Prague was a Premonstratensian foundation ; the Church of the Assumption belonged to it. Its organ was restored and improved by the prebendary and director of music, Johann Lohelius Oelschlägel (1744–88) in 1774.—Prebendary Norbert Loehmann (born 1750) was a member of the foundation from 1774 and a good organist.—Franz Xaver Brixi (Prague, 1732–71) ended his career as Kapellmeister in the cathedral in Prague ; he seems to have composed only one Requiem.

FROM JOHANN DEBROIS'S " URKUNDE ÜBER DIE VOLLZOGENE KRÖNUNG
. . . LEOPOLD DES ZWEITEN . . .", PRAGUE, 1818

. . . For the evening of this festal day [6 September 1791] a great opera seria was prepared by the Estates. The public was informed on 3 September by a printed announcement in what manner the tickets would be distributed.

The distribution itself took place on 5 September and in the morning of
the 6th . . . Moreover, a special ordinance concerning the arrangements
for the arrival and departure of carriages was also published on 3 September.
The Estates had chosen the Singspiel *La Clemenza di Tito* with text by the
hitherto unrivalled Italian opera poet Abbate Metastasio, and commissioned
the music for it from the composer at the Imperial Court, Wolfgang Mozart,
whose name every connoisseur of music utters with awe. The first three
sets were the product of the ingenuity of Peter Travaglia, who was in the
service of His Excellency, Anton, Prince Esterhazy ; the fourth was of
the invention of Preisig, of Coblenz. The costumes, designed by Cherubin
Babbini of Mantua, were remarkable for their novelty and richness. The
performance of this Italian serious Singspiel began at 7 o'clock. The usual
theatre guard was doubled, a division of Carabinieri was in occupation of
the proper posts, and the fire-fighting arrangements were strengthened.
Their Majesties the King and Queen with the Royal Family honoured the
National Theatre with their presence, and were welcomed with acclamation.
The house was as full as it could be without occasioning a crush, the best
places being made over to visitors in accordance with Prague's well-known
courtesy. The Singspiel itself was received with the applause which poet,
composer and singers, especially the famous Todi, most thoroughly deserved ; and it seemed that Their Majesties left the Theatre well pleased.

    Pp. 109 f.—Freisauff, *op. cit.*, p. 123.—The famous Luzia Todi returned to
her native land of Portugal in 1789 ; she never sang in Prague.

FROM JOSEPH WEIGL'S AUTOBIOGRAPHY, 1819

    . . . As I felt no interest in medicine, he [my father] allowed me to
study law. At that time the Director of Studies was Baron van Swieten,
who was at once a great connoisseur of music & had himself studied composition with the famous Prussian Kapellmeister Kirnberger. Every Sunday
at 12 noon there was music at his apartments. Only compositions by Bach,
Haendel & Graun, & by the earliest & most famous masters were given.
Mozart accompanied at the fortepiano, Salieri, Starzer, Teiber & the Baron
sang.
No one can imagine this pleasure. To hear Mozart play the most difficult
scores with his own inimitable skill, & sing the while, & correct the mistakes of the others, could not but excite the greatest admiration. . . .
    . . . Thus it was that I accompanied Mozart's *Figaro*, *D. Juan* etc. for all
rehearsals & to his satisfaction, & after the first 3 performances, which
Mozart himself directed from the keyboard, I had to take over his place
for all subsequent performances. . . .

    Copy in the National Library, Vienna.—*Jahresbericht des Wiener Konserva-
toriums für Musik*, New Series, Vol. VII, 1866–67, pp. 4 f.—This autobiography,
which Weigl's son copied, had been concluded on 23 May 1819.—Weigl
was a pupil of Salieri, who had introduced him into the Opera orchestra in

1785. When Mozart in 1787 took over the direction of van Swieten's orchestra after Joseph Starzer's death (22 April), Weigl succeeded him as clavier player. (But at the performances of C. P. E. Bach's cantata *Auferstehung und Himmelfahrt Jesu* on 26 February and 4 March 1788 the clavier was played by Umlauf.) —That Weigl took over the conducting of *Figaro* from Mozart was widely known ; but it is probably not generally known that this was also the case with *Don Giovanni* ; in that of *Così fan tutte* there can be no certainty.—The Gesellschaft der Musikfreunde in Vienna possesses a MS. biography of Weigl by Eduard von Lannoy, based on the autobiography. We read there in place of our second paragraph :

> " Those who never saw Mozart play Handelian scores of 16 or more staves with inimitable dexterity, and at the same time heard him sing and correct the other singers' faults, do not know him thoroughly, for he was as great there as in his compositions. One always heard a whole orchestra."

MARIANNE VON BERCHTOLD TO JOSEPH SONNLEITHNER

Sir,

I received your esteemed letter of 23 June on 26 June, I take pleasure in lending you one of the three portraits for copying, but as I do not know the artist Kraft personally, nor can judge her skill, and also do not feel I can undertake such a task because of my rather poor health and my age, I asked Councillor von Drossdick to take over this matter completely. He sent the artist to me to see all 3 pictures, the one that was painted when he came back from the Italian journey is the oldest, he was then just 16 years old, but as he had just got up from a serious illness, the picture looks sickly and very yellow ; the picture in the family portrait when he was 22 years old is very good, and the miniature, when he was 26 years old, is the most recent I have, I therefore shewed this one to the painter first ; it seemed to me from her silence that it would not be very easy to enlarge it, I therefore had to shew her the family portrait and the other one too ; as she was comparing the miniature with the representation in the family picture, and looking at them, she said they were both quite alike, only that the little one looks rather older ; and because it is painted in profile, the lineaments and colour being otherwise quite alike, she wants to take her copy from the family portrait and introduce only those features from the small picture which make him look somewhat older than in the big picture.

The artist on leaving me went straight to Councillor von Drossdick to tell him ; you will therefore perhaps receive a letter from him by the same post to which I entrust this letter of mine. What I do not like at all in this matter is the fact that the painter cannot copy the picture from the family portrait at my home, but it must be taken to her, it is very difficult to take it away without any damage being done to it, especially down the narrow stairs, [but] she is prepared to guarantee its safety. – – You must send Councillor von Drossdick the measurements of the height and breadth, you must have forgotten to enclose them in [your] letter, for I did not find them

It delights me really very much that you knew my brother personally, Sir, and that he accorded you pleasant hours . . .

Forgive me this long letter and my inadequate writing, it is my custom to write quickly and thus words always get left out.

I am, Sir, your obedient servant

> Maria Anna, Baroness Berchtold zu Sonnenburg
> widow of the Councillor and Prefect for St. Gilgen

Salzburg, the 2nd July, 1819

[Address :]

To the Imperial Court Agent and Councillor in the Lower Austrian Administration, Herr Joseph von Sonnleithner

Vienna

residing in

the Graben, No. 1200

> Autograph collection of the late Karl Geigy-Hagenbach, Basle.—O. E. Deutsch in *Bergland* (Innsbruck, August 1936), Year XVIII, No. 8, pp. 2-5, with reproduction in colour of Barbara Krafft's Mozart portrait on the title-page.—The letter, which had until then been but partly known, was quoted as having been addressed to Leopold (later von) Sonnleithner, Joseph's nephew.—Joseph Sonnleithner owned a collection of portraits in oils of well-known composers, which passed to the Vienna Gesellschaft der Musikfreunde. The portrait of Mozart by the prominent woman painter, who was then living in Salzburg, has in recent times become well known. Although not painted direct from life, it is today regarded as one of the few faithful likenesses of Mozart.—The " family portrait " is that by Johann Nepomuk della Croce, the " miniature painting " probably the lost small version of Joseph Lange's portrait, and the " earliest ", which was owned by Marianne, perhaps the miniature on ivory said to have been painted by Martin Knoller in Milan in 1773. (This and the group portrait are in the Mozart Museum at Salzburg.)

FROM CHARLES BURNEY'S MOZART ARTICLE IN ABRAHAM REES'S
" CYCLOPÆDIA ", LONDON, 1819

(in English)

During his residence in London we had frequent opportunities of witnessing his extraordinary talents and profound knowledge in every branch of music at eight years old, when he was able to play at sight in all clefs, to perform extempore, to modulate, and play fugues on subjects given in a way that there were very few masters then in London able to do.

> Percy A. Scholes, *The Great Dr. Burney* (London, 1948), Vol. I, p. 123.—*The Cyclopædia ; or, Universal Dictionary of Art, Science, and Literature* originally came out in parts between January 1802 and September 1819. Burney's articles on the Mozarts appeared early in 1813; he died in the following year.

In the autumn of 1820 Nissen and Constanze left Copenhagen for Salzburg.

> The couple at first stayed at Gastein, where Nissen took the cure for the first time. They then moved to the house of the Salzburg Burgomaster Anton Heffter on the Marktplatz (now Alter Markt 5).

M.—17 *a*

FROM JOHANN PETER ECKERMANN'S " GESPRÄCHE MIT GOETHE ",
23 APRIL 1823

With Goethe alone in the evening . . . We spoke . . . about the text
of *Die Zauberflöte*, of which Goethe wrote the sequel, but for which he
has not yet found a composer able to treat the subject adequately. He
admits that the well-known first part is full of improbabilities and jokes
which not everyone is capable of understanding and appreciating ; but it
must in any case be admitted that the author understood to a high degree
the art of making effective use of contrasts and of producing great theatrical
effects.

> Goethe, who in his epic poem *Hermann und Dorothea* of 1797 mentioned *Die
> Zauberflöte*, had begun a sequel to it as early as 1795 ; in the following year
> he corresponded with Paul Wranitzky, the " orchestra director " (Konzert-
> meister) of the Vienna Court Opera about its musical setting. His libretto,
> however, remained unfinished.

★   FROM BEETHOVEN'S " KONVERSATIONSHEFTE ", NOVEMBER 1823

Johann Schickh : Salieri has cut his own throat, but is still alive.

> German State Library, Berlin, Heft 95.—Friedrich Kerst, *Die Erinnerungen an
> Beethoven*, 2nd edn. (Stuttgart, 1925), Vol. II, pp. 282 f. (These references
> are also valid for the three further quotations from entries written by visitors
> to the deaf Beethoven—end of 1823, 1824, and May 1825.)—Schickh was the
> publisher of the *Wiener Zeitschrift für Kunst, Literatur, Theater und Mode.*—
> Salieri's mind failed in the autumn of 1823, and his attempt to cut his own
> throat was probably the first symptom of his last illness.

★   IBID., END OF 1823

Johann Schickh : The odds are one hundred to one that Salieri's conscience has spoken the truth ! The manner of Mozart's death confirms this
statement !

> For sources, see November 1823 ; Heft 124.—The old rumour of Mozart's
> having been poisoned had arisen again.

Between 1823 and 1827 Da Ponte's *Memorie* were published in four volumes in
New York (see 1829–30).

DR EDUARD GULDENER VON LOBES TO GIUSEPPE CARPANI, VIENNA,
10 JUNE 1824
(in Italian)

LETTER FROM COUNSELLOR GULDNER, AUSTRIAN FIRST PHYSICIAN.

It is with pleasure that I communicate to you, most excellent Sir, all
that is known to me of the illness and death of Mozart. He fell sick in the
late autumn of a rheumatic and inflammatory fever, which being fairly
general among us at that time, attacked many people. I did not know
about it until a few days later, when his condition had already grown

much worse. I did not visit him for some reason, but informed myself of his condition through Dr Closset, with whom I came in contact almost every day. The latter considered Mozart's illness to be dangerous, and from the very beginning feared a fatal conclusion, namely a deposit on the brain. One day he met Dr Sallaba and he said positively, " Mozart is lost, it is no longer possible to restrain the deposit ". Sallaba communicated this information to me at once, and in fact Mozart died a few days later with the usual symptoms of a deposit on the brain. His death aroused general interest, but the very slightest suspicion of his having been poisoned entered no one's mind. So many persons saw him during his illness, so many enquired after him, his family tended him with so much care, his doctor, highly regarded by all, the industrious and experienced Closset, treated him with all the attention of a scrupulous physician, and with the interest of a friend of many years' standing, in such a way that certainly it could not have escaped their notice then if even the slightest trace of poisoning had manifested itself. The illness took its accustomed course and had its usual duration ; Closset had observed it and recognized it with such accuracy that he had forecast its outcome almost to the hour. This malady attacked at this time a great many of the inhabitants of Vienna, and for not a few of them it had the same fatal conclusion and the same symptoms as in the case of Mozart. The statutory examination of the corpse did not reveal anything at all unusual.

That is the sum of what I am in a position to state concerning the death of Mozart. I shall have the greatest pleasure if this can contribute to giving the lie to the horrible calumny on the excellent Salieri. It remains for me only to beg you, most illustrious Sir, to excuse me for not communicating to you at once these few lines. My preoccupation with new cases, and an extended indisposition which was somewhat allayed only by a blood-letting, have constantly opposed new obstacles to my better intentions.

> With the greatest respect
> Dobling, 10 June 1824.   Your obdt. servant
>   Guldner.

Biblioteca Italiana (Milan, August 1824), Year IX, No. XXXV, p. 275.—Nissen, pp. 575 f. ; Jahn, Vol. II, p. 702.—Carpani, one of the first biographers of Joseph Haydn, lived in Vienna and published in this Italian quarterly a defence of the mentally deranged Salieri against the rumour, then gaining ground, of his having poisoned Mozart. (*Cf.* O. E. Deutsch in *Schweizerische Musikzeitung* [Zürich], January 1957.) One of the appendices to his article was this letter from Guldener, which Nissen incompletely and imperfectly retranslated into German, and which Jahn quoted from his version. Guldener, who lived in the Vienna suburb of Döbling in the summer, must have occupied an official medical post about 1791 the nature of which has not so far been determined ; in 1797 he became junior City Health Officer and rather later the senior one, being appointed Medical Superintendent for Lower Austria in 1814.—See 25 May 1825. For Closset and Sallaba *cf.* 28 November 1791.

Karl van Beethoven : Salieri maintains that he poisoned Mozart. Anton Schindler : Salieri is very ill again. He is quite deranged. In his ravings he keeps claiming that he is guilty of Mozart's death and made away with him by poison.—This is the truth—for he wants to make confession of it—, so it is true once again that everything has its reward.

> For sources, see November 1823 ; Heft 125.—Beethoven's nephew and his factotum agree in their versions of the rumours that were then circulating in Vienna. The report that Salieri is alleged to have desired to confess his crime has recently led to the unauthenticated claim that Salieri's confession is preserved in a Vienna church archive.

SOPHIE HAIBEL TO NISSEN, A CONTRIBUTION TO HIS MOZART BIOGRAPHY

D. [Djakovo], the 7th April 1825.

. . . Now to Mozart's last days. M:t became ever more fond of our late mother and she of him too, so M. often hurried over to the Wieden suburb (where our mother & I lodged at the Golden Plough) with a bag under his arm in which were coffee and sugar, handed it to our good mother and said, " Here, dear mother, is a little snack for you." This delighted her as it would a child. This happened very often. In brief, M. never again came to us empty-handed.

Now, when Mozart fell ill, we both made him a night-shirt which he could put on from the front, for he could not turn over because of the swelling ; and as we did not know how very ill he was, we also made him a quilted dressing-gown (for all of which his good wife, my dear sister, gave us the material) so that he would be well protected when he got up, and so we visited him diligently ; he made it plain that he was greatly delighted by the dressing-gown. I went to visit him in the city every day, and once when I went in on a Saturday, M. said to me, " Now, dear Sophie, tell Mama that I am getting on very well, and that I will be coming out to her in the octave of her name-day to give her my congratulations." Whose joy could be greater than mine when I brought my mother such glad tidings, after she could scarcely expect the news ; so I hurried home to calm her fears, after he had really seemed to me to be cheerful and well. The next day was a Sunday, then ; I was still young and, I admit it, vain —and I liked dressing up, but I never liked walking from our suburb into the town in my best clothes, and I had not the money for going by carriage ; so I said to our good mother, " Dear Mama, I shan't go in to Mozart today —he was so well yesterday, so he'll be better still today, and one day more or less will make no difference." She then said, " I'll tell you what, make me a cup of coffee, and then I'll tell you what you can do." She was rather concerned to keep me at home, for my sister knows how much she always wanted me to be with her. So I went into the kitchen. The fire had gone out ; I had to light a taper and kindle the fire. But Mozart was still constantly on my mind. My coffee was ready, and my candle was still burning. I then saw how wasteful I had been to have burnt so much of my candle. The candle was still burning brightly, and I stared straight at my candle and thought, " I wonder how Mozart is?", and as I was thinking this, and looking at my candle, the candle went out, it went out as if it had never been alight. Not even a spark remained on the big wick, there was no draught, to that I can swear ; I shuddered, ran to our mother, and told her. She said, " All right, hurry up and take those clothes off and go in [to see him], but come and tell me straight away how he is. Now don't be long." I hurried as fast as I could. My God ! how frightened I was when my sister, half demented yet trying to control herself, came to meet me and said, " Thank God you've come, dear Sophie ; he was so bad last night that I never thought he would survive this day. Stay with me today, for if he gets bad again today, he will die in the night. Go in to him for a little and see how he is." I tried to control myself and went up to his bed, when he called to me at once, " Ah, dear Sophie, it is good of you to come. You must stay here tonight, you must see me die." I tried to be strong and to dissuade him, but he answered to all my attempts, " I have the taste of death on my tongue already", and " Who will look after my dearest Constance if you don't stay ? "—" Yes, dear Mozart, but I must first just go and tell our mother that you would like me with you tonight, or she will think some misfortune has happened."—" Yes, do that, but come back soon."—God, how awful I felt. My poor sister came after me and begged me for heavens' sake to go to the priests at St Peter's and ask [one of] the priests to come, as if on a chance visit. That I also did, though the priests hesitated a long time and I had great difficulty in persuading one of these inhuman priests to do it. – – Then I hurried to our mother, who was anxiously awaiting me ; it was already dark. How frightened the poor dear was. I persuaded her to go and spend the night with her eldest daughter, Hofer, who is now dead, and so it was ; and I ran back as fast as I could to my inconsolable sister. Sissmaier was there at M's bedside ; and the well-known Requiem lay on the coverlet, and Mozart was explaining to him how he thought he should finish it after his death. Then he commanded his wife to keep his death a secret until she had informed Albregtsberger of it ; for the post was his by right in the eyes of God and the world. There was a long search for Glosett, the doctor, who was found in the theatre ; but he had to wait till the play was over—then he came and prescribed *cold* compresses on his burning head, and these gave him such a shock that he did not regain consciousness before he passed away. The last thing he did was to try and mouth the sound of the timpani in his Requiem ; I can still hear it now. Then Müller came from the art gallery directly and took a plaster cast of his pale and lifeless face. Dear brother, I cannot possibly describe the boundless misery of his faithful wife as she threw herself on her knees and implored succour from the Almighty. She could not tear herself from him, beg her as I did ; if her grief had been susceptible of increase it must have been increased on the day after that dreadful night by people passing by in crowds, lamenting and weeping for him loudly. I never in all my life saw M. in a temper, much less really angry. . . . My dear, forgive me if I have been diffuse in my letter ; but I cannot recall if I ever related the incident with the light, which impressed itself so deeply upon my mind, to my sister, as I was always careful not to re-open her wounds. Oh, how attentive M-t was when something was wrong with his dear wife. Thus it was once when she was seriously ill and I nursed her for 8 long months. I was just sitting by her bed, Mozart too. He was composing at her side ; I was observing her sweet slumber, which had been so long in coming. We kept as quiet as the grave so as not to disturb her. Suddenly, an unmannerly servant came into the room. Moz. was terrified that his dear wife might be disturbed from her gentle sleep, tried to beckon the man to keep quiet, pushed the chair back behind him, but happened to have his pen-knife open in his hand. This impaled itself between the chair and his thigh in such a way that it dug in up to the handle in the thick flesh. Moz., who usually made such a fuss, did not stir but, biting back his pain, he only signalled to me to follow him. We went to the room in which our mother was living secretly, for we did not want the good Mozart [Constanze] to realise how ill she was, and that her mother was there in case of need. She bound him up and put oil of cubebs into his very deep wound ; with this St John's oil she succeeded in healing him, and although he had to limp somewhat from the pain, he managed to conceal it and keep it from his dear wife. Write and tell me if you knew all [this] already.

Original in the possession of the Gesellschaft der Musikfreunde in Vienna.—
Nissen, pp. 573-5, 687 f.—*Mozarteums-Mitteilungen* (Salzburg, November 1918), Year I, No. 1, pp. 21-3.—The orthography is not exactly reproduced in the German edition, but the Salzburg reprint is literally accurate, as is also that in the new complete edition of the Mozart family correspondence, IV, 460-463 (1963).—Sophie, the youngest of the four Weber daughters, lived in Slavonia, where Jakob Haibel was choirmaster at the Cathedral of Djakovo, until she went to Salzburg to live with her sister after Nissen's death in 1826.—In about 1791 she was living with her mother in the main thoroughfare of the Wieden suburb (now No. 23), but her sister Josepha, like many members of the Schikaneder company, himself included, lived in the Freihaus.—Saturday was 3 December 1791.—(Maria) Cäcilia (Cordula) Weber celebrated her name-day on 22 November.—St. Peter's Church, off the Graben, was near "The Eye of God", where the Webers had lived in about 1780. The clergy are said to have hesitated about administering extreme unction because the patient had not himself asked for it (Nissen, p. 575). Mozart received extreme unction, but not the last sacrament. (Nissen's collectanea in the Mozarteum at Salzburg, partly published by Rudolf von Lewicki in *Mozarteums-Mitteilungen*, November 1919, p. 28.) Mozart's "post" was his appointment at St. Stephen's as assistant and successor to the Cathedral Kapellmeister.—Count Joseph Deym, alias Müller (see 26 March 1791) took Mozart's death mask,

which Constanze inadvertently broke later on.—In Nissen's biography of Mozart, pp. 575 and 627, other recollections of Sophie Haibel's are printed as well. The latter are cited under 1828, but the former, which relate to the letter and are in indirect speech, are given here :

" My sister-in-law thinks Mozart was not sufficiently well looked after in his illness, for instead of driving out the fever by other methods, they bled him and applied cold compresses to his head, whereupon his forces visibly forsook him and he lost consciousness, which he never again recovered. Even in his serious illness he never became impatient, and at the end his fine ear and feeling were still sensitive to the song of his pet, a canary, which even had to be removed from the next room, because it overtaxed his emotions."

* FROM BEETHOVEN'S " KONVERSATIONSHEFTE ", MAY 1825

Karl van Beethoven : Even now people still claim very forcefully that Salieri was Mozart's murderer.

For sources, see November 1823 ; Heft 25.—Salieri died on May 7 after nearly two years' confinement in his ward. *Cf.* following note.

FROM THE " ALLGEMEINE MUSIKALISCHE ZEITUNG ", LEIPZIG, 25 MAY 1825

Vienna. Music Diary for the Month of April.

Our worthy Salieri, to use the popular phrase, just can't die. His body suffers all the pains of infirm old age, and his mind has gone. In the frenzy of his imagination he is even said to accuse himself of complicity in Mozart's early death : a rambling of the mind believed in truth by no one other than the poor deluded old man himself. To Mozart's contemporaries it is unfortunately all too well known that only over-exertion at his work, and fast living in ill-chosen company, shortened his precious days !

Vol. XXVII, No. 27, col. 349 f.—*Cf.* 10 June 1824.—Carpani's article in defence of Salieri was also accompanied by the attestation of the two keepers who were with him day and night : neither of the two had ever heard such a self-accusation.—Carpani had died on 22 January 1825, Salieri on 7 May.

FROM JOHANN NEPOMUK HUMMEL'S SKETCH FOR A BIOGRAPHY OF MOZART, *ca.* 1825

. . . He was small of stature and of a rather pale complexion ; his physiognomy had much that was pleasant and friendly, combined with a rather melancholy graveness ; his large blue eyes shone brightly. In the circle of his good friends he could grow quite merry, lively, witty, even at times and on certain subjects satirical ! . . .

Karl Benyovszky, *J. N. Hummel* (Bratislava, 1934), pp. 32 and 186.—*Cf.* 20 and 21 May 1789, also 1873 and 1880.

* FROM JAKOB NEUKÄUFLER'S AUTOBIOGRAPHY, *ca.* 1825

[Vienna, 1782 :]

In addition Herr Compositeur Mozart had a copy of the *Entführung aus dem Serail* made for me ; I had only to pay the copyist's fee. I had got to know Herr Wolfgang Mozart in Salzburg, when he was still at his father's. He was always very friendly towards me.

> Konrad Schiffmann, *Aus dem Leben eines Wanderschauspielers : Jakob Neukäufler (1751–1835)* (Linz, 1930), pp. 73 f.—From the autumn of 1780 to Lent 1781 Neukäufler was with Schikaneder in Salzburg ; after a short time in Linz he came to Vienna in the autumn of 1781, and worked at the Leopoldstadt Theatre. In the autumn of 1782 he went to Strasbourg, where he passed on the score of Mozart's opera to the director, Joseph Koberwein.—It was performed there before the end of 1783 (and in 1801 in French).—The dates in Neukäufler's dictated autobiography are unreliable and have been corrected in our account. —He and his son Ferdinand (1785–1860) were engaged from 1795 at Schikaneder's Freihaus Theatre, where the boy, aged eight at the time, sang one of the Genii in *Die Zauberflöte*.

FROM THE MANUSCRIPT BIOGRAPHIES OF JOHANN GEORG ROSER VON REITER AND HIS SON FRANZ DE PAULA (COMPILED BY THE LATTER), VIENNA, *ca.* 1825

. . . A very pleasing little incident concerning Mozart deserves to be mentioned here. Whilst [Johann Georg] Roser was fulfilling his first function in the [Linz] Cathedral, performing a Mass for double choir of his own composition, Mozart came into the choir after the Gloria and asked Roser if he might be permitted to take over at the organ console. Roser, who did not know Mozart personally, asked him if he could play the organ well, as several fugal passages occurred in this Mass. Mozart assured him that he could, and they began the Credo. When it was finished, after the big fugue at " et vitam venturi ", Roser went over to the hero at the organ, and told him that he could be none other than Mozart ; Mozart's answer was : he was indeed none other. Roser had the good fortune to be able to entertain Mozart and his father in his own house for 11 days. Just at this time Roser was completing the pianoforte he had invented, which he called *Harmonie pour la parfait* [recte *l'harmonie parfaite*] . . . Mozart wrote 2 small pieces for this instrument during his sojourn with him ; unfortunately his manuscript fell a victim to the flames during the Linz fire of 1799.

. . . At Mozart's advice he [Franz de Paula Roser] came to Vienna in 1789 to study Latin, and furthermore to avail himself of Mozart's tuition ; but as Mozart often had to travel, and was later prevented by reasons of health from giving further tuition, he had only 32 lessons.

> MSS. in the Archives of the Gesellschaft der Musikfreunde, Vienna. Used by Aloys Fuchs for his article in the *Wiener allgemeine Musikzeitung*, 8 September 1842, and by Constant von Wurzbach in his *Lexikon*, Vol. XXVII, pp. 38 ff. (Vienna, 1874).—Unfortunately these statements can scarcely be

reconciled with the facts. Herr Roser senior, recommended by Leopold Mozart, became first cathedral Kapellmeister at Linz in 1787, that is, after Mozart's last visit (November 1783, with Constanze ; they stayed with Count Thun). The first six-manual pianoforte, invented by Herr Roser senior, was built in Brussels in 1785. The son left a description of the instrument and a copy of a rondo, part of the two compositions which Mozart is said to have written for this instrument.—Credence cannot be placed in the assertion that Herr Roser senior sang the first Papageno song to Mozart on his deathbed and was present at his burial (according to a journalistic article on *Die Zauberflöte* signed H-n and published in 1857).—Johann Georg Roser (1740–97) was never a theatre Kapellmeister, though his son Franz de Paula Roser (1779–1830), a many-sided composer, did hold this position. He was only ten when he came to Vienna, and about six when Mozart is reputed to have stayed with his father in Linz. (*Cf.* 20 November 1791 and Köchel-Einstein, p. 736.)—It is also to be remarked here that Franz de Paula Roser mentions in these recollections a Ludwig Gall (who in 1796 saw the second instrument built in Vienna by Roser's father) as having been a pupil of Mozart's ; Aloys Fuchs addresses him in this way in his dedication of a Mozart autograph. (*Cf.* Köchel/Einstein, p. 832.) Of Gall we know only that he was a civil servant *ca.* 1825 and that he arranged several works by Mozart for two pianofortes.

On 24 March 1826 Nissen died at Salzburg.

Constanze had him buried at the St. Sebastian cemetery, in Leopold Mozart's grave, where her aunt Genoveva Weber had also been laid.

FROM MAXIMILIAN STADLER'S " VERTHEIDIGUNG DER ECHTHEIT DES MOZART-ISCHEN REQUIEM " [DEFENCE OF THE AUTHENTICITY OF MOZART'S REQUIEM], VIENNA, 1826

. . , I enjoyed a friendly relationship with Mozart himself, and after his death was able to render his widow some assistance in respect of the manuscripts which her husband had left. She asked me in fact to put these papers in order. She wanted to send them to me at my lodgings. I declined, promising to visit her as often as time would allow me and, in the presence of her neighbour Herr von Nyssen, to go through, put in order and make a catalogue of all the music in the estate of the deceased. This did not take long, I read everything out, Herr von Nyssen carefully wrote everything down, and quickly brought the catalogue into being. It is well known that Herr André of Offenbach later purchased the entire estate . . .

> Pp. 9 f.—Stadler did not remove to Vienna till 1796 ; Nissen and he undertook the first sorting of the music in Mozart's estate in 1798, and a second, lesser, one in 1799, shortly before Johann Anton André acquired it. Nissen, who had come to Vienna in 1793, lived in the Franziskaner-Platz in the Inner City in 1799, and we know that Constanze had become his neighbour and housekeeper in 1798. The catalogue here mentioned by Stadler is printed in the appendix of his Mozart biography of 1828, where it appears as " Verzeichnis der in Mozarts Verlassenschaft gefundenen musicalischen Fragmente und Entwürfe, wie es grösstenteils von Abbé Maximilian Stadler verfasst worden " [" List of the musical Fragments and Sketches found in Mozart's

Estate, largely compiled by Abbé Maximilian Stadler "], and also as " Verzeichnis derjenigen Compositionen, welche Mozart ausser den hier angeführten
noch vollendet hinterlassen hat " [" List of Compositions, apart from those
entered here, which Mozart left in a finished state "].   The works entered
were those in Leopold Mozart's list of his son's early works and those enumerated in Mozart's own list of his works from 1784 till 1791. *Cf.* Köchel-
Einstein, p. XXVII.

FROM MICHAEL KELLY'S " REMINISCENCES ", LONDON, 1826
(in English)

. . . I went one evening to a concert of the celebrated Kozeluch's, a
great composer for the piano-forte, as well as a fine performer on that
instrument.   I saw there the composers Vanhall and Baron Dittersdorf ;
and, what was to me one of the greatest gratifications of my musical life,
was there introduced to that prodigy of genius—Mozart.   He favoured the
company by performing fantasias and capriccios on the piano-forte.   His
feeling, the rapidity of his fingers, the great execution and strength of his
left hand particularly, and the apparent inspiration of his modulations,
astounded me.   After his splendid performance we sat down to supper,
and I had the pleasure to be placed at table between him and his wife,
Madame Constance Weber, a German lady, of whom he was passionately
fond, and by whom he had three children.   He conversed with me a good
deal about Thomas Linley, the first Mrs. Sheridan's brother, with whom
he was intimate at Florence, and spoke of him with great affection.   He
said that Linley was a true genius ; and he felt that, had he lived, he would
have been one of the greatest ornaments of the musical world.   After supper
the young branches of our host had a dance, and Mozart joined them.
Madame Mozart told me, that great as his genius was, he was an enthusiast
in dancing, and often said that his taste lay in that art, rather than in music.
He was a remarkably small man, very thin and pale, with a profusion of
fine fair hair, of which he was rather vain.   He gave me a cordial invitation
to his house, of which I availed myself, and passed a great part of my time
there.   He always received me with kindness and hospitality.—He was
remarkably fond of punch, of which beverage I have seen him take copious
draughts.   He was also fond of billiards, and had an excellent billiard table
in his house.   Many and many a game have I played with him, but always
came off second best.   He gave Sunday concerts, at which I never was
missing.   He was kind-hearted, and always ready to oblige ; but so very
particular, when he played, that if the slightest noise were made, he instantly
left off.   He one day made me sit to the piano, and gave credit to my first
master, who had taught me to place my hand well on the instrument.—He
conferred on me what I considered a high compliment.   I had composed
a little melody to Metastasio's canzonetta, " Grazie agl' inganni tuoi ",
which was a great favourite wherever I sang it.   It was very simple, but

had the good fortune to please Mozart. He took it and composed variations upon it, which were truly beautiful ; and had the further kindness
and condescension to play them wherever he had an opportunity. Thinking that the air thus rendered remarkable might be acceptable to some of
my musical readers, I have subjoined it.

Encouraged by his flattering approbation, I attempted several little airs,
which I shewed him, and which he kindly approved of ; so much indeed,
that I determined to devote myself to the study of counterpoint, and consulted him, by whom I ought to be instructed.—He said, " My good lad,
you ask my advice, and I will give it you candidly ; had you studied
composition when you were at Naples, and when your mind was not
devoted to other pursuits, you would perhaps have done wisely ; but
now that your profession of the stage must, and ought, to occupy all your
attention, it would be an unwise measure to enter into a dry study. You
may take my word for it, Nature has made you a melodist, and you would
only disturb and perplex yourself. Reflect, ' *a little knowledge* is a dangerous
thing ' ;—should there be errors in what you write, you will find hundreds
of musicians, in all parts of the world, capable of correcting them ; therefore do not disturb your natural gift."

" Melody is the essence of music," continued he ; " I compare a good melodist to a fine racer, and counterpointists to hack post-horses ; therefore
be advised, let *well alone*, and remember the old Italian proverb—' Chi sa
più, meno sa—Who knows most, knows least '." The opinion of this
great man made on me a lasting impression.

My friend Attwood (a worthy man, and an ornament to the musical world)
was Mozart's favourite scholar, and it gives me great pleasure to record
what Mozart said to me about him ; his words were, " Attwood is a young
man for whom I have a sincere affection and esteem ; he conducts himself
with great propriety, and I feel much pleasure in telling you, that he par-
takes more of my style than any scholar I ever had ; and I predict, that
he will prove a sound musician." Mozart was very liberal in giving praise
to those who deserved it ; but felt a thorough contempt for insolent mediocrity. He was a member of the Philharmonic Society of Bologna and
Verona ; and when at Rome, the Pope conferred on him the Cross and
Brevet of Knight of Lo Sprone d' Ora [Speron d' oro] . . .

. . . Just at the same period, the celebrated Paesiello arrived at Vienna,
on his way to Naples, from Petersburg, where he had been some years,
and amassed very great wealth. I had the pleasure of seeing him introduced to Mozart ; it was gratifying to witness the satisfaction which they
appeared to feel by becoming acquainted ; the esteem which they had for
each other was well known. The meeting took place at Mozart's house ;
I dined with them, and often afterwards enjoyed their society together. . . .
. . . Storace gave a quartet party to his friends. The players were tolerable ; not one of them excelled on the instrument he played, but there was

a little science among them, which I dare say will be acknowledged when I name them :

The First Violin .	.	.	*Haydn.*
„ Second Violin	.	.	Baron *Dittersdorf.*
„ Violoncello .	.	.	*Vanhall.*
„ Tenor	.	.	*Mozart.*

The poet Casti and Paesiello formed part of the audience. I was there, and a greater treat, or a more remarkable one, cannot be imagined.

On the particular evening to which I am now specially referring, after the musical feast was over, we sat down to an excellent supper, and became joyous and lively in the extreme. . . .

. . . I had the pleasure, about this time, to be introduced to Monsieur Martini. He was a very old man. His sister, nearly his own age, kept his house for him. She was reckoned a deep blue, and very well versed in all the arts and sciences. The great poet Metastasio had lived *sixty years* in her brother's house, upon the most friendly terms, and died in it. The colleges of Bologna and Pavia gave her the title of Dottoressa ; and deputations came from both those places, with her diploma. When I was admitted to her conversaziones and musical parties, she was in the vale of years, yet still possessed the gaiety and vivacity of a girl, and was polite and affable to all. Mozart was an almost constant attendant at her parties, and I have heard him play duets on the piano-forte with her, of his own composition. She was a great favourite of his. . . .

. . . There was a very excellent company of German singers at the Canatore [Kärntnertor] Theatre ; it was more spacious than the Imperial Court Theatre. The first female singer was Madame Langé, wife to the excellent comedian of that name, and sister to Madame Mozart. She was a wonderful favourite, and deservedly so ; she had a greater extent of high notes than any other singer I ever heard. The songs which Mozart composed for her in *L'Enlèvement du Sérail*, shew what a compass of voice she had ; her execution was most brilliant. . . .

. . . Paesiello's *Barbiere di Siviglia*, which he composed in Russia, and brought with him to Vienna, was got up ; Signor Mandini and I played the part of Count Almaviva alternately ; Storace was the Rosina. There were three operas now on the tapis, one by Regini [Righini], another by Salieri (the *Grotta of Trophonius*), and one by Mozart, by special command of the Emperor. Mozart chose to have Beaumarchais' French comedy, *Le Mariage de Figaro*, made into an Italian opera, which was done with great ability, by Da Ponte. These three pieces were nearly ready for representation at the same time, and each composer claimed the right of producing his opera for the first. The contest raised much discord, and parties were formed. The characters of the three men were all very different. Mozart was as touchy as gunpowder, and swore he would put the score of his opera into the fire, if it was not produced first ; his claim was backed by a strong party : on the contrary, Regini was working like a mole in the dark to get precedence.

The third candidate was Maestro di Cappella to the Court, a clever shrewd man, possessed of what Bacon called, crooked wisdom ; and his claims were backed by three of the principal performers, who formed a cabal not easily put down. Every one of the opera company took part in the contest. I alone was a stickler for Mozart, and naturally enough, for he had a claim on my warmest wishes, from my adoration of his powerful genius, and the debt of gratitude I owed him, for many personal favours.

The mighty contest was put an end to by His Majesty issuing a mandate for Mozart's *Nozze di Figaro*, to be instantly put into rehearsal ; and none more than Michael O'Kelly, enjoyed the little great man's triumph over his rivals.

Of all the performers in this opera at that time, but one survives,—myself. It was allowed that never was opera stronger cast. I have seen it performed at different periods in other countries, and well too, but no more to compare with its original performance than light is to darkness. All the original performers had the advantage of the instruction of the composer, who transfused into their minds his inspired meaning. I never shall forget his little animated countenance, when lighted up with the glowing rays of genius ;—it is as impossible to describe it, as it would be to paint sunbeams.

I called on him one evening ; he said to me, " I have just finished a little duet for my opera, you shall hear it." He sat down to the piano, and we sang it. I was delighted with it, and the musical world will give me credit for being so, when I mention the duet, sung by Count Almaviva and Susan, " Crudel perchè finora farmi languire così ". A more delicious morceau never was penned by man ; and it has often been a source of pleasure to me, to have been the first who heard it, and to have sung it with its greatly-gifted composer. I remember at the first rehearsal of the full band, Mozart was on the stage with his crimson pelisse and gold-laced cocked hat, giving the time of the music to the orchestra. Figaro's song, " Non più andrai, farfallone amoroso ", Bennuci gave, with the greatest animation and power of voice.

I was standing close to Mozart, who, *sotto voce*, was repeating, Bravo ! Bravo ! Bennuci ; and when Bennuci came to the fine passage, " Cherubino, alla vittoria, alla gloria militar ", which he gave out with Stentorian lungs, the effect was electricity itself, for the whole of the performers on the stage, and those in the orchestra, as if actuated by one feeling of delight, vociferated Bravo ! Bravo ! Maestro. Viva, viva, grande Mozart. Those in the orchestra I thought would never have ceased applauding, by beating the bows of their violins against the music desks. The little man acknowledged, by repeated obeisances, his thanks for the distinguished mark of enthusiastic applause bestowed upon him.

The same meed of approbation was given to the finale at the end of the first act ; that piece of music alone, in my humble opinion, if he had never composed any thing else good, would have stamped him as the greatest master of his art. In the sestetto, in the second act, (which was Mozart's favourite piece of the whole opera,) I had a very conspicuous part, as the Stuttering Judge. All through the piece I was to stutter ; but in the sestetto, Mozart requested I would not, for if I did, I should spoil his music. I told him, that although it might appear very presumptuous in a lad like me to differ with him on this point, I did ; and was sure, the way in which I intended to introduce the stuttering, would not interfere with the other parts, but produce an effect ; besides, it certainly was not in nature, that I should stutter all through the part, and when I came to the sestetto, speak plain ; and after that piece of music was over, return to stuttering ; and, I added, (apologising at the same time, for my apparent want of deference and respect in placing my opinion in opposition to that of the great Mozart,) that unless I was allowed to perform the part as I wished, I would not perform it at all.

Mozart at last consented that I should have my own way, but doubted the success of the experiment. Crowded houses proved that nothing ever on the stage produced a more powerful effect ; the audience were convulsed with laughter, in which Mozart himself joined. The Emperor repeatedly cried out Bravo ! and the piece was loudly applauded and encored. When the opera was over, Mozart came on the stage to me, and shaking me by both hands, said, " Bravo ! young man, I feel obliged to you ; and acknowledge you to have been in the right, and myself in the wrong ". There was certainly a risk run, but I felt within myself I could give the effect I wished, and the event proved that I was not mistaken.

I have seen the opera in London, and elsewhere, and never saw the Judge portrayed as a stutterer, and the scene was often totally omitted. I played it as a stupid old man, though at the time I was a beardless stripling. At the end of the opera, I thought the audience would never have done applauding and calling for Mozart ; almost every piece was encored, which prolonged it nearly to the length of two operas, and induced the Emperor to issue an order, on the second representation, that no piece of music should be encored. Never was anything more complete than the triumph of Mozart, and his *Nozze di Figaro*, to which numerous overflowing audiences bore witness.

One morning, while we were rehearsing in the grand saloon of the palace, His Majesty, accompanied by Prince Rosenberg, entered the saloon, and addressing himself to Storace, Mandini, and Bennuci, said, " I dare say, you are all pleased, that I have desired there shall be no more encores ; to have your songs so often repeated, must be a great fatigue, and very distressing to you." Storace replied, " It is indeed, Sire, very distressing, very much so ; " the other two bowed, as if they were of the same opinion. I was close to His Majesty, and said boldly to him, " Do not believe them,

Sire, they all like to be encored, at least I am sure I always do." His Majesty laughed, and I believe he thought there was more truth in my assertion, than in theirs. I am sure there was. . . .

. . . I went to take leave of the immortal Mozart, and his charming wife and family ; he gave me a letter to his father, Leopold Mozart, who was at the Court of Saltzbourg. I could hardly tear myself away from him ; and, at parting, we both shed tears. Indeed, the memory of the many happy days which I passed at Vienna will never be effaced from my mind.

In the first week of February 1787, I quitted it with a heart full of grief and gratitude. Storace, her mother, her brother, Attwood, and myself, not forgetting Signora Storace's lap-dog, filled the travelling carriage, and with four horses we started for England Ho !

Were I to recount the *désagrémens* of a German journey, my task would be endless. I shall therefore content myself with mentioning the different places at which we stopped : the first, worthy of observation, was Saltzbourg, which would be celebrated, if for nothing else, as the birth-place of Mozart, who was born there in the year 1756. As I viewed its lofty spires from a distance, I felt a kind of reverential awe. The morning after our arrival, escorted by a *lacquais de place*, I waited upon Mozart's father, and delivered his son's letter. I found him a pleasing, intelligent little man ; he called upon Signora Storace, and offered to be our guide to every thing worth noticing ; he was, as I have before mentioned, in the service of the reigning Sovereign, the Archbishop, who was passionately fond of music, and a distinguished amateur ; he had also in his service Michael Haydn, brother of the celebrated Haydn, who was by many competent judges reckoned even superior to his brother in the composition of church music. . . .

. . . The Archbishop sent one of his attendants to invite Signora Storace and her party to hear a concert at his palace ; we felt ourselves highly honoured, and, of course, went. The Archbishop was a very fine looking man, particularly gallant and attentive to the ladies, of whom there was a splendid show ; it was conceived that he was very partial to the English, and English manners. The music was chiefly instrumental, admirably performed ; the band numerous and excellent. . . .

Vol. I, pp. 222-5, 234 f., 237 f., 249, 250, 253-9, 273-5, 275 f.—Kelly, as an Irishman often called O'Kelly, had been engaged at the Italian Opera in Vienna as Michele Ochelli from 1783 to 1786 and had sung Basilio and Don Curzio in *Le nozze di Figaro*.—His memoirs were written by Theodore Hook and are often unreliable.—Albert Leitzmann translated the passages relating to Mozart (1914, pp. 64 ff. ; 1926, pp. 72 f.).—For Linley see 4 April 1770. His eldest sister, Eliza Ann, married Richard Brinsley Sheridan.—Kelly's melody to Metastasio's canzonetta *La libertà a Nice*, for two sopranos and pianoforte accompaniment, is in the original quoted at the end of the second paragraph ; Mozart's variations have not come to light (cf. Köchel-Einstein, p. 682).—For Attwood see 23 August 1785.—For Paisiello see 23 August 1784 ; for Mozart's meeting with Paisiello, cf. the former's letter to his father of 9-12 June 1784.—For

Stephen Storace see 26 September 1785 and later entries.—For Martini read Martinez ; for Marianne Martinez (otherwise Martines) see 14 October 1762. Nicolò Martines (1689-1764), Master of Ceremonies to the Apostolic Nuncio in Vienna, had two daughters and several sons. Marianne was born in 1744, and was thus about forty in 1785. Her eldest brother, Joseph, Director of the Court Library, was born in 1729 and lived with another brother in the Herrengasse. Metastasio lived from 1730 to 1782 in the Grosse Michaeler-Haus on the Kohlmarkt, where Fräulein Martines also lived. There is no record that Mozart visited this house at this time.—Paisiello's *Barbiere* had been given in Vienna since 1783, in 1784 in the composer's presence.—Salieri's *La grotta di Trofonio* was first performed in 1785. Righini's *Il Demogorgone* went into the Burgtheater repertory after *Figaro* in 1786.

FROM A POSTHUMOUS TRIBUTE TO BENEDIKT SCHACK, 1827

. . . After he had made his bow in some of the provincial theatres in the Austrian states, he came to Schikaneder in Vienna and there became friend, confidant and neighbour of the unforgettable Mozart, and was thus able to relate a host of traits and anecdotes, which depict his artistic and domestic life and his generous soul. Tamino was written for him, he could tell how and on what occasion, at what time and in what place, every number of *Die Zauberflöte* was conceived, altered and finally perfected. The composing of the Requiem was not unknown to him, he was constantly near the master while the latter was busied with this work. To be with him was therefore entertaining and instructive. We learnt the right and also the wrong roads that even the greatest talent has to walk in the harsh reality of life . . .

And now for a word about the Mozart Requiem.

The story of the mysterious commissioning of it, and that the master did not complete his work, was known in Munich immediately after Mozart's death. It was known that the composition of the Sanctus and the Agnus Dei is the work of Herr Süssmayr, who may also have arranged and orchestrated many another number which had been left unfinished. But that Mozart, open, honest Mozart, accepted the fee but threw together the work itself in part from early products of his youth, and the whole without zeal, without interest, without love, simply out of necessity—not one of us would have wanted to express this strange opinion, even if it had entered into his mind. And simply because it refers to this matter, we relate what the good, truth-loving Schack told us on so many occasions, long before the appearance of *Cäcilia*. Mozart, so he related among much else that is not here relevant, received fifty ducats for the composition of the Requiem, half of it paid in advance. As no urgency for this work was pressed upon him, he travelled to Frankfurt in the meantime. The greatest part of his Requiem he wrote in the Laimgrube suburb, in Trattner's garden. As soon as he had completed a number, he had it sung through, and played the instrumental accompaniment to it on his piano. On the very eve of his death he had the score of the Requiem brought to his bed, and himself (it was two o'clock in the afternoon) sang the alto part ; Schack, the family friend, sang the soprano line, as he had always previously done, Hofer, Mozart's brother-in-law, took the tenor, Gerle, later bass singer at the Mannheim Theatre, the bass.   They were at the first bars of the Lacrimosa when Mozart began to weep bitterly, laid the score on one side, and eleven hours later, at one o'clock in the morning (of 5 December 1791, as is well known), departed this life.

> *Allgemeine musikalische Zeitung* (Leipzig), 25 July 1827 (Year XXIX, No. 30), pp. 519-21.—Anonymous report from Munich, where Schack had died on 11 December 1826.—In the periodical *Cäcilia*, published by Schott of Mainz, Gottfried Weber had in 1825 called the authenticity of the Requiem in question. —It was not to Frankfurt but to Prague that Mozart travelled in 1791.— Trattner's garden was not in the Laimgrube suburb, but at Alt-Lerchenfeld. —Novello published the vocal score of a Mass by Schack in London in 1831 ; it was supposed to contain additional music by Mozart.—For Schack, see also 1811.

FROM SOPHIE HAIBEL'S MEMOIRS, 1828

He was always good-humoured, but even at his most good-humoured he was very pensive, looking one straight in the eye the while, pondering his answer to any question, whether it be gay or grave, and yet he seemed the while to be working away deep in thought at some thing quite different. Even when he was washing his hands when he rose in the morning, he walked up and down in the room the while, never standing still, tapped one heel against the other the while and was always deep in thought.   At table he often took the corner of a napkin, crumpled it up tightly, rubbed it round below his nose, and seemed in his reflections to know nothing of what he was doing, and often he would grimace with his mouth the while. In his pastimes he was always passionately attached to the latest of them, and so it was with riding, and also with billiards.   To keep him from intercourse of an unworthy kind his wife patiently took part in everything with him.   Also, his hands and feet were always in motion, he was always playing with something, *e.g.* his hat, pockets, watch-fob, tables, chairs, as if they were a clavier.

> Nissen (published 1828), pp. 627 f.—*Cf.* 7 April 1825.

FROM THE TRAVEL DIARIES OF VINCENT AND MARY NOVELLO, SALZBURG, 14–17 JULY 1829
(in English)

[Visit to Constanze Nissen and Wolfgang Mozart junior]
July 14th.
Question. Whether he [Mozart] was in the habit of playing and singing much, and what particular pieces he most frequently performed, or whether

he generally played *extempore* when alone—any particularities in his mode of performance.

Vincent. He did not play much in private, but would occasionally extemporise when he was sitting alone with her, and would often play over the songs which he wished her to learn ; nor did he like playing to strangers, except he know them to be *good judges*, when he would exert himself to the outmost for their gratification.

Mary. He seldom played on the Pianoforte, scarcely in company unless he found someone who could appreciate him, but he would sometimes extemporise when alone with her.

Question. In composing, whether he sat at the instrument and tried over different passages as they occurred to him, or whether he deferred writing down any piece until he had completely constructed and finished it in his own mind, and then *scored* it at once ?—Whether it was necessary for him to be alone when he wrote, or if he could abstract himself so as to compose with many persons present ?

Vincent. He seldom went to the Instrument when he composed . . . In composing, he would get up and walk about the Room quite abstracted from everything that was going on about him. He would then come and sit down by her, tell her to give him his inkstand and paper and say " Ma chère femme, ayez la bonté de me dire de quoi on a parlé " ; then went on writing by her side while she talked to him, without the conversation at all impeding his occupation.

Mary. When some grand conception was working in his brain he was purely abstracted, walking about the apartment and knew not what was passing around, but when once arranged in his mind, he needed no Piano Forte but would take music paper and whilst he wrote would say to her, " Now, my dear wife, have the goodness to repeat what has been talked of ", and her conversation never interrupted him, he wrote on, " which is more ", she added, " than I can do with the commonest letter ".

Question. How many portraits, busts, engravings, etc., have been made of him and which does Mme. von Nissen consider the *best* likeness of him ?

Vincent. By far the best likeness of him in [Madame] Nissen's opinion is the painting in oils by the Husband of Madame Lange (the eldest sister of Mrs. Nissen) from which the portrait of Mozart contained in her Biography —is *unfinished* but admirably done . . . in a wooden case as if it had [been] travelling.—Some good Likeness done in Wax, by an Artist at Berlin.

Question. Whether his general disposition was lively and playful—or melancholy—whether he could draw, or paint well—or possessed any particular talent for any other art or pursuit than his own science ?

Vincent. She said " Il etoit toujours si gai ".—Was fond of Painting—Sculpture—and could draw himself. " Indeed " she added—he had " superior talents for all the Arts ".

Mary. She told us that he drew a little and was very fond of the arts, that he had indeed a talent for all the arts—that he was always in good humour, rarely melancholy but of a very gay humour, indeed he was an angel she exclaimed, and is one now—there was no affectation about this, but said quite simply.

Vincent. The King of Prussia (Frederick II) offered Mozart 16 hundred zechins a year to come [and] live at his Court, but Mozart was so much attached to the Emperor (Joseph II) that he preferred remaining with the latter from whom, however, Mozart received no salary whatever.

July 15th.

Question. Who were his most intimate and cordial friends amongst his brother professors, etc., and which seemed most completely to appreciate his incomparable genius?

Mary. Haydn he [Wolfgang] thinks his father's greatest admirer, and said he never saw him [Haydn] as a child but he wept.

Vincent. Spoke highly of Haydn—never saw him but he wept . . . Haydn told him that if he (Mozart) went to England first (as Salomon at one time wished) it would be of no use for him (Haydn) to go there as "nothing would do after Mozart's compositions". Haydn often visited them and repeatedly declared that Mozart was the greatest musical genius that ever existed.

Mary. She told us that Mozart when he finished an opera brought it to her and begged she would study it, after which he would play it over and sing with her, so that not only the songs but the words she knew by heart, but one air in the *Idomeneo* he preferred to hear her sing and on that account she prefers it also, " se il Padre perdei " . . . The most happy time of his life was whilst in Munich during which he wrote *Idomeneo* which may account for the affection he entertained towards the work.

Vincent. The widow seemed pleased when I mentioned so many pieces out of his operas—" Oh, I see you know them all by heart as I do "—she knows all the words by memory as well as the music . . . told me that " Non so più " in *Figaro* was a great favourite with Mozart also " Riconosci a questo amplesso ".

Question. Whether he was fond of reading, and what kind of literature he preferred—Poetry, prose, fiction or history?

Mary. Mozart was fond of reading and well acquainted with Shakespeare in the translation. One of his favourite authors is at present in her possession and which she most frequently peruses, it is in 9 volumes but being a forbidden fruit in the Austrian states she did not name it—I suspect some of the French revolutionary works.

Question. Was he a great performer on any other Instrument than the Piano Forte?—Whether he occasionally attended to play the organ, or accompany any of his own Masses, and if so, at what churches?

Vincent. Widow told me that Mozart's favourite Instrument was the Organ —upon which she said he played with the most incomparable skill.

Mary. He played upon several of the organs both at Salzburg and Vienna, the Cathedrals of both—the organ was his favourite instrument.

Question. Which were his favourite amusements, when he wished to relax from his severe studies, and intense application to composition and his other professional avocations ?—Whether he was an early riser, and if he generally composed late at night or early in the morning ?

Mary. It is quite evident that Mozart killed himself with over-exertion. He could never entirely abstract himself from his musical thoughts. Billiards he was very fond of, but he composed whilst he played, if he conversed with his friends, he always was at work in his mind. Necessity and the duties of his situation induced this habit, which evidently wore out the system and would have produced death had he not been attacked with the fever which killed him suddenly . . . —Madame confirmed the truth of her sitting up all night with him whilst he wrote the overture to *Don Giovanni.* He frequently sat up composing until 2 and rose at 4, an exertion which assisted to destroy him.

Question. On what occasion was the *Davidde Penitente* written, and which of the movements were originally composed as a Mass ?

Vincent. The *Davidde Penitente* originally a grand Mass which he wrote in consequence of a vow that he had made to do so, on her safe recovery after the birth of their first child—relative to whom he had been particularly anxious. This Mass was performed in the Cathedral at Salzburg and Madame Mozart herself sang all the principal solos. Mozart thought so highly of this production that he afterwards made several additions and adapted new words to make it a complete Cantata, or rather Oratorio, for the former is too modest a title for so elevated, elaborate and masterly a work.

Mary. She said his death was at last sudden, but a few moments before he had spoken so gaily, and in a few moments after he was dead—she could not believe it, but threw herself on the bed and sought to catch the fever of which he died, but it was not to be. There were moments, she declared, when she not only prayed sincerely to die but that she did not love her children, every thing was hateful to her in the world, yet here I am still, and have gone through all this suffering . . .

The Emperor asked him why he did not marry a rich wife—he said he hoped he should be able always to gain sufficient by his genius to maintain the woman he loved. He repeatedly told her he should not have known what to do with a rich wife—she would have expected his undivided attention and he must have neglected his compositions. He frequently compared the two Haydns, Joseph and Michael " But no one is so happy as I am in a wife " he would exclaim.

July 17th.

Question. Whether he was well acquainted with the works of the English composer Purcell, and the oratorios of Handel ?—Whether he ever began or finished any oratorios like Handel's, and if so, what is become of them ?

Vincent. Mozart [was a] great admirer of Handel, well acquainted with his works especially his oratorios.

Mary. He contemplated writing oratorios in the style of Handel and it seems as if fate had determined the latter should remain single in that department by removing the one who could best have outshone him.

Question. What kind of *speaking* voice, whether high or low, loud or soft, and his singing voice, whether contralto, tenor or bass—powerful or delicate ?

Mary. His singing voice was a tenor, his speaking voice gentle, unless he was directing, then he was energetic and would occasionally stamp with his feet, and once he was so loud in the Cathedral that Madame heard him at an immense distance.

Vincent. His voice was a Tenor, rather soft in speaking and delicate in singing, but when anything excited him, or it became necessary to exert it, it was both powerful and energetic. His usual exclamation was " Saperlotte ", and occasionally [he] would stamp with his foot when impatient, or things did not go correctly in the orchestra. With him at the opera *Il Seraglio* when they took the time of one of the Movements too fast—he became quite impatient and called out to the Orchestra without seeming to fear or to be aware of the presence of the audience.

> *A Mozart Pilgrimage. Being the Travel Diaries of Vincent & Mary Novello in the year 1829,* ed. Rosemary Hughes (London, 1955, Novello and Company Ltd.), pp. 77-82, 92, 94-8, 112-13. Quoted by kind permission of the publishers.—Published in excerpt by Mrs. Mary Novello in *The Musical World* (London, August-September 1837).—Constanze's younger son, Wolfgang, was staying in Salzburg in the summer of 1829.—She conversed mainly in French with the Novellos because her English was not good enough.—Nissen's Mozart biography was brought out by Constanze in 1828.—The wax relief was that by Posch, who at the end of his life lived in Berlin.—The King of Prussia who encouraged Mozart was Frederick William II.—Joseph II had granted Mozart a sinecure of 800 gulden per annum in 1787.—Constanze probably visited Joseph Haydn more often than he her.—*Idomeneo* was composed and performed before Mozart's marriage ; the aria mentioned is that of Ilia in Act II.—The *Figaro* numbers mentioned are the aria of Cherubino in Act I and the sextet in Act III.—The Shakespeare translation was Wieland's prose one, published in Zürich in eight volumes between 1763 and 1766.—The C minor Mass, performed in the church of St. Peter's Monastery in Salzburg, is connected with a vow made by Mozart before his marriage.—The Haydn brothers were unhappily married.—Henry Purcell was practically unknown on the continent in the eighteenth century.—It is not clear whether the cathedral referred to in the second instance is that of Vienna or Salzburg.

FROM LUDWIG BERGER'S ESSAY ON MUZIO CLEMENTI, 1829

. . . I believe I shall attain my object most directly if, in describing the contest between the two artists which took place in 1781 in the presence of Emperor Joseph II, I simply reproduce here, as far as I can recall them, Clementi's own words :

" Having been in Vienna but a few days I received an invitation from the Emperor to perform on the fortepiano in his presence.

On entering his music-room I found there someone whom, because of his elegant appearance, I took for one of the Emperor's chamberlains ; but scarcely had we begun a conversation than it turned at once towards musical matters ; and we soon recognised each other as Mozart and Clementi, brother artists, and greeted each other in the most friendly manner."

From the continuation of Clementi's narrative (entirely in agreement with Mozart's account), it became clear how deeply the artistic achievements of the latter impressed and delighted him.

" Until then I had never heard anyone play with so much spirit and grace. Especially did an Adagio and several of his extemporized variations surprise me, for which the Emperor chose the theme on which we, accompanying each other by turns, had to play variations." To my question, whether at that time he played the instrument in his present style (it was the year 1806), he answered *no*, adding : " That at that early date he took particular delight in great and brilliant dexterity, and especially in those double-chorded passages and extemporized ornaments that were not in common use before his time ; and that only subsequently did he come to favour the more melodious, nobler style of performance which he acquired through careful attention to then famous singers, and also through the gradual perfecting of the *English* concert grand fortepiano in particular, the earlier faulty construction of which had practically excluded the possibility of a more singing, more legato style of playing.

Thus, it seems to me, must we explain Mozart's judgement that called him [Clementi] " tasteless and insensitive ", and could only lead to misunderstandings to the disadvantage of Mozart—but it is to a certain extent understandable.

At least we cannot presume, remembering the latter's well-known honesty and his uprightness, that any ulterior motive influenced that judgement.

In no wise does it affect or harm the subsequent and now generally recognised creator and perfector of true fortepiano style.

Also worthy of notice here is Clementi's original practice of extemporising quite long, very interesting and thematically developed interludes and cadenzas following the fermatas in his sonatas ; this is what led him at that contest to choose a sonata which, though certainly suited to his purpose, yet in other respects was inferior to several of his earlier compositions in this genre. It was the following (Œuvres de Clementi, Cahier VI, Son. II, Allegro con brio)

and it is to this theme that we perhaps owe the genial and in its way unsurpassed Allegro of the overture to *Die Zauberflöte*.—

> *Cäcilia* (Mainz), July 1829, Vol. X, No. 40, pp. 238-40.—Berger, the Berlin composer, had gone to St. Petersburg with Clementi in 1804 and also stayed with him in London about 1814.—For the competition between Clementi and Mozart, *cf.* 24 December 1781.

On 29 October 1829 Marianne von Berchtold zu Sonnenburg died at Salzburg. She had been blind since 1825.

FROM MAXIMILIAN STADLER'S AUTOBIOGRAPHY, VIENNA, BEFORE 1830

As I had frequent intercourse with Mozart and Joseph Haydn, I could relate much about them. But as you already know the most important matters, I consider it superfluous to relate insignificant things.

I heard Mozart in his eighth year play the organ at a Vespers service in the Monastery of Melk in a way that one can expect [only] from a very gifted organist. When he came to Vienna and had his 6 sonatas for clavier and violin engraved by Artaria and dedicated to Fräulein Auernhammer, he took me to the rehearsal, Artaria brought the first printed copy with him, Fräulein Auernhammer played the F.P.—Mozart accompanied on a 2nd fortepiano that stood at hand, instead of on the violin, and I was wholly enchanted by the playing of master and pupil, and I never in my life heard it performed so incomparably again. In the art of free improvisation Mozart had not his equal. His improvisations were as well-ordered as if he had had them lying written out before him. This led several to think that, when he performed an improvisation in public, he must have thought everything out, and practised it, beforehand. Albrechtsberger thought so too. But one evening they met at a musical soirée ; Mozart was in a good mood and demanded a theme of Albrechtsberger. The latter played him an old German popular song.—Mozart sat down and improvised on this theme for an hour in such a way as to excite general admiration and shew by means of variations and fugues (in which he never departed from the theme) that he was master of every aspect of the musician's art. Albrechtsberger was so delighted that he was now fully convinced that Mozart had no need to prepare himself for an extemporized improvisation.

> Original in the Archives of the Gesellschaft der Musikfreunde, Vienna.— *Jahresbericht des Conservatoriums* (Vienna, 1864–65). Robert Haas in the *Mozart-Jahrbuch 1957* (Salzburg, 1958), p. 83 (inexact).—Mozart was eleven years old when he played at Melk. The Artaria named was evidently Pasquale Artaria, a Viennese freemason.—For Stadler's reminiscences see also 1826.

FROM LORENZO DA PONTE'S MEMOIRS, NEW YORK, 1829–30
(in Italian)

. . . It was not long before various composers came to me for libretti. But there were only two in Vienna such as to deserve my esteem. Martini, at that time the favourite composer of Joseph, and V. Mozzart, whose acquaintance I at that time had occasion to make in the house of Baron Vetzlar, his great admirer and friend, and who, although endowed with talents perhaps superior to those of any other composer of the world past, present or to come, had never been able, thanks to the cabals of his enemies, to exercise his divine genius in Vienna, and remained unknown and hidden, like a precious stone which, buried in the bowels of the earth, conceals the bright worth of its splendour. I can never recall to mind without exaltation and pleasure that it was to my perseverance and firmness alone that Europe and the whole world in large measure owes the exquisite vocal compositions of this admirable genius . . .

. . . So, after the considerable success of the *Burbero*, I went to the above-mentioned Mozzart and told him of the things that had happened to me both with Casti and Rosemberg, and also with the Sovereign, [and] asked him if it would please him to set to music a drama written for him by me, " I would do it very gladly ", he at once replied, " but I am certain that I will not obtain permission."—" That ", I added, " will be my concern." . . .

. . . So I calmly began to think about the dramas that I was to write for my two dear friends Mozzart and Martini. As for the first, I readily saw that the immensity of his genius demanded a broad, many-sided, sublime subject. Conversing with him on this subject one day, he asked me if I could easily reduce to an opera Beaumarchais's comedy called *Le Nozze di Figaro*. The proposition pleased me well enough, and I promised him that I would do it. But there was one very great difficulty to overcome.

The Emperor had a short time before forbidden the German theatre company to perform the comedy, which was written, he said, too outspokenly for a genteel audience : so how could it be proposed to him as an opera ? Baron Vetzlar with a fine generosity offered to give me a very reasonable sum for the words, and then to have this opera performed in London or in France if it could not be given in Vienna ; but I refused his offer and proposed that we should write the words and the music in secret, and await a favourable opportunity to shew it to the theatre directors or to the Emperor, which task I courageously dared to take upon myself. Martini was the only one who knew of this my fine plot, and he, very generous by reason of the esteem that he had for Mozzart, consented that I should postpone writing for him until I had finished the libretto of *Figaro*.

I therefore set to work, and as I wrote the words, so he set them to music. In six weeks all was ready. Mozzart's good fortune so willed it that the theatre lacked scores. I accordingly seized the opportunity, and without saying a word to anyone, I went along myself and offered *Figaro* to the Emperor. " What ? ", he said, " You know that Mozzart, very fine in instrumental music, has written but one vocal drama in his life, and that was nothing very special ! "—" I myself ", I replied humbly, " would, were it not for Your Majesty's favour, have written but one libretto in Vienna."—"It is true," he replied, "but I have forbidden this *Nozze di Figaro* to the German company."—"Yes," I rejoined, "but in composing a drama for music, and not a comedy, I had to join together many scenes and cut them fairly radically, and I have run together and omitted all that could offend the refinement and decorum of a spectacle at which Your Sovereign Majesty will be present. Now, as to the music, as far as I can judge, it seems to me to be of a marvellous beauty."—"Good, if it is as you say; I trust your taste as to the music, and your discretion as to the morals. Have the score given to the copyist."

I hastened to Mozzart at once, but I had not finished giving him the good news, when a footman came from the Emperor and handed him a note in which he commanded him to go at once to the Royal Palace with the score. He obeyed the royal command; he let him hear various pieces which pleased him marvellously and, without any exaggeration, positively astounded him. He was of an exquisite taste in matters of music, as he was indeed in all the fine arts. The great success which this theatrical performance had all over the world clearly shewed that he had not erred in his judgment. This news did not please the other composers in Vienna; it did not please Rosemberg, who did not like this kind of music; but above all it did not please Casti, who after *il Burbero* no longer dared say that Da Ponte could not write libretti, and began to perceive that it was not impossible that in the end I might write one that would please as much as his *Teodoro*.

The Count meanwhile, having in vain tried every underhand means, dared openly to seek for his own Petronius the post of Imperial Court Poet. And as the manner was very strange, I imagine that it will give pleasure to my readers to hear of it. The Emperor had given a very fine feast for the ladies of Vienna in the Palace of Schoenbrun, at the little theatre of which the Director of Entertainments had had a little German comedy given, and also an Italian opera, the words of which had, on his recommendation, been written by Casti. It bore the title *Le Parole dopo la musica*. To be assured that it was a true pastiche, without wit, without taste, without refinement, without real characters, it will be enough to know that nobody other than the Count had the hardihood to praise it. To make the success of their intrigues the more certain, they thought they would make a galant little satire on the actual Theatre Poet, and it can readily be believed that Signor Casti was not as galant towards me as was Apelles towards Antigonus. But even if he wore my clothes, and copied the way in which I wore my hair, the rest was closer to Casti than to me. He spoke among other things of my liaisons with the ladies of the theatre, and the best of it was that he himself was the protector and Cicisbeo of the two ladies who sang in this comedy. On the day after the feast, the Count, in his dignity as Joseph's Great Chamberlain, was commanded by

the Sovereign while passing him his shirt to write on a sheet of paper
the names of the singers and actors, and to affix to each name, in accordance with his merit, a certain number of sequins, as a mark of his Sovereign's
pleasure.—Now, while the Emperor was dressing, the Count was writing ;
as soon as the list was completed, he presented it to him. The Emperor
glanced at it, smiled, and taking the pen to his hand, he added a nought
to the various amounts entered by the Count, so that a ten became a
hundred, a 15 one hundred and fifty, and so on. Then, returning the list
to him, he said, " It is not Count Rosemberg who gave the feast, it is the
Emperor ". . . .

. . . Let us turn to Rosemberg. He had not yet had time to recover from
the mortification and surprise caused him by this nought. The Emperor,
who had already moved away from him, went up to him again to ask him
why the name of Casti was not on the list. " Casti ", rejoined the Count,
" and I with him, hope that Your Majesty will see fit to honour him with
the coveted title of imperial Poet."—" My dear Count," replied the Emperor, " I have no need of poets for myself, and for the theatre Da Ponte
is enough." That same day I heard this excellent anecdote from Maestro
Salieri, to whom our Sovereign told it, and a few days afterwards, I heard
it from our Sovereign himself. This repulse, however, only served to
increase their hatred of me. Thus both Mozzart and I were not without
a well-grounded fear of being obliged to suffer new intrigues from these
our two good friends. They have not been able to do much, but what
they could do, they have done. A certain Bussani, master of the theatre
wardrobe and also stage manager, and who knew how to perform all
trades except that of being a gentleman, having heard that I had inserted
a ballet into *Figaro*, at once ran to the Count and in a tone of disapproval
and surprise said to him, " Your Excellency, the poet has introduced a
ballet into his opera." The Count sent for me at once and in rather a
sinister manner opened the following little dialogue, which is quite as
good as the ' Barnabotic Excellency ' one. Count : " So you have
introduced a ballet into *Figaro*, Mr Poet ? "—Da Ponte : " Yes, Your
Excellency."—Count : " You are unaware, Mr Poet, of the fact that the
Emperor does not want ballets in his theatre ? " Da P. : " No, Your
Excellency."—C. : " Well, Mr Poet, let me inform you of this now."—
D.P. : " Yes, Your Excellency."—C. : " And let me tell you furthermore
that you must remove it, Mr Poet." (This ' Mr Poet ' was repeated in
an expressive tone, which seemed to signify ' Mr Donkey ', or something of the kind. But my ' Your Excellency ' too was not without its
due meaning.) Da P. : " No, Your Excellency."—" Have you the libretto
with you ? "—D.P. " Yes, Your Excellency."—C. : " Where is the scene
with the ballet ? "—D.P. : " Here it is, Your Excellency."—C. : " Do
you know what we shall do with it ? " So saying, he removed two sheets
from the opera, gently tossed them into the fire, gave me back the libretto,
saying, " You see, Mr Poet, that I am all powerful ", and honoured me

with a second " Vade ". I went at once to Mozzart, who was in despair
to hear this little piece of news from me. He wanted to go to the Count,
abuse Bussani, appeal to the Emperor, recall the score—in truth, I had
a hard task to calm him. In the end I begged him to give me just two
days and to leave the matter to me. This same day was fixed for the
dress rehearsal of the opera. I went personally to tell the Emperor, and
he told me that he would appear at the appointed hour. In fact he did
come, and with him half the nobility of Vienna. The Abbé also attended
with him. The first act was given amid general applause. At the end of
it there occurs a mimed scene between the Count and Susanna, during
which the orchestra plays and the dance is executed. But as His I-am-all-
powerful Excellency had cut this scene, the Count and Susanna could only
be seen gesticulating, and the orchestra being silent, it seemed to be only
a puppet-show. " What is this ? " the Emperor said to Casti, who was
sitting behind him. " You must ask the poet ", the Abbé answered with
a malicious little smile. I was accordingly sent for, but instead of answer-
ing the question put to me, I presented him with my manuscript in which
I had replaced the scene. The Sovereign read it and asked me why the
dance had been omitted. My silence gave him to understand that there
must be some little intrigue. He turned to the Count, asked him for an
account of the circumstance, and he, half muttering, said that the dance
was missing because the opera house had no dancers. " Are there none ",
he asked, " at the other theatres ? " They told him that there were.
" Well, let Da Ponte have as many as are needed."

In less than half an hour 24 dancers, or *figuranti*, arrived, at the end of the
second act the scene that had been cut was played, and the Emperor cried,
" Now it is all right." . . .

. . . Meanwhile Mozzart's opera was produced, and notwithstanding the
" We'll hear's " and the " We'll see's " of all the other musicians and their
partisans, notwithstanding the Count, Casti and a hundred devils, it met
with general approbation and was held by the Sovereign, and by all true
connoisseurs, to be sublime, almost divine. The libretto, too, was found
good ; and my most chaste critic was the first to remark its beauties. But
what were these beauties ?—" It is true that it is only a translation of
Beaumarchais's comedy ; but it has some fine verses and some fine arias.
Take these two very delicate lines, for instance :

> ' Non più andrai farfallone amoroso,
> Notte e giorno d' intorno girando.' "

All the merit of this opera consisted, then, according to him, in some
fine verse, or, at the very most, in some fine arias. . . .

. . . I thought, however, that it was time to reawaken my poetic muse,
which had completely withered when I was writing for Reghini and
Peticchio. The three renowned Maestri, Martini, Mozzart and Salieri,
gave me the opportunity ; all three came at the same time and asked me

for a libretto. I liked and esteemed them all three, and from all three I hoped to make amends for past failures and to win some increase to my slight theatrical glory. I wondered whether it would not be possible to satisfy them all three and to write three operas at one and the same time. Salieri did not require an original book of me. In Paris he had written the music for the opera *Tarar*; he now wanted to refashion it to the character of an Italian libretto and opera, and accordingly asked of me only a free translation; Mozzart and Martini left the choice entirely to me. For the former I chose *Don Giovanni*, a subject which pleased him infinitely, and for Martini, *l'arbore di Diana*—for him I wanted a gentle subject, suited to his very sweet melodies, which are felt in the soul, but which very few are capable of imitating. Having found these three subjects, I went to the Emperor, revealed my thoughts to him, and informed him that my intention was to write these three operas simultaneously. "You won't succeed!", he replied. "Perhaps not," I answered, "but I shall try. For Mozzart I shall write at night and shall account it reading Dante's *Inferno*—I shall write during the morning for Martini, and that will be like studying Petrarch. [In] the evening [I shall write] for Salieri, and he shall be my Tasso." He found my parallel very good, and scarcely had I got home than I began to write. I went to my writing table and sat there twelve hours on end. A small bottle of Tokay on my right, the inkstand in the middle, and a box of Seville snuff on my left. A beautiful sixteen-year-old girl, whom I had meant to love only as a daughter, but . . . was staying in my house with her mother, who looked after the house-keeping; she came to my room at the sound of the bell, which in sooth I rang rather often, and especially when it seemed to me that my inspiration was beginning to grow cool. . . .

. . . On the first day, however, between the Tokay, the Seville snuff, the coffee, the bell, and my young Muse, I wrote the first two scenes of *Don Giovanni*, two others of *l'arbore di Diana*, and more than half of the first act of *Tarar*, a title I changed to *Assur*. In the morning I took these scenes to the three composers, who could scarcely believe that what they read with their own eyes could possibly be achieved; and in 63 days the first two operas were entirely finished, and almost two-thirds of the last. *L'arbore di Diana* was the first to be given. It had a very happy reception, at least as good as that of the *Cosa Rara*. . . .

. . . After only one performance of this work, I was obliged to leave for Prague, where Mozzart's *D. Giovanni* was to be given for the first time, on the occasion of the arrival of the Princess of Tuscany in that city. I stayed there for a week in order to direct the actors who were to perform in it, but before it was staged, I was obliged to return to Vienna by reason of a fiery letter which I received from Salieri, in which, whether or not it was true, he told me that *Assur* was to be given immediately for the wedding of Francis, and that the Emperor had commanded him to recall me. . . .

. . . I had not seen the performance of *D. Giovanni* in Prague, but Mozzart informed me at once of its wonderful reception, and Guardassoni wrote these words to me : " Long live Da Ponte, long live Mozzart ! All the impresarios, all the virtuosi ought to bless them. As long as these two are alive, misery will be banished from the theatre." The Emperor sent for me, and loading me with gracious expressions of praise, made me a present of another hundred sequins, and told me that he was looking forward keenly to seeing *Don Giovanni*. Mozzart returned, at once gave the score to the copyist, who hastened to produce the parts, because Joseph was about to leave. It was staged, . . . and must I say it ? DON GIOVANNI WAS NOT A SUCCESS ! All but Mozzart thought that something was lacking. Additional numbers were inserted, some of the arias were changed, it was put on again—and *D. Giovanni* was not a success. And what did the Emperor say ? " The opera is divine, and perhaps it is finer than *Figaro*, but it is not food for the teeth of my Viennese." I told this to Mozzart, who replied unperturbed, " Let us give them time to chew it." He was not mistaken. On his advice I managed to have the opera frequently repeated ; at each performance the applause grew, and little by little the Viennese with their bad teeth came to enjoy its savour and appreciate its beauty, and placed *Don Giovanni* among the most beautiful operas ever performed on any dramatic stage. . . .

. . . I wrote *Il Pastor Fido* for her [Adriana Gabrieli del Bene, called ' La Ferrarese '], and also *la Cifra*, with music by Salieri, two operas which were not exactly epoch-making among his musical triumphs, although they are very fine in certain parts ; and *la scola degli amanti* with music by Mozzart, the opera which holds third place among the three sisters born to that most famous father of harmony . . .

. . . I had already written to Martini that they had refused my resignation and that I would not therefore have been able to go to St. Petersburg for several months. Suspecting, therefore, that they had already written to Italy for another poet, I conferred with Mozzart and endeavoured to persuade him to go to London with me. But he, having shortly before received a pension for life from the Emperor Joseph as a reward for his divine operas, and who was then setting to music a German opera (*Il flauto incantato*), from which he hoped for new glories, asked for six months in which to make up his mind, and I had meanwhile to face vicissitudes which obliged me almost by force to take quite a different path. . . .

. . . I arrived in Prague and stayed there some days in the hope (which was to prove vain) of receiving some news from the Abbé [of a purse which Da Ponte's wife had lost]. However, I did have the opportunity of going to see performances of the three operas written by me for Mozzart, and it is not easy to depict the enthusiasm of the Bohemians for this music. The numbers which are least admired in other countries are by this people considered divine ; and what is even more remarkable is that those great beauties of the music of this rare genius, which only after many, many performances are perceived by other nations, were perfectly understood by the Bohemians at the first hearing. . . .

> From the second, corrected and enlarged edition (the first, in 4 volumes, had appeared in 1823–27) of the *Memorie* in 3 volumes.—Vol. I, pp. 68-74, 81-3, 84 f., 99 f., 101, 103 f., 105 f., 111, 124 ; Vol. II, pp. 5 f.—The best critical edition is the German one by Gustav Gugitz (Dresden, 1924), where the passages quoted here are to be found as follows : Vol. I, pp. 227 f., 229 f., 231-7 249-53, 254 f., 278-80, 281 f., 286, 288 f., 299 ; Vol. II, pp. 26 f., 95.—" Martini " is Martín y Soler.—*Il burbero di buon cuore* by Martín, libretto by Da Ponte after Goldoni, had been produced on 4 January 1786.—Giovanni Battista Casti was another librettist of the Court Opera.—Mozart's first opera for Vienna had been *Die Entführung*.—Paisiello's *Il rè Teodoro in Venezia*, libretto by Casti after Voltaire, had been produced in Vienna in 1784.—The correct title of the opera written for the festivity at Schönbrunn in 1786 was *Prima la musica, poi le parole* ; the music was by Salieri, the women singers were Coltellini and Storace.—Antigonus the One-Eyed was one of Alexander the Great's generals.—Francesco Antonio Piticchio's opera *Il Bertoldo*, libretto by Da Ponte, was produced on 22 June 1787, Martín's *L' arbore di Diana* on 1 October 1787 and Salieri's *Axur, rè d' Ormus* on 8 January 1788 ; in between, on 29 October 1787, came the world première of *Don Giovanni* in Prague ; it was performed in Vienna on 7 May 1788. Salieri's *Il pastor fido* followed on 11 February 1789 and *La cifra* on 11 December 1789 ; and Mozart's *Così fan tutte ossia La scuola degli amanti* on 26 January 1790.—Martín was appointed to the Italian Opera of St. Petersburg in 1788.—For Rosenberg, Salieri and Casti, *cf.* spring 1786.

FROM J. P. ECKERMANN'S CONVERSATIONS WITH GOETHE,
3 FEBRUARY 1830

Dinner with Goethe. We spoke about Mozart. " I saw him when he was a seven-year-old boy ", said Goethe, " when he gave a concert on his way through. I myself was about fourteen years old, and I can still quite clearly remember the little fellow with his wig and his sword."

Cf. 25 August 1763.

FROM JOHANN SCHENK'S AUTOBIOGRAPHY, COMPLETED ON 28 JULY 1830

I composed three operas . . . for the Theater auf der Wieden . . . In the same year [1791] and on the same stage Mozart produced his *Zauberflöte*, which continues to bloom in the eternal freshness of youth. Memory leads my mind back in the friendliest way to that wonderful time when Salieri, Haydn and Mozart walked side by side in the happiest rivalry. Mozart, so merry, generously always bade me welcome in his house. I was witness of so many of the arts of his masterly hand when he sat at the piano. Rich in invention and dazzling as his fantasias were, they yet never lacked the greatest clarity in their perfect contrapuntal purity. This remarkable man had scarcely passed the 35th year of his life when he was surprised by death. If Mozart had reached a greater age, verily he would with ease have attained the highest goal of his art. As the stars twinkle in a still summer's night, and suddenly the moon spreads its full, clear radiance, thus Mozart might stand, alone and unique, in highest glory, before all his fellow-artists. So deep, so clear, so all-embracing, so rich in invention was his noble mind.

> Göttweig Monastery, Aloys Fuchs Collection (Schenk wrote this autobio-graphical sketch for Fuchs ; the Beethoven passage from it is well known). —*Studien zur Musikwissenschaft* (Vienna, 1924), No. XI, pp. 80 ff.—Jahn, 1859, Vol. IV, p. 593, note 3, and after him Abert, Vol. II, p. 752, note 2, state, presumably using this same source, that Schenk " had a seat in the orchestra at the first performance [of *Die Zauberflöte*] ; after the overture he crept along to the conductor's chair, beside himself with delight, seized Mozart's hand and kissed it, while the latter, continuing to beat time with his right hand, looked kindly at him and stroked his cheek ". This passage is not preserved in the MS. Schenk, moreover, was not a member of the Freihaus Theatre orchestra.

*   FROM THE " WAHRE UND AUSFÜHRLICHE GESCHICHTE DES REQUIEMS VON
    W. A. MOZART " BY ANTON HERZOG, WIENER-NEUSTADT (1839)

. . . On the question of how far this Requiem is Mozart's work or Süssmayer's, we have every reason to place the fullest confidence in the evidence of Abbé Stadler ; for after Mozart's death he put all the composer's writings in order for his widow, and set in train the completion by Herr Süssmayer of the partly composed Requiem . . .

Franz, Count Walsegg, owner of the estates of Schottwien, Klam[m], Stuppach, Pottschach and Ziegersberg, situated in Austria below the Enns, V.U.W.W., after his marriage to Anna, née von Flammberg, lived at his country-house at Stuppach as a loving husband and a true father to his dependents. He was a passionate amateur of music and the theatre ; hence each week, on Tuesdays and Thursdays, a full three hours was given over to the playing of quartets, and on Sunday there would be a dramatic performance . . .

But in order that there should be no lack of new quartets for such frequent performances, the Count not only acquired all published music of this kind, but also made an arrangement with many composers (but always without giving his name) that they should supply him with works, of which he was to hold the exclusive ownership, and he paid them generously for this. And in particular Hr. [Franz Anton] Hoffmeister supplied many flute quartets, in which the flute part was quite practicable but the other three parts uncommonly hard, so that the players had to work right hard at them, which made the Count laugh.

But because the Count never liked to play from printed music, he had everything copied out handsomely on ten-stave music paper, but always without the composer's name. The scores he had obtained secretly he usually copied out with his own hand, and then handed them over to have the separate parts copied. We never got to see an original score. The quartets were then played, and we had to guess the composer. Usually we guessed the Count himself, because he did in fact occasionally compose a few trifles ; he would smile at that and be pleased that he had (or so he believed) succeeded in mystifying us ; but we laughed because he thought us so credulous.

We were all young folk, and considered that we were giving our master an innocent pleasure. And in such manner the mutual deception continued for several years.

I feel that I must first set out these circumstances in order to reach a better judgement of what people have called mysterious about the origins of the Requiem.

On 14 February 1791 death deprived Count Walsegg of his dearly beloved wife, in the very prime of her life. He wished to erect for her a double memorial, and of an exceptional kind. He had his agent, Dr. Johann Sortschan, a Vienna lawyer, order from one of the finest sculptors in Vienna a monument, and from Mozart a Requiem, of which he would again, as usual, have the exclusive ownership.

The former, which cost more than 3000 fr., was in fact soon afterwards set up in the meadows near Schloss Stuppach, and the body of the deceased lady removed from the family vault at Schottwien and placed within it.

But the Requiem, which was to be performed each year upon the anniversary of the Countess's death, took longer ; for death overtook Mozart in the midst of this famous work. Now there was need of good counsel. Who would take upon himself to finish the work of a Mozart ? And yet the work must be finished, for the widow Mozart, who, as is well known, was not in the easiest of circumstances, was to receive the sum of a hundred ducats for it. Whether there had already been an advance payment is not known to us for sure, but there is reason to think so.

Eventually Süssmayer undertook to finish the work, and he states in his letter to the Leipzig music publishers Breitkopf & Härtel, 8 February 1800, " that while Mozart was still alive he had often played and sung through the sections that had already been composed, namely the Requiem, Kyrie, Dies irae, Domine, etc., that he had often discussed the completion of the work with him and informed him of his intentions about the instrumentation " . . .

The Count tried to explain to us the fact that his score had a different Agnus Dei from that in the Leipzig edition by saying that he was a pupil of Mozart's and that he had sent the score to him in Vienna piece by piece to be looked through. Shortly before Mozart's death he said that he had sent him the completed Benedictus for this purpose ; after Mozart's death the score, from the beginning up as far as the Agnus Dei, had been found, and people had believed it was a composition of Mozart's, so deceptively similar were their handwritings.

The Count, according to his own story, had then completed the Requiem by adding the Agnus Dei and the rest ; but the same sections had also been set to music by Süssmayer. And it was for this reason that the Count had a different Agnus Dei from the one in the Leipzig score.—From all this however we may conclude how completely the noble patron himself had been deceived, for he must certainly have been told that Mozart had completed the Requiem as far as the Agnus Dei, and that this was all Süssmayer had added, in order to make the work more valuable.

It is hard to blame the Count for playing a joke on us, his servants, by passing off the Requiem as his own composition (but only in our presence), for a much more blameworthy joke had been played on him in regard to his hard-won property. . . .

It is possible too that the widow Mozart and her circle may not have known of the contract into which her late husband had entered with Dr. Sortschan, to the effect that Count Walsegg should have the exclusive ownership of the commissioned Requiem ; otherwise they would surely not, at the same time as they sent the score to the Count, have sent a copy, without his knowledge, for sale to the Leipzig music publishers. It may be imagined what the Count thought when he discovered that the score of his property had appeared at Leipzig in public print.—

In fact the Count at first intended to take serious measures against the widow Mozart, but the matter was eventually patched up, through his goodness of heart.

So after Count Walsegg had received the score of the Requiem, he immediately wrote out a fair copy of it, note by note in his own hand in his usual fashion, and passed it on, section by section, to his violinist [Johann] Benaro to copy out the parts.

During this task I often sat for hours at a time at Benaro's side, and followed the progress of this exceptional work with mounting interest ; for at that time I had already learned the previous history of the Requiem from Herr Oberbeamter [Anton] Leitgeb, who had had to see to the payment of the honorarium from the Gypsum Agency in Vienna.

And as soon as all the parts had been copied, preparations for its performance were begun. But since it was not possible to find all the necessary performers in the neighbourhood of Stuppach, it was decided that the first performance should take place in Wiener-Neustadt. The performers were chosen so as to give the solos and the most important parts to the best, wherever they came from : thus the solo parts were taken by the male soprano Ferenz of Neustadt, the contralto Kernbeiss of Schottwien, the tenor Klein of Neustadt and the bass Thurner of Gloggnitz. The rehearsal took place on the evening of 12 December 1793 in the choir of the Cistercian abbey and parish church at Wiener-Neustadt, and on the 14th at 10 o'clock a Mass for the Dead was celebrated in the same church, at which this famous Requiem was performed for the first time, for its intended purpose.

Count Walsegg himself directed the whole performance. Of all the

M.—18 a

performers who took part the only living survivors, to the best of my knowledge, are myself and Herr Anton Plaimschauer, now a master turner here in Wiener Neustadt.

On 14 February 1794, the anniversary of the Countess's death, the Requiem was performed at the church of Maria-Schutz at Semmering, of which the Count was the patron, and from this time on the Count made no further use of it, except to arrange it for string quintet, of which version I had the score for several years . . .

That score of the Requiem which was said to be in Süssmayer's hand has never been seen by myself or anyone else except the Count, and no-one knew what he did with it or with the other original scores of various kinds that he owned. But the score that the Count gave me for preparing the work with the singers was written in his own hand, and I would still recognize it at the first glance.

We all knew that the Count wanted to make a mystery out of the Requiem, just like the quartets ; for when he claimed, in our presence, that it was a composition of his own, he always used to smile.

When I went out from Wiener Neustadt with his physician, Doctor Fink, to visit the Count during his last illness, a fortnight before his death, which took place on 11 November 1827, I led the conversation round to the music and theatre of those far-off days, for I knew he liked to speak of them, and at the same time to the Requiem. I also asked him whether he knew the pamphlets that Abbé Stadler had written about it.

He said he did, thought a while and then asked me if I knew a Herr [Franz Sales] Kandler of Vienna. I replied that I did not know Herr Kandler personally but that, if I was not mistaken, I had read some articles on music by him in the old *Wiener musikalische Zeitung*. Whereupon the Count said that when he was in Baden the previous summer, Herr Kandler had come to him for information about the origins of the Requiem. I said, Did you give it to him, your Excellency ? Upon which he replied, They are just as wise as before. — Herr Kandler will no doubt remember this meeting. I only mention it here in order to show that I am familiar with what happened at Stuppach concerning the Requiem down to the least details. That takes the story up to the Count's death. After he died, his entire musical collection was bought from his sister and sole heiress, Countess [Karoline] Sternberg, by Leitner, the estate manager. Among it there are no doubt many valuable pieces of music.

In the summer of 1838 the estate clerk, [Karl] Haag, died at Schloss Stuppach, naming the court usher of the place [Josef Adelpoller] as the sole heir to his property. Included in this there was a small collection of music. And wonder of wonders !, there came to light among this collection the score of Mozart's Requiem, which was at once recognised as the original score, written in Mozart's own hand.

The affair came to the notice of His Excellency Count Moriz von Dietrichstein, as also to that of Councillor [Ignaz] von Mosel, and steps were at once taken to send this score to Vienna so that it might be bought for the Imperial Library, where indeed it is now to be found, and where we may presume it has found its permanent resting-place . . .

The Countess's beautiful marble and granite tomb was so defaced by profane hands, especially at the time of the hostile invasion, and so completely ransacked in the hope of finding valuables, that those remains, so dear to the Count, had to be removed once more and taken back to the family vault at Schottwien . . .

Peace be with the ashes of the Master, and also with those of the honoured patron to whose generosity we owe so priceless a work of art.

> Wiener-Neustadt, Municipal Archives, in the museum.—Found by Otto Schneider and published by O. E. Deutsch in the *Österreichische Musikzeitschrift*, February 1964.—The writer, Anton Herzog, was in 1839 the headmaster of the district high school and choirmaster in Wiener-Neustadt.—The sculptor who worked on the Countess's monument was Johann Martin Fischer.

IGNAZ VON SEYFRIED TO GEORG FRIEDRICH TREITSCHKE, VIENNA, 1840 ?

I return with most grateful thanks the manuscript which you entrusted to me ; it gave me a great, and to a certain extent a rejuvenating, joy, & it is sure to have an historical interest for every art-lover.—In accordance with your wishes I permit myself the following observations, which I am prepared to attest on affidavit.—Schikaneder's personal acquaintance with Mozart, and his later acquaintance with Zitterbarth, dates from a masonic lodge—to be sure, not that famous lodge of Born's, which is said to have numbered Vienna's leading worthies & the élite of the literary caste of that period among its members—but merely a so-called peripheral or eating lodge, where the brethren busied themselves at the weekly evening meetings with games, music & the many pleasures of a well-covered table, as Gieseke often told me, who introduced Sch. to Wieland's *Dschinnistan*, from which he took the material for several of his operas. The composition of *Die Zauberflöte* was very probably begun in the spring of 1791, as M. never worked long at the same work, & invariably worked quickly. He usually wrote in Gerl's lodgings, or in Sch.'s garden, just a few steps from the theatre ; I myself often ate at the same table & took many rehearsals in the same salon, or to be more exact, wooden hut. The prompter Haselbeck had the task of versifying Sch.'s prose sketches ; much of the verse may well have come from his own factory, such rhymes for instance as : " schön Mädchen jung und fein—viel weisser noch als Kreide ", to the preceding : " Aha ! hier seh ich Leute,—gewagt, ich geh' hinein ! "—The libretto was complete as far as the first finale when *Die Zauberzither*, or *Kaspar der Fagottist*, was given in the Leopoldstadt. Perinet had also used the same Wieland fairy-story, but, apart from introducing local colour, he had kept faithfully to the original. That certainly rather vexed our Emanuel ; but he soon knew what to do, and altered the entire plan.

This saved & made the fortune of the whole, for M. could otherwise have hardly left us such a wonderfully fine, poetically romantic model and pattern in this, his dramatic swansong.—M. visited the Frankfurt coronation on his own initiative, to give concerts in order to stop the little hole which kept draining his chaotic finances ; when he entered upon the Prague journey rendered necessary by the invitation of the Bohemian Estates, all the concerted numbers of *Die Zauberflöte* apart from the last finale were ready ; that is, the vocal parts, the bass line, and the main instrumental motifs ; from this short score my friend Henneberg got busily to work on the rehearsals. After Mozart's return—10 or 12 September—he quickly got down to the task of scoring & of catching up with the small numbers which had not yet been composed ; not till the 28th, as the autograph thematic catalogue shews, did the Priests' March & the Overture flow from his pen ; the written parts for the latter, indeed, came wet to the dress rehearsal. . . . On the evening of 4 December M. lay delirious, imagining he was attending *Die Zauberflöte* in the Theater auf der Wieden ; almost his last words, which he whispered to his wife, were, " Quiet, quiet ! Hofer is just taking her top F ;—now my sister-in-law is singing her second aria, ' Der Hölle Rache ' ; how strongly she strikes & holds the B flat : ' Hort ! hört ! hört ! der Mutter Schwur ! '—".

Mozarteum, Salzburg : the end and the date are missing.—Paul Nettl, *Mozart und die königliche Kunst* (Berlin, 1932), pp. 93 ff.—Seyfried (1776-1841) is said to have been a piano pupil of Mozart's. It was 1799 before he joined Emanuel Schikaneder's Freihaus Theatre company as second Kapellmeister, later moving to the Theater an der Wien. Johann Baptist Henneberg was Kapellmeister in Mozart's day. Treitschke, who arranged the *Fidelio* text in 1814, wrote an article on *Die Zauberflöte* in 1841 in the Vienna almanac *Orpheus* ; he had evidently given Seyfried his MS. to read.—The merchant Bartholomäus Zitterbarth did not become Schikaneder's partner till 1799. Born's lodge was " The True Concord " (till 1785). Zitterbarth belonged to " The Three Fires " from 1786 ; Schikaneder, however, did not belong to any Viennese lodge. Gieseke was a member of the " New-Crowned Hope ".—Franz Xaver Gerl, the first Sarastro, lived not far from the theatre. The summer house from one of the courtyards of the Freihaus now stands behind the Mozarteum in Salzburg. Joseph Anton Haselbeck was one of the theatre poets ; the prompter was Biedermann.—The quotations from the libretto of *Die Zauberflöte* are from Act I, scene 12 and Act II, scene 9. Josepha Hofer, Mozart's sister-in-law, was the first Queen of Night. Perinet's Singspiel *Der Fagottist oder Die Zauberzyther*, music by Wenzel Müller, had been performed for the first time on 8 June 1791 in the Theatre in the Leopoldstadt ; it was based on the tale *Lulu oder Die Zauberflöte* in Wieland's collection *Dschinnistan*.—Mozart had been invited to compose and conduct *La clemenza di Tito* in Prague. His journey to Frankfurt took place in 1790.

On 6 March 1842 Constanze Nissen died at Salzburg.

FROM KAROLINE PICHLER'S MEMOIRS, VIENNA, 1843–44

One day when I was sitting at the pianoforte playing the " Non più andrai " from *Figaro*, Mozart, who was paying a visit to us, came up behind me ; I must have been playing it to his satisfaction, for he hummed the melody as I played and beat the time on my shoulders ; but then he suddenly moved a chair up, sat down, told me to carry on playing the bass, and began to improvise such wonderfully beautiful variations that everyone listened to the tones of the German Orpheus with bated breath. But then he suddenly tired of it, jumped up, and, in the mad mood which so often came over him, he began to leap over tables and chairs, miaow like a cat, and turn somersaults like an unruly boy . . .

Mozart and Haydn, whom I knew well, were men in whose personal intercourse there was absolutely no other sign of unusual power of intellect and almost no trace of intellectual culture, nor of any scholarly or other higher interests. A rather ordinary turn of mind, silly jokes and, in the case of the former, an irresponsible way of life, were all that distinguished them in society ; and yet what depths, what worlds of fantasy, harmony, melody and feeling lay concealed behind this unpromising exterior ! Through what inner revelations came their awareness of how they must set about the task of producing such mighty effects, and of expressing feelings, thoughts, passions in music, so that every hearer is obliged to feel them with them, and finds his soul responding deep within him ?

. . . In my youth I heard Händel's oratorio *Acis und Galathea* when Baron van Swieten in conjunction with Prince Dietrichstein and Prince Schwarzenberg had it performed for the delectation of the public, along with several other compositions of this great master, under the direction of Mozart, who had added wind parts to these essentially simple compositions . . .

. . . There was much music-making in our house, according to my father's wishes ; great Mozart, though not my teacher, gave me many a lesson, I often had the opportunity of hearing him play and of perfecting myself by means of his instruction.

> 1st Paragraph—*Allgemeine Theaterzeitung* (Vienna, 15 July 1843), p. 750 : " Ein Abend bei Karoline Pichler ", by Anton Langer. The rest appeared in Pichler's *Denkwürdigkeiten aus meinem Leben* (Vienna, 1844), new ed. by Emil Karl Blümml (Munich, 1914), Vol. I, pp. 293 f., Vol. II, pp. 184 and 410 f. Karoline Pichler, a prolific writer (1769–1843), was the daughter of the Councillor Franz Sales von Greiner, who lived in the house " Zur Mehlgrube " on the Neue Markt.—For van Swieten's Society of Noblemen and Mozart's arrangement of *Acis and Galatea* (K. 566), *cf.* November 1788.

On 29 July 1844 Franz Xaver Wolfgang Mozart died at Carlsbad.

> He was a pianoforte virtuoso and composer, made concert tours in Europe and lived for thirty years at Lwów (Lemberg) as music teacher.

FROM JOHANN BAPTIST GÄNSBACHER'S " DENKWÜRDIGKEITEN AUS MEINEM LEBEN ", VIENNA, 1844

. . . Before I removed to Prague with the Firmian family [1804] I very often visited Mozart's widow ; I there got to know old Baron van

Swieten, who took much interest in her son [Wolfgang]. The latter was already an excellent pianist, who could among other things transpose Bach fugues into another key at sight ; at that time Neukom was his teacher. I was often asked for my opinion on his compositions for the piano, and I always gave it to him frankly. On New Year's Eve 1807 I visited Joseph Haydn in his home in Gumpendorf in the company of Mozart's widow and another artist. We found him very neatly attired and with a newly dressed wig, sitting at a little table on which lay his three-cornered hat and stick, as if he had the intention of driving out directly. The whole room was hung with little plates in black frames. When Haydn saw that we were looking at them and wanted to observe them more closely, he asserted that they were his copper-plates ; they consisted in fact entirely of canons and solo songs which he had composed. He sadly lamented that he was too weak to compose now, although he had no lack of ideas. He spoke of Mozart with great veneration . . .

> Innsbruck, Museum Ferdinandeum.—*Allgemeine Wiener Musik-Zeitung*, 19 September 1844, p. 449 (the autobiography published by Karl Magnus Gross under the pseudonym Athanasius).—See 13 April 1808.—Gänsbacher (1778–1844) was cathedral organist and a composer of church music ; his first appointment was to the family of Count Firmian in Vienna and Prague. —Sigismund von Neukomm was Haydn's favourite pupil.—The canons, fair copies in an unknown hand, passed from Haydn's estate to Esterháza Palace, but they have since disappeared.

FROM THE ANONYMOUS BIOGRAPHY OF ADALBERT GYROWETZ, VIENNA, 1848

On his arrival there [in Vienna, ca. 1785] he was presented at the house of Hofrath von Käss, who was known as the leading musical connoisseur and dilettante in Vienna, and who gave society concerts in his house twice a week, at which the leading virtuosi at that time in Vienna, and the leading composers, viz : Joseph Haydn, Mozart, Dittersdorf, Hoffmeister, Albrechtsberger, Giarnovichi etc. etc. were gathered together ; Haydn's symphonies were performed there.—Mozart was most usually to be heard performing on the fortepiano, and Giarnovichi, at that time the most famous virtuoso on the violin, generally played a concerto ; the lady of the house sang. One evening it so happened that Mozart did not appear right at the beginning of the concert, and everyone had been waiting for him for some time, for he had promised to bring a new song for the lady of the house. Several servants were sent to look for him ; at last one of them found him in a tavern and asked him to come at once, because everyone was waiting for him and looking forward to the new song. Mozart then remembered that he had not yet composed the song ; he at once asked the servant to bring him a sheet of music paper—when this had been done, Mozart began to compose the song in the inn itself, and when he had it ready, he took it to the concert, where everyone was waiting with the keenest expectancy. He was received in the most joyful manner, after a few gentle reproaches for his considerable lateness, and when he at last sat down at the pianoforte, the lady of the house sang the new song with a voice that admittedly trembled a little, but it was none the less received enthusiastically and applauded. It was in this company, then, that Gyrowetz had the good fortune to make the acquaintance of Vienna's most famous masters, by whom he was also received and treated in the friendliest and most affable manner.

Mozart seemed to be the kindest of them all; he gazed at Gyrowetz, who was then still very young, with a very sympathetic expression, as if to say, " Poor young man, you are entering the ways of the great world for the first time and are anxiously awaiting from your Destiny what the future will bring ! "—His gaze made a very great impression on the mind of young Gyrowetz, whose heart at that first moment went out to him entirely. . . . He visited . . . Mozart, and was received by him in the friendliest way; cheered by his affability and kindness, he asked him to cast a glance at his youthful works, which consisted of six symphonies, and to give him his opinion on them. Mozart agreed to his request like the kind-hearted man he was, looked the pieces through, praised them, and promised the young artist that he would have one of these symphonies performed at his concert in the music room in the Mehlgrube, where Mozart was giving six subscription concerts; and thus it actually came to pass one Thursday. The symphony was performed in the music room in the Mehlgrube by the full theatre orchestra, and received general applause. Mozart with his innate goodness of heart took the young artist by the hand and presented him to the audience as the author of the symphony. . . .

[Gyrowetz then went to Italy as secretary to Prince Ruspoli.]

. . . One day before his departure he by chance met the kind and generous-hearted Mozart, to whom he once again paid his humble respects, and when he heard that Gyrowetz was really going to Italy, he said to him, " You lucky man ! Ah, how glad I would be if I could go with you !— But see, I must go and give another lesson so as to earn something ! "— Those were the last words which Mozart spoke to Gyrowetz.—With tears in their eyes and with a hand-shake they bade each other farewell.

Pp. 9 f., 11 and 13.—Gyrowetz (Jírovec), born at Budějovice (Bohemia) in 1763, studied music in Vienna, Naples and London; from 1805-31 he was Kapellmeister of the Court Opera. He was a prolific composer and died in Vienna in 1850.—The book is regarded as an autobiography.—Franz Bernhard von Keess (the father of Franz Georg) lived in the Bauernmarkt; his second wife was the singer Karoline, *née* von Mercier.—Giovanni Mane Giarnovichi (known as Jarnowick) lived in Vienna about 1785.—The concerts at the hall

" Zur Mehlgrube ", the programmes for which have not been preserved, took place on Fridays.

Original German opera libretti were . . . *Die Zauberflöte*, a genuinely German work, by Schikaneder and his chorus singer Gieseke, who gave him the outline of the plot, the division into scenes and the naïve and well-known rhymes. This Gieseke—a one-time student from Halle (born in Brunswick)—was the author of several magic operas, and also of *Die Zauberflöte* (after Wieland's *Lulu*), which Schikaneder merely altered, cut, and put together again, taking to himself the title of its author. Poor Gieseke led a penurious existence in Schikaneder's theatre . . . as a member of the chorus and in small parts. After a time he disappeared ; whither, no one knew. One day in the summer of the year 1818, an elegant old gentleman in a blue coat and white cravat, and wearing a decoration, sat down at the table in the tavern in Vienna at which Ignaz von Seyfried, Korntheuer, Julius Laroche, Küstner, Gned and I met for luncheon each day. His venerable snow-white head, his meticulous way of speaking, and his whole bearing, made a favourable impression on us all. It was the former chorus singer Gieseke, now a professor at Dublin University ; he had come from Iceland and Lapland straight to Vienna with a natural history collection formed from the plant, mineral and animal kingdoms, which he intended to present to the Imperial Natural History Collection. Seyfried was the only one to recognize him. The old gentleman's joy at being in Vienna and at the Emperor Francis's recognition (he gave him a really valuable gold snuffbox shining with solitaires and filled with brand new Kremnitz ducats) was the recompense for many years of privations and suffering. On this occasion we learnt so much about the old days ; among other things we learnt that he (who was at that time a member of the banned order of Freemasons) was the real author of *Die Zauberflöte* (although Seyfried already had a suspicion of this). I relate this according to his own statement, which we had no reason to doubt. He gave us this explanation when I sang the cavatina interpolated into *Der Spiegel von Arkadien*. Many thought that the prompter Helmböck had been Schikaneder's collaborator. But in this also Gieseke disabused us ; Gieseke attributed to Schikaneder only the figures of Papageno and his wife.

O. E. Deutsch, *Die Musikforschung*, Vol. V, 1952, pp. 152 ff.—Practically all the statements about Gieseke are incorrect.—Wieland was not the author of the tale *Lulu oder Die Zauberflöte*, which appeared in his collection *Dschinnistan* ; it was by A. J. Liebeskind.—Cornet's witnesses were all members of the Theater an der Wien, of which he himself had been a member in 1817–18. —Christoph Helmböck had been property man, not prompter, in Schikaneder's company.—Cf. Seyfried's letter to Treitschke, 1840.

FROM THE MEMOIRS OF DR JOSEPH FRANK, JANUARY 1852

I found Mozart to be a little man with a broad head and fleshy hands (des mains potelées) ; he received me rather coldly. " Now ", he said, " play me something ! " I played him a fantasia of his own composition. " Not bad ", he said, to my great astonishment, " now I'll play it for you." What a wonder ! The piano became a completely different instrument under his fingers. He had had it amplified by means of a second keyboard, which he used as a pedal. Mozart then made a few observations about the way in which I should play his fantasia. I was fortunate enough to understand him and to satisfy him.—" Do you play other pieces of my composition ? "—" Yes, sir ", I replied, " your variations on the theme ' Unser dummer Pöbel meint ', and a sonata with violin and violoncello accompaniment."—" Good, I will play the piece to you ; you will derive more benefit from hearing me than from playing it yourself."—I soon became intimate with Mozart. As I always found him busy studying the scores of French operas, I was bold enough to ask him if he would not do better to devote his attention to Italian scores. " In respect of melody yes, but in respect of dramatic effectiveness, no. Moreover, the scores which you see here are, apart from those of Gretry, by Gluck, Piccini, Salieri, and there is nothing French about them but the words." Once when we were speaking about instruments Mozart said that he loathed the flute and the harp. That is practically all I can remember having heard from this great composer. The twelve lessons which I had from him are not enough to let me call myself his pupil.

> *Deutsches Museum*, edited by Robert Prutz and Wilhelm Wolfsohn (Leipzig, January 1852), Vol. II, Part i, pp. 27 f. : " Aus den ungedruckten Denkwürdigkeiten der Aerzte [From the Unpublished Memorabilia of the Doctors] Peter und Joseph Frank ", communicated by G. E. Guhrauer.—Johann Peter Frank was a famous physician ; his son Joseph in 1798 married Christine Gerardi, who had sung the Archangel Gabriel in Haydn's *Creation*. The couple also knew Beethoven. Christine was an excellent amateur singer, Joseph a modest amateur composer.—For the pedal pianoforte, *cf.* 10 March 1785.—The variations on a theme by Gluck are K. 455.—Despite his dislike of the flute and the harp Mozart had written a concerto for these instruments (K. 299) in Paris in 1778 (in Mannheim he also wrote two concertos and an andante for flute, K. 313-15). All these works were commissioned.

★ MAX KELLER TO KARL EMIL VON SCHAFHÄUTL, 23 OCTOBER 1852

It was in the monastery at Seeon that I saw Mozart for the first time— and also the last, for in that year he went away to Vienna. At that time (so far as I remember) he looked rather pale and puffy. Of his wonderfully beautiful organ-playing I understood nothing then, for I was only just 10 years old.

Munich, Bavarian State Library.—Robert Münster in the *Mozart-Jahrbuch 1960–1* (Salzburg, 1962), p. 203. Keller (1770–1855) had been a choirboy at the Benedictine Monastery of Seeon from 1780 ; he became organist there and later at Altötting.—Schafhäutl, professor of geology in Munich, also wrote on music.—Mozart seems to have visited Seeon briefly at the beginning of November 1780, before he was summoned from Munich to Vienna in March 1781.

FROM LUDWIG TIECK'S MEMOIRS, LEIPZIG, 1855

. . . How often did he [Tieck] hear musical performances, conversations on music, judgements about the worth or lack of worth of particular compositions ! If he himself even now felt no inclination to take part in performances, he at least began to grow aware of the secrets of music in classical works. Here too he went counter to fashion in that he instinctively turned towards Mozart's great works, and refused to be led astray by ephemeral critical opinions, or even by voices as important as that of Reichardt. Mozart's victorious opponent was Dittersdorf, whose comic operas were given in Berlin too before large and enthusiastic audiences. *Doctor und Apotheker* was preferred to *Figaro* and *Don Juan*, and it was possible to praise *Die Liebe im Narrenhause* in public announcements as the greatest work of the musician's art.

Ludwig's regard for Mozart was to be rewarded in a surprising way. One evening in 1789, entering the dimly-lit and still empty theatre long before the beginning of the performance, as was his wont, he caught sight of a man in the orchestra pit whom he did not know. He was small, rapid of movement, restless, and with a stupid expression on his face : an unprepossessing figure in a grey overcoat. He was going from one music-desk to the next and seemed to be looking carefully through the music on them. Ludwig at once entered on a conversation. They spoke of the orchestra, the theatre, the opera, the public's taste. He expressed his views openly, but spoke of Mozart's operas with the deepest admiration. " So you often hear Mozart's operas and are fond of them ? " the stranger asked, " that is very good of you, young man." They continued their conversation for some time, the auditorium slowly filled, and finally the stranger was called away by someone on the stage. His words had strangely moved Ludwig ; he made enquiries. It was Mozart himself, the great master, who had spoken with him and expressed his appreciation to him.

Rudolf Köpke, *Ludwig Tieck : Erinnerungen aus dem Leben des Dichters nach dessen mündlichen und schriftlichen Mitteilungen*, Vol. I, pp. 86 f.—Tieck was born in Berlin in 1773 and died there in 1853.—*Doctor und Apotheker* was produced in Vienna in 1786 and in Berlin in 1787 ; *Die Liebe im Narrenhaus* was given in Vienna in 1787 and in Berlin in 1791 (16 May).—Tieck's meeting with Mozart may have taken place on 19 May 1789, before the performance of *Die Entführung* in Berlin.

FROM JOSEPH DEINER'S (?) MEMOIRS, VIENNA, 1856

It was on a cold and cheerless November day of the year 1791 that Mozart entered the " Silver Snake " tavern in Vienna, where he was a frequent visitor. This tavern was in the Kärnthnerstrasse and was then No. 1112 ; it is now No. 1074. Actors, singers and musicians often met there. On the said day Mozart found several strangers in the special parlour, so he at once entered the next and smaller room where there were only three tables. The little room had trees painted on the walls, a style of decoration that was kept when the owner of the house later turned this room into a small shop.
The optician Herr Josef Rospini is the present owner of this shop. When Mozart entered this little room, he threw himself wearily on to a chair and let his head sink, supported on his right hand. Thus he sat for quite a long time, and then ordered the waiter to bring him wine, whereas he normally only drank beer. When the waiter placed the wine in front of him, Mozart continued to sit there motionless and did not even taste his drink.—Then the landlord, Josef Deiner, entered the parlour through a door which led into the little courtyard. He knew Mozart well and the latter always took him into his confidence. When Deiner caught sight of the composer he stood still and looked at him long and carefully. Mozart looked unusually pale, his powdered fair hair was in disarray and the little pigtail was carelessly tied. Suddenly he looked up and noticed the landlord. " Well, Josef, how are you ? " he asked.—" I should be asking you that question ", answered Deiner, " for you look quite ill and wretched, Maestro. I heard you were in Prague, and the Bohemian air has not done you any good. So much is quite clear. You are drinking wine now, that's good ; you probably drank a lot of beer in Bohemia and upset your stomach. You'll be all right, Maestro ! "
" My stomach is better than you think," said Mozart, " I've learned to swallow all sorts of things ! " A sigh accompanied these words.
" That is lucky ", Deiner replied, " for all illnesses begin in the stomach, as our General Laudon said when we were outside Belgrade and Archduke Franz was sick for a few days. But I need not tell you anything about Turkish music today, you've often enough had a laugh at that ! "
" No," Mozart answered, " I feel that there won't be much more music-making. I've got a chill coming on that I can't account for. Deiner, you drink my wine, and take this coin (a 17-kreutzer piece). Come and see me tomorrow morning. Winter is coming on and we need wood. My wife will go along with you to buy some ; I'll have a fire lighted this very day."
Mozart thereupon summoned the waiter, pressed a silver coin into his hand, and then left.—Deiner, the landlord, took Mozart's wine with him to the best parlour, sat down, and said to himself : " A young man like that, and thinking of death ! Well, that'll come in time, but not yet

awhile ! But I mustn't forget the wood, for it's very cold in November."
—Then a crowd of Italian singers came into the " Silver Snake " ; Deiner
hated them, for they were always attacking his " dear Maestro ", and for
that reason he too went off.

The following morning at 7 o'clock Deiner went to No. 970 in the
Rauhensteingasse, the so-called " kleines Kaiserhaus ", where the present
Mozarthof No. 934 stands. When he knocked on the door of Mozart's
lodgings on the first floor, it was opened by the maid, who knew him and
accordingly let him in. She told him that she had had to fetch the doctor
in the night as the Herr Kapellmeister was very ill. Deiner was nevertheless
called into the room by Mozart's wife. In one corner of the room was
the bed, covered with a white coverlet, in which Mozart lay. When he
heard Deiner talking he opened his eyes and said only just audibly, " Josef,
there's nothing doing today ; today we're going to be busy with doctors
and apothecaries."

Josef Deiner left the house. He remembered that he had been at Mozart's
house a year earlier at the same time, also on the subject of wood. On
that occasion he had found Mozart and his wife in his study, which had
two windows looking on to the Rauhensteingasse and one on to the
Himmelpfortgasse. Mozart and his wife were dancing merrily round the
room. When Deiner asked if Mozart was teaching his wife to dance,
Mozart laughed and said, " We're only getting warm, it's freezing in here
and we can't afford any wood." Deiner hurried away and at once brought
them some of his own firewood. Mozart accepted it and promised to
pay generously for it when he had some money.

On 28 November the doctors held a consultation on Mozart's condition.
Dr Elossek [Closset], who was at that time quite famous, and Dr Sallaba,
head physician of the General Hospital, were present.

None of Mozart's operas was performed during his illness ; the progress
of the great master's condition was awaited with anxious expectancy.
Most painfully affected of all by Mozart's condition was Fräulein Anna
Gottlieb, who was born in Vienna on 29 April 1774. She became a member of the Court Opera in her earliest youth and she remained there until
her sixteenth year. At this age she was engaged by Baron Braun for the
Theatre in the Freihaus auf der Wieden and she later became the first
interpreter of the role of Pamina in Mozart's Zauberflöte ; in 1792 Fräulein
Gottlieb joined the Theatre in the Leopoldstadt, where she excelled as the
" Nymph of the Danube " [Hensler's Das Donauweibchen] and had considerable successes in comic opera. At the time of writing, this lady (as
we have already mentioned) is still living in Vienna.

As Mozart's illness took on a graver character with each minute, his wife
summoned Dr Sallaba again on 5 December 1791. He came, soon followed
by Kapellmeister Süssmeyer, to whom Sallaba secretly confided that Mozart
would not survive the coming night. Dr Sallaba also prescribed a medicine

for Mozart's wife, as she too was unwell, and after he had had another look at Mozart, he took his leave.

Süssmeyer remained at the side of the dying composer. At 12 o'clock in the night Mozart raised himself in his bed, his eyes staring, then he sank back with his head towards the wall, and seemed to fall asleep again. At 4 o'clock in the morning he was a corpse. At 5 o'clock in the morning the front door bell of the " Silver Snake " was violently rung. Deiner opened. Mozart's maid, Elise, stood before the door, sobbing. The landlord asked what she wanted.—" Herr Deiner ", said the maid, " please come and dress our master ! "—" To go for a walk ? "—" No, he is dead ; he died an hour ago ; please hurry ! "

Deiner found Mozart's widow dissolved in tears, and so weak that she could not stand upright. He performed for Mozart the services which it is usual to pay to the dead. In the morning Mozart was laid on the bier and covered with a black drapery from the burial society, as was then the custom, and which usage continued until the year 1818. The corpse was taken into the study and placed near his pianoforte.

Mozart's funeral took place at 3 o'clock in the afternoon of 7 December in St Stephen's Cathedral, not in the body of the church, but in the Crucifix Chapel on the north side, where the Capistrano pulpit stands. The committal was performed in the manner appropriate to a third-class funeral, at a cost of 8 fl., 36 kr. The hearse cost an extra 3 fl.

The night of Mozart's death was dark and stormy ; at the funeral too it began to rage and storm. Rain and snow fell at the same time, as if Nature wanted to shew her anger with the great composer's contemporaries, who had turned out extremely sparsely for his burial. Only a few friends and three women accompanied the corpse. Mozart's wife was not present. These few people with their umbrellas stood round the bier, which was then taken via the Grosse Schullerstrasse to the St Marx Cemetery. As the storm grew ever more violent, even these few friends determined to turn back at the Stuben Gate, and they betook themselves to the " Silver Snake ". Deiner, the landlord, was also present for the funeral. He then went up to Mozart's wife and asked her if she did not want a cross erected for her dead husband. She answered, " They will give him one any way."—When in the year 1832 King Ludwig of Bavaria visited Mozart's widow in Salzburg (she drew a pension from him), he asked her how it had come about that she had had no memorial stone erected to her husband. She replied to the King, " I have often visited cemeteries both in the country and also in big towns, and everywhere, especially in Vienna, I have seen very many crosses in the cemeteries. I was accordingly of the opinion that the parish in which the funeral takes place is also responsible for the provision of a cross."

This error is the reason why we cannot today accurately determine the place where lie the remains of this great musician.

Morgen-Post (Vienna, 28 January 1856), p. 2.—These recollections, written down for the centenary of Mozart's birth, were the editorial version of a report from " an ordinary man " who had been " in personal contact " with Mozart. Jahn thinks it possible that they are the work of Deiner. They had a great effect and this may still be felt after a further century and more.—The house, No. 12 in the Kärntnerstrasse, which in 1856 bore the number 1074 in the Inner City, did not correspond to No. 1112 in 1791, but to Nos. 1083-84 ; the sign of No. 1083 was " Zur goldenen " not " Zur silbernen Schlange " (The Golden, not the Silver Snake). The landlord of the beer-house was Joseph Preisinger. The houses 1083-84 were rebuilt into one in 1797.—Among the small Austrian silver coins were pieces of 5, 7, 10, 17 and 20 kreuzer, of which those of 7 and 17 kr. were later worth only 6 and 15 kr. (A gulden contained 60 kreuzer)—Fräulein Gottlieb died a few days later, on 4 February 1856.—Peter von Braun was lessee of the two court theatres from 1794 to 1806 and had nothing to do with the Theater auf der Wieden.—The funeral took place on 6, not on 7 December.—The weather was fine on 6 December (as on the 5th) ; *cf.* Zinzendorf's Diary.—The Grosse Schulerstrasse, where Mozart lived from 1784 to 1787, is now called simply Schulerstrasse.—The funeral cost 8 gulden 56 (not 36) kreuzer.

FROM AMBROS RIEDER'S AUTOBIOGRAPHY, VIENNA, 1856

. . . As a young man I admired many an excellent virtuoso of both the violin and the pianoforte ; but who can imagine my astonishment when I was fortunate enough to hear the immortal, mighty W. A. Mozart not only perform variations on the pianoforte, but also fantasias, before a numerous and eminent gathering. This was for me a new-created world with a nature entirely different from anything I had previously been accustomed to hear and see. The bold flight of his fantasy, which soared to the highest regions and then plunged into the depths of the abyss, was something which even the most experienced master of music could not sufficiently admire and wonder at. Even now as an old man I can hear those heavenly and unforgettable harmonies resound within me, and I move towards my grave in the fullest conviction than there has only ever been one Mozart.

Neue Wiener Musik-Zeitung, 29 May 1856, p. 97 f. The anonymous necrology was written on the basis of the autobiography written by Rieder for Joseph Sonnleithner in 1826 (Gesellschaft der Musikfreunde, Vienna).—Ambros Rieder (1771–1855) was from 1802 choirmaster of the Parish Church at Perchtoldsdorf in Lower Austria, and a prolific church composer. He and his two sons were on friendly terms with Schubert.

★ FROM XAVER SCHNYDER VON WARTENSEE'S " NOTIZEN ÜBER DIE ZAUBERFLÖTE VON MOZART " (PUBLISHED 25 JULY 1856)

When, in 1832, I made the acquaintance in Prague of Kapellmeister Trübensee, now dead for many years, he told me that he had been employed as second oboist at Schikaneder's theatre in Vienna, and had taken part in the first performance of *Die Zauberflöte* under Mozart's own direction. At first the opera was not well received. The overture, the introduction and so forth, obviously roused no enthusiasm at all, and the good Mozart, who had pinned great hopes of bettering his affairs on the reception of the *Zauberflöte*, went as pale as death. It was the duet " Bei Männern, welche Liebe fühlen" that first received definite applause, and from then on the brilliant success of the opera was assured. Moreover Trübensee told me that it was known that Schikaneder had rejected Mozart's original version of the duet, all written in the most lofty style, but that at that time it was still in circulation, and in the many performances of the work that followed they used to alternate the two settings, and on the posters it read : with the old duet, or with the new duet.

> *Neue Zeitschrift für Musik* (Leipzig), Vol. 45 No. 5, p. 43.—Josef Triebensee was engaged for several years at the Freihaus Theatre.—In the surviving posters this phrase does not occur. However, on 4 January 1802, when *Die Zauberflöte* was performed for the first time at the new Theater an der Wien, Schikaneder announced two unpublished pieces, of which one was doubtless the first version of the duet, which he had originally rejected.

FROM THE " BLÄTTER FÜR MUSIK, THEATER UND KUNST ", PUBLISHED
BY L. A. ZELLNER, VIENNA, 30 SEPTEMBER 1856

Among the guests [at the Salzburg Mozart Centenary celebrations] was that most excellent object of general curiosity and sympathy, Carl Mozart, the son of the great composer. Of Mozart's two sons Carl is the elder, the younger . . . died a few years ago in Carlsbad, as is well known. Carl Mozart, a small, thin man with black eyes and slightly greying hair, simple and extremely modest in his manner, was only seven years old when he lost his father. In spite of that he assured me when I asked him that he remembered his father very clearly, and that he recalled two circumstances in particular. Firstly, that his father often had to take him out for walks, because his mother Constanze had at that time long been ailing and had to keep to the house. Thus he was often taken to the theatre by his father, a pleasure that later he strangely enough never again sought out.

> Rudolf von Lewicki in *Mozarteums-Mitteilungen* (Salzburg, November 1919), Vol. II/1, p. 16.—Mozart took Karl to *Die Zauberflöte* on 13 October 1791.

FROM THE REMINISCENCES OF THE VIOLA PLAYER FRANZ XAVER SEMLER
(PUBLISHED 11 MARCH 1857)

[Mozart in Potsdam, 1789]
He was once requested to extemporize there. Willing as he always was, he made no exception on this occasion. He sat down at the keyboard ;

two themes were supplied for him by the musical connoisseurs present. The singer placed herself near his chair so as to watch him play. Mozart, who enjoyed joking with her, looked up to her and said, " Well ? Have you got a little tune on your conscience ? " She sang him one. He now began to play most delightfully, now with this theme, now with that, and in conclusion he combined all three, to the greatest pleasure and wonder of those present.

> *Vossische Zeitung* (Berlin, 11 March 1857), supplement, p. 7.—Abert, Vol. II, p. 631.—The singer was Semler's sister, Sophie Niclas.

On 13 October 1858 Karl Thomas Mozart died in Milan.

> Mozart's elder son, who like his brother remained unmarried, had become an official of the State Accountancy in Austrian Lombardy.

FROM IGNAZ FRANZ CASTELLI'S " MEMOIREN MEINES LEBENS ", VIENNA, 1861

The late bass singer Sebastian Meyer told me that Mozart had originally written the duet where Papageno and Papagena first see each other quite differently from the way in which we now hear it. Both originally cried out " Papageno ! ", " Papagena ! " a few times in amazement. But when Schikaneder heard this, he called down in to the orchestra, " Hey, Mozart ! That's no good, the music must express greater astonishment. They must both stare dumbly at each other, then Papageno must begin to stammer : ' Pa-papapa-pa-pa ' ; Papagena must repeat that until both of them finally get the whole name out." Mozart followed the advice, and in this form the duet always had to be repeated.

Further, when the priests were assembling in the second act, this happened as late as the dress rehearsal without any musical accompaniment, but Schikaneder asked that a solemn march be composed for it. Mozart is reported to have then said to the musicians, " Give me your music folders ! " and to have at once written this splendid march into their parts.

> Vol. I., pp. 232 f.—Friedrich Sebastian Mayer, or Meyer, married Mozart's sister-in-law Josepha Hofer, *née* Weber, in 1797. He was a member of Schikaneder's company from 1793, *i.e.* after the composition of *Die Zauberflöte*. The duet is sung at the second meeting between Papageno and Papagena. (The " Pa Pa Pa " letter in the Vienna City Library, reputedly written by Schikaneder to Mozart on 5 September 1790, is a forgery.) The priests' march and the overture were indeed written as late as 28 September 1791, but it is certain that not even the former was composed during the dress rehearsal.

FROM DORIS STOCK'S MEMOIRS, 1871

. . . Mozart himself, during his short stay in Dresden, was an almost daily visitor to the Körners' house. For the charming and witty Doris he was all aflame, and with his south German vivacity he paid her the naïvest compliments. He generally came shortly before dinner and, after he had poured out a stream of gallant phrases, he sat down to improvise at the pianoforte. In the next room the table was meanwhile being set and the soup dished up, and the servant announced that dinner was served. But who could tear himself away when Mozart was improvising ! The soup was allowed to grow cold and the roast to burn, simply so that we could continue to listen to the magic sounds which the master, completely absorbed in what he was doing and unaware of the rest of the world, conjured from the instrument. Yet one finally grows tired even of the highest pleasures when the stomach makes known its demands. After the soup had grown cold a few times while Mozart played, he was briefly taken to task. " Mozart ", said Doris, gently laying her snow-white arm on his shoulder, " Mozart, we are going in to dine ; do you want to eat with us ? "—" Your servant, Mademoiselle, I shall be with you in a moment." But it was precisely Mozart who never did come ; he played on undisturbed. Thus we often had the rarest Mozartian musical accompaniment to our meal, Doris concluded her narrative, and when we rose from table we found him still sitting at the keyboard.

Gustav Parthey, *Jugenderinnerungen* (Berlin, 1871), Vol. II, p. 51.—For Körner and Stock see 16 April 1789. Doris (Dora, Dorothea) Stock, the daughter of a Leipzig copper engraver, lived from 1760 to 1852. The assertion that Mozart visited the Körners almost daily is an exaggeration. The house was in the street later known as the Körnergasse (No. 7) ; the Theodor Körner Museum was later established in the house where the poet had been born on 23 September 1791.

JOHANNES HUMMEL ON HIS SON JOHANN NEPOMUK (1873)

[Young Hummel became Mozart's pupil in 1786]

Mozart was hard at work when we entered, but in spite of that he received me with the friendly words, " Ah look ; it's my dear Hummel ; where have you been, and how are you ? It's good to see you. Sit down ; and you, my young friend, find yourself a chair."—I had to sit down on the sofa next to the little man.—" What brings you here ? " he then asked me. With some slight embarrassment I brought out my request. He listened to me with patience, but when I had finished he looked a bit doubtful and said, " You know, my dear friend, I don't much like taking on pupils ; it takes up too much of my time and disturbs me in my work. But let's see and hear what the boy's like, and whether he's worth helping —Sit down at the piano, then, and show us what you can do ", he said to Nepomuk. The latter came out with a few small pieces by Bach which he had carefully practised, and spread them out. Mozart left him alone and he began. Wolfgang had sat down beside me again and listened with his arms crossed. He became ever more still, his expression ever more

rapt ; his eyes shone more brightly and joyously. During the performance he nudged me gently with his arm a few times and nodded appreci-
atively towards me. When my boy had finished the Bach, Mozart placed
another and not exactly easy composition before him, one of his own
this time, to see how good his sight-reading might be. It went very well.
Wolfgang's attention grew from minute to minute. Suddenly, with a
look that sparkled and twinkled for joy, he put his hand on my knee,
pressed it gently, and whispered to me, " You must leave the lad here with
me, I shan't let him out of my sight—something can be made of him ! "
—My Nepomuk had just about finished the movement when Mozart
got up, hurried over to him, put his hand on his head, and said, " Bravo
bravo ; you're a splendid lad. Carry on like that and you'll get on all
right ! "—He then took him by the hand, led him to the sofa, put him
on his lap, and petted him continually. And to me he said, " It's agreed,
then, I'll teach the lad, but he must live with me so that I can always have
my eye on him. He shall have everything free, lessons, lodging, food.
You will not have any of the cares of looking after him. Agreed ? "
—My eyes were moist with tears as I pressed the dear man's hand and
thanked him from an overflowing heart. For I knew that something really
would come of him, as Mozart had put it. Shortly after, my son Nepomuk
moved to Mozart's house, where he was treated like a son of the family.
He was as comfortable and well cared for as possible ; Wolfgang looked
after him like a father, and Konstanze cared for him like a mother.

> Moritz Müller, " Ein alter Musikmeister " in *Europa* (Leipzig, 1873), No. 37.
> (There is a copy of this periodical in the Bavarian State Library, Munich.)
> —Benyovszky, *op. cit.*, pp. 27-9.—Hummel must have been a pupil of Mozart's
> in 1786 and 1787. His father died in 1828.—See 20 and 21 May 1789.—*Cf.* the
> following memoir.

FROM FERDINAND HILLER'S " KÜNSTLERLEBEN ", COLOGNE, 1880

. . . Hummel took me to another building [in Vienna, 1827]—perhaps
there are people here who still know which—I neglected to write it down
because its significance occupied me too fully—it was the self same house
in which as an eight year old boy he had lived with Mozart and received
instruction from him. The master was completely absorbed in his
memories. As he led me through the various rooms, which seemed not
to have undergone any alteration, he described their former furnishings to
me. " Here ", he said, " stood Mozart's pianoforte, at which I had lessons,
—here was the writing desk at which he composed—here in this little room
stood my clavier and there in the middle of the room was a billiard table.
One day I tried to wield the cue and tore a hole in the cloth. The punish-
ment (he mimed it) was not slow in coming."

P. 52.—Hiller's reminiscences are based on a lecture which he gave in Vienna on 22 December 1879.—The house was the one in the Schulerstrasse which Mozart in fact left in the spring of 1787.—The anecdotes about young Hummel in Mozart's house which Edward Holmes gives in his Mozart biography of 1845, pp. 258 ff., have been passed over here.

* FROM WILLIAM JACKSON'S MEMOIRS, PUBLISHED 1882
(in English)

An anecdote of him may be worth preserving. When he was a mere infant (I think under six years of age) he was exhibited as a great performer on the harpsichord, and an extraordinary genius for music. John Bach took the child between his knees and began a subject on that instrument, which he left, and Mozart continued—each led the other into very abstruse harmonies, and extraneous modulations, in which the child beat the man. We were afterwards looking over Bach's famous song " Se spiego " in *Zanaida*. The score was inverted to Mozart, who was rolling on the table. He pointed out a note which he said was wrong. It was so, whether of the composer or copyist I cannot now recollect, but it was an instance of extraordinary discernment and readiness in a mere infant.

> *The Leisure Hour* (London, 1882), p. 274.—Discovered by Dr. Stanley Sadie. William Jackson, of Exeter (1730–1803), musician and composer, published in 1782 and in 1798 two books on various subjects, but extracts from his Memoirs were not printed before 1882. He apparently was present at one of the meetings between the Mozarts and John Christian Bach in London, 1764–65. Arias from Bach's opera *Zanaida* were published in 1763.

FROM JOHANNA VON BISCHOFF'S " JUGENDERINNERUNGEN ",
VIENNA, 1891

In the summer of 1825 we lived in one half of the [Villa] Bertramka outside Prague ; the other half was occupied by Herr Dussek, the landlord, and the heir of Mozart's friend Frau Dussek, who had lived here at the same time as Mozart. Dussek shewed Frau von Pichler the place in my room where Mozart's spinet had stood, and told her how, when *Titus* was about to be performed just at the time of the reception of Emperor Leopold, messenger after messenger was sent out by the Vienna orchestra for the missing overture. Mozart paced up and down in the room ; but when his friend Frau Dussek (who was constantly urging him on) spied the leader of the orchestra among those panting up the hill, and Mozart calmly answered the reiterated injunction with " Not a single idea will come ", she shouted at him, " Then for heaven's sake begin it with the cavalry march ! " He flew to the spinet and after the first two bars of the cavalry march, with which the overture really does begin, the melodies tumbled into place, the overture was finished, was quickly orchestrated, and the messengers hurried off with the sheets, still wet.

 Part IV, second section, p. 6.—Supplied by Dr. Franz Glück.—Frau Bischoff, *née* Kuh (1798–1891), married the doctor Professor Ignaz Bischoff von Altenstern in 1818 ; she lived with him in Prague until the year 1825, when they removed to Vienna.—Her reminiscences are entirely credible, and are further borne out by Karoline Pichler's *Denkwürdigkeiten* (see 1843–44). (New ed. 1914, Vol. II, pp. 203 f.) The only doubt concerns the name of the owner of the Villa Bertramka *ca.* 1825 : Frau Josepha Dušek had in fact sold, not bequeathed, the house in 1799 after her husband's death.—It was the Prague orchestra that played at the first performance of *La clemenza di Tito* in September 1791.

APPENDIX I

(Mozart's list, originally in French, has here been rearranged alphabetically. His spelling of surnames, where it differs, is given in quotation marks. More precise identifications follow after the colon.)

Aichelburg, Frau von (" Eichelbourg ") : Regine Josepha, *née* Wetzlar (afterwards Baroness Wetzlar von Plankenstern), wife of Maria Ferdinand, Baron Aichelburg, official in the head office of the Department for the accounts of charitable institutions and the municipality.

Althann, Countess, *née* [Countess] Batthyány (" Althan "—" Batiany ") : Eleonore, later senior lady-in-waiting ; wife of Michael Max, Count Althann ?

Apponyi, Countess (" Apumoni ") : *née* Nogarolla, wife of Anton Georg, Count Apponyi ?

" Arenfeld ", see Ehrenfeld.

Arnstein, von (" Arensteiner ") : Nathan Adam von Arnstein, Knight (later Baron), wholesale merchant and banker, consul general.

Auersperg, Prince Karl : Army officer.

Auersperg, Princess : Marie Josepha, *née* Countess Trautson.

Auersperg, Prince Adam : Johann Adam, Prince of the Realm.

Auersperg, Count Karl : Later Prince. Chamberlain, army officer, finally Lieutenant-General, Knight of the Order of Maria Theresa.

Auersperg, Count Wilhelm : later Prince Wilhelm.

Bánffy, Count (" Banffi ") : Georg, Count Bánffy, Baron Losontz, deputy Vice-Chancellor of the Hungarian-Transylvanian Chancellery, Commander of the Order of St. Stephen, Chamberlain in actual service.

Batthyány, Count Anton (" Batiany ") : Chamberlain ?

Bedekovich : Anton Bedekovich von Kumur, Knight of the Order of St. Stephen.

Beöthy, Councillor (" Bötti ") : Joseph Beöthy von Bessenyö, draftsman at the Hungarian-Transylvanian Chancellery.

Beöthy, Frau (" Betty ") : his wife.

" Bergen ", see Pergen

" Betty ", see Beöthy.

Binnenfeld, Joh. Adam (" Bienenfeld") : Johann Adam Binnenfeld, wholesale merchant.

Born, von : Ignaz von Born, nobleman, mineralogist, Councillor in the Department for the Mint and the Mines.

" Botti ", see Beöthy.

" Brandau ", see Prandau.

573

Braun, Baron : Karl Adolf von Braun, Baron of the Realm and Aulic Councillor.

Braun, von : Johann Gottlieb von Braun, Councillor in the Court of Audit and in the Commission for the control of taxes ; or Johann Nepomuk von Braun, official in the head fiscal accounts department ; or Ferdinand Augustin von Braun, Councillor to the Elector Palatine and agent for the Aulic Council.

Burkhardt, Baron (" Burkardt ") : ?

Burkhardt, Frau von (" Burkart ") : his wife.

Chotek (" Gotek ") : Johann Rudolf Chotek, Count of the Realm, deputy Chancellor of the Bohemian-Austrian Chancellery ?

Czernin, Count : Johann Rudolf, Count Czernin zu Chudenitz, Chancellor, Knight of the Order of the Golden Fleece, later Chamberlain-in-Chief and Supreme Director of the Court Theatres, nephew of Archbishop Hieronymus of Salzburg (Count Colloredo).

Dalberg, Baron : Johann Friederich Hugo, Baron Dalberg, amateur composer ?

Deglmann, Baron (" Tœgelman ") : Bernhard, Baron Deglmann, Councillor in the Bohemian-Austrian Chancellery.

Dietrichstein [Count], Joseph.

Ditmar, Baron : Gottfried Rudolf von Ditmar, Baron of the Realm, Aulic Councillor.

Drossdick, von (" Drostik ") : Johann Baptist von Drossdick, Hungarian-Transylvanian agent.

Dzierzanowsky, Count (" Dzierzanowschy ") : Count Michael ?

Edlenbach, von : Benedikt Schlossgängl von Edlenbach, agent.

Ehrenfeld (" Arenfeld ") : Joseph Frech von Ehrenfeld, draftsman to the Privy Council ; or Ignaz Frech von Ehrenfeld, assistant at the Registry of incoming correspondence at the Department for Finance and Austro-Bohemian Affairs.

" Eichelbourg ", see Aichelburg.

Engelsperg, Frau von (" Engelsbourg ") : wife of Joachim Mechtel von Engelsperg, High Steward ?

Engeström, Baron (" Engelstrom ") : Lars von Engeström, Swedish chargé d'affaires.

Erdödy, Count Ladislaus (" Ertödy ").

Esterházy, Count Franz : Esterházy von Galántha, Hungarian-Transylvanian Chancellor.

Esterházy, Count Johann : Councillor in the Lower Austrian Government.

Esterházy, Countess : Maria ; or Nicolette Franziska, née Richard de la Potréau, wife of Franz, Count Esterházy, previously married to Baron Durville.

Fechenbach, Herr von : Baron Fechenbach, Dean of Mainz, or a kinsman ?

Fichtl, von, Agent : Johann Baptist, agent for the Aulic Council, and agent for the Cathedral Chapter of Salzburg.

Finta, Baron (" Findak ") : Joseph von Finta, Lieutenant-Colonel of the Hungarian Noble Guards.

Fries, Count : Johann Fries, Count of the Realm, authorized depository agent, industrialist and banker ?

Galitsin, Prince (" Gallizin ") : Demetrius [Dmitryi Michailovich], Prince Galitsin, Russian Ambassador Extraordinary and Plenipotentiary, Privy Councillor and Chancellor.

Gebsattel, Baron : ?

Gleichen, Baron : ?

Gontard, Baron (" Gondar ") : Johann Jakob, Baron Gontard, later companion to Count Moritz [1] Fries.

" Gotek ", see Chotek.

Graneri (" Grenieri ") : Peter Joseph, Count Graneri, Sardinian Chancellor, Ambassador Extraordinary of Sardinia.

Greiner, Councillor : Franz Sales von Greiner, Councillor in the Bohemian-Austrian Chancellery, member of the Education Commission.

" Grenieri ", see Graneri.

Grezmüller, von, the elder : Erasmus, agent for the Aulic Council.

Grezmüller, von, the younger : Johann Nepomuk, adviser on accountancy to the Department for salt production.

Hall, Chevalier : Theodor, Baron Hallberg, Electoral Privy Councillor to the Bavarian Palatinate and Minister Plenipotentiary ?

Häring, von (" Härring ") : Johann Baptist von Häring (see 9 April 1790).

Harrach, Count, the elder : Johann Nepomuk Ernst, or Leonhard, Count Harrach.

Harrach, Ernst : Ernst Christoph, Count Harrach.

Hartenstein, von : Franz Zacharias von Hartenstein, Deputy Postmaster General.

Hatzfeld, Countess (" Hazfeld ") : Maria Anna Hortensia, née Countess Zierotin, wife of Clemens August Johann Nepomuk, Count Hatzfeld, Privy Councillor to the Elector of Cologne, and Lieutenant-General.

Henikstein, von (" Hönikstein ") : Adam Adalbert Hönig von Henikstein, nobleman, wholesale merchant, later adviser to the government and director of the salt works at Wieliczka.

Hentschell, von (" Hentschl ") : Leonard von Hentschell, nobleman, secretary in the Bohemian-Austrian Chancellery.

Herberstein, Bishop : Johann Karl, Count Herberstein, Bishop of Laibach [Ljubljana].

Herberstein, Count : Joseph Franz Stanislaus, Count Herberstein ?

Herberstein, Count Joseph : Joseph Herberstein, Count of the Realm,

Supreme Provincial Judge in Lower Austria, Hereditary Chamberlain and Hereditary High Steward of Carinthia, Privy Councillor and Chamberlain.

Herberstein, Count Nepomuk : Johann Nepomuk Thaddäus, Count Herberstein ?

Hess, Frau von, *née* von Kannegiesser : wife of Joachim Albert von Hess Aulic Councillor ; daughter of Hermann Joseph, Baron Kannegiesser, Councillor of State ?

Hess, Frau von, *née* von Leporini : Maria Theresia, *née* von Leporini, wife of Franz Joseph von Hess, Knight of the Realm, member of the Lower Austrian Government. [Parents of Field-Marshal Heinrich, Baron Hess.]

" Hochstatter ", Baron : Baron Hochstätten ?

" Honikstein ", see Henikstein.

Hoyos, Leopold : Johann Leopold Innozenz, Count Hoyos ?

" Hugart", Ugarte, Councillor to the Supreme Judiciary ?

Izdenczy (" Isdenczy ") : Joseph Izdenczy-Monostor, Hungarian-Transylvanian Councillor, Knight and Treasurer of the Order of St. Stephen.

Jacobi, von : Konstantin Philipp Wilhelm Jacobi (later Baron Klöst), Privy Councillor to the Legation, Prussian Resident Minister, later Ambassador.

Jacomini : ?

Jahn, Herr von : Ignaz Jahn, Court Purveyor ?

Jungwirth, Baron : Franz Joseph, Baron Jungwirth, member of the Lower Austrian Government.

" Kas ", see Keess.

Kaunitz, Dominik : Dominik Andreas [III], Prince Kaunitz-Rietberg-Questenberg, diplomat, later Vice-Master of the Horse, Knight of the Order of the Golden Fleece ?

Keess, Herr von (Käs) : Franz Bernhard von Keess, nobleman, Councillor to the Court of Appeal and to the Lower Austrian Provincial Court, and a lover of music ; or Franz Georg, his son.

Keglevich, Count (" Keglowitz ") : Joseph, Count Keglevich von Buzin, Commander of the Order of St. Stephen ; or Karl, Count Keglevich von Buzin, Privy Councillor, formerly Director of the Burgtheater and Kärntnertor Theatre.

Khevenhüller, Countess (" Kevenhüller ") : wife of Joseph Khevenhüller-Metsch, Count of the Realm, Major-General, Commander of the Order of St. Stephen ; or wife of Johann Joseph Franz Quirin, Count Khevenhüller-Metsch, Lieutenant-General.

" Kluschofsky ", Count : Kluszewsky ?

Knecht, von : Johann Anton Knecht, Privy Secretary to the Court ; or Karl Knecht, Privy Councillor to the Cabinet.

Koller, Count : Franz Xaver, Count Koller de Nágy-Mánya, Commander of the Order of St. Stephen.

Kollonitz, Count (" Kollnitsch ") : Karl Joseph, Count Kollonitz, Major-General.

Kuefstein, Count (" Kuffstein ") : Johann Ferdinand [III], Count Kuefstein, Court Councillor in actual service, later Commander of the Vienna City Militia, member of the Lower Austrian Government, provisional Vice-President of the Lower Austrian Government, and nobleman in charge of court music [*Hofmusikgraf*].

Lamezan, Herr von : Joseph, Count Salins von Lamezan, later Major-General.

Lewenau : Joseph Arnold von Lewenau, Knight, economic adviser to Prince Alois Liechtenstein.

Lichnowsky, Princess (" Lignowsky ") : Christine, *née* Countess Thun, wife of Prince Karl Lichnowsky.

Liechtenstein, Prince Louis (" Lichtenstein ") : Alois Joseph, Prince Liechtenstein, Knight of the Order of the Golden Fleece ?

" Lignowsky ", see Lichnowsky.

Lobkowitz, Prince Joseph : Field-Marshal, Chamberlain in actual service, Knight of the Order of the Golden Fleece.

Lüerwald, von (" Lucrewald ") : Ferdinand von Lüerwald, nobleman adviser to the War Council.

Lutz, von : Johann Lutz, authorized depository agent.

Madruzzi, von (" Madruce ") : Joseph, Baron Madruzzi, Councillor to the Lower Austrian Provincial Court.

Mandelslohe, Baron (" Mandelsloh ") : . . . . Lünikshausen von Mandelslohe.

" Marchal ", see Marschall.

Margelick, Frau von (" Margelique ") : wife of Joseph Wenzel von Margelick, Knight of the Order of St. Stephen, Councillor in the Bohemian-Austrian Chancellery, the Treasury and the Ministerial Sub-committee on Banking, doctor juris.

Marschall, Count (" Marchal ") : Count Marschall von Bieberstein.

Martini, Baron : Karl Anton von Martini, Baron of the Realm, Knight of the Order of St. Stephen, Councillor of State in the Ministry of the Interior.

Mayenberg, von (" Meyenberg ") : Anton Joseph von Mayenberg, nobleman, Estates Representative in the Lower Austrian Government, Councillor to the Lower Austrian Court of Appeal, High Steward.

Mecklenburg, Prince of (" Meklenbourg ") : Georg August, Duke of Mecklenburg-Strelitz, Major-General.

" Meyenberg ", see Mayenberg.

Montecuculi, Count : Ludwig Franz, Margrave Montecuculi.

Morton, Mylord : George Douglas, 16th Earl of Morton ?

M.—19

Müller, Councillor : Johann Christian Müller von und zu Mülleg, Councillor to the Lower Austrian Government, Court Agent (for Salzburg
and other cities).

Nádasdy, Count, General (" Nadasty ") : Franz Leopold, Count Nádasdy-
Fogáras, Field-Marshal and Ban of Croatia.
Neipperg, Count (" Neiperg ") : Leopold Johann Nepomuk, Count
Neipperg, later Aulic Councillor.
Neuhold, Frau von : wife of Johann Baptist Neuhold von Sövényháza,
Knight of the Order of St. Stephen, Hungarian-Transylvanian Coun-
cillor.
Nevery (" Nèvery ") : Alexius Leopoldus von Nevery, draftsman to the
Hungarian-Transylvanian Council.
Nimptsch, Count : Ferdinand, Count Nimptsch, army officer ; or Joseph,
Count Nimptsch, Baron Fürst und Kupferberg, Major, later General of
Cavalry and Knight of the Order of Maria Theresa.
Nimptsch, Countess : his wife.
Nostitz, Count (" Nostiz ") : Joseph Wilhelm or Franz Anton, Count
Nostitz und Rieneck (the former, chamberlain, the latter, burgrave,
both resident in Prague).
Nostitz, General : Friedrich Moritz von Nostitz und Rieneck, Count of
the Realm. Chamberlain in actual service, General of Cavalry, Captain
of the Lifeguard of Gentlemen-at-Arms.

Oettingen, Count ("Ötting ") : Philipp Karl, Count Oettingen-Waller-
stein, Knight of the Order of the Golden Fleece, later Aulic Councillor
and President of the Aulic Council.
Oeynhausen, Count : . . . later Portuguese Ambassador and Minister
Plenipotentiary.
Ott, von : Joseph Anton Ott, official at the Legation of the Franconian
Province.

Paar, Count : Wenzel, Count Paar, Chamberlain.
Paar, Prince : Wenzel Johann Joseph, Prince Paar, Supreme Postmaster-
General of the Realm and the Hereditary Lands.
Pálffy, Joseph (" Palfy ") : Joseph Franz, Prince Pálffy, Councillor in the
Hungarian-Transylvanian Chancellery, later Hereditary Overlord of
the Comitat of Pressburg [Bratislava].
Palm, Prince : Karl Joseph [II], Prince Palm-Gundelfingen.
Palm, Princess : Maria Josepha, née Baroness Gumpenberg, divorced from
Count Törring-Jettenbach.
Passowitz, Countess : ?
Passthory (" Paszthory ") : Alexander von Passthory, Hungarian-Transyl-
vanian Councillor.

Penzenstein (" Pentzenstein ") : Johann Penzeneter von Penzenstein, Major-General, later Lieutenant-General, in 1784-85 Commander of Artillery in the Netherlands.

Pergen, Count (" Bergen ") : Johann Anton Pergen, Count of the Realm, Grand Cross of the Order of St. Stephen, Privy Councillor, Chamberlain, Minister of State for the Interior, High Sheriff of Lower Austria, later President of the Lower Austrian Government and Minister of Police.

Ployer, Agent : Gottfried Ignaz von Ployer, nobleman, agent for Salzburg, Treasury representative to the Department for the Mint and Mines, and an honorary member of the Salzburg Princely Council.

Podstatzky, Count Joseph (" Potztazky ") : Joseph Podstatzky-Liechtenstein.

Poncet, Frau von : ?

" Potztatzky ", see Podstatzky.

Prandau, Baron (" Brandau ") : Franz, Baron Prandau, adviser to the Committee of the Lower Austrian Estates, later Privy Councillor.

Prandau, Baron : Joseph Ignaz, Baron Prandau, industrialist ?

Pufendorf, Frau von (" Puffendorf ") : Anna, née Baroness Posch, wife of Konrad Friedrich von Pufendorf, Aulic Councillor.

Puthon, von : Johann Baptist von Puthon, Knight [later Baron and Baron of the Realm], wholesale merchant, later an industrialist, and Director of the National Bank.

Raab : Ignaz, court advocate, doctor juris [kinsman of Leopold Mozart's housekeeper at Salzburg].

Rosty, von : Ignaz, Colonel, District Commandant in the Quartermaster's Department.

Rottenhan, Count : Heinrich, Count Rottenhan, Chamberlain in actual service, Councillor in the Bohemian-Austrian Chancellery.

Salburg, Count (" Sallabourg ") : Christoph, Count Salburg ; or Rudolf, Count Salburg, Major-General.

Sauer, Count : Wenzel Ferdinand Kajetan, Count Sauer, Councillor in the Bohemian-Austrian Chancellery, later Governor and head of civil administration [Bezirkshauptmann] in the Tyrol ; or Kajetan, Count Sauer von und zu Ankerstein, Chamberlain, Privy Councillor, Vice-President in pleno of the Government of the Interior.

Sauer, Countess : wife of Kajetan, Count Sauer von und zu Ankerstein.

Sauer, Countess : wife of Wenzel Ferdinand Kajetan, Count Sauer.

Schaffgotsch, Countess, née [Countess] Kollonitz (" Schafgotsch "—" Kollnitsch ") : Maria Anna, Countess Schaffgotsch, wife of Anton Gotthard, Count Schaffgotsch, Knight of the Order of the Golden Fleece.

Schleinitz, von : ?

Schwab, P. J. : Philipp Schwab, member of the Lower Austrian Government, and Ignaz Schwab [later ennobled], both wholesale merchants.

Schwarzenberg, Prince : Johann Nepomuk, Prince Schwarzenberg, Knight of the Order of the Golden Fleece ?

Seilern, Count August : Karl August, Count Seilern ; or Christian August, Count Seilern, President of the Supreme Judiciary, and a Privy Councillor.

Seilern, Count Joseph : Chamberlain, Aulic Councillor.

Smitmer, von : Jakob or Valentin Smitmer, noblemen [brothers], wholesale merchants ; or Matthias Joseph von Smitner ; or Andreas Benedikt von Smitner, nobleman, draftsman at the Bohemian-Austrian Chancellery ; or Joseph Stanislaus von Smitner, nobleman, draftsman in the Registry of incoming correspondence at the Department for Finance and Austro-Bohemian Affairs ; or Franz von Smitner, Knight, and canon.

Soltyk, Count ("Soldyk") : August ? (In 1794 he was suspected of being a "Jacobin".)

Sonnenfels, von : Joseph von Sonnenfels, Councillor in the Bohemian-Austrian Chancellery, member of the Education Commission.

Sonnfeld, von ("Sonnenfeld") : Leopold Kleinhans von Sonnfeld, official at army commissariat headquarters.

(Spanish Ambassador = Yriarte.)

Starhemberg, Countess, née Countess Neipperg ("Staremberg"—"Neiperg") : Wilhelmine Josephine Therese, Countess Starhemberg.

Sternberg, Count : Franz [Christian] Philipp, Count Sternberg, Knight of the Order of the Golden Fleece, Privy Councillor, Chamberlain, deputy High Steward.

Sternberg, Count Adam.

Sternberg, Count Gundacker : Count of the Realm, Chamberlain, Aulic Councillor.

Stöckel, Frau von ("Stökel") : wife of Joseph Adrian Stöckel, Municipal Councillor ; or of the art dealer Franz Xaver Zacharias Stöckel.

Stockmayer, Baron : Jakob Friedrich von Stockmayer, Knight of the Realm, Resident Minister of the Margrave of Baden.

Stopford, Lord : James George, Viscount Stopford, later 3rd Earl of Courtown, army officer ?

Streeruwitz ("Strurrewitz") : Johann Nepomuk von Streeruwitz, Councillor in the Bohemian-Austrian Chancellery.

Swieten, Baron van ("Suiten") : Gottfried van Swieten, Director of the Court Library, President of the Education Commission.

Thun, Countess, née [Countess] Uhlefeldt ("Ulfeld") : Wilhelmine, Countess Thun.

"Tœgelman", see Deglmann.

Trattner, Frau von : Therese von Trattner(n), wife of the printer Johann Thomas von Trattner(n), nobleman, landlord of the house in which the concerts were held.

Türkheim, Frau : wife of Ludwig [later Baron] von Türkheim, member of the War Council [about 1795 a member of the Secret Investigation Commission].

Ugarte, see " Hugart ".

Urmenyi (" Ürmeny ") : Joseph von Urmenyi, Knight of the Order of St. Stephen.

Vasseg (" Waseige ") : Edmund Maria, Count Arzt-Vasseg, Count of the Realm and Provost of Vienna Cathedral ?

Vockel, Baron : Friedrich Wilhelm, Baron Vockel, Legation Councillor and Resident Minister of the Duke of Brunswick-Lüneburg-Wolfen-büttel, and of the Prince of Orange-Nassau (Hereditary Stadholder of the United Netherlands).

Waldstätten, Baroness (" Bar.") : Martha Elisabeth, wife of Hugo, Baron Waldstätten, Sheriff, High Steward, and Councillor to the Lower Austrian Provincial Court.

Waldstein, Count : Franz de Paula or Ferdinand, Count Waldstein.

Waldstein, Count Georg : Georg Christian, Count Waldstein.

Waldstein, Countess, née [Countess] Uhlefeldt (" Ulfeld ") : Marie Elisabeth, Countess Waldstein, wife of Georg Christian, Count Waldstein.

" Waseige ", see Vasseg.

Weinbrenner, Joseph von (" Weinbremes ") : authorized depository agent.

Wetzlar, Baron, father : Karl Abraham Wetzlar von Plankenstein, Baron of the Realm, wholesale merchant and banker.

Wetzlar, Baron Raimund (" Wezlar ") : son of the preceding.

Wilczek, Count (" Wolschek ") : Franz Joseph, Count Wilczek, Privy Councillor and Chamberlain ; or Johann Joseph, Count Wilczek, Minister Plenipotentiary in Austrian Lombardy ?

Winkler, Baron : Joseph Johann Winkler von Mohrenfels, author ?

Wölkern, von, Aulic Council[lor] : Lazarus Karl von Wölkern.

" Wolschek ", see Wilczek.

Wrbna, Count (" Würm ") : Joseph zu Wrbna und Freudenthal, Count of the Realm, Chamberlain and Aulic Councillor ; or Rudolf zu Wrbna, etc., Count of the Realm, statesman, later Chamberlain-in-Chief and Supreme Director of the Court Theatres.

Wrbna, E. (" Würm ") : Eugen Wenzel Joseph zu Wrbna, etc., Count of the Realm, statesman, Knight of the Order of the Golden Fleece, later Privy Councillor and Marshal-in-Chief of the Imperial Household.

Wrbna, [Count] Louis (" Würben ") : ?

Württemberg, Prince (" Würtemberg ") : Ferdinand Prince of Württemberg ?

Yriarte, Don Domingo (" L'Ambassadeur d'Espagne ") : secretary and chargé d'affaires at the Spanish Embassy.

Zichy, Count Karl (" Zitchi ") : Karl, Count Zichy von Vásonykö, Chamberlain, Hungarian-Transylvanian Councillor, governor of the Comitat of Raab.

Zichy, Count Stefan : Chamberlain, later a member of the theatre management board.

Zinzendorf, Count : Karl, Count Zinzendorf, Privy Councillor and Chamberlain, President of the Court of Audit and of the Commission for the control of taxes.

" Zitchi ", see Zichy.

Zois, Baron : Joseph, Baron Zois von Edelstein ?

Mozart's original list is in the National Library, Vienna. Enclosure in a letter to his father at Salzburg written in Vienna on 20 March 1784.—Repeatedly printed in its original haphazard order, more or less accurately and with some misreadings of names often erratically spelt by Mozart (Schiedermair, Vol. II, pp. 246-48 ; Anderson, Vol. III, pp. 1297-1300 ; Müller von Asow, Vol. III, pp. 224 f.).—Alphabetically arranged, with identification of the persons where possible, by O. E. Deutsch in *Music & Letters*, London, July 1941 (partly translated) ; here reprinted again with some improvements.—For Trattner's Hall and Mozart's Wednesday concerts see 17 March 1784.—The subscription was 6 gulden per person ; the receipts exceeded 1,000 gulden, *i.e.* more than 167 persons. The list contains the names of 176 subscribers.—Mozart's use of " de " [= von] does not always denote nobility but, according to an old Austrian custom, merely a person of some standing (Wohlgeboren = well-born).

APPENDIX II

DOCUMENTS PERTAINING TO MOZART'S ESTATE

Suspense Order

Notification of death.
In the City.
Name of the deceased Herr Wolfgang Amadeus Mozart
Occupation Imperial & Royal Kapellmeister and Chamber Composer
State married, age 36 years
Address No 970 in the Rauchensteingasse, the Little Kaiserhaus
Date of Death 5 December 1791
Surviving spouse Konstanzia by name
Surviving children. Of age, and present whereabouts of same.—
Minors, and present whereabouts of same, 2 boys, viz. Karl, 7 years, and Wolfgang, 5 months, both at home.
Whether a Will is extant: none, but a Marriage contract enacted 3 August 1782.
Whereabouts of same. in the possession of the widow relict.
Next of kin. the widow will propose a trustee at the earliest opportunity.
N.B. Trustee : Michael Puchberg, Imperial and Royal Warehouse Supervisor in the Hohe Markt, at Count Walsegg's house.
The *Estate* to be legally inventoried in consideration of the minors, intestate heirs, concerning which the decree of the hon. Council is awaited. Furthermore the suspension has been instantaneously applied.

Dominic Crammer Magistrate
Commissary for Suspensions

Josef Odilo Goldhann/as invited witness, but/neither to my detriment
nor/disadvantage

Constance Mozart
née Weber

[Endorsement :]
Magistracy
of the I & R Residence and Capital
City of Vienna.
Suspense Order.
in re Herr Wolfgang Amadeus Mozart, deceased

fol[io]3305
7 December 1791

42059.
4

Cramer

The widow to be summoned to appear on 12 January, when the same shall propose a trustee ; also the inventory should be drawn up forthwith, of which the Commissary for Suspensions should be advised ex officio.

<table>
<tr><td>despatched</td><td>Ex cons[ilio] mag[isteriale] Vien[nensi]</td></tr>
<tr><td>15 December 1791</td><td>9 December 1791</td></tr>
<tr><td></td><td>Hofmann</td></tr>
</table>

. . . .

Delivery to the said Madam Mozard in person on 20 December 1791 : the summons of the 16th ditto

2144.   Delivered to Mme Mozart in person

. . . .

The widow to be summoned once more for the 19th inst., with the injunction that she shall appear without fail, and propose a trustee, as in the event of her failure to comply, a fine of 3 Imperial thalers shall be immediately imposed without further notice.

Ex cons : mg : Vien.
12 January 1792
Hofmann

Delivery to Frau Mozardt in person
17th inst. Koch
3703 F. 2
1791

To be retained and a copy to be supplied ; moreover the decree should be made available to the proposed trustee and also ex officio to the nominated representative of the children under age, Herr Doktor Ramor.

Decree despatched ex officio
Decree despatched to trustee and representative
30 January 1792.

Led.   Ex cons : mag : Vien.
copies despatched 10 February 1792   19 January 1792
Sch.   Hofmann

★

Inventory and valuation.

Concerning the personal estate of Herr Wolfgang Amadeus Mozart, intestate, Imperial & Royal Kapellmeister and Chamber Composer, of the Little Kaiserhaus, No. 970, Rauchensteingasse ; carried out pursuant to the Summons A, in the presence of the deceased's widow Maria Konstanzia, by the undersigned, viz. :   florins   kreuzer

in cash
Found after the decease of the above   60   —
out of which the burial and other expenses were defrayed.

in debts owing to the deceased
Arrears of the annual salary of 800 fl.   133   20

in ditto [debts owing to the deceased] presumed lost
1 recognisance enacted 23 August 1786 made out by
Herr Franz Gilowsky in favour of the deceased in
respect of a property bond received, for: 300 fl.—.

By Herr Anton Stadler, I & R Court Musician without liability, owing   500 fl.—.

Total—800 fl.—.

carried forward   193   20

	fl.	kr.
In silver		
3 poor spoons, at	7	—
In clothing and underclothing		
1 white cloth coat with manchester waistcoat	6	—
1 blue ditto	2	—
1 red cloth ditto	1	30
1 ditto of nankeen	—	45
1 brown satin ditto with breeches, silk embroidered	3	—
1 black cloth suit	1	30
1 mouse-coloured overcoat	4	—
1 cloth ditto	1	15
1 blue cloth fur coat	2	—
1 ditto fur-lined fur coat	3	—
4 waistcoats, various, 9 breeches ditto	8	—
2 plain hats, 3 pairs boots, 3 pairs shoes	3	—
9 pairs silk stockings	4	30
9 shirts	4	30
4 white cravats, 1 nightcap, 18 pocket handkerchiefs	6	—
8 underpants, 2 night-dresses, 5 pairs understockings	2	30
Household and bed linen		
5 table-cloths, 16 table napkins, 16 towels	6	—
10 linen sheets	8	—

carried forward   76   —

NB. the matrimonial bed, and 1 child's bed

	fl.	kr.
1 ordinary servant's bed	3	—
in household goods, in the first room		
2 hardwood chests of drawers	11	—

M.—19 a

1 sofa with canvas cover, 6 ditto chairs, 2 stools	8	—
1 softwood corner cabinet, 1 commode	1	—
1 Venetian blind, 2 curtains	1	—

In the second room.

3 hardwood tables	2	30
2 divans with canvas covers, 6 ditto chairs	50	—
2 small lackered cabinets	3	—
1 looking-glass in gilt frame	12	—
1 ordinary centre candelabrum	6	—
the papier-maché screen in this room	4	—
3 porcelain figures, 1 ditto casket	5	—

In the third room

1 hardwood table	1	—
1 green cloth billiard table with 5 balls, 12 cues, one lantern and 4 lights	60	—
1 iron stove with pipes	3	—

carried forward	170	30
	fl.	kr.

In the fourth room

1 hardwood table, 1 couch, worn damask, 6 chairs ditto	8	—
1 roll-top writing desk	8	—
1 clock, clockwork, in gilt case	5	—
1 forte-piano with pedal	80	—
1 viola in case	4	—
1 lacquered despatch box	1	8
2 softwood book cases	2	—

60 pieces china, various	12	—
1 small brass mortar, 3 ditto candle-sticks	2	30
2 coffee mills, 2 glass candle-sticks, 1 tin teapot, 1 lacquered tray, a few ordinary glasses	3	—

In the hall and kitchen

2 softwood tables, 1 old ditto wardrobe, 1 screen	1	30
2 softwood bed-steads, 1 small lacquered cabinet, and the small quantity of kitchen equipment remaining	1	30

In books and music

According to list B these amount to	23	41

carried forward	152	19

Sum total of the entire property, as listed, five hundred and ninety-two
gulden, 9 kreuzer *i.e.* 592 fl.—9 kr.

Consisting of :

in cash	60	—
in debts owing to the deceased	133	20
in ditto presumed lost—800 fl.		
in silver	7	—
in clothing and underclothing	55	—
in household and bed linen	17	—
in household goods	296	8
in books and music	23	41
Total, as above	592	9

Enacted Vienna 9 December 1797 [recte 1791]

Joseph Schlipfinger   Dominic Crammer, Magistrate
as witness   Commissary for Suspensions & Inventories
Johann Georg Graseller   Johann Pfeiffer,
as witness   Assessor of Property, under oath
                    Balthasar Müller
                    Assessor of Property, under oath

[Endorsement :]

Inventory and Valuation
of the estate of Herr Wolfgang Amadeus Mozart, I & R Kapellmeister and
Chamber Composer of this place, deceased, intestate.

A :
P.p. I & R Accounts Department of the City
of Vienna.
Checked, and found correct as to the calcu-
lations.
Vienna, 19 December 1791
Vidi Czernich
                    Plank

★

750.

List and valuation of the books of the late Herr W. A.
Mozart, Imperial Kapellmeister.

Quarto

No.

	Valuation fl. kr.	Selling price fl. kr.
1. Maskow's Einleitung zu den Gesch[ich]ten des Deutschen Reichs, Leipzig, 1763 8° et 12°	7.	

2. Almanach musikalischer für Deutschland
1782–1783. 1784 9.
3. Percy a Tragedy. London. 1778 6.
4. Forestier illuminato della Citta di Venezia
c[on] fig[uri]. Venez. 1765 7.
5. Faustin. 1783 8.
6. Der Gesellschafter, oder Sammlung unbekannter Anecdoten. Magdeburg. 1783 10.
7. Magazin der Musick by Cramer. 7 vols.
Hamburg. 1783 12
8. Friedrichs II., Königs in Preussen hinterlassene Werke. 4 vols. 1788 24.
9. Weiss's lyrische Gedichte, 3 parts. Leipzig.
1772 21
10. Atlas des Enfans, avec fig. illum. Amsterdam
1760 10

Carried forward 1. 54

	Valuation fl. kr.	Selling price fl. kr.

Octavo et 12°
No.

    Brought forward 1. 54
11. Ovid's Trauerlieder translated by Lory 4.
12. Molier's Lustspiele 3rd part, with copper
engraving. 1753 6.
13. Gessner's Schriften, parts 1 & 2. Zürich
1762 15.
14. Reisebuch geographisch und topographisches, durch alle Staaten der oesterreichischen
Monarchie, nebst der Reiseroute nach
Petersburg durch Pohlen. Vienna 1789. 20.
15. Skizen aus den Charakter und Handlungen
Joseph II. 2 parts. Halle 1783 7.
16. Sonnenfels's gesamelte Schriften. Vols 1, 2,
3, 4. Vienna 1783. 20
17. Smith's philosophische Fragmente über die
practische Musick. Vienna 1787. 3.
18. Punktierkunst. Leipzig 1754 7.
19. Ebert's Vernunftlehre. 1774. 3.
20. Blumen auf dem Altar der Grazien. Leipzig
1787. 15
21. Osterwald's Erdbeschreibung. Strasburg
1777. 12.

22. Ebert's Naturlehre, with engraving. Leipzig
    1775.   7.
23. Nebentheater. Leipzig 1786. 6 vols.   1. 30.
24. Kinderbibliothck, kleine, Vols 1, 2, 4, 5. Ham-
    burg 1783   12.

_____

                    Carried forward   5. 35

                              Valuation   Selling Price
                              fl. kr.   fl. kr.

        Octavo et 12⁰
No.
                    Brought forward   5. 35
25. Kleist's Werke, 2 parts. Vienna 1765   7.
26. Automathes or the Capacity of the human
    Understanding. London 1761.   12.
27. Diogenes von Sinope. Carlsruhe 1777   7.
28. Wieland's Oberon. Reutlingen 1781   7.
29. L' Arcadia in Brenta. Cologne 1674   3.
30. Braun's Götterlehre. Augsburg 1776.   6.
31. Die Metaphysick in der Connexion mit der
    Chemie, by J. Ortinger, Schwäbisch Halle   10
32. Spengler's Rechenkunst und Algebra. 1779   5.
33. Blumauer's Gedichte. Vienna 1784.   15.
34. Biblia Sacra : Colonio 1679.   17.
35. Phädon by Mendelsohn. Berlin 1776.   15.
36. Krebel's europäische Reisen, parts 2, 3, 4   6.
37. Collection of some Lettres, Anecdotes,
    Remarks etc. by W. Streit. 1774   7.
38. Schönberg's Geschäfte des Menschen, Zierde
    der Jugend, und lehrreiche Gedanken in
    Begebenheiten. 3 parts   9.
39. Opere del Sig. Metastasio. Tomo 1, 2, 4, 5.
    Venezia 1781   30.
40. Sechs Komedien Bände   36

_____

                    Carried forward   8. 47

                              Valuation   Selling price
                              fl. kr.   fl. kr.

        Octavo et 12⁰
No.
                    Brought forward   8   47
41. Der lustige Tag, Die Begebenheiten auf der
    Jagd. Die Entführung aus dem Serail.   6.

Music

42. L' Endimione Serenata dal Sig. Mich. Hayden.
    2 vols. Ms.   40.
43. Prologus del Sig. M. Hayden. folio   24.
44. Litania de Venerabili Sacramento di Sig.
    Hayden   24.
45. Sei fughi Preludie per Organo dal Sig. Al-
    brechtsberger. folio   15.
46. Jesus der sterbende. Ein Oratorium von
    Rosetti. folio Vienna   1. —.
47. Die Dorfdeputierten set to music by Schu-
    baur. folio Mannheim.   17.
48. Simphonie grande periodique en plusieurs
    Instrumens par Mozart. folio Vienna   24.
49. Concerti a Quatro di Sig. Leo   12
50. Le Barnvelt francais Comedie en Music   17
51. Concerte pour le Clavecin en piano forte par
    Hofmeister   12

                            Carried forward   12. 58

	Valuation fl. kr.	Selling price fl. kr.

Octavo et 12°
No.

                            Brought forward 12. 58
52. VIII Fughe per l' Organo dal Pasterwiz.   12.
53. Motetten und Arien, vierstimige in Partitur,
    by Hiller, Part 1. Leipzig 1776   6.
54. Bach's S. Clavierübungen : 2nd part. Ms.   12.
55. Poloneso con Variazione del Cl. Wohanka   7.
56. Ariette avec variations pour le Clavecin par
    Mozart, Nos 2 & 9   12.
57. Grand Concert pour le Clavecin par Mozart.   20.
58. Terzetto del Sig. Gasman. Ms.   10.
59. Labyrinth, klein harmonisches, by Bach   10.
60. Quintette del Figaro. Ms.   15
61. Winterlieder für Kinder und Kinderfreunde.
    Vienna 1791.   20
62. Zemire et Azor. Comedie Ballet. Ms.
    Mozart.   17
63. Arianna a Naxos Cantata par G. Hayden   20.
64. Sonates II pour le forte piano, par Duschek   15.

                            Carried forward   15. 54

	Valuation fl. kr.	Selling price fl. kr.

Octavo et 12⁰

No.

	Brought forward	15. 54	
65. Partition du Diable a Quatre par Chev. Gluck. Ms.		17.	
66. ———— des Airs de l'Arbre enchanté Opera comique par Chev Gluck. Ms.		15.	
67. Musickpränumeration Hofmeisterische. 22 Nos.		4. 30.	
68. Lieder fürs Klavier by K. Friberth 3rd Collection. Vienna 1780.		10	
69 Sonati sei a violino, solo col Basso composte di Fr. Ostad.		20	
70. Kantate über Gellerts Lieder, ich komme vor dein Angesicht, by Doles. Leipzig 1780.		12	
71. Fantasie et Sonate, pour le Forte piano par Mozart		12	
72. Verschiedene einzelne Musikalien	1. 30		

Carried forward   23. 20

	Valuation fl. kr.	Selling price fl. kr.

Music

No.

	Brought forward	23. 20
73. Blätter, dramaturgische, by Knigge. 2 parts, Hanover 1789		6.
Various Miscellanea		15

Total   23. 41

Joh. Georg Binz
Assistant Valuer of Books

*

List

1792.

of accounts rendered to my husband Wolfgang A. Mozart and
paid for him after his death, viz.

	fl.	kr.
No.		
1. To Herr Georg Dümmer, master tailor, his account No. 1, at	282.	7
2. To Anton Reiz, decorator, by account No. 2.	208.	3.
3. To the I & R Court Apothecary, by account No. 3.	139.	30.

4. To Herr Johann Heydegger, merchant, according to account
   No. 4.   87. 22.
5. To Herr Friedrich Purker, tradesman, his account No. 5.   59. —
6. To Frau Regina Hasel, apothecary at the sign of the Moor,
   by account No. 6.   40. 53.
7. Further, in settlement of her account for 74 fl. 53 kr., by
   account No. 7.   34. —
8. To Michael Anhamer, master cobbler, by bill No. 8.   31. 46
9. To Herr Georg Mayer, master tailor, his bill No. 9   13. 41.
10. To the merchant Reuter, by bill No. 10   12. 54.
11. To Herr Andre Igl, chirurgeon, by his receipt No. 11.   9. —

                                                          Total   918. 16
                                                   Konstanzia Mozart, Widow

*

Edict

By the present edict from the Magistracy of the I & R
Residence and Capital City of Vienna, notice
is hereby given : in consequence of the decease of Herr Wolfgang Andre
Mozart, I & R Kapellmeister and Chamber Composer, it has been found
necessary, in order that the administration of the estate may proceed in
proper manner, to summon all those who deem that they have claims
or demands on the aforementioned estate. The same must accordingly
appear on 19 March at ten o'clock in the forenoon before this Magistracy,
either in person or through persons having competent authority, and prove
their claims ; otherwise the settlement of the estate will be executed and
surrendered to the widow of the deceased. Vienna, 17 February 1792.
Joseph Georg Hörl, I & R   Franz Edler von Koffler, Magisterial Councillor
Councillor, and Burgomaster
L. Edler von Mossbach, I & R   Johann Nepomuk Edler von Reser,
Councillor and Deputy Burgomaster   Magisterial Councillor

*

[Summons to creditors]

In consequence of the decease of Herr Wolfgang Andre Mozart, I & R
Kapellmeister and Chamber Composer, it has been found necessary, in
order that the administration of the estate may proceed in proper manner,
to summon all those who deem that they have claims or demands on the
aforementioned estate. The same must accordingly appear on 19 March
at 9 o'clock in the forenoon before this Magistracy, either in person or
through persons having competent authority, and prove their claims ;
otherwise the settlement of the estate will be executed and surrendered to
the widow of the deceased.
Vienna, 17 February 1792

*

[Report on above edict]

[To the] Hon. Magistracy of the Royal Residence and Capital City of Vienna.

At the Convocation of Creditors on the 19th ult. in re W. Andre Mozart, Herr Dr Ramor has registered a claim through Herr Dr Rössler as representative in the name of the deceased's widow Anna Konstanzia for 1,500 florins in pursuance of a marriage contract drawn up on 3 August 1782, and further on a list of various expenses, for 918 florins, 16 kreuzer.
Hereby protocolled.
Vienna, 29 March 1792

Friedrich Hofmann
Secretary

*

[*Release*]
[To the] Hon. Magistracy
Pursuant to my declaration delivered to the court on 17 December 1792, I wish to deposit in court for each of my two children under age, namely Karl and Wolfgang Mozart, 200 florins as their paternal inheritance, by means of the appended Civic Upper Chamber 4% Bond A, No. 9234, in my name, Konstanzia Mozart, drawn up on 7 February 1793, for 400 fl. May it please the Hon. Magistracy to accept this my declaration and cause it to be protocolled.

Konstanzia Mozart
Widow

[Endorsement :]
[To the] Civic Magistracy   presented 11 February 1793
Konstanzia Mozart, relict of I & R Kapellmeister
For accepting and protocolling of the notified deposition of 400 fl. for her two children under age.

Franz Anton Weiss Solicitor

E. von Rösler Dr.   as
   5390   depositor

Approved, and the Upper Chamber Bond A, No. 9234, enacted 7 February 1793 in the name of Konstanzia Mozart, at 4% on 400 gulden, to be deposited at the proper department.

Ex cons : mag : Vien
11 February 1793
von Passel

The aforementioned Upper Chamber Bond No. 9234 for 400 fl. has been duly deposited at the Magisterial Trust Office.   Vienna, 11 February 1793

Johann Nepomuk Haderolt
Commissary
Anton Joseph Hörl
Comptroller
Niklas Hilger
Sub-Comptroller

3703
1791
F: 2 s

*

Statement of Property

Concerning the decease of Herr Wolfgang Amadäus Mozart, late I & R Kapellmeister and Chamber Composer.

	Assets	fl.	kr.
According to the contents of the legally drawn-up inventory A the estate consists of the following, viz. :			
In coin		60	—
Debts owing to the deceased		133 .	20
Silver		7 .	—
Clothing and underclothing		55 .	—
Household and bed linen		17 .	—
Household goods		296 .	8
Books and music		23 .	11
Total		fl. 592 .	9 .

Liabilities

From these are to be deducted the expenses resulting from illness, and other costs, according to statement B, defrayed by the widow relict, namely

918. 16.

According to the marriage contract C the widow could claim 500 fl. ; however, since the same has not proven the due payment of the dowry, her claims on the estate cannot be deducted. Apart from these two claims here mentioned, notified by the widow by the agreed fixed term of convocation according to edict D, no other creditor has presented himself according to the terms of writ E.

	Total :
	[left blank]
If the liabilities, namely	918 fl. 16 kr.
be now compared with the assets,	592 9

it becomes evident that the costs defrayed by the widow Frau Konstanzia Mozart exceed the estate by 326   7.
In consequence the estate is to be made over and released to the same against settlement of the trustee's charges ; to which there can be even less cause for objection in that the widow has, in accordance with the settlement F and deposition G, already deposited in the hands of the court 400 fl. as security in lieu of paternal inheritance for the 2 minors Karl and Wolfgang Mozart.

Document of this my enactment. Vienna, 1 March 1793.

Nicklas Ramor, Dr
as the legally appointed
guardian of the 2 children under age
of Wolfgang Mozart

*

Assessment to Estate Duty

Concerning the estate of Herr Wolfgang Amadeus Mozart, I & R Kapellmeister and Chamber Composer, deceased.

Assets

According to the contents of the official inventory the estate consists of
the following, viz. :

	fl.	kr.
In coin	60	—
,, debts owing to the deceased	133	20
,, silver	7	—
,, clothing and underclothing	55	—
,, household and bed linen	17	—
,, household goods	296	8
,, books and music	23	41
Total	fl. 592	9

Liabilities

From these are to be deducted the expenses resulting from the illness, and other costs defrayed by the widow, namely :	918	16
Personal clothing and underclothing exempt from estate duty	55	—
The marriage settlement stipulated for the surviving partner	500	—
Total	fl. 1473	16

If the liabilities, namely	1413 fl.	16 kr.
be compared with the assets, namely	592	9

it becomes evident that the widow's claims exceed the estate by 881 7
in consequence whereof the widow is not required to pay estate duty on
the marriage settlement of 1,000 fl., as she does not receive this amount
from the estate of her deceased husband, as has been shewn. Document of
this my enactment. Vienna, 1 March 1793.

> Nicklas Ramor, Dr
> As guardian of the 2 children
> under age of Wolfgang Mozart

★

[*Declaration of inheritance*]
[To the] Hon. Magistracy of the I & R Residence
and Capital City of Vienna

enclosed
with
the

A.
The undersigned, as the legally appointed
guardian, according to decree A, of the
children under age, Karl and Wolfgang Mozart,
as the only intestate heirs of their father,

petition
for
administration

B.

Herr Wolfgang Amadäus Mozart, I & R Kapellmeister and Chamber Composer, deceased, as seen in the terms of the Suspense Order B, is desirous of claiming the said estate, *cum beneficio legis et inventarii*, in the name of these his wards, with the most obedient request

that it please the Hon. Magistracy to accept and to protocol this declaration of inheritance. Vienna, 2 March 1793

Nicklas Ramor, Dr
as the legally appointed
guardian of the
2 children under age of
Wolfgang Mozart.

[Endorsement :]
166

3703
1791
F. 2 s.

To be retained,
and copies to be supplied.

Ex cons : mag : Vien

4 March 1793

Hofmann

350

[To the] Civic Magistracy
Niklas Ramor D^r
as the legally appointed guardian of the minors Karl and Wolfgang, being the sole intestate heirs of their father Wolfgang Amadäus Mozart, I & R Kapellmeister and Chamber Composer, deceased.

The within-mentioned statement of inheritance presented, cum beneficio legis et inventarii, with the most obedient request that the same be accepted and protocolled. Ramor Dr Presented 2 March 1793
8087

*

[*Application for release of the estate*]
[To the] Hon. Magistracy of the I & R Residence
and Capital City of Vienna

A.

The undersigned, as the legally appointed guardian, according to decree A, of the children under age, Karl and Wolfgang Mozart, as the only intestate heirs of their father, Herr Wolfgang Amadäus

Mozart, I & R Kapellmeister and Chamber Composer, deceased, as seen in the terms of the Suspense

B. Order B has now under today's date made a declaration of inheritance under this estate, in the name of these his wards, *cum beneficio legis et inventarii*, as under

C. C, and presents herewith the documents in this estate, and the

D. E. enclosed declarations D and E respectively, with the most obedient request :

that it please the Hon. Magistracy to ratify the same, and thus release the estate to the widow, Frau Konstanzia Mozart, in part payment of her claims, and against settlement of the expenses of the administration.

Niklas Ramor, Dr, as guardian of the children under age and intestate heirs of Herr Wolfgang Amadäus Mozart, deceased

[Endorsement :]
[To the] Civic Magistracy
Niklas Ramor, Dr, as legally appointed guardian of the children under age and intestate heirs of Herr Wolfgang Amadäus Mozart, I & R Kapellmeister and Chamber Composer, deceased.
Fol. 3305.   Vidi von Geer   vidit Accounts Department
                                                        Seelaus
                                                        Withalm

The documents of the administration, and also the within-mentioned declarations, herewith presented with the request for decision and for release of
Ramor Dr.   the estate to the widow relict.
        No. 58728
    10193
                                        16 March 1793.
                        Ex cons : mag : Vien.
                            4 March 1793
                                Hofmann

The copy of the declaration of inheritance
to be enclosed.
Duty 3 kreuzer
Settled

This application along with the declaration of the estate and of probate
duty, the statement of expenses, and the original marriage contract to be
retained and copies to be supplied ; the Magistracy also desires that the
estate of Wolfgang Amadeus Mozart, I & R Kapellmeister, Court and
Chamber Composer, amounting to 592 fl. 9 kr., be made over, and decreed
to be released forthwith, to his widow relict, Konstanzia Mozart, *ex conto* of
the illness and burial expenses defrayed by her, amounting to 918 fl. 16 kr.,
and also other debts settled, subject to provisional satisfaction of the guardian,
and payment of the outstanding administration fees.

Copy 15 April 1793	Ex cons : mag : vien.
despatched Eber.	2 April 1793
Cs	E. von Kayserstein

3703
1791
F : 2 s

★

[Direction for administration in full]
of 2 April 1793

Guardian of the two children under age and heirs intestate of Wolfgang Amadäus Mozart, I & R Kapellmeister and Court Chamber
Composer, to whose estate he has laid claim, *cum beneficio*,
for administration of the estate.

According to the official inventory the estate amounts to 592 fl. 9 kr. Against
this the widow, according to her statement, verified by receipts, has paid
in expenses arising from the illness and burial and in other proven debts,
the sum of 918 fl. 16 kr., that is 326 fl. 7 kr. more than the estate amounts to ;
and she has also deposited for each of the two children two hundred gulden ;
hence there is no objection to making the estate over to her against payment
of the outstanding administration fees, and with the consent of the guardian.

Direction

This application along with the declaration of the estate and of
probate duty, the statement of expenses, and the original marriage
contract, to be retained, also a special copy of them to be supplied.
The Magistracy also desires that the estate of Wolfgang Amadäus
Mozart, I & R Kapellmeister and Court Chamber Composer,
amounting to 592 fl. 9 kr., be made over, and decreed to be released
forthwith, to his widow relict, Konstanzia Mozart, on account of the
illness and burial expenses defrayed by her, amounting to 918 fl.

16 kr., and also other debts settled, subject to provisional satisfaction of the guardian, and payment of the outstanding administration fees.

Kanjowitz

*

[*Second application for release*]
[To the] Hon. Magistracy of the I & R Residence
and Capital City of Vienna

Since the widow Frau Konstanzia Mozart, as beneficiary of the estate of her husband Herr Wolfgang Amadäus Mozart, I & R Kapellmeister and Chamber Composer, deceased, has guaranteed my expenses as guardian, and since no administration fees remain marked as outstanding, and since otherwise the hon. Taxation Office would have charged these on the Direction for Administration A ; in consequence the said Direction A has already been carried out in every particular ; accordingly I request that it may therefore please the hon. Magistracy to agree to the release of the estate, and in what concerns the removal of the judicial closure, to direct the Commissary for suspensions concerned.

Niklas Ramor, D^r, as guardian of the children under age and intestate heirs of Wolfgang Amadäus Mozart.

*

[*Release*]

[To the] Hon. Magistracy

A. The undersigned has in consequence of Direction A annulled the Suspense Order imposed on the estate of Herr Wolfgang Amadäus Mozart, I & R Kapellmeister and Chamber Composer, deceased, and has duly surrendered said estate to the widow relict Frau Konstanzia Mozart.

Dominic. Crammer
Commissary for Suspensions

[Endorsement :]
33b

3703
1791

F. 2 s.

Inventory missing
Hiller
To be retained, and copies
to be supplied.

Magistracy
Certificate
Domini[c]   Crammer
Commissary for Suspensions

Ex Cons : Mag : Vien.   The Suspense Order annulled and the
        23 August 1793   estate of Herr Wolfgang Amadeus
            Seznagl   Mozart, I & R Kapellmeister and
                                     Chamber Composer, released
Copy made out Ort, 29 August 1793
Coll.
Copy despatched Jans [?]   Estate
1245   29687   Protocolled 22 August 1793.

Archives of the City of Vienna (copy in the Mozarteum, Salzburg).—*Deutsche Musik-Zeitung* (Vienna, 9 September 1861), pp. 284-6 ; Johann E. Engl in *Jahresbericht des Mozarteums*, Vol. XIV (Salzburg, 1894), pp. 31-9 ; Friedrich Kerst, *Mozart-Brevier* (Berlin, 1905), pp. 284-6 ; Arthur Schurig, *Konstanze Mozart* (Dresden, 1922), pp. 151-4 ; *id.*, *W. A. Mozart*, 2nd ed. (Leipzig, 1923), Vol. II, pp. 453-9 ; Albert Leitzmann, *W. A. Mozart* (Leipzig, 1926), pp. 489-93.—The reprint here is complete, including the indications of content and official remarks on the verso or last pages of the documents.—The following identification of the books and music left by Mozart amplifies and occasionally corrects the attempt in Schurig's biography.—Dr. Rudolf Geyer and Dr. Hanns Jäger-Sunstenau, of the Vienna City Archives, gave very kind assistance in the deciphering of the manuscripts.

SUSPENSE ORDER

   The property of every deceased person was subjected to an official closure or suspension (*Sperre*) ; in Vienna this was done by the Magistracy, whose Commissary for Suspensions drew up a Suspense Order and eventually annulled it. The Statement was entered on a printed form.—Constanze, who had to be summoned three times, at last nominated Puchberg as her representative in the matter. He did not press his claim to some 1,000 gulden, though in 1785 and 1787 he had distrained Anton Stadler for 1,400 gulden and in 1799 his wife for 150 gulden. Puchberg, whose place as representative was taken by Franz Xaver Flamm on 23 February 1792, himself died in poverty. According to Nissen (p. 686 of his biography), Puchberg demanded the money he had lent Mozart from his widow several years after 1791, and actually received it.—Not Puchberg but the Court and Civic Advocate Dr. Niklas Ramor, who lived in the Weihburggasse, City No. 941, became the legal guardian of the two boys. (In 1791 Mozart was on friendly terms with Flamm, his wife Barbara, *née* Stögern, and his daughter Antonie, a singer.)

INVENTORY AND VALUATION

   It was in the interest of the heirs to have the deceased's property valued as low as possible, chiefly on account of probate duty, and the experts took due consideration of this fact, especially in the case of needy families. (This answers the usual sentimental interpretation of the smallness of Mozart's estate ; it must be added that manuscripts had no market value.)—The arrears of salary for the post of Kammer-Kompositeur were computed for two months (a gulden contained 60 kreuzer).— Franz Anton Gilowsky's whereabouts were and remained unknown (see 2 May 1787).—For Anton Stadler see the remark on Puchberg above.—Herr Lackenbacher (see 1 October 1790) does not appear among Mozart's creditors, this debt having evidently been discharged.

LIST . . . OF BOOKS

1. Johann Jakob Mascow, *Einleitung zu den Geschichten des römisch-deutschen Reichs, bis zum Absterben Kaiser Karls VI. in 10 Büchern* [Introduction to the Histories of the Roman-German Empire, to the Death of the Emperor Charles VI, in 10 Volumes], Leipzig, 1747, new editions 1752 and 1763.

2. *Musikalischer Almanach für Deutschland*, ed. by Johann Nikolaus Forkel, Leipzig, 1782–84, with references to Mozart. *Cf.* pp. 199, 211, 220.

3. Hannah More, *Percy, A Tragedy in 5 acts in verses*, London, 1778, with Prologue and Epilogue by David Garrick.

4. Giambattista Abbrizzi, *Forestiero illuminato* [The Enlightened Visitor] . . . *della città di Venezia*, Venice, 1765 (published anonymously, bought by Leopold Mozart in 1770).

5. Johann Pezzl, *Faustin oder Das aufgeklärte philosophische Jahrhundert* . . . [or The Enlightened Philosophical Century], published anonymously without place-name, Zürich, 1788.

6. *Der Gesellschafter, oder Samlung grösstenteils unbekannter Anekdoten* [The Companion, or Collection of Mostly Unknown Anecdotes], 6 Parts, Magdeburg, 1783–88.

7. *Magazin der Musik*, ed. by Karl Friedrich Cramer, Hamburg, 1783–89 (with several references to Mozart). *Cf.* pp. 213, 214, 219, 229, 281, 290, 295, 349.

8. *Friedrich II. Hinterlassene Werke* [Posthumous Works of Frederick II], 15 Parts, Berlin, 1788 (also published in French).

9. Christian Felix Weisse, *Kleine lyrische Gedichte* [Short Lyric Poems], 3 Parts, Leipzig, 1772 (see K. 472–4 and 518).

10. *Atlas des enfans, ou méthode nouvelle, courte, facile et démonstrative, pour apprendre la géographie* . . . , Amsterdam, 1760 (copy in the Library of Congress, Washington).

11. *Ovids Trauerlieder* [*Tristia*] *aus dem Lateinischen in deutsche Verse gebracht von* [Ovid's *Tristia*, translated from the Latin into German verse by] *Michael Lori*, Augsburg, 1758 and 1762.

12. J.-B. P. Molière, *Sämtliche Lustspiele* [Complete Comedies] translated by Friedrich Samuel Bierling, 4 Parts, Hamburg, 1752 (present from Fridolin Weber, Mannheim, 1778). *Cf.* p. 174.

13. Salomon Gessner, *Schriften* [Writings] 4 Parts, Zürich, 1762. *Cf.* p. 60.

14. *Geographisches und topographisches Reisebuch durch alle Staaten der österreichischen Monarchie nebst der Reiseroute nach Petersburg durch Polen* [Geographical and Topographical Travel Book through all the States of the Austrian Monarchy, with the Travel Route to St. Petersburg through Poland], Vienna, 1789.

15. *Skizzen aus dem Charakter und den Handlungen* [Sketches of the Character and Actions of] *Josephs II*, 2 Parts, Halle, 1783.

16. Joseph von Sonnenfels, *Gesammelte kleine Schriften* [Collected Shorter Writings], 10 vols, Vienna, 1783–86.

17. Amand Wilhelm Smith, *Philosophische Fragmente über die praktische Musik*, Vienna, 1787 (published anonymously, with mention of Mozart). *Cf.* p. 358.

18. *Punktierkunst*, Leipzig, 1754 (consisting of casually scattered dots which are then joined together to form figures ; these are interpreted with the aid of " Dotbooks "—probably of Arab origin).

19. Johann Jakob Ebert, *Unterweisung in Anfangsgründen der Vernunftslehre* [Instruction in the First Principles of the Science of Reason], Leipzig, 1774 (2nd ed., 1775).

20. Georg Schatz, *Blumen auf dem Altar der Grazien* [Flowers on the Altar of the Graces], Leipzig, 1787 (epigrams published anonymously).

21. F. Osterwald, *Historische Erdbeschreibung zum Nutzen der Jugend* [Historical Description of the Earth for the Benefit of the Young], Strasburg, 1777 (and 1791).

22. Johann Jakob Ebert, *Naturlehre für die Jugend* [Natural Science for the Young], 3 vols., Leipzig, 1776–78.

23. Johann Gottfried Dyk, *Nebentheater* [Minor Plays], 6 Vols., Leipzig, 1786–1788.

24. *Kleine Kinderbibliothek* [Little Library for Children], ed. by Joachim Heinrich Campe, 12 Vols., 2nd edition, Hamburg, 1782–84.

25. Ewald Christian von Kleist, *Sämtliche Werke* [Complete Works], 2 Parts, Vienna, 1765 (reprint of the 1760 Berlin edition).

26. John Kirkby, *Authomates or the Capacity of the human Understanding*, London, 1761 (an imitation of Robinson Crusoe).

27. Christoph Martin Wieland, *Die Dialogen des Diogenes von Sinope*, Leipzig, 1770 (not 1777).

28. Wieland, *Oberon. Ein Gedicht* [a Poem], Reutlingen, 1781 (reprint of the 1780 Weimar edition).

29. Giovanni Sagredo, *L' Arcadia in Brenta, ovvero la Melanconia Sbandita* [. . . . or Melancholy banished], Cologne, 1674. (First published in 1667 under the name Ginnesio Gavardo Vacalerio. It is a collection of 45 novellas and 400 aphorisms presented within a framework, in the manner of the *Decameron*.)

30. Heinrich Braun, *Kurze Götterlehre* [Brief Mythology], Augsburg, 1776.

31. Friedrich Christoph Oetinger (not J. Ortinger), *Die Metaphysik in der Konnexion mit der Chemie*, Schwäbisch-Hall, 1770.

32. Joseph Spengler, *Anfangsgründe der Rechenkunst* [First Principles of Arithmetic] *und Algebra*, Augsburg, 1772 (and 1789, not 1779).

33. Alois Blumauer, *Gedichte* [Poems], Vienna, 1784 (2nd ed. ; first published in 1782). *Cf.* p. 260 f.

34. *Biblia Sacra*, Cologne, 1679.

35. Moses Mendelssohn, *Phädon, oder über die Unsterblichkeit der Seele* [. . . The Immortality of the Soul], Berlin, 1767 (4th ed. 1776).

36. Gottlob Friedrich Krebel, *Die vornehmsten europäischen Reisen* [The Foremost European Travels], 3rd ed. in 4 parts, Hamburg, 1783–85 (Part i contains Prague, Dresden, Leipzig and Berlin).

37. Friedrich Wilhelm Streit, *An Attempt to facilitate the learning of the English language by publishing a collection of some letters, anecdotes, remarks and verses, wrote by several celebrated English authors*, etc., Gera, 1774.

38. Matthias von Schönberg, *Das Geschäfte des Menschen, Die Zierde der Jugend und Lehrreiche Gedanken in kleinen Begebenheiten* [The Affairs of Man, the Ornaments of Youth and Instructive Thoughts in Small Events], 3 parts, Munich, 1773 and 1775 (Viennese reprint, 1777–79).

39. Pietro Metastasio, *Opere*, 7 vols., Venice, 1782–84. *Cf.* p. 110.

40. 6 vols. of comedies (perhaps those sold by Viennese theatre ushers).

41. P. A. C. de Beaumarchais, *Der lustige Tag oder Die Hochzeit des Figaro* (one of two translations published anonymously in 1785 : one by Müller at Kehl, the other by Strobl in Munich) ; Anselm von Edling, *Die Begebenheiten auf der Jagd oder über die Unschuld hält die ewige Vorsicht den Schild* [The Events of the Chase, or Over Innocence Eternal Providence holds a Shield], comic opera in 3 acts, Klagenfurt, 1789 ; Gottlieb Stephanie the Younger, after C. F. Bretzner, *Die Entführung aus dem Serail*, Vienna, 1782.

Music (partly in MS. copies) :

42. Michael Haydn, " Endimione ", Serenade.

43. Michael Haydn, " Prologus " (presumably the overture to a Latin comedy written for Salzburg University).

44. Michael Haydn, " Litaniae de venerabili [altaris] Sacramento " (probably the work from which Mozart himself copied the " Pignus futurae gloriae ", K. App. 239, KE. App. 109^{lv}).

45. Johann Georg Albrechtsberger, " Sei fughe e preludie per l' organo ", Vienna, 1787.

46. Francesco Antonio Rosetti (recte Rössler), *Der sterbende Jesus*, oratorio, Vienna, 1786.

47. Johann Lukas Schubaur, *Die Dorfdeputierten*, Singspiel, Mannheim, 1783 (produced at Munich in 1783).

48. Mozart, Symphony in B♭ major (K. 319) or in D major (" Haffner ", K. 385), probably both, Vienna, 1785.

49. Leonardo Leo, " Concerti a Quattro ", probably MS. copy.

50. *Jeuneval, ou Le Barneveldt français*, translation of George Lillo's *The London Merchant*. Put into French by L. Sebastian Mercier and thence into German (*Die Gefahren der Verführung*) by F. L. Schröder (Burgtheater, Vienna, 1781. A translation direct from the English by Christian Gottlob Stephanie the Elder had been given there in 1778). The hero of the play was a George Barnwell.

51. Franz Anton Hoffmeister, " Concerto pour le Clavecin ou Pianoforte " (probably that in C major, Op. 8, Vienna, 1784).

52. Georg Pasterwitz, " VIII Fughe secondo l' ordine de Toni Ecclesiastici per l' organo o clavicembalo ", Op. 1, Vienna, 1789.

53. *Vierstimmige Motetten und Arien in Partitur, von verschiedenen Componisten, zum Gebrauch der Schulen, gesammelt und herausgegeben von* [Four-part Motets and Arias in Score, by various Composers, collected and edited for the Use of Schools by] *Johann Adam Hiller*, Part i, Leipzig, 1776.

54. Johann Sebastian Bach, *Zweyter Theil der Clavier-Übung* (published 1735, in MS. copy).

55. Cl. Wohanka, " Polonaise con Variazione " (?).

56. Mozart, " Ariette avec Variations pour le Clavecin ", Nos. 2 and 9 of 12 Variations on " La Belle Françoise " (K. 353), and Concert Rondo (K. 382) arranged for pianoforte (K. App. 209), Vienna, Artaria & Co., 1786 and 1787.

57. Mozart, Pianoforte Concerto in F major (K. 413), Vienna, Artaria & Co., 1785.

58. Florian Leopold Gassmann, " Terzetto " (in MS. copy).

59. J. S. Bach, " Kleines harmonisches Labyrinth " for organ (doubtful work : BWV 591).

60. Mozart, *Le nozze di Figaro*, probably arranged for string quintet, MS. copy. Cf. p. 294.

61. *Liedersammlung für Kinder und Kinderfreunde am Clavier*, ed. by Placidus Partsch, section *Winterlieder*, Vienna, 1791. (Mozart's three children's songs, K. 596-98, appeared in the section *Frühlingslieder*.)

62. A. E. M. Grétry, *Zémire et Azor*, comédie-ballet (Fontainebleau, 1771 ; Schönbrunn, 1775), copy of a pianoforte score (?) in Mozart's hand (?).

63. Joseph Haydn, *Arianna a Naxos*, cantata for one voice with pianoforte accompaniment, Vienna, 1790.

64. František Dušek, " II Sonates pour le Forte Piano " (?).

65. *Le Diable à quatre, ou La double métamorphose*, opera in 3 acts, by F. A. Philidor (Paris, 1756), with arias by Gluck (Laxenburg, 1759). Score in MS. copy.

66. C. W. Gluck, *L'Arbre enchanté, ou Le Tuteur dupé*, opera in 1 act (Schönbrunn, 1759 ; 2nd version, Versailles, 1775), score in MS. copy.

67. *Prénumération pour le Forte Piano ou Clavecin*, a series of pieces by various composers, Vienna, F. A. Hoffmeister, 1785–87. Includes K. 511, 521, 526, etc.

68. Karl Friberth, " Lieder für das Klavier ", Part iii of *Sammlung deutscher Lieder für das Klavier*, Vienna, 1780 (see 6 January 1790).

69. Fr. Ostad (*recte* Franz Stad), " Sei sonate a Violino solo col Basso ", Paris, *ca.* 1775, published by the composer.

70. Johann Friedrich Doles, Cantata *Ich komme vor Dein Angesicht* (C. F. Gellert), Leipzig, 1790 (not 1780). Dedicated to Mozart and Naumann. *Cf.* p. 381.

71. Mozart, " Fantaisie et Sonate pour le Forte-Piano ", Op. XI (K. 475 and 457), Vienna, Artaria & Co., 1785. (Mozart in the end possessed only four out of some 70 original editions of his works.)

72. Various single items of music.

73. *Dramaturgische Blätter*, ed. by Adolph, Baron Knigge, Hanover, 1789 (2 parts). *Cf.* pp. 327, 332, 343.

Various miscellanies. (There was no list of Mozart autographs.)—Binz, who acted as valuer of the books and music, was a second-hand bookseller of repute. The Ewing Collection, Glasgow University, contains a book bearing Mozart's mark. It is Giovenale Sacchi, *Della divisione del tempo nella musica, nel ballo e nella poesia*, etc., Milan, 1770.

PAID ACCOUNTS

Of the two tailors, Mayer had probably only done repairs.

EDICT

The two lines below the heading are part of the printed form. The format is oblong.

SUMMONS TO CREDITORS

This appeared in almost the same words in the *Wiener Zeitung* for 7 March 1792. *Cf.* p. 443 f.—Nobody applied.

REPORT ON ABOVE EDICT

Constanze's dowry and Mozart's marriage settlement together amounted to 1,500 gulden.

RELEASE

Weiss was a solicitor. Haderolt was the director, Hörl the creditors' representative, and Hilger the cashier of the Trust and Tax Office of the City of Vienna.

STATEMENT OF PROPERTY

The marriage contract is now in the Stefan Zweig Collection, London (deposited in the British Museum). *Cf.* pp. 203 f.

ASSESSMENT TO ESTATE DUTY

This document exists in two copies.

DIRECTION FOR ADMINISTRATION

Ignaz Kanjowitz was a Councillor of the Viennese Magistracy.

SECOND APPLICATION FOR RELEASE

The Suspense Order was annulled after a delay of nearly two years. Dominikus Crammer, the Commissary for Suspensions, was instructed by the Magistracy on 20 August 1793 to release the estate.

ADDENDA

Page 293 :

* from the records of the greater marian congregation, salzburg
[28 May 1787] On the same day there took place the funeral of that worthy
gentleman our beloved colleague Leopoldus Mozart, *Vice* (as they say)
Kapellmeister.

> Salzburg, Provincial Archives, Universitäts-Akten.—Communicated by Dr
> Herbert Klein.—Leopold Mozart had probably been a member of this body
> from his university days. The full title of the record reads : Protocollum
> Congregationis majoris Beatae Virginis Mariae in coelos assumptae in univer-
> sitate Salisburgensis.

Page 409 :

On 10 October 1791 Giuseppe Gazzaniga's opera *Don Giovanni Tenorio*
was performed at the Théâtre Feydeau, Paris ; the conductor, Luigi Cherubini, inserted some numbers from Mozart's opera.

BIBLIOGRAPHY

T H I S bibliography is not to be considered a critical selection of the Mozart literature but rather as a list of the books most commonly referred to in the text, and of other works of a biographically important nature.

Abert, Hermann, see under Jahn and *Mozart-Jahrbuch*.

Acta Mozartiana, edited by Erich Valentin. Augsburg, published quarterly since 1954.

Anderson, Emily, *The Letters of Mozart and His Family*, 3 vols. London, 1938.

Augsburger Mozartbuch (Vol. 55/56 of *Zeitschrift des Historischen Vereins für Schwaben*, edited by Heinz Friedrich Deininger. Augsburg, 1943).

  Neues Augsburger Mozartbuch, ibid., 1962.

Barblan, Guglielmo, see under *Mozart in Italia*.

Bauer, William A., and Deutsch, Otto Erich, *Mozart. Briefe und Aufzeichnungen. Gesamtausgabe*, 4 vols. Kassel, 1962–63.

Blümml, Emil Karl, *Aus Mozarts Freundes- und Familien-Kreis*. Vienna, 1923.

Bory, Robert, *Wolfgang Amadeus Mozart. Sein Leben und seine Werke in Bildern*. Geneva, 1948. (Also published in French and English.)

Buff, Adolf, *Mozarts Augsburger Vorfahren* (Vol. 18 of *Zeitschrift des Historischen Vereins für Schwaben und Neuburg*. Augsburg, 1891).

Caflisch, L., and Fehr, M., *Der junge Mozart in Zürich* (Neujahrsblatt 140, published by the Allgemeine Musikgesellschaft Zürich. Zürich, 1952).

Corte, Andrea della, see under *Mozart in Italia*.

Deininger, Heinz Friedrich, *Wolfgang Amadeus Mozarts Augsburger Ahnen* (in the periodical *Schwabenland*, Year 9 [Mozart Number], 1942 ; see also *Augsburger Mozartbuch*).

Deiters, Hermann, see under Jahn.

Deutsch, Otto Erich, *Mozart and his World in Pictures*. Kassel and London, 1961.

Deutsch, Otto Erich, *Mozart und die Wiener Logen*. Vienna, 1932.

Deutsch, Otto Erich and Paumgartner, Bernhard, *Leopold Mozarts Briefe an seine Tochter*. Salzburg, 1936.

Einstein, Alfred, see under Köchel.

Engel, Erich W., *Wolfgang Amade Mozart*, a calendar. Vienna, 1914.

Farmer, Henry George, and Smith, Herbert, *New Mozartiana*. Glasgow, 1935.

Fehr, Max, *Die Familie Mozart in Zürich*. Zürich, 1942 ; see also under Caflisch, L.

Freisauff, Rudolf von, *Mozart's Don Juan 1787–1887*. Salzburg, 1887.

Genée, Richard, see under *Mitteilungen*.

Hadamowsky, Franz, see under Mozart exhibitions, Vienna.

Hammerle, A. J., *Mozart und einige Zeitgenossen*. Salzburg, 1887.

Hummel, Walter, *W. A. Mozarts Söhne*. Cassel, 1956.

  Nannerl Mozarts Tagebuchblätter mit Eintragungen ihres Bruders Wolfgang Amadeus. Salzburg, 1958.

Jahn, Otto, *W. A. Mozart*, 4 vols. Leipzig, 1856–59; 2nd edition in 2 vols, 1867; 3rd edition, edited by Hermann Deiters, 2 vols., 1889–91 (the edition quoted in this book) ; 4th edition also edited by Deiters in 2 vols., 1905–7 ; 5th edition, edited by Hermann Abert, 2 vols. Leipzig, 1919–21 (referred to as Abert in this book).

King, A. Hyatt, *Mozart in Retrospect*. London, 1955.

Köchel, Ludwig Ritter von, *Chronologisch-thematisches Verzeichnis sämtlicher Tonwerke Wolfgang Amade Mozarts*. Leipzig, 1862 ; 2nd edition edited by Paul, Count Waldersee, Leipzig, 1905 ; 3rd edition edited by Alfred Einstein, Leipzig, 1937. (Abbreviations : K.=Köchel's original numbering, KE.=Köchel-Einstein.)

Lewicki, Rudolf von, see under *Mozarteums-Mitteilungen*.

Mitteilungen für die Mozart-Gemeinde in Berlin, edited by Richard Genée and (after 1912) by Fritz Rückward. 43 nos. in 4 vols., Berlin, 1895–1925.

Mozart in Italia, edited by Guglielmo Barblan and Andrea della Corte. Milan, 1956.

Mozart exhibitions in 1956 (catalogues) :
London : Mozart in the British Museum
Milan : Mozart in Italia (Guglielmo Barblan and others)
Munich : Mozart in München (Alfons Ott and Hans Reuther)
Paris : Mozart en France
Vienna : Mozart. Werk und Zeit (Franz Hadamowsky and Leopold Nowak)

Mozart-Jahrbuch, edited by Hermann Abert, 3 issues. Leipzig, 1923–29.

Neues Mozart-Jahrbuch, edited by Erich Valentin, 3 issues. Regensburg, 1941–43.

Mozart-Jahrbuch, published by the Internationale Stiftung Mozarteum, Salzburg (edited since 1955 by Géza Rech). Salzburg, published annually since 1950.

Mozarteums-Mitteilungen, edited by Rudolf von Lewicki, 3 volumes. Salzburg, 1918–21.

Müller von Asow, Erich H., *Gesamtausgabe der Briefe und Aufzeichnungen der Familie Mozart*, 3 vols. Berlin, 1942. (The facsimiles are numbered as vol. 1 of this edition, the two parts of the [incomplete] collection of letters are vols. 2 and 3 and are cited thus in the present book; however, they have also been issued separately as vols. 1 and 2.)

Nettl, Paul, *Mozart in Böhmen*. Prague, 1938.

Niemetschek, Franz, *Leben des K.K. Kapellmeisters Wolfgang Gottlieb Mozart*. Prague, 1798 ; 2nd edition (author's name given as F. X. Nemetschek), Prague, 1808. (An earlier edition was allegedly published in 1797 under the initial N**.)

Nissen, Georg Nikolaus von, *Biographie W. A. Mozarts, herausgegeben von Constanze, Witwe von Nissen, früher Witwe Mozart*. Leipzig, 1828.

Nottebohm, Gustav, *Mozartiana*. Leipzig, 1880.

Nowak, Leopold, see under Mozart exhibitions, Vienna.

Ostoja, Andrea, *Mozart e l' Italia*. Bologna, 1955.

Ott, Alfons, see under Mozart exhibitions, Munich.

Paumgartner, Bernhard, see under Deutsch.

Pohl, C. F., *Mozart in London*. Vienna, 1867.

Procházka, Rudolf Freiherr von, *Mozart in Prag*. Prague, 1892.

Rech, Géza, see under *Mozart-Jahrbuch*.

Reuther, Hans, see under Mozart exhibitions, Munich.

Rückward, Fritz, see under *Mitteilungen*.

Schenk, Erich, " Mozarts mütterliche Familie ", *Bericht über die musikwissenschaftliche Tagung der Internationalen Stiftung Mozarteum in Salzburg, 1931*. Leipzig, 1932. *Wolfgang Amadeus Mozart*. Vienna, 1955.

Schiedermair, Ludwig, *Die Briefe W. A. Mozarts und seiner Familie*, 4 vols. Munich and Leipzig, 1914.

   Mozart-Ikonographie (5th vol. of *Die Briefe* . . .). Munich and Leipzig, 1914.

Schmid, Ernst Fritz, *Ein schwäbisches Mozart-Buch*. Lorch-Stuttgart, 1948.

Schurig, Arthur, *Wolfgang Amade Mozart*, 2 vols. Leipzig, 1913; 2nd edition, 1923.

   Leopold Mozarts Reise-Aufzeichnungen 1763-1771. Dresden, 1920.

   Konstanze Mozart. Dresden, 1922.

Smith, Herbert, see under Farmer.

Valentin, Erich, see under *Acta Mozartiana* and *Neues Mozart-Jahrbuch*.

Waldersee, Paul Graf von, see under Köchel.

Wurzbach, Konstantin von, *Mozart-Buch*. Vienna, 1869.

CATALOGUE OF THE WORKS BY MOZART
MENTIONED IN THIS BOOK

In conformity with English usage, the word
" Klavier " has been translated as " piano "
throughout this catalogue.

I. BY KÖCHEL AND EINSTEIN NUMBERS

IN the following list the revised numbers (KE.) proposed for many works by Alfred
Einstein in his edition of the Köchel Catalogue (Leipzig, 1937) are interpolated in
their numerical order into Köchel's original series (K.). Under each of these KE.
numbers will be found a cross-reference to the appropriate K. number, where one
exists (e.g. KE.386ª=K.414). All relevant entries in the book are given under the
K. numbers (in this instance, therefore, under K.414). In the text of the book only
he original Köchel numbering, as being the more familiar, appears except where the
new Einstein numbers are indispensable.

K.1 Minuet and trio for piano in G, 13
K.6 Sonata for piano and violin in C, 29, 31, 42-44, 48, 52, 199
K.7 Sonata for piano and violin in D, 29, 31, 38, 42-44, 48, 52, 199
K.8 Sonata for piano and violin in B flat, 31, 32, 38, 42-44, 48, 52, 199
K.9 Sonata for piano and violin in G, 31, 32, 42-44, 48, 52, 199
K.10 Sonata for piano and violin (or flute) and violoncello in B flat, 38-40, 42-48, 52, 56, 98, 199
K.11 Sonata for piano and violin (or flute) and violoncello in G, 38-40, 42-48, 52, 56, 98, 199
K.12 Sonata for piano and violin (or flute) and violoncello in A, 38-40, 42-48, 52, 56, 98, 199
K.13 Sonata for piano and violin (or flute) and violoncello in F, 38-40, 42-48, 52, 56, 98, 199
K.14 Sonata for piano and violin (or flute) and violoncello in C, 38-40, 42-48, 52, 56, 98, 199
K.15 Sonata for piano and violin (or flute) and violoncello in B Flat, 38-40, 42-48, 52, 56, 98, 199
K.16 Symphony in E flat, 494
K.19 Symphony in D, 494

KE.19ª=K.App.223
KE.19ᵈ Sonata for piano duet in C, 45, 352, 360
K.20 " God is our refuge ", motet, 46
K.22 Symphony in B flat, 51
K.24 Eight variations for piano in G on a Dutch air by Graaf, 52, 53
K.25 Seven variations for piano in D on " Willem van Nassau ", 52, 53, 494
K.26 Sonata for piano and violin in E flat, 53, 54, 56, 75, 78, 199
K.27 Sonata for piano and violin in G, 53, 54, 56, 75, 78, 199
K.28 Sonata for piano and violin in C, 53, 54, 56, 75, 78, 199
K.29 Sonata for piano and violin in D, 53, 54, 56, 75, 78, 199
K.30 Sonata for piano and violin in F 53, 54, 56, 75, 78, 199
K.31 Sonata for piano and violin in B flat, 53, 54, 56, 75, 78, 199
K.32 Galimathias musicum, instrumental quodlibet, 53, 66
K.32ª The third sketchbook (the so-called " Capricci "), 52
K.33ᵉ Stabat mater, 66
KE.33ˡ=K.36

2. BY CATEGORIES

With a few exceptions the following list adheres to the arrangement of the *Neue Mozart-Ausgabe*. Sections I (3 and 4), II and III are arranged alphabetically, the remainder in order of Köchel numbers (K.). Einstein numbers (KE.) are here given in brackets after the respective Köchel numbers, e.g. K.414 (386ᵃ).

I. SACRED VOCAL WORKS

1. Masses and Requiem

(a) MASSES

Missa (solemnis), K.47ᵃ   84, 85
Missa brevis in D minor, K.65 (61ᵃ)   86
Mass in C (Dominicus Mass), K.66   93, 94, 146
Missa brevis in F, K.192 (186ᶠ)   151, 461
Missa brevis in D, K.194 (186ʰ)   9, 151, 461
Mass in C (Credo Mass), K.257   464
Missa brevis in C (Spaur Mass), K.258   464
Missa brevis in C, K.259   175, 464
Missa (longa) in C, K.262 (246ᵃ)   156
Missa brevis in B flat, K.275 (272ᵇ)   169, 398
Mass in C (Coronation Mass), K.317   368, 464
Missa solemnis in C, K.337   464
Mass in C minor, K.427 (417ᵃ)   219, 240, 307, 464, 540, 541

(b) REQUIEM

Requiem, K.626   312, 415, 425–427, 430, 432, 439, 467, 468, 481, 488, 494–496, 500, 501, 509–512, 515, 525, 536, 537, 551–555

2. Litanies

Litaniae de venerabili altaris sacramento, K.125   150, 441
Litaniae de venerabili altaris sacramento, K.243   156, 175, 185, 214, 441

3. Smaller liturgical works (motets, offertories, antiphons)

" Ave, verum corpus ", motet, K.618   397
" Exultate, jubilate ", motet for soprano, K.165 (158ᵃ)   144
" God is our refuge ", motet, K.20   46

" Misericordias Domini ", offertory, K.222 (205ᵃ)   151
Offertory, K.47ᵇ   84, 85
" Quaerite primum regnum Dei ", antiphon, K.86 (73ᵛ)   127
Stabat mater, K.33ᶜ   66

4. Oratorios, sacred plays and cantatas

Betulia liberata, oratorio in two parts, K.118 (74ᶜ)   154, 271, 441
Davidde penitente, cantata, K.469   219, 236, 240, 540
" Dir, Seele des Weltalls ", cantata, K.429 (420ᵃ)   485
Little Masonic Cantata (*Eine kleine Freimaurer-Kantate*), K.623   309, 413, 440, 465, 512
Die Maurerfreude, cantata for tenor and male chorus, K.471   245, 247, 255, 257, 383, 406
Passion cantata (*Grabmusik*), K.42 (35ᵃ)   75, 101
Die Schuldigkeit des ersten Gebots, sacred play in three parts (first part only by Mozart), K.35   72–74, 101

II. STAGE WORKS

1. Operas and *Singspiele*

Apollo et Hyacinthus, musical intermezzo to a Latin comedy, K.38   75, 76
Ascanio in Alba, serenata in two acts, K.111   135–137, 460
Bastien und Bastienne, singspiel in one act, K.50 (46ᵇ)   84, 85, 159
La clemenza di Tito, opera seria in two acts, K.621   307, 363, 394, 398, 401, 403–406, 411, 428, 432, 433, 470, 471, 473–480, 482, 483, 485–488, 497, 509, 510, 515, 516, 519, 556, 572
Così fan tutte, opera buffa in two acts, K.588   144, 211, 307, 359, 361–364, 366, 368, 394, 395, 397, 398, 409, 508, 514, 515, 520, 549, 550.

III. Songs, Part-songs, Canons and Solfeggi

1. Solo songs with piano accompaniment

String quartet in D minor, K.421 (417[b]) 236, 250, 259-261, 292, 505, 516

String quartet in E flat, K.428 (421[b]) 236, 250, 259-261, 292, 505, 516

String quartet in B flat (Hunt), K.458 236, 250, 259-261, 292, 505, 516

String quartet in A, K.464 236, 250, 259-261, 292, 505, 516

String quartet in C, K.465 236, 250, 259-261, 292, 505, 516

String quartet in D, K.499 414, 415, 496

String quartet in D, K. 575 346, 366, 427, 428, 436, 465, 496
  Arrangement of string quartet K.575 as trio for piano, violin and violoncello, K.App.148 465

String quartet in B flat, K.589 346, 366, 427, 428, 436, 496

String quartet in F, K.590 346, 366, 427, 428, 436, 496

Adagio and Fugue for two violins, viola, violoncello (and double bass) in C minor, K.546 307

(b) QUARTETS WITH ONE WIND INSTRUMENT

Quartet in A for flute, violin, viola and violoncello, K.298 300, 301

Quartet for flute, violin, viola and violoncello in C, K.App.171 (285[b]) 321

3. Trios and duos for strings

(a) TRIO

Divertimento for violin, viola and violoncello in E flat, K.563 339, 365

(b) DUOS

Duo for violin and viola in G, K.423 319, 321, 464

Duo for violin and viola in B flat, K.424 319, 321, 464

4. Quintets, quartets and trios with piano (or glass harmonica)

(a) QUINTETS

Quintet for piano, oboe, clarinet, horn and bassoon in E flat, K.452, 223, 225

Adagio in C minor and Rondo in C major for glass harmonica, flute, oboe, viola and violoncello, K.617 496

(b) QUARTETS

Quartet for piano, violin, viola and violoncello in G minor, K.478 269, 317, 319, 331

Quartet for piano, violin, viola and violoncello in E flat, K.493 284, 295, 308, 319, 331, 414, 415

(c) TRIOS

Divertimento (trio) for piano, violin and violoncello in B flat, K.254 165, 169, 212, 251

Trio for piano, clarinet and viola in E flat, K.498 327, 331

Trio for piano, violin and violoncello in B flat, K.502 330, 351

Trio for piano, violin and violoncello in E, K.542 330, 351

Trio for piano, violin and violoncello in C, K.548 330, 351

Trio for piano, violin and violoncello in G, K.564 376

5. Sonatas and variations for piano and violin

(a) SONATAS

Sonata for piano and violin in C, K.6 29, 31, 42-44, 48, 52, 199

Sonata for piano and violin in D, K.7 29, 31, 38, 42-44, 48, 52, 199

Sonata for piano and violin in B flat, K.8 31, 32, 38, 42-44, 48, 52, 199

Sonata for piano and violin in G, K.9 31, 32, 42-44, 48, 52, 199

Sonata for piano and violin (or flute) and violoncello in B flat, K.10 38-40, 42-48, 52, 56, 199

Sonata for piano and violin (or flute) and violoncello in G, K.11 38-40, 42-48, 52, 56, 199

Sonata for piano and violin (or flute) and violoncello in A, K.12 38-40, 42-48, 52, 56, 199

Sonata for piano and violin (or flute) and violoncello in F, K.13 38-40, 42-48, 52, 56, 199

Sonata for piano and violin (or flute) and violoncello in C, K.14 38-40, 42-48, 52, 56, 199

Sonata for piano and violin (or flute) and violoncello in B flat, K.15 38-40, 42-48, 52, 56, 199

Sonata for piano and violin in E flat,
K.26   53, 54, 56, 75, 78, 199
Sonata for piano and violin in G, K.27
53, 54, 56, 75, 78, 199
Sonata for piano and violin in C, K.28
53, 54, 56, 75, 78, 199
Sonata for piano and violin in D, K.29
53, 54, 56, 75, 78, 199
Sonata for piano and violin in F, K.30
53, 54, 56, 75, 78, 199
Sonata for piano and violin in B flat,
K.31   53, 54, 56, 75, 78, 199
Sonata for piano and violin in C, K.296
198, 200, 214, 254, 292
Sonata for piano and violin in G, K.301
(293^a)   179, 181, 197, 199, 461
Sonata for piano and violin in E flat,
K.302 (293^b)   179, 181, 197, 199, 461
Sonata for piano and violin in C, K.303
(293^c)   179, 181, 197, 199, 461
Sonata for piano and violin in E minor,
K.304 (300^c)   179, 181, 197, 199, 461
Sonata for piano and violin in A, K.305
(293^d)   179, 181, 197, 199, 461
Sonata for piano and violin in D, K.306
(300^l)   179, 181, 197, 199, 461
Sonata for piano and violin in F, K.376
(374^d)   198, 200, 214, 254, 292
Sonata for piano and violin in F, K.377
(374^e)   198, 200, 214, 254, 292
Sonata for piano and violin in B flat,
K.378 (317^d)   198, 200, 214, 254, 292
Sonata for piano and violin in G, K.379
(373^a)   195, 198, 200, 214, 254, 292
Sonata for piano and violin in E flat,
K.380 (374^f)   198, 200, 214, 254, 292
Sonata for piano and violin in B flat,
K.454   224-228, 267, 268, 280
Sonata for piano and violin in E flat,
K.481   322, 323, 496
Sonata for piano and violin in A, K.526
376, 496, 603

(b) VARIATIONS

Twelve variations for piano and violin
in G on "La bergère Célimène",
K.359 (374^a)   247, 249, 251, 252, 279,
292
Six variations for piano and violin in
G minor on an Andantino "Hélas, j'ai
perdu mon amant", K.360 (374^b)
247, 249, 251, 252, 279, 292, 322, 323

VII. PIANO MUSIC

1. Works for two pianos and for
piano duet

(a) FOR TWO PIANOS

Fugue in C minor, K.426   307
Sonata in D, K.448 (375^a)   197, 225,
349, 464, 465

(b) FOR PIANO DUET

Sonata in C, KE.19^d 45, 352, 360
Sonata in B flat, K.358 (186^c)   215, 292
Sonata in D, K.381(123^a)   188, 215, 292
Sonata in F, K.497   308, 368, 376
Sonata in C, K.521   360, 603

2. Sonatas, fantasias and rondos for
piano

(a) PIANO SONATAS

Sonata in C, K.279 (189^d)   168
Sonata in F, K.280 (189^e)   168
Sonata in B flat, K.281 (189^f)   167, 168
Sonata in E flat, K.282 (189^g)   168
Sonata in G, K.283 (189^h), 166, 168
Sonata in D (Dürnitz), K.284 (205^b)
154, 167, 168, 225-228, 267, 268, 280,
286
Sonata in C, K.309 (284^b)   169, 212
Sonata in A minor, K.310 (300^d)   212
Sonata in D, K.311 (284^c)   212
Sonata in C, K.330 (300^h)   227, 228, 292
Sonata in A, K.331 (300^i)   227, 228,
242, 292, 385
Sonata in F, K.332 (300^k)   227, 228, 292
Sonata in B flat, K.333 (315^c)   225-228,
267, 280
Sonata in C minor, K.457   255, 272, 292,
604
Sonata in C, K.545   464, 465
Sonata in B flat, K.570   464, 465
Sonata in D, K.576   464, 465

(b) FANTASIA

Fantasia in C minor, K.475   167, 255,
272, 292, 342, 604

(c) RONDOS

Rondo in F, K.494   307
Rondo in A minor, K.511   603

3. Variations for piano

Eight variations in G on a Dutch air by Graaf, K.24   52, 53
Seven variations in D on " Willem van Nassau ", K.25   52, 53, 494
Twelve variations in C on a minuet by J. C. Fischer, K.179 (189ª)   166, 168, 221, 242
Six variations in G on " Mio caro Adone " from La fiera di Venezia by Salieri, K.180 (173ᶜ)   221, 253, 254
Nine variations in C on the arietta " Lison dormait " from the opéra-comique Julie by Dezède, K.264 (315ᵈ) 242, 261, 272, 279, 292, 346
Twelve variations in C on " Ah, vous dirai-je, Mamam ", K.265 (300ᵉ)   246
Eight variations in F on the chorus " Dieu d'amour " from Les mariages samnites by Grétry, K.352 (374ᶜ)   242, 247, 279, 292
Twelve variations in E flat on " La belle Françoise ", K.353 (300ᶠ)   242, 247, 279, 292, 342, 603
Twelve variations in E flat on the air " Je suis Lindor " from Le barbier de Séville by Baudron, K.354 (299ª)   195, 221, 242, 342, 347
Six variations in F on " Salve tu, Domine " from the opera I filosofi immaginarii by Paisiello, K.398 (416ᵉ) 213, 234, 246, 247, 279, 292
Ten variations in G on " Unser dummer Pöbel meint " from Gluck's Die Pilgrime von Mekka (La rencontre imprévue), K.455   213, 246, 251, 264, 279, 292, 561
Eight variations in A on Mingone's aria " Come un' agnello " from Sarti's opera Fra i due litiganti il terzo gode, K.460 (454ª) (probably not by Mozart), 227
Nine variations in D on a minuet by Duport, K.573   340
Eight variations in F on " Ein Weib ist das herrlichste Ding " from Der dumme Gärtner by Schack (?), K.613 367, 396

4. Separate pieces for piano and for mechanical organ

Minuet and trio for piano in G, K.1   13

The third sketchbook (the so-called " Capricci "), K.32ª   52
Allegro for piano in G, K.72ª   103
Little Funeral March for piano in C minor, K.453ª   294
Allegro in F and Andante in B flat for piano, K.533   307
Adagio in F minor and Allegro in F major for mechanical organ, K.594 389

VIII. ARRANGEMENTS AND COPIES OF WORKS BY OTHER COMPOSERS

Handel's Acis and Galatea, re-orchestration, K.566   330, 557
Handel's Messiah, re-orchestration, K.572   335, 338, 339
Handel's Alexander's Feast, re-orchestration, K.591   339, 370, 469
Handel's Ode on St. Cecilia's Day, re-orchestration, K.592   339, 370, 468, 469
Holzbauer's Miserere, arrangement, K.App.1 (297ª)   175, 215
C. P. E. Bach's Auferstehung und Himmelfahrt Christi, re-orchestration of an aria, K.App.109ᵍ, No. 19   311
" Pignus futurae gloriae ", copy of part of a Litany by Michael Haydn, K.App.239 (App.109ᴵⱽ)   603

IX. CADENZAS TO WORKS BY OTHER COMPOSERS

Cadenzas to piano concertos by Schröter, K.624 (626ª) App.D. (= K.App.61ª), F, G, H   169

X. SPURIOUS WORKS

" Wiegenlied ", solo song with piano accompaniment (by Flies), K.350 (App.284ᶠ)   447
Nine country dances or quadrilles for orchestra, K.510 (App.293ᵇ)   464, 465
Piano sonata in C minor (by Eberl), K.App.284ª   487
Twelve variations for piano in D on an Andantino " Freundin sanfter Herzenstriebe " from Dittersdorf's Der Gutsherr (by Eberl), K.App.287   487, 501

INDEX